SOCIAL CHANGE IN THE INDUSTRIAL REVOLUTION

SOCIAL CHANGE
IN THE
INDUSTRIAL
REVOLUTION

*An Application of Theory
to the British Cotton Industry*

BY

NEIL J. SMELSER

THE UNIVERSITY OF CHICAGO PRESS

THE UNIVERSITY OF CHICAGO PRESS, CHICAGO 60637
Routledge and Kegan Paul Ltd., London E.C.4, England

International Standard Book Number: 0-226-76311-0
Library of Congress Catalog Card Number: 59-10743

TO MY PARENTS

WHO KINDLED A PREOCCUPATION
WITH IDEAS AND SOCIETY

CONTENTS

ILLUSTRATIONS

PREFACE

The Society of Fellows of Harvard University ranks high among those who have facilitated my progress in this study. Their generous purse not only sent me abroad for research in 1956–7, but also, during my term as Junior Fellow between 1955 and 1958, relieved me of all necessity to earn a living. Less tangible, but more important, I feel, was the Society's general atmosphere, which breeds a faith in free and imaginative inquiry.

Those who read these pages will be aware of the gratitude which I now record for Talcott Parsons. Over a number of years—as teacher, critic, and collaborator—he contributed in innumerable ways to this study, both before its inception and during its development. Professor W. W. Rostow of the Massachusetts Institute of Technology offered particularly clear and helpful direction in the early stages of research and in the later revisions. To him I owe thanks for the advice to limit the study to a single industry. In somewhat extended conversations, both at Harvard and in London, with H. L. Beales, formerly of the London School of Economics, I gained many substantive suggestions and a mountain of source references. I should like also to include conversations, helpful in a variety of ways, with the following men: E. J. Hobsbawm of Birkbeck College, London; K. E. Berrill of St. Catharine's College, Cambridge; P. Mathias of Queens' College, Cambridge; M. M. Postan, Professor of Economic History, Cambridge; W. H. Chaloner, H. A. F. Turner, A. E. Musson, and A. B. L. Rodgers, of Manchester University. Bernard P. Cohen, now at Stanford University, reviewed some of the statistics in the appendices. More generally, I should like to extend long-overdue thanks to my tutors at Oxford, G. D. N. Worswick and Kenneth Tite of Magdalen College. Between 1952 and 1954, when I was their pupil, they imparted a great sense of curiosity over many issues in British social and economic history —a curiosity which extended through this study and which continues.

Quiet though indispensable contributors to the long research were the staffs of several libraries: the British Museum; the British Library of Political and Economic Science; the Manchester Central Library; Chetham's Library, Manchester; the Manchester University Library; the University of London Library, Senate House, especially the Goldsmith's Library of Economic Literature; and Widener Library, Harvard University. I harbour a special attachment to the reading-

Preface

rooms of the British Museum, where I spent many months huddled over its endless supply of invaluable books, pamphlets, and documents. Its halls of treasures and its Bloomsbury environs also afforded excellent recess from study.

A special kind of thanks is due to the *fondateurs* of *Rustique Olivette*, especially Daniel Guérin. *Rustique Olivette* is a villa in the hills above La Ciotat, a maritime port on the French Mediterranean. Its purpose is to harbour—temporarily—wayward scholars, artists, and intellectuals. In the spring of 1957 I composed a draft of the last half of the manuscript in this villa. It was a magnificent experience. If my interpretation of the social conditions of the British working classes is perhaps less dismal than others', possibly it may be attributed, in the end, to the sun and sea of La Ciotat.

My wife, Helen, listened and criticized patiently throughout; her readiness to master the drier bits of the history of the cotton industry went, in my opinion, well beyond the call. Toward the end of the last revisions she dissected, with me, each sentence and phrase of the manuscript. This was immensely helpful, since my editorial imagination had long since been dulled. And finally, our first son, Eric, obliged by making his appearance just five days before an earlier version of this book was submitted to Harvard University as a Ph.D. dissertation. His birth added an air of creativity to the event. I shall always be grateful for his sense of timing.

NEIL SMELSER

BERKELEY, CALIFORNIA
June 1959

CHAPTER I

INTRODUCTION

When comparing a society with its past or with another society, we often employ a dichotomy such as "advanced vs. backward," "developed vs. underdeveloped," "civilized vs. uncivilized," or "complex vs. simple." Sometimes these words yield too little information, because they claim simply that one society is superior to another. Sometimes they yield too much, for terms like "advanced" shroud a galaxy of vague connotations. Hence to use such words may generate conflicts of pride and conflicts of meaning, both of which subvert intelligent discourse.

The dichotomies are, however, not completely useless. Common to all are the dimensions of *complexity* and *differentiation*. In other words, an "advanced" or "developed" society possesses a complex organization of differentiated social and cultural components. To illustrate, a religion becomes a religious tradition only after it shakes off its undifferentiated tribal elements and develops a complex, independent organization. A military machine is more developed than spontaneous warfare because it operates under specific, explicit, and sometimes autonomous rules. Bureaucratic administration is more advanced than a household staff not only because it is more complex but also because it is less mingled with personal loyalties.[1] A highly developed economy has a complexity of organization and a differentiation of units which do not characterize underdeveloped forms.[2] Political behaviour "advances" when it is carried on within political institutions free from nepotism, tribal loyalties, and bald economic interests. In short, one element in "growth," "advancement," and "civilization" is that the social structures in question become *more differentiated* from each other.

[1] M. Weber, "Bureaucracy," in *From Max Weber: Essays in Sociology* (London, 1947), pp. 198–9.
[2] These elements are implied in Adam Smith's view of an economy. Book I of *The Wealth of Nations* (New York, 1937) is entitled: "Of the Causes of Improvement in the Productive Powers of Labour . . . ," or we might say, of the causes of economic growth. Chapter I, "Of the Division of Labour," and Chapter III, "That the Division of Labour is limited by the Extent of the Market," contain the twin ideas of complexity and differentiation from the market.

1

This implicit concept underlies much of our discourse about social development. We seldom ask, however, whether the *very process* of passing from a less differentiated to a more differentiated social structure possesses definite regularities, and whether the sequence itself produces phenomena which can be analysed systematically. It is my assertion that such regularities do exist, and can be extracted from societies in flux.

In the following study I shall analyse several sequences of differentiation. Above all I shall be attempting to apply social theory to history. Such an analysis naturally calls for two components: (1) a segment of social theory; and (2) an empirical instance of change. For the first I have selected a model of social change from a developing "general theory of action"; for the second I have chosen the British industrial revolution between 1770 and 1840. From this large revolution I have isolated the growth of the cotton industry and the transformation of the family structure of its working classes. Let us sketch the model and the historical processes in turn.

The model of structural differentiation is an abstract theory of change. When *one* social role or organization becomes archaic under changing historical circumstances, it differentiates by a *definite and specific sequence of events* into *two or more* roles or organizations which function more effectively in the new historical circumstances. The new social units are structurally distinct from each other, but taken together are functionally equivalent to the original unit. The differentiation of an economy's distribution system into "retail" and "wholesale" is an example. These branches of distribution differ, of course, but together they fulfil the same function as a more primitive distribution system. Another example is the differentiation of courtship from kinship. In a system of classificatory marriage (e.g., cross-cousin), the basis for marriage is simply extended kinship. When, on the other hand, the basis for marriage is personal acquaintance outside the family circle, courtship has become *differentiated* from the structure of kinship. Any sequence of differentiation is set in motion by specific disequilibrating conditions. Initially this disequilibrium gives rise to symptoms of social disturbance which must be brought into line later by mechanisms of social control. Only then do specific ideas, suggestions, and attempts emerge to produce the more differentiated social units. We shall elaborate this statement presently; for the moment let us apply it sketchily to an industrial structure and to a family economy.

Industrial differentiation implies that under certain market, value, and other conditions, the existing industrial structure becomes inadequate to meet productive requirements. A sequence enters its first stage when elements in the population express dissatisfaction with industrial productivity. This dissatisfaction appears in the form of complaints concerning the misuse of resources or the faulty performance of economic roles which control these resources, or both. In either case the dissatisfaction is legitimized by reference to the dominant value-system of the time. The immediate responses to dissatisfaction are undirected or misdirected symptoms of disturbance. Initially these disturbances are "brought into line" by a series of holding operations which prevent the outbursts from reaching explosive proportions. Simultaneously there is a reiteration of established values and an encouragement of ideas which promise to carry the implications of these values into practice. These ideas are implemented by inventions and experiments with methods of production. Finally, entrepreneurs turn these suggestions into action to overhaul the productive system. If successful, the entrepreneurial attempts produce a new industrial structure and an extraordinary growth of production, capitalization, and profits.

The family economy—those organized roles which govern production and consumption in the family—is a social structure distinct from any industry, but the principles regulating its reorganization are identical. The family may become, under specific pressures, inadequate for performing its defined functions. Dissatisfaction occurs when it is felt either that performance of roles or utilization of resources falls short of expectations. The symptoms of disturbance resulting from these pressures are first handled by mechanisms of social control. Gradually, as the energy is harnessed, it is diverted to the more positive tasks of legitimizing and specifying ideas for social action, and transforming these ideas into social experiments. If successful, these experiments produce one or more new social units. In this study we shall apply the model of structural differentiation to several changes in the family and community life of the British working classes in the early nineteenth century; among these changes were the reorganization of the economic roles of the family, the consolidation of friendly societies, the rise of savings banks and co-operative stores, and the evolution of trade unions.

We might note two general implications of this model at the outset: (1) It is applicable to *many* types of social structure. Separate models are not required for analysing changes in the economy, the family, the class system, etc. Even though unique conditions naturally govern the behaviour of different social units, the growth *pattern* of each should follow the same model. (2) Because structural differentiation is a *sequence*, its components appear in a temporal relationship to each other. For instance, symptoms of disturbance erupt when the obsolescence of the old structure is apparent but before the mobilization of resources to overhaul this structure begins. These disturbances, moreover, bear a symbolic relationship to the specific points of obsolescence; for these reasons social disturbances are not simply random outbursts. In this study I shall analyse several symptoms of disturbance—pleas for economic protection, strikes, attempts to restrict factory hours, and Utopian movements. By employing the model of structural differentiation it is possible to shed light on both the content and timing of these eruptions.

Why choose the cotton industry and the family economy of its working classes? First, because Britain was the cradle of modern industrialism and because cotton was, in a certain sense, the cradle of British industrialism.[1] Second, the changes in the cotton industry were rapid and dramatic between 1770 and 1840.[2] What is true of the industry is true of the family economy of its workers. In the late eighteenth and early nineteenth centuries, child, female, and male labour were reorganized dramatically, thus occasioning a thorough modification of the family structure. In addition, this period saw the creation of a number of social units—trade unions, co-operative stores, savings banks, etc.—which evolved as cushions for the family in its new industrial environment.

The final reason for choosing this period is a practical one. Historians have combed over the British industrial revolution from many points of view. This availability of historical research is necessary because of the broad scope of the present study. Though I have utilized many primary sources, I have relied more heavily on secondary sources than is customary in a traditional historical study.

Why, one might ask, if the economic and social history of the period is so familiar, should we attempt to improve the history of Baines, Mantoux, Marx, the Webbs, the Hammonds, Cole, and others? Why review the industrial and social revolution in cotton from the standpoint of a theory of structural differentiation?

---

[1] W. W. Rostow, "The Take-off into Self-sustained Growth," *Economic Journal*, LXVI (1956), pp. 44–5.

[2] The industry had begun its rapid growth many decades before the industrial revolution. Below, pp. 53–60. Though international competition became apparent in the 1830's and intensified thereafter, the British cotton industry continued to grow rapidly throughout the century, falling only after its peak in 1913. Even the industry's gloomiest prophets did not date its decline before the 1880's. G. von Schulze-Gaevernitz, *The Cotton Trade in England and on the Continent* (London, 1895), pp. 48–9; G. Armitage, *The Lancashire Cotton Industry from the Great Inventions to the Great Disasters* (Manchester, 1951); Bonami (pseud.), *The Doom of the Cotton Trade and the Fall of the Factory System* (Manchester, 1896), p. 5.

Introduction

Each time one looks to the past he is guided by certain assumptions or presumptions about what should be lifted from the chronicle of recorded history. Such assumptions are necessary to select from history's endless facts. They are ideas, concepts, abstractions, or notions which permit the observer to reconstruct meaningful relationships among the facts which interest him. No matter how avid the historian's concern for "facts," he must use such assumptions. Sometimes these are elaborately defined and self-consciously applied, as in Marx' *Capital*; sometimes they are more implicit, as in the work of the Hammonds or Cole. The value of *re*considering historical phenomena is to bring *new* ideas to bear on history. When, for instance, the concept of bureaucracy appears as an important element in modern social thought, it is important to consider the development of bureaucracy, even though historians may hitherto have neglected its significance. Similarly, when theories of social change elicit new historical relationships, it is important to reconsider history in the light of these theories.

The various approaches to history are not, however, always independent of each other. Sometimes they "compete" because they purport to explain the same facts. Thus the Marxist history of capitalism differs from *laissez-faire* history, even though both attempt to assign meaning to the same historical phenomena. Which explains them better? By comparing several approaches to a historical period, we might judge their relative analytical value, and hence generate criteria for preferring one or the other as an explanation for the facts in question. The grounds for preference concern the number and kinds of omissions, inconsistencies, distortions, and limitations which a given scheme implies. Hence a second value in applying a new interpretive device to history is to compare and contrast its explanatory value with that of existing approaches.

There is a third, more special reason for applying the model of structural differentiation. In the development of the model there have been indications that its applicability is exceedingly wide, e.g., to fields as diverse as economic development, small groups, and psychological processes of learning and socialization.[1] To apply it rigorously to another empirical field, therefore, provides evidence as to the generalizability of this model.

For these reasons I shall devote a later chapter to a critical examination of several approaches to the social history of the early nineteenth century. If I may preview my own analysis a little, I shall

[1] See T. Parsons, R. F. Bales *et al.*, *Family, Socialization, and Interaction Process* (Glencoe, Ill., 1955); Parsons and N. J. Smelser, *Economy and Society* (London and Glencoe, Ill., 1956).

5

Introduction

be less critical of the purely *industrial* aspects of the history of cotton. The model incorporates the usual elements of an industrial history— invention, innovation, reorganization, capitalization and production —in a very systematic way. In addition, however, it is necessary to consider systematically several "non-industrial" aspects of the industrial change, such as the burst of Nonconformist religious values in the eighteenth century, the rise of the Society of Arts and the Patent Office, the movements for protection and favouritism, etc.

Our analysis of the *social* history of this period will be both more novel and more controversial. The model of structural differentiation is novel because it deviates very radically from conventional interpretations of the social history of the period. Furthermore, because social historians have tended to "take sides" in the highly charged atmosphere of working-class misery, trade unionism, violence, and factory agitation, their approaches leave a residue of confusion and controversy over the correct interpretation of social conditions and movements. I shall therefore supplement this study with a brief critical analysis of three interpretations of social history in the industrial revolution: (1) Marx' *Capital*, in which many social phenomena are traced to the system of capitalist production and the resultant conflict between classes; (2) the work of the British Socialist historians, who attribute the rise of many social movements to the oppression and misery of the working classes, and (3) the work of a historian who recently has revived some of the assumptions of the *laissez-faire* ideology. I shall ask whether these approaches conform to the historical facts and whether their concepts have wide explanatory scope.

CHAPTER II

SOME EMPTY THEORETICAL BOXES

One of the most famous and fruitful—yet in one respect futile—
controversies ever to appear in the economic journals was a dispute
over the respective roles of theory and fact between two giants of the
tradition of economics, A. C. Pigou and J. H. Clapham.[1] The controversy began when the latter launched an attack on economic
theory. He complained specifically about the contemporary version
of diminishing return, constant return, and increasing return
industries. He preferred to discard such concepts because, first, "the
Laws of Returns have never been attached to specific industries . . .
the boxes are, in fact, empty . . . we do not, for instance, at this
moment know under what conditions of returns coal or boots are
being produced."[2] Even if filled with facts, such terms are not
translatable into useful directives for public policy. And finally, any
hope one might entertain actually to fill the boxes and thereby to
establish empirical conclusions is "not very encouraging."[3] The
empty boxes of economic theory are, in sum, both unfilled and useless if filled; these weaknesses, however, are unimportant in the end
because the boxes are virtually unfillable.

Pigou's counter-offensive was likewise multi-pronged. General
categories have proved useful elsewhere, e.g., in mathematics.
Indeed, to speak in general terms at all presupposes some kind of
empty box; a term such as "commodities," and nothing less general,
is necessary to analyse certain characteristics of hats *and* gold
watches *and* onions at the same time. Since the time of Adam Smith
theorists have employed such terms to "disentangle and analyse the
causes by which the values of different things are determined."[4]

I shall discuss neither the particular concepts of diminishing,
increasing, and constant returns, nor the question of theory's

---

[1] *Economic Journal*, XXXII (1922), pp. 305–14 and 458–65. Reprinted in
American Economic Association, *Readings in Price Theory* (London, 1953), pp.
119–39.
[2] AEA, *Readings in Price Theory*, p. 127.
[3] *Ibid.*, p. 128.
[4] *Ibid.*, p. 134.

7

applicability to policy. On methodological grounds, however, one must join Pigou. Theory, if it is to be theory, must include a number of empty boxes, i.e., categories which refer potentially to a wide range of facts. These categories maintain consistent logical relations among themselves; they possess a stable *structure*. Moreover, definite yet abstract propositions govern the *interaction* among the categories under conditions of change. Finally, to fill the boxes correctly, one must isolate empirical instances to accept or reject the logical relationships among the categories.

Following this logic, we may speak of two sorts of propositions, analytical and empirical. The first are "if . . . then" statements about the behaviour of the empty boxes. Empirical propositions, on the other hand, fill the boxes by specifying appropriate empirical areas in which the analytical relationships should hold. Empirical propositions are "tested," naturally, by referring to the empirical data which the propositions themselves call into question.[1] To state the laws of gravity in abstract formulas, for example, would be to create analytical propositions. To predict the course of planets, the speed of falling objects, and the sequence of tides would be to generate several sets of empirical propositions. The latter then would be tested by reference to astronomical, experimental, and natural data.

The controversy between Clapham and Pigou is futile, therefore, because it is impossible to discuss whether empty boxes are desirable or undesirable in theory. Theory cannot exist without them. For any *specific* set of categories Clapham's objections of "unfilled," "useless if filled," and "unfillable" may hold. This, however, is not the issue of theory vs. no theory, but of good vs. bad theory. To say that empty boxes are in principle unfillable is an illegitimate extrapolation based on objections to particular bad theories. This results in a general methodological position which rules out scientific explanation.

The controversy—and the reason for its futile aspect—suggest an approach to the present study. Application of theory might proceed by three steps: (1) to generate or assemble some empty theoretical boxes and to formulate analytical propositions; (2) to fill the boxes in several ways and thereby generate some empirical propositions; (3) to examine the relevant empirical phenomena themselves as a limited "test" for the empirical propositions.

Following this outline, I shall present, in this chapter, some of the segments of a general theory of action as it has developed in the past

1 J. O. Wisdom, *Foundations of Inference in Natural Science* (London, 1952), pp. 46–59.

several years.[1] Elsewhere these segments have been applied to the behaviour of small groups, the socialization of the child, and the development of economic institutions. While this theory of action is still relatively undeveloped methodologically, it is presumed that it is applicable to these and many more empirical areas. In this study I shall develop a further "case study" of its applicability.

For the moment I shall treat these theoretical segments as empty boxes, which possess a structure and interact with each other, but which do not refer to any *particular* human action. Consequently this chapter contains a minimum of empirical illustration. I shall also relegate some of the more elaborate theoretical refinements to appendices and to footnotes marked by asterisks (*) throughout the study. For a general appreciation of this research it is not necessary for the reader to pursue all these refinements. A full grasp of the technical arguments requires, however, a careful reading of all the theoretical material.

In the next chapter I shall fill these boxes by defining an industry—using cotton textiles in Great Britain—in terms of the general categories, and simultaneously translate the analytical propositions into empirical statements about industrial change. In Chapters IV–VII, I shall investigate the industrial developments in cotton textiles between the 1770's and the 1840's in Britain, in order to examine the workability of the propositions.

In Chapter VIII, I shall *re*fill the empty boxes and restate the abstract propositions with reference to the family economy. Naturally a family differs from an industry empirically; they are distinct institutionalized sub-systems and cannot be reduced to each other. The *pattern* of structural differentiation governing both, however, is identical. Having outlined these principles of change for the family economy, I shall turn to an analysis of its historical development during the industrial revolution (Chapters IX–XIII). In particular I shall analyse its changing division of labour, the trade union, the friendly society, the savings bank, and the co-operative society. In part I shall be reinterpreting material from economic and social history by means of a body of specifically sociological theory which has seldom commanded the attention of historians or economists.

[1] Particularly in T. Parsons and E. A. Shils (eds.), *Toward a General Theory of Action* (Cambridge, Mass., 1951); Parsons, *The Social System* (Glencoe, Ill., 1951); Parsons, R. F. Bales and Shils, *Working Papers in the Theory of Action* (Glencoe, Ill., 1953); Parsons, Bales, *et al.*, *Family, Socialization and Interaction Process*; and Parsons and Smelser, *Economy and Society*. Since the main purpose of this chapter is not to build theory but to collect and arrange already-formulated elements, I shall not discuss these elements in detail. Ample reference will be made to the works of action theory, however.

SOME CATEGORIES OF THE GENERAL THEORY OF ACTION

A System of Action. A system of action is generated by the inter-action of two or more units in a certain environment or situation. Inherent in this definition is the notion of the interdependence of the units; they influence and adjust to each other and to the external situation. This mutual influence and adjustment is not random, how-ever; all systems of action are governed by the principle of equili-brium. According to the dominant type of equilibrium, the adjust-ments proceed in a certain direction: if the equilibrium is stable, the units tend to return to their original position; if the equilibrium is partial, only some of the units need adjust; if the equilibrium is unstable, the tendency is to change, through mutual adjustment, to a new equilibrium or to disintegrate altogether.

The units of a system of action vary widely, according to the system in question. In a personality system the units are needs, drives, skills, etc. In a cultural system the units are value-orientations, beliefs, expressive symbols, and the like. A social system, finally, is composed of a set of interrelated roles, collectivities, etc., organized into sub-systems and subject to institutionalized controls at several levels. It is important to remember that the roles, collectivities, etc., not individuals, are the units in this last case.[1] Since this is a study of social systems, the following remarks refer only to that type of system of action.

The Units of Analysis of a Social System. At the more concrete levels the units of a social system are three: (*a*) sets of activities; (*b*) roles; and (*c*) organizations or collectivities composed of sub-roles. Analytically all three are identical; they are sectors of action of individuals or collectivities, and they *perform*, or contribute to the continuous functioning of the social system. In all three cases, furthermore, other units within the system *sanction* this contribution. The relative predominance of these units depends largely on the social system's degree of differentiation and its degree of crystalliza-tion. For instance, in an experimental small group, the units of analysis often are the *types of activities*—supplying information, making suggestions, etc.—performed by the group members, whether or not these activities have crystallized into definite roles. Once they become subject to relatively stable expectations for per-formance, however, we speak of the emergence of *roles*. Formally, of course, these roles are analysable in the same terms as the relatively uncrystallized activities. If organized sub-groups such as

---

[1] For an extended discussion of these three types of systems of action, cf. Parsons and Shils, *Toward a General Theory of Action*, Parts 1 and 2.

cliques and coalitions appear in the group, we may speak of *collectivities* as units of the social system. In large-scale society, the same three elements—sets of activities, roles, and collectivities—constitute the stuff of social systems, though on this level the latter two types predominate, because of the highly differentiated character of society and its sub-systems. For purposes of verbal economy, the term "role" hereafter will characterize the concrete units of a social system; in fact, however, it refers to all three types of units.

A social system is not, however, simply a conglomeration of activities, roles, and collectivities. At higher levels it is subject to a number of controls. It is governed by a value-system which defines and legitimizes the activities of the social system. Second, these values are institutionalized into regulatory patterns which govern the interaction of the more concrete units. Third, the more concrete units specialize in social sub-systems which cluster around functional imperatives governing the social system. Hence when we treat an industry as an institutionalized sub-system, it must be remembered that an industry is not simply an aggregate of firms, roles, and activities, but is a *system* which may itself have relationships with other social systems.

The Functional Analysis of a Social System. Roles are the units which contribute at the more concrete levels to the functioning of a social system. By what criteria may we assess this contribution? Or in other words, what *functions* do these roles fulfill in the system?

According to the theory of action which I shall utilize in this study,[1] all social systems are subject to four functional exigencies which must be met more or less satisfactorily if the system is to remain in equilibrium:

(1) Latent pattern-maintenance and tension-management. Every social system is governed by a value-system which specifies the nature of the system, its goals, and the means of attaining these goals. A social system's first functional requirement is to preserve the integrity of the value-system itself and to assure that individual actors conform to it. This involves socializing and educating individuals, as well as providing tension-control mechanisms for handling and resolving individual disturbances relating to the values. These functions are "latent" because the maintaining and managing activity proceeds continuously and independently of the system's larger adjustments.

(2) Goal-attainment. Given the value-system and its relatively stable institutionalization, the social system must establish certain

[1] Parsons, Bales, and Shils, *Working Papers in the Theory of Action*, Chapters III, V.

11

relationships with the external situation; that is, the system's activities must be directed toward a goal or set of goals. These goals differ, of course, from system to system.

(3) Adaptation. Since goals are not automatically realized, there arises an interest in establishing a supply of facilities by which a variety of goals may be pursued at different times and in different situations. It is important that these adaptive facilities be more *general* than any one goal, i.e., they must constitute an available store for attaining a plurality of goals.

(4) Integration. Harmony of purpose and lack of conflict are not necessarily guaranteed in the specialized pursuit of goals. That function which deals with maintaining the smooth interaction *among* individual units is integration.

The concrete stuff of social systems is *not* these functions. Individual actors and definite collectivities organized into sub-systems—not the functions—interact with each other. What then do the functions signify? They are, on the one hand, *dimensions* by which the behaviour of units is classified, described, and analysed. They are, second, *functions* which these units must perform if the social system is to operate with any degree of efficiency and effectiveness. For this reason the activities, roles, and collectivities of a social system tend to cluster into sub-systems around these functional dimensions. Finally, as we shall explain below, these functions define the *bases* upon which the units in a social system interact.

Figure 1 illustrates the relationship between the functional dimensions and the concrete units of analysis for any Social System *S*. The circles within each functional area represent activities, roles, or collectivities which contribute *primarily* to the function in which they are placed. Units specialized according to the latency and integrative sub-systems are oriented toward the cultural patterns and norms governing the system. Units specialized according to the adaptive and goal-attainment sub-systems are oriented toward the external situation.

The concept "unit of analysis" thus cuts across the concept "function." The functions are constant over time, no matter what the composition of a given social system. Indeed, the purpose of this study is to utilize the functional dimensions to account for empirically observable *changes* in the concrete organization of roles in social systems. Yet the concepts cross-cut in still another way. Given the primary specialization of a role, this contribution does not exhaust the role's entire functional significance; it may contribute to other functions in some measure. The problem is to assign functional *primacy* to any given role.

12

Some Empty Theoretical Boxes

An on-going social system utilizes various kinds of resources. An obvious example is an industry which uses the factors of production—land, labour, capital, and organization. Similarly, a problem-solving small group utilizes information, support of members, etc., as resources. When we discuss the problem of dissatisfactions with the functioning of social systems, we shall analyse the significance of resources.

FIGURE 1

FUNCTIONAL DIMENSIONS OF SOCIAL SYSTEM S^1

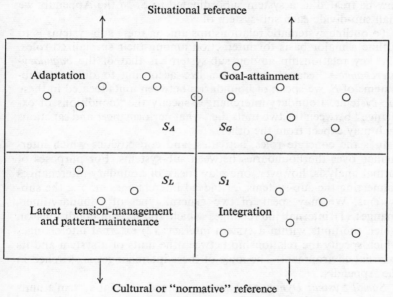

Relations among the Units of a Social System. So far only the composition of a Social System S has been outlined: a determinate number of roles analysable by a determinate number of functional dimensions. These functions define certain relationships among the units. To say of two roles, for instance, that one has adaptive primacy and the other goal-attainment primacy is to state a *relationship* between the units: the former creates generalized facilities which the latter employs to attain S's goals. Such relationships are, however,

1 The figure is taken from Parsons, Bales, and Shils, *Working Papers in the Theory of Action*, p. 182. It is applied to the economy and to the society as a whole in Parsons and Smelser, *Economy and Society*, pp. 39–53.

extremely general. How do the units actually *interact* with each other?

One characteristic of a social system is that it is divisible into sub-systems. This division takes place primarily along functional lines. The adaptive dimension, for instance, while it supplies facilities to the larger Social System *S*, *may itself be treated as a social system*, because in performing its defined function it must meet corresponding functional exigencies at its own level. Hence we may divide S_A into the same four functional dimensions, thus outlining in detail the *adaptive sub-system* of *S*. For many analytical purposes, it may now be treated as a system subordinated to *S*. In the Appendix we shall sub-divide each sub-system of *S*.

To outline systematic relationships among these sub-systems is to outline a major basis for interaction among their specialized roles. The key relationship among sub-systems is that of the *boundary-interchange*.[1] Because roles specialize according to different sub-systems of *S*, we speak of boundaries between units located in these sub-systems. Boundary-interchanges specify the "conditions of exchange" between the two units, i.e., what performances and sanctions each may expect from the other.

It is the concrete roles, activities, and collectivities which interchange over the boundaries between sub-systems. For purposes of formal analysis, however, one may speak of boundary-interchanges connecting the sub-systems, or indeed interchanges among the sub-systems. We may speak of two general types of boundary-interchange: (1) internal interchanges which specify the conditions on which the units within a system interact; (2) external interchanges which specify the relationship between the units of a system and its external environment. The logic of these interchanges is sketched in the Appendix.

Social System Dynamics. Having outlined a social system's units of analysis, the functional dimensions underlying these units, and its interactive bases, let us now inquire into the behaviour of units over time. In this operation we shall generate several analytical propositions, i.e., propositions about the dynamics of the empty boxes.

In general we might distinguish between two types of social system dynamics: (1) adjustments of the system which do not involve any reorganization of the roles; (2) structural changes which involve the disappearance, re-creation, and reorganization of the social system's roles. These types are distinguished in the first instance by the presence or absence of reorganization of the units. We also presume

[1] Parsons and Smelser, *Economy and Society*, Chapters II, IV.

that the second type is more complex than the first, and extends over a longer period of time. While short-term adjustments are of interest in any study of social change, and while the early nineteenth century supplies an abundance of short-term adjustments—trade cycles, ebbs and flows of public opinion, etc.—we must omit them for lack of space. This study deals with long-term change almost exclusively.

Only one type of long-term change—structural differentiation—is to be investigated. This type of change is especially characteristic of growing and developing social systems.[1] As outlined in the last chapter, the model of structural differentiation states that certain social phenomena proceed in definite *sequence* to produce specific types of structural change. In terms of action theory the sequence begins with a dissatisfaction with the goal-achievements (S_G) of the system. Frequently this dissatisfaction is caused by an external pressure which prevents the system from functioning satisfactorily.

Simultaneously there is a prospect of facilities (S_A) to correct this imbalance. Signs of disturbance then appear, which are "handled" by mechanisms of social control and "channelled" into mobilization of resources. In a series of steps these resources are incorporated into more and more specific proposals to innovate. Favourable innovations are rewarded by extraordinary sanctions and then gradually routinized.

The sequence has been broken into seven steps:

(1) Dissatisfaction with the goal-achievements of the social system or sub-system in question and a sense of opportunity for change in terms of the potential availability of facilities.

(2) Symptoms of disturbance in the form of "unjustified" negative emotional reactions and "unrealistic" aspirations on the part of various elements in the social system.

(3) A covert handling of these tensions and a mobilization of motivational resources for new attempts to realize the implications of the existing value-system.

(4) Encouragement of the resulting proliferation of "new ideas" without imposing specific responsibility for their implementation or for "taking the consequences."

(5) Positive attempts to reach specification of the new ideas and institutional patterns which will become the objects of commitments.

(6) "Responsible" implementation of innovations carried out by persons or collectivities which are either rewarded or punished,

---

[1] Hence the model is not meant to account, e.g., for the decline of the British cotton industry since 1914.

depending on their acceptability or reprehensibility in terms of the existing value-system.

(7) If the implementations of Step 6 are received favourably, they are gradually routinized into the usual patterns of performance and sanction; their extraordinary character thereby diminishes.

These concepts are empty boxes; they state nothing about specific social systems. In the next chapter we shall refine them theoretically and fill them with reference to industrial change. At this time we might consider two formal features of the model: (*a*) What is meant by dissatisfaction? (*b*) What is the place of the value-system in structural differentiation?

A social system is a number of concrete *units* which specialize according to certain *dimensions* and which utilize certain *resources*. Dissatisfactions may be phrased in terms either of roles or resources: (1) Many dissatisfactions boil down to the feeling that role-performance is inadequate. As we shall see, these dissatisfactions may be classified according to the functional dimensions of the social system. (2) Dissatisfactions may rest on a feeling that resources are being misused or misallocated. In the next chapter we shall classify dissatisfactions according to "role-performance" and "resources"; we shall see that all specific dissatisfactions deal with both implicitly.

What is the place of the value-system? It is first the source of the criteria for perceiving, evaluating, and controlling the achievements of the social system. It specifies the conditions under which members of the system should express dissatisfactions and prepare to undertake change. A value-system does not initiate change in the absence of other conditions; as the seven-step outline shows, there also must be an actual or perceived situational pressure and the promise of facilities to overcome this pressure.

Later in a sequence of structural differentiation the value-system occupies a similar position. It supplies standards for legitimizing and approving new ideas and plans. The value-system thus limits the directions and degrees of change; on the other hand, is it more than a simple "barrier to change."

The assumption that the major value-system remains constant during a single sequence of differentiation implies, above all, that the *criteria* for assessing the units' performance do not vary. This does not imply that values never change. It does imply, however, that the change of values is a separate analytical problem, and that the model of structural differentiation does not explain such changes in a simple way. It implies also that values generally change more slowly than social structure; this implication underlies our analysis.

Some Empty Theoretical Boxes

Since the value-system is so crucial in structural differentiation, its contents must be characterized carefully in any analysis. Because its elements are complex and frequently implicit, to outline the appropriate value-system poses extremely delicate interpretative problems.

During a sequence of structural differentiation, *reorganization* occurs in several ways. Relationships among the social system's roles and collectivities are restructured; old units disappear, new ones form, and new combinations arise. In order for this to happen, the system's resources—individual motivation, facilities, and integration—must be reorganized as well. Since the concept of resources is still relatively undefined, we shall discuss it in greater detail only when we attempt to put some empirical flesh on these theoretical bones in later chapters.

APPENDIX

THE LOGIC OF BOUNDARY-INTERCHANGES

To specify boundary-interchanges within Social System S, one must dissect the system in more detail than in Figure 1. The possibility of this dissection rests on a fundamental principle of action theory: what is treated as a *functional dimension* of S also is a focus of a primary *functional sub-system*, itself subject to the same functional exigencies as S, though at a different level. Thus S_A, the adaptive function of S, contributes generalized facilities to the pursuit of S's goals. In so doing, S_A faces functional problems logically identical with those of S—goal-attainment, adaptation, integration, and latent tension-management and pattern-maintenance. Because these problems are subordinated to S_A instead of S, however, they have different concrete definitions. The same logic applies to S's other sub-systems, S_G, S_I, and S_L. These are four separate social sub-systems, each meeting a function subordinated to S as a whole. Figure 2 shows this further functional sub-division of S. By the resulting sixteen bases we may classify and analyse the contribution of the concrete units of S to its goals.

How are these four sub-systems interrelated? What are the boundary-interchanges among them? Elsewhere it has proved fruitful to assume that each sub-system interchanges with every other sub-system primarily at *one* boundary only (though secondarily at others), yielding a total of six primary boundary-interchanges:[1]

[1] Parsons and Smelser, *Economy and Society*, Chapters II, IV, The *l*-boundary, for reasons developed there, is treated as "closed."

17

Some Empty Theoretical Boxes

(1) S_A offers S_G a repository of adaptive facilities to pursue the sub-goals of S_G, and vice versa. Hence the point of interchange between the two is the a sub-sector of each. The resulting boundary-interchange is S_{Aa}–S_{Ga}. (2) Likewise, the boundary-interchange between S_L and S_I is the mutual supply of adaptive facilities. The relationship is thus S_{La}–S_{Ia}. (3) S_G and S_I stand in a relationship of mutual goal-satisfaction. The performance of each is simultaneously a

FIGURE 2

THE FUNCTIONAL DIMENSIONS TREATED AS SUB-SYSTEMS OF S

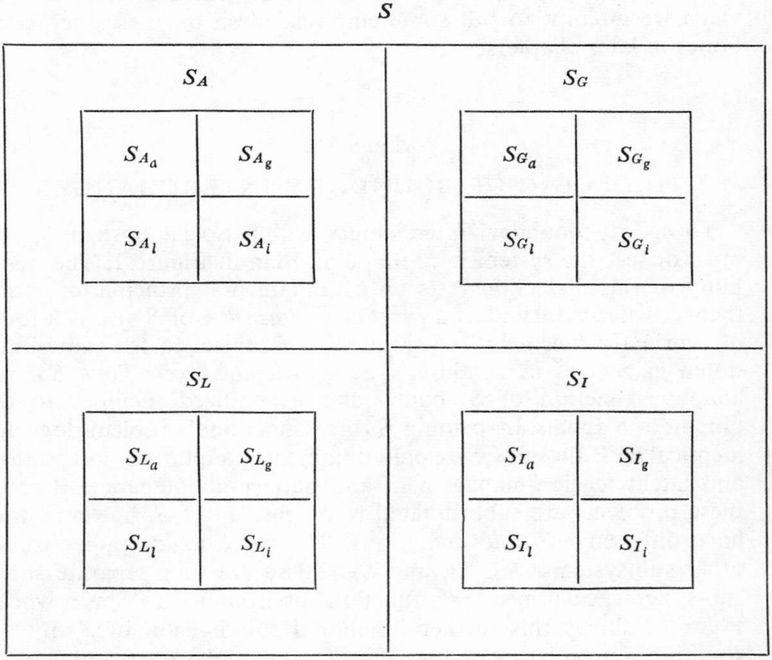

S

reward for the goal-attainment (g) of the other. Hence the boundary-interchange is S_{Gg}–S_{Ig}. (4) Similarly, between S_A and S_L the relationship is one of mutual goal-gratification, with the resulting boundary-interchange of S_{Ag}–S_{Lg}. (5) S_G offers S_L those resources which are prerequisite for the integration of S_L and vice versa. This interchange is S_{Gi}–S_{Li}. (6) The interchange between S_I and S_A is also mutually advantageous from the standpoint of the integration of each. The resulting interchange is S_{Ai}–S_{Ii}. If we add these bound-

18

ary-interchanges to Figure 2, the result is Figure 3.[1] These internal boundary-interchanges state the principles on which the concrete units within S are organized and by which they interact with each other in order to maintain the system in equilibrium or account for its disturbances.

FIGURE 3

THE BOUNDARY-INTERCHANGES WITHIN S

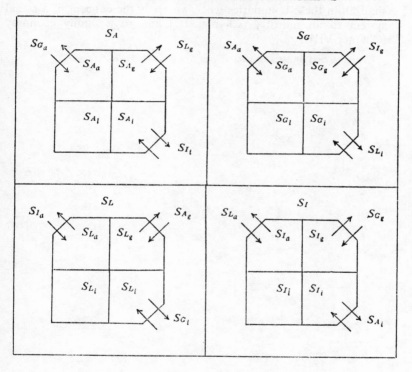

In addition to these internal exchanges the system maintains certain relationships with its external situation.[2] We use the concept of boundary-relationship to characterize these external relationships.

[1] *Ibid.*
[2] Parsons and Shils, *Toward a General Theory of Action*, pp. 4–6; Parsons, Bales, and Shils, *Working Papers in the Theory of Action*, pp. 172–9.

With its environment the social system exchanges performances and sanctions similar to those just outlined. By means of these interchanges it obtains the resources necessary for its own functioning and supplies resources for other systems of action. Elsewhere the resources of land, labour, capital, and organization—the factors of production for the economy—have been analysed as the elements exchanged at the external boundaries of the economy.[1] At present the statement of both the internal and external boundary-relationships must remain cryptic, for we are dealing with empty boxes. We shall fill in these boundaries when we apply the concept of a social system to an industry (Chapter III) and to a family economy (Chapter VIII).

[1] Parsons and Smelser, *Economy and Society*, pp. 51–78.

CHAPTER III

FILLING THE BOXES

This chapter parallels the preceding in outline. Instead of dealing with abstract units, relationships, and functions, however, we shall clothe the anonymous Social System S in empirical dress by applying it to an Industry C—specifically the cotton-textile industry. The empty analytical propositions of Chapter II will thereby become empirical propositions concerning the industry, which will serve in turn as a framework for analysing its historical development.

The Units of Analysis of an Industry. An analysis of an industry should include units at several levels—a value-system, an ideology, institutional patterns such as contract, differentiated industrial sub-systems, and concrete units such as firms. Since, however, we are analysing differentiation at the concrete levels of social structure, we shall concentrate on the industry's organizations, roles, and activities. We shall nevertheless refer frequently to the industrial value-system, as well as its functional dimensions.

At the more concrete levels, the industrial units are roles and organizations specialized in producing the industry's goods and services. Examples of such units are workers, managers, entrepreneurs, capitalists, boards of directors, etc. To analyse these roles as parts of a social system does not break with economic analysis in the least. Indeed, many problems in this study might be posed by an analytical economic historian. It is hoped, however, that social system analysis relates these units to a wider range of social phenomena than does "straight" economic history.

What are the cotton-textile industry's products? How immediately must a role contribute to their production in order to be treated as part of the industry? Does production include the cultivation of cotton? Is the entrepreneur "part" of the industry, or an external force with occasional influences on industrial organization? Are creditors part of the industry? Are engineering firms which supply fixed capital also units?

These questions demand that we establish appropriate definitional limits for the industry. Some limits will follow from the functional analysis of the industry; others must be established by referring to

21

the empirical peculiarities of the British cotton industry between 1770 and 1840. Even if we answer these questions satisfactorily, another, more troublesome set arises. Are we not studying the *change* of units over time? Are we not forced to identify new units each time the industry changes its structure? Suppose one role disappears and several new ones appear; can the industry still be discussed in the same terms? The functional analysis of the industry will clarify some of these problems. The theory of structural differentiation, or the principles of *how* the roles change, should clarify still more. The exact identification of units will unfold, therefore, as we analyse the cotton industry and its dynamics.

The Functional Analysis of an Industry. "The object of all industry is the production of goods, or to be more explicit, of articles of consumption which are not directly provided by nature."[1] The goal of any specific industry is to add value to its typical products. For the cotton industry in our period, therefore, the industrial goal is the *control over those processes which begin (in terms of value-added) with the acquisition of raw cotton and end with the marketing of cotton cloth.* Empirically these processes include the preparation—such as slubbing, carding, and roving—spinning, and weaving. The activities, roles, and/or organizations controlling the production of value at these various stages constitute the industry's *goal-attainment sub-system* (C_G). Within this sub-system there are several elements such as decisions to produce, budgeting for production, and co-ordination of production. In Appendix A we shall discuss the analytical relations among these elements. Finally, the C_G sub-system forms one of the bases for differentiated activities, roles, and organizations. Since the cotton industry has many products and several stages of value-added,[2] we should expect roles to proliferate to a greater degree than in industries like open-face coal mining, which has more homogeneous products and fewer preparatory stages.

To characterize an industrial goal raises several general problems. Empirically the units of an industry do not coincide with the analytical categories exactly. To illustrate this point, let us consider the educational system for a moment. Empirically this concept refers to an aggregate of schools, academies, and institutes. These units form a social system whose primary goal is to transmit the culture's cognitive elements. Glaring cut-off problems appear at once, however. The school system does not exhaust the society's educational

[1] P. Mantoux, *The Industrial Revolution in the Eighteenth Century* (London, 1955), p. 25. The theoretical basis for considering production to be the goal of the economy is developed in Parsons and Smelser, *Economy and Society*, pp. 20–25.
[2] Below, pp. 51–2 and 57–8.

system; the family, churches, industries, government, peer groups, etc., all educate. In analysing concrete problems, however, we generally select an aggregate of roles and organizations with educational *primacy* and ignore the rest.

In the case of the cotton industry, to exclude various border-line activities is in one way not justified, because we exclude some "industry" which contributes value to textile products. When faced with problems of historical analysis, however, one must isolate an empirical clustering of roles, activities, and collectivities governed *primarily* by this goal. To establish cut-off points is, again, not completely arbitrary. To eliminate spinning from the industry by some quick gesture would influence the validity of any subsequent conclusions. Activities judged to be secondary must *be* secondary, or else the treatment of the industry as a social system becomes useless.

With this principle in mind, I should like to exclude the following activities from our definition of the cotton industry: (1) The problem of hybrid products disappears about the beginning of our period. From 1735, when an Act of Parliament (9 Geo. II, c. 4) permitted the manufacture of mixed cotton-linen products but not pure cotton, the linen and cotton industries were closely linked. A common combination was linen warp and cotton weft. With the introduction of spinning machinery in the late eighteenth century, cotton yarn became hard enough for warp, and cotton-linen mixtures dwindled into insignificance. (2) By-products, scraps, cotton waste, etc., are relatively unimportant, so their elimination poses no difficult problems.[1] (3) For some purposes, cotton cultivation may be treated as part of the industry, especially if manufacturers engage in cotton cultivation themselves, as in India or Egypt before industrialization. Since all of Britain's cotton was imported, and since vertical integration controlling cultivation was absent, it is convenient to treat the acquisition of raw cotton stocks as a cut-off point for the industry. (4) The tailoring and dressmaking industries contribute a stage in the "value-added" process. Since, however, the assembly of garments was organized separately from textile manufacturing during our period, we exclude tailoring and the domestic cloth industry. (5) The timber, brick, iron, and engineering industries supplied the industry's fixed capital. Since they supplied other industries as well, it is inappropriate to include them in the cotton industry. I shall refer in passing, however, to changes in the engineering industry which can be linked to the cotton industry. (6) We must exclude, finally, the

[1] Not until the late nineteenth century was cotton waste devoted to a separate manufacture. Certainly its production was negligible in our period. T. Thornely, *Cotton Waste, Its Production, Manipulation, and Uses* (London, 1912), pp. 1–3.

finishing processes such as bleaching, dyeing, and printing. Since these operations often were separate from textile production, their omission is not too serious.

The adaptive sub-system of a social system involves the procurement of generalized facilities for the attainment of a plurality of goals. For an industry, as for the entire economy,[1] these facilities coincide with the concept of *capital*. Capital, which is a major factor in industrial productivity, permits more flexible adaptation of output at different times and in different market conditions. The roles, activities, and organizations dealing with the acquisition and control of capital comprise the adaptive sub-system of the cotton industry (C_A). The elements of this sub-system—fixed, working, and fluid capital, as well as the co-ordination of these types—are discussed in Appendix A.

Capital in cotton textiles was moderately intensive, at least from 1770 to 1840—more so than in agriculture as a rule, but less so than in producers' goods industries such as iron. Second, cotton products are semi-durable—more so than perishables or services, but less so than steel goods. This permits the storage of working capital (and consequently commodity speculation and inventory cycles). Third, because cotton is not cultivated in the British Isles and was imported from great distances, roles tended to proliferate around the acquisition and control of stocks of raw cotton.

An industry's integrative sub-system concerns its *organization* (C_I), or the roles controlling the combination of the factors of production. Above all this involves the problem of entrepreneurship—the introduction of new products, new types of organization, new techniques, new markets, etc.[2] Naturally the integrative sub-system is important for any study of industrial *re*organization, of which structural differentiation is one type. In Appendix A we shall outline the components of the C_I sub-system.

The goal-attainment, adaptive, and integrative sub-systems deal with decisions to produce, decisions to capitalize, and decisions to organize, respectively. The latency sub-system (C_L) implements these decisions; hence we term this sub-system "technical production." Most of its roles (e.g., workers, foremen, even plant managers) involve little responsibility for higher-level decisions. While it is incorrect to identify the latency function with specific social structures, "technical production" is roughly coterminous with the activities at the industry's "plant" level. The latency sub-system thus

[1] Parsons and Smelser, *Economy and Society*, p. 25.
[2] J. A. Schumpeter, *Theory of Economic Development* (Cambridge, Mass., 1934), p. 66.

24

provides a foundation of lower-level "processes" which exercise controls over many roles in the industry. For this reason we call the C_L sub-system latent. Its components are analysed in Appendix A.

Several conditions which influence C_G also influence C_L. The heterogeneity of products and the several stages of value-added make for an extensive segmentation of roles, which in turn creates delicate problems of integration and co-ordination. As we shall see, dissatisfactions with imbalances of productivity among these stages initiated many of the structural changes in the British cotton industry.

These sub-systems—control of production (C_G); procurement of capital facilities (C_A); control of industrial organization (C_I); and

FIGURE 4

THE FUNCTIONAL DIMENSIONS OF INDUSTRY C

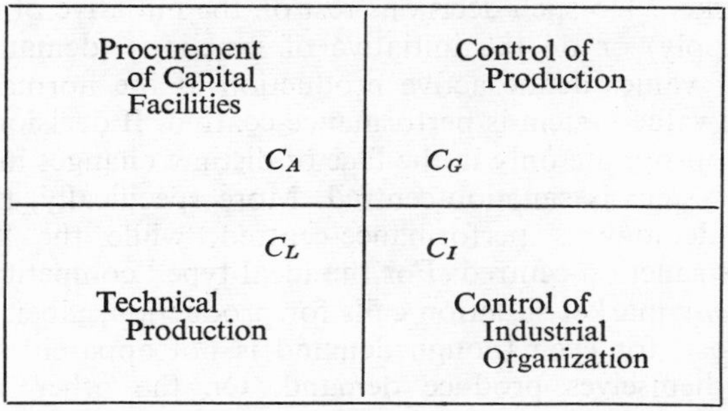

Procurement of Capital Facilities C_A	Control of Production C_G
C_L Technical Production	C_I Control of Industrial Organization

technical production (C_L)—are the four functional dimensions of Industry C. Figure 4 shows them graphically. They are the bases upon which the industry's concrete units—firms, workers, managers, entrepreneurs, etc.—are classified, described, and analysed. These sub-systems also constitute the broad bases for classifying the *dissatisfactions* with the performance of roles, dissatisfactions which are crucial in the genesis of social change.

Each sub-system shown in Figure 4 is a social system in itself. In Appendix A we shall dissect each into functional sub-systems and outline the relationships among them. Such an elaboration will provide us with a more detailed basis for classifying dissatisfactions and outlining the probable directions of subsequent structural change. Because of the technical nature of this analysis of sub-systems, we relegate it to an appendix.

Because C_G^-, C_A, C_I, and C_L are social systems in themselves, each is governed by a value-system. Among other things, these values define the conditions under which it is appropriate to express approval or dissatisfaction with the ways in which each system is operating. Without outlining the empirical content of any value-system, I should like to specify one dimension of all value-systems which is important in the discussion of social change. Any value-system places legitimate action at some point between two poles: *performance-centred* and *sanction-centred*. The defining characteristic of this dimension is the degree to which social action should be responsive to external sanctions. If a value-system is sanction-centred, performance is dependent only on the cognizance of definite and explicit sanctions from outside; if it is performance-centred, performance of the system's function is appropriate over a wider range of sanctions. Let us apply this general dimension to each industrial sub-system:

C_G. Control of production. On what basis should products be put on the market? Do such decisions rest on the initiative of industrial agents (supply) or on the initiative of sanctions (demand) in the market? If values define active production as the normal state of affairs, the value-system is performance-centred. If decisions to produce are appropriate only in the face of distinct changes in demand, the value-system is sanction-centred. More specifically, the "competitive" ideology is performance-centred, while the "security" ideology is sanction-centred. For the ideal-type "competitive" businessman, *any* market situation calls for production, albeit at lowest possible cost, for even though demand is not apparent, low-price products themselves produce demand. On the other hand, the "security-minded" businessman assumes that unless changes in demand are forthcoming, it is safer to maintain or reduce production. Furthermore, once sanctions are perceived, this businessman simply adjusts his production, taking care not to overstep the change in demand. Empirically, of course, value-systems lie between the extremes of this dimension.

Such a value-dimension does not, in any narrow sense, *determine* the entire performance of C_G. It defines the criteria for assessing and criticizing its performance. Furthermore, if defective performance is evident, the value-system suggests the broad lines for modifying roles and organizations.

C_A. Procurement of capital facilities. The value-system for capitalization also may be placed on a dimension with performance-centred and sanction-centred extremes. A ready example of the latter is the "conservative" approach to financing, which calls for traditional rates of depreciation, and traditional methods of advancing funds, and capitalization only under obvious conditions. At the other extreme, the emphasis is not on "what is required" by some objective situation, but on the initiative of investors. A "flexible" approach calls for capital commitment, speculative build-up of stocks, heavy credit assumption, and readiness to manoeuvre with capital resources. This value-dimension provides criteria for judging capitalization to be satisfactory or unsatisfactory, and hence for initiating or inhibiting structural change in the control of capitalization.

C_I. Control of industrial organization. If the emphasis is on external market demands for improving products, the integrative values are sanction-centred—to maintain and protect the existing arrangements for production. This implies little exploitation of anticipated demand and little response to actual demand. The performance-centred extreme legitimizes the reorganization of resources even in the absence of a clear demand for new or better products.

C_L. Technical production. The performance-centred extreme is close to the "rationality" attitude, which leads to continuous improvement of the means of production, even though obvious sanctions are absent. On the other hand, the "traditionalistic" or sanction-centred pole implies a reluctance to change the methods of production.[1]

Because Industry C is a social system, it maintains certain relationships with the *external* social environment. Of these relationships I shall consider only one—that related most closely to the family economy—and I shall merely mention the others.[2]

The industrial goal (C_G) is to control the production of cotton goods and services. At the external boundary of C_G there is one primary output and one primary input. The output is cotton textile products to be sold in the market. The major input is labour services which are solicited or commanded by those responsible for decisions to produce. Each of these "exchangeables" is sanctioned by money payments; cotton textiles are sold for money, and labour services are offered for wage payment. The following interchange results:

	Cotton Textile Products	
	←	
	Price Payments →	
Households	← Wage Payments	C_G
	Labour Services to Industry →	

[1] This is similar to Max Weber's contrast between "traditionalistic" and various kinds of "rational" behaviour. *The Theory of Social and Economic Organization* (London, 1947), pp. 105–7. Weber's dimension, with appropriate modification, applies at several levels and hence overlaps with the dimension of performance-centred vs. sanction-centred.

[2] For a detailed examination of the economy's external boundaries, cf. Parsons and Smelser, *Economy and Society*, pp. 46–79.

What is the external environment with which the industry exchanges? What are the units? In economic theory households purchase goods and services and offer labour services to the economy. Households or families are units which specialize in transmitting cultural patterns through socialization and the management of individual tensions. Hence the household specializes in the pattern-maintenance and tension-management sub-system of society as a whole,[1] and the above interchange links units of the industry with units—primarily households—of the latency sub-system of society.

Certain consequences follow from the fact that the interchanges involve a particular industry. If we consider the two sub-interchanges at the level of the economy as a whole, it is possible to link the two by some relatively simple function. For instance, the Keynesian consumption function is a series of ratios between the level of wages and the level of spending at different wage-levels.[2] Such a function is inapplicable to a single industry; an increase in wages of textile workers need not lead to a significant increase in the demand for cotton products. For present purposes, therefore, I consider the wage-level of a single industry to be virtually independent of the level of consumer demand for the same industry.[3]

Cotton textiles are by and large non-luxury, with the exception of laces, delicate prints, etc. Furthermore, by virtue of cotton's use in garments, bedclothes, etc., the product is relatively divisible. Hence one would expect somewhat less severe fluctuations in demand for cotton goods than in demand for luxury products such as silk, consumer durables such as carriages, or capital goods such as ships.

A large export market in our period also complicates the C_G boundary. Some have judged the rise of the cotton industry between

[1] Parsons, Bales, and Shils, *Working Papers in the Theory of Action*, pp. 264–7; Parsons and Smelser, *Economy and Society*, pp. 53–5. Families do not, of course, exhaust the latency system of society. Educational and religious institutions have this primacy as well. See Chapter VIII for further discussion of the family economy and its functions.

[2] J. M. Keynes, *General Theory of Employment, Interest, and Money* (London, 1936), Chapters 8, 9.

[3] I assume this even when an industry plays a major role in the economy, as did the cotton industry itself in the 1770–1840 period. William Radcliffe, writing in 1828, noted, " . . . cotton has attained a decided pre-eminence over every other substance . . . and by magnitude of its manufacture, must now justly rank as the staple trade of this kingdom . . . the fluctuations of this gigantic manufacture naturally tend to raise or depress not merely every other species of manufacture, but even the whole property of the kingdom which is at all times more or less affected by the prosperity or depression of the cotton trade." *Origin of the New System of Manufacture* (Stockport, 1828), p. 9.

1793 and 1811 to be "largely dependent" on a rapid increase of exports.[1] While the upward trend of exports levelled later, the foreign market continued to be important for the industry.

The industry's adaptive boundary (C_A) deals with the supply of credit and the corresponding control of the industry's productivity by banks, governmental agencies, or other bodies with "political" primacy. The third major boundary (C_I) deals with the supply of industrial organization through entrepreneurship and the creation of new or improved products through the recombination of the factors of production. I shall refer to these latter two boundaries only casually in this study.

Structural Differentiation in the Industry. At the outset, let us fill the empty boxes of the seven steps outlined in the last chapter with terms appropriate to Industry C. Industrial differentiation proceeds, therefore, by the following steps:

(1) Dissatisfaction with the productive achievements of the industry or its relevant sub-sectors and a sense of opportunity in terms of the potential availability of adequate facilities to reach a higher level of productivity.

(2) Appropriate symptoms of disturbance in the form of "unjustified" negative emotional reactions and "unrealistic" aspirations on the part of various elements in the population.

(3) A covert handling of these tensions and a mobilization of motivational resources for new attempts to realize the implications of the existing value-system.

(4) Encouragement of the resulting proliferation of "new ideas" without imposing specific responsibility for their implementation or for "taking the consequences."

(5) Positive attempts to reach specification of the new ideas which will become the objects of commitments by entrepreneurs.

(6) "Responsible" implementation of innovations carried out by persons or collectivities assuming the role of entrepreneurs, either rewarded by entrepreneurial profit or punished by financial failure, depending on consumers' acceptance or rejection of the innovations.

(7) Gains resulting from innovation are consolidated by their acceptance as part of the standard of living and their incorporation into the routine functions of production.

What does this model say? In general it states that when the division of labour becomes more complex, it follows a course in time outlined by the seven steps. As it stands, however, the model reveals little about the development of the British cotton industry between

[1] A. D. Gayer, W. W. Rostow, and A. J. Schwartz, *The Growth and Fluctuation of the British Economy, 1790–1850* (Oxford, 1953), p. 767.

29

1770 and 1840. We must discuss each step in detail; and most important, we must hold the model against the complex history of these decades to test its ability to account for observable changes in social structure.

First let us ask a number of formal questions about the model. What is the relationship between the seven analytical steps and time? Must the sequence be complete, or are "fits and starts," "regressions," "skipped steps," etc., possible? Does one sequence follow another in neat order, or do several sequences overlap or occur simultaneously? What are the units which differentiate? How is structural differentiation related to the functional analysis of Industry *C*?

The seven steps do not proceed in an orderly sequence, each appearing for a period, then disappearing to make way for the next. When the disturbances of Step 2 appear, for instance, the dissatisfactions of Step 1, which give rise to these disturbances, certainly do not disappear. Nor do they vanish when the symptoms of disturbance are "handled and channelled." The dissatisfactions persist, at least in part, until the system changes sufficiently to remove the initial disturbing conditions. Further, though the symptoms of disturbance in Step 2 apparently disappear during the "handling and channelling," their reappearance is probable until the original sources of dissatisfaction are removed or modified.

Figure 5 represents the relationship between the analytical steps of structural differentiation and simple time. The units on the vertical axis refer to phenomena corresponding to the seven analytical steps. Thus 1 is a certain level of dissatisfaction; 2 is a related set of symptoms of disturbance; 3 refers to the handling and channelling of this disturbance; and so on. The solid horizontal lines indicate the manifest appearance of these types of phenomena in time; the dotted horizontal lines indicate that the phenomena are latent but likely to reappear in the case of a renewal or augmentation of dissatisfaction. On the horizontal axis seven hypothetical periods of time are indicated. The dissatisfactions of Step 1 continue until the sixth or seventh step, when concrete differentiations appear. Symptoms of disturbance of Step 2 appear *after* the dissatisfaction is apparent, i.e., in the second period of time, but they disappear in Period 3 under the influence of handling and managing. As long as dissatisfaction is felt, however, both the disturbances and the methods of handling are likely to reappear. Again, Step 4 appears after the disturbances have been channelled. After providing new ideas it recedes into the background, ready to reappear, however, if the earlier steps recur. The same holds for Step 5; its point of incidence is not until Period 5, and it tends to disappear after this time, though it may reappear under the appropriate conditions. Step 6, which overlaps empirically with both Steps 5 and 7, appears at first in Period 6. The original dissatisfactions tend to disappear during Step 7, presumably because the original "sore spots" of the social structure have been modified during the course of structural differentiation.

Thus regression is possible, even likely, during a sequence of structural differentiation. For instance, if a sequence has reached Step 4 or 5, and some crisis exaggerates the original sources of dissatisfaction, an explosive regression back to the disturbances of Step 2 is probable.

FIGURE 5

THE RELATIONSHIP BETWEEN STEPS IN STRUCTURAL DIFFERENTIATION AND UNITS OF TIME

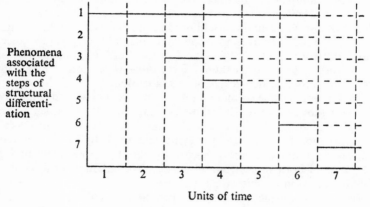

Units of time

These symptoms of disturbance must be handled and channelled anew to overcome the sources of dissatisfaction. We shall illustrate the phenomenon of regression in connection with the industrial revolution in cotton and the reorganization of the working-class family.

A sequence of differentiation also may be truncated. If the initial dissatisfactions are minor, the more explosive Steps 2 and 3 may not appear at all. Further, if channels for expressing disturbance are well institutionalized, uncontrolled outbursts may not be so apparent. Even further, when roles are institutionalized for the purpose of initiating change, dissatisfaction is often conveyed directly to the incumbents of these roles; only if they fail to establish new methods are symptoms of disturbance likely to appear. Thus we shall find

31

instances of regression (repeating steps) and truncation (skipping steps) under the appropriate historical conditions.

Since history cannot be controlled as in a laboratory, several more complexities arise in historical analysis. Because many sources of dissatisfaction are possible, several sequences of structural differentiation occur simultaneously. If we can pin-point the starting points of dissatisfaction, however, and identify the expected types of sequences, the analytical model may unravel such complex phenomena as industrial development and family reorganization. Further, what appears to be one sequence of differentiation may be a compound of several sequences resulting from a plurality of dissatisfactions. As we shall see, the appearance of the factory system concealed several distinct processes of differentiation.

The units which differentiate are sets of activities such as entrepreneurial innovation, distinct roles such as manager and worker, and distinct collectivities such as factories, trade unions, boards of directors, etc. These units should not be confused with the functional bases of the industry. It is not "control of capital" (C_A), for instance, which differentiates from "technical production" (C_L) in the rise of the factory system; rather these are the *dimensions* along which concrete units move to new levels of specialization.

Having noted these formal qualifications, we may now outline one complete sequence of structural differentiation. Not all sequences are complete or successful, of course. If at any step the mechanisms fail —e.g., if the "handling" of the symptoms of disturbance is inadequate—the sequence barely leaves the ground. We shall find a multitude of both successful and unsuccessful attempts at structural differentiation in the historical material.

Step 1. Dissatisfaction with the productive achievements of the industry or its relevant sub-sectors and a sense of opportunity in terms of the availability of adequate facilities to reach a higher level of industrial productivity. This initial step poses several questions. To what "social environment" are the industry's productive achievements related? By what criteria are these achievements judged satisfactory or unsatisfactory? What are the specific foci at which the dissatisfactions are felt? What are the possibilities of adjusting *within* the existing industrial framework, i.e., without structural change? What is meant by "opportunity" and "facilities"?

The industry's goals are defined in terms of the *relation* between industrial performance and the market demand for this performance.[1] The market conditions, since they constitute the major "environ-

[1] For the relational basis of production, see Parsons and Smelser, *Economy and Society*, pp. 20–21.

ment" for an industry, must be assessed when analysing a sequence of structural change. Particularly important are recent changes in demand which exert pressure on industrial capacity.

Simply to outline the conditions of demand, however, is not sufficient. There must exist criteria whereby demand is felt to be significant for industrial performance. Unresponsiveness to demand is a familiar concept to economists of imperfect competition and underdeveloped economies. Whether changes in the market are felt to be significant depends largely on the industry's value-system. It will be recalled that four industrial value-sub-systems were isolated— valuation of production, of capitalization, of innovation, and of implementation. Unless there is a substantial emphasis on the performance-oriented pole of one or more of these dimensions, dissatisfaction with the performance patterns themselves is not likely, even in the face of changes in demand.

Once these preconditions are determined, we must then classify certain *structural foci* in the industry toward which dissatisfaction is directed. I should like to classify these foci of dissatisfaction in terms of the use of industrial *resources*. I shall use a conceptual scheme developed previously in action theory.[1] These foci are also classifiable in terms of *roles*, i.e., the social units which control the resources. In Appendix B we shall show the formal parallels between dissatisfactions with the use of resources and dissatisfactions with role-performance. At present, however, we shall speak only in terms of resources.

Society is endowed with four general types of resources: (1) values by which social action is legitimized (L); (2) motivation of individual actors (G); (3) facilities which actors utilize (A); (4) integration (or cohesion, or solidarity) by which the interaction among actors is assured (I). Before these resources can be put to use in concrete collectivities such as firms, bureaucracies, families, and voluntary associations, they must be shaped into appropriate form for each collectivity. It is convenient to view this shaping process in terms of a *hierarchy of diminishing generality of resources*. At the most general level the resources are "unproductive," because they are too fluid to be utilized concretely. For instance, one cannot consider "motivation" in general to be a practical resource; it must be motivation *to do something*. By means of a number of stages, however, these general resources undergo greater and greater specification until ready to be incorporated into definite action.

To illustrate: "Labour" is one of the economic factors of production. Yet labour does not spring into finished form automatically.

---

[1] *Ibid.*, pp. 119–23 and 133–9.

33

It must be "conditioned" outside the economy before it can perform in accordance with economic requirements. At the most general level there must be a basic motivation to adhere to role expectations; we might call this "socialized motivation" (*G*). Second, this generalized motivation must be attached to definite areas of competence; at this point the motivation to labour is in a state of "generalized performance capacity." Third, in addition to this capacity, the individual must acquire requisite skills and abilities for appropriate roles; at this point he possesses "trained capacity." Only at the next (fourth) level is the individual able to offer his services to the economy and thereby assume "membership in the labour force." Still, labour is not in the limited sense "productive," for the labourer must be hired by firms (the fifth level of particularization), assigned to roles within firms (the sixth level), and assigned to tasks within the context of his role (the seventh and lowest level). Only after these stages of diminishing generality is the factor of labour in full readiness to perform economic tasks.

Figure 6 shows the seven levels of generality for the factors of labour (*G*), capital (*A*), and organization (*I*). Because values (*L*)[1] are assumed to be stable during a sequence of structural differentiation—and hence are not restructured—they are omitted from the series of diminishing generality. The figure also shows the nature of the transitions between each level. In the case of facilities (*A*), the most general level is a number of presumptions about the "given data" of the empirical world. These presumptions determine which elements of the real world are built into a system of language, cultural preferences, etc. In order for these presumptions to be brought to bear on specific problems, they must be codified into principles (second level), which are applied to technological problems (third level). In the next transformation, this technological know-how is attached to generalized purchasing power—usually liquid funds—in order to procure capital resources (fourth level).[2] This capital must be invested in firms (fifth level) and transformed into particular capital goods (sixth level), which are set to work in productive tasks (seventh level).

At the most general level, organization (*I*) is defined as a balance between self-interested action and action in the interest of some collectivity. Given a basic commitment to the latter, however, certain other specifications of the nature of organization must be made. Two of the most important are the kind of hierarchy and the kind of

[1] The fourth factor, land, is associated with relatively stable value commitments. *Ibid.*, pp. 25–6.
[2] *Ibid.*, pp. 131–2.

qualitative differentiation of effort to be pursued within the collectivity (second level).[1] Further (level three), the major situation for organized action must be specified. Should it deal with impersonal elements of the environment or with human relations primarily? Should it be oriented primarily to the maintenance of cultural traditions or to organizational responsibility? At this level the

FIGURE 6

THE LEVELS OF GENERALITY OF LABOUR, CAPITAL,
AND ORGANIZATION

Level	G (*Motivation*)	A (*Facilities*)	I (*Organization*)
1	Socialized motivation	Cultural presumptions regarding the "given data" of empirical world	Primary commitment to collectivities as such (self-collectivity balance)
	[Specification of motivational or cultural goals]		
2	Generalized performance capacity	Codified empirical knowledge ("science")	Organizational principles of hierarchy and qualitative differentiation
	[Specification and definition of situational objects]		
3	Trained capacity	Technological know-how	Organizational goals: cultural vs. organizational responsibility and impersonal vs. human relations
	[Assignment of economic significance to resources]		
4	Membership in labour force (labour)	Generalized purchasing power (capital)	Economic organization (entrepreneurship)
	[Commitment of resources to organizations]		
5	Commitment to firm (employment)	Investment in particular firms	Patterns of resource allocation (contract)
	[Differentiation of categories within organizations]		
6	Functions within firm (division of labour)	Acquisition of capital goods	Patterns of responsibility (authority)
	[Definition of and adjustment to situational exigencies]		
7	Task utilization of labour	Task utilization of capital goods	Operative rules for task utilization

general category of "organization" has been specified sufficiently to be available for concrete collectivities. For the economy it is available as entrepreneurial effort (fourth level). Once within the economy, the entrepreneurs undertake to specify patterns of resource allocation (fifth level), patterns of authority (sixth level), and various

[1] These two dimensions are the basic axes on which the family, as a small group, is based. Parsons, Bales, *et al.*, *Family, Socialization and Interaction Process*, Chapter II.

operative rules whereby tasks may be more or less harmoniously performed (seventh level).

Levels one, two, three, and four will provide a set of reference points to characterize the *re*structuring of resources during a sequence of structural differentiation. For the moment, however, we shall classify only the foci of dissatisfactions with resources *within* the industry. Using levels five, six, and seven for the bases of classification, the dissatisfactions resolve into the following nine types:

A-5. Investment. Dissatisfaction may arise in connection with the mode of transferring funds to the firm. Particular empirical foci of the dissatisfaction include too high payment of interest, unsatisfactory conditions of return, too high a degree of risk, etc.

A-6. Capital goods. As the capital goods are committed to more concrete forms, there may be dissatisfaction over the type of fixed or working capital. There may also arise dissatisfaction with the terms of exchange in acquiring these goods.

A-7. Task utilization of capital goods. While the transactions of acquiring capital goods may be satisfactory, there may arise concern over the utilization of capital goods for purposes of production. This may involve dissatisfactions over standards of performance, rates of depreciation, or adaptability of the capital goods to a number of tasks.

G-5. Employment. Dissatisfaction may be either in terms of the level of remuneration or in terms of conditions of labour such as the length and kind of contract under which the labour services are being offered.

G-6. Labour roles within the firm. There may arise dissatisfactions with the distribution of roles within organizations. Examples of such dissatisfactions would be the improper performance of some function (such as sales), the overloading of one role with too many functions, etc.

G-7. Utilization of labour in tasks. Concern may arise in connection with the performance within the role context, e.g., with the quality of skill and performance of the labourer.

I-5. Allocation of resources within the industry. Examples of such dissatisfactions include disparities of productivity in various branches of the industry, the withholding of liquid funds from investment, monopolistic restraints on the utilization of resources, etc.

I-6. Patterns of responsibility. Important foci of dissatisfaction include the overloading of certain roles with too much authority, the improper enforcement of authority, resistance against authority, etc.

I-7. Operative rules for task performance. There may be dissatisfactions with the ways in which men and capital resources are co-

ordinated on the task level, for instance, in the liaison between foremen and workmen, among workmen, etc.

We shall illustrate these dissatisfactions concretely in the chapters
which follow. Let us note at the moment that every dissatisfaction
has three components: (*a*) specific value-criteria; (*b*) a dissatisfaction
at specific points in the industrial structure; (*c*) a market context.
The value-criteria must be relevant primarily to the industry, and not
some other social system. For instance, while labourers might be dis-
satisfied with the conditions of the job (too long hours, too hard
work, etc.) we would *not* include this as a dissatisfaction with industrial productivity, because it refers to another set of values—those
of tension-management and pattern-maintenance, probably within
the family of the worker.

These nine foci of dissatisfaction are not independent of each
other. As one reads *across* in Figure 6, i.e., labour, capital, and
organization, dissatisfaction with labour implies some dissatisfaction with the organization of resources, and hence with capital.
Thus, dissatisfaction with one factor implies a dissatisfaction with
the others.[1] Proceeding *down* the hierarchy, however, there is a
possibility of dissatisfaction with the operative tasks of labour, for
instance, without any necessary dissatisfaction over the method of
recruiting labour. But dissatisfaction with the latter implies dissatisfaction with the use of labour. Generalizing these relationships,
we may say that higher-level dissatisfactions imply lower-level
dissatisfactions, but not vice versa.

Given this interdependence of levels, of what use are the nine
separate categories? By breaking the several resources into several
levels, we may speak of the *salience* of certain dissatisfactions, even
though these might imply dissatisfactions elsewhere in the industrial
structure. By isolating the salient dissatisfactions, furthermore, we
may gather clues as to the probable directions of subsequent
sequences of differentiation.

Dissatisfactions may be cushioned by the flexibility of existing
institutional arrangements. Thus, sheer exertion and longer hours can
alter production somewhat; a few more labourers can be recruited
at short notice; credit reserves can be lowered, and so on. These
adjustments, however, all of which stop short of structural change,
provide only temporary relief to the industry in times of pressure, but
cannot yield long-term solutions.

[1] Bert F. Hoselitz outlined this interlocking effect among factors in a pamphlet
written in 1956 in connection with the Social Science Research Council Conference on the Role of the State in Economic Growth: *Economic Policy and Economic
Development*, p. 6.

Always accompanying the dissatisfactions must be a general prospect that facilities are available to attack the sources of dissatisfaction. This promise usually means an availability of credit and encouragement from those who control the extension of credit.

Step 2. Symptoms of disturbance in the form of "unjustified" negative emotional reactions and "unrealistic" aspirations on the part of various elements of the population. Sooner or later, if dissatisfactions continue or increase and if the flexibility of the existing industrial structure reaches a limit, the structure "gives way" to symptoms of disturbance.

We may classify these symptoms with reference to Figure 6. When disturbance arises, social controls are broken; responses regress, as it were, to a more generalized level of behaviour. Thus we may read "up" the ladder of the levels of generality to trace the course of disturbances. Certain dissatisfactions with industrial performance may be overcome merely by tapping the existing resources of labour, capital, and organization at Level 4. On the other hand, perhaps new skills and knowledge are required; in this case the "regression" goes back to Level 3, from which it is brought "back down" to overcome the sources of dissatisfaction. In cases of serious dissatisfaction, however, responses generalize to the highest levels. In fact, we judge a response to be a "symptom of disturbance" in so far as it moves "beyond Level 1."

Three classic symptoms of disturbance are anxiety, aggression, and phantasy behaviour.[1] (*a*) Aggression is "unsocialized motivation," or the relaxation of the most primitive controls over behaviour (G-1); (*b*) Phantasy goes beyond the cultural definitions of the "given data" of the empirical world (A-1) in so far as there is a denial of certain elements, such as accepted means of attaining social goals, and a commitment to unacceptable elements, such as a belief in the impossible "if only" someone would do something; (*c*) Anxiety involves the diffuse fear that the person or group in question will be excluded from the social system altogether (I-1). Sometimes all these symptoms crystallize into a "movement," characterized by a deep pessimism about the present, unrealistic blame heaped on one individual or class (anxiety and aggression). On the other hand, there is frequently the promise of a paradise, often within the near future; its attainment frequently rests on one charismatic leader (phantasy and Utopia).

We are using the terms "unjustified" and "unrealistic" in a very restricted sense. By labelling behaviour in this way, we mean only

---

[1] Parsons, Bales, *et al.*, *Family, Socialization, and Interaction Process*, pp. 205–6.

that it is either misdirected or undirected *with regard to correcting the institutional conditions which give rise to it.* Thus we define these concepts in terms of our own assumptions concerning social behaviour and do not claim in any way that such behaviour is "unjustified," "unrealistic," or "wrong" *from all points of view.* We consider a Utopian phantasy which transforms institutional patterns magically to be unrealistic if, at the time it is produced, it is either undirected or misdirected as to appropriate means. This is not to say that the expression of this Utopia does not lead ultimately to the transformation of institutional structure. Indeed, the model of structural differentiation demonstrates how early "irrational" responses are eventually brought to bear successfully on the sources of dissatisfaction, but only after they are "handled and channelled" through several further stages. We consider aggression and anxiety to be unjustified if they are either so general as to be completely without objects or if they are directed at objects which are not responsible in any immediate sense for the sources of dissatisfaction. For all such behaviour, however, we must take it upon ourselves to demonstrate the unrealism or lack of justification in the light of available historical evidence.

Furthermore, by virtue of the presence of some deviance in all societies at all times, we may always locate a certain level of dissatisfaction and its accompanying disturbances. For any phenomena which we judge to be expressions of disturbance, therefore, we must trace an *appropriate symbolic relationship* between the phenomena and the set of conditions producing them. This may be done in two ways, both necessarily indirect: (*a*) by analysing the content of the symptoms of disturbance (e.g., what problems the Utopias "solve") and relating the content to social conditions; (*b*) by correlating the rise and fall of these symptoms with the social conditions which presumably give rise to them.

The criteria for defining a symptom of disturbance, therefore, are that it be sufficiently undirected or misdirected to be considered unrealistic; that its occurrence can be correlated with conditions which give rise to it; and that it bear a plausible symbolic relationship to these conditions.

Step 3. A covert process of handling these tensions and mobilizing motivational and other resources for new attempts to realize the implications of the existing value-system. Step 2 unleashes the unbridled energy of disturbance; Step 3 "brings it back into line." Aggression is brought back to the level of "socialized motivation" (*G*-1); anxiety is relieved by assurance of the basic security of the threatened person or group (*I*-1); and those committed to phantasies are encouraged to take account of the society's values and "given data" (*A*-1). These "holding operations" usually involve the police, the courts, religious leaders, and others specializing in social control.

Step 4. Encouragement of the resulting proliferation of "new ideas," without imposing specific responsibility for their implementation or for "taking the consequences." This step specifies more clearly the types of goals which must be pursued in order to erase or modify the initial sources of dissatisfaction. During this step, which corresponds to Level 2 of Figure 6, there is: (*a*) a specification of the sorts of motivation required to effect changes (*G*-2); (*b*) an encouragement to produce knowledge (*A*-2); and (*c*) speculation on the revision of authority and the division of labour required for some "new method" of production (*I*-2). The important element at this stage is that the authors of the ideas are not held responsible for implementing these contributions within the industrial structure itself. Hence the question of the "profitability" of the ideas from an economic standpoint has not arisen as yet. Rewards for promising ideas are prestige and honour, not profits.

Step 5. Positive attempts are made to reach specification of the new ideas which will become the objects of commitment by entrepreneurs. Empirically this stage is often indistinguishable from those steps immediately preceding and following. Analytically, however, Step 5 brings the resources to the threshold of commitment to production. Labour skills which are to be incorporated into the productive process are specified (*G*-3); technological possibilities are exploited (*A*-3); and the goals of proposed organizations are outlined (*I*-3).

Step 6. Positive and responsible implementation of innovation is carried out by persons or collectivities assuming the role of entrepreneurs. At this point the reorganized labour, capital, and organization are brought to bear on the industrial structure. The input of each factor is *new*, i.e., restructured by the mechanisms of Steps 1–5. The result of Step 6 is a *new level of differentiation of industrial roles* and consequently a *qualitatively new method of production*. During this step there is an extraordinary input not only of entrepreneurial activity but also of capital (*A*-4) and labour (*G*-4) as well. Wages will rise accordingly to attract labour on new terms, and if the industrial change is significant enough, the rate of interest will increase.

The following phenomena cluster in Step 6: attempts to improve the cost and quality of products by reorganizing the factors of production; reallocation of credit to new lines of investment; a jump in capitalization, as facilities are assembled; a jump in production; and extraordinary profits resulting from the gap in productivity between the old and new methods. This hive of activity begins, of course, only if the earlier steps have been successful. If not, entrepreneurs fail, and a "regression" to an earlier stage may occur.

Other things being equal, the salience of the new structural change parallels the salience of the dissatisfactions of Step 1. Thus the new methods focus at one or more of the following points: the structure of investment (*A*-5); the type of capital goods and the terms on which these are acquired (*A*-6); the utilization of capital in productive processes (*A*-7); the structure of the contract of labour (*G*-5); the allocation of roles within the firm (*G*-6); the utilization of labour in concrete tasks (*G*-7); the allocation of resources (*I*-5); the authority structure (*I*-6); and operative rules for the performance of tasks at the lower levels (*I*-7).

Step 7. Gains resulting from innovation are consolidated by their acceptance as part of the standard of living and their incorporation into the routine functions of production. This step marks the routinization of the new methods. As the new structure takes over the industry, the older elements are wiped out. The extraordinary rewards of Step 6 thus drop; wages find a somewhat lower level, profits level off, and perhaps the interest rate drops. Capitalization and innovation decrease sharply because of the "excess capacity" created in the previous step. Because of the productive advantages of the new structure, however, production may continue to climb during this step.[1] The routinization in Step 7, furthermore, does not mean that all is stabilized in the industry. The previous sequence of differentiation may create new disequilibria which touch off new sequences in other industrial sectors.

We may summarize the sequence of differentiation in two ways: (1) in terms of *roles*, older, more diffuse roles become the subject of dissatisfaction in the face of historical circumstances. After a period of general disturbance and social control, the dissatisfactions are harnessed and brought to bear on the problem of fashioning a new and more specialized social structure. (2) In terms of *resources*, the sequence begins with a perception that the existing organization of resources is inadequate for functioning in its new social environment. As these resources are restructured, they first generalize "up the ladder" of resources into a state of fluidity, from which they are worked gradually into the new social structure in a series of more specific steps.

Such are the relationships among the many phenomena involved in a single sequence of structural change. In abstract outline one

[1] J. A. Schumpeter, *Business Cycles* (New York, 1939), p. 254.

event follows another with neat regularity. When we apply the model to historical changes, the analytical neatness blurs. Wars, riots, strikes, embargoes, etc., elongate certain phases and truncate others. Furthermore, the recorded history frequently is not adequate for meeting all the requirements of this highly developed scheme. To illustrate the model, as well as its modifications in application, let us turn first to the industrial revolution in cotton.

APPENDIX A

THE INTERNAL ORGANIZATION OF INDUSTRY C

Functional Analysis. Let us now dissect the industry internally as outlined in the Appendix to Chapter II. *Each* industrial sub-system —C_G, C_A, C_I, and C_L—has goals, adaptive and integrative exigencies, and pattern-maintenance functions. These elements are in Figure 7, which parallels Figure 2. While the boxes of Social System S are empty, however, those of Industry C refer to a specific system.

C_G. Control of production. The character of C_G as a whole defines its *goal*, C_{G_g}.[1] Hence roles with C_{G_g} primacy specialize in decisions to produce goods and services. These roles assume many forms empirically—the independent producer, the master manufacturer, the cotton-spinning capitalist, the manager, the powerful consignee, etc. One object of this study is to outline how one such unit develops into more differentiated units.

The C_{G_a} sub-system allocates facilities to implement goal-oriented (C_{G_g}) decisions, particularly by *budgeting* available facilities among competing needs. In general, money or monetary commitments constitute the facilities for social systems with economic primacy.

Specialized roles in the C_{G_i} sub-system—"co-ordination of production"—smooth over conflicts which arise in the execution of production plans and assure relative harmony in the "policy" of the industry or its firms. Often these "liaison" roles are aspects of other roles in the C_G sub-system.

The value-system for C_G—one dimension of which has been discussed—refers most directly to the latency sub-system C_{G_l}. Roles in this latency cell assure a degree of conformity to these values and "handle" deviations with a minimum of disruption to the other processes in C_G. As such the latency cell constitutes a system of lower-level "processes," on which the C_G sub-system operates.

1 This is true for social systems in general, and not simply for an industrial system.

C_A. Procurement of capital facilities. C_{Ag}, the goal-attainment sub-system, includes the roles which control the industry's fixed and

FIGURE 7

DETAILED FUNCTIONAL ANALYSIS OF INDUSTRY C

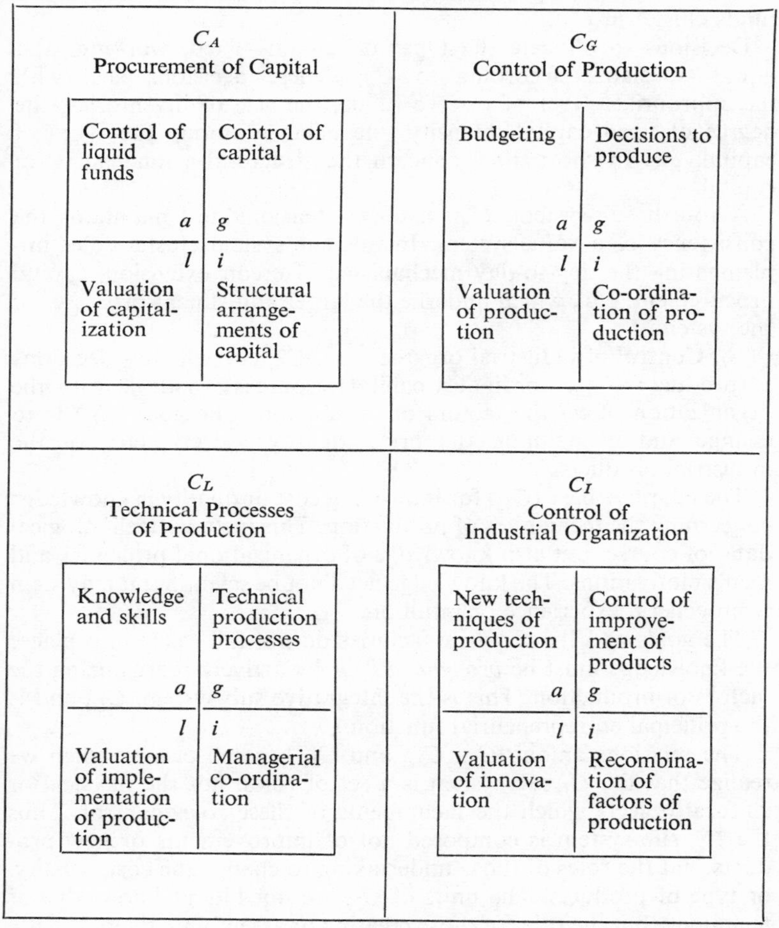

C_A Procurement of Capital		C_G Control of Production	
Control of liquid funds	Control of capital	Budgeting	Decisions to produce
a	*g*	*a*	*g*
l	*i*	*l*	*i*
Valuation of capitalization	Structural arrangements of capital	Valuation of production	Co-ordination of production

C_L Technical Processes of Production		C_I Control of Industrial Organization	
Knowledge and skills	Technical production processes	New techniques of production	Control of improvement of products
a	*g*	*a*	*g*
l	*i*	*l*	*i*
Valuation of implementation of production	Managerial co-ordination	Valuation of innovation	Recombination of factors of production

working capital at various levels. Functional analysis deals with *roles*, not bales of cotton or numbers of machines in any physical sense. While decisions to capitalize are followed by the appropriate

43

capital goods after a lag, we must distinguish between the two, since a social system is composed of roles and not physical objects.

In order to supply *various* capital needs, a level of more generalized resources, usually money, is required. Money can procure many types of capital—bales of cotton, power-looms, etc.—which are turned to particular productive tasks. Roles controlling such liquid funds cluster in C_{A_a}.

Decisions to allocate the types of capital—fixed, working, and liquid—specialize according to C_{A_i}. These decisions deal with the appropriate level of reserve funds, the size of inventories, the degree of fixed capital intensity, the balance among the types of capital, etc. In short, they concern the structural arrangements of capital.

A fourth sub-system, C_{A_l}, manages tensions and maintains the consistency of a value-system. In this sub-system cluster roles implementing the day-to-day mechanisms of credit extension, capital procurement, etc., which underlie the larger adjustment processes of the system.

C_I. Control of industrial organization. C_{G_i} co-ordinates decisions to produce; C_{A_i} co-ordinates capital resources. C_I deals with the organization of *all* the factors of production. The goal (C_{I_g}) is to change and/or maintain the price, quality, variety, etc., of the industrial products.

The adaptive base (C_{I_a}) for improving cost or quality is knowledge concerning the techniques of production. This includes technological data, of course, but also knowledge of organizational principles and men's motivations. The knowledge need not be scientific; it may stem from general experience or intuition.

The goals and the requisite facilities do not fall easily into place; the knowledge must be *brought to bear* by actively reorganizing the factors of production. This is the integrative sub-system, C_{I_i}, and is the principal entrepreneurial function.[1]

The relations among C_{I_g}, C_{I_a}, and C_{I_i} become clearer when we realize that the C_I sub-system is a set of roles, not the physical or cultural objects which the incumbents of these roles control. Thus the C_{I_g} sub-system is composed not of improvements or new products, but the roles of those undertaking to change the cost, quality, or type of products. The units of C_{I_g} are not bits of knowledge or technique, but the roles of those creating or assembling them. Finally the C_{I_i} sub-system is not the factors of production themselves, but the roles involved in their recombination. To view industrial organization as a social sub-system permits us to treat a variety of

[1] Schumpeter, *Theory of Economic Development*, pp. 74–94.

social structures as entrepreneurial—the individual innovator, the less colourful but diligent engineer, the government, the board of directors, etc.

C_L. Technical production. The C_L sub-system subsumes the productive processes which do not involve decisions to produce (C_G), decisions to modify the capital resources (C_A), or decisions to improve the cost-quality balance of products by means of industrial reorganization (C_I). The level of responsibility and control in this C_L sub-system is therefore low.

The goal (C_{Lg}) is composed of roles dealing with the immediate processes of production—the labourers and their supervisors who process the materials, run the machines, load goods for shipment, etc.

Adaptive facilities for these processes (C_{La}) are knowledge and skills applicable at the plant level, such as the mechanic's abilities. This sub-sector is not identical with C_{Ia}. In the latter the problem is to accumulate and generate principles; at the C_{La} level the problem is to apply these principles to the day-to-day processes of production.

The integrative sub-system (C_{Li}) might be termed managerial responsibility. Empirically such roles overlap with those in C_{Gi}. Analytically, however, they are separable; roles in C_{Gi} co-ordinate production at the *market* level, whereas those in C_{Li} operate at the *plant* level.

Boundary-interchanges. A second step in filling the empty boxes of Social System S is to introduce content into the boundary-interchanges. Figure 8—which parallels Figure 3—shows the following performance-sanction interchanges for Industry C:[1]

$C_{Gg}-C_{Ig}$, or the interchange between those responsible for decisions to produce and those responsible for changes in the cost or quality of products. Clearly the entrepreneur of C_{Ig} offers new opportunities for producing and marketing goods. In return he receives the profits realized by innovation. This interchange is between *roles*, not particular agents. Hence the introduction of new products for profits may involve an exchange between two individuals, between individual and firm, between two firms, between two departments of one firm, or indeed between two roles in the same individual, if he is simultaneously producer and innovator.

$C_{Ga}-C_{Aa}$, or the interchange between those responsible for budgeting funds and those responsible for the control of liquid funds available to the industry. By this interchange credit is allocated within the industry. The main contribution of holders of liquid funds

[1] Chapter II, Appendix, for a general outline of boundary-interchanges.

45

is to release them to potential producers. They receive in return certain "rights to intervene" in the supply of these funds, above all rights to withdraw them under specific conditions.[1]

FIGURE 8

INTERNAL BOUNDARY-INTERCHANGES OF INDUSTRY *C*

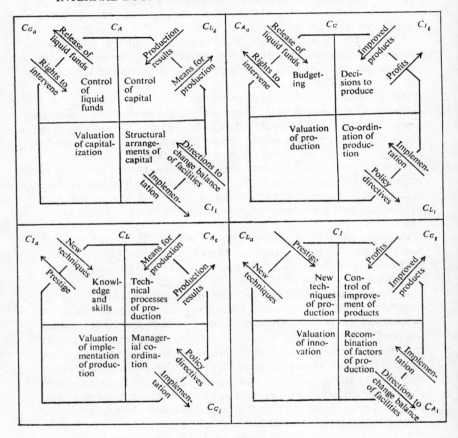

[1] This interchange is parallel to the general relationship between economy and polity. Parsons and Smelser, *Economy and Society*, pp. 56–64, 72–8. The C_{A_a}–C_{G_a} interchange, therefore, is a focus of political control within the industry.

46

$C_{G_i}-C_{L_i}$, or the interchange between those responsible for co-ordination of production at the market level and those responsible for co-ordination at the plant level. Even though this interchange occurs in an industrial context, it is not "economic" in so far as it deals with lines of authority. The co-ordinator of production (C_{G_i}) gives the manager (C_{L_i}) policy directives; in return the manager supervises at the plant level to implement these policies. In un-differentiated organizations the same individual is both "producer" and "manager", but middlemen in authority chains are common.

$C_{A_g}-C_{L_g}$, or the interchange between those in control of capital and those in control of technical production. This relationship is "give us the tools and we will do the job." Mere technical knowledge (C_{L_a}) and managerial co-ordination (C_{L_i}) do not produce goods and services without an input of material. This material is, of course, the industry's fixed and working capital. Those in control of this capital supply the means—raw materials, machines, etc.—for the "plant" (C_{L_g}) to transform the material and thereby achieve the desired pro-duction results.

We may clarify this interchange by recalling the definition of the C_L sub-system as production *processes*. Its major environment is *not* the market for industrial goods; that is the situation for C_G. The C_L sub-system is responsive to decisions taken in higher-level industrial sub-systems. Hence it is gauged to decisions to produce (C_G), decisions to alter the capital base (C_A), etc. Its members achieve pro-duction results when supplied with the appropriate orders ($C_{G_i}-C_{L_i}$), capital goods ($C_{A_g}-C_{L_g}$), and appropriate technical knowledge ($C_{I_a}-C_{L_a}$).

$C_{A_i}-C_{I_i}$, or the interchange between those responsible for the structural arrangements of capital and those responsible for the new combinations of the factors of production. Like $C_{G_i}-C_{L_i}$, this inter-change is primarily integrative; the elements of authority are out-standing. Entrepreneurs in C_{I_i} supply orders to modify the capital structure; in return a compliance is given.

$C_{L_a}-C_{I_a}$, or the interchange between those responsible for new techniques of production and those responsible for the application of these techniques at lower levels. As in the $C_{G_a}-C_{A_a}$ interchange, this is an exchange of facilities; in this case, however, the facilities are knowledge and information, not purchasing power. Inventors in C_{I_a} supply C_{L_a} with knowledge of the principles of production. Their reward is a kind of approval, in which monetary rewards play more the role of symbols of honour or prestige than the role of economic profits; profits accrue only when entrepreneurs apply these techniques to the modification of products.

THE RELATIONSHIP BETWEEN ROLES AND RESOURCES

Figure 6 shows how *resources* are incorporated into Industry C. Figure 8 shows the boundary-relationships, or the bases of inter-action for the *roles* which control these resources. In fact, the two categories are two aspects of the same industrial action. There is a point-for-point correspondence between the boundary-interchanges and the lower levels of generality of resources.

In the first place, Level 4 of the table of resources corresponds to the major *external* boundaries of the industry. The transition whereby a labourer becomes a member of the labour force (G-4) corresponds to the C_G external boundary, in which labour services are offered to the industry in return for wage payments. The transition which yields generalized purchasing power as capital (A-4) corresponds to the C_A external boundary, in which capital is supplied to the industry. And finally, organization (I-4) corresponds to the entrepreneur's offer to recombine resources for a profit at the C_I external boundary. The table of resources shows the status of resources; the boundary-interchanges state the principles of role-interaction which govern the flow of resources.

Once the resources are within the industry, there is a further correspondence between Levels 5 and 6 on the one hand, and the *internal* boundaries of the industry on the other, as follows:

I-5. Patterns of resource allocation. This level parallels the C_{Ii}–C_{Ai} boundary, at which decisions to recombine the factors of production are applied to the capital structure of the industry. Hence a dissatisfaction with the allocation of resources (I-5) is simultane-ously a dissatisfaction with the way in which this allocation is effected via the C_{Ii}–C_{Ai} boundary.

I-6. Patterns of authority. This level corresponds to authority patterns clustering at the C_{Gi}–C_{Li} boundary, which co-ordinates production at the market level with production at the plant level.

A-5. Investment in particular organizations. The boundary-interchange which controls capital at this level is C_{Ga}–C_{Aa}, or the offer of liquid funds for "rights to intervene." By this boundary, industrial capital is distributed among firms.

A-6. Acquisition of capital goods. This level corresponds to the boundary C_{Ag}–C_{Lg}, which brings the capital facilities closer to the production process. Those roles which control the acquisition of capital goods cluster at this boundary.

G-5. Commitment of labour services to specific organizations.

Those in control of production (C_{G_g}) allocate the labour services to productive endeavour in accordance with the composition of products in the industry (C_{I_g}). This involves the relationship between "decisions to produce" and "product composition" ($C_{G_g}-C_{I_g}$).

G-6. Allocation of labour within firms. This allocation depends above all on the techniques of production, which include knowledge of the division of labour, the motivation of men, etc., as well as material techniques. The internal division of labour, therefore, expresses the relationship between technological knowledge and its application at the plant level ($C_{I_a}-C_{L_a}$).

Finally at Level 7—task utilization of labour (*G*-7), task utilization of capital (*A*-5), and operative rules for task utilization (*I*-7)—the reference is primarily to the intralatency (C_L) level, at which the processes of production are performed.

The following correspondences thus hold between the table of resources and the boundary-relationships:

Resource-level	Boundary-interchange
I-5	$C_{I_i}-C_{A_i}$
I-6	$C_{G_i}-C_{L_i}$
I-7	Intra-C_L
A-5	$C_{G_a}-C_{A_a}$
A-6	$C_{A_g}-C_{L_g}$
A-7	Intra-C_L
G-5	$C_{G_g}-C_{I_g}$
G-6	$C_{I_a}-C_{L_a}$
G-7	Intra-C_L

Any concrete empirical dissatisfaction implies a dissatisfaction both with the *utilization of resources* and with the *roles responsible for controlling this utilization*. We shall observe this double reference when we consider the cotton industry and the family economy of its working classes.

CHAPTER IV

STRUCTURAL DIFFERENTIATION IN SPINNING

INTRODUCTION

In this and the next three chapters I shall implant the model of differentiation on the development of the British cotton industry between 1770 and 1840. The elements of this model are the organized roles of an industry, its value-system, dissatisfactions, symptoms of disturbance, handling and channelling, entrepreneurship, the gross movements of production, capitalization, innovation, profits, etc. To employ the empirical propositions developed in the last chapter is to account for the *direction of change* of these variables and their *temporal relationship to each other*.

Two features of the historical evidence complicate this task. First, the data are inadequate. Quantitative indices of production and capitalization, to say nothing of innovations, are absent, especially for the late eighteenth century; usually we must accept questionable substitutes. For profits, dissatisfactions, disturbances, etc., only qualitative evidence such as verbal testimony is available. Second, this evidence conceals many simultaneous processes. To cite one example, we shall use raw cotton consumption as an index of production; this is sometimes the only available index. Some of the empirical propositions, however, require the isolation of the components of total production, such as the production of muslins, calicoes, power-loom cloth, etc., which the figures of cotton consumption do not reveal. In such instances we shall rely on plausible movements of the general indices, and strengthen or weaken our impressions by other indirect evidence.

To interpret the facts of this period raises the inevitable question of the historical status of these facts. Did they occur, and if so, were they correctly recorded? Because of the wide scope of this study, it is impossible to assume a professional historian's concern with facts except in certain cases. In many instances I shall rely on what appear to be intelligent assessments by accepted authorities—Baines,

Daniels, Chapman, Wadsworth and Mann, and others [1]—of the history of cotton manufacturing.

Stages of Production in Cotton Manufacturing. Without recounting the minutiae of a treatise on textiles, one must review the processes necessary for transforming bales of cotton into textiles, since the divisions among these processes constituted some of the main bases for industrial differentiation in our period.

The number of stages varies, of course, with the level of technology and the complexity of machinery.[2] In the early nineteenth century, however, the following operations were important. Initially the raw cotton must be *opened* and *cleaned* of impurities; the cleaning operation is sometimes called *scutching*, *batting*, or *blowing*. Next the material is *spread* flat, more or less evenly. In *carding*, the next operation, the cotton fibres are raked parallel to each other. Then follow several stages of attenuating and twisting the cotton into thread. First the slivers delivered by the carding process are *doubled* and *drawn out*. This operation is essentially repeated in the *roving* or *slubbing* stages, in which the fibres are drawn out further and given a slight twist to increase their cohesion. The product is a loose and coarse thread, ready for *spinning*, by which it is again drawn out to varying degrees of hardness or fineness. This fineness is graded by a "count" signifying the number of standard-length hanks of thread to one pound. Thus Number Forty means forty hanks of thread per pound; Number One Hundred, naturally a finer yarn, has one hundred hanks of the same length per pound.

After the thread is *wound*, *doubled*, and *singed*, it is ready for weaving. Part of the yarn must be *warped*, i.e., set on the loom in long parallel threads through which the shuttle is thrown. Warping involves *beaming*, or rolling the warp regularly upon the cylindrical roller of the loom, and *dressing*, or applying a flour or other paste to

---

[1] E. Baines, jun., *History of the Cotton Manufacture in Great Britain* (London, 1835); G. W. Daniels, *The Early English Cotton Industry* (Manchester, 1920); S. J. Chapman, *The Lancashire Cotton Industry* (Manchester, 1904); A. P. Wadsworth and J. Mann, *The Cotton Trade and Industrial Lancashire, 1600–1780* (Manchester, 1931).

[2] Chapman broke the process into cleaning, carding, drawing and roving, spinning, and weaving. On the other hand, Ure mentioned ten distinct phases, and Baines and Fairbairn "not less than ten or twelve distinct operations." S. J. Chapman, *The Cotton Industry and Trade* (London, 1905), p. 22; A. Ure, *The Cotton Manufacture of Great Britain* (London, 1861), Vol. I, pp. 301–2; T. Baines and W. Fairbairn, *Lancashire and Cheshire, Past and Present* (London, 1868), Vol. II, pp. clxviii–clxix. Also G. Dodd, *The Textile Manufactures of Great Britain* (London, 1844), pp. 24 ff.; R. Guest, *A Compendious History of the Cotton Manufacture* (Manchester, 1823), pp. 6–7; Baines, *History of the Cotton Manufacture in Great Britain*, pp. 242–3.

smooth and stiffen the threads in place. In the familiar process of *weaving*, the shuttle is shot alternately across the threads of warp, pressed hard against the previous shot of weft, thus producing a woven piece of cloth. Finally, the cloth undergoes various *finishing* processes, which include *bleaching*, *dyeing*, and *printing*.

These operations may be isolated or combined; one worker or one machine may be responsible for one or several processes. No matter what the precise division of labour, however, the difficulty of transforming the raw cotton into textiles requires many stages of "value-added." These stages form one of the major bases on which activity segments and differentiates into concrete roles; still other roles crystallize around the delicate problems of balancing production at the various stages.

STRUCTURAL CHANGES IN THE COTTON INDUSTRY PRIOR TO 1765

If the analysis of structural change in the cotton industry is to be complete, one should begin centuries before the industrial revolution in cotton. From about the beginning of the seventeenth century the industry creaked and groaned to a fairly advanced level of capitalist organization, so that by the eve of the industrial revolution it conformed closely to the "putting-out" system.[1] I shall merely sketch the development of the industry before 1765, emphasizing changes in the division of labour according to the functional categories in Figure 4.

By the late seventeenth century,[2] the cotton industry was still comparatively tiny,[3] and the differentiation of distinct role types was limited. Most of the production (C_L) was carried on domestically by weavers and their families. Furthermore,

masters commonly participated in the labours of their servants. Commercial enterprise was exceedingly limited . . . the Manchester chapmen used occasionally to make circuits to the principal towns and sell their goods to the shopkeepers,—bringing back with them

[1] For a brief description of the system in Lancashire, cf. T. S. Ashton, *The Industrial Revolution, 1760–1830* (London, 1954), p. 31.

[2] Price found bits of evidence locating the origin of the cotton manufacture in England well before 1621. Still more recent discoveries of documents indicate that the cotton manufacture was in existence even earlier, possibly in the late 1500's, in Westhoughton. W. H. Price, "On the Beginning of the Cotton Industry in England," *Quarterly Journal of Economics*, XX (1905–6), pp. 608–13; *Manchester Guardian*, May 17, 1957; also Daniels, *The Early English Cotton Industry*, pp. 1–16.

[3] Baines listed the annual cotton imports at 1,985,868 lb. in 1701, in contrast to 56,010,732 lb. one hundred years later. *History of the Cotton Manufacture in Great Britain*, p. 215.

sheep's wool, which was disposed of to the makers of worsted yarn at Manchester, or to the clothiers of Rochdale, Saddleworth, and the West Riding of Yorkshire.[1]

This fusion of master's and workman's labour and the sporadic marketing illustrate a fuzzy differentiation between roles in C_L (technical processes of production) and in C_G (control over decisions to produce). In addition, "the capital of merchants was generally very small,"[2] and the control over capital (C_A)—looms, spinning-wheels and distaffs, and the funds to finance their installation—was not clearly differentiated from the roles of the producers.[3]

Around the beginning of the eighteenth century, the industry received what proved to be a mixed blessing and curse. Until this time it had suffered from competition from Indian calicoes.[4] In 1700 Parliament, under pressure from woollen interests, prohibited the importation of printed calicoes from India, Persia, and China (11 & 12 Wm. III, c. 10). Apparently this did not bring the desired results, for in the early 1700's agitation began anew, this time against both imports and imitations manufactured in Britain.[5] Thus in 1721 a second Act (7 Geo. I, c. 7) prohibited the use or wear of printed calicoes—with certain exceptions—printed in England or elsewhere. This prohibition gave an immediate boost to cotton-mixtures and pure linen products, which were substitutes for calico. In 1735 Parliament clarified the 1720 provision by exempting mixed cotton-linen goods from this restriction (9 Geo. II, c. 4). The effects of these Acts on the cotton manufacture were mixed. On the one hand Indian fabrics were ruled out of competition; but on the other British attempts at imitation to meet the demand for calicoes were throttled. The total effect of the legislation stimulated the trade, however, for it encouraged the manufacture of calico substitutes. These conditions continued until 1774 when Parliament repealed all prohibitions against calico-printing.[6]

---

[1] *Ibid.* p. 105.

[2] *Ibid.* Butterworth noted that "few capitals of £1,000 acquired by trade existed in this part of the country before 1690." E. Butterworth, *Historical Sketches of Oldham* (Oldham, 1856), p. 104.

[3] Credit extended over working capital to a degree, but scarcely over fixed. Wadsworth and Mann, *The Cotton Trade and Industrial Lancashire*, p. 33.

[4] *Ibid.*, p. 125.

[5] Mantoux, *The Industrial Revolution in the Eighteenth Century*, pp. 205–7.

[6] For a commentary on these legislative developments, cf. Daniels, *The Early English Cotton Industry*, pp. 20–24; Mantoux, *The Industrial Revolution in the Eighteenth Century*, pp. 203–8; Wadsworth and Mann, *The Cotton Trade and Industrial Lancashire*, pp. 129–44; and Baines, *History of the Cotton Manufacture in Great Britain*, pp. 259–62.

Under these circumstances the industry advanced considerably during the first three-quarters of the eighteenth century. As shown in Table 1, the imports of cotton fluctuated irregularly, then jumped toward the middle of the century. In 1717 an account of the inhabitants of Manchester, the centre of the Lancashire cotton trade, listed an approximate 8,000; in 1757 another estimate for Manchester and Salford indicated 19,939. When an actual enumeration was taken in 1773, the total for Manchester and Salford came to 27,246.[1]

TABLE 1

COTTON IMPORTS FROM 1701 TO 1764
IN SELECTED YEARS [2]

Years	Lb.
1701	1,985,868
1701–5	1,170,881
1710	715,008
1720	1,972,805
1730	1,545,472
1741	1,645,031
1751	2,976,610
1764	3,870,392

The eighteenth century also saw a number of organizational changes in the cotton manufacture; furthermore, by the 1760's great pressure began to weigh on the industrial structure. Without applying the model of differentiation in full, I shall merely list several major structural changes which had run their course or were in progress by the 1760's. It is necessary, of course, to eliminate many local exceptions and minor developments.

Most processes of production (C_L) were fused with the nuclear family. Under this domestic system, the father wove and apprenticed his sons into weaving. The mother was responsible for preparatory processes; in general she spun, taught the daughters how to spin, and

[1] T. Percival, *Observations on the State of Population in Manchester and other adjacent Places* (Manchester, 1773), pp. 1–2; also J. Aston, *The Manchester Guide* (Manchester, 1804), p. 4.

[2] From Baines, *History of the Cotton Manufacture in Great Britain*, p. 215. These only approximate the level of output, for during the eighteenth century there were no measures of stored raw cotton and other working capital (which were no doubt significant, given the long distances and slow transportation). The figures are, however, "representative" of output. W. Hoffmann, *British Industry 1700–1950* (Oxford, 1955), pp. 254–5.

Structural Differentiation in Spinning

allocated the picking, cleaning, drying, carding, etc., among the children.[1]

Cotton production also was linked with farming, especially during the early eighteenth century. "In South Lancashire . . . the number of persons was comparatively small who devoted themselves exclusively to artizan labour; the manufacture of clothing being for the most part regarded as subordinate to other employments . . . the 'gudeman' worked at his farm-patch in summer-time . . . in winter plying the hand-loom. . . ."[2] In and around Oldham "the number of fustian weavers who were cottagers working for manufacturers, without holding land, were few; but there were a considerable number of weavers who worked on their own account, and held at the same time small pieces of land."[3] There are no statistical data on the proportions of full-time weavers and farmer-weavers, respectively, or the amount of time spent in each activity. We may surmise, however, that toward the 1760's the pressure to devote more time to textiles mounted because of the increasing volume of trade. Certainly this was true by the last quarter of the century.[4]

Tendencies to differentiate productive activity *within* the family became apparent early in the eighteenth century. According to Kennedy,

[after the beginnings of foreign trade, and its attendant growths and fluctuations] the manufacturers soon found that they could not supply the increased demand for cloths, and the first consideration was, how they were to produce a greater quantity in their respective families. It naturally occurred to them that, if they had another loom, or another hand to spin, they might be able to supply this additional demand. But, if they were all employed before, this could not be done, unless they could make some arrangement, by which the same number of hands might produce a greater quantity of cloth. By separating their different operations, and dividing them, with some order, between the different members of the family, they found, that

[1] I. Pinchbeck, *Women Workers in the Industrial Revolution, 1750–1850* (London, 1930), p. 113; Radcliffe, *Origin of the New System of Manufacture*, pp. 8–9.

[2] H. Ashworth, "Statistical Illustrations of the Past and Present State of Lancashire," read before the British Association in Manchester in 1840–41, pp. 47–8.

[3] Butterworth, *Historical Sketches of Oldham*, p. 101.

[4] Radcliffe, for instance, reported that of the fifty or sixty farmers of Mellor in 1770, "there were only 6 or 7 who raised their rents directly from the produce of their farms; all the rest got their rent partly in some branch of trade; such as in spinning and weaving woollen, linen or cotton. The cottagers were employed entirely in this matter, except for a few weeks in the harvest." *Origin of the New System of Manufacture*, p. 59. Also Chapman, *The Lancashire Cotton Industry*, pp. 10–11.

more could be produced. But in the small compass of a single family, division of labour could not be carried far.

The next consideration was, could they get a neighbour to card or spin for them, they might then be able to weave a still greater quantity.[1]

Thus production began to move outside the miniature factory of domestic labour. Generally cleaning and carding remained in the home, while rovings were sent out to wives and daughters of neighbourhood farmers and craftsmen.[2] The weaver often assumed "managerial responsibility" * for the quality of workmanship outside his home, even paying spinners and carders for work completed.[3] In addition, several other modifications of production hinted at a factory system. Since none of these modifications really developed on a large scale, and since some were outright failures, I shall merely enumerate them.

Late in the seventeenth century, shortly after the introduction of the "Dutch loom" for smallwares, groups of weavers began to gather in sheds to work looms. These looms were owned by important weavers and weaver-farmers who paid the less important weavers; this arrangement differentiated more sharply between the processes of production themselves (C_L) and the control of fixed capital (C_A). This development did not mean that the master weavers became "capitalists," for the merchant-employers still controlled production at a higher level. The important weavers merely supervised the completion of work;[4] hence their role was more "manager" than "producer." **

In 1738 Lewis Paul patented a spinning machine which embodied the principle of spinning by rollers later to be incorporated into Richard Arkwright's water-frame. Two years later Paul and John Wyatt set up a small factory with these machines, run by mule-power and employing ten female workers. The factory failed after a couple

[1] J. Kennedy, "Observations on the Rise and Progress of the Cotton Trade, in Great Britain, particularly in Lancashire and the adjoining Counties," *Memoirs of the Literary and Philosophical Society of Manchester*, Second Series, III, pp. 117–18 (read November, 1815).

[2] Pinchbeck, *Women Workers in the Industrial Revolution*, p. 114.

* Analytically this specialization is along the C_{L_i} dimension. Above, p. 45.

[3] Butterworth, *Historical Sketches of Oldham*, p. 103.

[4] Wadsworth and Mann, *The Cotton Trade and Industrial Lancashire*, pp. 105–6; Butterworth, *Historical Sketches of Oldham*, p. 104. In the 1750's and 1760's this system began to spread to the manufacture of sailcloth, especially around Warrington. Wadsworth and Mann, *The Cotton Trade and Industrial Lancashire*, pp. 302–3. For a discussion of later hand-loom "factories," below, pp. 141–3.

** That is, they specialized along the C_{L_i} rather than the C_{G_i} dimension. Above pp. 42 and 45.

of years, and an attempted revival in Northampton, using water power to drive Paul's spinning and carding machines, struggled along profitless until its demise in 1764.[1]

By the middle 1760's carding also began to differentiate from other preparatory activities. John Kay is supposed to have developed a carding and spinning machine, but the extent of its use is unknown. In 1748 Lewis Paul patented two carding machines. These were confined to wool until 1760 when a man named Morris introduced one of them into Lancashire for carding cotton. As early as 1762, Robert Peel adopted this machine, with James Hargreaves' modifications. While the carding engine thus never entered the factory to a great extent before Arkwright's subsequent improvements, experiments began to isolate this branch of activity.[2]

The distribution of products was complex even in the eighteenth century. The Manchester merchant-employers remained in control of decisions to distribute the goods (C_G), but between 1730 and 1770 they began to send "riders-out" to various market towns to take orders for cloth. Local retailing was done in markets and by individual salesmen and hawkers who took goods from the travelling merchants or dealers. Early in the century goods for foreign trade were sold directly to London merchants, who distributed them abroad. About 1770, however, numerous riders and factors appeared in "every part of Europe," and foreigners began to reside in Manchester to do their own buying.[3]

By 1765 or 1770, therefore, the cotton trade had differentiated extensively with respect to the processes of production alone. This was accompanied by an equally extensive differentiation of products; in 1769 Arthur Young counted 13 distinct products in the fustian manufacture, nine in checks, and "numerous little articles" in the smallwares branch.[4]

---

[1] Mantoux, *The Industrial Revolution in the Eighteenth Century*, pp. 213–20; Wadsworth and Mann, *The Cotton Trade and Industrial Lancashire*, pp. 431–48.

[2] Ashworth, "Statistical Illustrations of the Past and Present State of Lancashire," p. 50; Baines, *History of the Cotton Manufacture in Great Britain*, p. 175; J. Butterworth, *A Complete History of the Cotton Trade* (Manchester, 1823), pp. 79–80; Kennedy, "Observations on the Rise and Progress of the Cotton Trade," *op. cit.*, pp. 118–19. Below, pp. 98–9, for a further account of the carding improvements.

[3] J. Aiken, *A Description of the Country from thirty to forty Miles round Manchester* (London, 1795), pp. 181–2; R. B. Westerfield, "Middlemen in English Business, 1660–1770," *Transactions of the Connecticut Academy of Arts and Sciences*, XIX (1915), pp. 313–18; Chapman, *The Lancashire Cotton Industry*, p. 6.

[4] *A Six Months Tour Through the North of England* (London, 1771), Vol. III, pp. 187–92. For an account of the introduction of new products, new dyes, etc.,

How specialized were the roles *controlling* the level of production (C_G)? What degree of control did they exercise? The answers to these questions rest in the "putting-out" system, under which the master gave out raw materials to weavers and others, who usually worked them up at home and returned them to the master for payment. This system probably appeared in the late seventeenth century and solidified during the first three-quarters of the eighteenth.[1] In terms of industrial structure, putting-out meant a differentiation of roles *from* the processes of production (C_L) in two directions: the manufacturer gained greater control over decisions to produce (C_G) and greater control over working capital (C_A), even though the latter was physically in the workers' hands.

Even before the putting-out system, merchants controlled production to a degree, simply by refusing to purchase finished work from the weavers. On the other hand, the semi-independent weaver who owned his own goods could gauge his own output freely. Furthermore, he was under no obligation, beyond the pressure of the market, to meet definite schedules. When the merchant-employers began to give out raw materials, however, *without actually relinquishing ownership*, their control of production became more definite. Their claim upon goods rested not merely on a money offer which could be accepted or rejected. Now they could exercise a legal right of ownership. In short, this change meant a sharper differentiation between roles in C_G (control of decisions to produce) and those in C_L (technical production).

In some cases the master manufacturer controlled spinning directly; in others the weaver hired spinners to produce yarn, which he subsequently wove and returned to the master. In the latter the differentiation was still between decisions to produce (master manufacturer) and processes of production (spinners, etc.), but the weaver's role as middleman between master and spinner represented a greater differentiation of roles.[2] Yet another middleman, the

---

cf. W. E. A. Axon, *The Annals of Manchester* (Manchester, 1886), pp. 91–9, and J. Ogden, *A Description of Manchester by a Native of the Town* (Manchester, 1783), pp. 73–9.

[1] Certainly the independent weaver who bought his own materials had disappeared by the early eighteenth century. Daniels, *The Early English Cotton Industry*, pp. 36–7; Wadsworth and Mann, *The Cotton Trade and Industrial Lancashire*, pp. 79–91. Of course he did not vanish overnight in all places. In Oldham, for instance, "it was not until 1740 that the Manchester tradesmen began to give out warps and raw cotton to the weavers, receiving them back in cloth, and paying for the carding, roving, spinning, and weaving." Butterworth, *Historical Sketches of Oldham*, p. 103.

[2] Wadsworth and Mann, *The Cotton Trade and Industrial Lancashire*, pp. 275–6.

"fustian master" or country putter-out, appeared around 1750. In many cases he was merely a country agent for a larger Manchester manufacturer. His appearance in the fustian branch, and not in checks or smallwares, was undoubtedly associated with the fact that the latter clustered in and around Manchester, whereas fustians were scattered throughout the villages and rural areas of Lancashire.[1]

In many respects the differentiation of roles controlling fixed and working capital (C_A) before 1770 paralleled the differentiation of those controlling production (C_G). By definition the putting-out system implies that the working capital remains under the master manufacturer's control. Thus, as the independent weaver-producer gave way to the weaver who received wages for working up raw material, the control of working capital was differentiated more sharply from the processes of production (C_L). One limitation on the masters' control of raw material, however, lay in the credit which the importers of raw cotton extended to the manufacturers.[2] Also, at the other "end" of the production process, the master manufacturer often relinquished control of the finished goods by selling cloth "in the grey" to Manchester merchants who dyed and finished it before marketing.[3]

The control of fixed capital—looms, spinning-wheels, carding equipment, etc.—continued to rest largely with those who processed the raw materials (C_L) through most of the eighteenth century.[4] The sheds for warping, for Dutch looms, and later for sailcloth manufacture, were exceptions; the capital equipment and premises were owned by small masters. Another exception to domestic ownership was the expensive draw-boy loom for fancy designs, which, after its invention in 1760, was often erected in workmen's homes at the employers' expense; the latter frequently supplied parts for these looms as well.[5]

Thus during the eighteenth century various elements of the workman's control of capital began to slip from his grasp through the

---

[1] Guest, *A Compendious History of the Cotton Manufacture*, pp. 10–11; Daniels, *The Early English Cotton Industry*, p. 56.

[2] S. Dumbell, "Early Liverpool Cotton Imports and the Organization of the Cotton Market in the Eighteenth Century," *Economic Journal*, XXXIII (1923), pp. 362–73.

[3] Butterworth, *Historical Sketches of Oldham*, p. 105. His remarks refer primarily to 1740–60.

[4] By the beginning of the nineteenth century it was common to hire looms as part of the "furniture" of cottages. In this case the ownership rested with neither manufacturer nor weaver, but with the *rentier*. Chapman, *The Lancashire Cotton Industry*, pp. 23–4.

[5] *Ibid.*, pp. 22–3; Daniels, *The Early English Cotton Industry*, p. 74.

processes of differentiation. Raw materials came more under the control of the master manufacturers in the putting-out system; the employers occasionally supplied looms on the workers' own premises; sometimes they supplied both looms and premises. One particularly dramatic feature of the subsequent factory system is that these pressures to differentiate the control of capital—raw materials, tools, and premises—unfolded all at once and in a relatively short time. As we shall see, the factory system arose from many pressures and hence was differentiated simultaneously along several lines.

Finally, we must say a word regarding the differentiation of roles controlling industrial organization (C_I). During the first three-quarters of the eighteenth century there was much inventive activity by men like John Kay, Lewis Paul, and John Wyatt. Furthermore, new and improved products made their appearance. And as the preceding discussion shows, the industrial resources underwent many recombinations.* Clearly there was much entrepreneurial *activity*; but the responsibilities for innovation were not yet differentiated into institutionalized *roles*. Perhaps the technical skills of the carpenter, clockmaker, and millwright were required to apply new techniques to production. It is permissible, however, to treat entrepreneurial activity in cotton during the early and middle eighteenth century as an aspect relatively undifferentiated from other parts of the industry.

So much for the background. Within several decades after the middle 1760's, the cotton industry experienced a revolution in almost every sense. Output soared to astronomic heights; the labour force multiplied; and industrial organization underwent a great meta-morphosis. What led to this revolution in cotton? What were its preconditions? What course did the reorganization take, and why? How were these structural changes related to changes in output? In short, what were the origins and nature of the industrial revolution in cotton?

A NOTE ON THE "CAUSES" OF INDUSTRIAL CHANGE

The subject of the "causes," "conditions," "determinants," or "underlying factors" leading to the industrial revolution in cotton (or the entire industrial revolution) is seldom neglected by historians and others; yet the highest confusion reigns both in the definition of

* That is to say, specialization occurred in all three integrative sub-systems—C_{I_a}, C_{I_g}, and C_{I_l}. Above, pp. 42–5.

these terms and in the search for appropriate empirical conditions to fit the definitions. By way of introducing this important subject, let us first list a number of observations on the causes of the industrial revolution.

In seeking so-called primary causes for the Industrial Revolution one may conceivably choose any one of three: the mechanical achievement; the commercial changes; or physiographic factors that were in a sense the basis of both the commercial change and the development of the mineral industries. It is wiser, perhaps, to abandon the search for a single cause, recognizing that the interplay of factors was in reality essential. The commercial changes that underlay the industrial transformation were not specifically associated with England; they might have stimulated industrial development in France. The intensity and importance of the changes in England were due to the unusual conjunction of factors making for change in a number of related industries. All the factors favourable to change were present in England, and the conjunction of factors did not occur in any other country (Usher).[1]

The causes which have most powerfully contributed to promote the progress of the population and wealth of the north-western district of England during the last hundred years:

1. Improvement of means of transport by construction of navigable canals, good roads, of railways, and the introduction of steam navigation to the most distant countries.

2. The development of the great mineral wealth of Lancashire and Cheshire.

3. The application of steam power to manufacturing purposes, and to locomotion, by sea and land.

4. The invention of numerous and most ingenious machines, applied to the industry.

5. An immense increase in the supply of cotton and of other raw materials of industry.

6. The opening of new and extensive markets for the products of the industry of this district in every part of the world.

7. Great improvements in shipping, and in the art of navigation.

8. The application of large and increasing capitals to the carrying out of public works of all kinds, as well as to every branch of private industry.

9. The rapid increase of people within the limits of the two counties, and a continual influx of numbers, industry, and intelligence from every part of the United Kingdom (Baines and Fairbairn).[2]

[1] A. P. Usher, *An Introduction to the Industrial History of England* (London, 1921), p. 252.

[2] *Lancashire and Cheshire, Past and Present*, Vol. II, p. 202.

The essence of the Industrial Revolution is the substitution of competition for the mediaeval regulations which had previously controlled the production and distribution of wealth (Toynbee).[1]

The arts are the daughters of peace and liberty. In no country have these blessings been enjoyed in so high a degree, or for so long a continuance, as in England. Under the reign of just laws, personal liberty and property have been secure; mercantile enterprise has been allowed to reap its reward; capital has accumulated in safety; the workman has "gone forth to his work and to his labour until the evening"; and, thus protected and favoured, the manufacturing prosperity of the country has struck its roots deep, and spread forth its branches to the ends of the earth (Baines).[2]

. . . certainly, nothing has so directly contributed to the pre-eminence of Great Britain in manufactures, as her race of laborious, skilful, and inventive artisans, cherished as they have been by the institutions of a free country, which opened to the possessors of talents and knowledge, in however humble a station, the amplest career of honour and fortune to stimulate effort and dignify success. The reformation of religion, in spreading knowledge through the middle and lower classes of society, has distinguished the Protestant population even in Catholic countries for their superior skill in the useful arts . . . (Ure).[3]

Clearly most if not all these factors are significant in the genesis of economic growth at some level and at some stage. One cannot deny the place of coal, steam, water, and climate; nor can one eliminate commercial and technological features; and enough is known of values and ideology to admit their importance in industrial development. In addition, however, these factors do not constitute a simple list of conditions, each logically co-ordinate as a "cause" or "determinant." The significance of each appears *at different stages of development*. For this reason the notion of simple cause or determination may be misleading because it implies a "before-after" relationship. In fact industrial development involves an interplay of qualitatively different factors which "add their value" to growth at different stages and in different weights. It is hoped that the model of structural differentiation, which characterizes industrial change as an unfolding sequence whereby various "determinants" operate *only* under specific conditions, will provide a framework in which the value-system, technology, natural resources, capital, and so on, may be relegated to their appropriate contributory roles.

[1] A. Toynbee, *Lectures on the Industrial Revolution of the Eighteenth Century in England* (London, 1908), p. 64.

[2] *History of the Cotton Manufacture in Great Britain*, pp. 88–9.

[3] *The Cotton Manufacture of Great Britain*, Vol. I, p. 220–21.

THE EARLY STAGES OF STRUCTURAL DIFFERENTIATION IN SPINNING AND ALLIED ACTIVITIES

During the first four steps of structural differentiation—dissatisfaction, disturbance, handling, and encouragement of ideas—there is no appreciable change in industrial organization, capitalization, or output. During these steps, the industry and other elements in society prepare for a frontal attack on the sources of dissatisfaction. Only in the fifth, sixth, and seventh steps do the factors of production and the output change markedly. I shall use this division between the early stages and the frontal attack to organize the remainder of this and the next two chapters. First I shall discuss the Steps 1–4 as they related to spinning and allied activities in the middle and late eighteenth century; next I shall reapply Steps 5, 6, and 7 several times in accordance with the several sequences of reorganization in the industry during the following decades—the introduction of the jenny, the water-frame and the mule; the rise of steam power; the advent of carding machinery, etc. When it is necessary to refer back to the first four steps, I shall do so.

Step 1. Dissatisfaction and a Sense of Opportunity. We will discuss the five questions outlined in the last chapter in order: (1) What market pressures, if any, generated pressures on the existing industrial structure? (2) What were the foci of dissatisfaction with this structure in terms of the utilization of resources? (3) What value-criteria underlay these dissatisfactions? (4) What was the flexibility of the existing industrial structure? (5) What were the prospects of facilities, if any, to overcome the sources of dissatisfaction?

Market Pressures. Successful British wars and treaties made possible an enormous expansion of the foreign market for British goods in the eighteenth century:

Gibraltar gave access to the Mediterranean. The Methuen Treaty of 1703 . . . opened up Brazil. The Treaty of Utrecht partly opened up the Spanish market of Central and South America. There was also the Indian market, and the markets of North America, and access to the German market through Hanover and Bremen. England never had such a market, and all through the century there was no competitor.[1]

For cotton, this expansion was reflected in the gradual increase of exports before 1750 and their rapid growth after that date, as shown

[1] L. S. Wood and A. Wilmore, *The Romance of the Cotton Industry in England* (Oxford, 1927), pp. 124–5.

63

in Table 2. Domestic demand was rising, though less dramatically.[1]
Table 3 shows domestic cotton consumption, calculated by subtracting exports from imported cotton.

TABLE 2

EXPORTS OF COTTON PIECE GOODS EVERY
TEN YEARS, 1699–1769 [2]

Year	Exports (£)
1699	13,138
1709	5,182
1719	7,853
1729	9,605
1739	14,324
1750	19,667
1759	109,358
1769	211,606

TABLE 3

AVERAGE ANNUAL CONSUMPTION OF COTTON IN
GREAT BRITAIN, 1698–1770 [3]

Years	Lb.
1698–1710 (1705 missing)	1,095,084
1711–1720 (1712 missing)	1,476,107
1721–1730 (1727 missing)	1,505,273
1731–1740	1,717,787
1741–1750	2,137,294
1751–1760	2,759,916
1761–1770	3,681,904

[1] Phyllis Deane, in a study of contemporary sources, estimated a growth in
population from approximately 5½ million in the late seventeenth century to over
7 million in 1771. Crude estimates of the approximate total national income are
£48,000,000 for 1688–1695 and £130,000,000 (possibly too high) in 1770.
Throughout the period there were fluctuations in price level for consumers' goods,
but no overall trend. "The Implications of Early National Income Estimates for
the Measurement of Long-term Economic Growth in the United Kingdom,"
Economic Development and Cultural Change, IV (1955), p. 36.

[2] From Wadsworth and Mann, *The Cotton Trade and Industrial Lancashire*, p.
146. The year 1750 is substituted for 1749, an abnormal year because the African
trade had not recovered from the war and the reorganization of the company.
Though the amounts are given in sterling, the figures are a fair index of the
volume of exports, since "official values" used in this table were based on fixed
1696 prices. The figures, drawn from Custom House Accounts, are "notoriously
unreliable" (*ibid.*, p. 145), but probably illustrate the general trend of exports.

[3] From Wadsworth and Mann, *The Cotton Trade and Industrial Lancashire*,
p. 170. The figures, which show the amount retained in the country after deduc-
tion of exports, are based on Custom House Accounts.

Foci of Dissatisfaction. So rapid a rate of growth, particularly after 1750, exercised a mounting pressure on the industrial structure. Correspondingly, in the generation before 1770, there appeared several complaints reflecting dissatisfaction with industrial productivity. The most salient of these dealt with the shortage of cotton yarn. The spinning-wheel and distaff simply could not keep up with the loom. In the mid eighteenth century, one loom provided work for five or six common wheels. Around 1760 John Kay's fly-shuttle (which approximately doubled the productivity of the loom) found its way into the cotton manufacture. After this time the yarn shortage must have been very serious indeed.[1] This disequilibrium within the industry became the source of concern to manufacturers and the source of enforced unemployment among weavers.[2]

Those weavers whose families could not furnish the necessary supply of weft had their spinning done by their neighbours, and were obliged to pay more for the spinning than the price allowed by their masters; and even with this disadvantage, very few could procure weft enough to keep themselves constantly employed. It was no uncommon thing for a weaver to walk three or four miles in a morning, and call on five or six spinners, before he could collect weft to serve him for the remainder of the day. . . .[3]

The shortage of spinning hands was worst in harvests, when the families of farmer-craftsmen turned to their second source of income. Besides driving up the cost of spinning, the yarn shortage drove weavers to accept inferior qualities of cotton weft to mix with linen warp. This generated a second complaint among the manufacturers— diminishing quality of output.[4]

In addition to the yarn shortage, several sources of dissatisfaction arose from the putting-out system itself. Even though this system augmented the manufacturer's control over working capital, his command was not absolute. Theft and embezzlement of raw materials probably concerned the employers most. In 1702 an Act of

[1] Pinchbeck, *Women Workers in the Industrial Revolution*, p. 115; Mantoux, *The Industrial Revolution in the Eighteenth Century*, p. 213.

[2] Mantoux, *The Industrial Revolution in the Eighteenth Century*, p. 213.

[3] Guest, *A Compendious History of the Cotton Manufacture*, p. 12.

[4] This diminished quality is probably related to the fact that when the demand for cotton weft rose, all ages and skills were recruited to the spinning-wheel. Pinchbeck, *Women Workers in the Industrial Revolution*, p. 130. In the early 1780's before the introduction of machine spinning in Scotland, the directors of the Chamber of Commerce of Glasgow showed concern with such spinning faults as "slack twine, ill thum'd and dry spun, hard twine, thumb knots, different colours in the same hank, slip ekes, coarse pieces, roaney, or having the shows or straw adhering, spun beyond the grist and hairy, check spales, lumpy, low spun, &c " G. Stewart, *Progress of Glasgow* (Glasgow, 1883), pp. 25–6.

Parliament specified penalties for persons "embezzling and purloining" materials on which they were working. This Act covered cotton and several other trades. It was made perpetual in 1710 and extended in 1740. In 1749 the scope of the Act was revised to specify "linen, fustian, cotton," and others.[1] These regulations signify the masters' struggle to consolidate their control over working capital. Yet the Acts were difficult to enforce. The weaver continued to take his almost traditional cut from the woven piece, and the spinner to relinquish her weft to a hawker for a bribe.[2] Furthermore, we may assume that the masters' consternation over these practices mounted as the demand for cotton goods increased at home and abroad.

Even if the workpeople had been impeccable, however, the putting-out system would have had its bottlenecks. Inherent in the system is an inordinate amount of "fetching and carrying"—cotton distributed around the countryside to the spinners; yarn collected by or for the weavers; and cloth collected from the weavers. Such bottlenecks led to a great "irregularity of employment in the domestic industries," and failures of delivery "which might involve some days' idleness." It goes without saying that the manufacturers' dissatisfaction with these delays was widespread.[3]

How may we formalize these dissatisfactions in terms of the table of resources? Clearly the most important complaint focused on the I-5 level, or the allocation of resources; there was a shortage of spun yarn and no promise of augmenting the supply in the near future. In the second place, the kind and amount of authority over workmen (I-6) was the source of misgivings, especially with respect to the workmen's standards of honesty and punctuality. A third salient dissatisfaction dealt with the inadequacies of capital equipment—the distaff and common spinning-wheel (A-6). Naturally these dissatisfactions implied others—with the use of capital equipment (A-7); the terms on which labour was recruited (G-5); its allocation to various roles (G-6); and its performance in these roles (G-7). The major dissatisfactions, however, concerned the organization of resources, the authority relationships, and the inadequacies of fixed capital.

Value Background. Why were these institutional bottlenecks a source of dissatisfaction? Why did not the masters and workmen let well enough alone, particularly in good times? Why did the masters

1 M. Postlethwayt, *The Universal Dictionary of Trade and Commerce* (London, 1751), Vol. II, pp. 128–9.

2 Wadsworth and Mann, *The Cotton Trade and Industrial Lancashire*, p. 199; W. C. Taylor, *The Hand Book of Silk, Cotton and Woollen Manufactures* (London, 1843), p. 105.

3 Wadsworth and Mann, *The Cotton Trade and Industrial Lancashire*, p. 404; Wood and Wilmore, *The Romance of the Cotton Industry in England*, pp. 62–3.

complain about deliveries on schedule? Why did they object to a loss of material through semi-traditionalized theft and embezzlement? Could they not assume this as a "cost" to be met by stiffening their terms of exchange with the weavers? In short, what *values* made dissatisfaction with the existing state of affairs a legitimate and appropriate response?

In connection with these questions, much has been made of the "Weber thesis" connecting ascetic protestantism and capitalistic economic development. The essence of this thesis is that this value-system is a particularly fruitful breeding ground for a social structure and for individual motivation which encourage the development of bourgeois capitalist institutions.[1] Without analysing the content of these values in detail,[2] I should like first to sketch some of their explicit and implicit elements relevant to motivation in the economic sphere.

Common to a number of the nonconformist doctrines is the notion of *personal responsibility* as the basis of human behaviour. The legitimization of action lies in the individual's personal relation to God, not in an infallible church or state.[3] In order to exercise this responsibility effectively, life should be thoroughly and methodically *disciplined*. "[The Puritan] disciplines, rationalizes, systematizes his life; 'method' was a Puritan catchword a century before the world heard of Methodists. He makes his very business a travail of the spirit, for that too is the Lord's vineyard, in which he is called to labour."[4] Closely associated with discipline is a kind of rational attitude toward experience, a scepticism toward magic and a strong denial of impulse expression.[5] These circumscriptions for individual behaviour were united in the notion of a *calling*, which meant the rational pursuit of duty as a sort of sacred performance in the service of God.

---

[1] The supposed connection is not simply between ascetic protestantism and the desire for gain or riches. Rather it is between this value-system and a system of economic endeavour "based, not on custom or tradition, but on the deliberate and systematic adjustment of economic means to the attainment of the objective of pecuniary profit." R. H. Tawney, in the introduction to M. Weber, *The Protestant Ethic and the Spirit of Capitalism* (London, 1930), p. 1 (e).

[2] For extended discussions, cf. Weber, *The Protestant Ethic and the Spirit of Capitalism*; R. H. Tawney, *Religion and the Rise of Capitalism* (New York, 1954); R. K. Merton, *Science, Technology, and Society in Seventeenth Century England* (Bruges, 1938); E. Bebb, *Nonconformity and Social Life, 1660–1800* (London, 1935); R. F. Wearmouth, *Methodism and the Common People of the Eighteenth Century* (London, 1945).

[3] Bebb, *Nonconformity and Social Life*, pp. 89–90.

[4] Tawney, *Religion and the Rise of Capitalism*, p. 167.

[5] Weber, *The Protestant Ethic and the Spirit of Capitalism*, pp. 139–43.

When these principles of conduct were applied to everyday life, the result was a relative permissiveness and even encouragement of the systematic pursuit of economic gain. Puritan writers took a fairly lenient stand on selling at the best possible price, on borrowing, and on profits for the tradesman. John Wesley's sermons show his dislike of wealth as such, but also indicate his positive encouragement of diligent labour, of the investment of savings, and even of "experiments and adventures" which foster economic gain. Wesley forbade luxury spending, however, and emphasized giving to the poor on Christian principles.[1] In short, these socio-economic elements of seventeenth- and eighteenth-century Nonconformity emphasize the "performance-centred" extremes of economic values: the positive valuation of production (C_G), of saving and—more important—capitalizing on this saving (C_A), of the search for opportunities for economic gain (C_I), and of "exertion" (C_L).

Thus there is, broadly speaking, an "intimate connexion between the tenets peculiar to Nonconformity and the rules of conduct that lead to success in business." [2] For our purposes it would be desirable to demonstrate that a disproportionately large number of those who expressed active dissatisfaction with the economic bottlenecks of the mid eighteenth century held the values of the Nonconformist economic ethic. Of course this is impossible; we do not even know the religious and social beliefs of most of the initiating agents in the economic advances of the eighteenth century.[3] Given these obstacles, we must attempt a more indirect demonstration of the place of religious values in the genesis of dissatisfaction with economic arrangements. We shall ask the following questions: Was Nonconformity prevalent in the manufacturing districts during the eighteenth century? What was its course during the industrial revolution, 1770–1840? To what specific social and geographical groups did Nonconformity appeal? What particular values did religious agents preach to the populace? Were these values established in religious

---

[1] For an analysis of the socio-economic tenets of leading Protestants, cf. Bebb, *Nonconformity and Social Life*, pp. 101–23; Wearmouth, *Methodism and the Common People in the Eighteenth Century*, pp. 231–3 and 240–41.

[2] Quoted from Ashton, *The Industrial Revolution*, p. 18.

[3] I attempted to locate the religious preferences of business personalities of the late eighteenth- and early nineteenth-century cotton trade in the *Dictionary of National Biography* and other standard biographical sources. Only a tiny proportion of the businessmen, for example, from the list that petitioned Parliament for Samuel Crompton in 1812, are listed, and religious preference is seldom given. Furthermore, available biographies "are always concerned more with the externals of achievement than with the psychological make-up of their subjects." F. W. Taussig, *Inventors and Money-Makers* (New York, 1915), fn., p. 21.

and educational institutions and if so, how? Is there evidence of Nonconformity among entrepreneurs, inventors, etc.?

After thriving in the seventeenth century, English Nonconformity experienced a decline in the early eighteenth century.[1] Toward 1740, however, Methodism, while itself remaining in the Establishment, initiated a revival of interest in Dissent, which reached its height in the first decades of the industrial revolution, from 1760 to 1800. "The figures for Methodism present an almost uninterrupted story of growth especially marked in 1778 and after, from which time most of the other Nonconformist bodies took a new lease of life."[2]

Methodism spread rapidly in the manufacturing districts and slowly in the rural areas. By 1802, of those counties "where Methodism had less than ten centres only two had felt the impact of industrialism and them but slightly."[3] During the third quarter of the eighteenth century, Dissent as a whole increased "nearly everywhere along a line drawn from Wiltshire almost due north to Northumberland, with a notable increase in Lancashire, while south of a line between London and Bristol, but excluding Wiltshire, there [was] an almost uninterrupted decrease."[4] To be sure, a general population movement toward the northern counties had already begun in the second half of the eighteenth century. The increase in the towns and manufacturing districts has been attributed more to migration than to changes in local rates through natural causes.[5] But in the agri-

[1] Bebb, *Nonconformity and Social Life*, pp. 45–7. Major sects of Nonconformity (often called Dissent) are Presbyterian, Independent, Quaker, Baptist, Congregational, Unitarian, and later Methodist.

[2] *Ibid.*, pp. 43–4. The following estimates are from the circuit records of Wesleyan Methodism. "The absolute accuracy of these statistics may be questioned —in the original printed copy of the Minutes in which they first appeared, they are sometimes inaccurately totalled—but as to their substantial accuracy there seems to be little doubt."

Year	Circuits	Members
1765	39	—
1770	49	29,496
1775	50	34,997
1780	64	43,880
1785	76	52,431
1790	108	71,463
1795	138	90,347
1800	161	109,961

[3] Wearmouth, *Methodism and the Common People in the Eighteenth Century*, pp. 182–3.
[4] Bebb, *Nonconformity and Social Life*, p. 42.
[5] A. Redford, *Labour Migration in England, 1800–1850* (Manchester, 1926), pp. 15–16.

cultural southern and eastern counties there was *not* a decrease in total population between 1750 and 1800. In fact there was an absolute increase in Somerset, Dorset, Hampshire, Sussex and Kent.[1]

We are presented, therefore, with three facts: (1) a general drift of population toward the northern industrial counties; (2) a rapid absolute increase of Dissenters in the northern counties and an absolute decrease in the southern counties; (3) an absolute increase of population in the southern and eastern counties, though not so rapid as in the northern. What were the components underlying these facts? First a greater social and psychological receptiveness to Dissent in the manufacturing districts and second a selective drifting of Dissenters into these districts. Since these components are not separable, we cannot gauge the strength of each. Together, however, they fit plausibly with the facts. In some instances such drifting can be traced definitely. After the middle of the eighteenth century, for example, an impetus was given to Congregationalism in Lancashire by the migration of Scottish weavers and traders into that county.[2] This is not to suggest that great blocks of Dissenters moved into the manufacturing districts. Indeed, the primary type of migration in the early nineteenth century, and probably earlier, was by very short distances only.[3] We may assume, however, that there was an overall drift of Dissenters or those receptive to Dissent to the northern manufacturing districts.

Within these areas the larger towns were the greatest breeding grounds for Methodism. After conducting a service in Manchester in 1783, John Wesley said, "Such a sight as, I believe, was never seen in Manchester before. I believe that there is no place but London where we have so many souls so deeply devoted to God."[4] Local histories show the singular successes of Methodism in Oldham, Stockport, Rochdale, and Preston, all in the cotton manufacturing district.[5]

[1] Mantoux, *The Industrial Revolution in the Eighteenth Century*, pp. 357–63.

[2] R. Halley, *Lancashire: Its Puritanism and Nonconformity* (Manchester, 1869), Vol. II, p. 434.

[3] Redford, *Labour Migration in England*, pp. 157–8.

[4] Axon, *The Annals of Manchester*, p. 109.

[5] Wearmouth, *Methodism and the Common People in the Eighteenth Century*, p. 184; H. Fishwick, *History of the Parish of Rochdale* (Rochdale, 1889), p. 259 ff., and *The History of the Parish of Preston* (Rochdale, 1900), pp. 170–1. In Stockport it has been shown that the development of Methodism was closely connected with the tradesmen and manufacturers of the town. H. Heginbotham, *Stockport: Ancient and Modern* (London, 1882), Vol. II, pp. 25, 62–3, and G. Unwin, A. Hulme, and G. Taylor, *Samuel Oldknow and the Arkwrights* (Manchester, 1924), pp. 39–40.

Structural Differentiation in Spinning

Methodism attracted the poor especially in the manufacturing areas. The Vicar of Bolton observed in 1753 that "most" of the strolling Methodist preachers were "men brought up in laborious employments . . . miners, weavers, carriers, soldiers, petty schoolmasters, and such like." [1] Warner has singled out "industrial workers, weavers, skilled artisans, and the day-labourers of the towns" as particularly receptive classes. Even more so, perhaps, were those "workers who migrated to the centres where economic opportunity offered a livelihood." [2]

Among these converts in the poorer classes, the weavers were particularly visible:

When Wesley and Whitefield unfurled the standards . . . the Weavers flocked . . . and shewed as much zeal and ardour in favour of the new Religion, as their predecessors had previously shewn at the Reformation, or in the succeeding period of puritanism. The great mass of Weavers are now [1823] deeply imbued with the doctrines of Methodism, and form a great proportion of the whole number of persons who profess that religion. [3]

In another passage the same writer characterized the market behaviour of the weavers as follows:

The facility with which the Weavers changed their masters, the constant effort to find out and obtain the largest remuneration for their labour, the excitement to ingenuity which the higher wages for fine manufactures and skilful workmanship produced, and a conviction that they depended mainly on their own exertions, produced in them that invaluable feeling, a spirit of freedom and independence, and that guarantee for good conduct and improvement of manners, a consciousness of the value of character and of their own weight and importance. [4]

In so far as this historian's observations are accurate, there seemed to be an intimate association between "performance-centred" economic behaviour and a vigorous alignment to Methodism.

Thus the manufacturing districts partook heavily of the Methodist revival and the associated invigoration of Nonconformity. This is to assert neither that Dissent caused the industrial revolution nor that

[1] J. C. Scholes, *Memoir of the Reverend Edward Whitehead* (Bolton, 1889), p. 17.

[2] W. J. Warner, *The Wesleyan Movement in the Industrial Revolution* (London, 1930), p. 165. For a discussion of some of the possible reasons for this attraction of the poor, cf. Wearmouth, *Methodism and the Common People in the Eighteenth Century*, p. 217, and Bebb, *Nonconformity and Social Life*, pp. 53–4.

[3] Guest, *A Compendious History of the Cotton Manufacture*, p. 43.

[4] *Ibid.*, p. 38.

71

incipient economic developments caused Nonconformity to be revitalized. The logic of the model of structural differentiation does not require that we accept either position. It is sufficient that there existed, in substantial strength, certain *criteria* whereby bottlenecks in the existing industrial structure were deemed unsatisfactory on the one hand, and whereby motivation to modify this structure was encouraged on the other. Methodism and the other branches of Dissent seem clearly to fulfil this requirement in the late eighteenth century.

During the first half of the nineteenth century Nonconformity not only sustained but also strengthened its hold in the manufacturing districts. In 1843 Edward Baines enumerated the number of sittings in churches and chapels, Sunday Schools, etc., in the manufacturing counties. The numerical increase in Episcopal Church sittings between 1800 and 1843 was from 176,752 to 377,104, or 113%, whereas the increase in chapel sittings was from 135,036 to 617,479, or 357%.[1] Of course the number of sittings reveals neither the rate of attendance nor the convictions of the faithful. In 1851, however, when some attempt was made to assess the number attending, there was still a predominance of Nonconformity in the manufacturing counties.[2]

The values of industry, prudence, and economic rationality were evident to a certain degree in the Establishment as well. In this connection the efforts of two leading figures in Lancashire are particularly instructive—Rev. John Clayton, chaplain at the Collegiate Church in Manchester, and Rev. Edward Whitehead, Vicar of Bolton from 1737 to 1789.

In 1755 Clayton, a friend of John Wesley, issued a pamphlet entitled *Friendly Advice to the Poor*. From the preface it is clear that Clayton was supported in his enterprise by the business-dominated local officials of Manchester. Hence the pamphlet is perhaps typical of the attitudes of the manufacturers "in the generation before the inventions and the first factories." [3]

---

[1] E. Baines, jun., *The Social, Educational and Religious State of the Manufacturing Districts* (London, 1843). The Establishment had seats for 40·3% of the inhabitants of Lancashire, the lowest figure for any county. R. F. Wearmouth, *Methodism and the Working Class Movements of England, 1800–1850* (London, 1937), pp. 19 ff. For further figures, cf. Ashworth, "Statistical Illustrations of the Past and Present State of Lancashire," p. 14; J. Wheeler, *Manchester: Its Political, Social and Commercial History, Ancient and Modern* (Manchester, 1836), pp. 373–6; *Parliamentary Papers*, 1852, XI, Manchester and Salford Education, p. 477.

[2] *Parliamentary Papers*, 1852–3, LXXXIX, Census of Religious Worship, pp. cxci–ii.

[3] Wadsworth and Mann, *The Cotton Trade and Industrial Lancashire*, p. 386.

Clayton attributed "those woefull Distresses under which the Poor do sadly labour" to the slovenly habits of the workpeople themselves.[1] First among the vices was idleness. "One [who is slothful in his work] is extravagant in the Use of *Time*, that most precious Talent; and neglects the appointed Means of providing Necessaries, Comforts and Conveniences for himself and his Dependents." [2] He traced this idleness to two sources primarily: the fact that "common Custom has established so many Holy-days, that few of our Manufacturing Work-folks are closely and regularly employed above two-third Parts of their Time . . ." and "that slothful spending the Morning in Bed . . . in Winter Time especially." [3] Conjoined with idleness was dissipation:

The Holy Ghost by the Mouth of wise King *Solomon*, hath taught us that *the Drunkard and Glutton shall come to Poverty*, as surely as *Drowsiness will cloath a Man with Rags*. And yet these Vices of Intemperance and Excess are, God knows, as common, as they are scandalous. And they are such close Attendants upon Sloth, that they may fairly be esteemed Sister Sins, and are commonly observed to go Hand in Hand with each other.[4]

The final sins were extravagance, or living from hand to mouth, and "bad Management and want of Economy amongst [the poor]." [5]

These exhortations drew forth a counter-attack from Joseph Stot, a Manchester cobbler, in the following year. Stot focused the blame for poverty in the Manchester region not on the poor but rather on the pride of the wealthy and their failure to set good examples.[6] On the subject of idleness, however, Stot admitted that

Not . . . every Thing which [Mr. Clayton] has said . . . is so liable to Censure, as the few Expressions which We have noticed; on the contrary, wou'd the Poor take his Advice in the Main, I am persuaded, they wou'd live with more Credit to themselves, as well as Comfort to their Families; especially, if they made the proper Use of what he has said under . . . Extravagance; which is well calculated for their Good, if they will mind it.[7]

[1] *Friendly Advice to the Poor*, p. 23.
[2] *Ibid.*, pp. 6–7.
[3] *Ibid.*, pp. 13, 36.
[4] *Ibid.*, pp. 16–17.
[5] *Ibid.*, pp. 23–4.
[6] J. Stot, *Sequel to the Friendly Advice to the Poor* (Manchester, 1756). Many Wesleyans felt that one of the basic causes of poverty was the absence of the virtues of frugality, industry, etc. This was a characteristic of all classes, but if anything the Wesleyans agreed with Stot in feeling that the wealthy members of society were indolent and slothful. Warner, *The Wesleyan Movement in the Industrial Revolution*, p. 163.
[7] Stot, *Sequel to the Friendly Advice to the Poor*, p. 16.

Edward Whitehead's sermons in Bolton, a cotton manufacturing centre, show an agreement on these values. In 1753 Whitehead delivered a sermon entitled "The Use and Importance of Early Industry" to the Society of Weavers and Manufacturers of Bolton:

[He spoke upon] the advisability of artizans, by means of regular contributions to the Sick and Burial Clubs, to prepare for days of distress and adversity.

. . . . .

The preacher then encouraged his audience to industry . . . and dissuaded them from sloth and idleness, observing that sloth was the fruitful parent of many crimes, and of those atrocious ones of robbery and murder, so much practised, and so much complained of in those days. . . . The preacher did not condemn and forbid all sorts of recreation, but all those who led a sedentary life, and studious persons, ought to indulge themselves at proper seasons in some cheerful exercise in the open air in order to refresh their bodies, to unbend their minds, to expel melancholy humours, and to preserve or restore to health and vigour their whole frame.[1]

About twenty years later Whitehead delivered a second sermon on the same subject. His agreement with the Wesleyan Methodists and Nonconformists is remarkable, as the following excerpts show:

What Numbers could I recount, Members of this and other Societies whom when overtaken by Sickness, Age, or Accident, the seasonable Relief of their boxes, like the provident Bee's Summer Store, hath saved from impending Misery and Ruin? Whilst others dissipated, idle, and improvident have, when in the like Circumstances, either perished thro' Want, and entail'd Misery on their wretched Offspring; or been forced to pass the Remainder of their Days in the Filth and Penury of a parish Cell?

. . . . . .

. . . let us turn our Attention now to a few of those domestic Duties, which Prudence, or *Self-love*, from Persons in your Stations, more immediately calls for.

And 1st. If you love *yourselves*, you must love your Wives and Children which are *Part of yourselves*, and this suggests to you the Demand they have upon your Labour and Industry, in order to make a decent and comfortable Provision for them.

Indeed, no Man living can plead a Right to be *idle*; it is contrary to one of the first Laws of God; Labour is our Lot, but such a Lot as is capable of being improved to the most beneficial Purposes, respecting ourselves, our Families, and Society. . . .

[1] Scholes, *Memoir of the Reverend Edward Whitehead*, pp. 17–19.

... the Apostle exhorts such poor Persons, whose Abilities are not equal to their kind Wishes, to *labour working with their Hands the Thing that is good*, that they may enjoy this singular Felicity *of having to give to him that needeth.*

And to deter Men from the baneful and destructive Vice of Idleness, he another Place declares, that *he that provideth not for his own, and specially for those of his own House, hath deny'd the Faith, and is worse than an Infidel.*

As therefore you would not, instead of enjoying the god-like Pleasure of doing good, bring yourselves and Families to depend upon the Mercy and Charity of others; as you would not incur the infamous Character of being Drones in the Creation; of being Assassins to your Children, and Rebels to your God, resolve *before the Day is far spent*; in your young and healthful Days to be diligent and industrious; to acquit yourselves like Men, in doing your Duty in that State of Life unto which it hath pleased God to call you.

And in order to make yourselves still more independent, to provide better for your Families, and to be more useful in your Generation; to the aid of *Industry*, call in her Sister Virtue *Frugality*; which *latter* will enable you to preserve and keep together what the *former* hath acquired.

. . . . . .

What generally brings on this great Distress is a Vice which in this trading Country is almost epidemical, and against which I cannot on this Occasion but think it my Duty to caution you; you will anticipate in your own Minds the Vice I mean, which is *Intemperance* or *Drunkenness.*

This if it were no *Crime*, is a Practice as opposite to what Frugality or Economy would recommend, as Light is to Darkness, and the utmost Exertions of both Art and Industry cannot build as fast as it demolishes. . . .[1]

In addition to the churches and chapels, the Sunday Schools instructed the young in the values of the day. Begun by Robert Raikes in 1784 and praised both by Adam Smith and John Wesley, these schools were "the product of a quite remarkable wave of Puritan reform in which the prudential motives were uppermost."[2]

[1] E. Whitehead, *The Duty of bearing one another's Burdens. A Sermon preached before a Society of Weavers . . . in Bolton* (Manchester, 1874), pp. 9–10, 14–17.
[2] A. P. Wadsworth, "The First Manchester Sunday Schools," *Bulletin of the John Rylands Library*, Vol. 33 (1950–51), pp. 300, 305.

The schools managers seemed to have a keen sense of their practical effects; "[Sunday Schools were] the cheapest way to civilize the poor, to make them less dangerous to society, to render them more useful workers, and, incidentally, to save their souls." [1] These schools were virtually the only education for the working classes during the first two generations of the industrial revolution.[2]

The Sunday Schools developed fastest in Lancashire and the other manufacturing districts. "In no other part of the country is there more zeal and devotedness to the work of Sunday school instruction, nor is there any part of the kingdom where the contributions are so large for the support of them." [3] In 1835 a committee of the Manchester Statistical Society concluded that "notwithstanding the short time necessarily devoted to instruction in the Sunday Schools, they must, nevertheless, be regarded as forming a most important feature among the means at present existing in Manchester for the education of the lower classes of people." [4]

Nonconformist Sunday Schools came quickly to predominate in the manufacturing districts. For a time in the 1790's the Dissenting (including Roman Catholic) children in Sunday Schools were in a minority, but by 1821 they were double the number of Anglican.[5] In 1843 Baines' count of Sunday Schools in the manufacturing counties yielded a ratio in favour of Nonconformity similar to that for the number of church and chapel sittings.[6]

Finally, many inventors and early entrepreneurs were Nonconformists. In addition, there are instances of contacts between Nonconformity and business; for example, the Manchester Literary and Philosophical Society—of Unitarian origin—had many cotton spinners and manufacturers as members.[7] Because counter-examples

[1] A. P. Wadsworth, *Ibid.*

[2] Unwin, *Samuel Oldknow and the Arkwrights*, p. 41.

[3] H. Ashworth, *Cotton: Its Cultivation, Manufacture, and Uses* (Manchester, 1858), p. 12. In 1843 Baines calculated that in Lancashire there was one Sunday scholar to every $5\frac{2}{3}$ inhabitants. Similar proportions held in the other manufacturing counties, whereas, in all London, the proportion was one scholar to twenty inhabitants. *The Social, Educational and Religious State of the Manufacturing Districts*, p. 23.

[4] Manchester Statistical Society, *Report on the State of Education in Manchester in 1834* (London, 1835), p. 20.

[5] Wadsworth, "The First Manchester Sunday Schools," *op. cit.*, p. 319.

[6] *The Social, Educational and Religious State of the Manufacturing Districts*, p. 45. Also Wheeler, *Manchester: Its Political, Social and Commercial History, Ancient and Modern*, pp. 386–8, and *Parliamentary Papers*, 1852, XI, Manchester and Salford Education, p. 476.

[7] E. Mendelsohn, Seminar Paper for History 234a, Harvard University, January, 1956, entitled "The Scientific Spirit and the Industrial Revolution: A

may be found,[1] however, and because the entire evidence is so sketchy, these examples are not conclusive.

In general, however, the evidence is sufficiently strong to establish the association between "performance-centred" emphasis in economic activity and the religious values characteristic of (but not limited to) the Nonconformist sects of Protestantism. Because of these values, it was not only appropriate to feel dissatisfaction with industrial bottlenecks, but also it was *legitimate* to express it. Thus the values of the day gave a legitimate stamp to the manufacturers' increasing despair and the growing condemnation of theft and embezzlement in the cotton trade.

The Flexibility of the Existing Industrial Structure. Could output expand freely under the putting-out system, and if so, how much? At what point did the rigidities of the institutional structure reach a breaking point?

The fusion between farming and textile manufacturing allowed a certain transfer of labour from one type of work to the other as the occasion demanded. Because of the need for agricultural labour at harvest,[2] however, and because of the high status associated with land ownership,[3] this transfer was limited. Furthermore, it was not the heads of households (weavers) who were under pressure to give up farming in the 1760's, but rather their dependents (spinners, carders, etc.). The latter certainly could not migrate from the farms without their husbands. This immobility of spinning and preparatory labour perhaps contributed to the fact that the demand crisis came to a head first in the spinning and allied branches.

Within the domestic system a limited increase of numbers of spinsters probably occurred before the advent of the factory system. Pinchbeck inferred from parish account books and from contemporary observations in the mid eighteenth century that "every farm house and most of the cottages had a wheel or a distaff as part of the ordinary household furniture." [4] Similarly, the labour of the young was probably pushed to its maximum. Child and even infant labour was

Study of the Origins of the Manchester Literary and Philosophical Society." Also Ashton, *The Industrial Revolution*, p. 21.

[1] Edmund Cartwright, inventor of the power-loom, for instance, was an Anglican clergyman.

[2] In 1761 the Society for the Encouragement of Arts, Manufactures, and Commerce prefaced an advertisement of a premium for the invention of a spinning-wheel with a complaint that the shortage of yarn became particularly acute during harvest seasons. F. Espinasse, *Lancashire Worthies* (First Series: London, 1874), p. 319.

[3] Wadsworth and Mann, *The Cotton Trade and Industrial Lancashire*, p. 318.

[4] *Women Workers in the Industrial Revolution*, p. 133.

widespread in the eighteenth century [1]; it seemed to reach a high point, however, in the years preceding the industrial revolution. W. Cooke Taylor, for instance,

> conversed with very old persons who remember when the weavers, or their factors, travelled about from cottage to cottage with their packhorses, to collect yarn from the spinsters, often paying a most exorbitant price for it, which absorbed the profits of weaving. This was the commencement of the system of infant labour, which was at its worst and greatest height before anybody thought of a factory. Spinning was so profitable, that every child in the cottage was forced to help in the processes—picking the cotton, winding the yarn, and arranging the card-ends. When the father was a weaver, and the mother a spinner, which was very commonly the case, the tasks imposed upon the children were most onerous. . . .[2]

Such expansion within the domestic system had its limits; it would have required a tremendous transfer of population to spinning and its allied processes to meet the rapidly climbing demand. The adjustments of labour *within* the putting-out system probably reached these limits shortly after the introduction of the improved fly-shuttle into the cotton trade around 1760.

The Sense of Opportunity and the Prospect of Facilities. If historical commentators are to be trusted,[3] all Lancashire was buzzing with the opinion that giant fortunes were to fall to individuals lucky enough to stumble upon a solution for the yarn shortage, Furthermore, the general supply of capital was probably more favourable than it had been in generations. Interest rates had undergone a series of decreases from as early as the seventeenth century, so that by the 1760's funds were sometimes available at as little as 3 per cent.[4] Also, Britain, unlike most of the continental countries, emerged from the Seven Years War of 1763 in a remarkably sound financial position.[5] In addition, there had been a great increase in the number of country banks about the time of the American war, though Lancashire lagged in this development.[6] And finally, if we may assume that the values of industry and frugality were taken seriously, there undoubtedly had accumulated substantial capital in the personal

[1] Wadsworth and Mann, *The Cotton Trade and Industrial Lancashire*, pp. 405–8; R. Bayne-Powell, *The English Child in the Eighteenth Century* (London, 1939), pp. 28–44.

[2] *The Hand Book of Silk, Cotton, and Woollen Manufactures*, pp. 105–6.

[3] Mantoux, *The Industrial Revolution in the Eighteenth Century*, pp. 221–2; J. H. Crabtree, *Richard Arkwright* (London, 1923), pp. 17–18, 20–21.

[4] Ashton, *The Industrial Revolution*, pp. 8–11.

[5] Ure, *The Cotton Manufacture of Great Britain*, Vol. I, pp. 218–19.

[6] Wadsworth and Mann, *The Cotton Trade and Industrial Lancashire*, p. 92.

savings of enterprising weavers and manufacturers.[1] Probably the most important source of capital lay, however, in the credit extended by manufacturers and dealers, which permitted the expansion of capital and the acquisition of time.[2]

Thus in the 1760's the several components of the first step of structural differentiation had converged. The international and domestic markets for cotton textiles had expanded to the point of creating bottlenecks in the existing industrial structure. This pressure gave rise to mounting dissatisfaction with both individual performance and the utilization of resources. A strong value-system, which placed a premium on economic rationality, provided the weight of legitimization to these dissatisfactions. A general availability of facilities gave men a sense of promise. Now we must continue the story of how this pressure broke in the following decades and how the industry moved to a higher level of organization to meet the crisis in productivity.

[1] In this connection, cf. W. J. Ashley, *The Economic Organization of England* (London, 1914), pp. 156–8, and Radcliffe, *Origin of the New System of Manufacture*, p. 10.

[2] Wadsworth and Mann, *The Cotton Trade and Industrial Lancashire*, pp. 95 ff.

CHAPTER V

STRUCTURAL DIFFERENTIATION
IN SPINNING (*Continued*)

Step 2. Symptoms of Disturbance. In the period between the crisis in yarn supply (early 1760's) and the initial steps to relieve it (1764–70), a full-fledged "disturbed movement" did not develop. From the very limited evidence, however, we may extract several signs of disturbance in these years: (1) We may assume that friction between spinners and weavers developed, particularly when the latter were spending long periods in search of yarn to keep them occupied.[1] (2) In Lancashire in the early 1760's there was excited speculation about instantaneous fortunes for the man lucky enough to stumble upon the right invention. To be sure, such dreams came true in later decades, *but only after* great trial and error in the assembly and reassembly of resources. Dreams of overnight riches are too general, because they neglect, or perhaps deny the necessaries which have to be overcome ploddingly before any invention can reap fortunes. (3) The eighteenth century was a century of browbeating the poor over lack of discipline, immorality, theft, drunkenness, holiday-keeping, etc. In certain respects this was unjustified. Even though the consumption of alcohol increased during the early part of the century, it decreased in the second half [2]; it is not probable, furthermore, that leisure or dishonesty among workmen increased during this period.[3] More important, in so far as critics—such as John Clayton and Edward Whitehead—blamed poverty and industrial inefficiency on the poor, they were expressing misplaced aggression. Even if the workers had stretched their work-day, delivered their goods punctually, etc., the fact remains that the system of production was outmoded. Any realistic solution required more than augmented individual exertion and responsibility.

This last point, incidentally, illustrates the delicate interpretive problems in assessing symptoms of disturbance. The phenomenon of exhorting the population to follow the code of economic rationality

[1] Guest, *A Compendious History of the Cotton Manufacture*, pp. 12–13. Ogden referred to the "insolence" of the spinners. *A Description of Manchester*, p. 87.
[2] M. D. George, *London Life in the Eighteenth Century* (London, 1930), p. 307.
[3] Wadsworth and Mann, *The Cotton Trade and Industrial Lancashire*, p. 399.

had a place in the initiation of change, as our analysis of Nonconformist values indicated. Yet in so far as these sentiments were
directed at human behaviour, which, *even if perfected within the
existing institutional framework*, could not overcome the sources of
dissatisfaction, this exhortation displayed elements of disturbance.

*Steps 3 and 4. Handling and Channelling Disturbances; Tolerance
of "New Ideas."* While these two steps are analytically distinct,
historically they mesh; hence we will discuss the phenomena associated with both in the same section.

Probably the most immediate action taken in Step 3 is to manage
the aggression associated with the symptoms of disturbance. Thus in
the eighteenth century, a number of mechanisms operated by which
individuals could express antagonism legitimately and peacefully.
The prime instance was procedure through the law-courts.[1] The
fact that merchants and manufacturers used the courts instead of
more direct means to challenge the workers' supposed habits of
idleness and dishonesty is a clear case of "handling"—the presence
of an intermediary agency specializing in social control to mediate
conflicts. The Press served a similar function; while hostility was
expressed through this medium, the fact that antagonists chose to
write it meant that the hostility was moving into institutionalized,
relatively peaceful channels rather than extra-institutional lines.

Closely linked with the channelling of potential conflict is the encouragement of attempts to direct energy into more productive
channels. Undoubtedly much encouragement took place informally
among the workmen themselves, or between manufacturers and
workmen,[2] but by and large such information is unavailable. Two

---

[1] Wadsworth and Mann outlined the sanctions applied to wayward workmen
as the legal provision for preventing embezzlement, the successful prosecutions
carried out under this legislation, and employers' associations for black-listing
workmen known to have embezzled. *The Cotton Trade and Industrial Lancashire*,
pp. 395–401. William Rowbottam occasionally mentioned in his diary a prosecution for keeping goods beyond the statute time or for stealing cotton twist.
Giles Shaw Manuscripts, Vol. 93, pp. 30, 91. George White, the parliamentary
agent who drafted the repeal of the combination laws in 1824, felt that the law
punishing workmen who did not finish work after having taken it (5 Eliz., c. 4)
was the "chief mill-stone round the neck of the worker." M. D. George, "The
Combination Laws Reconsidered," *Economic Journal* (*Economic History Supplement*), I (1929), p. 215.

[2] Kennedy refers to gatherings in public houses in which workers boasted about
improvements that they might have made in their domestic apparatus. This
boasting was a claim for prestige on the basis of producing "new ideas." "On the
Rise and Progress of the Cotton Trade," *op. cit.*, p. 119. Robert Peel's retainment
of James Hargreaves to attempt improvements on the carding engine is another
more explicit instance of "encouragement." Butterworth, *A Complete History of
the Cotton Trade*, pp. 79–80.

agencies, however—The Society for the Encouragement of Arts, Manufactures, and Commerce, and the Patent Office—illustrate the phenomena of Steps 3 and 4 clearly.

The Society of Arts, founded in 1754, aimed from the outset at "bestowing Premiums for . . . Productions, Inventions, or Improvements, as shall tend to the employing of the Poor, and the Increase of Trade." It was sponsored by "several of the Nobility and Gentry of this Kingdom." [1] The Society offered rewards in commerce, manufacturing and fine arts,[2] and in 1783 it began to publish annual transactions making past awards and new offers public.

In 1761 the Society announced premiums of £50 and £25 for the "invention of a machine that will spin six threads of wool, flax, hemp, or *cotton*, at one time, and that will require but one person to work and attend it (cheapness and simplicity in the construction will be considered part of its merit)." [3] Six such awards were granted between 1761 and 1766, and some £544 12s. were awarded between 1754 and 1776 for "improving several machines used in manufacture, viz., the Comb Pot, Cards for Wool and Cotton, Stocking Frame Loom, Machines for Winding and Doubling, and Spinning Wheels." [4]

It is not necessary to observe that the Society's concern for improvements in the spinning-wheel coincided with the extreme yarn shortage of the 1760's. That this concern diminished after the introduction of spinning machines in the 1770's also exemplifies the occurrence of "mobilization of motivation" and "encouragement of ideas" in the early stages of differentiation. Three questions arise, however, in connection with the Society of Arts. Why were the advertised premiums limited to the spinning-wheel and not machine spinning? Why were the awards so comparatively small? Why were the major inventors of successful spinning machinery—Hargreaves, Arkwright, Crompton, etc.—absent from the lists of the Society's awards?

The answer to the first is relatively simple. Because of the earlier failures in spinning by rollers, which had cost the experimenters

[1] *The Plan of the Society for the Encouragement of Arts, Manufactures, and Commerce* (London, 1755).

[2] In the first volume of the Society's *Transactions* (1783), there were 113 premiums for planting and husbandry; eleven for chemistry, dyeing and mineralogy; twenty-five for promoting the polite arts; nine for encouraging and improving manufactures; ten for inventions in "Mechaniks"; and seven for the advantage of the British colonies. The number of premiums for each category changed from time to time, as did the categories themselves.

[3] Quoted from Espinasse, *Lancashire Worthies* (First Series), pp. 319–20.

[4] Society of Arts, *A Register of the Premiums and Bounties Given, 1754–1776* (London, 1778), p. 23.

"sixty or seventy thousand pounds," the Society held a partially justified prejudice against spinning machinery. To most of its members, improvements in the common spinning-wheel seemed to promise the best results.[1]

With regard to the second question, the Society presented two types of awards—"premiums" granted for ideas and inventions previously advertised, and "bounties" granted for ideas and inventions not called for but nonetheless possessing merit. For both types, there were honorary awards (a gold or silver medal) and pecuniary awards (usually £20 to £50, though sometimes greater or less). Certainly the latter were small, considering the inventions' potentiality. The Society of Arts seemed to justify Baines' lamentation on the fate of inventors:

It is melancholy to contrast with the sanguine eagerness of inventors, the slowness of mankind to acknowledge and reward their merits,— to observe how, on many occasions, genius, instead of realizing fame and fortune, has been pursued by disaster and opposition,—how trifling difficulties have frustrated the success of splendid discoveries, —and how these discoveries, snatched from the grasp of their broken-hearted authors, have brought princely fortunes to men whose only talent was in making money.[2]

The Society's funds were limited, and rewards naturally could not be both widespread and large. In addition, however, the smallness of its grants is not inconsistent with the type of function peculiar to such agencies at this stage of the innovative process. They do not offer monetary rewards in the sense of profits; these are appropriate at the entrepreneurial stage of the sequence (Step 6). Rather, the assets which accrue to the inventor and producer of ideas are prestige, honour and publicity.[3] True, some inventors die unknown; but if we examine the rewards granted to inventors in this age (as in others) the bifurcation between profits and prestige appears. By examining these rewards, we shall consider also the conspicuous absence of famous names from the Society's lists.

Beyond the awards from the Society of Arts was the possibility of patents for the inventor. Very few were given in these years—only fourteen in 1765—and generally patents were distrusted on the grounds that they gave the holder an artificial monopoly. So strong

---

[1] H. T. Wood, *A History of the Royal Society of Arts* (London, 1913), p. 258. Above, pp. 56–7.

[2] *History of the Cotton Manufacture in Great Britain*, pp. 114–15.

[3] Thus the commencement of the publication of names of inventors and their patents in the *Annual Register* in 1794 was not merely information, but also an implicit reward to inventors and an encouragement to invention in general.

was this sentiment that in 1765 the Society of Arts prohibited awards to any inventor who had submitted his idea to the Patent Office.[1] Hence the Society probably excluded many "entrepreneurial" inventors such as Arkwright. Despite this "competition" between the Society of Arts and the Patent Office in their encouragement of new ideas, neither agency imposed upon the inventor any specific responsibility for implementing his ideas in practice. The Society effectively discouraged this by insisting that the invention be made public upon submission; the Patent Office merely allowed the author to attempt to realize a fortune from the invention, or control the attempts by licence. Hence both agencies are appropriate at Steps 3 and 4 of the sequence of structural differentiation—"the encouragement of new ideas without imposing specific responsibilities for their implementation and for taking the consequences." [2]

A second reason for the absence of major inventors from the Society's lists stems from the extremely *general* level of encouragement given by such agencies. It is imperative that encouragement be fairly vague at this early stage, simply because the appropriate means for overcoming unsatisfactory productive arrangements are unknown. The agencies send out a call for general ideas, not ready-made solutions; in the nature of the case the call cannot be specific. This characteristic is illustrated by the Society's general wording of the announcements of premium awards and its announcements of completely non-specific bounty awards.

This is not to excuse the Society for its mistakes in the late eighteenth century. Sometimes it seemed curiously behind the times; for instance, in its call for an improvement on the common spinning-wheel in 1795, a quarter-century after the successful introduction of spinning machinery.[3] Nonetheless, many of the criticisms of the Society's effectiveness, as well as the belligerent assertions of its practical value,[4] are misguided, because such agencies in the pre-

[1] This prohibition continued until the mid nineteenth century. Wood, *A History of the Royal Society of Arts*, pp. 240 ff.

[2] For a suggestion of a similar scheme of rewards and publicity in the realm of invention, cf. T. Barnes, "On the Affinity between the Arts, with a Plan for promoting and extending Manufactures, by Encouraging those Arts, on which Manufactures principally depend." *Memoirs of the Literary and Philosophical Society of Manchester* (Warrington, 1785), Vol. I, pp. 72–89; also Vol. II. pp. 510–11.

[3] *Transactions of the Society for the Encouragement of Arts, Manufactures, and Commerce*, XIII (1795), p. 271.

[4] Ure, for instance, dismissed the Society's influence as "feeble." *The Cotton Manufacture of Great Britain*, Vol. I, p. 219. Wood launched an attack against *ex post facto* criticism of the Society's success with regard to spinning machinery. *A History of the Royal Society of Arts*, pp. 240 ff.

liminary stages of structural change offer general encouragement for general ideas, and should not be expected to produce detailed solutions.*

Hence we would expect only a loose correspondence between rewards and ultimately successful inventions.[1] Frequently there were compensations of "prestige" for inventors after the importance of their inventions became apparent. Richard Arkwright was knighted in 1786 and appointed High Sheriff of Derbyshire the following year.[2] Parliament voted grants to Edmund Cartwright, inventor of the power-loom, in 1809 (£10,000), and to Samuel Crompton, inventor of the mule, in 1812 (£5,000). These rewards, while more substantial monetarily, parallel those of agencies such as the Society of Arts in the sense that they were primarily rewards of prestige, with the monetary element mainly a symbol of this prestige.

At the end of Step 4 in the sequence of structural differentiation, more attention is turned to the problems of industrial structure. In Step 5 the lines of differentiation are outlined, in Step 6 they are implemented, and in Step 7 they are routinized. In the 1760's and 1770's there were three major reorganizations in the spinning and allied branches—the introduction of the spinning jenny and the accompanying readjustments in household labour; the introduction of the water-frame and the advent of the factory system; and the incorporation of the carding engine into the factory. I shall specify Steps 5, 6, and 7 for each sequence.

THE SPINNING JENNY AND THE REVOLUTION IN HOUSEHOLD INDUSTRY

Step 5. Attempts to Specify. The circumstances of James Hargreaves' invention of the spinning jenny are obscure. By 1764, however,[3] he had brought it to a state of workability. Besides the jenny, we have noted several less spectacular improvements of the common spinning-wheel rewarded by the Society of Arts between 1761 and 1766. Undoubtedly there were many more unrecorded attempts.

These inventions clustered in the early and middle 1760's; or more exactly, *their serious consideration* commenced at this time. It goes

* Formally, according to Figure 6, this encouragement of ideas occurs at Level 2 of the table of resources. Hence resources are still at a relatively "fluid" level.

[1] The undeveloped system of communications of the day probably added to this inexact correspondence. Most of the interest in improving textiles was centred in Lancashire and the other manufacturing counties; the Society of Arts had its headquarters in London.

[2] Guest, *A Compendious History of the Cotton Manufacture*, p. 28.

[3] Even this date is uncertain. Baines, *History of the Cotton Manufacture in Great Britain*, pp. 155-6.

without saying that many of the ideas underlying the inventions were not new. The principles of both the spinning jenny and the water-frame derived from the spinning machine patented in 1738.[1] The critical element of Step 5 is that these technological specifications must be created *or* assembled *or* rearranged—in any case seriously considered—at approximately this stage.[2]

Step 6. Implementation by Entrepreneurs. During this step production, capitalization, organizational innovation, and profits increase extraordinarily. Let us trace the course of these familiar indices as far as the statistics of the 1760's and 1770's permit.

For some reason James Hargreaves delayed his attempt to put the jenny to use until 1767, when he offered some machines for sale in Lancashire.[3] Despite a vicious popular uprising against the jenny on the part of some Lancashire workpeople who feared unemployment, and despite Hargreaves' belated patent in 1770 and his attempt to sue various manufacturers for breaking the patent,[4] the jenny swept rapidly over the countryside after 1767. In this minor revolution the entrepreneurs were neither large capitalists nor industrial leaders, but rather weavers in need of yarn who had accumulated some capital. Since the jenny required only human power, and since its cost and size were relatively small, it could be erected in cottages without disrupting the traditional domestic arrangements.

The years following 1767 involved a "leap-frog" relationship between improvement of the jenny (Step 5) and rapid incorporation (Step 6). With each addition of spindles,[5] there occurred a fresh burst of activity to incorporate these models; then within a short period, a new and enlarged jenny would appear. Twelve spindles were "thought a great affair" at first. Hargreaves' patented model in

[1] Mantoux, *The Industrial Revolution in the Eighteenth Century*, pp. 216–17.

[2] Schumpeter distinguished between invention, or the creation of technique, and innovation, or the positive attempts to realize profits by applying the technique. *Business Cycles*, pp. 85–7. I should like to add another distinction, namely the "serious consideration" of the invention, which occurs in Step 5. Invention may occur at any time before or during Step 5; serious consideration of the industrial potential of the invention occurs in Step 5, and innovation occurs in Step 6.

[3] Mantoux, *The Industrial Revolution in the Eighteenth Century*, p. 222.

[4] Baines, *History of the Cotton Manufacture in Great Britain*, pp. 161–2; Wadsworth and Mann, *The Cotton Trade and Industrial Lancashire*, p. 481; Daniels, *The Early English Cotton Industry*, pp. 93–4.

[5] Addition of spindles was almost the only means of improving the jenny. Ure noted that "the Jenny received some slight improvements, first from Hargreaves, and afterwards from other mechanicians; but in fact it is too simple a scheme of spinning to afford much scope for modifications." *The Cotton Manufacture of Great Britain*, Vol. I, p. 224.

1770 contained sixteen. As early as 1771 Thomas Highs constructed a "double jenny" with twenty-eight spindles on each side of the central driving power. By 1784 a single jenny contained as many as eighty spindles and promised to increase still more.[1]

While statements of the jenny's productivity are usually simple extrapolations from the number of spindles, the effects on productivity were nevertheless staggering. In its early days, not only did the jenny multiply the spinner's power by eight, but it became clear that children could operate it more easily than adults. Soon the machine, operated by a woman or child, could spin sixteen, twenty or thirty times as much as a common spinning-wheel.[2] By the time the machine reached eighty spindles, the productivity differential must have been even more impressive.

With the introduction of the jenny came a great increase in profits; that is, the earnings of the jenny-spinners—women and children primarily—rose rapidly.[3] In 1780, petitioners to Parliament claimed that "about Sixteen Years ago a Woman could earn from Ten Pence to Fifteen Pence a Day by the Single Spindle . . . those who then worked upon Jenneys of Twenty-four Spindles earned from Eight to Nine Shillings a Week." [4] Larger jennies undoubtedly yielded more.

Exact production figures beyond the rate of increase of cotton imports are not available. From 1771 to 1781, when the jenny predominated, imports increased $75\frac{3}{4}\%$, compared with $21\frac{1}{2}\%$ from 1751 to 1761 and $25\frac{1}{2}\%$ from 1761 to 1771. These figures reflect the influence of Arkwright's water-frame and carding machine as well as the jenny; still, the movement is plausible. Furthermore, the facts that complaints about the supply of weft ceased and that fustian goods received a boost reveal the increased production stimulated by the jenny.[5]

Capitalization figures are equally vague. However, "[in spite of] the popular resistance, the spinning 'jenny' had been adopted to a great extent by spinners in Lancashire" by 1771.[6] The first numerical estimate of hand jennies in 1788 showed 20,070 machines of eighty spindles each, or 1,605,600 spindles. Since jennies were generally

[1] Ogden, *A Description of Manchester*, p. 87; Crabtree, *Richard Arkwright*, p. 41; Pinchbeck, *Women Workers in the Industrial Revolution*, p. 116.

[2] Ure, *The Cotton Manufacture of Great Britain*, Vol. I, p. 233.

[3] D. Ramsbotham, *Thoughts on the Use of Machines in the Cotton Manufacture* (Manchester, 1780), pp. 14–15.

[4] *Parliamentary Papers*, 1780, V, Paper 38, Petition of Cotton Spinners, p. 4.

[5] Baines, *History of the Cotton Manufacture in Great Britain*, p. 348; Ure, *Cotton Manufacture of Great Britain*, Vol. I, p. 233; Ogden, *A Description of Manchester*, pp. 87–93.

[6] W. A. Abram, *A History of Blackburn* (Blackburn, 1877), p. 207.

located in country cottages, this number is a sheer guess, and is probably inaccurate;[1] it is, however, the only indication of what was undoubtedly a rapid process of capitalization.

Step 7. Routinization. Since the jenny was soon superseded by the mule, it is difficult to estimate whether this step ever ran its course. In 1780, however, the petitioners mentioned above complained that jenny earnings had dropped from the eight or nine shillings a week sixteen years earlier to four or six a week. It is difficult to know whether this decline in profits resulted from competition with other types of machines, or from the competition among jennies associated with Step 7. There is a presumption in favour of the latter, however, because Arkwright's patent machines did not compete with the jenny, and the mule was not yet in existence.[2]

Given the inadequacies of historical data, these seven steps conform in broad outline to the abstract model of structural differentiation. The movements of production, capitalization, profits, productivity, and the assembly of techniques are plausible. Figure 9 illustrates the seven steps, the approximate dates of each, and the gross movement of the major indices of differentiation.

What role differentiation accompanied the introduction of the domestic jenny? The reorganization of labour was not drastic; the domestic system remained intact. The activities connected with weft spinning merely differentiated more sharply from the other activities of cotton textile production within the C_L sub-system. There also was a limited re-allocation of family labour, with the children spinning more than before. No new roles emerged with respect to the control of production (C_G), the control of capital (C_A), and the control of industrial organization (C_I).[3]

[1] P. Colquhoun, *An Important Crisis, in the Callico and Muslin Manufactory in Great Britain, Explained* (London, 1788), p. 4. W. Bowden, *Industrial Society in England towards the End of the Eighteenth Century* (New York, 1925), pp. 78–9.

[2] *Parliamentary Papers*, 1780, V, Paper 38, Petition of Cotton Spinners, p. 4. For some time the jenny and the water-frame complemented each other, the former producing weft in cottages, and the latter warp in factories. Pinchbeck, *Women Workers in the Industrial Revolution*, p. 116.

[3] In and around Glasgow, an interesting compromise along the lines of capital control was suggested by the Glasgow Chamber of Commerce during the shortage of weft yarn in the middle 1780's. In these years the Scottish manufacture was carried on by using warp from the English mills and hand-spun weft. Shortly before the opening of David Dale's famous works in Lanarkshire, a committee of the Glasgow Chamber of Commerce suggested presenting sums to spinners to assist them in purchasing jennies to supply badly-needed weft. The control of the jennies was undefined, but presumably it would have remained in the hands of the spinners. Since Scotland was soon to initiate factory production, this financial adventure probably did not materialize. Stewart, *Progress of Glasgow*, pp. 31–3.

The jenny underwent a second, truncated sequence of differentiation which did not influence production so dramatically, but which involved a more extensive differentiation of roles than the domestic jenny. As the number of spindles continued to multiply, neither children nor women had the strength to run the larger jennies. At the same time, increased capital requirements began to limit the number of workers who could finance them. In addition, the jennies

FIGURE 9

THE DOMESTIC PHASE OF SPINNING BY THE JENNY

Steps in Structural Differentiation	Approximate Dates of Steps	Output	Capital	Innovation	Profits	New Techniques
1	Several decades before 1765, accelerating after 1760	—	—	—	—	—
2	Several decades before 1765, gradually mounting	—	—	—	—	—
3	Particularly noticeable, 1760–66	—	—	—	—	—
4	1760–66	—	—	—	—	Considerable increase
5	Later 1760's, continuing into mid-1770's	Beginning to rise	Beginning to rise	Beginning to rise	Beginning to rise	Rapid rise
6	1768–middle 1770's	Rapid rise	Rapid rise	Rapid rise	Rapid rise	Rapid falling off
7	Mid-1770's to c. 1785	Maintained at high level	Falling off	Rapid falling off	Falling off	—

began to outgrow the small upper rooms of their cottages. And finally, it was convenient to link jenny-spinning to machine-carding, which was also being centralized in the 1770's and 1780's.[1] These pressures underlay the migration of the jenny into the factory.

As early as 1768 Hargreaves and James set up a small factory for carding, slubbing, and jenny-spinning. Not until the number of spindles increased, however, did groups of skilled male operatives

[1] In fact, the various types of carding machines often formed the original nucleus of the earlier mills in which jennies were employed. Wadsworth and Mann, *The Cotton Trade and Industrial Lancashire*, p. 492.

begin to gather in workshops or factories. Even these were minor in scale and only supplementary to the domestic manufacture of weft.[1] And in fact, the "factories" were not well-defined, but were "of all sizes, from the small shop with nothing but a hand-carding engine, to the more elaborately organized factory in which all the operations from the cleaning and picking of the cotton to warping, were carried on, and in which horse or water power was used."[2]

Because these mills were soon replaced by the water-frame and mule factories, we shall postpone our discussion of the factory system until the next section. Nevertheless, the movement of the jennies into the factory was not unimportant, both because it represents a case of structural differentiation, and because the mill jenny lasted well into the nineteenth century, though it had its competitive woes; "there were still plenty of wooden spinning jennies, turned by hand, in the Lancashire mills in 1824, though the drawing process, preparatory to spinning, was always done by power. But nine years later, 'those that are now jenny-spinners are getting, I think, into the decline of life,' so quickly was the industry moving."[3]

THE WATER-FRAME AND THE FACTORY SYSTEM

The jenny and the corresponding readjustment of roles relieved the shortage of weft, and erased this source of dissatisfaction. The shortage of cotton warp, however, plus those continuing dissatisfactions over authority, task performance, and faulty equipment, lay at the basis of a reorganization which shook the industrial framework much more dramatically than had the jenny. The shortage of warp was attacked in a preliminary way by applying the jenny to finer counts. This movement was nipped in the bud, however, by the new water-frame, which "produced such excellent twist for warps, that they soon out-rivalled the makers of warps on the larger jennies."[4] We must turn our attention, therefore, to the problem of spinning by rollers, which underlay the water-frame.

Step 5. Attempts to Specify. The subject of the invention of the water-frame has commanded endless controversy among historians of the cotton trade. Though considerable doubt still remains, it is probable that Highs (or Hayes) invented a water-frame about 1767 and

---

[1] Chapman, *The Lancashire Cotton Industry*, pp. 52, 57, 61; Wadsworth and Mann, *The Cotton Trade and Industrial Lancashire*, p. 481; Pinchbeck, *Women Workers in the Industrial Revolution*, p. 148.

[2] Wadsworth and Mann, *The Cotton Trade and Industrial Lancashire*, pp. 492–3.

[3] J. H. Clapham, *An Economic History of Modern Britain* (Cambridge, 1926), Vol. I, p. 237.

[4] Ogden, *A Description of Manchester*, p. 93.

Richard Arkwright invented, assembled, or purloined it in 1768, and patented it in 1769. For our purposes, however, the exact inventor is not so important as the fact that "the roller-spinning scheme was of common notoriety about the year 1766."[1]

Step 6. Implementation by Entrepreneurs. The early stages of this step coincide roughly with the personal history of Arkwright, who undertook to push the machine to its practical limits. Beginning his search for financial support in 1768, he finally joined forces with Samuel Need, a manufacturing hosier from Nottingham, and Jedediah Strutt, the recent inventor of an improvement on the stocking frame.[2] Hoping that the water-frame would produce yarn for the hosiery manufacture that the jenny and common wheel could not, these men provided partnership and financial backing for Arkwright. Their first attempt, a Nottingham factory run by horse power, was so promising that they established a water-mill at Cromford with frames of fifty to a hundred spindles each in 1771. Though extremely successful, the Cromford works did not begin to return profits on their £12,000 investment until 1774. By this time, however, Arkwright was able to supply the yarn for the stocking manufacture with ease; indeed, he began to accumulate stocks of yarn which he deemed as useful as the linen warps then in use in Lancashire. In 1774, therefore, he persuaded Parliament to repeal the statutes prohibiting the use and manufacture of pure cotton cloth.

From 1774 to 1785 the development of factories around his water-frame and carding engine showed the increase in production, capitalization, productivity, and profits associated with Step 6 of a sequence of structural differentiation. The average level of cotton imports between 1771 and 1775, inclusive, was 4,764,589 lb.; between 1776 and 1780, inclusive, 6,766,613 lb. Again these figures, while plausible, reflect the simultaneous influence of the jenny and the carding engine. In 1773 Arkwright and his partners built a factory specifically for calico at Derby. Another manufactory went up at Belper in 1776. By 1780 there existed between fifteen and twenty water-frame factories, either the property of Arkwright and his partners or of proprietors paying him sums for permission to use the patented machine. It was estimated that these factories contained 30,000 spindles, each capable of spinning twelve hanks of 24's in a week. By

---

[1] Ure, *The Cotton Manufacture of Great Britain*, Vol. I, p. 246.

[2] The productivity of this improved stocking frame was high, and, like the fly-shuttle, it probably aggravated the yarn shortage. For an account of Arkwright's search for funds between 1768 and 1770, cf. Ure, *The Cotton Manufacture of Great Britain*, Vol. I, pp. 250–1, and *Dictionary of National Biography*, Vol. II. p. 82.

1782 the value of their concerns totalled £200,000, and the number of their employees five thousand.[1]

Arkwright's productivity advantage over his competitors was enormous. After 1774 he was "able to supply . . . every kind of cloth manufactured in Great Britain . . . at very reasonable prices." The water-frame produced Number 40's best, but he could supply higher counts at higher prices.[2] His profits were gigantic, and he was already becoming one of the richest commoners in England.[3] Normally we would expect a gradual levelling off of profits in Step 7. Arkwright himself, however, attempted to prevent this decrease by monopolistic control. He was careful to protect his patent by adding token improvements.[4] By virtue of such tactics, ". . . he compelled the Lancashire spinners . . . to submit to his dictation. For several years he fixed the price of cotton twist, no one venturing to vary from his prices." [5]

In terms of structural differentiation, the failure of Step 6 to resolve into routinization means that the dissatisfactions of Step 1 are unresolved and that many opportunities for profit remain unexploited. The interruption of a sequence, moreover, is an occasion for "regression" to symptoms of disturbance. I should like to interpret some of the phenomena which appeared in Lancashire in the 1770's and early 1780's as regressive responses which were gradually directed toward overthrowing Arkwright's patents, thereby closing the sequence of structural differentiation.

The infringements upon his patents in the late 1770's [6] show the first signs of pressure. In 1781 Arkwright instituted nine actions against infringers, only one of which came to trial. In connection with this trial,[7] a group of Lancashire manufacturers donated a

[1] Guest, *A Compendious History of the Cotton Trade*, p. 31; Daniels, *The Early English Cotton Industry*, p. 100; Wadsworth and Mann, *The Cotton Trade and Industrial Lancashire*, pp. 489–90.

[2] Crabtree, *Richard Arkwright*, p. 43.

[3] Schulze-Gaevernitz gives the difference between prices of yarn and prices of raw cotton (which yields the sum for expenses and profits) at 8s. 11d. in 1784, as contrasted with 4s. 2d. in 1797 and 1s. in 1812 for each pound of cotton. *The Cotton Trade in England and on the Continent*, pp. 34–5. Arkwright left a half-million pounds, an almost unheard-of sum for a commoner. Mantoux, *The Industrial Revolution in the Eighteenth Century*, p. 238.

[4] Mantoux, *The Industrial Revolution in the Eighteenth Century*, pp. 230–1.

[5] W. C. Taylor, *Illustrated Itinerary of the County of Lancaster* (London, 1842), pp. 46–7.

[6] These were probably substantial. Daniels, *The Early English Cotton Industry*, p. 92.

[7] The action dealt with the infringement upon the patent for a carding engine granted in 1775. The defence rested upon the claim that the patent was inadequately specified.

Structural Differentiation in Spinning (continued)

large subscription to fight Arkwright. Eventually the case went against him. The following year he asked for a further extension of his patent, due to expire in 1783. Parliament did not act on this request. In 1785 he brought another case and his patent was renewed after he gained a favourable verdict. Manchester was again thrown into a turmoil, particularly since a number of manufacturers, acting on the results of the first trial, had gone ahead with plans to develop factories along Arkwright's lines. Immediately a movement crystallized to reverse the verdict on grounds that the carding patent was insufficiently specified and that Arkwright was not the inventor of the spinning machine. After an interesting trial, his patents were made public in 1785.

In so far as Arkwright's claims to invention may have been dubious,[1] and his specifications inadequate, the Lancashire manufacturers were right to insist that the patents be laid aside. In addition, however, there developed—simultaneously with Arkwright's period of monopoly—several symptoms of disturbance traceable to the continuing industrial disequilibrium.

In the first place, in 1772 the Lancashire manufacturers, anxious

to participate in the advantages to be derived from so admirable an invention . . . entered into a combination, and raised an action to have the patent set aside, on the ground that Sir Richard Arkwright was not the original inventor. But the evidence brought forward at the trial was quite insufficient to support this allegation. A verdict was accordingly given in Sir Richard Arkwright's favour.[2]

Second, the manufacturers conducted a more or less organized boycott of Arkwright's yarn for warp, which probably led to his request that the laws prohibiting the manufacture of calico be repealed so that he might organize a manufacture himself.[3] When Arkwright made this application in 1774, there was a concerted opposition among the manufacturers. Once the laws were repealed, furthermore, the Lancashire manufacturers immediately produced a panic measure to prevent the export of cotton machinery.[4]

The manufacturers' opposition to Arkwright's patents between 1781 and 1785 carried this fear of foreign competition to extreme lengths. The opposition grew out of a committee which had earlier

[1] There was plenty of doubt. Mantoux, *The Industrial Revolution in the Eighteenth Century*, pp. 234–9.

[2] J. R. McCulloch, "An Essay on the Rise, Progress, Present State, and Prospects of the Cotton Manufacture," *Edinburgh Review*, XLVI (1827), pp. 9–10.

[3] Baines, *History of the Cotton Manufacture in Great Britain*, p. 167, and Ure, *The Cotton Manufacture of Great Britain*, Vol. I, pp. 263–4.

[4] Wadsworth and Mann, *The Cotton Trade and Industrial Lancashire*, p. 485.

represented the textile manufacturers of the Manchester districts. The main purpose of this committee, even before the patent trials had begun, was "keeping the inhabitants of the town on tenter-hooks regarding the presence of foreigners, who had come for the purpose of carrying away trade secrets, and who, apparently, adopted the most dramatic methods to discover them." [1] During the patent proceedings in 1785 this organization produced predictions that the entire industry would remove to Scotland and Ireland if the patents were not broken, and that "this great manufactory, the envy of Europe, will in great degree lie at the mercy of one man, who has already received by far, greater emoluments than any other individual, or united body of discoverers ever did." [2]

Certain manufacturers' reactions to the tax on fustians in 1784–5 also are interesting. This tax was not prohibitive, but it caught the fustian manufacturers at a time when calico—that branch which profited most from the water-frame—was gaining rapidly, and when the manufacturers themselves could not produce calico except on Arkwright's terms or illegally. Consequently, when the tax on fustians was enacted in 1784, a delegation departed from Manchester to secure its immediate repeal. One of its spokesmen predicted mass emigration to Germany and other lands; ". . . if the late oppressive Act of Parliament on the making of cotton goods is continued, there is not the shadow of a doubt remains, but that a transmigration of thousands will soon take place. *If the spirit of migration taketh root in the minds of discontented men—where, or when, will its growth terminate?*" [3] Furthermore, the alternatives of positive or negative Utopia awaited the nation:

If [the fustian branch] is suffered to grow, it will arrive at gigantic size—become a bulwark of national support—and a better fund for our opulence, than if an inexhaustible gold mine of twenty-four carats, were opened in the heart of our island. Suffer me but to inform you that the Swiss, French, Germans and Spaniards, too sensible of this, are making rapid strides to rival us in the Manchester trade; that great encouragement is given by the wisest ministers of these countries to procure our machines; to allure our workmen to migrate into their territories; and to incite ingenuity amongst themselves.[4]

As a result of vigorous agitation by these manufacturers, the fustian tax was repealed in 1785.

[1] Daniels, *The Early English Cotton Industry*, p. 101.
[2] *Ibid.*, pp. 105–6, quoted from the *Manchester Mercury*.
[3] J. Wright, *An Address to the Members of Both Houses of Parliament on the late Tax laid on Fustian, and other Cotton Goods* (Warrington, 1785), pp. 16, 60.
[4] *Ibid.*, p. 7.

Structural Differentiation in Spinning (continued)

Why do we call these manufacturers' outburst in the 1770's and 1780's "symptoms of disturbance"? In addition to the familiar gloominess and despair which they contain, their predictions were fixed on objects not entirely responsible for the disturbing conditions —foreign agents and Richard Arkwright himself. In what sense were these persons inappropriate? First, the threat of foreign domination was grossly exaggerated. The fear that the industry would move to Scotland apparently was based on a single arrangement that Arkwright had made with Scottish manufacturers to open mills in Lanarkshire.[1] Furthermore, competition from abroad was virtually nonexistent. A leading authority in the industry stated in 1833,

> When I first knew the cotton manufacture in this country, which was in 1787, and when I first entered into business extensively, which was in 1792, there was no manufacture of cotton of any importance in any part out of Great Britain. . . . In those times there was no cotton manufacture in France at all, none in Switzerland worth speaking of, none in any part of Germany.[2]

Nor could I locate any evidence as to an unusual emigration of British artisans or manufacturers in this period. Surely the manufacturers' anxieties were unjustified in the light of the domestic and foreign conditions of the trade.

Second, the virulent attack on Arkwright himself was in part justified, for he had tried to control prices and supply for some time. But the gloomy prediction that the entire industry would fall into his hands was clearly unrealistic. In any case the patents were to expire in a few years. Furthermore, one case had already gone against him, and Parliament had ignored his first appeal for some time. Certainly the Government had not shown Arkwright the extraordinary favour that it had shown, for instance, Boulton and Watt, the manufacturers of steam-engines, who enjoyed an unchallenged monopoly under patent from 1769 to 1800.[3] This fear of long-term domination by one man was rather an unwarranted generalization. The exaggerated fears resulted from a short-term obstacle to the realization of economic opportunities in the field of machine-spinning.

Finally, in the case of the fustian tax, there were familiar signs of disturbance presumably based upon a fiscal measure which was by no means prohibitive, and whose enactment and repeal made no great difference in the progress of the fustian manufacture. The disturbance

[1] *Ibid.*, p. 7.
[2] Kirkman Finlay, quoted by G. W. Daniels, "The Cotton Trade During the Revolutionary and Napoleonic Wars," *Transactions of the Manchester Statistical Society*, 1915–16, pp. 56–7.
[3] Baines, *History of the Cotton Manufacture in Great Britain*, p. 225.

surrounding the fustian tax makes more sense, however, when we examine the underlying institutional pressures on the fustian branch stemming from the changing machine technology.

In addition, these disturbed responses commenced with Arkwright's partial monopoly and ceased when his patents were thrown open. This provides further evidence that they resulted from the interrupted sequence of differentiation associated with the waterframe and carding machinery.

Once the patents were open, Step 6 resumed; Lancashire cotton manufacturing burst into several years of rapid expansion, the feverish pace of which had never been known and has never been repeated since. One likely cause of this explosion is that the manufacturers, supercharged by their disturbed opposition to Arkwright, had developed an exaggerated awareness of opportunities for expansion and consequently pushed the development of the new factory system faster than would have been suggested even by casual economic calculation. Whatever the causes, "capital and labour rushed to this manufacture in a torrent . . . all classes of workmen in this trade received extravagantly high wages; such as were necessary to draw from other trades the amount of labour for which the cotton trade offered profitable employment."[1]

Production rocketed, if we may rely again upon cotton import figures. From 1776 to 1780 average imports amounted to $6\frac{3}{4}$ million lb.; from 1786 to 1790 the average was $25\frac{1}{2}$ million. Baines calculated a 320% increase of imports between 1781 and 1791.[2] This was reflected in the prices of imported raw cotton, which, having dropped slightly since 1782, jumped in 1786, then gradually began to fall again. Exports, according to official values, virtually doubled between 1785 and 1790.[3] On the basis of Postlethwayt's estimate of £600,000 for the value of manufactured cotton goods for 1767, and on the basis of the ratio of exports to total manufactures, Baines put the 1787 level at £3,304,371, or a multiple of $5\frac{1}{2}$ over 1767.[4]

With regard to capitalization after 1785, Baines reported simply that "numerous mills were erected, and filled with water frames."[5] In

[1] *Ibid.*, p. 214.

[2] *Ibid.*, p. 348. Daniels, *The Early English Cotton Industry*, p. 132.

[3] For West India and Berbice cotton (the greatest proportion of imports at the time), Mann said the prices "appear to have been as follows": 1782, 31*d.*/lb.; 1783, 25*d.*; 1784, 19*d.*; 1785, 21*d.*; 1786, 32*d.*; 1787, 31*d.*; 1788, 23*d.*; 1789, 17*d.*; 1790, 17*d.* Mann's figures for exports are, for 1785, £864,710; 1786, £915,046; 1787, £1,101,457; 1788, £1,252,240; 1789, £1,231,537; 1790, £1,662,369. J. A. Mann, *The Cotton Trade of Great Britain* (London, 1860), pp. 23, 97.

[4] *History of the Cotton Manufacture of Great Britain*, pp. 217–18.

[5] *Ibid.*, p. 214.

1787, there were 143 factories of the water-frame type engaged in spinning warp thread.[1] In 1790 a similar estimate showed 155 water mills in England and Scotland, with some 310,000 spindles.[2] Profits during these years were "unequalled."[3] Except for the figures on water-frame factories, however, the above must be tempered by the fact that this period coincided with the domestic phase of Crompton's mule.

Step 7. Routinization. "It was impossible to maintain [all the resources] for any lengthened period,"[4] after the 1785 explosion. The enormous profits on No. 40's began to diminish in the 1790's,[5] and the water-frame, even though it was to become the "throstle" when attached to steam, was not to be modified significantly after its incorporation in the 1780's.[6] It took its place as a routine element in the industry.

In terms of future developments—the mule, steam power, and the power loom—the industrial revolution had barely commenced by the late 1780's. By that time, however, when the jenny had run its innovational course and the water-frame was in the same process, we reach a temporary resolution of disequilibrium in the production of certain varieties of cloth. The two new types of organization—the cottage built around the jenny and the early factory built around the water-frame—had struck a balance:

The water-frame spun a hard and firm thread, calculated for warps; and from this time the warps of linen yarn were abandoned, and goods were, for the first time in this country, woven wholly of cotton. Manufactures of a finer and more delicate fabric were also introduced, especially calicoes, imitated from the Indian fabrics of that name. The jenny was peculiarly adapted for spinning weft; so that the two machines, instead of coming in conflict, were brought into use together.[7]

---

[1] Colquhoun, *An Important Crisis . . . Explained*, p. 4. Bowden feels that there is "no sufficient reason for believing that the number of . . . water frames was exaggerated." *Industrial Society in England toward the End of the Eighteenth Century*, p. 79.

[2] P. Colquhoun, *Case of the British Cotton Spinners and Manufacturers of Piece Goods, Similar to the Importations from the East Indies* (London, 1790), Appendix. For the same year Guest estimated some 150 mills for England and Wales. *A Compendious History of the Cotton Manufacture*, p. 21.

[3] Baines, *History of the Cotton Manufacture in Great Britain*, p. 214.

[4] *Ibid.*

[5] Footnote, p. 92. Cf. also Mercator, *A Letter to the Inhabitants of Manchester on the Exportation of Cotton Twist* (Manchester, 1800), p. 5.

[6] *Dictionary of National Biography*, Vol. II, p. 83.

[7] Baines, *History of the Cotton Manufacture in Great Britain*, pp. 163–4.

Macpherson testified in 1785 that these low-priced cotton fabrics were becoming part of the standard of living of all classes. Indirect evidence of this change in the consumption pattern is seen in complaints of competition from the new cotton products by other textile manufacturers.[1]

THE INTRODUCTION OF CARDING MACHINERY

Since the outstanding dissatisfactions with spinning extended to all the preparatory processes in the middle eighteenth century, the complaints touched carding as well. The first spinning factories in the early 1770's naturally heightened this dissatisfaction; it would have been awkward to continue to put out raw cotton for carding, especially since rovings and yarn were being produced on the water-frame.

Step 5. Attempts to Specify. In 1748 Lewis Paul had patented two carding machines, only two months after Daniel Bourne had patented a rotary system of carding. Paul's cylindrical design was introduced into Lancashire about 1760. About this time John Kay is supposed to have developed a carding engine. Ainsworth noted the invention—probably one of many—of a hand carding engine in 1772 by John and Ellen Hacking. Around 1760 James Hargreaves is said to have doubled the productivity of carding with an improvement on the old hand method. John Lees introduced a feeder to the carding machine in 1772 and the following year Hargreaves invented the crank and comb. The machine ultimately adopted, however, was improved by Arkwright; in 1775 he took out a patent which was to lead to dispute in the trials of the early 1780's. His final design was to be modified only slightly in the next several generations.[2]

Step 6. Implementation by Entrepreneurs. By the early 1770's sufficient modifications had been made in carding machinery to permit its competitive use. Again it was Arkwright who incorporated it successfully into the factory system just at the time that the jenny and

1 D. Macpherson, *Annals of Commerce, Manufactures, Fisheries, and Navigation* (London, 1805), Vol. IV, p. 81. F. Moore, *The Contrast, or a Comparison between our Woollen, Linen, Cotton, and Silk Manufactures* (London, 1782), and W. Muggliston, *A Letter on the Subject of Wool Interspersed with Remarks on Cotton* (Nottingham, 1782).

2 For a history of carding improvements, cf. E. Leigh, *The Science of Modern Cotton Spinning* (Manchester, 1873), pp. 77 ff.; Wood, *A History of the Royal Society of Arts*, pp. 261 ff.; R. Ainsworth, *History and Associations of Altham and Huncoat* (Accrington, 1932), pp. 187–8; Butterworth, *A Complete History of the Cotton Trade*, p. 79; Baines, *History of the Cotton Manufacture in Great Britain*, pp. 172–9; Also *Dictionary of National Biography*, Vol. LIX, p. 277, and E. Baines jun., *History of the County Palatine and Duchy of Lancaster* (London, 1868), Vol. II, Appendix VI, p. 706.

the water-frame pushed the demand for cardings beyond the capacity of the old methods.[1] In Arkwright's larger factories, or those of his licensees, carding was an adjunct to the water-frame. In the 1770's, moreover, it often constituted the core of small country mills which combined carding engines with a variety of operations.[2] Figures on the speed of incorporation of carding machinery and the level of profits it created are almost unavailable. In 1779, however, an apologist for workmen who destroyed carding and other machines in Lancashire hesitatingly submitted a "low computation" (presumably for Manchester) of two hundred carding machines with twenty pairs of cards each.[3]

The productivity advantages of the spinning machines and carding engines over the old methods were estimated by the same apologist as follows:

Patent Machine costs per lb. of cotton

Picking	$1\frac{1}{4}d.$
Carding and Roving	$\frac{3}{4}d.$
Spinning	$1\frac{1}{2}d.$
Reeling	$1d.$
Wear and tear and overlooker	$1\frac{1}{2}d.$
TOTAL	$6d.$

Hand Spinning per lb. of cotton: 3s.

This estimate of a six-fold advantage for the factory in spinning and allied activities about 1780 cannot be taken literally. In the light of Arkwright's reported profits, however, it is probably not far off the mark. These figures apply, furthermore, to those years just before the explosive attempt to annul Arkwright's patents. If the profit differential even approached the above estimate, it is not surprising that those "regressive" symptoms of disturbance broke in the early 1780's.

THE EARLY FACTORY SYSTEM: FIRST APPROXIMATION

What were the characteristics of the new spinning factories? How were these characteristics related to the dissatisfactions which gave rise to them? In discussing these questions, we shall attempt to relate the *structural* features of the new factory system in the 1780's and 1790's to the *dynamic* sequences which led to its formation.

[1] Guest, *A Compendious History of the Cotton Manufacture,* p. 18.
[2] Wadsworth and Mann, *The Cotton Trade and Industrial Lancashire,* pp. 492–3. Above, pp. 89–90.
[3] *Ibid.,* p. 502.

Structural Differentiation in Spinning (continued)

The first point of departure is to reject explicitly the notion that "technology" explains the rise of the factory system. According to this view, the rise of factories is attributed to the physical characteristics of fixed capital, such as the size of machines, the need for a centralized power source, etc. These characteristics do account for *several* features of the factory system. Some, however, must be related to other than technological conditions.

The second point of departure is the fact that "the factory" is, in many respects, variable. The functional dimensions of an industry provide several bases for organizing industrial action, and roles along these dimensions vary considerably in degree of differentiation, e.g., in the degree of control over fixed and working capital (C_A) by certain agents, the control over decisions to produce (C_G), etc. We have seen that in pre-factory modifications of industrial structure—weaving sheds, the putting-out system, installing looms in workers' homes, etc.—the differentiation along these functional lines varied considerably. This variability extends to the factory system as well; the early factory based on the water-frame, carding engine, and/or spinning jenny is only one type. Our problem is to relate this particular *type* of factory to the institutional conditions which gave rise to it.

One approach to the problem is to construct an *ideal type* for purposes of comparison and analysis, such as Weber's outline of the conditions for the maximum formal rationality of capital accounting. Three of Weber's conditions are: (1) Complete appropriation of all non-human means of production by the owners. This means a maximum differentiation of roles controlling capital (C_A) from those engaged in the technical processes of production (C_L). (2) Absence of appropriation of jobs by workers and conversely absence of appropriation of workers by owners (formally free labour). In other words, the worker should neither own his job (C_L) nor be owned by those in control of production (C_G). (3) Calculability of the technical conditions of the productive process, including labour discipline. This implies a complete differentiation along the dimension connecting C_G (co-ordination of production at the *market* level) and C_L (co-ordination of production at the *plant* level).* There should be no intervening elements in the relationship between the former and those under his discipline. Of course such conditions are never realized empirically; nevertheless they constitute an analytical aid in understanding various empirical arrangements.[1]

I assume the following: (1) the conditions outlined by Weber are closer to the standards of economic rationality than their less dif-

---

* This relationship is summarized by the C_{G_i}–C_{L_i} boundary-interchange.

[1] Weber, *The Theory of Social and Economic Organization*, pp. 252–3.

ferentiated counterparts; (2) the modern factory system approximates these conditions more closely than other types of capitalist organization, such as the independent producer, the putting-out system, etc. Even with these assumptions, Weber's conditions for economic rationality—maximum differentiation along several axes—lead only to a certain analytical point. The conditions, being static, have little explanatory force for the dynamics of the development of various historical instances of industrial organization. Such dynamics are complicated and irregular; the cotton industry, for instance, twisted, spiralled, reversed, and creaked as it accumulated the elements which carried it nearer to Weber's conditions of extensive role differentiation. By utilizing the model of structural differentiation, it is possible to account, in part at least, for the *selective* rise of these conditions. In this way a dynamic dimension is added to Weber's comparatively static analysis of social structure.

The dynamic proposition is that the salient features of the structure emerging after a process of differentiation correspond to the salient structural foci of the initial dissatisfactions. Let us first summarize the salient dissatisfactions in the middle eighteenth century in terms of the table of resources (Figure 6):

Dissatisfaction	Resource level
Misallocation of resources in the industry, with emphasis on shortages in the spinning and other preparatory processes	*I*-5
Ineffective means of disciplining labour with regard to honesty, punctuality, motivation, &c.	*I*-6
Inadequacy of the common spinning-wheel and ineffective control over raw cotton, weft, and other working capital	*A*-6*

What were the major structural characteristics of the new factories? First, the factory system marked a dramatic *centralization* of industrial effort. In part this arose from the misallocation of resources (*I*-5), for centralization occurred first in the spinning and allied branches. A second generating factor was the dissatisfaction with the existing level of control over fixed and working capital (*A*-6). To bring working capital to the owner's premises reduced the amount of "fetching and carrying" and enhanced his control over workers' dishonesty and lack of punctuality. Furthermore, it later became apparent that the carding engine and the water-frame required a power source greater than human power. All these dissatisfactions hastened the centralization of capital. Thus by the process of

* In terms of boundary-interchanges, I-5 corresponds to $C_{I_i}-C_{A_i}$; I-6 to $C_G - C_{L_i}$, and A-6 to $C_{A_g}-C_{L_g}$. Above pp. 48–9.

centralization the spinning branch moved closer to Weber's first condition—the appropriation of all non-human means of production by owners. This differentiation relieved the salient dissatisfactions with the putting-out system.[1]

We should not push the notion of centralization too far, however. Centralization of machinery and workers does not imply that workers necessarily cease to appropriate their own jobs; nor does centralization as such discipline the labour force. In the case of the water-frame and carding engine, of course, a centralized power source required a certain punctuality and constancy of attention from labour. But on the other hand, hand spinning on jennies, and several operations associated with power-spinning—scavenging, cleaning machinery, reeling, etc.—did not require a regular work-day, so long as the jobs were completed. We should not, therefore, attempt to solve Weber's other conditions automatically by reference to the requirements for centralized machinery. A number of *other* factors—also identifiable in the sequence of differentiation—contributed to the degree to which these latter conditions were fulfilled.

Some of these factors are to be found in a preliminary discussion of the labour supply for the new factories. The early mills were "thinly strewn over the country," and hence situated in sparsely populated areas.[2] Furthermore, the attractiveness of the weaving-farming complex in the country areas undoubtedly posed resistances to entering a new employment, especially when weavers' wages had been boosted by the advent of the factory system itself. And finally, on grounds which we shall discuss later, there were general resistances to the simple recruitment of women and children into factories, which

[1] Cf. Baines' characterization of the factory system: "The use of machinery was accompanied by a greater division of labour than existed in the primitive state of the manufacture; the material went through many more processes; and of course the loss of time and the risk of waste would have been much increased, if its removal from house to house at every stage of the manufacture had been necessary. It became obvious that there were several important advantages in carrying on the numerous operations of an extensive manufacture in the same building. Where water power was required, it was economy to build one mill, and put up one water-wheel, rather than several. This arrangement also enabled the master spinner himself to superintend every stage of the manufacture: it gave him a greater security against the wasteful or fraudulent consumption of the material: it saved time in the transference of the work from hand to hand: and it prevented the extreme inconvenience which would have resulted from the failure of one class of workmen to perform their part, when several other classes of workmen were dependent upon them." *History of the Cotton Manufacture in Great Britain*, pp. 184–5.

[2] *Parliamentary Papers*, 1816, III, Children employed in the Manufactories, p. 258.

would have disrupted traditional family arrangements.[1] Consequently much early factory labour was a casual compromise between full-time differentiated labour and undifferentiated, semi-agricultural labour.

... [the] casual, transient character of the early factory population is seen ... in the readiness with which workers were transferred from one occupation to another, sometimes within the mill, sometimes outside. . . . Agricultural workers had found domestic industry a profitable method employing their spare time in the slack winter months; and industrial workers had, from time immemorial, deserted their looms or frames during the summer to help with the harvest ... this looseness of differentiation persisted in the country districts for some time after the introduction of the factory system.[2]

How did factory-owners meet this crisis in labour supply? In some of the country works of Scotland, "the first supply was chiefly from the Highlands, where, from the introduction of sheep, the farmers and small cotters were forced away to seek employment in such establishments." In general, it was the "roving and dissolute characters" who sought work.[3] There was also a successful effort to import Irish labour into such centres as Glasgow and Paisley. Finally, some of the Scottish entrepreneurs in Lancashire probably encouraged labourers to migrate from Scotland by paying their cost of transportation.[4]

The most widespread solution lay, however, in the recruitment of child labour from the parish workhouses in the large towns. The old apprentice system was maintained formally intact, with an indenture of the traditional seven years or more,[5] with the master presumably providing housing, clothing, food, and a certain amount of religious

1 "Alfred," *The History of the Factory Movement* (London, 1857), Vol. I, p. 16. The father who allowed his child to enter a mill "made himself the town's talk, and the unfortunate girl so given up by her parents in after life found the door of household employment closed against her,—Because she had been a factory girl."

2 Redford, *Labour Migration in England*, pp. 19–21. For further information on the labour scarcity, cf. *Parliamentary Papers*, 1816, III, Children employed in the Manufactories, p. 259; 1839, XIX, Factory Inspectors, p. 530. Because the cities such as Manchester were already manufacturing centres and had grown considerably in the decades before the introduction of machinery, the problem of labour supply was never so critical in the crowded centres. F. Collier, *The Family Economy in the Cotton Industry* (Manchester, 1921), Chapter II, p. 1. On the other hand, concentration of factories in the cities did not characterize the industry until the early decades of the nineteenth century.

3 *Parliamentary Papers*, 1839, XIX, Factory Inspectors, p. 530.

4 Redford, *Labour Migration in England*, pp. 131, 118.

5 *Parliamentary Papers*, 1814–15, V, Parish Apprentices, p. 1573.

and educational training. Clearly this method of employment was economically irrational from certain standpoints. Wages were low, but this was counterbalanced in part by cost of maintenance. Furthermore, the troublesomeness of the diffuse responsibility for the apprentices' welfare must have been a source of continuous distraction from the economic management of the mill. And finally, the employment on the basis of indenture, which forbade the employer to discharge apprentices even in times of slack business, marked the furthest deviation from Weber's requirement of formally free labour.

The accepted reasons for the apprenticeship system of child labour in these mills are that the machinery required simple attentiveness rather than skill and that the factory owners desperately needed cheap labour. However, the continuing system of apprenticeship owes its existence also to the fact that it was not *yet* the subject of salient dissatisfaction in the minds of millowners in the late eighteenth century. Because apprenticeship had not been widely discredited, the system seemed a reasonable basis on which to recruit labour. Had it been at the core of the institutional bottlenecks of textile production—as it later became—it undoubtedly would not have been adopted on such a large scale by the early manufacturers. They probably would have relied on the other methods—recruiting the casually unemployed, the foreign, and the transient in the first period of factory labour, and their offspring in later generations.[1]

As the industry developed, it became evident that the characteristics of the new factory system conflicted with the old apprenticeship system, and that the two systems could not continue long side by side. In the first place, apprenticeship implies the acquisition of a fairly high-level skill. The tasks for the young in the early factories—piecing, picking, cleaning, batting, and scavenging—were at such a low level that it scarcely could be argued that the children were being brought into a skilled craft. Even if they were taught spinning (few young males continued into adulthood as spinners before the introduction of the mule), seven years or more was superfluous. Furthermore, the old controls of limiting apprentices' entry into the trade were being superseded completely, since recruitment was wholesale and uncoordinated. And finally, it became apparent that the care and worry for a community of apprentices contributed to the diminishing

[1] This latter phenomenon did in fact tend to displace the massive recruitment of parish apprentices. Ashton, *The Industrial Revolution*, p. 115. The largeness of scale of parish apprenticeship should not, however, be exaggerated. After examining the evidence from several factories, Redford concluded that "the apprentices, even in country mills, were not usually more than one-third of the total workers employed, and were often not more than one-quarter." *Labour Migration in England*, p. 25.

competitive abilities of the country mills. During the next several decades, therefore, from the 1780's through the Napoleonic War, the formal apprenticeship system became the source of dissatisfaction, and consequently was replaced by a system of child labour which approximated more closely—but not completely—the conditions of Weber's requirement of formally free labour.[1]

Among the most widely discussed characteristics of the early factory system is the moral character of the masters. Usually the factories are divided into two types—those run by brutal, heartless capitalists who flogged their employees, especially the apprentices;[2] and those run as "model" communities by humanitarian masters.[3] Empirically the distinction is valid, if we view the outward behaviour of the capitalists and possibly their psychological makeup. From the standpoint of control of labour, however, both types of factory management display a concern with the enforcement of discipline, which was one of the most salient points of dissatisfaction with the earlier modes of production (*I*-6).

This preoccupation with discipline [4] rested on (1) a long history of dissatisfactions with worker discipline under the putting-out system; (2) the exaggerated importance of discipline arising from the earlier scapegoating of the working populace; (3) the transient, marginal, and probably deviant character of many of the earlier adult labourers; (4) the fusion of specific economic management of apprentices with diffuse authority and concern for their welfare.

The cruel manufacturers approached the problem of discipline in a primitive and direct manner. Often this was encouraged by the structure of incentives.

A vicious and most reprehensible practice existed in those days, of paying the overseers or overlookers of the mills according to the quantity of work they could turn off in the week or month; an

[1] For a discussion of the decline of the apprenticeship system, below, p. 187.
[2] Mantoux, *The Industrial Revolution in the Eighteenth Century*, pp. 480–6; Ashton, *The Industrial Revolution*, pp. 113 ff.; and J. L. and B. Hammond, *The Town Labourer, 1760–1832* (London, 1949), Vol. I, pp. 30–47.
[3] *Annual Register*, 1792, p. 27; One Formerly a Teacher at New Lanark, *Robert Owen at New Lanark* (Manchester, 1839); R. Owen, *The Life of Robert Owen, Written by Himself* (London, 1857); *Dictionary of National Biography*, Vol. XLIV, p. 209; F. Collier, "An Early Factory Community," *Economic Journal (Economic History Supplement)*, II (1930), pp. 117–24; Unwin, *Samuel Oldknow and the Arkwrights*, pp. 159–75; *Parliamentary Papers*, 1839, XIX, Factory Inspectors, pp. 528–9.
[4] For Richard Arkwright's struggles with discipline, cf. *Dictionary of National Biography*, Vol. II, p. 85, and Ure, *The Cotton Manufacture of Great Britain*, Vol. I, pp. 258–9.

incentive to long hours of labour, which caused frequent cases of overworking and cruelty.[1]

The case of the humanitarian managers is more subtle. The literature of these masters illustrates, however, an abiding concern with improving the moral habits of the working populace in the matter of orderliness, punctuality, regularity, and temperance. Samuel Greg the younger, for instance, established a Sunday School, games and gymnastic exercises, drawing and singing classes, parties during the winter evenings, warm baths, a library, a day-school, a band, and flower-shows.[2] Greg conceived that he was making a "*home* . . . losing by degrees that restless and *migratory* spirit, which is one of the peculiar characteristics of the manufacturing population, and perhaps the greatest of all obstacles in the way of permanent improvement among them."[3] Robert Owen's efforts to help the working people included low-cost housing, retail stores, a democratic attempt at enforcing justice, and an infant education school.[4] But Owen was also looking toward the discipline and character of his workpeople, as the following anecdote, related by his son, illustrates:

Within the mills everything was punctiliously kept. Whenever I visited them with my father, I observed that he picked up the smallest flecks of cotton from the floor, handing them to some child near by, to be put in his waste-bag.

"Papa," said I one day, "what *does* it signify,—such a little speck of cotton?"

"The value of the cotton," he replied, "is nothing, but the example is much. It is very important that these people should acquire strict habits of order and economy."[5]

This concern with discipline included a general and diffuse concern for education, leisure, housing, clothing, etc., of the workpeople. In a number of cases, the factory-owners took an interest in their workers' religious welfare. In addition to Samuel Greg, we might mention Samuel Oldknow in Mellor, in whose mill the following notice appeared in 1797:

1 *Parliamentary Papers*, 1836, XXIX.1, Second Report of the Poor Law Commissioners, p. 414.

2 S. Greg, *Two Letters to Leonard Horner* (London, 1840), pp. 5–13; *Dictionary of National Biography*, Vol. XXIII, pp. 87–8.

3 Greg, *Two Letters to Leonard Horner*, p. 6.

4 F. Podmore, *Robert Owen* (London, 1906), pp. 88–9; One formerly a Teacher, *Robert Owen at New Lanark*, pp. 4–5; Owen, *Life*, pp. 232–3; and R. Owen, *A New View of Society* (London, 1813), p. 24.

5 R. D. Owen, *Threading My Way* (London, 1874), p. 73; Owen, *Life*, pp. 30–31 and 83–5.

WHEREAS The horrid and impious Vice of profane CURSING and SWEARING,—and the Habits of Losing Time,—and DRUNKEN-NESS,—are become so frequent and notorious; that unless speedily checked, they may justly provoke the Divine Vengeance to increase the Calamities these Nations now labour under.

NOTICE is hereby given, That all the Hands in the Service of SAMUEL OLDKNOW working in his Mill, or elsewhere, must be subject to the following RULE: That when any person, either Man, Woman or Child, is heard to CURSE or SWEAR, the same shall forfeit One Shilling.—And when any Hand is absent from Work, (unless unavoidably detained by Sickness, or Leave being first obtained), the same shall forfeit as many Hours of Work as have been lost; and if by the Job or Piece, after the Rate of 2s. 6d. per Day.—Such Forfeitures to be put into a Box, and distributed to the Sick and Necessitous, at the discretion of their Employer.[1]

Such concern for the general well-being and discipline of the workmen drew high praise from contemporary observers.[2] Thus several of the major characteristics of the early factory communities are traceable to the problem of establishing appropriate discipline (*I-6*, or in Weber's terms, "calculability of the technical conditions of the productive process"). Further, this concern can be related to the earlier dissatisfactions which initiated the structural differentiation resulting in the factory system itself.

To summarize, the water-frame factory of the late eighteenth century moved only "part way" toward the ideal conditions of economic rationality. Workers were segregated from their means of production, but the remnants of job appropriation by workers remained in the form of a modified apprenticeship system and family hiring.[3] Discipline posed a major problem to the early capitalists, but its enforcement had not differentiated entirely from the more diffuse community ties of the pre-factory social structure. Furthermore, by referring to the specific dissatisfactions which gave rise to the factory system, we may account in part for those structural features which were most dramatically modified and those elements of economic "irrationality" which persisted despite its rise. The most salient foci of dissatisfaction before the 1770's were the same foci which differentiated most sharply in the new factory system. Other elements such as the apprenticeship system and family hiring were

[1] Unwin, *Samuel Oldknow and the Arkwrights*, p. 198.
[2] W. C. Taylor, *Notes on a Tour in the Manufacturing Districts of Lancashire* (London, 1842), p. 163.
[3] On the problem of the recruitment of many members of the same family, below, pp. 185–93.

theoretically as incompatible with economic rationality as workers' appropriation of tools and ineffective discipline. Yet the former disappeared only when a *new* set of dissatisfactions later showed them to conflict with the industrial methods. The factory system, therefore, did not unfold all at once; it crept forward irregularly and piecemeal. By isolating the salient dissatisfactions with the earlier forms of industry and following these dissatisfactions through sequences of differentiation, we may read a degree of regularity into this discontinuous rise.

CHAPTER VI

STRUCTURAL DIFFERENTIATION
IN SPINNING (*Concluded*)

THE INTRODUCTION OF MULE SPINNING

Early Steps. The spinning jenny, the water-frame, and the carding engine boosted the fustian and calico branches of the cotton trade enormously. Muslins,[1] however, still could not compete effectively with the finer goods imported from India. The water-frame was strictly limited on higher yarn counts; in addition, it could not produce an even yarn because it lacked the jenny's "stretch" principle. The jenny, however, could produce only soft yarn suitable for weft. Samuel Crompton, subsequently the inventor of the mule, was aware of this shortcoming, as well as the inconvenience of attaching broken ends when spinning on the jenny. A brief attempt to simulate Indian muslins by using the jenny's yarn as weft failed in Lancashire around 1780.[2]

In formal terms, the primary dissatisfaction preceding the invention of the mule concerned a misallocation of resources, namely a shortage of *fine* and *regular* yarn for luxury goods (*I-5*).[3] Furthermore, the existing spinning machines were inadequate to correct this shortage (*A-6*). The records of Samuel Oldknow's firm show these dissatisfactions. In 1784 Oldknow used counts no higher than No. 44 in twist and No. 47 in weft for calicoes, shirtings, and sheetings; even for muslins he did not normally use as high as No. 66 in twist and No. 86 in weft. In 1786 Oldknow's London merchant wrote to him, "Arkwright . . . must spin finer. Tell him the reputation of our country against Scotland is at stake . . . Great Revolutions we think will

---

[1] This is the generic term for the finest quality cotton goods at the time. Unwin, *Samuel Oldknow and the Arkwrights*, p. 43.

[2] Usher, *An Introduction to the Industrial History of England*, pp. 296–7; Daniels, *The Early English Cotton Industry*, p. 117; *Dictionary of National Biography*, Vol. XIII, p. 148; Baines, *History of the Cotton Manufacture in Great Britain*, p. 334.

[3] The connection between this shortage and the subsequent incorporation of the mule is illustrated by the fact that Crompton's invention was called the Muslin Wheel for some time after its introduction. Baines, *History of the Cotton Manufacture in Great Britain*, p. 202.

happen in Lancashire amongst the Manufacturers of Cotton Yarn." [1] Through 1786 Samuel Oldknow attempted in vain to capture the English market for luxury cottons, his main stumbling-block being the supply of fine thread.

Step 5. Attempts to Specify. In 1779, after Crompton had experimented with the mule for a number of years, he brought a machine of thirty or forty spindles into operation. Its potentialities for spinning fine yarn were immediately apparent.

Crompton . . . obtained 14/– per lb. for the spinning and preparation of Number 40 . . . a short time after he got 25/– a lb. for . . . Number 60; and . . . he then spun a small quantity of Number 80 to show that it was not impossible, as was supposed, to spin yarn of so fine a grist, and for the spinning and preparation of this he got 42/– per lb.[2]

For reasons not entirely clear, Crompton never patented the mule. Perhaps he lacked the entrepreneurial temperament. It has also been suggested that a number of Lancashire manufacturers, in their anxiety to overcome Arkwright's monopoly in twist production, induced him to make the machine public by presenting him a small subscription.[3] The fact that this grant was inadequate—and in the end only half-paid—was probably one of the reasons that led Parliament to compensate Crompton in 1812.

Step 6. Implementation by Entrepreneurs. From 1779 to around 1785, mules spread over the countryside. The entrepreneurs were again domestic workers who had sufficient capital to finance its construction. "All these machines were yet worked by hand; they were erected in garrets or lofts, and many a dilapidated barn or cowshed was patched up in the walls, repaired in the room, and provided with windows to serve as lodging room for the new muslin wheels." It spread around Bolton and the other manufacturing districts, particularly Scotland, "where the peculiar yarn of this machine was in the highest degree useful." [4]

The shortage of rovings[5]—which up to 1785 were subject to Arkwright's monopolistic control—and the early mules' limited potentialities retarded this development. Mules seldom exceeded

[1] Unwin, *Samuel Oldknow and the Arkwrights*, pp. 70–72. This was written just about the time mule-spun yarn was coming into use. Its competitive power probably had provided sufficient concern to Arkwright for him to lower his prices in 1786.

[2] J. Dakeyne, *Samuel Crompton* (Bolton, 1921), p. 19.

[3] Espinasse, *Lancashire Worthies* (Second Series: London, 1878), p. 48; Daniels, *The Early English Cotton Industry*, p. 120.

[4] G. French, *Life and Times of Samuel Crompton* (London, 1859), p. 89.

[5] The loose twist prepared before actually spinning the yarn. Above, p. 51.

forty spindles, and they were not producing enough to allay the concerns of Oldknow and others over the supply of fine yarns. Hence " . . . up to 1785 . . . there were [not] a thousand spindles in existence of Crompton's construction," and by 1786, it was only "tolerably well known." [1] Around this time, however,

. . . as Arkwright's contrivances for making rovings became available to the public and were of the utmost importance to Crompton's machine, the door was opened wide for the exertions of ingenuity in preparing the cotton roving, as all could avail themselves of the advantage displayed by Arkwright's method of preparing the cotton for spinning; and the consequence was, that every one who had the slightest talent for constructiveness or appropriativeness fell to work to improve this process.[2]

It appeared, therefore, that the mule was beginning to take over the cottage spinning industry in the middle and late 1780's. In his 1787 estimate, Patrick Colquhoun listed 550 mules of 90 spindles each, or a total of 49,500 spindles.[3] Statements for profits are not available, but reports of high wages for mule-spinners, and Oldknow's growing interest in finer quality goods in 1785–6 indicate the initial successes of the mule.[4]

The *structural features* of this sequence of differentiation parallel the introduction of the domestic jenny, in so far as mule-spinning represented primarily a differentiation *within* the C_L sub-system whereby the spinning of finer yarns differentiated further from the other processes of manufacture. Until the 1790's the mule remained in the cottage, and hence within the confines of the domestic system of labour. One interesting feature, to which we shall return, is that the mule, like the later jenny, required the labour of a skilled adult male.[5]

[1] J. Kennedy, "A Brief Memoir of Samuel Crompton, with a description of his Machine called the Mule, and of the subsequent improvement of the Machine by Others," *Memoirs of the Literary and Philosophical Society of Manchester*, Second Series, V (1831), pp. 330, 335.

[2] *Ibid.*, pp. 330–31. In 1786 the "Billy" appeared, which was a mule modified to produce rovings at reduced cost. Henry Stones, a mechanic familiar with the water-frame, superimposed metal rollers on the mule. A man by the name of Baker also introduced several important modifications. By 1786 the number of spindles upon an individual mule had risen to 108, at least in the Bolton area. *Ibid.*, pp. 329–32. French, *Life and Times of Samuel Crompton*, p. 101. Formally these improvements and specifications represent "regressions" to Step 5, occurring because of the difficulties the mule encountered in Step 6.

[3] *An Important Crisis . . . Explained*, p. 4. Like the estimate for jennies, this figure is probably based on guesswork.

[4] Kennedy, "A Brief Memoir of Samuel Crompton," *op. cit.*, p. 335, and Unwin, *Samuel Oldknow and the Arkwrights*, pp. 43–5.

[5] Pinchbeck, *Women Workers in the Industrial Revolution*, p. 186.

Midway in the mule's "take-off" period, however, in the summer of 1787, a severe trade depression set in, possibly because of the frenzied activity following the freeing of Arkwright's patents in 1785. For the finer branches, this depression worsened when the East India Company marketed muslin and calico cloth 60% more than its average annual imports for the past seven years.[1] During the next few years these circumstances produced a number of "regressive" symptoms of disturbance, handling and channelling, and attempts to establish a better competitive basis for muslin manufacturing.

A movement for protection crystallized shortly after the onset of the depression. Manufacturers from Lancashire and the Glasgow area selected Patrick Colquhoun of Glasgow[2] to head a delegation to agitate for relief in London. In 1788 and for several years following, Colquhoun produced a number of fiery pamphlets, reference to which illustrates the manufacturers' disturbed state of mind. In the earliest of these documents, Colquhoun bemoaned: "the pressure of the occasion makes it of the utmost importance that the nature and extent of the danger which at present threatens nearly *one half* of the Cotton Trade in Great Britain should be well understood. The case is sudden and without example." In contrast, he saw a blissful future if relief were granted. ". . . [Nothing] is wanted but a fine raw material, to fix in Great Britain, *for ever*, a decided *pre-eminence in the manufacture of Muslins.*"[3] The obstacle to advance, moreover, was clear:

It is not a crisis in the Manufacture of that nature, which often arises in every branch of trade, where a temporary stagnation is succeeded by a brisk demand. The evil has a much deeper root. From the rapid increase in trade, it is plain to demonstration, that in the common articles of apparel there is not room in the British markets both for the home Manufactures, and for the same species of goods imported from India.[4]

To remedy this apparent stranglehold on the British market, Colquhoun suggested "a TOTAL restriction of the East India calicoes and muslins for home-consumption," and the establishment of a General Hall in London for displaying British goods, the

---

[1] For a discussion of this depression, cf. Unwin, *Samuel Oldknow and the Arkwrights*, pp. 87–96.

[2] For an account of Colquhoun's activities in the 1780's, cf. Iatros (pseud.), *The Life and Writings of Patrick Colquhoun* (London, 1818), pp. 9–14.

[3] *An Important Crisis . . . Explained*, pp. 11–12, 8–9.

[4] *Ibid.*, pp. 14–15. For further attacks on the East India Company, cf. *Case of the British Cotton Spinners*, pp. 1, 6.

issuance of catalogues, and the establishment of machinery for promoting sales abroad.[1] The opposition to the East India Company was particularly vociferous in Glasgow, a centre of muslin manufacturing.[2] The high feelings in Lancashire spilled over into a standing controversy between the calico and muslin manufacturers on the one hand and the fustian manufacturers on the other.[3]

In 1788 the East India Company responded in kind by producing a paper which claimed that seventeen-twentieths of its calicoes and three-fifths of its muslins were re-exported and hence did not compete domestically. Parliament intervened in this incipient conflict of interests. With regard to the manufacturers' appeal for marketing advantages, it exempted British cotton manufactures from the auction duty, thus placing them on the same basis as the East India Company in public sales. With regard to direct restrictions on the Company, however, Parliament hesitated, believing the distress to have resulted not from competition but from temporary overstocking and speculating. "On such Occasions, Distress will induce Men to catch at every means for Relief; conceiving that if the Company could be prevented from importing, they should be enabled to dispose of their Surplus Stocks."[4]

In this way Parliament acted as a "handling" agency in a period of disturbance. It received all the complaints and recommendations from a distressed group, studied them, allowed some but cancelled others. In the meantime other agencies were involved in "channelling" energy toward solutions consonant with the performance-centred value-system.* Samuel Oldknow, a leader in the muslin

---

[1] *Considerations Relative to a Plan of Relief for the Cotton Manufactory, By the Establishment of a General Hall in the City of London* (London, 1788), p. 9; *Observations on the means of extending the Consumption of British Callicoes, Muslins and other Cotton Goods, and of giving pecuniary Aids to the Manufacturers, under Circumstances of the highest Respectability and Advantage* (London, 1788), p. 2 ff. Also *An Important Question, shortly stated: Relative to the Present Competition between the Callico and Muslin Manufactures of Great Britain; and the same Species of Goods Imported from the East Indies* (London, 1788); *A Representation of the Facts Relative to the Rise and Progress of the Cotton Manufacture in Great Britain, with Observations on the Means of Extending and Improving this valuable Branch of Trade* (London, 1789).

[2] Each time the question of renewing the East India Company's charter was discussed in the following decades, the Glasgow Chamber of Commerce raised noisy opposition—in 1792, 1812, and finally in 1831, two years before the Charter was finally abrogated. Stewart, *Progress of Glasgow*, pp. 37–41.

[3] A. Redford, *Manchester Merchants and Foreign Trade* (Manchester, 1934), p. 14.

[4] *Parliamentary Papers*, 1793, XXXVIII, Paper 774c, Cotton Manufacture, pp. 1–2.

* For a characterization of this dimension, above, pp. 25–7.

trade, joined the cry for protection against Indian goods. In this connection, he received the following note from his consignee in London in 1788:

We again repeat our Sentiments that we cannot see what mode of redress you can apply for to Govermt. Sir Richard Arkwright joins us in Opinion that you must make fewer Goods and make them better & this doctrine we preach to you in particular. Mind your own Manufacture and leave the rest to pursue whatever means they may in their wisdom think best . . . Good muslins and British are selling so very cheap that we are amazed from whence they come, but it is from Lancashire or Cheshire.[1]

The sequence of these events is instructive. When the innovation clustering around the mule was midway in Step 6, a number of obstacles—severe depression, overstocked inventories, and a stock of East Indian goods—arose simultaneously. Immediately a number of symptoms of anxiety and aggression appeared—to eliminate East Indian goods; to relieve domestic manufactures, etc. To right these disturbances, Parliament "handled" some of the tensions, and business leadership "channelled" energies into productive lines. The delicate interaction of these forces set aright the movement to complete the innovational sequence in accordance with the value-system which emphasized industrial *performance*. Considerations such as these justify the judgment that "the effect of the competition of India combined with that of Lancashire and Scotland was to give Oldknow a stronger impetus towards the adoption of the factory system." [2]

This sequence of events also illustrates the place of the value-system in structural differentiation. At the performance-centred extremes, the emphasis in an unstable situation is on active performance to overcome obstacles. The obstacles may differ from case to case. In the 1750's and 1760's these were over-demand and institutional bottlenecks; in the crisis of 1787–8 a temporary under-demand for accumulated stocks. Yet if the potential entrepreneur is predisposed to assess the situation in terms of his own performance, *both* types of disequilibrium are likely to produce innovational activity, since appropriate reactions are defined in terms of performance-centred values.

As soon as the worst of the trade depression had passed, the mule marched ahead. For 1789 Colquhoun estimated 5,000 mules in England and 1,000 in Scotland, with 700,000 spindles in all.[3] This

[1] Unwin, *Samuel Oldknow and the Arkwrights*, pp. 101, 45.
[2] *Ibid.*, p. 98.
[3] *Case of the British Cotton Spinners*, Appendix.

figure, while clearly inexact, not only dwarfed the figure of 59,500 spindles for 1787, but also raised the average number of spindles per mule from 90 in 1787 to 110–120 in 1789. Colquhoun also lowered his 1787 estimate of jennies from 20,070 with 1,605,000 spindles to 20,000 with 1,400,000 spindles for 1789, indicating possibly the early stages of supersession of the jenny by the mule.

Judgments of increases in production in the 1790's are unsatisfactory. The tripling of cotton imports between 1781 and 1791

TABLE 4

PATRICK COLQUHOUN'S ESTIMATES OF THE COMPOSITION
OF PRODUCTION, 1787–89

1787 Estimate

Branch	Lb. Consumed
Calicoes and muslins	10,440,000
Fustians	5,400,000
Mixtures—silk and linen	1,800,000
Hosiery	1,350,000
Candle-wicks	1,350,000
Cotton waste and dirt removed	2,260,000
TOTAL	22,600,000

1789 Estimate

Branch	Lb. Consumed
Calicoes and muslins	13,000,000
Fustians, etc.	6,500,000
Silk mixed goods, checks, etc.	1,500,000
Hosiery	1,800,000
Candle-wicks	1,700,000
Cotton waste and dirt removed	3,000,000
TOTAL	27,500,000

resulted from the opening of Arkwright's patent and the introduction of the mule. We may form an idea of the composition of this increase, however, by comparing Colquhoun's estimates for 1787 and 1789. For the latter, he included approximately a 10% loss in weight during the course of manufacture. In Table 4, I have produced his estimates for 1787 and 1789, the former total reduced by 10%.[1] In addition to the generally rapid growth, the table shows that even though all the

[1] I reduced this total on the suggestion of a criticism of Colquhoun by Ure, who felt that the 1787 totals were erroneous because they did not account for waste in production. *The Cotton Manufacture of Great Britain*, Vol. I, p. 298.

branches except cotton mixtures were growing, the finer fabrics subsumed under calico and muslin increased slightly faster (25% growth from 1787 to 1789) than fustians (20% growth). While these figures are necessarily approximate, the movement is consistent with the burst which mule-spinning gave to the finer branches in the late 1780's. This impression is corroborated by contemporary observers' comments[1] and by the report of the select committee on the cotton manufacture in 1793 that "every Shop offers British Muslins for Sale, equal in Appearance, and of more elegant Patterns, than those of India, for One Fourth, or perhaps more than One Third less in Price . . . the comparative Value of the Indian Goods consumed in this Country [is] totally insignificant."[2]

Notwithstanding this gigantic growth in muslins, several dissatisfactions pressed toward the centralization of the mule. The potentiality of spindle-multiplication was distinctly limited by the inadequacies of human power, by the small size of cottage facilities, and by the lack of capital of the small mule-spinners. Furthermore, all the difficulties of authority, enforcement of punctuality, guarantee of quality, prevention of embezzlement, etc., lingered.

Hence around the late 1780's the centralization of mule power began to appear in two forms: (1) Spinners gathered to work hand mules in sheds. In the Catrine works in Scotland, hand-mule spinning was carried on until 1801.[3] During the years 1795–9, hand-spinning in sheds was widespread around Manchester. The habits of domestic industry persisted in these sheds, however. "[The operative spinners] were very irregular, as the business at that time was done mostly by hand, and it was generally the practice to drink the first day or two of the week, and attempt to make it up by working very long hours towards the close of the week."[4] (2) In 1790 Mr. Kelley of Lanark first yoked the mule to water power. As a result "the mules were removed from the cottages to factories, were constructed more substantially and upon better mechanical principles, and produced yarn of a more uniform quality and at less expense."[5] Neither of these modifications developed fully, however, for just as they were introduced, steam invaded the cotton manufacture.

[1] Kennedy, "A Brief Memoir of Samuel Crompton," *op. cit.*, pp. 339, 344–5.

[2] *Parliamentary Papers*, 1793, XXXVIII, Paper 774c, Cotton Manufacture, p. 5.

[3] *Parliamentary Papers*, 1834, XX, Supplementary Report by the Factory Commissioners, p. 27.

[4] *Parliamentary Papers*, 1816, III, Children employed in the Manufactories, p. 472.

[5] Kennedy, "Rise and Progress of the Cotton Manufacture," *op. cit.*, p. 129.

THE INTRODUCTION OF STEAM POWER

Early Steps. Water power was not without its inconveniences. The river's flow varied by season, and the now-crowded streams made the supply of water from artificial reservoirs precarious, hence making constancy of water power and hours of work irregular.[1] Furthermore, water-wheels were known to be "ill-constructed, deficient in power, and constantly breaking down or getting out of repair," which was a "grievous drawback at a time when trade was good."[2] Besides the imperfections in the source of power itself, the increasing complexity of machines made for "difficulty in procuring an increase of machinery, or in repairing that already in use," because mills were removed from the machine manufacture and because skilled mechanics, such as "watch and clock-makers, white-smiths, and mathematical instrument-makers," were not available in the country districts.[3] In formal terms the dissatisfactions clustered at the levels of *A*-6, the procurement and quality of capital machinery, and *G*-6, the misallocation of skills.

It is significant, therefore, that the Society of Arts offered a premium for "Increasing Steam" in 1783,[4] and continued this offer through the feverish years of the industrial revolution. There were unsuccessful attempts, furthermore, to apply certain old and inadequate techniques of steam propulsion.[5] The ultimate improvement of the steam-engine rested primarily on the shoulders of Boulton and Watt; after they had made "essential improvements" in 1781, 1782, and 1784,[6] the problem of power rested on the ability to assure enough capital to construct and install an engine.

Step 6. Implementation by Entrepreneurs. The first steam-engine for cotton was installed in 1785; subsequently in the 1780's and early 1790's engines were erected primarily by men already in possession of ample capital—men like Drinkwater, Arkwright, Oldknow, and Peel.[7] Between 1785 and 1795 some forty-seven steam engines with a total of 736 h.p. were applied to cotton in England alone;

---

[1] E. Halevy, *History of the English People in the 19th Century* (London, 1949), Vol. I, pp. 275–6.

[2] W. Pole, *The Life of Sir William Fairbairn* (London, 1877), pp. 121–2.

[3] Kennedy, "Rise and Progress of the Cotton Manufacture," *op. cit.,* pp. 122, 124.

[4] *Transactions of the Society of Arts,* Vol. I, 1783, p. 179. The need for steam power was naturally tied to industries other than cotton.

[5] Kennedy, "Rise and Progress of the Cotton Manufacture," *op. cit.,* p. 126.

[6] Baines, *History of the Cotton Manufacture in Great Britain,* p. 225.

[7] Crabtree, *Richard Arkwright,* pp. 63–4; Unwin, *Samuel Oldknow and the Arkwrights,* p. 123; French, *The Life and Times of Samuel Crompton,* pp. 113–15.

between 1795 and 1800 another thirty-five engines, with 637 h.p., were installed. From 1785 to 1800 Scotland accumulated eight engines with 128 h.p.[1]

This innovation is interesting because it "did not create the modern factory system, but it lent that system its power, and gave it a force of expansion as irresistible as itself."[2] Beneath the surface, however, the roles imposed by the first factories were sharpened considerably by the steam-engine. For instance, since installing steam power meant an outlay of capital which excluded individuals possessing small amounts, the introduction of steam gradually tightened the control over capital and differentiated more sharply between roles involved in the control of capital (C_A) and those involved in the processes of production (C_L). By the same token, it differentiated more completely between those responsible for the decisions to produce (C_G) and those engaged in production (C_L). Workmen became more subordinated to a work discipline, because the power-source lay in steam, not in their own muscles; they could no longer pace their industry in the cottage or even work sixteen hours a day during the last days of the week in a hand-mule shed to make up for a leisurely Monday and Tuesday. The introduction of steam, therefore, did not create new roles, but pushed the old to a new level of specificity.[3]

With the heavy capitalization between 1785 and 1800, we would normally expect a comparable increase in production. In fact, however, the increase of imported raw cotton between 1791 and 1801 was $67\frac{1}{2}\%$, and between 1801 and 1811 only $39\frac{1}{2}\%$; sizeable to be certain, but tiny when compared to the 320% of the preceding decade and the bursts in the second and third decades of the nineteenth century. The explanation lies in the long and severe period of the Revolutionary and Napoleonic wars, which postponed the full rewards of steam and the factory mule for two decades, just as Arkwright's monopolistic practices had dampened Step 6 in the introduction of water-

[1] Figures taken from J. Lord, *Capital and Steam-Power, 1750–1800* (London, 1923), pp. 166–72. The English figures show an increasing average size of engine even before the end of the century. Between 1785 and 1795 the average was 15·9 h.p., as contrasted with 18·1 in the following five years.

[2] Mantoux, *The Industrial Revolution in the Eighteenth Century*, p. 345.

[3] *Parliamentary Papers*, 1816, III, Children employed in the Manufactories, pp. 472–3. Steam innovations and the growing complexity of machinery did, however, lie at the foundation of an entirely new industry. Heretofore the mechanical invention and maintenance of capital equipment had been performed primarily on an "on call" basis by the millwright, carpenter, clockmaker, etc. But as the machinery became more costly and complex, greater specialization along the C_{Ia}–C_{La} dimension began to appear. Thus an industry for the construction of steam-engines and textile machinery began to be differentiated. Cf. S. Smiles, *Industrial Biography* (London, 1863), pp. 299–300.

frame factories, and just as severe depression and competition had dampened Step 6 in the growth of the muslin manufacture. The cotton trade in the war period was suspended in the middle of Step 6, as it were, and did not realize its growth potential fully until after the wars.

If the years from 1793 to 1815 had been peaceful, there is every reason to believe that the cotton industry would have spiralled to new heights.

Export markets would have been more steadily available, and the supply of raw cotton would have been cheaper and more abundant. Further, to the extent that war-time conditions obstructed the flow of foreign wheat to Britain (helping to raise the cost of living, lowering real wages) the domestic demand for cotton goods was less than it would have been. Similarly, had there been no war, it is doubtful whether investment in agriculture would have been as large as, in fact, it was. A greater quantity of resources might have been freed for industrial investment.[1]

In fact, however, the war inhibited industrial development. Probably its effect on exports was the most significant. European buying, having expanded greatly during the latter half of the eighteenth century, was restricted as early as 1793, when the French government passed a series of measures prohibiting English goods, including textiles. By 1796 Napoleon had invaded Italy and threatened the Mediterranean. The fall of Spain and the capitulation of Portugal in 1800 closed many British markets. By 1801 the Commercial Society of Manchester, formed to protect commercial interests in the crisis, had become almost inactive, largely because "the home demand for manufactures was, under such circumstances, exceedingly small, and the foreign trade was highly hazardous and restricted by the perils of war, danger of capture or destruction of merchandise."[2] The peace of 1802–3 brought relief and a brief boom.[3] Exports rose slightly between 1805 and 1812, when the Orders in Council and the Continental System came to an end, but the fluctuations were enormous, as Table 5 shows.

Political difficulties created an unpredictable import supply as well. When the United States—the principal supplier of cotton—applied an embargo on exports to Britain in 1807, imports of raw

[1] Gayer, Rostow and Schwartz, *Growth and Fluctuation of the British Economy*, p. 649.

[2] E. Helm, *Chapters in the History of the Manchester Chamber of Commerce* (London, 1902), pp. 59–60. Also Redford, *Manchester Merchants and Foreign Trade*, pp. 15, 25–44.

[3] Daniels, "The Cotton Trade During the Revolutionary and Napoleonic Wars," *op. cit.*, p. 63.

119

cotton dropped from 53,180,000 lb. in that year to 7,993,000 lb. in 1808 and 13,366,000 lb. in 1809. During the war of 1812, American exports to Great Britain dropped from 38,073,000 lb. in 1811 to 23,461,000 lb. in 1812 and to 9,279,000 lb. in 1813.[1]

TABLE 5

EXPORTS OF COTTON GOODS, 1805-12 [2]

Year	Cotton Manufactured Goods	Twist and Yarn	Total Exports
1805	£8,619,990	£914,475	£9,534,465
1806	9,753,824	736,225	10,489,049
1807	9,708,046	601,719	10,309,765
1808	12,503,918	472,078	12,986,096
1809	18,425,614	1,020,352	19,445,966
1810	17,898,519	1,053,475	18,951,994
1811	11,529,551	483,598	12,013,149
1812	15,723,225	794,465	16,517,690

TABLE 6

CONSUMPTION OF RAW COTTON, 1801-15 [3]

Year	Lb.
1801	53,203,433
1802	56,615,120
1803	52,251,231
1804	61,364,158
1805	58,878,163
1806	57,524,416
1807	72,748,363
1808	41,961,115
1809	88,461,177
1810	123,701,826
1811	90,309,668
1812	61,285,024
1813	50,966,000
1814	53,777,802
1815	92,525,951

What was the effect of these extraordinary conditions on the industry? Porter reported that ". . . from the beginning of the century to the return of peace [1815] is marked by a striking sluggish-

[1] G. W. Daniels, "The Cotton Trade at the Close of the Napoleonic War," *Transactions of the Manchester Statistical Society* (1917–18), p. 5.

[2] Daniels, "The Cotton Trade During the Revolutionary and Napoleonic Wars, *op. cit.*, p. 76.

[3] G. R. Porter, *The Progress of the Nation* (London, 1912), p. 296. These figures, calculated by subtracting the quantity of raw cotton exported from that imported, give only the approximate course of production. Daniels, "The Cotton Trade at the Close of the Napoleonic War," *op. cit.*, pp. 18–20.

ness of trade. [The cotton trade] may almost be said to have stopped, and in fact the quantity of raw material manufactured in each of the two last years of the war was smaller than that consumed in 1801."[1] This statement is perhaps a little gloomy. The years 1813 and 1814 were exceptionally low, and in more prosperous years such as 1809, 1810, and 1811, the quantity consumed was almost double either 1801 or 1813–14, as Table 6 shows. These figures reveal extreme irregularity rather than simple stagnation. In a calculation of the fluctuations in the cotton trade between 1790 and 1850, Gayer, Rostow, and Schwartz found that fluctuations were more frequent during the Napoleonic war than afterwards.[2]

One effect of this irregularity is seen in bankruptcy figures. From 1786 to 1800, inclusive, the average annual number of bankruptcies in the cotton industry was 3·53 firms. Between 1801 and 1815, inclusive, the average was 13, while from 1816 to 1830, inclusive, a period including several "depression" years, the average was only 11·2.[3] Yet industrial capacity seemed to grow during the war, mainly in 1802 and 1803. The only available figures show 52 factories in Manchester in 1802, 64 in 1809, and 64 in 1816.[4] This investment, added to the burst in the 1790's, probably means that the industry was operating under conditions of excess productive capacity during the war.

Industrial composition changed as well during this period. Let us recall Colquhoun's estimate of spindles for 1789:

Jenny spindles	Water-frame spindles	Mule spindles
1,400,000	310,000	700,000

In 1812 Samuel Crompton took an extensive census of the cotton trade in order to bolster his petition for monetary compensation by the government. His count yielded the following figures:

Jenny spindles	Water-frame spindles	Mule spindles
155,880	310,516	4,209,570 [5]

[1] Porter, *The Progress of the Nation*, p. 296.

[2] *Growth and Fluctuation of the British Economy*, p. 672.

[3] R. Burn, *Statistics of the Cotton Trade* (London, 1847), Table 25. It should be kept in mind that the number of firms was expanding continually between 1786 and 1830.

[4] Daniels, "The Cotton Trade at the Close of the Napoleonic War," *op. cit.*, pp. 18–21. The 1802 and 1816 figures included several districts contiguous to Manchester. The 1809 figures included only Manchester proper. It is probable, therefore, that between 1809 and 1816 there was a slight decline in the number of factories in Manchester.

[5] G. W. Daniels, "Samuel Crompton's Census of the Cotton Industry in 1812," *Economic Journal* (*Economic History Supplement*), II (1930), pp. 108–11. Daniels judged the census to have been "fairly complete."

Structural Differentiation in Spinning (concluded)

The mule had superseded the jenny; water-frame spindleage probably had not grown much; but mule spindles had multiplied during the two war decades. The mule, furthermore, was linked to new steam installation; two-thirds of the steam engines in existence in 1812 turned mules.[1]

Despite the fact that investment followed the most productive lines—mules combined with steam-engines—the industry limped through the wars with a productivity gap among firms. The continuation through the wars of jenny-spinners at a clear productivity disadvantage to more advanced machines, illustrates this spotty composition. And because of the variable trade conditions the course of profits was irregular.

Sound anticipation was impossible, and what is revealed is a state of uncertainty, with consequent depressions and booms. With such a state of trade over a long period considerable development may take place; discreet individuals may, with much turmoil of soul, amass a fortune; but those whose comfort depends upon continuity of employment and regular wages will never be far from distress and privation. This was exactly the position of the cotton industry and those engaged in it during the period of the wars . . . during the war, profits were made by plunges and speculation.[2]

The war period, therefore, was a period of conflicting trends. Investment, which was high preceding and during the early part of the period (1785–1800), diminished but still progressed spottily during the difficult war years (1800–1815). Production climbed irregularly, though not so rapidly as might be expected from the earlier innovation and investment. Profits were irregular and bankruptcies high. The net result was the persistence of a variety of productivity levels within general conditions of excess productive capacity.

We may explain these divergent trends by one long-term and one short-term factor: (1) the imbalance of productive units resulting from the fact that the war interrupted the industry in the middle of Step 6 of the mule-steam complex; (2) the dramatic limitation of markets during the war period. The first factor explains the high level of investment which pushed into the 1790's. It also explains the direction of investment toward mules and steam-engines. But being interrupted by the war, this growth could not proceed rapidly. This

[1] McCulloch, "An Essay on the Rise, Progress, Present State, and Prospects of the Cotton Manufacture," *op. cit.*, p. 15.

[2] Daniels, "The Cotton Trade During the Revolutionary and Napoleonic Wars," *op. cit.*, p. 55.

122

Structural Differentiation in Spinning (concluded)

interruption explains also the persistence of high profit-levels.[1] Because Steps 6 and 7 had not yet wiped out the obsolete industrial elements, there was still a differential of productivity. Furthermore, bankruptcies were associated as much with the flukes of demand as with the persistent pressure of more productive firms on less productive ones. Demand would leap during a year when markets became available, and the entire industry would push its products; demand would drop the following year, and those firms which chanced to be in embarrassing inventory positions would collapse while the others tightened their belts. Then prosperity would return for a year or two, allowing the fortunate to profit, and permitting the industry to come up for air once more.

At the end of the war, therefore, the cotton industry possessed an excess capacity, a disparity of productivity levels, and consequently an opportunity for profits in the newer branches. If our analysis of the effects of the war period is correct, we should expect that, during the years following, the industry would gradually erase these older, less productive elements by consolidation, lowering of profits, and routinization associated with Step 7 of structural differentiation.

This long-term tendency certainly does not explain everything. Prices of yarn, for instance, fell continuously because prices of raw cotton fell continuously; some investigators judge this influence to have been more important than technological improvements in determining price-changes.[2] Furthermore, even though we treat the post-war period primarily as Step 7, technological innovation was proceeding apace. Power-loom weaving underwent great improvements in its own Step 6 from approximately 1822 to the middle of the century. Mules were expanding in size and number of spindles, and a self-acting mule entered the spinning branch. In addition, Ure listed 1,194 patents for improvements in "cotton-spinning, &c." from January 1800 to July 1860, inclusive; 854 of these cluster between 1850 and 1860. But most of these were "improvements . . . in the details and not in principle." [3] While they reduced spinning costs, they merely rounded out the basic lines which had been laid down by the earlier innovations. All these features and more contributed to

[1] Gayer, Rostow, and Schwartz, *Growth and Fluctuation of the British Economy*, p. 653.

[2] *Ibid.*, p. 838. For an attempt to assess the relative influence of the price of raw cotton, the improvements in spinning, and the improvements in weaving, respectively, cf. Chapter VII, Appendix.

[3] Ure, *The Cotton Manufacture of Great Britain*, Vol. I, pp. 317–52; J. Nasmith, "The Inventive Epoch in the Cotton Trade," *Transactions of the Manchester Association of Engineers* (Manchester, 1897), p. 22. Also *Parliamentary Papers*, 1833, VI, Manufactures, Commerce and Shipping, p. 41.

industrial development in the decades after 1815. I shall consider, however, only the gradual erasure of outmoded plant by the industrial centralization, particularly in Lancashire (Steps 6 and 7 of the steam-mule innovations), and declining profits associated with growing competition (Step 7).

Through the first decade of the nineteenth century, even though the introduction of steam-power had begun decades earlier, "water-power was still considered to be the more economical agent, except for its irregularity of working." Indeed, water-driven mills increased steadily up through the Napoleonic war.[1] Between 1811 and 1821, however,

> ... the increase in the number of cotton factories was causing local increases of population, not only throughout southern and central Lancashire, but also in Cheshire, Cumberland, Derbyshire, and the West Riding of Yorkshire. At the same period the establishment of cotton mills was leading to increased population in many towns and villages of Scotland from Dumfriesshire to Aberdeen. On the other hand, the failure of isolated cotton mills was being reported from Cumberland, Derbyshire, Staffordshire, and Warwickshire ... In Scotland the increases of population attributed to the expansion of the cotton trade were now mainly in Renfrew; and mills in the less accessible parts of the country were being abandoned.[2]

The demise of the less efficient firms was accentuated in periods of deep slump or depression. "One of the most characteristic features" of the depression of 1841–2, for instance, was the failure of the older firms.[3] Even in more prosperous times, when profits were better but still tending to fall, the firms with older plant felt the pinch sooner.[4]

Accompanying these "mopping-up" operations of Step 7 was the

---

[1] Redford, *Labour Migration in England*, p. 32; Ashton, *The Industrial Revolution*, pp. 73–4.

[2] Redford, *Labour Migration in England*, pp. 33–4. In 1780–90 less than one-third of the cotton mills were in Lancashire; by 1835 this had increased to more than a half. Furthermore, the Lancashire mills were comparatively more modern than those in other counties. R. Robson, *Structure of the Cotton Industry* (London, 1950), p. 27.

[3] R. C. O. Matthews, *A Study in Trade-Cycle History* (Cambridge, 1954), p. 145.

[4] "You have stated that the trade in cotton spinning, from 1826 to the present time [1833] has been unprofitable?—Generally so.

"Do you mean uniformly so?—I do not mean universally so; I think that those houses which labour under the disadvantages of having to purchase the material on credit, or who have old machinery, have not got a profit." *Parliamentary Papers*, 1833, VI, Manufactures, Commerce and Shipping, p. 557.

general decline of profits between 1815 and 1850.[1] As the antiquated firms were gradually extinguished, the productivity differential among the new and modern firms grew less and less. There are no indubitable figures establishing this decline. The several series in Table 7, however, show the differences between prices and costs in several finished products. The figures indicate neither profit percentages on capital invested nor total profits for the industry, but rather profit per unit. While inexact, therefore, the figures show a general downward trend of profits associated with Step 7. Verbal

TABLE 7

DECLINING PROFITS, 1802–44 [2]

	Difference between cost and selling price of calico		Difference between price of cotton and twist		Selling price of calico less price paid for weaving and cotton	
Annual average	Pence per piece	Index	Pence per lb.	Index	Pence	Index
1802–05	—	—	20·20	149	—	—
1806–10	—	—	16·49	122	—	—
1811–13	—	—	11·86	87	—	—
1814–19	7·96	100	13·57	100	217·50	100
1820–25	3·75	47	10·01	74	149·54	69
1826–30	−0·30	—	7·21	53	91·05	42
1831–33	1·33	17	5·72	42	77·33	36
1834–39	—	—	—	—	82·33	38
1840–44	—	—	—	—	58·65	27

evidence agrees with these quantitative estimates.[3] This decline is related to routinizing production, exhausting the opportunities for exploiting new methods, and consumers' acceptance of the improved products on a routine basis.[4] The industry, once again in

[1] Between 1850 and 1896 the profit margins in the industry were halved again, probably because of increasing structural differentiation of the cotton industry in Britain, and because of the effects of international competition. D. A. Farnie, *The English Cotton Industry, 1850–96* (Manchester, 1953), pp. iii, 419–27.

[2] Gayer, Rostow, and Schwartz, *Growth and Fluctuation of the British Economy*, p. 653.

[3] *Parliamentary Papers*, 1833, VI, Manufactures, Commerce and Shipping, pp. 39, 315, 556–8.

[4] This conclusion agrees with Schumpeter's theory of declining profits. *Theory of Economic Development*, Chapter IV. For further evidence, cf. Gayer, Rostow, and Schwartz, *Growth and Fluctuation of the British Economy*, pp. 155, 221–6.

loose structural equilibrium after its see-saw changes in the late eighteenth century, was filling out the new structural lines; investment followed the lines of expanding plant and equipment when required, but very few radical changes in industrial structure occurred.[1]

THE ADOPTION OF THE SELF-ACTING MULE

The application of steam completed the *major* structural innovations in spinning; on the other hand, there were frequently minor improvements, small reorganizations, and implementations. One of the more significant of these was the self-acting mule. It illustrates how a minor sequence of differentiation may be imposed upon a gradual process of routinization.

Early Steps. For some time before the 1820's a number of inventors had attempted an automatic spinning machine, since Crompton's mule required the attendance of a highly paid male worker and several assistants. William Strutt of Derby invented an automatic machine "at an early period" and in 1792 William Kelley took out a patent for a self-actor. These and several other attempts at automatic mule-spinning never proved competitive.[2]

Early in the nineteenth century, the mule-spinners formed a well-paid and powerful group in the new factory system.[3] Their behaviour in wage disputes was considered refractory by manufacturers, and considerable bitterness arose between the two.[4] In 1824, during a "long-continued strike," several manufacturers from the region around Stalybridge approached Richard Roberts, a famous Manchester engineer, and requested him to do something which would "render them in some measure independent of the more refractory class of their workmen."[5] Formally this set of dissatisfactions concerned the conditions of employment on which the manufacturers were forced to accept the mule-spinners (*G*-5) and the allocation of roles which gave the spinners so much control in the plant (*G*-6).

Step 5. Attempts to Specify. After several months of experimentation Roberts designed a self-acting mule, patented it in 1825, and

[1] This process of "routinization" did, however, occasion the most critical disturbances in the family economy of the working classes. Cf. Chapters IX and X.

[2] Daniels, *The Early English Cotton Industry*, p. 125; Baines, *History of the Cotton Manufacture in Great Britain*, p. 207.

[3] Cf. Chapter XII for the question of trade unionism.

[4] Cf. the belligerent tone of manufacturers' evidence in *Parliamentary Papers*, 1833, VI, Manufactures, Commerce and Shipping, pp. 322–3, 689.

[5] Smiles, *Industrial Biography*, pp. 267–8.

took out a patent with improvements in 1830. It is said that he and his partners spent close to £12,000 in perfecting this machine.[1] The invention illustrates an important trend in the industry. No longer was the inventor a simple weaver or barber who might persuade a carpenter to assist him in the construction of a machine which might revolutionize an entire industry. By the mid-twenties, the technical basis of the cotton manufacture was sufficiently complex to support an embryonic engineering industry. Entrepreneurs hesitated to tackle technical problems themselves, and began to consult experts who had not only knowledge but also capital to finance experiments and trials.*

Step 6. Implementation by Entrepreneurs. Though the success of the self-actor was not so immediate as the manufacturers might have hoped,[2] it increased productivity considerably. After its introduction, "one man could work, with the assistance of two or three boys, 1,600 spindles with as much ease as he could work 600 spindles by hand mules."[3] Schulze-Gaevernitz compiled an approximate comparison of the productivity of mules in 1812, of self-actors in 1830, and of hand-spinning in India: [4]

Counts of yarn	Costs per pound of yarn		
	1812 *(pence)*	1830 *(pence)*	*India (pence)*
40	12	7½	40
80	26	19½	82½
100	34	26½	143
150	78	59	300
200	200	138	535

The finer counts, heretofore available only at prohibitive cost, were thrown open to a larger proportion of the market at home and abroad.[5]

By early 1834 there existed some 520 self-acting mules containing

[1] *Dictionary of National Biography*, Vol. 48, p. 390.

* Thus the engineering industry was beginning to crystallize along the lines of assembling knowledge for techniques (C_{I_a}), supplying capital resources (C_{Aa}–C_{G_a}), and controlling to a greater degree the kind of fixed capital utilized in the industry (C_{A_g}–C_{L_g}).

[2] *Parliamentary Papers*, 1833, VI, Manufactures, Commerce and Shipping p. 331.

[3] W. Fairbairn, *Treatise on Mills and Millwork* (London, 1861), Vol. II, p. 178; *Parliamentary Papers*, 1842, XXII, Factory Inspectors, pp. 363–4.

[4] *The Cotton Trade in England and on the Continent*, p. 43; also Usher, *An Introduction to the Industrial History of England*, p. 313.

[5] Ultimately the self-actor had much to do with Britain's final conquest of the Indian market. Daniels, *The Early English Cotton Industry*, fn., p. 130.

200,000 spindles; these apparently doubled during the course of the year. In comparison with the total number of spindles, however, the number of self-actor spindles was very small.[1] Undoubtedly the high cost of self-actors discouraged all except the larger and more progressive firms from installing them; various technical difficulties, as well as a prejudice for the manually-operated mules, also retarded their installation.[2] The self-actor was not completely incorporated until the American Civil War.

What kind of differentiation accompanied the self-actor? From an industrial point of view it substituted the role of a "minder" for that of a highly skilled spinner.[3] This constituted a proliferation of roles within the C_L sub-system. Further, by virtue of its high capital cost and technical complexity,[4] the self-actor pushed the control of capital (C_A) further from the processes of production themselves (C_L). In general, however, the structural changes did not approach those of the earlier industrial developments.

At this point we must leave the spinning branches, even though they continued through various processes of differentiation later in the nineteenth century. Cotton imports, which were 686·4 million lb. in 1850, grew to 1409·9 million lb. by 1885. A typical cotton mill of the mid-1880's made the mill of the 1840's appear small, ill-ventilated, and archaic.[5] Furthermore, the combined spinning-weaving mills, which had often developed jointly in the early days of power-loom weaving, split into separate establishments later in the century.[6] We might well have attempted to apply the model of structural differentiation to these later changes. Since our aim is not to write a complete history, however, but rather to interpret analytically the development of the industry during a period of rapid change, we shall leave spinning at this point and turn to a similar analysis of changes in the structure of weaving during the industrial revolution.

[1] Baines, *History of the Cotton Manufacture in Great Britain*, pp. 207–8; J. Mortimer, *Cotton Spinning* (Manchester, 1895), pp. 98–9; Schulze-Gaevernitz, *The Cotton Trade in England and on the Continent*, p. 63.

[2] Chapman, *The Lancashire Cotton Industry*, pp. 69–70.

[3] From the standpoint of the family economy, however, the impact of this adjustment was enormous. Below, pp. 196–200.

[4] In 1842 a large Manchester spinner estimated that out of the 1·58 pence/lb. costs for spinning on the hand-mule in 1838, only 0·56 pence/lb. constituted fixed charges. For the 1·04 pence/lb. costs for self-actor spinning in 1841, 0·70 pence/lb. constituted fixed costs. *Parliamentary Papers*, 1842, XXII, Factory Inspectors, pp. 363–4.

[5] S. Andrew, *Fifty Years' Cotton Trade* (Oldham, 1887), p. 1 and Table opp. p. 12.

[6] *Victoria County History of Lancaster*, Vol. II, p. 391. Also below, p. 150.

CHAPTER VII

STRUCTURAL DIFFERENTIATION
IN WEAVING

In one sense the transition from hand-loom to power-loom weaving appears to be more straightforward than the jerky and sporadic advance of the spinning branches. Weaving machinery was not divided into so many major sub-types as the spinning machinery, and the power-loom, once it became competitive in the 1820's, marched irresistibly and cruelly over the helpless mass of hand-loom weavers. In addition to this relatively clear case of industrial displacement, however, we must consider also several minor developments between the 1770's and the 1840's such as structural changes within hand-loom weaving itself and the rise of "hand-loom factories" in the early nineteenth century. Neither of these is very important quantitatively, but each is instructive as an instance of structural differentiation.

In analysing these developments, we must neglect for the time being the social aspects of the decline of the hand-loom weavers. As in the preceding chapters, we shall consider structural differentiation only from the *industrial* standpoint. The weavers' sufferings belong to another sequence of change, namely the structural differentiation of the family. Until later chapters, therefore, we shall separate the strictly industrial aspects of the weaving trade from the "human" aspects.

Step 1. Dissatisfaction and a Sense of Opportunity. The dramatic arrival of spinning machinery in the eighteenth century reversed the yarn supply situation of twenty years earlier, and hence created new dissatisfactions with the allocation of resources in the industry (*I-5*):

The first great effect of the introduction of the spinning machinery, had been to produce yarn with such rapidity and quantity, as to cause an extreme demand for weavers to convert the articles into cloth; and the productive powers of machinery became so amazing, as totally to disable the hand-loom from maintaining a proportionate pace.[1]

[1] Butterworth, *Historical Sketches of Oldham*, pp. 157–8, 140–41. Also Baines, *History of the Cotton Manufacture in Great Britain*, p. 183, and R. MacIntyre, "Textile Industries," in A. McLean (ed.), *Local Industries of Glasgow and the West of Scotland* (Glasgow, 1901), pp. 137–8.

As late as 1800 Radcliffe complained that it was "impossible to get more weavers than were then employed, although many descriptions of goods, printing cambrics in particular . . . were in such demand that any quantity might be sold . . . we employed every person in cotton weaving who could be induced to learn the trade." [1] Because weavers' wages were forced up accordingly, this period, especially 1788 to 1803, came to be known as "the golden age of the hand-loom weaver," in which the operatives were brought to a state of "wealth, peace and godliness." [2]

In addition, several dissatisfactions lingered because weaving remained a putting-out industry through the first two decades of the nineteenth century and partially so for several decades thereafter. The major dissatisfactions with this system, it will be recalled, concerned the enforcement of schedules, work specifications, etc., when cloth was put out (*I*-6) and the master manufacturer's control over embezzlement, theft, delays, etc., in the processing of working capital (*A*-6). Both dissatisfactions probably were aggravated as the capacity of the hand-loom fell further behind the new spinning machinery.

Even though many of the weavers were endowed with the values of economic rationality,[3] the resistances to changing the *structure* of weaving were old and deep. Having the status of a craft, the trade produced men of status: "a fine body of men, full of the spirit of self-reliance . . . they sold their cloth and not their labour, and they were not servants but independent business men." [4] They were "as faithful, moral, and trust-worthy, as any corporate body amongst his Majesty's subjects . . . they wore their armorial bearings of merit . . . with as few stains upon their coat-armour as any individual or corporate body on whom these marks of Royal favour have ever been bestowed." [5] Furthermore, the attachment of weaving to farming constituted an obstacle to the desertion of the trade. Hence the growing dissatisfactions with weaving were counterbalanced by a vigorous attachment to the craft. These forces were later to contribute much to the social misery of the hand-loom weavers.

With regard to an appropriate sense of opportunity, the remarks on the general availability of capital hold even more for weaving than for the earlier spinning achievements, because of the wealth which had already accumulated with the rise of the spinning branches.

---

1 *Origin of the New System of Manufacture*, p. 12.
2 *Ibid.*, pp. 63 ff.
3 Above, p. 71.
4 Chapman, *The Lancashire Cotton Industry*, p. 36.
5 Radcliffe, *Origin of the New System of Manufacture*, p. 107.

In addition, some felt that the same revolution could be effected in weaving as had been in spinning. Shortly before Edmund Cartwright commenced work on the power-loom, he engaged several spinners in the following conversation:

Happening to be at Matlock, in the summer of 1784, I fell in company with some gentlemen of Manchester, when the conversation turned on Arkwright's spinning machinery. One of the company observed, that as soon as Arkwright's patent expired, so many mills would be erected, and so much cotton spun, that hands never could be found to weave it. To this observation I replied that Arkwright must then set his wits to work to invent a weaving mill. This brought on a conversation on the subject, in which the Manchester gentlemen unanimously agreed that the thing was impracticable; and in defence of their opinion, they adduced arguments which I certainly was incompetent to answer or even to comprehend, being totally ignorant of the subject, having never at that time seen a person weave. I controverted, however, the impracticability of the thing, by remarking that there had lately been exhibited in London, an automaton figure, which played at chess. Now you will not assert, gentlemen, said I, that it is more difficult to construct a machine that shall weave, than one which shall make all the variety of moves which are required in that complicated game.[1]

Step 2. Symptoms of Disturbance. As the weavers' inability to keep pace with spinning grew more pronounced, small exports of cotton twist began, probably around 1790.[2] This development soon touched off an anti-exportation "movement" among certain master manufacturers who feared weaving would thereby be transferred abroad. As early as 1794, the question of exporting twist arose in the Commercial Society of Manchester. Opinion was split, with master spinners favouring exportation and master manufacturers favouring prohibition. A little later some twenty-six members of the Society agreed that "the exportation of cotton twist is detrimental to the manufactures of this country." Six months later some members attempted to carry the issue before Parliament, but action was postponed, and the issue did not arise in the Society again.[3] Meantime exports continued to mount. The depression of 1799 touched off another flurry of activity which continued into the first years of the nineteenth century. A group led by William Radcliffe determined to take the question of prohibiting twist exports to Parliament. Several

---

[1] Quoted in Guest, *A Compendious History of the Cotton Manufacture*, pp. 44–5. Also Radcliffe, *Origin of the New System of Manufacture*, pp. 12–13.

[2] Guest, *A Compendious History of the Cotton Manufacture*, pp. 33–5.

[3] Helm, *Chapters in the History of the Manchester Chamber of Commerce*, pp. 18–20.

controversial pamphlets written by Radcliffe and his opponent, Mercator, circulated for a few years. Again in 1808 there was a flare-up of debate, controversy, and petitions. Radcliffe re-entered the conflict with a vitriolic pamphlet in 1811. The last serious burst of anti-export activity came in 1816–17, when four petitions from cotton manufacturers and merchants were signed by a total of 1,054 persons. J. B. Sharp published several letters opposing exportation in 1817. After this time the agitation subsided, though occasional assertions that exportation hurt weavers and manufacturers appeared later.[1]

Most of the "unjustified" aggression associated with this movement was directed against an unspecified "Anglo-Foreign Junto," a band of presumed conspirators who were scheming to remove the supply of yarn from domestic weavers by exportation and to drive down their wages through foreign competition. Walker suggested that foreigners were establishing themselves under fictitious names in England.[2] The conspirators' economic tactics presumably included an attempt to import cloth fashioned abroad from British twist; a scheme to gain control of the ships, colonies, and commerce of the world; price-cutting to drive down the price of weaving; and devious influence on the Board of Trade to continue the support of exportation. Some of the master spinners were behaving, in short, "as if it were for the *sole purpose of establishing the cotton trade on the continent.*"[3]

Radcliffe also saw political conspiracy lurking in the background. One of the direct effects of price-cutting, he held, was to provoke the weavers to participate in the blanket expedition in 1817, the Peterloo meeting in 1819, and the Scottish rebellion of 1820. Even more directly, the Junto stirred the hand-weavers to riot and to destroy

[1] For the history of the movement, cf. G. White, *A Practical Treatise on Weaving by Hand and Power Looms* (Glasgow, 1846), pp. 126–7; Mercator, *A Letter to the Inhabitants of Manchester on the Exportation of Cotton Twist*; a second letter appeared in 1800 and a third in 1803; J. Mortimer, *Mercantile Manchester Past and Present* (Manchester, 1896), pp. 41–2; W. Radcliffe, *Exportation of Cotton Yarns the Real Cause of the Distress that has fallen upon the Cotton Trade for a Series of Years Past* (Stockport, 1811); J. B. Sharp, *Letters on the Exportation of Cotton Yarns* (London, 1817); *Parliamentary Papers*, 1817, XIV, Memorials on the Exportation of Cotton Yarns, pp. 355–60; 1824, V, Artizans and Machinery, p. 543; 1834, X, Hand-loom Weavers, pp. 382, 415; and, of course, Radcliffe, *Origin of the New System of Manufacture.*

[2] G. Walker, *Observations founded on Facts upon the Propriety of Exporting Cotton Twist, for the Purpose of Being Manufactured into Cloth by Foreigners* (London, 1803), p. 8.

[3] Radcliffe, *Exportation of Cotton Yarns*, pp. 10, 12; *Origin of the New System of Manufacture*, pp. 85 ff., 113–17.

power-looms so that British weaving could not prosper; further, it attempted to agitate the weavers during the state trial of Queen Caroline in the 1820's. Radcliffe himself refused "with inward disdain" to deal with foreigners between 1794 and 1800, even though they offered better prices for his products. Finally, he attacked the "Chesterfields and Lockes of *our day*" (i.e., the political economists) who were blinding the Board of Trade to the true interests of the cotton manufacture with a flood of jargon.[1]

In addition to this hostility, the movement showed hints of alternating gloom and euphoria (anxiety and phantasy). One of the drafted resolutions of an anti-exportation meeting in Manchester in 1800 read as follows:

Resolved, that the exportation of cotton twist is highly injurious to the manufactures of this country, and unless some means are speedily adopted to restrict the exportation under certain regulations, it will ultimately end in the destruction of the cotton manufacture of the kingdom.[2]

The petitioners in 1816–17 complained that because of exportation "our workmen are driven out of employ, and your Memorialists to utter ruin."[3] On the other hand, hope was strong enough among Radcliffe and his friends to warrant a toast to "*The shuttle of the United Kingdom, and may it very soon consume ALL the produce of the British spindle.*"[4]

How were these outbursts related to the pressures on the weaving trade? The agitation commenced in earnest with the first major business failure (1799) after the water-frame, the mule, and steam-power had consolidated, thus widening the productivity gap between the spinning and weaving branches. Between 1780 and 1800, furthermore, there had been a great increase in numbers of hand-loom weavers.[5] Hence the old hand-loom weaving trade was becoming both outmoded and overcrowded. For these reasons weaving was vulnerable in times of depression. If we may judge by the appearance of pamphlets and petitions, the agitation against the exportation of twist coincided with periods of slack trade—1799–1800, 1808, 1811, and 1816–17. When, however, the power-loom invigorated the weaving branch later in the century, the manufacturers ceased such attacks on master spinners and foreigners and joined the ranks of

[1] *Origin of the New System of Manufacture*, pp. 10–11, 53–5, 11–19, 126–9.
[2] *Ibid.*, p. 11.
[3] *Parliamentary Papers*, 1817, XIV, Memorials on the Exportation of Cotton Yarns, p. 357.
[4] Radcliffe, *Origin of the New System of Manufacture*, pp. 13–14.
[5] Below, pp. 136–7.

free-traders. Hence the rise and fall of the agitation against exportation coincides with the period of precariousness in the manufacturers' industrial position.

Why were the outbursts "unrealistic," i.e., irrelevant to the exportation of twist? In the first place, as Mercator pointed out, " . . . three fourths at least of the yarns exported go to countries, where British piece-goods are prohibited, and were so, long before any yarn was sent thither from this country." [1] Hence competition from British twist woven abroad was not so great as might be expected. Furthermore, to prohibit twist exports would threaten the British cotton industry as much as exportation, since foreign powers presumably would be driven to establish their own spinning concerns.[2] The most telling argument, however, was Mercator's in 1800:

I readily admit that . . . the depression of our trade and the exportation of twist . . . have been concomitant; but a little consideration will convince you, that they have had no connection with one another,—It is a known fact, that none of the lower numbers of water-twist have been exported, and yet it so happens, that the part of our manufacture for which this quality of twist is required has been in a more depressed state than other branches. The muslin and calico trades on the contrary, have been in a rising and improving condition,[3] although the major quantity of twist exported, has been of a quality and fineness proper for the manufacture of these articles, and has actually been applied abroad to these purposes. If it were true, therefore, that our trade has suffered a decrease in consequence of the exportation of twist, exactly the reverse must have taken place. Our heavy articles would have been in great demand, and muslins and calicoes would have met with no sale.[4]

Around 1800 depression was *generally* due to the political effects of the war period [5]; the fact that weaving suffered *particularly* had to do with the long-term productivity position of this branch. These factors lay behind the depressed conditions of trade and the declining

[1] *A Third Letter to the Inhabitants of Manchester on the Exportation of Cotton Twist*, p. 7.

[2] Mercator, *A Letter to the Inhabitants of Manchester on the Exportation of Cotton Twist*, pp. 10–11.

[3] This statement is interesting in connection with the problem of declining profits of Step 7. At the time Mercator's letter was written, the water-frame, largely responsible for the coarser counts on which profits had fallen, had entered Step 7, whereas the mule, largely responsible for higher counts on which profits remained high, was suspended in Step 6. Above, pp. 97 and 118–23.

[4] Mercator, *A Letter to the Inhabitants of Manchester on the Exportation of Cotton Twist*, p. 5.

[5] Above, pp. 122–3.

wages of the weavers; the exportion of cotton twist was at the root of neither.

Still less could the woes of the weaving branch be traced to a conspiratorial group of foreigners, spinners, and perhaps political economists. There may have been, among the foreigners in Manchester, a few who were politically disloyal; even more improbably, a few of these disloyal felt that their aims could best be realized by exporting cotton yarn. Certainly there is no reliable evidence on the subject, but the accusations are sufficiently unlikely to justify the judgment of "unrealistic."

Step 3. Handling and Channelling. At every stage of the agitation against the exportation of twist, appropriate mechanisms of social control operated. During the 1790's certain disruptive tensions were handled, weighed, postponed, and finally dismissed within the rubric of parliamentary methods in the Commercial Society of Manchester. At the community level, a local authority—e.g., the boroughreeve or constable of Manchester—sanctioned and sometimes presided over meetings called to discuss the grievances of interested groups. In Parliament itself, committees heard, assessed, and sifted out grievances for governmental action. Radcliffe "had several interviews with the principal statesmen of the day—such as Sidmouth, Castlereagh, and others, and although the deputies were generally favourably received, nothing was ever recommended to be done by the Committees of the House of Commons. . . . " [1] Thus, even though Parliament never acted upon the manufacturers' grievances, it nevertheless "handled" these tensions by bringing them before responsible authorities in an orderly manner.

The tensions associated with the anti-exportation movement were managed in still another manner. "The press . . . groaned with pamphlets, letters, and papers upon the subject . . . with a degree of rancour and animosity not at all becoming so respectable and valuable a body of men: argument is drowned in aspersion, and fair discussion kept out of view." [2] While the language of these publications was certainly vitriolic, the fact of publication indicates that authors were expressing their hostility and fear through a channel which was relatively peaceable and relatively subject to rules of procedure.

These early steps—dissatisfaction, disturbance, and handling— gave rise to three distinct sequences of structural differentiation in the weaving branch: (1) the differentiation of hand-loom weaving

[1] White, *A Practical Treatise on Weaving by Hand and Power Looms*, p. 127.
[2] Walker, *Observations . . . upon the Propriety or Impropriety of Exporting Cotton Twist*, p. 2.

Structural Differentiation in Weaving

from the farmer-weaver complex; (2) the rise of hand-loom factories; and (3), by far the most dramatic, the rise of power-loom factories. We shall discuss these in order.

THE DIFFERENTIATION OF HAND-LOOM WEAVING INTO A FULL-TIME OCCUPATION

On the eve of the industrial revolution in cotton, hand-loom weavers could be broken into two sub-classes: (*a*) the full-time journeyman weaver and (*b*) the farmer-weaver who plied the loom in the winter and tilled the land in the summer.[1] Structurally, of course, the economic activity of the former is *more differentiated* than that of the weaver-farmer. One might expect, furthermore, that when the demand for weaving rocketed with the introduction of the spinning machinery in the 1780's and 1790's, the proportion of full-time weavers would increase. Did such a differentiation within the hand-loom weaving trade in fact occur in the late eighteenth and early nineteenth centuries?

In sheer numbers the hand-loom weavers multiplied during the first several decades of the industrial revolution. In 1769 Arthur Young estimated the number of "manufacturers [i.e., weavers] employed *out* of [spinning]" to be 50,000.[2] A decade later there were "three Times as many Looms employed [as a decade before] . . . and . . . if there were more Looms . . . the Manufacturers would be glad to employ them." [3] These quantitative estimates reveal little except the fact that the number of looms was expanding even before the golden age of the hand-loom weaver.[4] In 1788 an estimated 108,000 weavers were employed; by 1801 this had grown to 164,000. Table 8 shows the estimated rate of increase up to 1820, where the number apparently stabilized around 240,000 for more than a decade. Three distinct movements contributed to this gross increase: (1) the absorption of women and children into hand-loom weaving; (2) the weavers' gradual desertion of part-time agricultural pursuits; and (3) the immigration of Irish peasants and textile workers into the English hand-loom weaving trade. These movements overlap, of course, but together they made hand-loom weaving a more highly differentiated occupation.

---

[1] Above, p. 55.

[2] *A Six Months Tour through the North of England*, Vol. III, p. 192.

[3] *Parliamentary Papers*, 1780, V, Paper 38, Petition of Cotton Spinners, p. 5.

[4] Radcliffe claimed that the number of looms had diminished between 1770 and 1788. This apparent error probably stems from an unwarranted generalization from his own particular district. *Origin of the New System of Manufacture*, pp. 61–2.

136

In the golden age the demand for weavers was met partially by labourers unemployed by the spinning and carding machinery:

[About 1790] . . . carding, roving and spinning were now given up in the cottages, and the women and children formerly employed in these operations, applied themselves to the Loom. The invention of the Mule, by enabling spinners to make finer yarns than any the Jenny and Water Frame could produce, gave birth to the muslin manufacture, and found employment for this additional number of weavers.[1]

Around the turn of the century, dependent family members flocked to the looms. The combination of falling wages and the loss of

TABLE 8

NUMBERS EMPLOYED IN HAND-LOOM WEAVING, 1788–1820 (THOUSANDS) [2]

Year	Number	Year	Number
1788	108	1813	212
1801	164	1814	216
1806	184	1815	220
1807	188	1816	224
1808	192	1817	228
1809	196	1818	232
1810	200	1819	236
1811	204	1820	240
1812	208		

males to the military encouraged many householders to teach women to weave "rather than let their Looms stand." In 1808 the number of female weavers was contrasted with the "remarkably few" of two decades earlier.[3] In addition, it was complained in 1816 that children were put to the loom "of late years . . . at a younger period than any other business," universally under ten years for an apprenticeship of three, four or five years.[4] As late as 1839, an Assistant

[1] Guest, *A Compendious History of the Cotton Manufacture*, p. 31. This compensation for unemployed spinners and carders probably accounts for the short-lived opposition to the spinning and carding machines. Radcliffe, *Origin of the New System of Manufacture*, pp. 35 ff., 61–2.

[2] G. H. Wood, *The History of Wages in the Cotton Trade During the Past Hundred Years* (London, 1910), p. 125; Gayer, Rostow, and Schwartz, *The Growth and Fluctuation of the British Economy*, Microfilmed Supplement, p. 1587.

[3] *Parliamentary Papers*, 1808, II, Petitions of Cotton Manufacturers and Journeymen Weavers, p. 121.

[4] *Parliamentary Papers*, 1816, III, Children employed in the Manufactories, p. 408. Also B. L. Hutchins and A. Harrison, *A History of Factory Legislation* (London, 1903), p. 20.

137

Hand-Loom Weavers' Commissioner set the ratio of families to looms at five to nine in the West of Scotland. Thus the 51,060 looms working in that region engaged 28,366 families. Assuming that every head of these families occupied one loom, the remaining 22,694 looms were worked by women and youths.[1] If we may generalize from this estimate, between 30% and 50% of the looms were being operated by dependent members of the family, even after factories had begun to absorb this class of labour.[2] In terms of structural differentiation, the family was becoming more specialized as dependent members moved entirely to weaving and its allied activities; previously dependent members had been responsible for spinning and the preparatory processes.

A second source of differentiation was the farmer-weavers' gradual drift from the land. Shortly after the advent of the spinning inventions, the operative discovered that "his labour, when employed on his loom, was more profitable, and more immediate in its return, than when devoted to agricultural pursuits." [3] The movement away from the land probably quickened during the golden age (1788–1803), when "[weaving] was extending itself [and] there was a temptation held out to draw the people from agricultural labour. . . ."[4] As late as 1827 and even later, however, there was still the hand-loom weaver "with his cottage and loom who . . . represented a social order that was already obsolete."[5] By this time, however, the power-loom was hastening the decline of country weavers and full-time weavers alike.

Why did the country weaver decline? Chapman has given five reasons: (1) outdoor employment which roughened the weavers' hands; (2) the waste of expensive machines standing idle part of the year; (3) the weavers' spirit of enterprise which encouraged them to specialize in weaving at the expense of farming; (4) the pressure to desert farming because of increased demand for weaving; (5) the power-loom which began to drive down the wages of the hand-loom weavers.[6] Each of these reasons is probably correct in its own right. Yet together they do not form a list of co-ordinate factors. Each reason assumes significance *only at a specific point* in a sequence

[1] *Parliamentary Papers*, 1839, Hand-loom Weavers, pp. 6–7.
[2] Below, pp. 208–9.
[3] P. Gaskell, *Artisans and Machinery* (London, 1836), p. 25.
[4] *Parliamentary Papers*, 1810–11, II, Petition of Several Weavers, pp. 394–5.
[5] Chapman, *The Lancashire Cotton Industry*, pp. 47, 10. Also *Parliamentary Papers*, 1826–7, V, Emigration, pp. 11, 19, 26, 43, 50; 1834, X, Hand-loom Weavers, p. 483; 1835, XIII, Hand-loom Weavers, p. 209; 1839, Hand-loom Weavers, pp. 184–5.
[6] *The Lancashire Cotton Industry*, p. 10.

resulting in a more differentiated structure of hand-loom weaving. The "spirit of enterprise," for instance, is an element of the pre-existing value-system, and, as such, a defining criterion for dissatisfaction with the old structure of weaving. The first and second reasons are structural foci of dissatisfaction with the old farmer-weaver pattern: dissatisfaction with the performance of tasks (G-7) and with capital equipment (A-7). The expansion of trade, the fourth reason, is a market change which augmented the initial level of dissatisfaction. And finally, the power-loom pressed from still another direction; in its own Steps 6 and 7, it rendered the old weaving structure even more obsolete. Furthermore, in the model of structural differentiation, the "reasons" are interrelated. If the appropriate values had not been present, for instance, an increased demand for weaving would have been slower to create definite dissatisfactions with men and equipment. If these dissatisfactions had not developed, moreover, power-loom weaving itself would have been slower to develop and erase the old forms. *Thus only after one or more "reasons" are present do the others become significant.* The determination of social change is best conceived as a "value-added" sequence in which determinants rise to significance only after other definite conditions are realized. Merely to list several "reasons" does not reveal so much about the dynamics of social change.[1]

A third source of full-time hand-loom weavers was the mass migration from Ireland into the manufacturing districts. As early as 1825–30, "the Irish crowded into Lancashire and the West of Scotland." By 1835 there were an estimated 35,000 Irish in Manchester; in the 1841 census the number was established at 34,300. In the 1840's this number was swollen by the exodus from Ireland during the potato famine. The majority of these immigrants pushed into building, hand-loom weaving, and other unskilled trades.[2]

These various trends brought hand-loom weaving to the level of a full-time, relatively differentiated occupation. While there are no available statistics to trace the course of production, capitalization, etc., we may follow Steps 6 and 7 of this sequence by mapping the course of wages and profits in hand-loom weaving during the late eighteenth and early nineteenth centuries.

Step 6. Implementation by Entrepreneurs. In the years of the golden age and probably earlier, weavers' wages rose extraordinarily. Radcliffe said they "rose to five times the amount ever before

---

[1] For a statement of this methodological position, above, pp. 60–62.

[2] Clapham, *An Economic History of Modern Britain*, pp. 179–80; Redford, *Labour Migration in England*, pp. 134–5; D. C. Morris, *The History of the Labour Movement in England, 1825–1852* (London, 1952), pp. 347–8.

experienced . . . every family bringing home weekly 40, 60, 80, 100, or even 120 shillings a week." [1] Taking Radcliffe's base year of 1770, Unwin has shown that Samuel Oldknow's weavers had received only a 50% increase in wages during the years 1784–7.[2] Even after 1788 when more family members were employed in weaving, Radcliffe's estimate is still too high. Nevertheless, the rise in weavers' wages was enormous, and since the wages of cottage farmers did not rise accordingly, the profit differential between weaving and weaving-farming became apparent. The golden age of hand-loom weaving

TABLE 9

AVERAGE WEEKLY WAGES FOR HAND-LOOM WEAVING, 1797–1838 [3]

Year	s.	d.	Year	s.	d.	Year	s.	d.
1797	18	9	1811	12	3	1825	8	3
1798	18	9	1812	14	–	1826	7	9
1799	18	6	1813	15	–	1827	7	6
1800	18	9	1814	18	6	1828	7	3
1801	18	6	1815	13	6	1829	7	3
1802	21	–	1816	10	3	1830	6	3
1803	20	–	1817	8	9	1831	6	–
1804	20	–	1818	8	3	1832	6	–
1805	23	–	1819	8	3	1833	6	–
1806	20	–	1820	8	3	1834	7	–
1807	17	3	1821	8	3	1835	6	3
1808	13	3	1822	8	3	1836	6	3
1809	14	–	1823	8	3	1837	6	3
1810	14	3	1824	8	3	1838	6	3

constituted Step 6 in which extraordinary rewards were given for full-time activity in hand-loom weaving.

Step 7. Routinization. Around the turn of the century, average wages in cotton hand-loom weaving began to decline, as Table 9 shows. The decline begins definitely before the introduction of the power-loom on a competitive basis (early 1820's). There were only 2,400 power-looms in 1813, yet reductions before that date were greater than afterwards.[4] The decline of wages at first rested more on the forces of differentiation internal to hand-loom weaving than on

[1] *Origin of the New System of Manufacture*, pp. 61–2.
[2] *Samuel Oldknow and the Arkwrights*, pp. 112–13.
[3] Wood, *The History of Wages in the Cotton Trade*, p. 112. Wood felt that the series understates, if anything, the decline.
[4] Below, p. 148.

the competition of superior machinery. Profits followed a similar course. The hand-loom manufacturer, "as wealthy at the close of 1813 as he would [be] in any period of his life," complained thereafter that his profits declined continuously except in times of great prosperity.[1]

After the 1820's the decline of wages and profits was associated with the advance of the power-loom. Until the virtual disappearance of hand-loom weaving, however, there remained a difference between the city and country weaver. In 1827 a Parliamentary Committee noticed

two classes [of weavers], almost wholly distinct from each other: the one, who though they take in work in their own houses or cellars, are congregated in the large manufacturing towns; and the other, scattered in small hamlets or single houses, in various directions throughout the manufacturing country . . . though both are in a state extremely deplorable . . . [it is upon the country-weavers] that the distresses of the times have fallen with peculiar hardship.[2]

Country weavers earned five or ten per cent less than the city weavers; they also were apparently more willing to emigrate from England and Scotland.[3] Even though both city and country weaving were organized on the putting-out basis well into the nineteenth century, the former possessed structural advantages over the latter. The country-weaver roughened his hands in farm labour, thereby reducing his skill; his capital equipment lay idle for the summer season; and the country distances implied more "fetching and carrying" of raw materials, greater difficulties of communication between master and weaver, etc.[4]

THE RISE OF THE FACTORY SYSTEM IN HAND-LOOM WEAVING

In addition to the country–city difference in hand-loom weaving, the trade was characterized by another distinction which cross-cut the former. Work was taken either (*a*) by individual city or country

[1] *Parliamentary Papers*, 1833, VI, Manufactures, Commerce and Shipping, pp. 63, 560, 562; 1834, X, Hand-loom Weavers, pp. 23, 260–61; 1835, XIII, Hand-loom Weavers, p. 149.

[2] *Parliamentary Papers*, 1826–7, V, Emigration, pp. 5, 459–61.

[3] *Ibid.*, pp. 460, 472. Also 1834, X, Hand-loom Weavers, p. 62; 1839, Hand-loom Weavers, p. 9.

[4] For a description of the structure of weaving in the early nineteenth century, cf. Clapham, *An Economic History of Modern Britain*, pp. 179–80; *Parliamentary Papers*, 1826–7, V, Emigration, pp. 268–9; 1835, XIII, Hand-loom Weavers, pp. 117, 149.

weavers and worked at home or (*b*) by a master-weaver employing several weavers on his premises. It is impossible to determine the relative proportions of these two forms before and during the industrial revolution. Warping, smallware, and sailcloth manufacture persisted in sheds before the industrial revolution. In 1816 Kinder Wood of Oldham thought that "generally speaking" hand-weavers worked in their own houses in his district; later, however, he spoke of loom-shops in the same neighbourhood. The small Rossendale area had a great variety of loom-shops—living-rooms of cottages, the top story of a row of cottages, old barns, etc. Rural Scotland had an abundance both of individual weavers and masters' shops. In certain branches, such as fancy weaving in Paisley, shops of four to six looms predominated.[1]

Whatever the arrangements, however, certain disadvantages with the system of putting-out continued:

. . . the employer of domestic weavers can never tell within a fortnight or three weeks when every web sent out to the neighbouring villages will be returned . . . embezzlement of yarn . . . the risk of the work being taken out of the loom to be sold or pawned by a dishonest weaver . . . wrangling and dispute between the foreman and the men.[2]

In general, these chronic sources of dissatisfaction were erased by the power-loom factories. The simultaneous erection of large hand-loom factories, however, represents a minor sequence of structural differentiation based on the same set of dissatisfactions.

As early as the 1780's Samuel Oldknow gathered a number of weavers on his premises to work hand-looms, and "a loom-house formed part of the premises offered for sale in 1798." [3] A witness in 1827 described a successful hand-loom factory in which weavers gathered simply to drive the shuttle. In 1833 six such factories, some with more than two hundred looms, were said to exist in Manchester. By the 1840's there were two or three hand-loom factories for fancy work in Paisley. The major basis for hand-loom factories, however, was the "dandy-loom." Used primarily on coarser fabrics, this wider loom was superior to the ordinary hand-loom but inferior to a comparable power-loom. In 1834 a Bolton manufacturer said that "[dandy-looms] are setting up every day in our town," and in the

[1] *Parliamentary Papers*, 1816, III, Children employed in the Manufactories, pp. 40–41; 1843, XIII, Children's Employment Commission, pp. 347–8; G. H. Tupling, *The Economic History of Rossendale* (Manchester, 1927), pp. 207–8. *Lords Sessional Papers*, 1818, IX, Cotton Factories Bill, p. 72.
[2] *Parliamentary Papers*, 1840, Hand-loom Weavers, p. 45.
[3] Unwin, *Samuel Oldknow and the Arkwrights*, pp. 106–10.

same year a weaver noticed that dandy-loom weavers were increasing in numbers but ordinary hand-loom weavers were not. The dandy-loom was worked "by persons who employ men to come on to their premises to work, in a sort of factory." So small was its incorporation, however, that it was only beginning to be applied extensively to hand-loom weaving in the 1840's.[1]

In terms of structural differentiation, these hand-loom factories meant that the control of capital (C_A) and the control of production (C_G) had split from the processes of production themselves (C_L). In the first place, the masters of the factories owned both the premises and the looms; in the second place, they could control holidays and other absence from work and could enforce regular habits and prompt schedules—all difficult under the putting-out system. The hand-loom factories' productivity advantage was such that they could finish a hundred webs while domestic weavers finished fifty. Correspondingly, wages were uniformly two shillings to three shillings higher per week for hand-loom weavers in the factory than for those in the home.[2]

The full differentiation of domestic hand-loom weaving and the rise of hand-loom factories, while not too important quantitatively, nevertheless follow the model of structural differentiation. As far as the limited historical information indicates, each conformed to the following sequence: (1) dissatisfactions; (2) experimental modifications of the division of labour; (3) an early period of profits; (4) a longer period of declining profits, routinization, and elimination of outmoded elements. In terms of structural results, the full-time hand-loom weaver was more differentiated than the farmer-weaver, and the factory hand-loom weaver was more so than the full-time domestic weaver. The ratio of wages and profits in these three sub-branches, as well as their behaviour over time, reflect these long-term processes.

THE ADVENT OF POWER-LOOM WEAVING

Eventually the power-loom factories erased all the miscellaneous modifications of hand-loom weaving; but the *manner* in which they did so conforms to the same pattern of differentiation as the development of the minor forms themselves. Steps 1, 2, and 3—outlined in

[1] *Parliamentary Papers*, 1826–7, V, Emigration, pp. 292–3; 1833, XX, Factory Commissioners, p. 811; 1843, XIII, Children's Employment Commission, p. 347; 1834, X, Hand-loom Weavers, pp. 397–8, 432–3; 1835, XIII, Hand-loom Weavers, pp. 27–8; 1840, Hand-loom Weavers, p. 45.
[2] *Parliamentary Papers*, 1840, Hand-loom Weavers, pp. 9, 10, 591–2; 1826–7, V, Emigration, p. 292; 1835, XIII, Hand-loom Weavers, pp. 154–5; 1839, Hand-loom Weavers, p. 8.

the early part of the chapter—set the stage for the full industrialization. Let us now continue the story of the power-loom.

Step 4. Encouragement of "New Ideas." Early after the improvements of spinning machinery there appeared several encouragements for innovative ideas in weaving. In 1783, on the eve of the golden age of hand-loom weaving and two years before Cartwright's invention of the power-loom, the Society of Arts offered the following:

ENGINE FOR WORKING LOOMS. To the person who shall invent and construct an Engine for the purpose of working at one time, the greatest number of looms, not fewer than three, for weaving silk, woollen, linen, or cotton goods (equally well, and more expeditiously than by hand, or by any other method now in use), each piece to be not less than half a yard wide; the gold medal, or thirty guineas.[1]

In the following two years this offer was repeated and extended to 1786. The Society offered several awards for improvements both on the hand-loom and the power-loom during the next several decades.[2] In addition, there were probably similar encouragements at more informal levels. In 1811, for instance, Radcliffe formed a club of manufacturers, whose purpose was to exchange ideas for improving weaving, "either in the system itself, or in the teaching and management of the hands." [3]

Certain "encouragements" occurred after the inventions as well. Cartwright was elected to the Society of Arts in 1798 and became a candidate for office in the following year. In 1808 he petitioned Parliament, and in the following year he was granted £10,000 "for the good service he had rendered the public by his invention of weaving." [4] Similar appeals on behalf of William Radcliffe, who improved the weaving process, failed in 1825 and 1836, but after an appeal for aid throughout the trade in 1834, "several English and Scotch firms honourably continued to pay him a royalty for having used his patents." [5]

Step 5. Attempts to Specify. After Cartwright had patented his model of the power-loom in 1785,[6] he "immediately employed a

---

[1] *Transactions of the Society of Arts*, I (1783), pp. 217–18.

[2] Wood, *A History of the Royal Society of Arts*, pp. 263 ff.; *Transactions of the Society of Arts*, 1783–1830.

[3] *Origin of the New System of Manufacture*, p. 5.

[4] M. Strickland, *A Memoir of the Life, Writings, and Mechanical Inventions of Edmund Cartwright* (London, 1843), pp. 222–37.

[5] Heginbotham, *Stockport: Ancient and Modern*, Vol. II, p. 326.

[6] Earlier attempts at power-loom construction include that of M. de Gennes in 1678, notable "on account of its being the first known attempt at power weaving,

carpenter and smith. . . . As soon as the machine was finished, I got a weaver to put in the warp, which was of such materials as sail cloth is made of. To my great delight a piece of cloth, such as it was, was the produce." [1] Apparently Dr. James Jeffray of Glasgow invented a similar, possibly better loom independently of Cartwright in 1787, but this was never put into practice.[2]

As soon as Cartwright's loom reached the point of operation, inventors attempted to correct its obvious defects. Cartwright himself added specifications in 1786, 1787, and 1790. Improvements by "Thomas Clark, the Younger," Richard Gorton, John Austin, and Robert Miller also appeared in the 1780's and 1790's.[3] William Radcliffe and Thomas Johnson added an important improvement between 1802 and 1804. Convinced that the evils of exporting cotton twist could be overcome only by improving the weaving branches, Radcliffe "shut himself up" in 1802 with several joiners, filers, etc., determined to improve the power-loom, which was still far from a commercial success. Within a month he had split the activities of weaving and dressing altogether, thereby minimizing the time spent in passing from one operation to another. This turned his attention to dressing alone, and after two years he and his assistants had developed the "noiseless simple dressing machine" for sizing the warp.[4]

After the turn of the century, improvements on the power-loom were almost too numerous to count; many were not patented, and some were probably unrecorded. The features introduced by William

and not from any practical value it possesses"; that of Vaucanson in 1745, and that of Robert and Thomas Barber of Nottingham in 1774. A. Barlow, *The History and Principles of Weaving by Hand and Power* (London, 1878), pp. 230–33.

[1] Quoted in Guest, *A Compendious History of the Cotton Manufacture*, pp. 44–5. Also *Dictionary of National Biography*, Vol. IX, p. 222.

[2] White, *A Practical Treatise on Weaving by Hand and Power Looms*, p. 98.

[3] For a statement of the operational defects of Cartwright's machine, cf. Strickland, *A Memoir . . . of Edmund Cartwright*; White, *A Practical Treatise on Weaving by Hand and Power Looms*, p. 98; A. P. Usher, *A History of Mechanical Inventions* (New York, 1929), pp. 251–2; Barlow, *The History and Principles of Weaving by Hand and Power*, p. 235. For chronologies of improvements, R. Marsden, *Cotton Weaving: Its Development, Principles, and Practice* (London, 1895), pp. 69 ff.; E. J. Donnell, *Chronological and Statistical History of Cotton* (New York, 1872), Chs. III–IV; D. W. Snell, *The Managers' Assistant* (Hartford, 1850), p. 59; also the works by Strickland (p. 64), White (pp. 91–274) and Usher (pp. 249–61) cited in this note.

[4] *Origin of the New System of Manufacture*, pp. 20–24. Radcliffe's efforts illustrate the types of specifications in Step 5: changes in the division of labour itself (*I*-3); applications of knowledge to achieve technological capacity (*A*-3); specifying the skills necessary within this technology and division of labour (*G*-3). Above, pp. 33–7.

Horrocks in 1813 and 1821 and consolidated by Richard Roberts in 1822 probably brought the loom to a permanent competitive position. At any rate, Horrocks' design was in common use in 1835.[1] Many of these improvements were limited to the coarser grades of cloth. Not until the 1840's was Jacquard's loom for fancy weaving widely used in the weaving districts of England. In 1841 William Kenworthy and James Bullough introduced an improvement in the loom's motion by which ". . . the labour of weaving was reduced by nearly one half and a greater quantity of high grade cloth was produced."[2]

Step 6. Implementation by Entrepreneurs. This step overlaps with the preceding; once an improvement is made, entrepreneurs attempt to apply the new method. If it succeeds, Step 6 runs its course; if not, there is a "regression" to Step 5 or an earlier step to improve or reassemble the appropriate techniques. In power-loom weaving, this "leap-frog" relationship between Steps 5 and 6 was protracted, largely because of technical difficulties in power-loom weaving and because of the extremely low wages of hand-loom weavers which power-loom entrepreneurs had to overcome. Let us first record a few early entrepreneurial attempts, then turn to the full blossoming of Step 6 in the 1830's and 1840's.

Neglecting earlier scattered attempts at power-loom installation,[3] we detect the first signs of pressure to establish the power-loom in the 1780's and 1790's, when Cartwright's original patents were broken several times. In the meantime Cartwright himself attempted several applications. At Doncaster, the power for twenty looms was initially supplied by a bull, but in 1788 or 1789 he installed a steam-engine. The cloth was of "some excellence," but unsaleable, possibly because jealous competitors boycotted the cloth, but possibly because its quality was not up to standard hand-woven material. At any rate, "the establishment . . . was far from being profitable," and closed down.[4] Cartwright, who possessed an "ample fortune," had supplied the capital.[5] Shortly thereafter he licensed Messrs. Grimshaw of Gorton to build a factory, but this was apparently burned by workers

[1] Usher, *A History of Mechanical Inventions,* p. 251; Heginbotham, *Stockport: Ancient and Modern,* Vol. II, p. 327.

[2] G. C. Miller, *Blackburn: The Evolution of a Cotton Town* (Blackburn, 1951), pp. 332–3; Usher, *An Introduction to the Industrial History of England,* p. 302.

[3] Cf. the attempt of a Mr. Gartside of Manchester in mid eighteenth century as described in Wadsworth and Mann, *The Cotton Trade and Industrial Lancashire,* pp. 301–2.

[4] Strickland, *A Memoir . . . of Edmund Cartwright,* pp. 77, 80–82, 176–80.

[5] White, *A Practical Treatise on Weaving by Hand and Power Looms,* p. 93.

and the attempt not renewed.[1] Before 1800, therefore, the power-loom was apparently "both necessary and unpopular." On the other hand, the experiments of James Lewis Robertson in 1793, and John Monteith in 1798 and 1801, came closer to success.[2]

After Radcliffe and Johnson's improvements of 1802–4 and those of Horrocks in 1803, there were reports of several power-loom factories in and about Lancashire. Donnell placed the first successful power-loom establishment in 1806, when a Manchester factory was fitted with power-looms.[3] Yet in 1815 Kennedy could still say,

[weaving] remains nearly the same as it was 50 or 60 years ago, or indeed at any period, or in any country where the people have been in the habit of weaving for a subsistence; with the difference only of the application of the fly-shuttle, which was invented and introduced about the year 1750 . . . by John Kay. . . .[4]

As late as 1817 there were only 2,000 power-looms in Lancashire, of which only half were said to be in employment [5]; the total in England and Scotland in 1820 was 14,150.

In 1823, however, there were "large additions" and in 1824–5 "larger additions." [6] The upward trend seemed to falter in the crisis and depression of the late 1820's, yet there were 59,127 looms in England and Scotland by 1829 and 100,000 by 1833. Table 10 shows the rate of accumulation. Most of the expansion into the 1830's was composed of looms designed for weaving the coarser grades of cloth. By 1835 power-looms were conquering the field in fustians and cambrics, but fancy weaving still held its own. Some even felt that "each loom has its distinct province. True it is that in some cases the Power Loom has been applied to the weaving of cloth on which the Hand Loom is now employed, but the general dissimilarity of the goods manufactured by each is such as to warrant an affirmation that they stand on independent grounds."[7] The conquest of the fancier grades was delayed until the 1840's and later.

[1] Donnell, *Chronological and Statistical History of Cotton*, p. 50.
[2] Mantoux, *The Industrial Revolution in the Eighteenth Century*, p. 248; Donnell, *Chronological and Statistical History of Cotton*, p. 58.
[3] Donnell, *Chronological and Statistical History of Cotton*, p. 62; Mantoux, *The Industrial Revolution in the Eighteenth Century*, p. 249.
[4] "Rise and Progress of the Cotton Trade," *op. cit.*, p. 116.
[5] Donnell, *Chronological and Statistical History of Cotton*, p. 73.
[6] Wood, *The History of Wages in the Cotton Trade*, p. 123; also *Parliamentary Papers*, 1835, XIII, Hand-loom Weavers, p. 130.
[7] *A Letter . . . by the Committee of Manufacturers and Weavers of . . . Bolton* (Bolton, 1834), p. 9. Also *Parliamentary Papers*, 1833, VI, Manufactures, Commerce and Shipping, p. 709; 1835, XIII, Hand-loom Weavers, pp. 151–2, 168.

On the coarser grades, however, the calculated productivity difference between power- and hand-loom was impressive:

A very good *hand weaver*, 25 or 30 years of age, will weave *two* pieces of 9–8ths shirtings per week, each 24 yards long, containing 100 shoots of weft 40 hanks to the lb.

In 1823, a *steam-loom weaver*, about 15 years of age, attending two looms, could weave *seven* similar pieces in a week.

In 1826, a steam-loom weaver, about 15 years of age, attending to two looms, could weave *twelve* similar pieces in a week; some could weave fifteen pieces.

TABLE 10

NUMBERS OF POWER-LOOMS 1813–50 [1]

Year	England	Scotland	Total
1813	2,400	—	—
1819	—	—	14,000–15,000
1820	12,150	2,000	14,150
1829	55,000	14,127	69,127
1829–31	—	—	80,000
1833	85,000	15,000	100,000
1835	—	—	108,128
1844–6	—	—	225,000
1850	223,626	23,564	247,190

In 1833, a steam-loom weaver, from 15 to 20 years of age, assisted by a girl about 12 years of age, attending to four looms, can weave *eighteen* similar pieces in a week; some can weave twenty pieces.[2]

Even if correct, this calculation is likely to be misleading. Capitalization expenses and management were much higher on the power-looms; furthermore, the hand-loom weaver was often responsible

[1] The 1813 figures are from Usher, *A History of Mechanical Inventions*, p. 302. The figures for 1819, 1829–31, and 1844–6 are estimates from Kennedy and Ellison incorporated in Taylor, "Concentration and Specialization in the Lancashire Cotton Industry," *op. cit.*, p. 117. The figures for 1820, 1829, and 1833 are from Baines, *History of the Cotton Manufacture in Great Britain*, pp. 235–7. The 1835 figures are from *Parliamentary Papers*, 1836, XLV, Returns of Number of Power-looms, pp. 149–53. The 1850 figures are from *Parliamentary Papers*, 1850. XLII, Returns on Numbers of Factories, etc., pp. 456–7 and 466.
[2] Baines, *History of the Cotton Manufacture in Great Britain*, p. 240.

for dressing and other allied activities, while in the factory dressing was split from weaving and the dresser commanded high wages.

In order to assess the influence of the power-loom on costs, I have performed some computations based upon cost components in the Appendix, and have arrived at the following series of index numbers which indicate the decline in costs *traceable to innovations in weaving and allied activities* (1820 = 100).

1820	100
1828–30	101
1838–40	85
1848–50	81

The index numbers are approximate at best, yet they seem to justify the conclusion that the largest reductions traceable to power-loom weaving were felt only in the 1830's. Other figures seem to substantiate this conclusion. The number of looms installed between 1829 and 1833 almost equalled the number installed from 1820 to 1829. With regard to production, we must rely on the weight of twist consumed domestically—a very imperfect index of weaving production. In 1819–21, the average weight worked domestically was 87,096 lb. It rose slowly through 1823–5, fell in 1826, and by 1828–30 it had risen to 149,570 lb. (a gain of 72% from 1819–21). By 1838–40 it totalled 263,475 lb. (a 76% gain from 1828–30), and 1848–50 yielded an average of 403,771 lb. (a 53% rise from 1838–40). These figures undoubtedly dampen the influence of the power-loom, since the number of hand-loom weavers reached a maximum in the 1820's and declined especially in the 1830's and 1840's.[1] With regard to numbers employed, there was an average of 10,000 operatives employed in power-loom weaving in 1819–20. By 1829–31 this average had risen to 50,000, and an estimate in 1832 gives 75,000. The 1832 figure had doubled by 1844–6.[2] All these figures seem to indicate a rapid take-off into Step 6 in the late 1820's or early 1830's; certainly it was well under way in the 1830's. In general, however, the power-loom never matched the speed of incorporation of some of the major spinning improvements. This gradualness probably had much to do with the long, tortuous history of the hand-loom weavers during the first half of the century.

Since power-looms were an adjunct of spinning concerns into the 1840's,[3] separate profits for weaving were not adequately recorded.

[1] Figures from Gayer, Rostow and Schwartz, *The Growth and Fluctuation of the British Economy*, Microfilmed Supplement, p. 889.

[2] Wood, *A History of Wages in the Cotton Trade*, p. 123.

[3] J. Butterworth, *A History of . . . Stockport, Ashton-under-Lyne, etc.* (Manchester, 1827), pp. 284–5; *Parliamentary Papers*, 1833, VI, Manufactures, Commerce and Shipping, pp. 569, 681.

Witnesses in 1833 testified, however, that the joint concerns were faring better than those engaged in spinning alone:

Do you know any trade which requires permanent investment in machinery or manufactures that has been profitable?—Yes, I think spinning and power-loom weaving has been profitable down to the middle of last year.

Has the profit been sufficient to justify a prudent man to embark his capital in it?—I think it has in those branches of business united, but not separate.

When a combination of those trades has been brought to bear, they have been sufficient to insure a profit?—I think they have.[1]

Hence our limited information on production, capitalization, labour and profits—all of which grow rapidly in Step 6—leads to the conclusion that this step occurred in the late 1820's and extended through the 1840's in weaving.

Step 7. Routinization. Whether the profits of the joint spinning–weaving enterprises declined in later years is almost impossible to determine, for two reasons: (1) Profits in these joint firms reflected processes other than power-loom weaving; (2) Already in the 1840's, the signs pointed toward a future differentiation of weaving and spinning into separate establishments. Between January 1, 1844, and April 30, 1845, Leonard Horner, factory inspector, noted that of 78 new mills constructed, 27 were for spinning only, 30 for spinning and weaving, and 21 for weaving only.[2] After 1850 the independent weaving firms came even more into their own.[3] If, however, the calculations in the Appendix are indicative, power-loom weaving joined those branches with declining profits, since the radical cost reductions in this branch were becoming less impressive by the 1840's.

APPENDIX

STRUCTURAL DIFFERENTIATION AND PRICE CHANGES, 1820–1850

When the supply curve for a commodity shifts downward and to the right, demand remaining constant, the price of the commodity falls. This is the effect which successful structural differentiation,

[1] *Parliamentary Papers*, 1833, VI, Manufactures, Commerce and Shipping, p. 558.

[2] *Parliamentary Papers*, 1845, XXV, Factory Inspectors, pp. 453–6. Also 1843, XXVII, Factory Inspectors, p. 347.

[3] Taylor, "Concentration and Specialization in the Lancashire Cotton Industry, 1825–1850," *op. cit.*, pp. 114–22.

which improves supply conditions, has on price. The general movement of the prices of cotton yarn and piece goods during the industrial revolution in cotton is consistent with this relationship; both fell considerably up to 1850 and afterwards.

Several important questions arise in connection with this movement, however. What was the influence of the price of raw cotton on the price decline? What was the contribution of innovation in spinning and preparatory operations? What was the influence of innovation in weaving and allied activities?

In order to assess these effects I have performed a few operations on available statistics and estimates. The results suggest also the periods of the maximum impact of structural differentiation in each branch of the industry.

First, let us trace the actual course of several series of prices. In Table 11, Column (1) shows the annual average of monthly prices of imported *raw cotton* from 1814 to 1850 in pence per lb. (duty excluded); Column (3) shows the average declared value of *cotton yarn* from 1814 to 1850, also in pence per lb.; Column (5) shows the prices of *cotton piece goods exported* from 1820 to 1850 in pence per piece.[1] Price relatives based on 1820 for each series are shown in Columns (2), (4), and (6), respectively. The use of relatives based on the same year permits a comparison of the rate of change for each series. Thus, by the late 1840's, the price of yarn had fallen more than the price of raw cotton, and the price of piece goods had fallen more than either yarn or cotton since 1820. These movements are clouded, however, by the fact that price changes in raw cotton *contributed* to price changes in cotton yarn and that both raw cotton and cotton yarn *contributed* to price changes in piece goods. From the price-relatives alone, moreover, we cannot assess the relative strength of these contributions.

To estimate these respective contributions to final cost, a set of cost estimates drawn up in 1840 by James Montgomery, the superintendent of the York Factories, Saco, Maine, is available. Montgomery, the author of several technical works on cotton spinning,[2] left Scotland in 1836, where he had been in the cotton trade. His estimates compared the costs of manufacturing in America and Britain; he had been induced "to lay them before the public, especially as the most contradictory reports have been circulated in that

[1] The prices for all three series are taken from Gayer, Rostow, and Schwartz, *Growth and Fluctuation of the British Economy*, Microfilmed supplement, pp. 1270–74.

[2] *The Cotton Spinner's Manual* (Glasgow, 1850); *The Theory and Practice of Cotton Spinning* (Glasgow, 1836).

TABLE 11

PRICE AND PERCENTAGE CHANGES IN COTTON, YARN,
AND PIECE GOODS, 1814–50

Year	1	2	3	4	5	6
1814	27·5	227	52·41	157	—	—
1815	19·6	162	43·47	130	—	—
1816	18·3	151	40·08	120	—	—
1817	19·7	163	38·01	114	—	—
1818	20·4	169	38·99	117	—	—
1819	14·5	120	33·99	101	—	—
1820	12·1	100	33·44	100	11·51	100
1821	9·8	81	29·43	88	11·16	97
1822	9·1	75	25·71	77	10·03	87
1823	8·6	71	24·34	73	9·28	81
1824	8·2	68	23·02	69	9·08	79
1825	12·2	101	22·39	67	9·15	79
1826	7·2	60	23·58	71	7.78	68
1827	6·4	53	18·96	57	7·52	65
1828	6·0	50	17·09	51	7·12	62
1829	6·2	51	15·53	46	6·31	55
1830	6·4	53	15·35	46	6·43	56
1831	6·3	52	14·95	45	6·09	53
1832	6·6	55	14·98	45	5·42	47
1833	8·4	69	15·99	48	5·41	47
1834	8·8	73	16·35	49	5·51	48
1835	10·2	84	16·46	49	5·97	52
1836	10·0	83	16·66	50	5·91	51
1837	7·3	60	16·14	48	5·10	44
1838	7·1	59	15·56	46	4·82	42
1839	7·8	64	15·57	46	4·76	41
1840	6·4	53	14·39	43	4·32	38
1841	6·3	52	14·15	42	4·10	36
1842	5·3	44	13·57	41	3·63	32
1843	4·7	39	12·30	37	3·42	30
1844	5·0	41	12·11	36	3·49	30
1845	4·2	35	12·37	37	3·42	30
1846	4·7	39	11·68	35	3·22	28
1847	6·3	52	11·89	36	3·57	31
1848	4·3	36	10·47	31	2·92	25
1849	4·9	40	10·76	32	2·85	25
1850	7·3	60	11·66	35	3·07	27

country, by many who have visited America." [1] The estimates seem carefully drawn, and were submitted to the inspection of "several gentlemen in both countries, in whose judgment, experience, and practical knowledge of the Cotton Manufacture in all its details, the author has the utmost confidence." [2]

We shall consider Montgomery's "typical factory" in Great Britain only, engaged both in spinning and in weaving in 1840. Table 12 shows the costs for two weeks of production in this typical factory.

In order to arrive at an appropriate weighting of raw cotton costs, costs for spinning and allied activities, and costs for weaving and allied activities, we must distribute the General Charges and the On-cost Charges in Table 12 among these branches. I assume (1) the

TABLE 12

FORTNIGHTLY COSTS OF A TYPICAL FACTORY, 1840 [3]

	£	s.	d.
Preparation charges (carding, batting, etc.)	18	4	0
Spinning charges	25	17	4
Dressing and weaving charges	99	10	5
General charges (including mechanics, porter, book-keeper, superintendent or manager, hands for measuring and folding cloth, calenderer or packer, etc.)	21	4	0
On-cost (including capital and depreciation, coals, oil, twine, incidental charges, etc.)	69	6	11
NET CHARGES FOR TWO WEEKS	234	2	8

On-cost Charges, which are primarily depreciation costs, were proportional to the fixed capital devoted to spinning, weaving, etc., respectively; (2) the General Charges, which were spread more or less evenly over the whole series of operations, were divided equally between spinning and allied activities and weaving and allied activities.

Montgomery calculated the initial (capital investment) costs of the various parts of the plant, which we may use for distributing the On-cost Charges. For the preparatory machinery (carding, batting, etc.), the initial costs were £3,000 12s. 0d.; for the spinning machinery

---

[1] J. Montgomery, *The Cotton Manufacture of the United States of America and the State of the Cotton Manufacture of that Country Contrasted and Compared with that of Great Britain* (Glasgow, 1840), p. v.

[2] *Ibid.*, p. vii.

[3] *Ibid.*, p. 124.

the costs were £1,858 8s. 0d. Combining these (both types of machinery were involved in converting raw cotton to yarn), the machinery costs for preparation and spinning were £4,859 0s. 0d. Machines for weaving and dressing cost £1,714 0s. 0d. initially. Thus the cost ratio of preparation and spinning machinery to weaving machinery is £4,859 to £1,714, or 74 : 26. We might assume also that the initial building and gearing charges for the whole plant were devoted to these processes in the same ratio.

To assign the £69 6s. 11d. On-cost Charges, therefore, we add 74%, or £51 6s. 0d. to the spinning and preparatory charges, and 26%, or £17 1s. 0d. to the weaving and dressing processes. The *wage and capital* charges, therefore, for spinning and preparation, were £51 6s. 0d. plus £44 1s. 4d., or £95 7s. 4d., and, for weaving and dressing, £99 10s. 5d. plus £17 1s. 0d., or £116 11s. 5d.

To assign the £21 4s. 0d. General Charges to these two branches, we add half, or £10 12s. 0d. to each. This gives *total production costs*, exclusive of raw materials, of £105 19s. 4d. for spinning and preparation and £127 3s. 5d. for weaving and dressing.

For raw material costs, Montgomery took 7d./lb. as the price for raw cotton in 1840, which is higher than the average for 1840 in Table 11, but which seems an appropriate average for the years around 1840. Each "piece," the unit in which woven goods were calculated, consumed 8½ lb. of cotton. Hence the raw cotton for one piece cost approximately 4s. 11½d. Adding one-sixth for loss and waste as Montgomery suggested, the raw material for one piece totalled 5s. 9½d. Montgomery's "typical factory" produced some 1,408 pieces per fortnight in 1840, yielding a total of £407 14s. 8d. for raw cotton. Montgomery suggested the addition of 27·5% for cost of shipment, freight and insurance, importer's profit, duty on cotton, and inland carriage. This 27·5%, or £112 2s. 6d., when applied to the costs of spinning and preparation, yields a total two-weekly cost for this process of £218 1s. 10d.

In sum, the following totals are yielded for the two weeks' production:

Raw materials	Spinning and preparation	Weaving
£407 14s. 8d.	£218 1s. 10d.	£127 3s. 5d.

Considering yarn production alone, the raw materials (£407 14s. 8d.) comprise 65% of costs; and wages, capital, etc., for spinning (£218 1s. 10d.) comprise 35%. Considering production of piece goods, yarn production (£407 14s. 8d. *plus* £218 1s. 10d.) comprises 83% of costs; weaving and dressing (£127 3s. 5d.) comprise 17%.

Structural Differentiation in Weaving

These proportions give a rough percentage estimate of the cost components of the production of cloth at the stages corresponding to Columns (1), (3), and (5) of Table 11. By using these proportions, we should now be able to calculate the influence of changes in the cost of raw material upon the cost of producing yarn on the one hand, and the influence of changes in the cost of producing yarn upon the cost of producing cloth on the other. This calculation assumes, unrealistically of course, that the cost proportions remained the same during the period 1820–50. They altered because of the innovations themselves; but since all three components fell in cost during the period, the proportions did not vary so much as to invalidate the assumption. At any rate, the 1840 estimates seem to be the only satisfactory figures on costs available.

To calculate the influence of each component, let us take an example from Table 11. From 1820 to 1823 the price-relative of raw cotton fell from 100 to 71; for yarn production it fell from 100 to 73. Since the cost of raw material is considered to be ·65 of the cost of yarn production, we would multiply 29 (the number of points the price-relative of raw cotton fell) by ·65 to obtain, as a result, 19, or the fall in yarn prices to be *expected* by virtue of the fall in raw cotton prices. But in fact the price-relative for yarn fell by 27 points, or 8 more than 19. Hence the *corrected* price-relative for yarn (showing the influence of changes in production costs of spinning and preparation only) is 100 − 8, or 92. To calculate the corrected price-relatives for weaving, the same procedure is used, except that the change from the preceding years in yarn prices is multiplied by ·83 to achieve the expected fall or rise.

Using this method, I calculated the actual, expected, and corrected price-relative changes from the base year 1820 for the years 1828–30, 1838–40, and 1848–50, each group of years inclusive. In Table 13, therefore, Column (1) shows the price-relatives of raw cotton; Column (2) shows the price-relatives of yarn; Column (3) shows the direction and magnitude of change in yarn price-relatives *expected* from changes in the cost of raw cotton; Column (4) shows the *actual* change in yarn price-relatives; Column (5) gives the *corrected* price-relatives, showing the influence only of spinning and preparation; Column (6) gives the price-relatives of piece-goods; Column (7) gives the change in price-relative of piece-goods expected by virtue of price changes in raw cotton and yarn production costs; Column (8) shows the actual change in price-relatives for piece-goods, and Column (9) shows the corrected price-relatives for piece-goods, indicating the price-reducing influence of weaving and allied activities only.

155

We may interpret the crude results of Table 13 as follows: the price of raw cotton fell extremely rapidly between 1820 and the late 1820's, thus justifying the assertion that it contributed more to the falling costs of production than improvements in production techniques in these years.[1] Between 1828–30 and 1838–40, however, cotton costs rose irregularly; they resumed their fall, though not too rapidly, from 1838–40 onwards. Columns 5 (corrected price-relatives for yarn) and 9 (corrected price-relatives for piece goods) are more interesting. The price-relative for yarn dropped sharply before 1830, probably as a result of the extensive application of steam, speeding up machinery, and superior mules; from then until 1850, however, the downward trend slowed. The definite movement for piece goods (Column 9) apparently did not begin until after 1830, even though the application of steam-looms had begun to some degree in the '20's. The delay in price reduction caused by weaving

TABLE 13

CONTRIBUTIONS OF RAW COTTON, COTTON YARN,
AND PIECE GOODS TO PRICE CHANGES,
SELECTED YEARS

Years	1	2	3	4	5	6	7	8	9
1820	100	100	—	—	100	100	—	—	100
1828–30	52	48	−31	−52	79	58	−43	−42	101
1838–40	59	45	5	− 3	71	40	− 2	−18	85
1848–50	45	33	− 9	−12	68	26	−10	−14	81

improvements probably can be traced to three factors: (1) the gradualness of the improvement and application of the power-loom; (2) its restriction to coarse goods in its early years; (3) the low costs of hand-loom weaving which stemmed from overcrowding, etc., in the early years of the century.

In this elementary attempt to assess the relative contributions of various costs to final prices, we have ignored the effects of changes in demand on the price series. To justify this, we might note that (1) Of the years chosen—1820, 1828–30, 1838–40, and 1848–50—none was a year of extreme prosperity, such as 1825 or 1836, and each three-year period had one year of "deep" depression.[2] Hence the short-term speculative rises in raw cotton prices (as in the years 1825, 1835, and 1836) were eliminated in the calculation, as were the years of gloomiest depression (such as 1841 and 1842). (2) Taking the three-year averages for 1828–30, 1838–40 and 1848–50 tends to

1 Above, p. 123.
2 1829; 1837–8; 1848.

156

eliminate short-term fluctuations in demand, inventory adjustments affecting prices, etc. (3) In the long run, demand conditions influencing piece goods also influenced the prices of raw cotton and yarn. This is particularly true for British industry, which controlled a large share of the world's cotton trade between 1820 and 1850. Hence long-term changes in demand would be reflected in all three series, and would not distort the long-term *proportions* radically.

CHAPTER VIII

REFILLING THE BOXES

Introduction. At this point our study reaches a half-way mark. We first outlined several abstract dimensions by which the structure of *any* social system may be analysed, and next generated a series of abstract propositions concerning the sequence by which institutionalized activity becomes more differentiated along these dimensions (Chapters I, II). To fill these empty boxes, we described an industry—cotton textiles—in terms of the general dimensions, and re-phrased the abstract propositions of structural change as more specific propositions governing industrial change (Chapter III). Finally, we attempted to assess the workability of these propositions by unravelling the tangled history of structural change in the cotton industry between 1770 and 1840 (Chapters IV–VII). Now we must re-phrase these propositions once more, and apply them to the changes in the economic life of the working-class family in the same period. To carry out these operations on the family economy is to apply the same set of theoretical concepts to a different institutional complex without varying the logic of the theory.

First we shall apply the same formal functional categories to the family economy that we applied to the industry; furthermore, we shall apply the same formal principles of change to the family economy as to the industry. This is not to say that the family *is* or *is reducible to* an industry. Because its value-system, goals, and institutionalized roles differ radically from those of any industry, we must observe unique characteristics for the family. Nor is it to say that industrial change *automatically* induces change in the family economy, even though it may initiate such changes by generating dissatisfactions with the existing role-performance in the family economy. Any differentiation of familial roles, however, must be analysed in terms specific to the family.

With such an analysis of the family economy, we should be able to throw light on such historical developments as the agitation to limit factory hours, the emergence of trade unions, the evolution of friendly societies, the appearance of savings banks, and the early co-operative movement. All these illustrate the process of *structural*

158

differentiation at various stages. In each case a more specialized unit or units appear along the family economy's functional dimensions. Furthermore, many phenomena—dissatisfactions, disturbances ("movements"), handling and channelling, encouragement of ideas, etc.—run their course at certain points in the sequences. Naturally the empirical illustrations concerning the family economy will be vaguer than those for the cotton industry because its dimensions are more difficult to operationalize and because statistical data on the family are scarcer than industrial data.

The Units of Analysis of a Family Economy. The family is a multi-functional unit. It is a relatively permanent, face-to-face group (integrative function); it allocates authority within this group (political function); it allocates economic goods and services among its members (economic function); it is the seat of much expressive behaviour (pattern-maintenance function).[1] The family, however, like an industry, has a *primacy* of function. All the functions of an industry—authority, integration, production, etc.—are subordinate to its primary goal of adding economic value to products. The family's primary function is to transmit cultural values through socialization (pattern-maintenance) and to manage individual tensions within a small, face-to-face group (tension-management).[2] In particular, its *economic* functions are subordinated to these latency functions. This proposition is fundamental.

The family's *economic* functions include the generation of motivation for economic performance, and the generation, management, and disposal of wealth. Our concrete units of analysis are therefore labourer, breadwinner, consumer, saver, purchasing agent, etc. The economist or economic historian often uses such concepts in discussing price, production, or distribution. I shall treat these concepts as they relate to family structure primarily and as they influence market processes secondarily.

A Functional Analysis of the Family Economy. Let us now refill the boxes of Social System *S* with categories appropriate to Family Economy *E*. These categories are special cases of *S*, since filling the boxes involves placing certain empirical restrictions on *S*. Furthermore, Family Economy *E* does not differ *formally* from Industry *C* in so far as each has a primary goal; each meets adaptive and integrative exigencies and each perpetuates a value-system. These elements differ in *content*, however; the industry produces goods and

[1] For a similar classification of family functions, cf. M. J. Levy, *The Family Revolution in Modern China* (Cambridge, Mass., 1949), pp. 6–40.
[2] Parsons, Bales, and Shils, *Working Papers in the Theory of Action*, pp. 264–9.

services, whereas the family produces motivation appropriate to economic performance.

The goal of the family economy (E_G) is *to generate motivation appropriate to occupational performance* through the mechanisms of socialization of the child and the management of tensions of the family members. The resulting labour is often rewarded by wage payments in the labour market. The motivation to work and the rewards for work are not, however, reducible to each other. An independent set of processes must guarantee the state of readiness to *respond* to occupational rewards.

In a domestic economy, the bulk of economic performance remains in the household; in a factory economy, one or more persons take jobs elsewhere. In both cases, however, the family creates and manages motivation relative to these roles. In this study we shall consider only the transition from domestic to factory labour. In theory, of course, the family generates and maintains motivation over a whole range of roles, whether primarily economic or not, whether performed in the home or away, etc. In complex societies the family's major socializing and management roles are shared partially with educational, religious, business, and other organizations. In our analysis of factory legislation below, we shall see how some of the family's training functions began to pass into the school system. Responsibility for early motivation has remained, however, largely a family matter; in addition, the family remains an appropriate setting for "blowing off steam" generated in the workaday world.

Furthermore, the family must maintain a style of life whereby its resources are devoted to a continuous maintenance of occupational motivation. Marx recognized several essential conditions for the labourer's "continuous appearance in the market"—to procreate and provide for offspring, who will be future labourers; to expend wealth in training the labourer for a job, etc.[1] To meet these conditions is to build *adaptive facilities* for the family economy (E_A), i.e., a continuous and flexible basis for assuming occupational roles. Furthermore, these conditions are realized partially by means of the family's organized expenditures on a style of life. This naturally includes a standard package of basic necessities; it also includes, however, a level of spending on health, education and leisure,

[1] K. Marx, *Capital* (London, 1949), pp. 150–51. We cannot agree, however, that the "value of labour-power resolves itself into the value of a definite quantity of the means of subsistence. It therefore varies with the value of these means or with the quantity of labour requisite for their production" (p. 151). The family cannot be reduced to an input of economic goods and services which turn out labour.

160

symbolic spending based upon social class position, and a level of personal saving. Thus the family economy's adaptive function involves consumption in the economic sense. This consumption, however, is not simply individual gratification, but is definitely *structured* in relation to the family's larger goals, just as industrial capital is structured in relation to industrial goals of production. We shall examine the elements of the style of life in Appendix A.

The integrative sub-system of the family economy (E_I) deals with the *organization* of the family's economic roles. What is the division of labour in the family? Is it a co-operative economic enterprise, or is there one principal breadwinner who earns the entire family income? In what ways do the children contribute to the family economy, and how is this related to the socialization of the children? Who is responsible for purchasing and allocating goods and services in the family? Which family members represent its class and community roles symbolically? We shall examine this sub-system in more detail in Appendix A.

In one sense the E_L sub-system is the seat of the value-system governing the family economy as a whole. All latency sub-systems refer, however, to various maintaining and managing activities relative to these values as well. E_L concerns, therefore, the more intimate levels of family interaction. Given an institutionalized type of economic performance (E_G), a certain style of life (E_A), and an organization of family roles (E_I), the latency functions supply techniques of socialization and tension-management to implement these functions. Hence most of the concrete, day-to-day "activities" of the family cluster in the latency sub-system.

Figure 10 shows the major functions of the family economy. Empirically the family is "sorted" into these categories according to age and sex. In the typical textile family of the late eighteenth and early nineteenth centuries, for instance, husbands often were responsible for the major occupational duties of the family, though women and children contributed substantially (E_G). Women were responsible primarily for expenditures on necessaries and for personal saving. Males were responsible for much status spending, particularly in symbolizing the role of breadwinner and reinforcing the family's occupational status (E_A). We shall discuss these role-specializations and their changes in subsequent chapters. It should be remembered also that to represent the family economy as a social system does not exhaust all the functions of the family. We have isolated the major functional exigencies which must be met in performing only *one* of its major functions—to generate and maintain motivation appropriate to occupational performance.

Each of the major sub-systems of Figure 10 is governed by a value-system which may be described in terms of the "performance-centred" vs. "sanction-centred" dimension.[1]

E_G. "Valuation of industry" outlines the broad basis for occupational performance. If values call for a response to occupational opportunities in the absence of external pressures, they are performance-centred. The other extreme defines a readiness to respond to such situations only under definite sanctions. Commentators in the late eighteenth and early nineteenth centuries might have called these extremes "industrious" and "idle" respectively.

E_A. If we recall that consumption is one factor in producing motivation appropriate to occupational performance, we may speak

FIGURE 10

THE FUNCTIONAL DIMENSIONS OF FAMILY ECONOMY E

Consumption: utilization of goods and services to form and manage motivation E_A	Generation of motivation to assume occupational roles E_G
E_L Processing of motivation in family	E_I Organization of roles in family economy

of values as performance-centred or sanction-centred. For the former, families actively utilize their facilities to induce motivation geared to economic performance, e.g., by spending on health, education, training, etc. Such families are, in the words of the moralists of our period, "frugal," "prudent," and "provident." At the sanction-centred pole, spending tends to be devoted more to goods and services which are irrelevant to the generation of economic performance, e.g., gambling, drinking, etc. We shall analyse such values in connection with savings banks and co-operative societies in our period.

E_I. This value-system concerns the organization of economic performance. If performance-centred, there is a readiness to modify the

[1] For a general characterization of this dimension and its application to industrial sub-systems, above, pp. 25–7.

family organization in the interests of improving its economic performance; if sanction-centred, the family structure is closely guarded except in the face of the most apparent of external pressures.

E_L. We might call this value-system the evaluation of "training," because it implies processes at more intimate levels. If the values are performance-centred, motivation relative to training will be maximized in the absence of clear sanctions to do so. If values are sanction-centred, only obvious external pressure will initiate such activity. All these value-dimensions underlie and legitimize expressions of dissatisfaction with role-performance in the family economy, as we shall illustrate in later chapters.

We have used many of the same words to describe the family economy as the industry—labour, occupational role, goods and services, resources, etc. Indeed, the physical, social, and cultural objects utilized by the family economy do not differ from those utilized by an industry; both invest money, both handle products, etc. The objects differ in *functional context*, however. This distinction between an industrial and familial complex is one case of Weber's distinction between profit-making and budgetary units.[1] Both engage in rational activity; managers plan production and the family budgets its income. The former, however, is oriented toward profit as a substantive end, and the latter toward the distribution of resources in accordance with familial criteria. In Weber's terms the two types differ in meaningful orientation of economic activities; in terms of action theory, they have distinct functional primacies. The industrial enterprise is a profit-making unit, the family a budgetary unit.

External Boundaries. Because we shall analyse the impact of industrial change upon the family economy, let us consider that external boundary which is most closely related to the industry. Members offer labour services for wage payments, thus:

$$E_G \quad \xrightarrow{\text{Labour services}} \quad C_G$$
$$\xleftarrow{\text{Wage payments}}$$

Within a given industrial and family structure, there is an interest in maximizing input on both sides of the exchange. There are, however, relationships beyond this familiar economic one. What concerns us in this study is that a change in industrial structure means a change in the situation for E_G, and as such constitutes a *dissatisfaction* with the organization of the family economy. Given other appropriate

[1] *The Theory of Social and Economic Organization*, pp. 183 ff.

conditions, this dissatisfaction is likely to initiate structural differentiation of the roles of the family economy.

The other external boundaries of the family are the community-neighbourhood complex, the educational system, and the religious system, i.e., those systems with primary functions in the pattern-maintenance and tension-management functions of society. These spheres provide further fields for applying the model of structural differentiation during the industrial revolution. We shall refer to these spheres, however, only when we discuss the agitation to limit factory hours in the cotton industry. In part this agitation tried to establish limits on the economic functions of the family, and simultaneously to reassert the need for the remaining familial, as well as religious and educational functions. We shall analyse the symbolism of the factory movement to illustrate this interpretation.

Structural Differentiation of the Family Economy. The model of structural differentiation is a general statement of social development, and hence applies to industrial *and* familial systems, as well as many others. Thus we may *refill* the empty boxes of structural change with categories appropriate to Family Economy E:

(1) Dissatisfaction with the family economy or its sub-sectors and a sense of opportunity in terms of the availability of adequate facilities to attain a better style of life.

(2) Appropriate symptoms of disturbance in the form of "unjustified" negative emotional reactions and "unrealistic" aspirations on the part of various elements in the population.

(3) A covert handling of these tensions and mobilizing motivational resources for new attempts to realize the implications of the existing value-system.

(4) Encouragement of the resulting proliferation of "new ideas" without imposing specific responsibility for their implementation or for "taking the consequences."

(5) Attempts to specify institutional forms which will ease the dissatisfactions with the family economy.

(6) Attempts to establish institutional forms which will be "rewarded" by wide public acceptance or "punished" by public indifference or hostility.

(7) New institutional forms are consolidated as permanent features of the institutionalized family.[1]

---

[1] We must recall the several formal qualifications of the model of structural differentiation from Chapter III: (1) the relationship between the analytical steps of structural differentiation and simple time; (2) the possibilities of regression and truncation; (3) the possibility of several simultaneous sequences; (4) the possibility that one new collectivity or role may represent several discrete sequences of

What are the *units* which differentiate? Naturally we include the family roles of labourer, purchasing agent, breadwinner, wage-earner, etc. If one of these roles differentiates, its performance is more isolated from other roles in the family. An example is the switch from domestic employment—in which family relationships and work relationships are aspects of the same familial structure—to factory employment, which segregates work from family activity. In addition, we shall follow the differentiation of several units which are not family members in the narrow sense. For instance, the savings banks in the early nineteenth century grew partially out of the inflexibilities in saving and budgeting as performed by the friendly societies. Neither friendly societies nor savings banks are, of course, members of the nuclear family. Since, however, their functions were geared primarily to the family economy, we may treat them as differentiations in this area.

Step 1. Dissatisfaction with the family economy or its sub-sectors and a sense of opportunity in terms of the availability of adequate facilities to attain a better style of life. To assess the historical material relevant to this step, we must pose the same five questions as before: To what institutional context are the family economy's activities related? By what criteria are the family's achievements judged satisfactory or unsatisfactory? What are the structural foci of dissatisfaction? Is the family flexible enough to adjust to these dissatisfactions without structural change? What is meant by "opportunity" and "facilities" for the family economy?

If there is any segregation of family structure from productive activities—and this exists in all except certain primitive societies—the family's environment includes some system of economic exchange.[1] In practice this means that the markets for consumers' goods and for labour are of first importance to the family. Changes in the structure of these markets generally produce pressures on the family, and frequently constitute the initiating conditions for structural change.

Yet industrial and market forces do not automatically generate specific dissatisfactions with the performance of economic roles in the family. There must exist certain *value-criteria* for assessing, interpreting, and legitimizing dissatisfactions of this sort. Such dissatisfactions are ultimately phrased in terms of these values. We

differentiation. Above, pp. 29–32. While these formal qualifications were stated in terms of industrial change, the logic is directly applicable to other types of change.

[1] This differentiation lies behind the economists' famous distinction between "household" and "firm." Parsons and Smelser, *Economy and Society*, pp. 52–5.

isolated four major sub-systems for the family economy: industry (E_G), consumption (E_A), change in economic performance (E_I), and "training" (E_L). Each may be performance-centred or sanction-centred. If the former is strong, there will be initiative in the market; if the latter, there will be a rigidity of economic performance. In any sequence of structural differentiation, therefore, we must examine the dominant family value-system.

What are the structural foci of dissatisfaction? It will be recalled that for Industry C we classified dissatisfactions in terms of *resources*. We may do the same for the family economy.

For Industry C we considered the resources of labour, capital, and organization. We discovered, however, that these factors must be "conditioned" for economic use by several steps of increasing specification. Motivation, for instance, has to be shaped into definite attitudes and skills before it is available as "labour"; the facilities of society must be codified into knowledge and technology and given the strength of purchasing power before becoming "capital"; and the factor of organization must be defined before it is available as industrial organization. In short, only after the factors of motivation, facilities, and integration become *less general* do they emerge as labour, capital, and organization, respectively.

Yet not *all* the potential motivation, facilities, and integration in the society become factors of economic production. Some are devoted to military and political aims, some to monuments which symbolize the values of society, some to aesthetic objects, etc. In particular, some resources go into fulfilling the family's various functions—socialization, training, tension-management, etc. Hence by reclassifying the levels of generality of resources in terms of the family economy, we may outline the structure of its resources.

At Levels 1, 2, and 3 in Figure 11—before the resources enter *any* concrete organizations—the "preparation" of the resources does not differ from sub-system to sub-system of society. At Level 1, for instance, motivation (G) is subject to very general controls which produce "socialized motivation"; facilities (A) are defined only in terms of the "given data" of society; and integration (I) specifies only a general commitment to some collectivity. In short, at these general levels, the resources are "conditioned" in the same ways—though with different contents—no matter whether they eventually enter an industry, a family economy, a political party, or some other kind of organization.

The crucial point of divergence is between Levels 3 and 4. Facilities—which are now purchasing power—are diverted to the family economy as financial resources rather than to the industry as capital

166

or elsewhere; motivation is organized into occupational roles relative to the whole family economy; and the factor of integration is devoted to the family. At Level 4 this process of divergence "sorts" the general resources of society into the institutionalized sub-systems of the society. The family economy is one such sub-system.

FIGURE 11

THE LEVELS OF GENERALITY OF RESOURCES FOR THE FAMILY ECONOMY

Level	G (*Motivation*)	A (*Facilities*)	I (*Organization*)
1	Socialized motivation	Cultural presumptions regarding the "given data" of empirical world	Primary commitment to collectivities as such (self-collectivity balance)
	[Specification of motivational or cultural goals]		
2	Generalized performance capacity	Codified empirical knowledge ("science")	Organizational principles of hierarchy and qualitative differentiation
	[Specification and definition of situational objects]		
3	Trained capacity	Technological know-how	Organizational goals: cultural vs. organizational responsibility and impersonal vs. human relations
	[Assignment of resources to familial context]		
4	Occupational roles	Diversion of wealth to latency purposes	Organization of family economy
	[Commitment of resources to organizations]		
5	Assumption of work in occupational context	Maintenance of family economy in terms of its basic requirements	Integration of family's spending patterns with its position in the labour force
	[Differentiation of categories within organizations]		
6	Management of tensions generated in economic performance	Application of earnings to the training, guidance, and maintenance of family members	Integration of family spending with its socialization and tension-management functions
	[Definition of and adjustment to situational exigencies]		
7	Work capacity	Consumption activities	Rules for work, relaxation, expenditure, etc.

Before the resources become effective, however, they must be made even more specific. Occupational roles (*G*-4) alone do not realize the productive goals of the family economy. One must turn his labour to specific jobs for definite rewards (*G*-5). Once labour is thus committed, certain mechanisms are required to manage the tensions and frustrations which necessarily arise in the course of labour (*G*-6). The family is the prime agency for "blowing off steam," for obtaining a "hearing" on the decisions in connection with the workaday world, etc. The end process of the generation of motivation (*G*-7) is to guarantee the capacity to transform the motivation into concrete "work."

The *G*-series is clarified if we recall that the family economy's goal is not to "work" in the physical sense, but to generate and maintain *motivation* for economic performance at various levels. At each level a more specific "guarantee" for this motivation is added. At *G*-5 the motivation is committed to some sort of organization. At *G*-6 tensions generated in this commitment are brought into line to insure stability. By virtue of these specifications, continuous performance of work at the concrete levels (*G*-7) is made possible.

Similarly, the family economy's facilities are controlled at various levels; above all this means a restriction on the random expenditure of the family's financial resources. The first restriction provides for the basic requirements of the standard package and personal saving —basic necessities (*A*-5). Unless this requirement is met, the family cannot survive as a unit of social organization. Once guaranteed, however, the family's expenditures can then turn to motivational spending (*A*-6), or those types of expenditure geared particularly to socialization and tension-management, such as education, occupational training, health, leisure, etc. The concrete utilization of goods and services (*A*-7) means much the same as "consumption," or the utilization of commodities after the basic structure of expenditure has been determined at higher levels. It is the final stage of specification of the family economy's facilities.

The *I*-series is primarily integrative; furthermore, one reads *across* to *G* and *A* to observe "what is integrated." Family and community roles at the *I*-5 level balance the division of labour with the general spending patterns of the family, and thus consolidate the occupational and status positions of the family. At the next level down there is a more detailed regulation; overspending or underspending is checked, and positive goals (e.g., occupational training, education, leisure) are balanced with the family's level of occupational performance. Finally, certain normative rules assure the more or less harmonious proceeding of day-by-day family activity in work, relaxation, spending, etc. (*I*-7). Such rules define the "time and place" for various kinds of family activity.

We may now classify the nine salient foci of dissatisfaction which constitute the starting-points for structural change in the family economy:

G-5. Dissatisfaction with the economic performance in an occupational role. Instances in our period would be the dissatisfactions with

168

the status of the hand-spinner and the hand-loom weaver in the domestic economy.

G-6. Dissatisfaction with the means of handling and channelling tensions created in the occupational context.

G-7. Dissatisfactions with the economic performance itself, or "work." Perhaps "idleness" or "laziness" is an appropriate term for such complaints.

A-5. Dissatisfaction with the way the family is providing a standard package and personal savings from its earning capacity, e.g., "extravagance," "improvidence," "lack of independence and foresight," etc.

A-6. Dissatisfaction with the "motivational results" which are produced by the family's style of life, e.g., a complaint about the low proportion of persons who wish to "get ahead" at a certain level of society.

A-7. Dissatisfaction with the utilization of goods and services, e.g., wastefulness, inappropriate expenditures, etc.

I-5. Dissatisfaction with the expenditure of family resources relative to the division of economic roles within the family. Since the emphasis is on integration, this dissatisfaction refers to the whole pattern of family and community obligations. An instance is the complaint that the family is "spending above its head," i.e., going beyond that level permitted by its occupational and social status.

I-6. Discrepancies in spending patterns. The criticism in this case refers primarily to *misallocation* of funds rather than simple overspending or underspending. For instance, even though a family meets its general responsibilities, it still might be felt that impulsive spending or luxury spending "sets bad examples" for its children.

I-7. Dissatisfaction with the proportions of time devoted to leisure, work, overwork, etc.

Most dissatisfactions imply that the family or its members are performing inadequately at these focal points. In Appendix B we shall trace the parallels between dissatisfactions with resources and dissatisfactions with roles. In addition, one empirical dissatisfaction may refer to several foci. A dissatisfaction with the allocation of labour in the weaving trade* refers in the first instance to the industry, and hence is assessed in terms of production and profits. The *same* dissatisfaction may imply, however, a demand that the domestic worker change from hand-loom weaving to factory work of some sort.** The focus of the latter demand is the family division of labour.

* *G*-6 of the table of resources for the industry. Above, p. 35.
** *G*-6 of the table of resources of the family economy.

Some dissatisfactions may be "ironed out" without reorganization of the family economy; this depends primarily on the flexibility of the family structure. Temporary adjustments may be made, for instance, by dipping into savings, by borrowing, by transferring skills, etc. As we shall see, however, the flexibility of the family is limited because inherently it deals with deep and explosive emotions which cannot be manipulated freely.

If the dissatisfactions of Step 1 are to initiate a sequence of structural differentiation, there must exist a simultaneous sense of "opportunity," i.e., a prospect that if the family economy changes its organization, it will be able thereby to enhance its style of life (E_A). This promise is formally identical with the promise of capital facilities, which, if combined with dissatisfactions with industrial productivity, initiates a sequence of industrial differentiation.

Step 2. Appropriate symptoms of disturbance in the form of "unjustified" negative emotional reactions and "unrealistic" aspirations on the part of various elements in the population. When the family exhausts its flexibility, the resulting symptoms show a regression of response "up" the table of resources "beyond Level 1." *Formally* these disturbances resemble those appropriate to all other symptoms of disturbance—the undoing of the most primitive controls over socialized motivation (G-1), or the expression of *aggression*; the movement of perceptions beyond the "given data" (A-1) of the conventionally defined world into *phantasy behaviour*, both negative and positive; and the expression of *anxiety*, or fear of exclusion from the social system (I-1).

Disturbances traceable to the family economy differ from all other disturbances, however, in that they have a special symbolic reference to the family. It would be wrong to assign the agitation against the exportation of cotton twist, for instance, to family conditions primarily. On the other hand, agitations for legislation to limit factory hours were in many respects symbolically appropriate to the problems which faced the working-class family in the early nineteenth century.

Step 3. A covert handling of these tensions and mobilizing motivational resources for new attempts to realize the implications of the existing value-system. In this step responsible agents undertake "holding operations" against the unbridled energy of Step 2. Formally these operations do not differ from disturbance to disturbance. Because we are dealing with the family, however—which specializes in "security" in the deepest psychological sense—violent aggressive reactions such as property destruction, personal attack, and intimidation are especially frequent in periods of disturbance.

Since this is the case, more extreme controls such as the police and military must be used to handle these disturbances. Expressions of anxiety traceable to pressures on the family, furthermore, must be handled more "delicately" than, for instance, an agitation for tariff protection by industrialists.

Despite this uniqueness of disturbance and management, Step 3 brings the resources back to Level 1 by restoring basic controls over motivated behaviour (*G*-1), rendering phantasy productions intelligible in terms of the accepted "given data" (*A*-1), and assuring disturbed elements that their position is not unconditionally threatened (*I*-1).

Step 4. Encouragement of the resulting proliferation of "new ideas" without imposing specific responsibility for their implementation or for "taking the consequences." This period brings a vast production of plans, projects, and opinions about ways to modify the family economy, which are encouraged by specialized agencies. At this stage there is a reaffirmation of the basic goals toward which the family must continue to orient its performance (*G*-2), an emphasis on the appropriate knowledge or education to carry these goals to a new level (*A*-2), and a specification of levels of differentiation which new social forms should assume (*I*-2). As yet, however, these ideas do not have to "meet the test" of social experimentation. Hence the schemes of this step will include many projects and plans which may be judged later to be irresponsible or fanciful, but supply the background of more realistic developments.

Step 5. Attempts to specify institutional forms which will ease the dissatisfactions with the family economy. This step, which fuses empirically with the preceding and following, brings the plans and projects to a greater degree of specificity. For instance, if Step 4 specifies that "prudence" and "frugality" are cultural goals to be preserved in *any* new level of differentiation, Step 5 outlines institutional forms such as annuity schemes, savings plans, etc., appropriate to these goals. While change is still in the "planning stage," there are attempts to specify roles, rules, and methods (*G*-3). Any particular skills or knowledge necessary for future role incumbents is also emphasized at this level (*A*-3). Finally, any proposed roles are defined in terms of the kinds of responsibility to be assumed (*I*-3).

Step 6. Attempts to establish institutional forms which will be "rewarded" by public acceptance or "punished" by public indifference or hostility. At this point the resources which have been "prepared" in the earlier steps are brought to bear on family organization itself. New jobs are taken, new organizations formed, and

171

new relationships established among family members and family units. The result is a qualitatively new level of differentiation of social units built upon the functions peculiar to the family economy. Formally, the process descends to Level 4 in the table of resources.

Since the level is "new," the sanctions for forming such units should be extraordinary, and the "reward" for experimenters in institutional innovation should be unusually great. If the concrete experiment is a "success," there will be a rush to incorporate it; if a failure, it will be discredited or ignored.

One element which distinguishes Step 6 from earlier steps is that innovators are accountable for the success or failure of projects in a way in which earlier promoters of ideas are not. The board of trustees of a savings bank is responsible for its success or failure; the social planner for the success or failure of his ideas. The government which legislates is responsible for the law in a way in which agitators are not responsible for proposals, and so on.

The directions of differentiation in Step 6 are classifiable in terms of the nine structural foci of dissatisfaction. The salient characteristics of the newly-differentiated unit parallel the original dissatisfactions in the sense that they "solve the problems" posed by them.

Step 7. New institutional forms are consolidated by their incorporation as a permanent feature of the institutionalized family. At this level the new differentiation becomes a "usual" feature of the family; controversy over principles, basic experimentation, extraordinary rewards, etc., diminishes. Because no obvious indication is available to illustrate this process of routinization, we must rely on the disappearance of controversy, the *type* of concern voiced about institutional arrangements, and the course of public opinion. If discussion concentrates on amending the technical *details* of a new social unit, for instance, rather than upon the *principles* of its establishment, this is one sign of its routinization.

APPENDIX A

THE INTERNAL ORGANIZATION OF FAMILY ECONOMY *E*

Functional Sub-systems. Each major sub-system of the family economy—E_G, E_A, E_I, and E_L—may be treated as a system in itself, with the functions of goal-attainment, adaptation, integration, and pattern-maintenance.

E_G. Generation of motivation to assume occupational roles. Goal-attainment (E_{G_g}) is composed of the occupational roles of the

172

family members. The performance of these roles may be situated on or away from the household premises; it may involve the work of a single breadwinner or many family members.

Besides the attitudes and skills comprising an occupational role, there must be a level of *generalizability* in the occupational market as well. It seems appropriate to call this characteristic *earning capacity* (E_{G_a}). It includes intelligence and educational level, both of which facilitate the acquisition and improvement of skills; it includes the ability and willingness to transfer skill to new occupational settings. In academic, political, and popular writings the worker's labour has been referred to as his capital.[1] In a similar sense we use the term "earning capacity" to refer to the flexibility which permits or encourages movement in several productive contexts.

We might call the integrative function (E_{G_i}) a "balance of skills, levels of competence, and motivation for economic performance." Frequently this involves co-ordinating domestic labour of several family members, or perhaps setting limits to the economic perform-ance of one. A common integrative problem is to decide when education and training should give way to productive employment.

E_A. Utilization of goods and services to form and manage motiva-tion. The goal of this sub-system (E_{A_g}) includes types of expenditure closely related to motivation—education, training, medical care, etc. Such spending forms and controls motivation to fulfil economic roles and maintains the productive powers of family members.

The adaptive base (E_{A_a}) upon which this motivational spending is built is expenditure on basic necessities—food, clothing, shelter, etc. —required to maintain the family at a biologically and culturally defined level. The adaptive facilities also include a level of personal savings. These provide for indivisible family expenses such as sick-ness, death, maintenance in old age, etc., which cannot be met simply by the steady use of a steady income. Furthermore, unexpected fluctuations in prices and wages must be cushioned by a reserve of savings.

---

[1] This is implied by Adam Smith: "When the stock which a man possesses is no more than sufficient to maintain him for a few days or a few weeks, he seldom thinks of deriving any revenue from it. He consumes it as sparingly as he can, and endeavours by his labour to acquire something which may supply its place before it be consumed altogether. His revenue is, in this case, derived from his labour only. This is the state of the greater part of the labouring poor in all countries." *Wealth of Nations*, p. 262. William Huskisson "always maintained that labour was the poor man's capital." Quoted in *Annual Register*, 1825, p. 91 (Hist.). See also the popular Lancashire tract by Sally Bobbinwinder (pseud.), *A Conversa-tion between Peter Pickingpeg, and Harry Emptybobbin, carefully reported* (Barnsley, 1838), especially p. 10.

Consumption is consolidated by "status spending" (E_{A_l}), which includes much spending for luxuries and in formal and informal associations. Status spending also relates the various elements of family expenditure to each other.

E_I. Organization of family economy. The "organizational" aspects of the family economy may be invisible except in times of change. In this sense E_I resembles the entrepreneurial function for the industry (C_I), which is quiescent in periods of industrial stability. In times of pressure, however, great energy is devoted to revising family organization.

The goal of the E_I sub-system is the improvement of the family's occupational capacities by reorganizing its roles, consumption patterns, and socialization techniques (E_{I_g}). Often the pressure to improve originates in economic, moral, political, or other community pressures. While leaders in these spheres are not members of the family, we attribute their leadership roles to the family's integrative sub-system.

The facilities (E_{I_a}) for creating new occupational capacity or improving the old are the family's potential for creating, admitting, and handling new role behaviour. The integrative sub-system (E_{I_i}) involves the organization of family roles in all their economic aspects, just as the entrepreneurial sub-system (C_{I_i}) deals with the organization of all the factors of production.

E_L. Processing of motivation in family context. The E_{L_g} sub-system processes motivation relative to economic performance. Certain family members may be singled out for this role in child socialization and in the management of adult tensions. Frequently the woman bears primary responsibility in this sphere.

The facilities for this processing are the family's techniques of socialization and tension-management (E_{L_a}). If these are too narrowly defined, the potentiality of the family for processing motivation is limited; if many and flexible, the family unit can direct motivation over a wider range. The socialization techniques and their application are integrated (E_{L_i}) by means of the organization of family roles, e.g., the division of responsibilities between father and mother in applying discipline, supplying nurture, etc.

The value systems for each major sub-system—industry (E_G), consumption (E_A), change in economic performance (E_I), and "training" (E_L)—refer primarily to the *l* cell of each sub-system. These and the other detailed functional dimensions are shown in Figure 12.

Internal Boundary-interchanges. The boundary-interchanges of the family economy, shown in Figure 13, do not differ in principle from the industry's, in so far as both specify functional bases for role

FIGURE 12

DETAILED FUNCTIONAL BREAKDOWN OF FAMILY
ECONOMY E

E_A		E_G	
Consumption: utilization of goods and services to form and manage motivation		Generation of motivation to assume occupational roles	
Standard package and personal saving	Motivational spending: health, education, training, &c	Earning capacity	Assumption of occupational role
Consumption values	Status spending	Valuation of industry	Balance of skills, levels of competence, and motivation

E_L		E_I	
Processing of motivation in family		Organization of roles in family economy	
Techniques of socialization and tension-management	Processing of appropriate motivation	Channels of creating and handling new role-behaviour	Improvement of occupational capacities
Valuation of "training"	Organization of socialization and tension-management in family	Valuation of change in economic performance	Organization of family roles

FIGURE 13

INTERNAL BOUNDARY-INTERCHANGES OF FAMILY
ECONOMY *E*

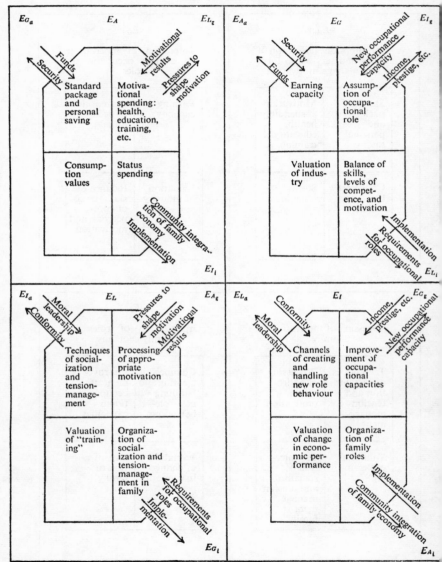

specialization and interaction. The major differences between the industrial and familial systems are (a) their value-systems, goals, and roles are distinct, and (b) the industry is often characterized by large-scale organizations, whereas family differentiation is naturally restricted to roles and sub-roles in the family. On the other hand, organizations geared to the family economy, such as the savings bank, may be relatively large.

E_{G_g}–E_{I_g}. This relationship leads to improvements in the family's economic performance. The reward for this new structure of occupational roles is enhanced income, prestige, etc., for the family unit, analogous to industrial profits. This interchange thus has an "extraordinary" character; the improvements in performance capacity and the resulting gains extend beyond the routine occupational give-and-take of a stable role. This interchange always involves a *reorganization* of family roles.

E_{G_a}–E_{A_a}. This concerns the balance between the family's earned income (E_{G_a}) and its spending–saving ratio (E_{A_a}). By devoting some of its income to the standard package and a level of personal savings, the E_{A_a} sub-system guarantees a level of economic "security" for the family. This interchange involves facilities; funds are facilities for consumption, and security is a major facility for the family's attainment of its culturally-defined goals.

E_{G_i}–E_{L_i} involves the relationship between occupational roles and the organization of socialization and tension-management. The family's occupational requirements are passed on to the "processing" level, and by the mechanisms of socialization and tension-release are geared to family life. A modern example is the adult male in an occupational role away from the household, which calls for a "concentration" of socialization in the female role, particularly in the early years of children's lives.

E_{A_g}–E_{L_g}. By "motivational spending" on health, education, training, and leisure (E_{A_g}), the pressures to shape motivation are conveyed to the "processing" levels of the family (E_{L_g}). If the interchange proceeds smoothly, certain "motivational results" should emerge. This interchange establishes concrete motivation for economic performance in the appropriate family members, such as the willingness to work, the desire to provide for a family out of one's own earning capacity, etc.

E_{A_i}–E_{L_i}, or the exchange between "status spending" and "organization of family roles." This reinforces both the work status and consumption behaviour of the family unit. For E_{A_i} it provides criteria to eliminate potential conflicts by emphasizing and de-emphasizing specific consumption patterns; for E_{I_i} the work status of family members is solidified. Often the social reinforcement of consumption and occupational standards occurs in associational groups which discuss work, shop matters, etc.[1]

E_{I_a}–E_{L_a}. The relationship between channels of creating new role patterns (E_{I_a}) and the techniques of socialization (E_{L_a}) implies a sort of "leadership" relation. E_{I_a} provides "moral leadership" for the more intimate levels of family structure. In response, the E_{L_a} sub-system provides a certain conformity. The rewards for this conformity are primarily "recognition" and "respect." A modern example of this interchange is the community social worker, who, by the exercise of supportive leadership, attempts to re-establish the distressed family as a unit which will continue to provide an income, rear its children appropriately, etc.

APPENDIX B

THE RELATIONSHIP BETWEEN ROLES AND RESOURCES

Figure 11 shows the family economy's resources at various levels of specificity; Figure 13 shows the boundary-relationships, or the bases on which its roles crystallize. The roles *control* the utilization of the resources at various levels. In fact, to represent roles and resources separately is to distinguish two aspects of social action which coincide empirically. Dissatisfactions with the status of resources, furthermore, imply dissatisfactions with the roles of agents who control resources, and vice versa. Let us indicate the points of correspondence between Figures 11 and 13.

G-5, or assumption of work in an occupational context, is controlled by roles organized around the E_{I_g}–E_{G_g} boundary, which allocates the responsibilities and rewards of occupational performance. E_{I_g} "gives" new patterns of occupational responsibility in return for enhanced income and/or prestige. This reallocation of occupational responsibilities in the family may result from an ambitious husband, an energetic wife, or may be "adjustments" to ever-tightening external pressures.

[1] Kennedy, for instance, referred to the conveyance of information about the conditions of work in public houses in the early days of the improvement of cotton-spinning machinery. "Observations on the Rise and Progress of the Cotton Trade in Great Britain," *op. cit.*, p. 119. See also *The Poor Man's Advocate*, Jan. 21, 1832: "When assembled [on social occasions] nothing could be more natural than to talk over and discuss the various matters which more particularly affected the workmen." Such "discussions" are never without normative overtones.

G-6 involves the control of motivational resources at more intimate levels. Work has already been assumed, and the problem is to control, manage, and keep the commitment to the job in good repair. This involves the use of tension-management techniques, and hence refers most directly to the $E_{I_a}-E_{L_a}$ boundary-interchange.

G-7 is the "consummation" of the motivation to work in the application of physical and mental skills to specific tasks. This occurs at the lowest or "processing" levels (intra-E_L). The reference is to the "end stage" of applying motivation which has been "prepared" or "structured" at higher levels.

At Level A-5 the problem is to fasten the family economy's facilities to basic articles of expenditure which maintain it as a family unit. If this fails, the family becomes "bankrupt," or is forced into dissaving and insecurity which hinders its functioning as a family unit. In terms of the boundary-interchanges, A-5 strikes a balance between the family's earning capacity and its basic expenditures ($E_{G_a}-E_{A_a}$) in order to maintain family security.

At Level A-6 expenditures turn to more detailed norms concerning education, training, health, and leisure. This parallels the interchange between motivational requirements and motivational results at $E_{A_g}-E_{L_g}$.

A-7, which also marks the "end stage" in the utilization of a structured series of resources, refers to sub-system E_L, or the lower-level processes of family interaction.

I-5 maintains a general balance between the family's occupational status and its general spending patterns. Concretely this involves the mutual influence among family units which regulates spending patterns through discussion, emulation, and other means of social control. This same balance is struck at the $E_{A_i}-E_{I_i}$ interchange between "organization of family roles" and "status spending."

At I-6 the socialization and tension-management roles are organized to meet the needs of the occupational structure of the family. The generation of "ambition," "laziness," "responsibility," etc., is important at this level, which parallels the $E_{G_i}-E_{L_i}$ interchange.

Finally, at I-7 the integrative emphasis involves the regulation of day-to-day family activities by rules and norms governing leisure, work, and spending activities. These are the "family customs" or "family rituals" which balance the family's economically productive interests with its other interests. Such norms refer primarily to the E_L or "processing" sub-system.

CHAPTER IX

PRESSURES ON THE FAMILY
DIVISION OF LABOUR

Introduction. From the industrial perspective the cotton-textile revolution appears as a dramatic rearrangement of all the factors of production. The revolution originated with a series of dissatisfactions legitimized by the dominant value-system of the day. In several sequences of differentiation the industry emerged with a structure more adequate to meet the demands of the foreign and domestic markets. Such a revolution naturally did not occur in a vacuum. It was initiated by non-economic elements such as religious values, political arrangements, and social stratification. At the same time, the industrial revolution in cotton created a *source of dissatisfactions*, which, when combined with other elements, initiated several sequences of differentiation in other social sub-systems.

In the rest of this study we shall analyse structural differentiation in one of the cotton industry's social neighbours: the family economy of its working classes. Because the *industrial* structure of labour changed in the late eighteenth and early nineteenth centuries, pressure began to weigh immediately upon the *family* division of labour.* The immediate dissatisfactions produced by these industrial changes might be characterized as follows: in order to offer industrial labour on new terms (e.g., to become a factory hand instead of a domestic worker) *and at the same time* maintain its functions of socialization and tension-management, the family economy required a series of drastic structural modifications. Historically the family rose to this challenge by a process formally identical with that of the industrial change itself—the process of structural differentiation.

Several sequences led to the emergence of a new form of family. For a convenient starting-point, however, we shall consider the sequence initiated most dramatically by the industrial revolution— the differentiation of new labour roles in the family economy.** In

* The immediate focus of this pressure is the E_G–C_G boundary. Above, p. 163.
** Even this starting-point conceals two separate processes of differentiation: (*a*) the differentiation of the family economy as a whole from textile production as a whole, by which the family unit was segregated from its traditional productive roles; (*b*) the differentiation of occupational roles *within* the family.

this chapter we shall consider only Step 1 of this sequence by pinpointing the pressures on the family division of labour and eliciting the meaning of these pressures in terms of the dominant value-system. We shall ask what happened when machinery threw some family members out of employment and employed others on a new basis. We shall also examine the related questions of female and child labour. In short, we shall retell the story of the industrial revolution, not in terms of its productive achievements but in terms of its impact on the working-class family.

In Chapter X we shall investigate the initial symptoms of disturbance which issued from these institutional pressures, specifically the destruction of machinery, early radical reform, early co-operative ideology, labour violence and strikes, and the early agitation to limit factory hours. Analytically these eruptions constitute Step 2 of the sequence of structural differentiation. From these turbulent disturbances sprang several new, more differentiated social units. In Chapter XI we shall trace the emergence of the new family, in which economic roles were segregated gradually from other family roles. Factory legislation played a crucial role in "guiding" the family in this sequence. We shall analyse the thunderous agitation for such legislation, the handling and channelling of this agitation, and the subsequent paths by which the family gradually moved to a structure more in harmony with the new industrial society.

Above all, this analysis concerns *family structure*, not the history of individual families. In some cases individual families moved from the old labour force to the new; in other cases there was no continuity of membership. In the transition from hand-loom to power-loom weaving, for instance, we shall observe that very few of the hand-loom weavers themselves moved into the factories, even though the family structure of hand-loom weavers was being revolutionized.

This evolution of the family in turn initiated several other sequences of differentiation, most of which had their roots in the friendly society. In the eighteenth century this type of club served as a protective buffer between the working-class family and its economic environment. One of the friendly society's functions was to save, or to withhold part of the labourers' income for inelastic expenditures such as funerals, sickness, and old age.* At the same time it was a close-knit club for communal drinking.** Further, it enforced

* Hence it regulated the interchange at the $E_{G_a}-E_{A_a}$ boundary.
** One function of this drinking and fellowship was to reinforce the occupational and social status of the members in the community ($E_{A_i}-E_{I_i}$).

standards for skill and occupational training among members,* and dealt with wages and other conditions of employment.** The early friendly society was thus an insurance company, savings bank, associational status grouping, and trade union all in one.

When industrial and urban growth began to make the small and intimate friendly society obsolete, there appeared a number of new social units. In Chapter XII we shall apply the model of differentiation to the textile trade union, which became a *more specialized* guardian of the conditions of labour in the nineteenth century than the friendly society had been in the eighteenth. It also took over the saving function for contingencies such as unemployment. The friendly society, while it "lost" some of its comprehensiveness, continued as a medium for status spending. During the same period many of the friendly society's functions of consumption and saving spread to a number of new social units which were geared more effectively to the new family economy. In Chapter XIII we shall trace the development of these units, particularly the savings bank and co-operative store; the rise of both conforms to the model of structural differentiation.

To illustrate these developments, the cotton industry is a fortunate choice, because it was characterized by two types of workpeople typical in periods of rapid industrialization. The first—spinners and other factory operatives—represent the "new" labour force which differentiated rapidly and shared fully in the new industrial world. Historians have treated the cotton-spinners, for instance, as the representative body *par excellence* of trade unionism in the early nineteenth century.[1] The hand-loom weavers, on the other hand, illustrate an "old," sick trade which was painfully eliminated amidst a display of symptoms of disturbance. In our analysis of working-class history between 1770 and 1840 we shall refer frequently to the instructive contrasts between these groups.

INSTITUTIONAL PRESSURES ON THE FACTORY OPERATIVES, 1770–1840

Historical Background. The typical textile family of the mid eighteenth century was a domestic enterprise within the putting-out system. The independent weaver was a thing of the past, of course; most weaving families depended on the putter-out both for the acquisition of raw materials and for the disposal of woven cloth.

---

* This function fits formally at the E_{G_i}-E_{L_i} boundary, mediating between occupational requirements and family organization.

** Thus the friendly society was a mediating body at the E_G-C_G boundary.

[1] S. and B. Webb, *The History of Trade Unionism* (London, 1894), pp. 40–41.

Pressures on the Family Division of Labour

Nevertheless, the weaving family maintained a certain isolation as a productive unit. The father was occupational head of the family. He himself wove and supervised occasional weaving by women and children.[1] Formally weaving was based on seven years' apprenticeship under a master, though this had decayed by mid eighteenth century. Most small weaving masters who had not been apprenticed in masters' shops, however, were taught weaving by their fathers or brothers.[2] Women and children were responsible for spinning and preparatory activities.

This family has been the subject of frequent romantic reminiscence.

... removed from many of those causes which universally operate to the deterioration of the moral character of the labouring man, when brought into large towns . . . [the working man] presented [an] orderly and respectable appearance. It is true that the amount of labour gone through . . . [and] . . . the quantity of cloth or yarn produced [were] small. . . . They were, however, sufficient to clothe and feed himself and family decently, and according to their station; to lay by a penny for an evil day, and to enjoy those amusements and bodily recreations then in being. He was a respectable member of society; a good father, a good husband, and a good son.[3]

Guest and Engels lingered over the benevolent squire, the wholesome outdoor sports, the communal holidays, the happy rural courtship, and the rest of village life. It is an open question whether these communities justify the romantic contrast with the industrial world of a half-century later; it nevertheless is true that work, religion, recreation, and amusements were confined to a small, relatively undifferentiated community.[4] Just as these domestic and putting-out systems were the starting-point for the *industrial* revolution, so the productive arrangements of the family constitute the starting-point for our analysis of changes in the *family* division of labour.

[1] Some women wove independently, but most of these around 1750 seem to have been widowed or in other special circumstances. Wadsworth and Mann, *The Cotton Trade and Industrial Lancashire*, pp. 332–3 and 336–7.

[2] Usher, *An Introduction to the Industrial History of England*, p. 353; T. Shuttle, *The Worsted Small-Ware Weavers' Apology* (Manchester, 1756), especially pp. 5–6; Wadsworth and Mann, *The Cotton Trade and Industrial Lancashire*, pp. 334–6.

[3] Gaskell, *Artisans and Machinery*, pp. 13–14.

[4] Guest, *A Compendious History of the Cotton Trade*, pp. 37–9; F. Engels, *The Condition of the Working-Class in England in 1844* (London, 1926), pp. 1–4. For an account of local feasts and other entertainment in the village during the era of domestic manufacture, cf. Butterworth, *Historical Sketches of Oldham*, pp. 106–8. Contrast this with Whittle's observations on the amusements of the working-classes in Blackburn one hundred years later. P. A. Whittle, *Blackburn as it Is* (Preston, 1852), p. 32.

183

Pressures on the Family Division of Labour

What dissatisfactions did the new industrial society create for this typical textile family? To sort out these pressures, we shall consider spinning and its allied activities separately from weaving. For spinning we shall isolate three stages: (*a*) from the introduction of the domestic jenny and mule to their incorporation into the factory (*c*. 1770 to *c*. 1790); (*b*) from the rise of the factory system to the 1820's, a period of transitional equilibrium for the family economy; (*c*) from the mid-1820's to the 1840's, when the family economy of the factory operatives moved to a new level of differentiation. For background material we shall devote Appendix A to the long-term course of factory operatives' wages as well as short-term fluctuations in their wages and employment.

Spinning 1770–1790. Two separate industrial changes in this period influenced the family economy: (*a*) the introduction of the jenny and mule, which merely rearranged labour within the domestic system, and (*b*) the beginning of the water-frame mills, which drew family members from the home.

The cottage machines were not without their dramatic consequences. Through 1780 the jennies "*increased* the *gains* of the *females* in a family, and of the *family in general*." [1] After this, women were displaced by the water-frame factories and the skilled male jenny and mule operatives. For a time the latter enjoyed the status of an "aristocracy of spinners." Apparently many were former weavers who had capital to invest in the new spinning machines. All these changes eclipsed the female hand-spinner, who, by the beginning of the nineteenth century, had disappeared almost entirely. In textile families her decline mattered less, for machine-spinning or weaving offset the drop in women's earnings. Indeed, one movement which probably complemented the exodus of wealthy weavers into machine-spinning was the drift of former female spinners into hand-loom weaving.[2]

From the standpoint of *social structure*, however, the cottage jenny and mule reshuffled rather than reorganized labour. The main earning power, at least after 1780, still rested with the husband,

[1] Ramsbotham, *Thoughts on the Use of Machines*, p. 15. In addition, the author held that for several years spinners had been earning more than weavers. P. 14.
[2] Wadsworth and Mann, *The Cotton Trade and Industrial Lancashire*, p. 404; J. L. and B. Hammond, *The Skilled Labourer, 1760–1832* (London, 1920), p. 53; D. K. Macdonald, *Fibres, Spindles and Spinning-Wheels* (Toronto, 1944), pp. 47–8; Gaskell, *Artisans and Machinery*, pp. 28–9; Pinchbeck, *Women Workers in the Industrial Revolution*, p. 149; B. L. Hutchins, *Women in Modern Industry* (London, 1915), pp. 40–41. For the impact of technological changes on female hand-spinners outside Lancashire, *Parliamentary Papers*, 1831, VIII, Lords Committee on the Poor Laws, p. 69.

whether spinner or weaver. Some women began to weave beside their husbands,[1] but in other cases the wife became more secondary economically because hand-spinning had been taken from her. Further, the new cottage machines did not disturb the traditional relationship between father and son; in either spinning or weaving the father continued to instruct his son in the trade. Perhaps more important, the other family functions of child-rearing and tension-management were relatively unaltered, because the family economy remained in the home. In many ways, therefore, the period between 1780 and 1790 was a "golden age" for the domestic spinner; his earnings increased, but the structure of his employment remained the same.

Side by side with the domestic jenny and mule came the water-frame and the mill. While we should not minimize the hardships in these early mills, particularly for parish apprentices,* we must remember the correctives which preserved many features of the traditional family. A clear example was the practice of hiring whole families in country mills. In general the proportion of adult males was low; perhaps they amounted to only one in ten employees at a typical mill in the 1780's or 1790's. Masters often hired the head of the family, however, for road-making, bridge-building, or plant construction while employing the wife and children in the mill.[2] Such an arrangement not only augmented the family income, but also allowed for the presence of a parent with the children during working hours.

Two sets of wage books illustrate this invasion of family standards into the manufactory. In the spinning mill of Robert Peel and his partners near Bury, very few of the 136 persons employed as free labour in 1801–2 were adult males. Ninety-five of the 136, however, belonged to twenty-six families, showing the opportunity for members of the same family to gather on the premises. Furthermore, "in every case [that employees took labour only on a casual basis] no other member of their families was employed there . . . their employment was very irregular and stands in striking contrast to the steady work of the majority of the families."[3]

The second set of books concerns women pickers in the firm of McConnell and Kennedy in Manchester in 1795. The work was

[1] Pinchbeck, *Women Workers in the Industrial Revolution*, pp. 162–4.

* Indeed, we shall see that conditions of bad health and overwork were much worse in the late eighteenth century than in the early decades of the nineteenth, when the problem came most forcefully to public attention. Below, pp. 273–87.

[2] Unwin, *Samuel Oldknow and the Arkwrights*, p. 167. Below, pp. 188–92.

[3] Collier, *The Family Economy in the Cotton Industry*, Chapter III, pp. 6–14.

disagreeable, and in general women worked only sporadically to augment their family earnings. Even though most of the total production was carried on in the mill,

this intermittent work was possible because picking was a hand process. Premises were provided near the mill but the pickers were not subjected to mill discipline; it appears to have been the custom to allow them to come and go as they pleased, or to take their work home if they chose. In short, as long as sufficient supplies were forthcoming they were free to do the work where most convenient to themselves. This degree of liberty attracted to the work women whose domestic duties prevented their leaving their homes for 12 hours a day, or whose health could not stand the strain of long hours of standing.[1]

In addition we have mentioned a number of humanitarian masters who provided several correctives—welfare, education, recreation, etc.—to pressures on the family and community within the factory setting. In 1802 an Act of Parliament extended this voluntary welfare by requiring masters to provide food, clothing, and a modicum of educational and religious training for parish apprentices.[2] Many capitalists disregarded this law, to be sure, but its minimal effect, plus the efforts of humanitarian millowners, benefited both free and apprentice labour and thereby softened the impact of the water-frame mill on the family.

The first sweep of spinning machinery was, therefore, indeed a revolution in terms of wages and technological unemployment. Yet at the same time the unique arrangements of labour around the jenny, mule, and water-frame allowed the family economy to ride this wave into the industrial revolution without severe discontinuity.

Spinning 1790–1820. Despite the industrial slowdown occasioned by the Revolutionary and Napoleonic wars, the pressures on the family reached a new level during these decades. Most of these rose from the migration of the jenny and the mule—especially the latter—into the mills. There were jenny workshops and manufactories in the 1770's and 1780's, and centralized mule-spinning commenced about 1790.[3] Because mules in sheds were powered mainly by hand in the early 1790's, however, workers in these sheds could attend them casually. On the other hand, most new spindles were being attached to steam-powered mules in larger factories run by "free labour"

---

[1] *Ibid.*, Chapter II, pp. 3–4.

[2] 42 Geo. III, c. 73. Below, pp. 269–70.

[3] T. Hopkins, *Great Britain for the Last Forty Years* (London, 1834), p. 134. M. Hovell, *The Chartist Movement* (Manchester, 1925), p. 11. Above, pp. 89–90 and 117–18.

entirely. In a classic statement in 1816, Robert Peel claimed that apprenticeship was no longer a basic concern in the cotton manufacture because of these steam factories with their free child labour.[1]

A decline in the water-frame mills exaggerated this trend. These manufactories continued strong throughout the war period; their autumn commenced only in the decade following. Their recruitment of labour, however, changed greatly. Because of the conflict between economic rationality and a general concern for child labour,[2] and because of the restrictions imposed by the Act of 1802, the recruitment of parish apprentices declined steadily after the turn of the century. In 1815 a parliamentary committee found that 1,493 of 2,026 apprentices bound during the ten years preceding had gone into the cotton manufacture. This proportion was large, but over a ten-year period the number was tiny. In fact, apprentices contributed only 1% to the Lancashire population increase during these ten years.[3]

Thus when Parliament negated the statute requiring seven years' apprenticeship to a skilled trade in 1814, and when it forbade workhouses in London to send apprentices outside a forty-mile radius in 1816,[4] these Acts scarcely applied to cotton. Apprentices had long since proved to be "of great trouble and anxiety to the master."[5] In 1835 James McConnell, a large Manchester spinner, purchased a Derbyshire factory with apprentices and decided to continue with them. In 1843 he complained that they had given him little else than headaches. He had foreseen a cost advantage because of their low wages, but the expenses for housing, the waste of food, the care of clothing, the apprentices' complaints that they were working for nothing, and their ineffective labour led McConnell to believe that "in reality [apprentice labour] is more expensive than paid-labour . . . and . . . troublesome, inconvenient . . . and objectionable in almost every point of view." He believed that there were almost no apprentices in cotton in the early 1840's, general experience having "decided against the system."[6]

[1] *Parliamentary Papers*, 1816, III, Children employed in the Manufactories, p. 371. For the course of investment during the war period, above, pp. 121–2.
[2] Above, pp. 103–8.
[3] *Parliamentary Papers*, 1814–15, V, Parish Apprentices, p. 1571; Redford, *Labour Migration in England*, pp. 28–9.
[4] 54 Geo. III, c. 96, and 56 Geo. III, c. 139.
[5] *Parliamentary Papers*, 1836, XXIX.1 Second Annual Report of the Poor Law Commissioners, p. 415.
[6] *Parliamentary Papers*, 1843, XIV, Children's Employment Commission, pp. 211–12.

The accent on urban factories meant an increasing drift of population toward the towns. Between 1801 and 1811 the population of Manchester and Salford increased by 22% (from 94,876 to 115,874), compared with a 14⅔% increase for all of England. Between 1811 and 1821 the rate was 40% (from 115,874 to 161,635), compared with 17⅞% for all of England. The cotton towns of Ashton, Preston, Oldham, Blackburn, and others also mushroomed. Because of the demand for children in the cotton trade, many large families could be counted among the migrants.[1] Thus the children of working people were pouring into the factories to fill the vacuum left by the vanishing apprentices and to meet the growing need for child labour in the steam-powered industry. The only available information on the industry's age–sex composition in these years shows that adult males constituted only 17·7% of the total employees listed in parliamentary returns in 1816, while for six mills in Nottinghamshire the figure was 18·54%.[2]

All these trends threatened to disperse the family through the factories at the cost of its tradition and its solidarity. The recruitment of women and children weakened the traditional domestic basis for child-rearing. Because the opportunities for the adult male in the industry were limited, his status as chief breadwinner in the family was in danger. Furthermore, it was becoming harder for him to train his children for a trade, particularly as the domestic spinning machinery became progressively less competitive.

These and other strains gave rise to some disturbances before the 1820's among the spinners, which we shall examine in the next chapter. If we consider the factory as a community, however, it is apparent that several corrective mechanisms prevented the family from disintegrating into a mere aggregate of individuals in a free labour market. In fact, if we may trust our limited evidence, the trend toward depersonalization and differentiation did not reach a critical point until the 1820's.

We have described the benevolent country capitalists' cushioning effect upon the family economy. What of the new city factories? Were there guarantees of family integrity even in this relatively large, impersonal setting?

Clearly the interests of the family invaded the recruitment of child labour. Witnesses before the parliamentary committees from 1816 through 1819 testified consistently that masters allowed the operative

1 J. R. McCulloch, *A Descriptive and Statistical Account of the British Empire* (London, 1847), Vol. I, p. 153; Redford, *Labour Migration in England*, pp. 55–6; *Parliamentary Papers*, 1816, III, Children employed in the Manufactories, p. 510.
2 Usher, *An Introduction to the Industrial History of England*, pp. 358–9.

spinners to hire their own assistants (piecers, scavengers, etc.) and that the spinners chose their wives, children, near relatives, or relatives of the proprietors.[1] Many children, especially the youngest, entered the mill at the express request of their parents.[2] One manager claimed that children under ten either were employed by their own parents or were the children of widows.[3] Finally, most of the early trade unions' rules explicitly prohibited members from recruiting assistants outside the narrowly defined classes of children, brothers, orphan nephews, etc.[4]

In the early 1820's, therefore, a child entered the factory at the age of eight or nine years as a scavenger who worked for his father; he cleaned machinery, gathered waste cotton, etc. If designated for future spinning he became a piecer, mending broken threads for a number of years. He was trained to spin until seventeen or eighteen when he finally became a spinner. If destined for the cardroom, he was transferred there after several years of scavenging.[5]

In general the spinner paid his assistants from his own wages; the

[1] *Parliamentary Papers*, 1816, III, Children employed in the Manufactories, p. 334; *Lords Sessional Papers*, 1819, XVI, Children in the Cotton Manufactures, pp. 84, 207, 228–9, 445.

[2] *Parliamentary Papers*, 1816, III, Children employed in the Manufactories, pp. 76, 178–9, 239, 341, 387.

[3] *Ibid.*, p. 502. Evidence of William Taylor, manager of a large Preston spinning concern. The figures in Appendix B for the Catrine Works in 1819 show this apparent favouritism to widows and their children. For a similar sentiment of thanks to cotton manufacture, that art which "glads the widow's and the orphan's heart," see a poem, "The Cotton Mill," written in 1821 by an operative spinner, and quoted in Collier, *The Family Economy in the Cotton Industry*, Chapter II, p. 21.

[4] In 1792 and again in 1795 the Friendly Associated Cotton Spinners of Manchester prohibited spinners from teaching anybody to spin except their own children or paupers who were in receipt of parish relief. Others were forced to pay the high price of £1 1s. The Stockport mule-spinners in 1795 and the Oldham spinners in 1796 made the same prohibitions. See *Articles, Rules, Orders and Regulations . . . of the Friendly Associated Cotton Spinners . . . of Manchester* (Manchester, 1792 and 1795), Article XVI in the 1792 Rules and Article XV in the 1795 Rules; *Articles, Rules, Orders and Regulations of the Friendly Associated Mule Cotton Spinners . . . of Stockport* (Stockport, 1795), p. 12; for the Oldham rules, cf. *Webb Manuscripts on Trade Unionism*, Vol. VII, p. 171. In the resolutions of the delegate meeting of the Operative Spinners of England, Ireland and Scotland drawn up in 1829, the restrictions specified only the son, brother, or orphan nephews of operatives, or poor relations of proprietors. Reprinted in *Webb Manuscripts on Trade Unionism*, Vol. XXXIV, p. 31. The Association of Operative Cotton Spinners of Glasgow and Neighbourhood were reported in 1838 to restrict training to sons and brothers of members. *Parliamentary Papers*, 1837–8, VIII, Combinations of Workmen, p. 303–6.

[5] This progression was described by Archibald Buchanan in *Lords Sessional Papers*, 1818, IX, Lords Committee on Cotton Factories Bill, p. 68. Adult male spinners were not employed in Buchanan's own works, however.

master did not deal with the assistants at all.[1] Adult spinners preferred this system both because they could supplement their own family wages by their children's labour and because, as one spinner put it, "working in a cotton-mill I could instruct them myself in their work."[2] The system perpetuated the traditional values of training children under parental authority for an occupation. Under this system an operative in the early nineteenth century was able to

live more generously, and clothe himself and his family better than many of the lower class of tradesmen . . . eat meat every day, wear broad cloth on Sunday, dress their wives and children well, furnish their houses with mahogany and carpets, subscribe to publications, and pass through life with much of humble respectability.[3]

Little wonder, then, that the conditions of child labour did not offend spinners interviewed by Factory Commissioners in 1833.[4]

Children other than sons, brothers, etc., of operatives—the exact proportion is a mystery in these early days [5]—*left their families* for the long hours of factory labour, returning at night and perhaps for meals.[6] Their lot was naturally less favourable from a family standpoint. We hope to show, in fact, that in the 1820's and 1830's the multiplication of this class of children and the concomitant disintegration of the operative spinner's position in the face of technological changes precipitated the real crisis in child labour. Up to that time, however, the persistence of safeguards maintained by the spinner's authority in the factory set limits on the isolation of numbers of young from their families.

In addition to his economic authority, the adult spinner exercised much *general moral authority* in the factory:

[Gross language] does not seem to arise altogether from the two sexes being mingled; and if you go into silk mills, where none but women

---

[1] *Parliamentary Papers*, 1837–8, Combinations of Workmen, p. 265; 1833, XX, First Report of the Factory Commissioners, p. 752.

[2] *Parliamentary Papers*, 1833, XX, First Report of the Factory Commissioners, p. 886.

[3] Baines, *History of the Cotton Manufacture in Great Britain*, p. 446. His characterization undoubtedly applied to fine spinners, who were better paid and more highly respected than coarse spinners. *Parliamentary Papers*, 1833, XX, First Report of the Factory Commissioners, p. 648.

[4] *Parliamentary Papers*, 1833, XX, First Report of the Factory Commissioners, p. 873.

[5] In the statistical breakdown of the Catrine Works in Appendix B, however, we see, besides the heavy representation of operatives' and widows' children, many weavers' children in the works. The Catrine Works did not, however, employ adult male spinners.

[6] *Parliamentary Papers*, 1816, III, Children employed in the Manufactories, p. 391.

are employed, I should say that the language was as gross, and it may be even more so, than in cotton factories. There is no doubt that males and females who work together much in the day will meet in the evenings; but though I have no doubt that the tone of morality is lowered by habits necessitated in factories, yet I cannot say to what extent, and I see several things which correct it. It is fathers or friends who work in factories, and they have all a common interest in checking immorality among the younger assistants, both boys and girls. Suppose a cotton factory contains forty spinners, each of whom employs four piecers, making 160 young persons of both sexes, and of ages varying from nine to twenty; I should say that thirty at least out of the forty spinners were married men, and that many of them had large families. Now, even if none of their own children were working with them, yet they have all a common interest as fathers in discountenancing indecencies of conduct and language: add to this, that Sunday schools have greatly increased during the last twenty years, and I should say, roughly, that there are upwards of 30,000 children who frequent Sunday schools alone in Manchester. The teachers in them are generally adult young men and women from the age of eighteen to about twenty-four or twenty-five: the female teachers will be working all the week as frame tenters, stretchers, piecers, reelers, &c., and the male teachers also as card-room hands, piecers, and in some instances spinners. Habits of decency, of order, of respect for religious observances, which they contract in their capacity of teachers, they naturally communicate by example and precept to their classes. I could give several instances of this.[1]

Married spinners "[gave] the tone to the conduct of such spinners who are not married, who again may be employing their own sisters and brothers to piece for *them*." [2] On such evidence the Factory Commissioners concluded that the factory operatives were in fact "distinguished from other classes by being collected together (both sexes, young and old,) in large numbers"; nevertheless, "the language and behaviour common to uneducated people, under such circumstances, is found to be checked in no inconsiderable degree by the presence of fathers, mothers and brothers." When "rude behaviour" and "obscene conversation" did appear in the spinning rooms, it was not married but single spinners who failed to check it.[3]

Thus a network of controls based upon kinship and community bonds permeated the apparently impersonal factory. Some even

[1] *Parliamentary Papers*, 1833, XX, First Report of the Factory Commissioners, p. 655. Evidence of John Redman, former spinner and Manchester overseer of the poor.
[2] *Ibid.*, p. 654.
[3] *Ibid.*, pp. 36, 659, 686–7.

blamed unsatisfactory conditions on parents who neglected these bonds in placing their children:

children are not ill-treated in mills. There are instances; but generally they are as well treated in mills as any where else ... those parents who now place their children, for the sake of higher wages, with spinners who ill-treat them, rather than with neighbours or friends, will, I suppose, treat them in the same way as they do now, that is, will neglect them ... there are parents who will take their children away from a kind master, and place the child with another, for the purpose of getting higher wages. There is a class of spinners who are morose to children, and they have to give higher wages to children than other spinners. Now, parents who look out for the highest wages are obliged to place their children with this kind of master.[1]

While this witness blamed parents for not assigning their children to neighbours or friends, the resulting "morose" behaviour no doubt stemmed also from the fact that the spinner had no kinship or community link with his assistants' parents.

In these years, therefore, labour in the cotton factories was scarcely free labour. Robert Peel had complained in 1816 that free were replacing apprentice children and that the former were without protection. While the first part of the proposition was true, the second required qualification, as a pamphleteer pointed out:

... the young persons for whose protection the bill is framed are, through some strange mistake, represented to be exposed, forlorn and unprotected, to any excess of labour which the avarice of their employer may exact, and to all the hardships which his inhumanity may inflict. Why bewail the forlorn state of those who have never felt their parental home? What is meant by talking of children being exposed to hardships without protection, who are constantly under the eye of their natural guardian, many of them even during the time when they are engaged in labour? How is there "not the slightest security for their good treatment," when their own parents have the unceasing superintendence of them, and thus can either prevent injury, or instantly remove them beyond the reach of its influence? What though they have no masters "obliged to maintain them in sickness, or during unfavourable periods of trade," when they have the cares of their own families to cherish them in the one, and support them in the other? These children are neither deserted nor unprotected, nor exposed to the tyranny and injustice of a master...[2]

[1] *Parliamentary Papers*, 1833, XX, First Report of the Factory Commissioners, p. 657; also p. 670 for similar evidence from six witnesses; also p. 689.
[2] *An Inquiry into the Principle and Tendency of the Bill now pending in Parliament, for Imposing Certain Restrictions on Cotton Factories* (London, 1818), pp. 2–3.

Other scattered evidence shows a communal atmosphere among the workers in the factory. Dunlop, a Scottish advocate of temperance, noticed the ceremonial whisky feasts when a spinner "changes his wheels, or gets new wheels" in a factory.[1] Related to this was the custom of "footing," which was observed when a new hand entered the factory; he bought a round of drinks for his shopmates "as a token of his desire to cultivate their friendship and goodwill." According to a defender of this custom, it had existed "time out of mind." [2] In addition, a new master apparently was expected to supply funds for the workmen to drink to his health. In Chorley in 1825, even though relations between the workers and the new master were strained, the latter gave the operatives £13, "which they spent that evening, and paraded the streets of Chorley with a band of music." [3]

Such evidence leads us to question some accepted views of urban-factory life. Almost as a matter of definition we associate the factory system with a decline of the family and the onset of social anonymity. Certainly the steam-powered mule created a new type of factory system. By virtue of an intricate set of controls based on kinship and community ties, and by virtue of the continuing authority of the spinner, however, the potential anonymity of factory life was postponed. The departure from the traditional working-class family was far from complete in 1820, even though the factory system had been prospering for four decades.

Spinning 1820–1845. Midway through the 1820's a number of simultaneous trends operated to disrupt the traditional family structure of the factory operatives. Some of these trends, such as industrial centralization and the concentration of population, had been in motion for some time. Others, such as the changing technology in spinning and weaving, were relatively sudden, and during the next few decades seriously threatened the surviving family economy. Let us review these trends in order.

After the Napoleonic war the Lancashire cotton towns showed an "extraordinary burst" in population. Between 1821 and 1831 Lancashire added almost 300,000 persons, an increase of 27%, while Manchester alone increased 47% in its growth from 154,807 to 227,808. In the following decade Lancashire increased from 1,336,854

---

[1] J. Dunlop, *Artificial Drinking Usages of North Britain* (Greenock, 1836), pp. 10, 101.

[2] *The Poor Man's Advocate*, Jan. 21, 1831. For a discussion of this custom in several trades in the eighteenth century, cf. George, *London Life in the Eighteenth Century*, pp. 291–3.

[3] W. Hall, *Vindication of the Chorley Spinners' Turn-out* (Manchester, 1825).

to 1,667,054, registering an increase of 24·7%. Manchester's rate slowed to 30%, but the other cotton towns accelerated.[1] Much of the migrating population no doubt entered the factories. The number of cotton factory operatives was 107,000 in 1815 (7,000 in power-loom operation). By 1832 this had grown to 208,000 (75,000 in power-loom weaving), and by 1844–6 the total was 340,000 (150,000 in power-loom weaving).[2]

Urbanization alone, of course, is not a sufficient condition for the disintegration of the family structure. On the other hand, this rapid growth of cotton towns was unsettling in so far as it created unstable neighbourhood populations, crowding into small spaces, bad health, and diminished opportunities for education. The Commission on Large Towns in 1845 singled out South Lancashire's particular inadequacies in draining and sewerage, cesspools and toilet facilities, water supply, cellar habitations, lodging-houses, conditions of schools, and so on.[3] In 1841 the Manchester Statistical Society suggested gloomily that the "superior class" was deserting Manchester proper and soon would leave perhaps 100,000 workpeople in the smoky, noisy, crowded interior of the city.[4]

To add to these disorganizing effects, the smaller country mills were beginning to decline. "By 1825 the country mill was losing, if it had not already lost, the predominance in the cotton industry which it had once enjoyed. During the next twenty-five years the preponderance of steam-power and of the town mill steadily increased." As water-mills and steam-mills any distance from the Manchester plain began to fail,[5] some country mills, such as those of the Ashworths and Gregs, survived, but these were "survivals rather than new creations." [6]

The combined spinning and weaving firms accentuated the concentration and largeness of scale. This combined form rose with the onset of power-loom weaving between 1825 and 1833, and reached

[1] Redford, *Labour Migration in England*, p. 58; McCulloch, *A Descriptive and Statistical Account of the British Empire*, Vol. I, p. 153.

[2] Wood, *The History of Wages in the Cotton Trade*, p. 123.

[3] *Parliamentary Papers*, 1845, XVIII, Large Towns and Populous Districts, Appendix, Part II, pp. 303–83. On the opportunities for relaxation in Manchester, cf. Wheeler, *A Political, Social and Commercial History of Manchester*, p. 349.

[4] T. S. Ashton, *Economic and Social Investigations in Manchester, 1833–1933* (London, 1934), p. 37. For an occupational breakdown showing the concentration of the working class in Manchester's poorer neighbourhoods, cf. *Manchester Guardian*, Nov. 8, 1834.

[5] Taylor, "Concentration and Specialization in the Lancashire Cotton Industry," *op. cit.*, pp. 114–16.

[6] W. Ashworth, "British Industrial Villages in the Nineteenth Century," *Economic History Review*, Second Series, III (1950), p. 378.

its zenith about mid-century.[1] The average combined firm was larger than the spinning firm, and much larger than the weaving concern. According to factory inspectors' figures in 1841, 548 spinning firms employed an average of 125 workpeople when working full time. Some 89 power-weaving concerns engaged an average of 100 operatives. On the other hand, 313 firms engaged in both spinning and weaving employed an average of almost 350 per firm. In cities the average size was even larger. In Manchester and Ashton, for instance, 133 spinning firms employed an average of 185 operatives, as compared with 125 for spinning concerns in general. For combined spinning and weaving, Manchester and Ashton had 65 mills employing an average of about 500 operatives, as contrasted with 350 for combined firms in general.[2] Clearly the combination of weaving and spinning in the same concern—plus the possible addition of sheds of self-actor mules—increased the average size of the firm from 1825 onwards. In addition to the general lack of intimacy associated with increasing scale, these combined firms possessed *structural* features, to be analysed presently, which undermined the traditional position of the adult spinner and brought the problem of child labour to a critical point.

Such were the general trends pressing toward depersonalization and anonymity. Two technological developments, however, bore more directly upon the family itself: (*a*) changes in the technology of the spinning machinery; (*b*) changes in the factory community resulting from the introduction of the power-loom. These developments constituted a "dissatisfaction" for the operatives' family economy in the sense that family members were no longer able to offer labour to the industry on the new terms and at the same time maintain the traditional organization of family life.

In the 1820's international and internal competition was increasing in the cotton industry. It will be recalled that the Napoleonic war prolonged the conditions of a limited rate of growth, high profits, and discrepancies in industrial productivity. A decade after the war, rapid growth began to iron out these profits and differentials in productivity. Foreign competition also began to add to the manufacturers' discomfort. While Edward Baines could write in 1835 that "no symptom has yet appeared, to indicate a decline, or even a stagnation, in the cotton manufacture of England," [3] both France

---

[1] Taylor, "Concentration and Specialization in the Lancashire Cotton Industry," *op. cit.*, p. 122.

[2] J. Jewkes, "The Localisation of the Cotton Industry," *Economic Journal* (*Economic History Supplement*), II (1930), pp. 93–5.

[3] *History of the Cotton Manufacture in Great Britain*, p. 507.

and the United States were growing fast. Between 1812 and 1826 British production increased by 270%, whereas the French—while only a fraction of the British total production—grew by 310%. American production increased by 65% between 1829 and 1834 while the British rose only 40%.[1] In addition to this strictly commercial competition, antagonism between masters and operative spinners was increasing in the early 1820's.[2] For these and other reasons, the cotton industrialists began to look for ways of increasing productivity in both spinning and weaving.

The first improvements in spinning were simply increases in the number of mule spindles and longer mules. This had been in process for some time, but in the 1820's the additions reached a point of discontinuity in terms of the organization of labour. Apparently the longer mules first drew the attention of the operative spinners in 1823 or 1824. "The next few years . . . witnessed the introduction of mules carrying a greatly increased number of spindles." [3] This, as well as "double-decking" of mules, continued into the 1840's and was particularly noticeable in the slump years of 1841–2.[4] In addition, the self-actor mule, which tended to displace the skilled adult male spinner, began to invade the industry in the 1830's and 1840's.

The longer mules with an increased number of spindles had the following general effects:

(1) To reduce the piece-rates of spinners on the more productive mules and hence to introduce a variety of piece-rates for the same count of yarn. Up to the early 1820's the operative received wages only according to the count of yarn. These wages were so customary that "yarns were frequently known by the amounts paid for weaving them—8's counts, e.g., were known as 'tenpenny,' and 5's as 'sixpenny.' " [5] Pieces rather than time determined the rate of wages. As long as the difference among machines was not enormous, however, differences in wages expressed differences in time worked. On the new and larger machines, some of which contained as many as 1,000 spindles, the masters varied the wages *for the same counts* depending on the size of machine and number of spindles. By 1834 in Man-

[1] A. Graham, *The Impolicy of the Tax on Cotton Wool, as Aggravated by the Progress and Capabilities of Foreign Countries in Cotton Manufactures* (Glasgow, 1836), pp. 4, 12, quoted from the 1833 Committee on Manufactures, Commerce and Shipping. The figures are naturally approximate.

[2] Above, pp. 126–7.

[3] *Webb Manuscripts on Trade Unionism*, Vol. XXXIV, p. 122. Below, pp. 231–3.

[4] Matthews, *A Study in Trade-Cycle History*, p. 145.

[5] S. J. Chapman, "The Regulation of Wages by Lists in the Spinning Industry," *Economic Journal*, IX (1899), p. 593.

chester "there [were] as many different prices paid for spinning as
. . . differences in the size of mules." [1]

(2) To increase the operative spinners' *weekly* wages while reducing their *piece-rate* wages. This followed because "six hundred
spindles on one machine [operated by one spinner] will produce
twist of nearly as good a quality, and within seven per cent of the
same amount that six hundred spindles on two machines [two
spinners] will produce." [2] Using figures from the Manchester price
list, Ure calculated that in 1829 the spinner produced 312 lb. of yarn
in the same amount of time needed to produce 648 lb. in 1833. Even
though the piece-rate fell from 4s. 1d. in 1829 to 2s. 5d. in 1833, his
time earnings were nevertheless 1,274s. in 1829 and 1,566s. in 1833.[3]
These figures require qualification, since the spinner had to pay for
an increased number of assistants, but the increasing productivity
still appeared in the operative spinners' wages.

(3) To create some technological unemployment through the
increased productivity of the machines. In 1842 a factory inspector
observed that "the number of adults employed in the spinning-rooms
has been greatly diminished by the introduction of self-actors, and
by coupling or double decking." [4] Matthews located some unemployment traceable to improvements in spinning and weaving
between 1835 and 1841, though general industrial growth absorbed
much of it.[5] The improved machinery thus threatened the employment of individuals or groups of spinners, at least in the short
run.

(4) To make the work on mules physically more arduous.[6]

(5) To increase the number of assistants per spinner. In 1819 a
Manchester spinner testified that for 504 spindles (on two mules) he
required two piecers, his wife and brother.[7] In 1832 another spinner
estimated that three children would be employed to assist one adult
in fine spinning.[8] The following year an example of four assistants

[1] Quoted in *Webb Manuscripts on Trade Unionism*, Vol. XXXIV, p. 120.
[2] *Ibid.*, Vol. XXXV, p. 285.
[3] A. Ure, *Philosophy of Manufactures* (London, 1835), pp. 324–5.
[4] *Parliamentary Papers*, 1842, XXII, Factory Inspectors, p. 453.
[5] *A Study in Trade-Cycle History*, p. 145.
[6] *Parliamentary Papers*, 1837–8, VIII, Combinations of Workmen, pp. 40, 70,
277–8; 1840, X, Regulation of Mills and Factories, pp. 693, 724–5. Because
evidence of this sort came most often from those active in the campaign to
shorten factory hours, their claims were probably sometimes exaggerated.
[7] *Lords Sessional Papers*, 1819, XVI, Children in the Cotton Manufactories,
p. 207. Another spinner working on wheels of unspecified size also used only
two, his sons of fifteen and ten years of age, pp. 445–6.
[8] *Parliamentary Papers*, 1831–2, XV, Bill to Regulate Labour of Children in the
Mills and Factories, p. 323.

per spinner was given for a hypothetical factory.[1] Also in 1833 a factory commissioner produced an even more extreme estimate after conversations with persons in the trade. By his estimates the improved mules would change the ratio of assistants to adult spinners from 4 : 1 to 9 : 1.[2] While these estimates cannot be taken literally,[3] it is clear that such alterations would distort the relative proportions of spinners and assistants.

In fact the proportion of spinners to the total working population diminished in the late 1820's and 1830's, and by 1838 there were complaints that the "great increase [in the cotton trade] is among the piecers."[4] Spinners were forced to hire "women and children to superintend and assist in several operations more or less connected with the use of machinery."[5] In 1833 the Factory Commissioners found that

Children employed in factories, as a distinct class, form a very considerable portion of the infant population. We have found that the numbers so employed are rapidly increasing, not only in proportion to the increase of the population employed in the manufacturing industry, but, in consequence of the tendency of improvements in machinery to throw more and more of the work upon children, to the displacement of adult labour. The children so employed are assembled together in large numbers . . . their daily entrance and dismissal from the factories take place with the regularity of military discipline.[6]

(6) To break up the old apprenticeship system based on kinship[7] and thus to undermine the traditional economic authority of the spinner.[8] With an increasing number of assistants required, a spinner

---

[1] Above, p. 191.

[2] *Parliamentary Papers*, 1834, XIX, Supplementary Report of Factory Commissioners, pp. 386–8.

[3] Cowell, for instance, admitted that not quite so many piecers would be needed for the improved machines because of their more convenient structure. *Ibid.*, p. 386. Also, since threads broke less frequently upon the new machines, the number of piecers would be reduced correspondingly. Ure, *Philosophy of Manufactures*, pp. 362–3.

[4] *Parliamentary Papers*, 1837–8, VIII, Combinations of Workmen, p. 263; 1833, VI, Manufactures, Commerce and Shipping, p. 327.

[5] *Parliamentary Papers*, 1830, X, Manufacturers' Employment, p. 223. Also J. Kennedy, "Observations on the Influence of Machinery upon the Working Classes of the Community," *Memoirs of the Literary and Philosophical Society of Manchester* (London, 1831), p. 29.

[6] *Parliamentary Papers*, 1833, XX, First Report of Factory Commissioners, p. 55.

[7] Chapman, *The Lancashire Cotton Industry*, p. 191.

[8] The qualification "economic" is important. There is virtually no evidence on the question of whether there was a general decline of the father's authority in

would seldom have enough children of his own at the appropriate ages. Therefore there was considerable impingement upon his control over "bringing his sons up to a trade." More important, perhaps, children were flooding into the industry, each a potential spinner. This compounded the threat of short-term technological unemployment by glutting the adult market with skilled spinners.

Fragmentary evidence indicates that the social relationship among spinners and piecers was on the decline. In 1838 a Glasgow lawyer affirmed that the restrictions of piecers to sons or brothers

has never been acted upon; they [the spinners] found it impossible to do so; and at this moment I have ascertained, from minute inquiry, there are no less than 1,305 children of hand-loom weavers employed as piecers to 950 spinners in Glasgow and its vicinity at this moment, so that [the Cotton Spinners' Association in Glasgow] is not of [an] exclusive character.[1]

The last two effects were particularly important from the standpoint of the differentiation of the family's economic roles. Because the semi-apprenticeship system based on kinship was on the wane, it was becoming more difficult to maintain that fusion between the economic authority of the parent and other socialization functions. Two other trends associated with increasing productivity in spinning and weaving aggravated this pressure. The first is the tendency for the factory operatives, whose real wages were rising almost continuously, to *withdraw* completely their own children from factory employment, thus splitting the economic connection between adult worker and child. The second is the tendency for hand-loom weavers to send their children into factories with greater frequency, thus eliminating the *kinship* element linking spinner and assistant in the factory.[2] Hence the social arrangements enforced by the new machinery pressed toward greater and greater *differentiation*, both in the factory and for the hand-loom weaving family. These pressures created the key dissatisfaction with the family economy of the working classes in the 1820's and 1830's.

This array of threats to the family's traditional organization underlay much of the turmoil among operatives and others between 1825 and 1850. We shall analyse these disturbances and their outcome in

the working classes in these years. For comment on the scanty literature on the subject, cf. M. Hewitt, *The Effect of Married Women's Employment in the Cotton Textile Districts on the Home in Lancashire, 1840–1880* (London, 1953), pp. 245 ff.

[1] *Parliamentary Papers*, 1837–8, VIII, Combinations of Workmen, p. 219; also pp. 63–4.

[2] There is very little evidence on these two tendencies. See, however, Appendix B and below, pp. 208–9.

the next two chapters. Let us note now that only after the changes of
the 1820's and later did the old family form begin to "break up,"
even though industrial factory labour was already many decades
old.[1]

Also between the 1820's and 1850 the structure of weaving underwent more dramatic changes, perhaps, than the structure of spinning.
What was the impact of power-loom weaving on the family economy?
Most immediately it accelerated the hand-loom weaver's decline,
which we shall trace presently. In the factories, moreover, power-
loom weaving demanded young persons and women, but very few
adult males. "The early power-loom weavers were all women or
boys . . . women and boys in factories replaced men who had worked
at home."[2]

. . . as far as the greater proportion of the hands in [power-loom
factories] are females and young persons, the erection [of them] does
not, in the case of adult male weavers, furnish an adequate extent of
employment to them which it deprives. . . . In [one] factory, I found
the number of hands 245, of whom were—

Females above 18 years of age . .	129
Females under 18	38
Males above 18	42
Males under 18	36

which is about the average of other establishments of this nature.
. . .[3]

The presence of women and children in factories does not necessarily ruin the family economy; mule-spinning continued thus for
many decades without disrupting its traditional organization radically. It seems, however, that the *structure* of factory weaving differed
from mule-spinning and thereby generated severe pressures on the
traditional family system.

The major difference was that, in weaving, the recruitment of
young persons and children fell into the hands of the masters, not the
operatives. In 1834 Samuel Stanway analysed returns from 151
Lancashire cotton mills. In spinning the operatives still recruited

[1] Thus it seems erroneous to associate factory labour *as such* with the deterioration of the family. Gaskell, for instance, felt that "the greatest misfortune" to
come from factory labour was "the breaking up of these family ties [of the old
domestic manufacture], the consequent abolition of the domestic circle, and the
perversion of all the social obligations which should exist between parent and
child on the one hand, and between children on the other." *Artisans and Machinery*, pp. 61–2.
[2] Hammond, *The Skilled Labourer*, p. 72.
[3] *Parliamentary Papers*, 1840, Hand-loom Weavers, p. 607.

most employees under eighteen, despite the inroads on their authority. Of 6,599 male employees under eighteen in spinning, operatives hired 5,852 and masters only 697 (50 employees unclassifiable). For females under eighteen, operatives hired 2,284 out of 2,654 and masters only 346 (24 unclassifiable). In weaving, on the other hand, the masters' recruitment predominated.[1] Of 1,631 males under eighteen, masters hired 986 and operatives 610 (35 unclassifiable). Of 3,674 females under eighteen, masters hired 2,538 and the operatives only 1,104 (32 unclassifiable).[2] With the introduction of the power-loom, the recruitment of young labour undoubtedly began to supersede those kinship and community ties which had operated so strongly in the spinning branches.[3]

Hence the economic authority, instruction, and control associated with the apprenticeship system were probably absent in the weaving rooms. Dressers were so few that it was virtually impossible to develop a system whereby young persons could move into a lifetime adult occupation. In the weaving rooms one manager superintended the whole mill and one overlooker superintended one department or room. The literature yields no mention of informal controls exercised by, e.g., the adult dressers, which paralleled those of the mule-spinners. One dresser complained, in fact, that

the sufferings of the children in the weaving department are as great as in any department in the factories; they are under the control of inconsiderate young people, who are themselves spurred to exertion both by the necessity of doing a certain quantity of work and by the expectation of getting money, and, as such, are indifferent to the condition or feelings of the children, who suffer very severely.[4]

The weaving innovations therefore altered the traditional form of the family economy more radically than did the spinning improvements.

The Factory Branches after 1830. Before considering the plight of the hand-loom weaver, let us fill in a background for our subsequent

[1] This goes counter to the opinion of Joseph Sadler, a yarn-dresser at Stockport, who said that the operatives engaged the children in the weaving department. *Parliamentary Papers*, 1831–2, XV, Bill to regulate the Labour of Children in the Mills and Factories. It is possible that Sadler was referring to a local situation in Stockport; or it is possible that he used the word "children" (under 13) to contrast with "young persons" (age 13–18).

[2] *Parliamentary Papers*, 1834, XIX, Supplementary Report of the Factory Commissioners, p. 426.

[3] The proportion of young males hired by operatives (37%) as contrasted with the proportion of females (30%) hints that there was an interest in apprenticing boys to warping or dressing, though this is by no means conclusive.

[4] *Parliamentary Papers*, 1831–2, XV, Bill to regulate the Labour of Children in the Mills and Factories, p. 279.

discussions by characterizing the factories according to age, sex, and occupational description. Trends and fluctuations in wages may be found in Appendix A.

The following age and sex percentages obtained among the cotton factory operatives between 1835 and 1850:[1]

	1835	1838	1847	1850
M & F under 13 or half-time	13·2	4·75	5·8	4·6
M, 13–18	12·5	16·6	11·8	11·2
M, over 18	26·4	24·9	27·1	28·7
F, over 13	47·9	53·8	55·5	55·8
TOTAL NUMBER	218,000	259,500	316,400	331,000

Between 1835 and 1838 the proportion of children (under thirteen) dropped radically and young persons (thirteen to eighteen) and females rose correspondingly. After 1838 the proportion of young persons dropped slightly, with male adults and females over thirteen rising slightly. These changes rested on two counteracting trends: (*a*) the technological changes described above, which increased the numbers of children, young persons and women; (*b*) the restrictions of factory legislation, which in 1833 limited the age of entry into the industry to nine years and restricted the hours of children (nine to thirteen), and later restricted the hours of adolescents and women.*

These pressures resulted in a squeeze in the supply of young labour in the 1830's. In 1834 when the cotton industry was enjoying a boom accompanied by great demands for labour, the Poor Law Commissioners initiated a scheme to encourage the migration of families into the manufacturing districts. Their concern with the size of migrants' families in this attempt reflects the great need for the labour of children and adolescents and the limited opportunities for adult males.

Widows with large families of children or handicraftsmen, such as shoemakers, tailors, blacksmiths, &c., &c., with large families, will be the most successful immigrants. Adult men could not acquire the requisite skill for the superior processes of the factories [i.e., spinning], and if employed in the mills at all, would not rise beyond the

---

[1] *Victoria County History*, Lancashire, Vol. II, p. 390.

* These two influences worked against each other with regard to numbers of children and young people employed in the factories. As we shall see when we analyse the effects of factory legislation upon the family economy, however, both influences worked toward the greater differentiation of family roles. Below, pp. 295–6.

blowing-room, or, at farthest, the card-room, which are the inferior and worst-paid occupations of adult labour in the trade.[1]

Millowners often agreed to hire the father as well as other family members, but generally as a carter or porter, or in some sort of day work, and "very rarely . . . in the factory." His wages were 10s. to 13s. a week, which was perhaps less than his wife or child might earn as a power-loom weaver or throstle-spinner.[2] In general, therefore, "the inducement to agricultural labourers to migrate into the cotton towns often lay less in the opportunity to increase their own earnings than the improvement in the earning power of their children." [3]

From the beginning of the migration experiment until mid-1837, when it flopped ignominiously in the depression, some 203 families totalling 1,660 persons migrated under contract procured through the Poor Law Commission, and 72 families with 345 individuals migrated without contract (though presumably with some encouragement by the Commissioners).[4] The average size of contracted families was almost eight, and that of non-contracted families was only five. The whole migration scheme illustrates both the selective labour needs of the middle 1830's and the pressure to minimize the husband's role as chief breadwinner in a cotton mill.[5]

In connection with the subject of age and sex, is it possible to speak of a typical "textile family"? How much did the jobs of father, mother, and children overlap? Only one bit of evidence is available on this point. In 1844 a number of Manchester proprietors and mill occupants prepared certain statistics which showed the occupations of husbands of married female factory operatives. In 412 factories a total of 61,098 females were employed; of these, 10,721 were married (about 18%). Of their husbands, 5,314 were in factory work, 3,927 in other trades, and 821 unemployed. This shows a certain overlap between the industrial employment of females and their husbands,

[1] *Parliamentary Papers*, 1835, XXXV, First Annual Report of the Poor Law Commissioners, p. 300.

[2] *Parliamentary Papers*, 1837, XVII.1, Poor Law Amendment Act, p. 75.

[3] Matthews, *A Study in Trade-Cycle History*, pp. 146–7.

[4] *Parliamentary Papers*, 1837, XXXI, Third Report of the Poor Law Commissioners, p. 221.

[5] Another reflection of the same squeeze on labour was the attempt of Poulett Thomson in 1836 to reduce the minimum defining age of the child from thirteen to twelve. This effort failed, but nevertheless shows the pressure upon the trade. *Parliamentary Debates*, Third Series, XXXIII, 1836, cols. 737–83, and XXXIV, 1836, cols. 306–7. Also *A Statement from the Master Cotton Spinners* (London, 1836). For a discussion of the origins and course of the migration scheme, as well as the general population movement in the 1830's, cf. Redford, *Labour Migration in England*, pp. 84–101.

and probably a high proportion of unemployed husbands. In the cotton industry in general, however, all women except widows tended to drop out of the factories after marriage.[1]

On the factory premises themselves, the mule-spinners, almost all strong, skilled, and highly paid men, occupied an important position in the 1830's.

> Some . . . who have intelligence enough to conduct themselves in a becoming manner, are clever and respectable men, making as good an appearance when out of their employ, as tradesmen generally make; and some of the more careful and better informed are welcomed in respectable company. But the great majority, wretched in the slavery of long and unremitting attention to the regularity of their machinery, make themselves still more wretched, in a voluntary slavery, by their misconduct in the alehouse, from Saturday afternoon until Monday morning.[2]

Assisting these spinners were piecers, mostly young men and women or children, and scavengers, young children of both sexes. The throstle spinners were almost entirely girls over fourteen. Male adult overlookers supervised all types of spinning.

In the cardrooms were persons of both sexes and all ages. Reeling was an intermediate process between spinning and weaving. This involved winding the yarn into hanks for the weavers and "[could be] and [was] frequently performed at home." Reeling was perhaps "the best part of the cotton mill employment." [3] In the weaving-room, both adults and non-adults tended the looms, and most were females. In Stanway's sample of Lancashire mills, weavers formed the largest single occupational group even as early as 1833.[4] Dressers were almost all adult males, and warpers were adult males and females. Adult male overlookers supervised the weaving-rooms.

Practically all these occupations required attentiveness rather than strength. The exceptions were mule-spinning for males and batting (cleaning raw cotton by beating it with switches) for females. Richard Carlile was "offended at the sight of women working at it. It gave

[1] Figures from McCulloch, *A Statistical and Descriptive Account of the British Empire*, Vol. I, p. 702. Also Clapham, *An Economic History of Modern Britain*, pp. 568–70. The high proportion of unemployed husbands in the prosperity year 1844 tallies with the conclusions below, pp. 306–8.

[2] Richard Carlile in *The Lion*, Vol. I., No. 9, p. 283.

[3] Redford, *Manchester Merchants and Foreign Trade*, p. 240; *The Lion*, Vol. I, No. 9, p. 284. Also above, pp. 185–6.

[4] *Parliamentary Papers*, 1834, XIX, Supplementary Report of the Factory Commissioners, p. 434.

that masculine, quarrelsome, and fighting appearance to women.
. . . " [1]

THE INSTITUTIONAL STRUCTURE OF HAND-LOOM WEAVING, 1770–1840

In one sense the story of the hand-loom weavers is simpler. In a sick trade, they experienced a gradual and painful decline in wages, comforts of life, and status. Nevertheless, we may discuss the fortunes of hand-loom weaving under three topics: (*a*) the golden age from the 1780's to the late 1790's; (*b*) the overcrowding of an outmoded field from the late 1790's to the early 1820's; (*c*) the extinction of the hand-loom weaver by the power-loom from the early 1820's to the 1840's.

The Golden Age. The economics of this period involved (*a*) a general shortage of labour caused both by prosperity and by the disappearance of weavers into the military; (*b*) the movement of women and children into weaving and allied activities; the gradual desertion of farming as a supplementary source of earnings; and the immigration of the non-industrial population of England and later of Ireland into hand-loom weaving.

Even with all this the golden age did not witness a definite *restruc-turing* of the weaving family. The father continued as the family's economic head, apprenticing his sons. His wife and children sub-stituted the subsidiary processes of weaving for the distaff, wheel, and carding equipment. Samuel Bamford wrote in 1843 that his "father was a weaver of muslin, at a time considered a fine course of work, and requiring a superior hand; whilst my mother found plenty of employment in occasional weaving, in winding bobbins or pins for my father, and in looking after the house and the children." [2] There is no definite information on the numbers of women who took up weaving. Certainly, however, the great expansion of weaving relieved the technological unemployment of hand-spinners and carders. The family in any case did not desert its domestic division of labour and its structure of economic authority; it merely turned to weaving alone instead of weaving and spinning.

Overcrowding an Outmoded Field. As the Hammonds sug-gested, the golden age ended before 1803, the date which William Radcliffe suggested. As early as 1798 weaving wages began their long and tortuous decline. While depressions exaggerated this decline from

---

[1] *The Lion*, Vol. I, No. 9, p. 282. Also W. C. Taylor, *Factories and the Factory System* (London, 1844), p. 38.
[2] *Early Days* (London, 1843), p. 27.

time to time, the history of the trade through the 1820's was that of
overcrowding accompanied by declining profits and wages.* The
capital structure of weaving probably exaggerated the overcrowding.
Capital costs for the manufacturer were for working capital (yarn
and cloth) and those for the weaver were a loom (the cost of which
might be £2). Hence entry into the trade was relatively easy.[1]

We have seen that the first response of the weavers was to encourage females to weave in greater numbers and to apprentice
children at an early age.[2] Weavers' children also began to enter the
factories in increasing numbers. In 1818 a witness attributed both
early apprenticeship and children in factories to the low wages of
weaving "of late years." The figures in Appendix B show a liberal
number of weavers' children in the Catrine Works. Certainly the
economic if not the social conditions of the factory encouraged child
labour. Even "little children" could make more money in the factory
than the father could earn on the loom. In 1824 a man and wife
together could earn 10s. or 11s. on the hand-loom, but a child of
fifteen years could earn 7s. in the factory, and one of ten years could
earn 6s., which together would exceed their parents' earnings.[3]
Already the father's status as breadwinner was being undermined.

The symptoms of overcrowding, overwork, and low pay were
clearly in evidence before the power-loom made its competitive
appearance. Furthermore, during the first real burst of power-loom
installation (1822–5), hand-loom manufacturers and weavers multiplied in a scramble for meagre profits.[4] Hand-loom weaving thus
continued to expand even after the power-loom threatened gradually
to remove it from the industrial scene.

The Advent of Power-Loom Weaving. The economics of competition between the power-loom and the hand-loom are relatively
simple; the increased productivity of the former rendered the latter
unprofitable,[5] first in the coarser grades and later in the fancy weaves.
By the early 1830's the number of hand-loom weavers had begun to

* This process constitutes Step 7 of the differentiation whereby the hand-loom
weaver became the full-time incumbent of an occupational role. Above, pp. 140–41.

[1] Hammond, *The Skilled Labourer*, p. 58; *Parliamentary Papers*, 1808, II,
Petitions of Cotton Manufacturers and Journeyman Weavers, p. 115; Collier,
The Family Economy in the Cotton Industry, Chapter II, pp. 23–4.

[2] Above, pp. 137–8.

[3] *Lords Sessional Papers*, 1818, IX, Lords Committee on Cotton Factories Bill,
p. 72; *Webb Manuscripts on Trade Unionism*, Vol. XXXVII, p. 20.

[4] Hammond, *The Skilled Labourer*, p. 123.

[5] For classical statements of this relationship, cf. R. Torrens, *On Wages and
Combinations* (London, 1834), pp. 37–8 and T. Twiss, *Two Lectures on Machinery*
(Oxford, 1844), p. 43.

decline. In 1838 they were reported as "a diminishing class, very considerably, for some years," and in the 1840's they dropped off rapidly. While they still numbered 23,000 in 1856, and while hand-loom weaving lasted much longer in scattered communities, the 1840's mark its effective demise.[1]

To worsen conditions, the Irish "crowded into Lancashire and the West of Scotland" between 1825 and 1830. The next two decades brought even more. Of the 20,000 inhabitants of cellars in Manchester in 1836, most were Irish and many were hand-loom weavers. In subsequent years commentators noted the great numbers of Irish descent in the hand-loom trade. These Irish, accustomed to a lower standard of living, seemed more willing to accept wage reductions than English or Scottish weavers.[2]

The legislation of the early 1830's also heightened the weavers' grievances. The New Poor Law of 1834, which reversed the policy of compensating distressed labourers by various kinds of outdoor relief, initiated a policy which "[refused] them relief altogether, except in a detestable workhouse, where they were separated from wife and children, with little prospect of ever getting out again."[3] Several weavers also complained that the Factory Act of 1833 diminished their income by restricting the entry of their children into the factories.[4] Certainly such policies appeared to the weavers as new attacks in society's war against their trade.

Hardships were not uniform for all weavers. Both strength and skill, especially the former, made for higher wages; hence wage levels varied considerably. Hours were extremely long, if irregular.

[1] The estimated course of numbers of hand-loom weavers is as follows: 1830, 240,000; 1831, 240,000; 1832, 227,000; 1833, 213,000; 1834, 200,000; 1835, 188,000; 1836, 174,000; 1837, 160,000; 1838, 147,000; 1839, 135,000; 1840, 123,000; 1841, 110,000. Gayer, Rostow, and Schwartz, *The Growth and Fluctuation of the British Economy*, Microfilmed Supplement, p. 1587. Also *Parliamentary Papers*, 1837–8, XVIII.1, Poor Law Amendment Act, p. 283. Among the surviving communities, Altham and Huncoat in 1848 had "hand-loom weaving [as] a household industry in most of the homes." Ainsworth, *History and Associations of Altham and Huncoat*, p. 286. Baines reported a certain amount of weaving by farmers' children in Ribchester parish in 1868. *History of the County Palatine and Duchy of Lancaster*, Vol. II, p. 109. As late as 1894, "the sound of [hand-loom weaving could] be heard in the cottage . . . within four miles of [Manchester]." W. A. Shaw, *Manchester Old and New* (London, 1894), p. 22.

[2] Clapham, *An Economic History of Modern Britain*, p. 180; Redford, *Labour Migration in England*, pp. 134–8; Gaskell, *Artisans and Machinery*, p. 82; *Parliamentary Papers*, 1840, Hand-loom Weavers, pp. 6–7. See also J. Adshead, *Distress in Manchester* (London, 1842), p. 31; C. R. Fay, *Life and Labour in the Nineteenth Century* (Cambridge, 1947), p. 217.

[3] Hovell, *The Chartist Movement*, pp. 80–81.

[4] *Parliamentary Papers*, 1840, Hand-loom Weavers, p. 45.

Estimates varied from twelve to thirteen hours per day for a seventy-hour week to fourteen, sixteen, and even eighteen hours for some days. In any case the weavers worked longer hours than factory workers.[1] Because the weaver remained at home, however, these disagreeable conditions may have had their advantageous side:

... their employment is in some respects *more agreeable*, as *laying them under less restraint than factory labour*. Being carried on in their own cottages, their time is at their own command: they may begin and leave off work at their pleasure: they are not bound punctually to obey the summons of the factory bell: if they are so disposed, they can quit their loom for the public-house, or to lounge in the street, or to accept some other job, and then, when urged by necessity, they may make up for lost time by a great exertion. In short, they are more independent than factory operatives; they are their own masters; they receive their materials, and sometimes do not take back the web for several weeks. ... .[2]

As the weavers' position deteriorated in the 1830's and 1840's, the practices of early apprenticeship, employment of the unskilled, employment of wives and children in home weaving, and employment of dependents in factories no doubt became more common. Complaints of early apprenticeship for early gains, especially in the country districts, were incessant in these decades. Furthermore, agricultural labourers and immigrants moved freely into coarse weaving because the skills could be acquired in a short time. Women in weaving families were forced to devote more of their home activities to weaving and less to other domestic duties. This probably led to a greater proportion of married women in hand-loom weaving than in the factory labour force.[3]

In addition, the weavers' readiness to send their children into the factories grew. While they complained, probably correctly, that "children of spinners are always preferred before the children of weavers, because they work with their parents," Parliamentary evidence shows that weavers often put their children into the factory,

[1] *Parliamentary Papers*, 1841, Hand-loom Weavers, pp. 2–3, 14, 18; 1839, Hand-loom Weavers, p. 8; 1826–7, V, Emigration, pp. 268, 446, 502; 1833, XX, First Report of the Factory Commissioners, p. 753.

[2] Baines, *History of the Cotton Manufacture in Great Britain*, p. 494.

[3] *Parliamentary Papers*, 1833, VI, Manufactures, Commerce and Shipping, pp. 567, 701, 707; 1834, X, Hand-loom Weavers, p. 179; 1837–8, XVIII.1, Poor Law Amendment Act, p. 284; 1839, Hand-loom Weavers, pp. 7, 53; 1840, Hand-loom Weavers, p. 601; 1841, Hand-loom Weavers, pp. 41, 45. Also Twiss, *Two Lectures on Machinery*, pp. 35, 37–8; Pinchbeck, *Women Workers in the Industrial Revolution*, p. 179; Hewitt, *The Effect of Married Women's Employment in the Cotton Textile Districts on the Home in Lancashire*, p. 84.

particularly in power-loom work. This probably accelerated as power-loom weaving advanced and as the spinners began to lose their control in the spinning branches.[1] Certainly contemporary observers noted with bitterness the reversal of traditional age and sex roles as wives and children went to the factory.

This condition, which unsexes the man and takes from the woman all womanliness without being able to bestow upon the man true womanliness, or the woman true manliness—this condition, which degrades, in the most shameful way, both sexes, and through them, Humanity, is the last result of our most praised civilization, the final achievement of all the efforts and struggles of hundreds of generations to improve their own situation and that of their posterity.[2]

Whether hand-loom weavers themselves could enter the factories is uncertain. Some individuals no doubt changed directly from hand-loom to power-loom weaving, but the different labour requirements of each argue against such changes on a large scale. Many weavers and others complained that while factories were open to their children, factory employment for themselves was almost unavailable because of their age and skill and because of the opposition of the spinners' unions. It is probably safest to assume that adults left hand-loom weaving primarily through aging and death, and that mostly children and young adults left for other occupations.[3]

THE VALUES UNDERLYING THE DISSATISFACTIONS WITH THE FAMILY ECONOMY

We have now outlined the structural foci of dissatisfaction with the family division of labour between 1770 and 1840 for both the spinners and the weavers. For the former the pressures were (a) to differentiate the labour of certain family members from that of others, and (b) to differentiate labour roles in the family from other family functions. The dissatisfactions stemming from power-loom machinery pressed the hand-loom weaving family to desert the domestic family economy in favour of the more differentiated industrial family.

[1] *Parliamentary Papers*, 1834, X, Hand-loom Weavers, p. 179, 84–5; 1839, Hand-loom Weavers, pp. 11–12; 1833, VI, Manufactures, Commerce and Shipping, pp. 681, 684, 701–2. Also Appendix B.
[2] Engels, *The Condition of the Working-Class in England in 1844*, p. 146. Also Hutchins, *Women in Modern Industry*, pp. 42–3. Below, pp. 280–83.
[3] For limited evidence on this subject, cf. *Parliamentary Papers*, 1824, V, Artisans and Machinery, p. 302; 1833, VI, Manufactures, Commerce and Shipping, pp. 701, 712; 1835, XIII, Hand-loom Weavers, pp. 162–3; 1841, Hand-loom Weavers, p. 31; Redford, *Labour Migration in England*, pp. 35–6.

Legitimizing these dissatisfactions were a number of dominant values. In fact, Step 1 of structural differentiation always implies a set of values which legitimizes the expression of dissatisfaction. For the family's division of labour, therefore, we should extract some new implications from the value-system of the late eighteenth and early nineteenth centuries.* Many values relevant to individual economic performance stem, of course, from the *same* value-system which generated dissatisfactions with industrial productivity. We noted that the values associated with Nonconformity emphasized the "performance-centred" extremes of the industrial values. What are the implications of these values for the economic roles of family members?

The broad values of personal responsibility, discipline, and the calling gave rise to the pleas of moral leaders on the subjects of industry, temperance, and the rational use of time and money. Many of these directives are translatable directly into those qualities desirable for an economic breadwinner. Reference to such virtues is found in the writings and sermons discussed above, and in other literature pertaining more directly to the family.[1] In terms of the valuation of industry (E_G), therefore, the implications of these admonitions are clearly performance-oriented in the extreme. Nor were the sentiments merely empty mouthings of religious leaders; many converts, especially Methodists, drove vigorously to realize the values of industry, prudence, temperance, and frugality.[2]

The concept of *independence* subsumes many of these elements. A grasp of this value is important for understanding the dissatisfactions with the family economy and for tracing the subsequent directions of its structural change in the nineteenth century. Independence includes, among other things, the freedom of the individual, responsibility, the notion of a calling, and the positive evaluation of industry. Just as a person is responsible only to God for his general behaviour, so in the worldly sphere his welfare depends on his personal responsibility. "The love of freedom and independence is natural to all, whether high or low; a spirit of *self-support* raises a man in his own estimation; he feels his consequence in society, and nobly

---

* This section refers only to the division of the family economy's labour (E_G in general, and particularly the E_{G_g}–E_{I_g} boundary-interchange). We shall discuss it further in Chapter XI, and discuss the "consumption values" (E_{A_i}) in Chapter XIII.

[1] For instance, the sermon of John Rogers, D.D., entitled "The Great Duty of Redeeming Time, and the Danger of Neglecting it," reprinted in V. Knox, *Family Lectures, or Domestic Divinity* (London, 1791), p. 196.

[2] Warner, *The Wesleyan Movement in the Industrial Revolution*, pp. 168, 176–8.

determines not to be obliged for any one for what his *own* industry can procure." [1]

Independence expresses, further, a direct relationship between an individual's productive activities and his economic self-sufficiency. Personal responsibility was so highly valued that Eden—perhaps the most sensitive observer of the poor of the time—nevertheless said in 1797 that "the miseries of the labouring Poor arise, less from the scantiness of their income . . . than from their own improvidence and unthriftiness. . . ." [2] The young tradesman should postpone marriage until after training and experience have given him "the pleasure of being his own master." [3] In short, a man should "seriously reflect . . . and ask himself—am I independent?" meaning by this "that feeling of conscious freedom which every man must experience who, by his own hands, provides for his daily wants, and who to the utmost of his power and ability discharges the several duties which his station imposes." [4] If he could answer in the affirmative, he possessed "the noblest attributes of social and civilized men." [5]

Because of the importance of independent responsibility, a man should be able to pursue his calling freely. Hence the antagonism to "interference" with industry and the artificial props which sustained the unproductive. The Poor Laws, for instance, were often conceived as temporary expedients rather than permanent features of a healthy society, as "Relief of the Poor within a Framework of Repression." Indeed, they were as much punitive measures for the economically unproductive as relief for the needy.[6] In the literature of the time addressed to the working classes, the cardinal sin (corresponding to the cardinal virtue of independence) was reliance upon the parish for support.[7]

Applied to the labouring family, then, independence meant a man at the head of his family, self-supporting, seeking the best opportunities

---

[1] W. Davis, *Friendly Advice to Industrious and Frugal Persons* (London, 1817), p. 10.

[2] F. M. Eden, *State of the Poor* (London, 1797), Vol. I, p. 495.

[3] T. Kelly, *Thoughts on the Marriages of the Labouring Poor* (London, 1806), pp. 6–7.

[4] H. Gregson, *Suggestions for Improving the Condition of the Industrous Classes* (London, 1830), p. 17.

[5] *Moral Instruction Addressed to the Working Classes* (London, 1834), p. iv. This pamphlet was "written between thirty and forty years ago, for the *mental* and *moral* improvement of the Working Classes at Birmingham; and . . . now offered to the Public . . . in the hope of benefiting others." P. iii.

[6] S. and B. Webb, *English Local Government: English Poor Law History. Part I: The Old Poor Law* (London, 1927), especially pp. 396–428.

[7] Gregson, *Suggestions for Improving the Condition of the Industrous Classes*, p. 17; Davis, *Friendly Advice to Industrious and Frugal Persons*, pp. 10–11.

the market offered, and experiencing the pride of independence which arose from this condition. That the breadwinner should be responsible for the economic independence of his family did not, of course, contradict the desire that his wife and children should contribute to the family's support. Neither did the traditional relationship between master and man contradict the value of independence. The employer's general concern for the welfare of his employees, and the employees' responsibility and obedience was limited to the *contracted work situation*. "The pursuit of economic ends, even though conditioned by the strictest moral standard, was a divinely sanctioned calling." [1]

Such a value-system legitimized a multitude of dissatisfactions with family conditions in the late eighteenth and early nineteenth centuries. Common to all these dissatisfactions was a man's inability to remain independent. When overcrowding and power-loom competition drove the domestic hand-loom weaver to the Poor Law authorities, there was dissatisfaction because he could no longer maintain his economic independence. When the spinner refused to assume semi-familial employment in the factory because of technological improvements, he was no longer economically independent under the old conditions. These dissatisfactions based on the value of independence thus constituted a *lever for social change*. Furthermore, they pointed in specific directions; any realistic solution had to leave the workers' independence and freedom intact. He was, after all, by definition an agent for his own self-sufficiency through the exercise of his own industry, frugality, and prudence.

Finally we must remark on the general flexibility of the family. In some respects its organization is extremely rigid, because it involves socialization and emotional expression at the deepest psychological levels.[2] By virtue of this characteristic it cannot adjust to outside pressures simply by adding more members, laying off or firing excess members, etc. (as is the case with an industrial firm). For such reasons the family organization under strain tends to break and not to bend. Even though the initial disturbances of Step 2 may be rapid and explosive, furthermore, the resulting structural change in the family is also likely to be long and painful because of the same inflexibilities. Despite these unique features, the sequence by which

[1] Warner, *The Wesleyan Movement in the Industrial Revolution*, pp. 147–51. For a statement of the kinds of responsibility incumbent upon a master, cf. T. Gisborne, *An Enquiry into the Duties of Men in the Higher and Middle Classes of Society* (London, 1794), pp. 562–5.
[2] E. Erikson, *Childhood and Society* (London, 1952), Chapters 2 7. Parsons, Bales, *et al.*, *Family, Socialization, and Interaction Process*, Chapter II.

the family differentiates does not differ formally from structural change in any other social system.

This concludes our discussion of Step 1 in the differentiation of the division of family labour. We have outlined several structural foci of dissatisfaction, the appropriate values underlying these dissatisfactions, and the inherent inflexibility of the family. When these elements combine, the stage is set for structural differentiation. The first reaction in Step 2 is a number of symptoms of disturbance traceable to the original dissatisfactions. To these disturbances we shall devote the next chapter.

APPENDIX A

LONG-TERM TRENDS AND SHORT-TERM FLUCTUATIONS IN WAGES

Factory Operatives. Writers on wages in the cotton industry have complained of the difficulties of their task, because "machine is always replacing machine; women replace men and children replace women," [1] and because of the inaccessibility of materials. Investigators like Wood and Bowley, however, have sketched average wage movements fairly clearly.

Before 1800 we know only that factory operatives' wages were better and fluctuated less than others in the working classes, often because of the augmented earnings of women and children.[2] Neglecting the heterogeneity and fluctuation of wages, Eden estimated that the manufacturing labourer's average wage was about 16s. in 1797; "but . . . they rarely work on Mondays, and . . . many of them keep holiday two or three days in the week. . . . Women earn from 6s. to 12s. a week: their clear weekly earnings may be stated at 8s. Children, of 7 or 8 years old, can earn 2s. a week; of 9 or 10 years, 4s. a week." [3]

The spinners of fine counts or on long mules always commanded high wages. In 1806 they earned 33s. 3d. per week, which rose in 1810, but fell to the earlier level between 1814 and 1822. Between 1833 and 1845–6 the level varied between 33s. 3d. and 42s. per week, and remained above 40s. after 1839. Medium counts or medium-length mules yielded wages which hovered around 30s. between 1806 and 1822, maintained a level of 26s.–28s. in the early and middle 1830's,

---

[1] Clapham, *An Economic History of Modern Britain*, p. 550.
[2] Collier, *The Family Economy in the Cotton Industry*, Chapter II, pp. 2, 5, 7, 17.
[3] *State of the Poor*, Vol. II, p. 357.

213

and ranged between 18s. and 25s. in the 1840's. Mule-spinners for coarse counts earned better than 20s. between 1806 and 1822, but after 1836 their wages were between 16s. and 20s. per week. Throstle-spinners, always a lower-paid group, could command 8s.–9s. in the years following 1810, and in the 1830's and 1840's their pay was between 7s. and 10s. 6d. per week.[1]

Piecers' pay varied according to their age and size. The first class, big piecers, earned 7s. in 1832; small piecers earned 4s. 7d., and middle piecers earned something half-way between the two. The average wage of piecers had not varied, furthermore, more than 6d. since 1813. After 1833 their wages rose slightly, with the first class ranging between 8s. and 11s., the second earning approximately 5s., and the third ranging from 3s. 6d. to 5s. 6d.[2]

Male adults in the carding and blowing rooms earned between 15s. and 18s. from 1806 to 1833. In 1833 they varied between 14s. 6d. and 17s. After this time the average dropped 1s.–3s. Women's wages in the same departments averaged around 9s. from 1806 to 1833, when they dropped about 1s. per week, with some year-to-year variation, of course. In 1833 persons under fifteen earned 6s. or 7s., and this figure remained much the same in later years. Throstle reelers earned 19s. per week in 1806, but by 1810 this had declined to 12s. and again to 10s. between 1815 and 1824. By 1833 they earned between 7s. and 9s., and after that time their wages varied between 8s. and 9s. 6d.

Power-loom weavers' wages varied according to the number of looms they attended. In 1824, for instance, an operative with two looms earned between 7s. 6d. and 10s. 6d.; the addition of a third loom would raise the figure to 14s. In 1846 a watcher of two looms earned 10s., and a minder of four, 16s. On the average, however, weavers' wages remained between 9s. 6d. and 11s. between 1824 and 1849. Up to 1836 they never fell below 10s. 2d., but between 1839 and 1841—years of depression—wages were 9s. 6d., before rising again to 10s. or 10s. 6d. during the 1840's. Warpers, on the other hand, after earning between 11s. and 12s. between 1824 and 1833, made 17s. 6d. in 1834, and often more than a pound between 1839 and 1849.[3]

For some time it was assumed that the operatives' *real* wages fell after the Napoleonic war, but wage statisticians have shown that the

1 Wood, *The History of Wages in the Cotton Trade*, p. 28. The figures refer to the Manchester district. Also Clapham, *An Economic History of Modern Britain*, pp. 550–51.
2 A. L. Bowley, *Wages in the United Kingdom in the Nineteenth Century* (Cambridge, 1900), chart opposite p. 118.
3 *Ibid.*, Also Redford, *Manchester Merchants and Foreign Trade*, p. 239.

living standards of cotton operatives (hand-loom weavers excluded) climbed steadily to mid-century.[1] According to Cole's rough calculations based on Wood's figures, real wages in 1800 were 19% of those of 1900. In 1810 they rose to 23%. Between 1810 and 1820 they jumped to 34% and between 1820 and 1830 to 43% of the 1900 figure.* Between 1830 and 1840, however, wages dropped to 40%, but by 1850 they had resumed their upward course, and in this year real wages stood at 54% of the 1900 wages. In general this rise rested on the decrease of prices between 1815 and 1850 more than the rise of the operatives' money wages.[2]

It is important to outline what is known on the subject of short-term fluctuations in unemployment in these years, since such fluctuations precipitated many social disturbances. Unfortunately we must rely almost entirely on the accounts of journalists, factory inspectors, and other observers for this information.

Karl Marx estimated that between 1770 and 1815 the cotton industry was depressed or stagnated in only five years.[3] While some bleak years, e.g., 1787–8, were the result of oversupply in brisk years followed by doldrums, many depression years were "accidental" in the sense that wartime restrictions cut off exports or imports. The crises of 1793, 1796–7, 1800–1, 1808, and 1811–12 fall into this category.[4]

The effect of such crises on the factory operatives is not clear. In 1797, however, Eden "confessed that at present, constant and regular employment cannot be procured by all who are inclined to work." Furthermore, he complained that the stagnation of business since the war (i.e., since 1793) had driven a great number of manufacturing labourers into the military, thereby throwing their families on poor relief.[5] When weavers and spinners were compared, how-

---

[1] Clapham, *An Economic History of Modern Britain*, p. 7. Also T. S. Ashton, "The Standard of Life of the Workers in England, 1790–1830," in F. A. Hayek, *Capitalism and the Historians* (London, 1954); D. Chadwick, "On the Social and Educational Statistics of Manchester and Salford," *Transactions of the Manchester Statistical Society*, Session 1861, pp. 13, 48.

* Paradoxically, it was in these years of greatest increase in real wages that the factory operatives became embroiled in their most serious disturbances. We shall examine this relationship in Chapters X, XI, and XIV.

[2] G. D. H. Cole, *A Short History of the British Working Class Movement, 1797–1937* (London, 1937), pp. 181–2. For various technical reasons—e.g., choice of base year—these figures should be treated as reflecting only the general *direction* of real wages. Also Gayer, Rostow, and Schwartz, *The Growth and Fluctuation of the British Economy*, pp. 657–8.

[3] *Capital*, p. 457.

[4] Above, pp. 112–14 and 119–21.

[5] *State of the Poor*, Vol. II, pp. 351, 357.

ever, the latter fared better both in crisis and prosperity.[1] Certainly the fortunes of the operative spinners were good in 1801–2 and 1810.[2] There were also difficult moments; in 1816 a prominent Manchester spinner said that employment in the cotton trade "has been of late very uniform; I have known it otherwise, much otherwise." [3] In general, however, "no class of people . . . had such constant and uniform employment [between 1790 and 1818] as [the spinners had. . . .]" [4]

A general characteristic of the Revolutionary and Napoleonic wars was that high prices, taxation, wartime shortages, high rents, high interest rates, and other inflationary features transferred income to "landlords, farmers, house-owners, bondholders, and entrepreneurs . . . and [this] almost certainly worsened the economic status of labour." [5] Between 1710 and 1765, the price of wheat had hardly ever been above 45s. a quarter, and sometimes as low as 25s. After a less certain series of years leading up to the beginning of war in 1793, the price of wheat rose giddily. In the years 1800, 1801, 1810, 1812, and 1813 it was above 100s. per quarter, and in 1795, 1796, 1805, 1806, 1807, 1808, 1809, 1811, and 1814 it was more than 70s. Such inflation made the war years probably the gloomiest of any between 1770 and 1840 for the working classes.[6]

From the standpoint of profits the industry was depressed between 1815 and 1821. Since production was expanding and prices of provisions had begun to fall after 1817–18, this depression may not have been severe for the operative groups. Possibly, however, their increase in real wages was offset by high unemployment. In the strike of 1818 spinners complained in an address to the public that wages were "inadequate to procure even the coarsest necessaries of life for ourselves and families." [7]

[1] E.g., the diary of William Rowbottom in *Giles Shaw Manuscripts*, Vol. 94, pp. 14, 18, 25–6, 30, 34, 57, 82–3, 102, 111; Vol. 95, pp. 5, 19, 29, 76, 106; Vol. 100, pp. 56, 82, and 110. Also *Annual Register*, 1818, p. 104 (Chr.).

[2] *Giles Shaw Manuscripts*, Vol. 95, pp. 106, 115; Vol. 97, p. 2.

[3] *Parliamentary Papers*, 1816, III, Children employed in Manufactories, p. 476a.

[4] *Annual Register*, 1818, pp. 103–4 (Chr.).

[5] Ashton, "The Standard of Life of the Workers in England, 1790–1830," *op. cit.*, p. 135. Also A. Prentice, *Historical Sketches and Personal Recollections of Manchester* (London, 1851), pp. 30–31.

[6] Mantoux, *The Industrial Revolution in the Eighteenth Century*, p. 437; W. W. Rostow, *British Economy in the Nineteenth Century* (Oxford, 1949), pp. 124–5. Prices after 1793 are actual annual averages.

[7] Quoted in R. F. Wearmouth, *Some Working-Class Movements of the Nineteenth Century* (London, 1948), pp. 28–30. The worst years were probably 1816 and 1819. Also *Annual Register*, 1820, pp. 59–60 (Hist.); Gayer, Rostow, and

Other evidence indicates that the spinners were less damaged by the stormy economic conditions of 1815–21. A Manchester newspaper singled the spinners from "every other class of manufacturers and labourers in Lancashire," for most of 1816 and 1817, noting that they "had full and constant work, and high wages during the whole of the time." [1] In 1818 a magistrate distinguished "very materially" between the weavers and the spinners. "The spinners is an occupation which has not been at all in a state of depression; I have here a sketch of the spinners for the last year, of whom very few have applied for relief; the utmost not being above two in any one week." On the other hand, weavers were earning only 6*s.* or 7*s.*, and sometimes as little as 4*s.* per week.[2] Between 1816 and 1821, therefore, the factory population experienced unemployment at times, but they should not be lumped with weavers and others into one mass of "depressed" workers.

The years between 1821 and 1825 brought "steadily increasing prosperity." [3] Not only was cotton booming, but conversions to reduce the national debt and the restoration of the gold standard breathed confidence into the economy. In 1824 a master spinner offered "constant Employment upon large Wheels, fine numbers at Good Prices" to mule-spinners.[4] This prosperity was reversed abruptly by the 1825–6 crisis. In mid-1826, mills were closing and working short-time. By the summer of 1827, however, the Manchester factory population was recovering from this severe crisis. Between 1828 and 1832 conditions were sometimes stagnant and sometimes positively depressed. While there were reports of unemployment in certain areas of Lancashire, especially in 1829 and 1830, little information on unemployment among factory operatives is available.[5]

In 1833 a "great number of mills in Lancashire [were] working only four days a week"; master spinners had no difficulty in securing hands, except for throstle-spinners.[6] Another witness reported, how-

Schwartz, *Growth and Fluctuation of the British Economy*, pp. 140–45, 167; Ashton, "The Standard of Life of the Workers in England, 1790–1830," *op. cit.,* p. 135.

[1] *Annual Register*, 1818, p. 103 (Chr.), quoting from *Wheeler's Manchester Chronicle.*

[2] *Parliamentary Papers*, 1818, V, Lords Committee on Poor Laws, p. 247.

[3] Redford, *Labour Migration in England*, p. 74.

[4] *Manchester Guardian*, Dec. 11, 1824.

[5] *Ibid.*, July 8, 1826; C. Driver, *Tory Radical: The Life of Richard Oastler* (New York, 1946), p. 49.

[6] *Parliamentary Papers*, 1835, XIII, Hand-loom Weavers, p. 188; 1833, VI, Manufactures, Commerce and Shipping, pp. 315, 689.

ever, that "the employment [in cotton mills] is regular and constant; it never varies; the prices do not vary . . . the labourers must be better off now in such employment than they were at almost any period I can name for many years back." [1] Whatever the exact conditions in 1833, the trend of employment was certainly upward. By 1834 there was "plenty of work," especially for women and children, in the cotton factories of Lancashire.[2] This demand for labour continued through 1837.

The years 1837–8 brought a depression, but by turning to the home markets to sell their produce, the manufacturers (and presumably the operatives) escaped the terrific loss that the merchants sustained in these years. The year 1839 was a "singularly disastrous year for manufacturer, spinner and merchant," and broke the steadiness of employment for factory workers. Unemployment, however, took the form more of short-time working than of outright dismissal.[3]

From the standpoint of unemployment, the years 1841–2 constituted probably the most serious depression ever experienced by the factory workers. Not only did dull trade enforce short-time working, but technological improvements forced many firms to close entirely and thereby throw whole families out of work.[4] In 1843 Leonard Horner counted 8,108 unemployed persons in his factory inspection district whose place of employment had not been working since January 1, 1842; 5,312 unemployed who had been working on that date but who had subsequently lost their jobs through the closing of factories, and 3,469 persons working short-time. On the other hand, some 3,490 were working in mills which had *opened* since January 1, 1842, indicating that the deep depression was probably over by 1843.[5]

[1] *Parliamentary Papers*, 1833, VI, Manufactures, Commerce and Shipping, p. 40. In general, however, "hardly anything is known about the early 1830's except that unemployment among the. . . . Ironfounders rose until 1833. Still in general it must have declined from the 1832 peak, though this may not have affected the men hit by technological changes." E. J. Hobsbawm, "Economic Fluctuations and Some Social Movements since 1800," *Economic History Review*, Second Series, V (1952), p. 11.

[2] *Parliamentary Papers*, 1834, XXXVI, Poor Law Commission, pp. 68, 69, 71, 73, 74.

[3] Matthews, *A Study in Trade-Cycle History*, pp. 137–9, 144.

[4] *Manchester Guardian*, Sept. 21, 1841; *Parliamentary Papers*, 1841, VI, Sess. 2, Factory Inspectors, p. 224; 1842, XXXV, Report on Distress in Rochdale, pp. 171–9, and Population of Stockport, pp. 210, 237–9; 1842, XIX, Eighth Annual Report of the Poor Law Commissioners, pp. 10–11; 1843, XXI, Ninth Annual Report of the Poor Law Commissioners, p. 5; Matthews, *A Study in Trade-Cycle History*, pp. 141–3; K. M. Lyell, *Memoir of Leonard Horner* (London, 1890), Vol. II, pp. 35–6.

[5] *Parliamentary Papers*, 1843, XXVII, Factory Inspectors, pp. 313–15.

By May, 1844, Horner reported that "the cotton trade is in a state of great activity; new mills are building, others long unoccupied have been taken by new tenants; and in some places it is difficult to find workers." [1] This feverish state continued through 1845 and 1846, but the familiar crisis and crash plunged the trade into another "unprecedented depression" which prevailed from late 1846 into 1848, again creating unemployment among the factory operatives.[2]

Hand-loom Weavers. We have sketched the upward course and fluctuations of weavers' wages during the golden age. After the turn of the century the trend was downward, as Table 9 shows. The social conditions accompanying this decline are familiar enough only to list—starvation, crowded conditions, crime, filth, and gradual withdrawal from religion, education, friendly societies, etc.[3]

Some years were worse than others. The weavers, like the spinners, had their earnings erased by high prices during the war period. Both 1798–1800 and 1807–8 were severe, but 1811–12 was worst, when "few masters could give employment, and none could give good wages." At one time in 1812, Bolton weavers earned as little as 5s. per week. Between 1816 and 1821 the weaving population was very depressed. The year 1816 was marked by the "high price of provisions" and "scarcity of employment" in the manufacturing districts. Conditions were little better in 1817, and the concentration of Irish and weavers on the relief lists in 1818 indicates that weaving was in distress. The year 1819 was even worse; wages continued low, and it has been calculated that the cost of diet for the weavers had actually risen during the past year.[4]

In 1826 there were reports of a "state of distress bordering upon actual famine" among the hand-loom weavers in many districts. Though 1827 and 1828 brought some relief, weaving, unlike spinning, never really recovered from the 1826 distress. In 1829 and 1830 Richard Carlile and William Cobbett lamented the condition of hand-loom weavers in their Lancashire tours. In 1829 approximately

[1] *Parliamentary Papers*, 1844, XXVIII, Factory Inspectors, p. 568.
[2] *Parliamentary Papers*, 1845, XXV, Factory Inspectors, p. 436; 1846, XX, Factory Inspectors, p. 577; 1847, XV, Factory Inspectors, p. 448; 1847–8, XXVI, Factory Inspectors, p. 107.
[3] In addition to the parliamentary publications of 1834, 1835, 1839, 1840 and 1841, cf. Gaskell, *Artisans and Machinery*, pp. 37–9, 78, and Ashton, *Economic and Social Investigations in Manchester*, pp. 20–21.
[4] Prentice, *Historical Sketches and Personal Recollections of Manchester*, pp. 36, 47, 83; A. Bryant, *The Age of Elegance* (London, 1950), p. 335; *Parliamentary Papers*, 1818, V, Poor Laws, pp. 13, 245, 257; D. Read, "The Social and Economic Background to Peterloo," *Transactions of the Lancashire and Cheshire Antiquarian Society*, 1954, p. 18; Wearmouth, *Some Working-Class Movements in the Nineteenth Century*, pp. 28–30.

one-fourth of the weavers in parts of Lancashire and Cheshire were without work.[1] After this time, anything approximating full employment—and that at starvation wages—occurred in boom periods when power-loom manufacturers supplemented their machinery by giving work to hand-loom weavers. Even in 1834, a year of increasing prosperity, a family could not survive on a weaver's wages. In 1835 it was reported that hand-loom weavers paid their rents by borrowing from their masters.[2] The crises of 1837–8 and 1841–2 simply aggravated the death-throes of the weavers.

APPENDIX B

THE CHANGING SOCIAL STRUCTURE OF A MILL: THE CATRINE COTTON WORKS

During the investigations and debates which terminated in the act to limit factory hours in 1819, the principal issue was the operatives' health. As we shall see, this subject was the source of exaggeration, claim, counterclaim, and prejudice. From a document submitted to Parliament in this controversy, however, we may reconstruct the Catrine Cotton Works in the county of Ayr, Scotland, with reference to the operatives' family economy. In 1819 Kirkman Finlay described the factory community to the Lords Committee on Children Employed in the Cotton Manufactories of the United Kingdom.[3] His documents emphasized matters of health; they compared the numbers of live and dead children per family of Catrine with those of several non-cotton communities and were accompanied by a surgeon's estimate of the health of the Catrine operatives. This demonstration contained incidentally, however, the names and occupations of heads of families (males and widows) with children in the Works, and the numbers and employment of all their children.

The Catrine Works themselves illustrate several conflicting trends in the cotton industry as of 1819. Situated in a village of only 2,100 or 2,200, they were nevertheless large, employing a total of 832 employees in December, 1818. The manager was Archibald Buchanan, a benevolent master with a personal interest in his workers' welfare.

[1] *Parliamentary Papers*, 1826–7, V, Emigration, pp. 4, 236–7; *Manchester Guardian*, Apr. 12, 1828; *The Lion*, Vol. I, No. 8, Aug. 21, 1829; W. Cobbett, *Rural Rides* (London, 1930), Vol. II, p. 596; Driver, *Tory Radical*, p. 49; *Annual Register*, 1829, pp. 171–2 (Chr.).

[2] *Parliamentary Papers*, 1834, XXXVI, Poor Law Commission, pp. 68, 69, 71, 73, 74 (especially questions 30, 35, 37, 39, 40, 41). Also 1835, XIII, Hand-loom Weavers, p. 5.

[3] *Lords Sessional Papers*, 1819, XVI, pp. 578–82.

In one sense, therefore, the Catrine Works represented the humanitarian type of country mill. Not limited to water-frame spinning, however, they engaged in coarse mule-spinning, and by 1819 had already installed power-loom weaving.[1] Again, however, women ran the small mules; the semi-apprenticeship system for training adult male spinners was absent.

In 1819 the Works employed 568 children from 276 families. Of the heads of these families, 100 (79 males and 21 widows) worked in the manufactory.[2] Since there were no male adult spinners, the men probably were overlookers, card-room employees, and mechanics. The remaining 176 heads of families having children employed in the mill were composed of 44 widows, 26 weavers, and 106 "others" (masons, clockmakers, labourers, etc.).

The differentiation of child labour from their parents' had reached a fairly advanced level in Catrine, partly because of conscious policy. "I have laid it down as a Rule, in our Works," said Buchanan, "that none of the Children of the Person who is Master of the Room, should work in his Room, for it gave rise to Jealousy; other Hands thought he was partial to his own Children; and it was necessary, therefore, to prevent that Person's Children from working under his particular Superintendence." [3] He noted, however, that the practice was "pretty general in other Works." [4] Since the Catrine Works provided no line of training into an adult male occupation,[5] the pressure to maintain a traditional apprentice relationship between parent and child was presumably less than in the firms with adult male spinners. In a "few instances" an exception to the separation of parent and child was made, when a "Widow Woman is employed in the Factory along with her Children." [6]

The social organization of the Catrine Works shows, in a roundabout way, the importance of the apprenticeship system in the mule-

[1] *Lords Sessional Papers*, 1819, XVI, pp. 492–3, 582; *Parliamentary Papers*, 1839, XIX, Factory Inspectors, pp. 529–36; 1816, III, Children Employed in Manufactories, p. 243.

[2] This makes a total of 668 persons in the Catrine Works in April, 1819. Archibald Buchanan said that the difference between this figure (668) and the one of December, 1818 (832), is contained in "Relatives of the above Families, and single Persons." *Lords Sessional Papers*, 1819, XVI, p. 582. For these remaining 146 employees we have no further information.

[3] *Lords Sessional Papers*, 1818, IX, p. 64.

[4] *Ibid.* Were not these other works those in which adult males overlooked or tended the mules and apprenticed their own children?

[5] Buchanan said that children (presumably including boys) left the manufactory "about the Time that they are fit to go as Apprentices to other Businesses.' *Ibid.*, p. 74.

[6] *Ibid.*, p. 67.

spinning branches employing adult males. At Catrine the children seemed to be segregated effectively from their parents. The possibly disruptive consequences of this arrangement on the family probably were softened in Catrine, a small village with close social ties, extended kinship, as well as humanitarian management. Without such correctives the dislocation of the traditional family economy would seem to have been fairly complete. In the city factories with large mules run by males, most spinners hired and trained their own piecers, often their own children or relatives. In an urban environment this relationship was the anchor point of family stability in the factory. In such factories, furthermore, the multiplication of assistants began to undermine this anchor point.

The information on the Catrine Works also illustrates an apparent trend which was important for the family's long-term equilibrium. This information concerns the employment of children from different occupational categories in the Catrine community:

(1) Male heads of families employed in the Works. These 79 men had a total of 373 children of all ages, or an average of 4·74 children per family. From this average number, 2·93, or 61·8%, were employed in all occupations. Of those working, furthermore, 58% worked in the mill itself.

(2) Widows employed in the Works. These 21 women had 100 children of all ages, or an average number of 4·76. An average of 3·71, or 77·1%, worked in some occupation. Of those working, 52·6% worked in the manufactory itself.

(3) Widows not employed in the Works. These 44 women had an average number of 5·23 children. An average of 4·46, or 85·3%, worked. Of the working children, 45·9% were in the manufactory.

(4) Weavers (hand-loom) in the community. These 26 weavers had an average of 5·31 children. An average of 4·15, or 7·63%, of these children worked. Of those working, 59% worked in the manufactory.

(5) Other heads of families in the community (masons, labourers, clockmakers, etc.). These 106 men had an average of 5·63 children per family. An average of 3·75, or 66·6%, worked. Of these, 60% worked in the manufactory.

First, the figures lend support to Buchanan's statement that he permitted widows to work with their children on occasion. Of those widows working *in* the manufactory, 52·6% of their employed children worked in the manufactory as well. For widows *not* thus employed, only 45·9% of their children found employment in the mill. While not striking, these figures show a slight favouritism in allowing widows to support their children maternally and economically at the same time.

It also appears that the percentage of working children per head of family was a function of the wage-level of the head of the family, even though exact wage figures are not available. In the first place, those males—overlookers, card-room operatives, mechanics—who held positions in the factory experienced a certain variability of wages, but in general theirs were higher than weavers'. In 1818, in fact, the wages of a child in the manufactory were often greater than those of a hand-loom weaver.[1] Further, from the standpoint of uniformity, wages in the Works were "equal to any, and much more than many." [2] It seems fair, moreover, to place the wage-level of "others" (masons, labourers, clockmakers) somewhere between the weavers and other male factory operatives. Factory workers' wages were generally better than artisans', and among the artisans, the weavers were perhaps the most distressed in 1819. Finally, it is reasonable to assume that widows employed in the Works earned more than those not working there, on the same general grounds. Hence the following rank, based on the probable wages of the head of the family:

Rank	Category	% of Children of all ages employed
1	Males in mill	61·8
2	"Others"	66·6
3	Weavers	76·3
4	Widows in mill	77·1
5	Widows not in mill	85·3

It is plausible to assume from these figures that families reaching a *more differentiated role* in the labour force as factory operatives (spinners, dressers, mechanics, overlookers, etc.) were *also* working their children less in general. Part of this effect is enforced by the fact of differentiation itself; if the economic role of the adult splits from the child, the processes of socialization probably were transferred more to the home. Another contributing factor was of course the wage-level. For adults whose factory employment meant a higher income, to employ children was no longer so necessary; they could afford the luxury of differentiation. On the other hand, those in economically precarious positions, either because of special circumstances (e.g., widows) or because of long-term pressures (e.g., weavers), were forced to send their children into the factories.[3]

[1] *Lords Sessional Papers*, 1818, IX, p. 80.
[2] *Parliamentary Papers*, 1816, III, Children employed in Manufactories, p. 241.
[3] *Lords Sessional Papers*, 1818, IX, p. 72.

One might extrapolate from these observations to comment anew on the changes in technology in spinning and weaving between the 1820's and the 1840's. One effect was to *break* the traditional economic ties of the spinner with his children. At the same time, however, because of this break and because his real wages were rising, there was less reason for him to send his children to work. In short, the technological changes promised greater rewards to the family member who would differentiate his labour from the family context.*

In the meantime, because of competition from the *same* technological improvements, the undifferentiated family economy of groups like the hand-loom weavers deteriorated more and more. One of their responses was to send more "dependents" into the factories. This arrangement, particularly when the dependents were sent into the power-loom departments which lacked the traditional kinship controls, disrupted the weavers' family by separating adults and children.

Thus the technological changes of the 1820's influenced the family economy in two ways: (1) directly, by endangering the traditional apprenticeship system between spinner and child and by bringing pressure on the non-economic familial functions; (2) indirectly, by encouraging the depressed non-factory classes to send more children into the factories. The first effect set off the stormy disturbances among the factory operatives to be analysed in the next chapter. The second effect, however, lifted the problem of child labour above the agitation of a single class of operatives and brought the problem of the family economy more generally to the public mind. We shall discuss this second effect in Chapter XI.

* For the theoretical rationale for this, above, pp. 171–2.

CHAPTER X

SYMPTOMS OF DISTURBANCE IN THE FAMILY

Any major sequence of structural change in the family, which touches the deepest of human sensitivities, is neither easy nor automatic. Early in such a sequence there occur periods of explosive "symptoms of disturbance" which constitute *Step 2* of the differentiation. In this chapter we shall trace these disturbances first among the factory operatives and second among the hand-loom weavers. Among the working-class turbulences of the period were appeals for relief, destruction of property, strikes, Utopian schemes such as Cobbettism and Owenism, and agitation to limit factory hours.*

INTRODUCTION: THE RELATIONSHIP BETWEEN STRUCTURAL PRESSURES AND SYMPTOMS OF DISTURBANCE

How far can working-class disturbances of the period be traced to the cotton industry? How far may we generalize to other industries? In this chapter we shall discuss movements which spread beyond the cotton industry. The early co-operative ideology, for instance, seemed to attract hand-loom weavers and other artisans more than factory spinners. To account for the full course of early co-operation, of course, we must refer both to other social groups and to other pressures than those on the family economy. I shall consider only two problems: (*a*) Why did the co-operative ideology appeal to certain groups in the cotton industry at certain times? (*b*) What parts of this ideology were appropriate in terms of the pressures on and dissatisfactions with the family economy? Any conclusions must apply only to the working classes of the cotton industry. The same holds for factory agitation. The cotton operatives fought to limit factory hours by law, particularly in the 1830's and 1840's. Much of the impetus for this movement came, however, from the Yorkshire woollen and worsted industries. Furthermore, industrialists, Tory

---

* We shall postpone a full discussion of the "disturbed" elements of factory agitation until Chapter XI.

Radicals, and clergymen joined the agitation. I shall inquire neither into the reasons which moved these latter groups, nor into the exact timing of the factory legislation itself, but only into the significance of the agitation for the cotton operatives.

We shall trace such disturbances to the dissatisfactions with family organization. Because disturbances are *generalized,** they frequently reflect diverse dissatisfactions. For instance, the early co-operative ideology promised solutions for hours of labour, family division of labour, level of income, consumption standards, religion, education, family harmony, master-servant relationships, and more. From these general promises we must isolate specific symbolic references to the family economy of the working classes. While the generalized nature of disturbances makes interpretation difficult, this lack of specificity aids us in identifying them as genuine disturbances. The generality of a movement's promises is usually a fair measure of its degree of disturbance. A scheme which promises to erase the whole system of labour by establishing ideal communities, for instance, has a different ring from a movement to reduce the hours of children without such elaborate ideological trimmings. Again, an agitation to limit factory hours which promises as an outcome an idyllic rural existence differs qualitatively from a similar agitation which holds out no such consequences. The former is a genuinely disturbed movement, whereas the latter belongs in a later stage of structural differentiation. The specificity of ideologies, in short, often parallels the stages of differentiation on the level of social structure. Later we shall trace the processes by which the factory-hours agitation and the co-operative movement became more specific in their promises of consequences and hence less "disturbed."

Because symptoms of disturbance may be so generalized and may refer to many sequences of differentiation, we must review each disturbance more than once. In this chapter, for instance, we shall discuss the co-operative ideology in terms of the family division of labour, and later we shall assess the same ideology in terms of the roles governing consumption and saving in the family. Because we shall treat a number of social movements, we must summarize each briefly. In an attempt to secure a representative statement, I have concentrated on three main sources: the writings of major exponents, periodicals and pamphlets which reached the working classes, and discussion of these movements in secondary sources.

Finally, any discussion of social disturbances must take account of fluctuations in wages and employment. Machine-breaking, trade-

* Above, pp. 38–9.

union activity, factory agitation, and political activity were correlated closely with business conditions in our period.[1] On the other
hand, the fact of depression itself does not explain why machine-
breaking occurs in one depression and factory agitation in another.
Depressions often *precipitate* regressive disturbances, but the qualitative differences *among* disturbances stem from long-term institutional
pressures.*

SYMPTOMS OF DISTURBANCE AMONG THE FACTORY OPERATIVES, 1770–1840

Destruction of Property. Several commentators have observed that
violence against machinery is the first sign of disturbance among
workers in a period of rapid industrial reorganization.[2] In one sense
such attacks are linked correctly to the cause of the workpeople's
misery.

Occasional unemployment resulting from the use of machines, a
frequent shifting and readjustment of labor, a natural lack of foresight as to the ultimate expansion of industry and increase of
employment, and knowledge of the dubious opportunities of the
workers for sharing the profits of industrial expansions,—such
circumstances combined to cause many local groups of workers to
fix their attention momentarily upon the machines as the cause
of their distress.[3]

On the other hand, from the standpoints of the rational means of
preventing the march of machinery, the legal consequences of
assaulting property, and longer-term gains to the wage-earner himself, these attacks are "misdirected," and represent a relaxation of
the most basic controls over socialized behaviour.**
  Though frequent in the late eighteenth century, such attacks were
scattered in the cotton-spinning branch. Generally they occurred
locally on the introduction or threatened introduction of a machine,
e.g., the fly-shuttle in the 1730's, a cotton reel in 1753, new jennies in
1768, and the mule in the early 1780's. Another precipitating factor

[1] Rostow, *British Economy in the Nineteenth Century*, pp. 123–5; Hobsbawm,
"Economic Fluctuations and Some Social Movements since 1800," *op. cit.*
  * The role of depressions in precipitating disturbances from the standpoint of
the family economy does not differ from their role in the industry itself. For
instance, we discovered that depressed conditions precipitated "regressions"
such as the agitation to prevent the exportation of cotton twist. Above, p. 133.
[2] E.g., Engels, *The Condition of the Working-Class in England in 1844*, pp. 213 ff.
[3] Bowden, *Industrial Society in England toward the End of the Eighteenth
Century*, p. 292.
**For the formal status (*G*-1) of such attacks, cf. above, pp. 38, 170.

was economic distress; high food prices, for instance, probably contributed to the outrage against the cotton reel.[1]

The wholesale destruction of machinery in Lancashire in 1779 reflects both influences. The new jennies, water-frames, and carding-engines seemed to imperil the livelihood of the domestic hand-workers. For years, furthermore, the American Revolutionary War had tightened economic conditions in the trade. Destruction began with an attack upon the "larger factories and more prosperous concerns," and within a few days mobs had destroyed much printing machinery and either smashed large jennies or pared them down to twenty spindles. The symbolism is interesting, for the mobs attacked machinery only of factory size; cottage machines were acceptable, because they had not altered the traditional arrangements of production radically.[2] Shortly after the attacks, workers claimed in a petition that old stock cards and smaller jennies could supply the necessary quantity of high-quality work. Several years later a petition from Leicester complained of technological unemployment, and cited the advantages of the domestic system for training children and attending the sick and aged.[3]

According to the Hammonds, "after these riots in 1779 the workers made no more attempts to check the introduction of machinery for spinning."[4] In the long run this is clearly incorrect, as our analysis of the strikes in the 1820's and 1830's will show. Even in the 1780's the Manchester magistrates strengthened the local police and circulated literature to convince the working classes of the advantages of the new machinery. Improved machines at Stalybridge brought such working-class opposition in 1796 that the owner locked and armed the mill for a time.[5] In general, however, attempts to resist new machinery by riot subsided by the turn of the century, both because of the authorities' repression and because the family was in a transitional equilibrium. The expansion of factory spinning ab-

[1] Espinasse, *Lancashire Worthies* (First Series), pp. 312–13; Axon, *The Annals of Manchester*, p. 90; Abram, *A History of Blackburn*, p. 205; Crabtree, *Richard Arkwright*, pp. 49–50, and French, *Life and Times of Samuel Crompton*, pp. 68–9.

[2] Daniels, *The Early English Cotton Industry*, p. 89; Crabtree, *Richard Arkwright*, pp. 52–3; Abram, *A History of Blackburn*, pp. 209–10; Mantoux, *The Industrial Revolution in the Eighteenth Century*, pp. 411–13; Chapman, *The Lancashire Cotton Industry*, p. 76. Also E. Butterworth, *An Historical Account of . . . Ashton-under-Lyne, Stalybridge, and Dukinfield* (Ashton, 1842), p. 81.

[3] *Parliamentary Papers*, 1780, V, Petition of Cotton Spinners, p. 4; *The . . . Petition of the Poor Spinners* (Leicester, 1788), pp. 1–3.

[4] *The Skilled Labourer*, p. 56.

[5] L. S. Marshall, *The Development of Public Opinion in Manchester, 1780–1820* (Syracuse, 1946), p. 40; Butterworth, *An Historical Account of . . . Ashton-under-Lyne, Stalybridge, and Dukinfield*, pp. 142–3.

sorbed much unemployment; the golden age of hand-loom weaving permitted families to devote their efforts entirely to domestic weaving; and the factory system possessed correctives which assured a certain continuity in family organization.[1]

Strikes and Parliamentary Reform, 1800–1820. Because the operatives moved through the first two decades without severe discontinuity in their traditional ways, the disturbances displayed by the factory groups show a certain moderation, especially when compared with other groups in the same period and with their own history in the 1820's and 1830's. In general the Combination Laws, which forbade combining to raise wages, obscure trade union activity between 1800 and 1825. Usually spinners' organizations were confined to specific localities, and their activities were "furtive, secret, and nervous." [2] Nevertheless, the operatives continued to concern themselves with wages and labour recruitment in this period. Of the recorded strikes and disturbances before 1820, however, none seems to have reflected any *structural pressure* of the sort which developed in the 1820's and 1830's in the spinning branches.[3] Even the "hordes of women and children" pouring into the industry apparently did not imperil the spinners' control of apprenticeship and related work conditions. Most disputes dealt with wage-levels, though occasionally the question of filling work vacancies arose. Most violence was directed not against machinery but against "knobsticks" (scabs) whom masters employed to break strikes. Most strikes, furthermore, occurred in good times when spinners desired a share of the prosperity and when their striking power was enhanced by the temporary shortage of labour.[4]

To illustrate, in 1798 cotton-spinners attacked a manufactory in Manchester for hiring workers below customary prices. Whether this minor riot followed the introduction of machinery is not known. In 1810 disturbances occurred in Glasgow and Manchester, both of which dealt with the conditions of employing adult operatives. The major cause of the Manchester strike, however, was the attempt to equalize the country spinning rate of 4*d.* with the Manchester rate of 4½*d.* This "most extensive and persevering strike" involved spinners from Manchester and outlying towns. The union's funds gave some

[1] Above, pp. 118–22, 137–8, and 184–6.
[2] Wearmouth, *Some Working-Class Movements of the Nineteenth Century,* p. 252.
[3] The opposition to women in the mills in Scotland in 1818 is an exception.
[4] Clapham, *An Economic History of Modern Britain,* p. 210; *Parliamentary Papers,* 1824, V, Artisans and Machinery, pp. 361, 484; Taylor, *Factories and the Factory System,* p. 94; E. C. Tufnell, *Character, Object, and Effects of Trades' Unions* (London, 1834), pp. 86–7.

relief, but after four months of idleness marked by sporadic rioting, men returned to work at either the old rates or lower ones. The strike dealt, therefore, not with structural dissatisfaction but with wages, though secondarily the workmen attempted to control the employment of adult operatives by submitting to the master a list of three candidates for employment each time a spinner was discharged. Apparently similar demands from the Scottish operatives precipitated the Glasgow lockout. Both these outbursts occurred in the period of relative prosperity sandwiched between the crises of 1808 and 1811–12. They thus seem to fit the pattern: dealing primarily with wage levels and occurring in a period of prosperity.[1]

The next major cotton strike was in 1818, when trade was relatively brisk and a number of trades were experiencing demands for higher wages. In Manchester the spinners demanded a wage advance; almost simultaneously the journeymen jenny-spinners of Stockport struck for their 1814 wages, which had been reduced several times since that date. In both disputes the operatives were tranquil; only one or two small outbursts of violence occurred. The Stockport spinners did not riot, though striking power-loom weavers rioted when knobsticks arrived to work at the old wage-level.[2]

Perhaps the most intense working-class turmoil after the Napoleonic war concerned the radical reform of Parliament. The spinners attended the giant reform meetings, but their active participation in violence was limited to a brief period following the disappointing strike of 1818, and a short flurry in Scotland and parts of Lancashire and Yorkshire in 1820. In any case the spinners' involvement in violence fell far short of the weavers'.[3] That they assumed only a moderate interest in social disturbances seems reasonable because, as we have seen, the pressures on this group were less severe than on other groups in the period 1800–20. They were interested in maintaining a wage-level, especially in prosperous times, and in

[1] *Annual Register*, 1798, p. 21 (Chr.); Tufnell, *Character, Object, and Effects of Trades' Unions*, pp. 13–17; Clapham, *An Economic History of Modern Britain*, p. 215; *Webb Manuscripts on Trade Unionism*, Vol. XXXIV, p. 15; D. Bremner, *The Industries of Scotland* (Edinburgh, 1869), p. 284.

[2] Hammond, *The Skilled Labourer*, pp. 92–6; Clapham, *An Economic History of Modern Britain*, p. 215; *Webb Manuscripts on Trade Unionism*, Vol. XXXIV, pp. 21–7; *Annual Register*, 1818, pp. 121, 123–4 (Chr.); F. A. Bruton, *The Story of Peterloo* (Manchester, 1919), p. 12; A. Aspinall, *The Early English Trade Unions* (London, 1949), p. 255; *Parliamentary Papers*, 1824, V, Artisans and Machinery, p. 413.

[3] Marshall, *The Development of Public Opinion in Manchester*, p. 155; Cole, *A Short History of the British Working Class Movement*, pp. 65 ff.; *Annual Register*, 1820, pp. 37–9 (Hist.).

protecting the adult operatives' control of outside recruitment of labour.

Structural Strikes, 1820–1845. In the 1820's and 1830's, by contrast, the spinners plunged headlong into a parade of "regressive" disturbances. These disturbances were mainly *structural* in the sense that they issued from the increasing pressure on the division of labour of the family. We outlined these pressures in the last chapter. Urbanization, community breakdown, and overcrowding intensified after the end of the Napoleonic war. More directly, changes in the spinning machinery threatened the spinners' economic, familial, and moral controls, which had been in equilibrium for some time. The resulting disturbances constitute Step 2 in the sequence which eventually brought the division of labour in the family of the factory operatives to a *more differentiated level* in the 1840's.

It will be recalled that the effects of the larger mules with more spindles in the 1820's were (1) to reduce spinners' piece-rates on the larger machines; (2) to increase spinners' weekly wages on these machines; (3) to threaten some technological unemployment, at least in the short run; (4) to increase the physical exertion of labourers on the larger machines; (5) to increase the number of assistants per spinner, and (6) to endanger the apprenticeship system based on kinship, and thus to undermine the economic authority of the spinner. Almost all the social turbulence which engulfed the factory operatives in the 1820's and 1830's reflects an attempt to minimize these effects and to restore the traditional ways. Let us analyse the timing and symbolism of these disturbances.

Between the 1820's and the 1840's the cotton industry experienced two types of strikes: (*a*) the familiar type limited to demands for wage advances in times of relative prosperity. Instances include the flurry of strikes in all industries between 1823 and 1825, the Oldham, Bolton, and Preston strikes of 1836, and various individual strikes in Manchester in 1844.[1] (*b*) "The most frequent cause of strikes in the cotton trade," however, was "the introduction of improved machinery, and especially the enlargement of mules, by means of which, the number of spindles a spinner is capable of superintending, has been continually increasing."[2] These strikes (plus those resisting the

[1] *Webb Manuscripts on Trade Unionism*, Vol. XXXIV, p. 272; *Manchester Guardian*, Oct. 19, 1836, and Feb. 22, Mar. 19, June 7, 1837; Feb. 10, Nov. 20, 1844; H. Ashworth, *An Inquiry into the. . . . Strike of the Operative Spinners of Preston* (Manchester, 1838), p. 2. The 1823–5 flurry is complicated by the repeal of the Combination Laws in 1824, which no doubt encouraged a number of trade groups to demand higher wages. The Preston strike also was complicated by other factors. Below, pp. 234, and 322–3.

[2] Tufnell, *Character, Object, and Effects of Trades' Unions*, p. 17.

entrance of women as spinners) we classify as structural; let us review them briefly.[1]

As early as 1818 the male spinners expressed the highest indignation when some masters attempted to introduce women spinners, probably on the smaller mules. The occasion precipitated several instances of mill-burning.[2] Six years later the same practice triggered a strike in Manchester. The *Manchester Guardian* chastised the men for preventing women from invading their monopoly.[3] A week later a union official responded passionately with an appeal to preserve the position of the head of the family.

"Are females quietly employed in any department of the cotton mills which the men wish to monopolize? The latter demand their discharge." In this charge, there is fortunately for you, sir, some shadow of truth. In one instance, where the master declared his determination to fill his mill with women *only*, the men left their employment. But, sir, this does not apply to the great body of spinners,—there are many instances where women are employed in the same mill, and actually occupy the best departments. We do not stand opposed to women working, but we do enter our protest against the principle on which they are employed. The women, in nine cases out of ten, have only themselves to support,—while the men, generally have families. This the employers know, and of this the unprincipled take advantage. The women can afford their labour for less than the men, and those masters who employ them are enabled to come into market on better terms than those employers who do not; thus the fair tradesman is injured and he is ultimately, though reluctantly forced to maintain families on the most inadequate means. We wish not to come forward as moralists, but if we could call the inhabitants of Manchester, the parents of children especially, to view the character and conduct of females in a cotton-mill, we think we could present them with an exhibition at once disgusting and appalling. Girls, many of them interesting ones, from 14 to 20 years of age, are thus rendered independent of their natural guardians, who in many cases, indeed, become *in consequence of this very employment*, dependent upon their children. In this unnatural and unwholesome state of things, the reins of government are broken, and the excited feelings of youth and inexperience let loose upon the world, a prey too often to pride, vice, and infamy.[4]

1 While fairly exhaustive, this information on strikes during the period is obviously not absolutely complete. In some cases the origin of the strike is clear, but in others we must rest on weak inferences because of the lack of available historical material.

2 *Webb Manuscripts on Trade Unionism*, Vol. XXXIV, p. 381.

3 Nov. 20, 1824.

4 *Ibid.*, Nov. 27, 1824.

Such hot feelings may be related to an incident a week later in which vitriol was thrown on a spinner who took employment on unfavourable terms, though the union disclaimed any connection with the incident.

Strikes to resist superior machinery began clearly in 1823 when "spinners [in Bolton] complain of reductions in the prices paid on large wheels when they have to keep more piecers and work harder themselves." Two years earlier a strike had broken out when masters had submitted a new list of prices. Both these Bolton strikes failed. In 1824 a larger strike developed in Hyde when spinners claimed they made only 3*s.* 7*d.* per 1,000 of No. 40's, whereas other spinners made 4*s.* 7*d.* On their improved machinery, however, these Hyde spinners were earning higher *weekly* wages than others. In the following year, one of the precipitating factors in a strike in Chorley was the possibility of reduced prices on the larger wheels. The years 1825–6 brought depression and "lack of cohesion and concerted action amongst the workers." One strike with violence, however, broke in Oldham after several mills introduced new prices.[1]

In 1829 the Manchester masters attempted to reduce their wages for counts above 80 to the Hyde level. In April about 1,000 fine spinners turned out. Negotiations dragged on until September, when some coarse spinners joined the striking fine spinners. Some violence occurred, mostly to prevent other spinners from accepting employment at the reduced rates. By October the spinners' funds apparently ran out, and they decided to return to work. During the same period the masters of Bolton contemplated reducing the wages of their fine spinners. In Oldham the spinners struck because the masters wished to abandon the weekly pay basis for rovers. In 1830 a strike accompanied by bomb-throwing occurred after a reduction of wages in Chorley. There was also a minor turnout, of unknown cause, in Stalybridge in mid-1830.[2]

This flurry culminated in 1830–31 with a gigantic strike against piece-rate reductions in Ashton-under-Lyne. This strike, which

[1] *Webb Manuscripts on Trade Unionism*, Vol. XXXV, pp. 37–8; Vol. XXXVI, p. 63; *Parliamentary Papers*, 1824, V, Artisans and Machinery, pp. 556–7; Tufnell, *Character, Object and Effects of Trades' Unions*, pp. 18–19; Hall, *Vindication of Chorley Spinners' Turn-out*, pp. 13, 25; Morris, *The History of the Labour Movement in England*, p. 26; *Annual Register*, 1826, pp. 151–2 (Chr.). For the 1826 strike, the report does not indicate whether prices were reduced because of depressed conditions or new machinery.

[2] *Manchester Guardian*, Feb. 28, Mar. 14, Apr. 4, 18, 25, May 23, June 6, July 4, 18, Aug. 22, Sept. 12, Oct. 3, 10, 24, 1829; Jan. 30, Sept. 11, 1830; Tufnell, *Character, Object and Effects of Trades' Unions*, p. 19; *Webb Manuscripts on Trade Unionism*, Vol. XXXIV, p. 61, Vol. XXXV, p. 272; *Annual Register*, 1830, p. 92 (Chr.).

occasioned violence, the bearing of arms, and assembly of troops, forced some 18,000 into idleness.[1] At its commencement, the central association of operative spinners declared:

We . . . do determine that a general strike of all those spinners who are receiving less than 4/2 per 1000 hanks for No. 40's (and other numbers in proportion) on *all* sizes of wheels, shall take place on Monday, the 27th instant; not one of whom shall return to work until the full price be given.[2]

Ultimately the strike collapsed when unemployed spinners accepted the lower rates. The new weekly wages, however, probably exceeded the old. When the masters claimed this, the union leader tacitly admitted it when he commented on the masters' claim: ". . . there is a more important point of view," namely that a spinner deserved even higher weekly wages because of his short average work life.[3] A minor strike occurred in 1831, possibly in connection with the same dispute over wage differentials. In the same year Preston workers caused some property damage when they attempted to check the introduction of new machinery.[4]

After unsuccessful strikes in 1833 and 1836–7, the Oldham union dissolved in confusion, but re-formed in 1842 to resist the practice of assigning one spinner to four or six mules. They attempted to demonstrate that one male spinner to each pair was more effective and more economical. The great Preston strike of 1836 commenced with the discharge of six insubordinate spinners, but immediately upon striking the spinners demanded the Bolton list. Some also complained that their piecers' wages were increasing, and that employers were changing the numbers on machines.[5]

The Glasgow strike of 1837 began with a reduction of wages during the crash of 1836–7, but it acquired a *structural* aspect before its termination. The Glasgow masters had advanced wages late in 1836, apparently because of the general prosperity. The principle of equality of wages for all mule-spinners, however, which had obtained for ten years, remained undisturbed. When the masters proposed to reduce piece-rate wages six months after the advance, the workmen struck.

[1] *Manchester Guardian*, Dec. 18, 1830, Jan. 1, 1831. *Webb Manuscripts on Trade Unionism*, Vol. XXXIV, pp. 134–8; Vol. XXXV, p. 156.
[2] *Webb Manuscripts on Trade Unionism*, Vol. XXXIV, pp. 134–5.
[3] John Doherty, quoted in *Webb Manuscripts on Trade Unionism*, Vol. XXXV, p. 156.
[4] *Manchester Guardian*, June 25, 1831; Hardwick, *History of the Borough of Preston*, p. 415.
[5] *Annual Register*, 1834, pp. 57–8 (Chr.); *Webb Manuscripts on Trade Unionism*, Vol. XXXIV, pp. 52–5; Ashworth, *An Inquiry into . . . the Strike of the Operative Cotton Spinners of Preston*, p. 5.

Shortly thereafter, the masters proposed second and third reductions, the last assigning lower prices to wheels with more than 300 spindles. Apparently the masters had begun to increase the size of their machines (and to introduce women into the mills as well). According to a representative of the operatives' association, the larger machine was objectionable because (*a*) "it increases the amount of labour," (*b*) "it brings a reduction of one per cent. upon every 12 spindles above 300," (*c*) "it will have the effect of throwing a great number of men idle," and (*d*) "it will destroy that equality in the price of labour which has tended to promote and continue that peace and happiness between the employers and the employed these 10 years back. . . ." [1]

The scattered strikes in the early 1840's—Wigan in 1840, Stockport in 1840, Blackburn in 1842—resulted by and large from wage reductions originating in the introduction of new machinery and the generally depressed state of trade.[2]

Many of these structural strikes initiated a vicious circle by creating the very technological conditions which the spinners were opposing. The incorporation of the self-actor mule, for instance, rested partially on the masters' indignation at what they considered refractory behaviour. Both the Manchester strike of 1829 and the Preston strike of 1836 hastened the introduction of self-actors, and the Glasgow strike of 1837 apparently stimulated the introduction of large machines and the recruitment of women for the smaller mules.[3]

These structural strikes, in my opinion, represented the operatives' attempt to resist the pressures of the improved machinery on the family division of labour—pressures to modify the traditional wage-structure, to multiply the number of assistants, to throw heads of families out of employment, and to hasten the general deterioration of the spinners' authority. The operatives' interest was to maintain these *more generalized* elements of the family economy.* The strikes alone, however, do not exhaust the evidence regarding such disturbances. Since strike demands almost always concerned the reduction or equalization of wages, they yield little direct information concerning the traditional relationship between father and child in the factory. To obtain supplementary evidence, therefore, let us analyse several other simultaneous disturbances: the operatives'

---

[1] *Parliamentary Papers*, 1837–8, VIII, Combinations of Workmen, pp. 19, 36, 41, 43; Chapman, *The Lancashire Cotton Industry*, p. 214.

[2] *Manchester Guardian*, Aug. 22, May 20, 1840; Mar. 26, 1842.

[3] *Webb Manuscripts on Trade Unionism*, Vol. XXXIV, p. 142; Ashworth, *An Inquiry into . . . the Strike of the Operative Cotton Spinners of Preston*, pp. 9–10; Chapman, *The Lancashire Cotton Industry*, p. 214.

* For a statement of the generalized nature of the factory family in the first two decades of the nineteenth century, above, pp. 188–93.

expression of attitudes toward female and child labour, their agitation for limiting factory hours, and their brief flirtation with the co-operative movement.

Attitudes toward Conditions of Labour. As the structural strikes proceeded, various statements expressing concern with uniform piece-rates were emitted from working-class circles. John Doherty, the leader of the unionists, complained that the low piece-rates on large mules drove the smaller machines out of business. "In Glasgow," he concluded, " the same price is paid on the largest as on the smallest wheels, and why there should be such an enormous difference [in Manchester] we cannot discover."[1] Occasionally these specific attacks generalized into protests against the march of machinery as a whole.

Could inspiration have unfolded to our fathers, who now moulder in their graves, the calamities which the invention of machinery was to bring upon their descendants;—could they have obtained but a faint glimmering of the havoc it has made upon the independence, the physical energies, and moral habits of Englishmen, what would they have thought, or how would they have acted? Would they have sung the praises of those who unintentionally were the authors of the pestilence; would they have permitted *"improvements,"* which have been a scourge to the country, to overwhelm the health and happiness of the people? Oh, no! Unless we greatly err in our estimation of the spirit of our forefathers, they would have raised up the standard of humanity, and under its sacred banners, have fought against *"improvements"* which have been, and are at this moment, the curse of the country . . . the "improvements" of machinery will soon enable them *to do without you*.[2]

The familiar elements of disturbance—anxiety, gloom, and the glorification of the past—were beginning to appear in the early 1830's.

In the same period the spinners were expressing the greatest hesitation on the subject of women workers. On occasion an article would lament the man displaced by a woman spinner. The earliest unions in the 1790's had included women as members. By 1829,

[1] *The Union Pilot and Co-Operative Intelligencer*, Apr. 3, 1830, pp. 35–6. The difference to which Doherty refers probably stems from the fact that Manchester introduced the new machinery much more rapidly than Glasgow, and hence created a more substantial basis for differential wage-payments. *Parliamentary Papers*, 1833, VI, Manufactures, Commerce and Shipping, pp. 314–15; 1837–8, VIII, Combinations of Workmen, p. 13. For a similar complaint on piece-rates, cf. *The Herald of the Rights of Industry*, Feb. 15, 1834.

[2] *The Union Pilot and Co-Operative Intelligencer*, Mar. 17, 1832. In the issue of Mar. 24 an article entitled "Machinery and Starvation" appeared.

however, no doubt because of the growing insecurity of the male spinner, there were no female members in the Manchester group. The Isle of Man Conference of spinners in 1829 prohibited women from joining the men's unions but encouraged them to form their own. The Scottish spinners had a long history of resisting women in their ranks. The Bolton Association of Cotton Spinners had female members, but only in the Piecers' Section.[1]

Child labour was the subject of even greater concern. We have cited the early trade-union restrictions on those classes of children suitable as apprentices. In 1829, when pressure on the spinners was beginning to mount, delegates assembled on the Isle of Man to amalgamate the spinners of England, Scotland, and Ireland. After preliminary organizational discussion, the delegates turned immediately to the question of spinning by piecers. The Manchester representatives expressed particular alarm at this invasion of the adult spinners' position. The Glasgow delegates, not so immediately concerned because in Glasgow "piecers were not suffered to spin on any account," nevertheless agreed that the practice was dangerous if allowed to spread. In the end the delegates decided to admit piecers into the union and to provide them with allowances during strikes (so they would be less tempted to take work from unemployed spinners). In addition they resolved that no piecer be allowed to spin "on any account whatever . . . except such as may be hereafter provided for, and they only while the spinners are in the wheelhouse or wheelgate, walking to and from with the wheels and attending their work." [2]

At the same meeting the delegates resolved that only sons, brothers, or nephews of spinners, or masters' poor relatives should be instructed in spinning. Again the contrast between Manchester and Glasgow is instructive. In the former, where the apprenticeship crisis had come to a head, the delegates wished to delay the minimum age for spinning instruction until seventeen. Glasgow felt its current practice of instruction at fifteen years was adequate.[3] In Manchester, where large machinery was coming in faster, the spinners were willing

---

[1] *United Trades Cooperative Journal*, Mar. 10, 1832, pp. 3–4; *Articles of Agreement. Rules, Orders and Regulations . . . of the Friendly Associated Cotton Spinners . . . of Manchester*, 1792; Chapman, *The Lancashire Cotton Industry*, pp. 213–15; Trades Union Congress, *Women in the Trade Union Movement* (London, 1955), pp. 22–4.

[2] *A Report on the . . . Delegate Meeting of the Operative Spinners of England, Ireland and Scotland* (Manchester, 1829), pp. 17–18, 48; *Webb Manuscripts on Trade Unionism*, Vol. XXXIV, p. 39.

[3] *A Report on the . . . Delegate Meeting of the Operative Spinners of England, Ireland and Scotland*, p. 44.

to adopt more extreme measures in order to perpetuate their traditional system of controls.

Early Factory Agitation. The agitation to limit factory hours in these years also lends support to the proposition that the workers were attempting to protect or restore the traditional division of family labour. In the next chapter we shall trace the course of factory legislation itself; at present we shall analyse the symbolic appropriateness of the agitation among the operatives in the 1820's and 1830's.

It is difficult to establish the origin of the factory operatives' interest in factory hours. Certainly a large-scale "movement" did not begin among the cotton workers until the early 1830's.* There were, however, signs of interest in the first two decades of the century.[1] Certainly the operatives submitted petitions for limiting the hours of "children and others" in 1816 and 1818.[2] The content of this early interest is more interesting than its strength, however. Sir Robert Peel summarized the operatives' attitudes in 1818:

The parents had no objection to this measure [limiting the hours of labour of children by law]. It appeared they were willing that the hours of labour in each day should be limited to eleven; but they had no alternative, as the masters said they must either remove their children altogether, which they could not afford to do, or they must let them work 12 to 14 hours, as the men did.[3]

The operatives wanted their children to work, because of existing family wage rates and because of the contemporary arrangements of apprenticeship and socialization. Long hours for children, moreover, were preferable to no hours at all, no doubt for the same reasons. It seemed as important to operatives as to masters that the labour of children be linked to that of adults. In 1825 the spinners supported an amendment to the Factory Act of 1819, but again their interest was weak and scattered in comparison with what was to come.[4]

---

* This delay in itself is interesting, since most of the issues in the agitation—the health and morals of the children—had been problems of a *more extreme order* several decades before the movement began. I shall treat these and other apparent paradoxes of factory legislation in the next chapter.

[1] J. Doherty, *The Ten Hours Bill* (Manchester, 1845), p. 3; Chapman, *The Lancashire Cotton Industry*, p. 97.

[2] *Parliamentary Debates*, First Series, XXXIV, 1816, cols. 2–3; XXXVII, 1818, cols. 265–8, 1182–3, 1188, 1259–63; Ure, *The Philosophy of Manufactures*, p. 288.

[3] *Parliamentary Debates*, First Series, XXXVIII, 1818, col. 354.

[4] *Ibid.*, Second Series, XIII, 1825, col. 1010; Hutchins and Harrison, *A History of Factory Legislation*, p. 44.

Symptoms of Disturbance in the Family

The British working classes plunged into an avalanche of disturbances of all sorts in the early 1830's—Parliamentary reform, the ten hour agitation, strikes, and co-operation. The cotton factory operatives joined many of these outbursts.

Many a northern operative professed to be a trade unionist, a radical, an Owenite co-operator, and a Ten Hours man all at the same time, actively serving (like John Doherty) in all four movements. There was thus a bewildering tendency for the various organizations to fade into one another; sometimes to vanish altogether and then reappear in another guise.[1]

From this maze we must now extract the spinners' attitudes toward factory hours and relate these attitudes to the operatives' institutional position.

The late 1820's saw a revival of interest in limiting hours on the part of the factory workers. In the spring and summer of 1829—during the Manchester strike—Doherty reported several masters for overworking children. About the time the Ashton-under-Lyne strike of 1830–31 was at the point of collapse, Doherty and many of his followers joined the agitation to limit the hours of children to ten. Meantime, Yorkshire woollen and worsted operatives had been waging a vigorous campaign for ten hours under Richard Oastler during 1830 and 1831. Michael Sadler, another leader in the movement, had introduced a bill into Parliament providing that no one under eighteen work more than ten hours a day, nor more than eight on Saturday, that no one under twenty-one be employed before 6 a.m. and after 7 p.m., and that no child under nine be employed in factories. By early 1832 Lancashire had joined the ten hour movement.[2]

While Lancashire, like Yorkshire, demanded the ten-hour day, the former recognized explicitly that if children's hours were limited to ten, so would adults' hours be,[3] because both were required to attend the machinery. This condition concealed several diverse aims: to limit adults' hours and spread the total employment over greater numbers; to keep children's wages high; to limit the flood of children into the factories by limiting the legal age of entry; and to maintain

[1] Driver, *Tory Radical*, p. 262. For other descriptions of the early 1830's, cf. G. D. H. Cole, *The Life of William Cobbett* (London, 1924), pp. 350–1, and Hobsbawm, "Economic Fluctuations and Some Social Movements since 1800," *op. cit.*, p. 6.

[2] *Manchester Guardian*, May 23, Aug. 1, 1829; *Webb Manuscripts on Trade Unionism*, Vol. XXXIV, p. 139; Hutchins and Harrison, *A History of Factory Legislation*, p. 51.

[3] Driver, *Tory Radical*, pp. 149–50.

that complex set of parental controls which could not be maintained if the child were absent from the mill all or part of the working day.[1] This complex of attitudes, which reappeared explicitly and implicitly in the agitation, shows that the ten hour movement, in the operatives' minds, would have achieved *much the same results* as the strikes against improved machinery—to halt the flood of children and to protect the traditional economic relationships between parent and child by linking their hours and consequently maintaining the existing conditions of work. The element common to the structural strikes and the ten hour agitation was a desire to maintain or revert to the less differentiated structure of the family economy.

After Sadler's bill was deflected into committee and Sadler himself was defeated in election in 1832, a second agitation for a ten hour bill began in the north. The agitation reached a feverish pitch in the spring of 1833, even though petitions to Parliament continued throughout 1831 and 1832.[2] While some operatives opposed the measure for fear of losing children's employment altogether,[3] it is clear that the operative spinners were the primary supporters of a ten hour bill.[4]

This second agitation also was unsuccessful. After Sadler's Com-

[1] Cf., for instance, the evidence of a former Bolton spinner: "What do you think would be the effect of a bill bringing about two relays of children?—I think it would be very injurious to both master and man; as to workmen, parents cannot keep their children without getting them employ; even if it was to perjure themselves, or thereabouts, they must work; they would change about from mills, and go fine counts in the morning and coarse counts in the afternoon, or a card-room hand would go piecing, and a piecer to card-room; they would work, that's my opinion; and if they had not two places to work at, then the other part of the day they'll be out; then they begin to find delight in all sorts of mischief, and . . . I think they'll not like to work at all; for children like play and idleness, and getting into mischief. Some boys and girls that are of a wildish nature, if they were to work only six or eight hours a day, would be running away from work altogether. It would never do at all, never." *Parliamentary Papers*, 1834, XIX, Supplementary Report of Factory Commissioners, p. 471.

[2] *Parliamentary Debates*, Third Series, IV, 1831, col. 502; X, 1832, cols. 20, 894, 1225; XII, 1832, col. 500; XV, 1833, col. 1160; XVI, 1833, cols. 640, 970, 1001.

[3] *Parliamentary Debates*, Third Series, X, 1832, col. 1222; *Poor Man's Advocate*, Mar. 10, 1832.

[4] Tufnell, *Character, Object and Effects of Trades' Unions*, pp. 28–9; *Manchester Guardian*, Jan. 26, 1832; *Poor Man's Advocate*, Jan. 28, Feb. 18, and Mar. 10, 1832, in which John Doherty attacked manufacturers for working night hours; *Parliamentary Papers*, 1833, XX, First Report of the Factory Commissioners, pp. 37–8; 1834, XIX, Supplementary Report of Factory Commissioners, p. 498; 1837–8, VIII, Combinations of Workmen, pp. 274–5. In 1866 Philip Grant devoted his small book, *The Ten Hours' Bill* (Manchester, 1866), to the Operative Fine Spinners of Manchester, the "active promoters" of factory legislation. Also Hutchins and Harrison, *A History of Factory Legislation*, pp. 50–51 and Driver, *Tory Radical*, p. 129.

mittee published its report in 1832, the manufacturers pressed for a Commission to investigate industrial conditions on the spot. This Commission recommended that children between nine and thirteen work no more than *eight* hours per day and prohibited the labour of children under nine altogether. Under such a limitation, children presumably would work under a system of relays, or shifts. The Commission also recommended that masters or others provide minimum education in schools for children between nine and thirteen. These recommendations passed into legislation in 1833.[1]

The ten hour act would have reduced labour of adult and child,[2] restricted the number of children, and continued to link the labour of adult and child. The Factory Act of 1833, with its relay system and its eight-hour limitation, achieved almost the opposite. If, on the one hand, master and operative accepted the relay system, *more* assistants per adult would be required, thus making for even more deterioration of the traditional relationship between adult and child. If, on the other hand, masters dispensed with children altogether because of the burdensomeness of the educational clauses, this would break the tie between adult and young child altogether and force the operatives to recruit assistants among women and juveniles. These classes required higher wages than children.[3] In short, the 1833 legislation, far from acceding to the operatives' demands, threatened to split the economic performance of adults and children. *This would have increased the differentiation of the labour roles in the family economy, the same differentiation imposed by the simultaneous improvements in machinery.* Little wonder, then, that after the Act of 1833 the operatives were "far more vehement for a ten hours' bill [for all labour] than before."[4] The first sign of their despair was a brief but explosive attempt to fuse the movements of co-operation, factory agitation, and trade-unionism.

Earlier in the 1830's the cotton operatives had "looked askance" at co-operation. John Doherty, their leader, had taken an interest in it, however, as the titles of his publications show: *The United Trades' Co-Operative Journal* in 1830 and *The Union Pilot, and Co-Operative Intelligencer* in 1832. During the spring and summer of 1832, his *Poor Man's Advocate* printed several articles outlining the advantages of co-operative communities. The years 1833 and 1834

[1] 3 & 4 William IV, c. 103.

[2] *Parliamentary Papers*, 1833, XX, First Report of Factory Commissioners, p. 38. Both masters and men agreed on this point.

[3] The second seemed to happen in the few years after 1833. Above, pp. 198, 202, and 214.

[4] N. Senior, *Letters on the Factory Act as it affects the Cotton Manufacture* (London, 1837), p. 19.

witnessed Robert Owen's gigantic Grand National Trades Union, some of the aims of which were co-operative projects. The spinners did not join the Grand National; nevertheless, the cotton operatives were deeply influenced by Owenism, and Owenite phrases "survived for years in [their] records." [1]

One manifestation of this interest in the co-operative movement was the fleeting history of the Society for National Regeneration. John Fielden, an agitator for the ten-hour day, organized this movement, which both Robert Owen and William Cobbett endorsed. In the first issue of the Society's journal, the Factory Act of 1833 was attacked as a "scandalous treatment of the earnest prayers of the operatives." The Society's more positive aims were to limit the working day of children *and* adults to eight hours, to maintain existing wage-levels and advance them as soon as practicable, and to begin a system of education to teach men industrial skills and women to "wash, bake, brew, make and mend clothes and stockings; all in all other duties appertaining to Cottage Economy." [2] The Society's literature refers repeatedly to co-operative notions such as the labour theory of value, the attack upon machine-owners who rob labourers of their fair share of this value, etc. There were also attacks upon "the fund-holder, dead weight men, army and navy men, jew, and capitalist." Scapegoating and Utopian idealization of the past were in clear evidence. [3]

In December, 1833, Fielden wrote to Cobbett that the Manchester Short-time Committee (the committee interested in shortened hours) was taking up the idea of limiting labour to eight hours. The journal of the Society for National Regeneration issued several appeals to hand-loom weavers and trade unions. On the practical side, the Society proposed to enter a universal strike demanding forty-eight hours a week at wage-levels current for sixty-nine hours. The date for this universal strike was deferred several times. In April, 1834, however, a short, violent, and unsuccessful strike for eight hours touched off several worker demonstrations in Manchester. The whole movement collapsed, however, within a week after the strike. [4]

[1] Chapman, *The Lancashire Cotton Industry*, p. 222; *The Poor Man's Advocate*, Mar. 10 and July 14, 1832; Webb, *History of Trade Unionism*, pp. 119–22.

[2] *Herald of the Rights of Industry*, Feb. 8, 1834. The reference to cottage economy no doubt shows the influence of William Cobbett's ruralism. Below, pp. 250–52.

[3] *Ibid.*, Mar. 8, 1834. Also Fielden, "Letter to Mr. Fitton," in *National Regeneration* (London, 1834), p. 14. For a more thorough analysis of the "disturbed" elements in the early co-operative ideology, cf. below, pp. 253–61.

[4] *The Pioneer*, Dec. 21, 1833; *Herald of the Rights of Industry*, Feb. 8, 1834; Webb, *History of Trade Unionism*, pp. 136–7, 142–3.

The success of the movement interests us less than the fact that the operatives turned at this time to an obviously impractical demand, shrouded in symptoms of disturbance, for exactly eight hours. The movement followed a long period of costly and unsuccessful strikes as well as the recent indifference and hostility to the operatives' entreaties for a ten-hour day. Furthermore, eight hours coincided with the number of hours which Parliament had recently established for children between nine and thirteen. One element in the abortive scheme for national regeneration, therefore, was to re-link the labour of adult and child, thus returning to a less differentiated family organization. The Society for National Regeneration marked a degeneration of earlier efforts—strikes and ten hour agitation—into an extremely disturbed Utopian movement. Its failure left the factory operatives disorganized and pessimistic.[1]

The characteristics of the operatives' activities during the next three years lend support to this interpretation. In late 1835 "in one town after another" gatherings of operatives voted by "a large majority" to press for a *twelve-hour day* for children, a figure coinciding with the average number of hours worked by adults. Many operatives were prepared to extend the labour of children, even though they had complained bitterly years before of the moral and physical distresses imposed by long hours. This little movement embarrassed some supporters of factory legislation because it threatened to unite employers and workers in opposition to the Act of 1833.[2]

"By 1837 the operatives' Short Time Committees [were] ready to extend young children's hours . . . to *ten* provided they [could] reduce every one else's to the same figure." This stand also troubled the humanitarian promoters of factory legislation in Parliament. Finally, one element of the short-time agitation of 1835–6 was the stipulation that machinery be limited to specified hours to prevent violations of the Act of 1833. While this feature would have assured only a ten-hour day, its advocates envisioned the prevention of any type of relay system.[3] In terms of the family division of labour, the

---

[1] In 1834 "many men who have hitherto been active and indefatigable in the cause of union, seem now to sink into dispair [sic], and give up all hopes of ever seeing the body rise to its former height of power and glory." This was John Doherty's opinion of the cotton operatives' spirits as expressed in *The Quinquarticular System of Organization* (Manchester, 1834), p. 1.

[2] Driver, *Tory Radical*, pp. 309–10. Below, pp. 296–7.

[3] Clapham, *An Economic History of Modern Britain*, p. 574 (italics mine); J. L. and B. Hammond, *Lord Shaftesbury* (London, 1936), pp. 40, 48; Hutchins and Harrison, *A History of Factory Legislation*, pp. 57–8; Alfred, *The History of the Factory Movement*, Vol. II, pp. 85–6, 104–10.

demands for a universal eight-, ten-, or twelve-hour day, and the restrictions on machinery promised to restore the traditional pattern of labour.

Finally, the *way* in which spinners and masters violated the Factory Act of 1833 shows, on the spinners' side, an attempt to restore a whole line of family controls weakened by the Act. Factory Inspectors complained in the 1830's of falsified certificates of age, shuffled relays, lies—in short, the "connivance of the surgeon, the parent, and the employer." The most frequent evasion was to introduce children into the factory at too early an age, working them more than eight hours, and thus eliminating the necessity of hiring adolescents at higher wages. These evasions attempted to restore the economic link between young children and parents, thereby achieving many of the "regressive" objectives which trade-union activity and factory agitation could not obtain. Masters often collaborated with or initiated such evasion for their own economic and administrative reasons. The operatives blamed the masters for the evasions, and the masters blamed the operatives. Both sides probably had a case.[1]

By 1837 it was becoming apparent that short of outright evasion of the law, the operatives themselves were failing in their attempts to restore the traditional division of family labour. Partly because of this frustration and partly because of widespread unemployment and distress between 1837 and 1842, the operatives' activities dispersed over a wide range of political and economic objectives. The opposition to the New Poor Law, which began in 1834, was assimilated to the Chartist agitation in 1838, but factory agitation itself lagged between 1837 and 1841.

In general, however, the spinners were not responsive to the more extreme elements of the turbulence of 1837–42; they assumed only a moderate interest in the branch of Chartism advocating physical force, the universal strike in 1839, and the violent "Plug Plot" of 1842. Several historical commentators have observed that trade-unionism, while coloured by Chartism during the bad times, was never really seduced by the more violent features of the movement. In 1842, W. Cooke Taylor found that all the idle and unemployed factory operatives, block printers and hand-loom weavers of Burnley adhered to the *principles* of Chartism. These factory operatives differed from the printers and weavers, however, because they "deprecated anything like an appeal to physical force" and did not

---

[1] *Parliamentary Debates*, Third Series, XLIV, 1838, col. 422; *Parliamentary Papers*, 1837–8, VIII, Combinations of Workmen, pp. 68–9; 1837, L, Manchester Short-Time Committee, pp. 203–8; Hutchins and Harrison, *A History of Factory Legislation*, pp. 72–7, 85–7.

unite "to their Chartism a hatred of machinery." Whatever "jealousy of machinery" they expressed seemed to be "directed only against the latest improvements; and even in this case it rarely amounts to direct hostility." [1]

In the late 1830's and early 1840's, therefore, the spinners' and other factory operatives' involvement in social explosions was limited, particularly when compared with their activities in the early 1830's and the excessive activities of other groups in 1837–42. One important reason for this is that the factory operatives were gradually approaching the completion of a sequence of differentiation whereby their family and community structure was entering the industrial era on a new basis. By contrast, as we shall see presently, the weavers and related groups were gasping for their very life.

SYMPTOMS OF DISTURBANCE AMONG THE HAND-LOOM WEAVERS

Analytically the hand-loom weavers' death in the nineteenth century parallels the hand-spinners' death in the late eighteenth century. Economic and social factors, however, made the weavers' decline infinitely more painful. In the first place, the spinning machinery conquered the field much more quickly than the power-loom. Equally important, though, is the fact that the hand-spinners and carders were mostly women and children; their reallocation did not dethrone a whole class of principal breadwinnners. The extinction of the adult male weaver displaced the economic head of the household and thus reorganized the occupational structure much more dramatically.

Two basic types of disturbance accompanied the decline of hand-loom weaving from the beginning of the nineteenth century: (1) open pleas and agitation for relief; (2) violence, political agitation, and Utopian movements. These two types alternated, probably cyclically. Unsuccessful pleas for relief often gave rise to expressions of hostility and phantasy. Moreover, there is reason to believe that the weavers themselves fell into classes corresponding to these types of disturbance in the early nineteenth century: (1) "loyal weavers" who desired relief in the form of minimum wages, boards of trade,

---

[1] *Notes of a Tour in the Manufacturing Districts of Lancashire*, pp. 16–17, 67–9; also Webb, *History of Trade Unionism*, pp. 158–63; Clapham, *An Economic History of Modern Britain*, pp. 583–4. On the Plug Plot, cf. G. D. H. Cole and A. W. Filson, *British Working Class Movements* (London, 1951), p. 396; *Manchester Guardian*, Sept. 28, 1842. On the weavers' involvement in the plot, below, pp. 261–2.

assistance for emigration, etc.; (2) weavers who persisted in the more violent and bizarre symptoms of disturbance.[1]

Applications for Relief. As we have seen, the weaving groups were always heavily represented on the poor-registers. Well-to-do citizens occasionally supplemented the poor-laws by direct subscriptions, as in 1796, 1819, 1826, and 1837. Appeals for direct relief reached Parliament from time to time, e.g., in 1810–11, 1820, and 1841. Most of these appeals were direct, desperate, and free from ideological trimmings.[2] Often, however, groups of distressed weavers pressed for some definite scheme which promised to relieve weavers more or less permanently, but which would not involve any reorganization of the trade itself. Nassau Senior warned in 1839 that the parliamentary investigators of the weavers' distress would have to "combat many favourite theories, and may disappoint many vague or extravagant but long-cherished expectations." [3]

The most persistent of these schemes involved the fixing of wages, either through legislation or regulatory boards. As early as 1799 weavers and some masters petitioned for legislative regulation. In the following year Parliament passed not a minimum-wage law but an arbitration act requiring workmen and masters to submit disputes to arbitrators chosen by both parties or to justices of the peace. For various reasons the act was a clear failure. Since it did not compel arbitrators to act, masters appointed them in distant places. Some magistrates interpreted the act as inapplicable to wage disputes. Finally, it became apparent that arbitration was extraordinarily unwieldy. After further appeals, Parliament amended the act in detail in 1803, but it was equally ineffective in keeping up wages.[4] In 1807–8, after a year of tremendous unemployment and wage-reductions, Parliament treated several demands for minimum wages summarily. Another agitation met the same fate in 1809. Again, in 1811, the weavers' appeals flowed in, and again Parliament responded

[1] Hammond, *The Skilled Labourer*, p. 119. The Hammonds date this grouping from the failure of the weavers' strike in 1818.

[2] Read, "The Social and Economic Background to Peterloo," *op. cit.*, pp. 3–4; *Parliamentary Papers*, 1810–11, II, Petition of Several Weavers, pp. 389–90; 1839, Hand-loom Weavers, p. 9; Hammond, *The Skilled Labourer*, pp. 82–4; *Parliamentary Debates*, Second Series, II, 1820, col. 16; Adshead, *Distress in Manchester*, pp. 39–40.

[3] N. Senior *et al.*, *Instructions to Assistant Commissioners* (1839), pp. 31–3.

[4] *Webb Manuscripts on Trade Unionism*, Vol. XXXVII, p. 6; Macpherson, *Annals of Commerce*, Vol. IV, p. 500; Hammond, *The Skilled Labourer*, pp. 63, 68; *Parliamentary Papers*, 1802–3, VIII, Disputes between Masters and Workmen in the Cotton Manufacture, pp. 891–2, 900, 911, 917, 926 ff., 997, 999; 1803–4, V, Differences between Masters and Workmen in the Cotton Manufacture, pp. 211–13.

with advice to be patient.[1] Such appeals were punctuated by violence and property destruction, which we shall analyse presently.

Other types of disturbance overshadowed the interest in wage regulation for the next two decades.[2] About 1832, however, the weavers began an outcry for various kinds of boards of trade to regulate weavers' wages; through the 1830's and 1840's, in fact, weavers felt that the universal remedy was to establish such boards. The promises of these schemes were almost miraculous—to prevent selfishness on the part of individual masters, to erase wage disputes, to check the evils of competition, to limit the hours of labour by raising wages and thereby reducing the supply of weavers, and to "extinguish [those societies called trade unions] ultimately and wholly." [3]

Why did such appeals for relief and regulation receive such summary treatment by the public authorities? It has been pointed out that the philosophy of laissez-faire dominated the social atmosphere in the late eighteenth and early nineteenth centuries.[4] What is noted less often is that this aspect of laissez-faire is a special case of the values of *independence* and *personal responsibility*.[5] The ideal of independence implied self-support and the pursuit of a calling. If an individual failed repeatedly in one line, he should have sought another line better geared to independent self-sufficiency. Artificial props such as minimum wages and boards of trade conflict with these values because they bind him unnaturally to unproductive activity. Little wonder, then, that weavers' appeals for assistance for the weavers should have fallen on deaf ears; they simply were not legitimate under the dominant value-system of the day.

Schemes to *limit* the productivity of other trades—blind opposition

[1] *Parliamentary Papers*, 1808, II, Petitions of Cotton Manufacturers and Journeymen Weavers, pp. 97–9, 119; 1809, III, Petitions of Cotton Manufacturers and Weavers, p. 311; 1810–11, II, Petition of Several Weavers, p. 399; Hammond, *The Skilled Labourer*, pp. 72–7, 82–4; A. E. Bland, P. A. Brown and R. H. Tawney, *English Economic History, Select Documents* (London, 1914), p. 500; Bremner, *The Industries of Scotland*, p. 283; Webb, *History of Trade Unionism*, p. 56; *Parliamentary Debates*, 1st Series, XX, 1811, cols. 239–40.

[2] Bolton and Stockport headed an appeal for minimum wages in 1819. Between 1821 and 1826 a manufacturers' scheme for minimum wages received consideration from time to time. Hammond, *The Skilled Labourer*, pp. 120–6; *Parliamentary Debates*, Second Series, IX, 1823, cols. 598–9.

[3] *Parliamentary Papers*, 1834, X, Hand-loom Weavers, pp. 3, 6–7, 68, 89, 104, 111, 118, 170, 209, 238, 469, 626–30; 1839, Hand-loom Weavers, pp. 23–4; 1840, Hand-loom Weavers, pp. 602–3; J. Maxwell, *Manual Labour versus Machinery* (London, 1834), p. 10; *Letter . . . by the Committee of Manufacturers and Weavers of Bolton*, p. 6.

[4] Webb, *History of Trade Unionism*, pp. 55–6.

[5] Above, pp. 71–5 and 209–13, for definitions of these values.

to machinery, proposals to tax machinery, prohibition of cotton twist exports—fall into the same category.[1] Like permanent relief for weavers, such schemes threatened to prolong sickness without cure by keeping men from more productive lines of endeavour. As such, they could not be tolerated on value grounds.

Miscellaneous notions rounded out the parade of disturbances among the weavers. Some attached their woes to the corn laws; others to the manufacturers' irresponsible behaviour; others to the burdens of the national debt, and still others to bad fabric design which might be overcome by establishing a school of design. In 1836 a bill was introduced into Parliament to publicize the hand-loom weavers' low wages, and in 1838 John Fielden proposed a law either to raise their wages or to provide them with a remission of taxation.[2]

Violence against Property. Interspersed with these applications for relief were several kinds of attacks upon property. While the potential for explosive regression was perpetuated by long-term pressures to force hand-loom weaving out of the economy, actual violence tended to occur during trade slumps.[3] As we shall see, business conditions determined the *timing*, structural pressures the *content* of the violence.

We have already mentioned several early attacks on the power-loom in the late eighteenth century. In the first decade or so of the nineteenth, almost every deep depression saw the destruction of some machinery. The successful weavers' strike of 1808 in Manchester broke out after Parliament rejected an appeal for wage regulation. During this outburst, strikers entered the houses and removed the shuttles of weavers willing to continue at the old rates. Some cloth was slashed and rioting was reported in Manchester, Rochdale, and Preston.[4] Again, after the failure of petitions in 1810–11 and during

1 "Man versus Machine," *The New Anti-Jacobin*, 1833; H. Rose, *Manual Labour versus Brass and Iron* (Manchester, 1825), p. 7; A Looker-on, *A Letter addressed to Farmers and Manufacturers* (York, 1826), pp. 8, 14–15; J. Maden, *Observations on the Use of Power Looms* (Rochdale, 1823), pp. 12–14; Heginbotham, *Stockport: Ancient and Modern*, Vol. I, p. 327; above, pp. 131–6.

2 *Parliamentary Papers*, 1834, X, Hand-loom Weavers, p. 3; 1840, Hand-loom Weavers, pp. 592–8; 1841, Hand-loom Weavers, p. 50; Taylor, *Notes of a Tour in the Manufacturing Districts of Lancashire*, p. 209; *Webb Manuscripts on Trade Unionism*, Vol. XXXVII, p. 46.

3 Love, for instance, claimed that Manchester's notoriety for rioting was justified only in so far as rioting was an index of bad times. B. Love, *Manchester as it Is* (Manchester, 1839), p. 26.

4 Hammond, *The Skilled Labourer*, p. 78; *Annual Register*, 1808, pp. 2, 51, 58; Fishwick, *History of the Parish of Rochdale*, p. 61; Hardwick, *History of the Borough of Preston*, p. 375.

the crisis of 1811–12, Lancashire weavers joined the violent Luddite movement which had been raging for some time. After threats to break machinery in Stockport, rioters ravaged steam-loom mills in Stockport, Westhoughton, and Middleton. This outburst accompanied raids for arms and money, provision riots, and reform meetings. Home Office reports indicate that weavers were largely responsible for the attacks on power-loom establishments. Driven to despair by the economic crisis of the day, the weavers directed their hostility toward the power-loom, the threat of which was becoming more apparent to the weavers.[1]

Between 1816 and 1822 attacks on machinery were rare,[2] possibly because of the hopes which the weavers placed in Parliamentary reform, possibly because of the extremely slow advance of power-loom machinery in these years. Between 1822 and 1825, moreover, when the first real burst of power-loom construction occurred, conditions were sufficiently prosperous for hand-loom weavers and manufacturers to feel no pinch. When prosperity ended abruptly with the crash of 1825–6, mobs of enraged hand-loom weavers flooded the countryside, destroying some 1,000 power-looms valued at £30,000 and clashing periodically with the military. Again in 1829 violence flared. In Manchester attacks were directed primarily at hand-loom *manufactories* (which were beginning to be established at this time), though in some instances the mobs destroyed power-loom machinery as well.[3]

In addition to this sporadic violence, pilfering and fraud apparently increased as the weavers' condition deteriorated. The *Manchester Guardian* complained of its recent increase in 1824. The following year a writer attributed the distress in the Blackburn region to the practice of dealing in embezzled materials. By 1834 a pamphlet claimed that whole manufactories were operating with embezzled goods, and in the same year several manufacturers testified to Parliament that embezzlement was on the increase. In 1839 the Assistant Hand-loom Weavers' Commissioners verified the existence of

[1] The Luddite outbreaks are described in F. O. Darvall, *The Luddite Disturbances and the Machinery of Order* (London, 1932), pp. 233–83.

[2] In these years I found only one instance of an attack on a steam-loom manufactory, that in Glasgow in the depression year 1816. *Annual Register*, 1816, pp. 115–18 (Chr.).

[3] *Annual Register*, 1826, pp. 63–7, 124–5, 128 (Chr.) and Ainsworth, *History and Associations of Altham and Huncoat*, pp. 160–61; *Manchester Guardian*, May 9, 1829; *Annual Register*, 1829, pp. 88–92 (Chr.); Prentice, *Historical Sketches and Personal Recollections of Manchester*, pp. 343 ff. In 1829 in Rochdale there was a repetition of the shuttle-gathering riots of 1808. R. D. Mattley, *Annals of Rochdale* (Rochdale, 1899), p. 13.

"regular and organized establishments" which purchased stolen materials.[1]

What is the significance of this aggression against property? Certainly the attacks were disturbed in the sense that they unleashed the most basic kind of unsocialized behaviour.* They were *misdirected*, moreover; they could not stop the march of capital, they invited severe legal and political repression, and they were irrelevant to the problem of changing an outmoded division of labour. Even though "disturbed" in these senses, however, the attacks were not completely random. Their timing was conditioned by business crises, and their content was conditioned by the most recent symbolic or real pressure to ease the weavers from their trade.

Reform and Cobbettism. In the years immediately after the Napoleonic war (though somewhat in 1811–12 as well) the movement to reform Parliament captured the weavers. That part of this agitation which embraced the outlook of William Cobbett was symptomatic of deep social disturbance.

The social ideology of Cobbettism idealized the division of family labour of the recent past. Cobbett visualized an independent yeoman or craftsman at the head of the family and a wife who rose early, worked hard, reared her children, baked and brewed. What prevented this Utopia was the whole commercial and industrial system—interest, paper money, money-lenders, Jews, rich and crude factory-owners, and sinecures.[2] Cobbett felt, furthermore, that radical reform of representation in Parliament would effect a miraculous achievement of this Utopia.

It all seemed so simple to Cobbett. He wanted a Reform which would create a Parliament really representing, and really responsible to, the whole people. That Parliament, once elected, would straightaway put an end to pensions and places, cut down the Army and Navy, sweep away the monstrous burden of debt, get rid thereafter safely of paper money and inflation, and bring back the good old England which he placed in a visionary past, before the coming of the Bank

---

[1] *Manchester Guardian*, July 17, 1824; Miller, *Blackburn: The Evolution of a Cotton Town*, p. 96; *Letter . . . by the Committee of Manufacturers and Weavers of Bolton*, pp. 10–11; *Parliamentary Papers*, 1834, X, Hand-loom Weavers, pp. 142, 396, 397, 481–2. One witness claimed in 1834 (p. 504), however, that embezzlement was not as serious as formerly. *Parliamentary Papers*, 1839, Hand-loom Weavers, p. 85; MacIntyre, "Textile Industries," *op. cit.*, pp. 137–8.

* Formally this is G-1 of the table of resources. Above, p. 170.

[2] For a critical analysis of these and other elements in Cobbett's thought, cf. C. Brinton, *English Political Thought in the Nineteenth Century* (London, 1949), pp. 65–71, and Cole, *The Life of William Cobbett*, pp. 10–12, 104–5, 144.

of England, the National Debt, the Pitt system, the stock-jobbers, and the hideous new factory towns. Parliamentary Reform, Radical Reform, was the one thing needful.[1]

In terms of the social division of labour, Cobbettism represented a *de*-differentiation of roles. The re-establishment of the domestic economy—which fused economic with other family functions— would erase that great complexity of "artificial" commercial and industrial roles. In this sense Cobbettism was regressive; it was an idealization of a *less differentiated* form of society. Such idealization appears frequently when social roles are under pressure to differentiate. The appeal had an unrealistic ring, furthermore, because of the sheer impossibility of such a mighty retrogression in the face of recent changes in population and social structure and in the face of the dominant English values of the day.

However unrealistic, the ideology of Cobbettism had an appropriate symbolic appeal for the weavers and other dying artisan groups after the war. The release of weavers from the military aggravated the effects of overcrowding, the wage-cuts, and the Irish immigrants.[2] The weavers, with some reason, attached their woes to the new industrial society. Furthermore, the radical reform of Parliament—for which there were some powerful arguments in any case—represented a simple yet grandiose appeal to restore a society in which the outmoded artisan could flourish.

To illustrate the weavers' interest in reform, let us examine the Hampden Clubs, the Blanketeer march, and the Peterloo massacre. The first were small societies to work for the reform of Parliament. The year 1816 in particular saw a flowering of these societies, just at the time when Cobbett's writings were being distributed in great numbers in the manufacturing districts. The Clubs saw several simple cures for the nation's woes—"Universal Suffrage, Annual Parliaments, and a Reform of the Currency." In 1817 the Committee on Secrecy reported that such notions "have been systematically and industriously disseminated amongst Mechanics and Manufacturers, discharged Soldiers and Sailors, and Labourers of all descriptions." We know little of the exact membership of the Clubs. In 1816, however, thirty-eight weavers were arrested in Manchester on political grounds; furthermore, in connection with the Hampden Club of Middleton, it was noticed that seven of the fifteen "radical leaders

[1] Cole, *Life of William Cobbett*, p. 199.
[2] For an examination of some of the causes of the labour surplus, cf. Baines, *History of the Cotton Manufacture in Great Britain*, pp. 493–9; for the rapid wage decline between 1813 and 1820, above, pp. 140–41.

of the region [who] were often seen together" were weavers.[1] These scraps of evidence prove nothing, but illustrate the sorts of people drawn toward Cobbettism and Reform in 1816.

In 1817, some 12,000 persons, presumably weavers for the most part, joined a march on Parliament to enforce radical reform. The marchers were dubbed "Blanketeers" because they carried blankets for sleeping along the road to London. The march collapsed around Stockport in an encounter with the yeomanry.[2]

After an equally dismal failure of their strike in 1818, the weavers turned to parliamentary reform in greater numbers than before. Meetings were held in January and June of 1819, and drilling was reported. The tragic meeting at St. Peter's fields in August of that year was attended by some 60,000 persons, of whom the greatest number were weavers.[3] The banners carried by the workers converging on Manchester for the Peterloo meetings show their kind of interest—"Unity and Strength"; "Liberty and Fraternity"; "Parliaments Annual"; "Suffrage Universal"; "The Royton Female Union —Let us DIE like Men and not be Sold like Slaves"; "Manchester Female Reformers."[4]

Such flare-ups died shortly after Peterloo, both because of improved economic conditions and because of political repression. I have tried to sketch the Reform turmoil of 1816–19 not in terms of justice or injustice to the workers.[5] My concern has been with its appropriate symbolic relationship to the institutional pressures on the weavers at this time. For them, Cobbettism and Reform meant a vague, but nevertheless rapid destruction of the harsh reality of the commercial and industrial world, and a restoration of the stable village and rural society of the not-too-distant past.

[1] Prentice, *Historical Sketches and Personal Recollections of Manchester*, pp. 83–9; Bruton, *The Story of Peterloo*, p. 10; *Parliamentary Papers*, 1817, IV, Committee on Secrecy, p. 3. The terms "mechanic" and "manufacturer" referred to artisan groups in the early nineteenth century.

[2] An observer in Macclesfield described the blanketeers as "weavers, unincumbered by arms, or baggage, except a few blankets," and again as "a host of hungry manufacturers." J. Corry, *The History of Lancashire* (London, 1825), Vol. II, p. 461; also Heginbotham, *Stockport: Ancient and Modern*, pp. 79 ff.; *Parliamentary Papers*, 1817, IV, Committee on Secrecy, p. 9.

[3] Prentice, *Historical Sketches and Personal Recollections of Manchester*, pp. 147 ff.; Bruton, *The Story of Peterloo*, p. 15. Of the 69 traceable signatures on the requisition for the Peterloo meeting, 46 were weavers; of the 200 killed and injured whose occupations are listed, 150 were weavers. Read, "The Social and Economic Background to Peterloo," *op. cit.*, p. 16.

[4] Bruton, *The Story of Peterloo*, pp. 20–21, 24.

[5] It is widely agreed that government officials, with the French Revolution fresh in their minds, were excessively sensitive to the possibility of revolution and hence excessively repressive.

Early Co-operation. One persistent feature of the weavers' decline was their withdrawal from community attachments. Membership in friendly societies declined, public worship fell off, the education of young adults and children decreased, and unions failed completely.[1] "Ever since their condition has deteriorated, they have in great measure lost heart; and because they have not the same outward look as other tradesmen, they generally stay at home [on Sundays] or take skulking walks in the country to get out of sight."[2] The weavers were failing, either by choice or economic necessity, in those very activities which were finding a new and more differentiated place in the lives of the newer classes of factory operatives.

Side by side with this withdrawal was an increasing interest in various Utopian schemes which promised to *maximize* the happiness associated with family and community life. Sometimes these Utopian expressions merely glorified the weavers' past life.[3] Occasionally one claimed to have invented a miraculous hand-loom to restore the status of hand-loom weaving.[4] The most widespread of these promises to revitalize community life, however, appeared in the form of the co-operative ideology of the 1820's and early 1830's.

The growth of co-operation is inseparable from Robert Owen's personal experience as a benevolent capitalist. We have noted his experiment in infant education, community management, and paternalistic welfare in New Lanark. In many ways his cure for society rested on a generalization of this experience:

On a territory agriculturally rich enough to support about 1,000 or 1,500 people, a new village will be built. The buildings will be constructed around a central parallelogram devoted to lawns and gardens. They will include living-quarters with common kitchens, dining-rooms, and recreation-rooms, but providing separate apartments for each family. A school, a community hall, and other necessary public buildings will complete the parallelogram. Barns and workshops will be a little apart. The community will be self-supporting as far as possible in regard to food. Owen even defends spade culture as the most productive form of agricultural labour. The machine is not wholly repudiated, however. Each community will manufacture in model factories what its resources best provide

---

[1] *Parliamentary Papers,* 1834, X, Hand-loom Weavers, pp. 45, 55, 61, 65, 100, 207, 761, 798–9; 1839, Hand-loom Weavers, pp. 22–4.

[2] *Parliamentary Papers,* 1834, X, Hand-loom Weavers, p. 45.

[3] W. Thom, *Rhymes and Recollections of a Hand-loom Weaver* (London, 1844), p. 32; Artisan, *Machinery* (London, 1843), p. 4.

[4] J. J. Sadler, *The New Invention of Double and Quadruple . . . Looms* (London, 1831), pp. 5–8, 10–11.

it with. Free trade between communities will then ensure an ample supply of such goods for all.[1]

Owen rendered his plan ideologically feasible with two assumptions concerning economic and social nature: (1) "Labour is the source of all wealth,"[2] or the radical labour theory of value. The capitalist or competitive system not only utilized labour inefficiently, but deprived labourers of their just rewards for producing real wealth. Co-operative communities promised to right this imbalance. (2) Human nature is completely pliable. "The will of man has no power whatever over his opinions: he must, and ever did, and ever will believe what has been, is, or may be impressed on his mind by his predecessors, and the circumstances which surround him."[3] Thus the co-operative community, the ideal environment, could produce ideal men. One feature of the community was to dissolve the family as a socializing unit. "Children are to be separated from their parents at the age of three, though of course they will see a great deal of them in normal community life."[4]

In many ways Owenism and Cobbettism were parallel ideologies, even though the adherents of each often antagonized the other in practice.[5] Each found industrial capitalism, factories, and urbanism distasteful. Each considered the urban-industrial family a perversion of human nature, Cobbett because it deviated from the rural or village model of the past, and Owen because it created vice in adult and child. The two ideologies differed, however, in their suggested cures. Cobbett proposed—albeit with a vague connection between parliamentary reform and social reform—to *destroy* the new way of life by means of a gigantic retrogression to a less differentiated community. Owen, on the other hand, promised to *absorb* and thereby cure the evil elements of capitalism by a proliferation of multi-functional communities. Everything would be assimilated to the parallelogram communities. Capital would not be a differentiated medium, but would be inseparable from the community. Labour roles would be less specialized. Above all, Owenism glorified the notion of union as such, which would eliminate—through happiness and love—all possible bases for conflicts of interest. Despite these differences, however, Owenism promised, like Cobbettism, a massive *de-differentiation* of social roles. Let us illustrate these promises of early co-operation.

[1] Brinton, *English Political Thought in the Nineteenth Century*, pp. 54–5.
[2] *Lancashire Cooperator*, June 11, 1831.
[3] Owen, *A New View of Society*, p. 47.
[4] Brinton, *English Political Thought in the Nineteenth Century*, p. 55.
[5] Cole, *Life of William Cobbett*, pp. 10–12.

The co-operative literature of the 1820's and 1830's—including the popular organ in Lancashire and Yorkshire—displayed a basic hostility to the existing use of machinery. "Under the present system of competition [machinery's] influence tends to degrade, to pauperize, and enslave mankind." [1] "You [labourers] have received no higher wages, although with your machine you may perform the work of ten men; although you may produce ten times the value of your own labour; therefore, machinery works against labour. . . . It works for the master, not for the workman." [2]

Under co-operation, however, machinery was to become "one of the greatest blessings of mankind." [3] It was not to be segregated from, but rather an *aspect of* collective effort. William Thompson, who felt that the wish to return to domestic manufactures was "utterly vain," nevertheless promised that the co-operative community had the advantages of both the machinery economy and the domestic economy:

Nothing but the voluntary agreement of *large numbers* of the industrious classes themselves . . . to settle together and supply each others' wants, agricultural and manufacturing, in a state of honest social equality, with all the *means* of happiness within the sphere of human regulation, can accomplish the great object of the union of knowledge and cheapness with domestic manufactures and virtuous habits. Thus only, by co-operative industry, can domestic manufactures be rendered compatible with machinery, can manufactures be again domesticated. [4]

Machinery was not to be associated with the artificial role of the capitalist. Such is an instance of the promised powers of absorption; the capitalist was to disappear, and his old function was to be reduced to an aspect of the co-operative community.

Co-operators promised also to obliterate many middlemen. By definition co-operation meant the "new power of industry, constituted by the equitable *combination* of worker, capitalist, and consumer." [5] Thompson advised to "let some . . . raise your own food,

[1] *Report of Proceedings . . . of the Society for the Promotion of Co-operative Knowledge* (London, 1829), p. 15.

[2] F. Baker, *Second Lecture on Co-operation Delivered . . . at . . . Bolton* (1830). Also *Lancashire Cooperator*, July 23, 1831; *Lancashire and Yorkshire Cooperator*, Nov. 12, 1831.

[3] *Report of Proceedings . . . of the Society for the Promotion of Co-operative Knowledge*, p. 15.

[4] *Practical Directions for the Speedy and Economical Establishment of Communities* (London, 1830).

[5] G. Holyoake, *The History of Cooperation in England* (London, 1875), Vol. I, p. 2. (Italics mine.)

let others on that land erect your work-houses and dwellings, let others fabricate linen, woollen, and cotton articles for your clothing," etc.[1] This simple community had a division of labour, but certainly retreated from the advanced differentiation between agricultural and industrial labour in the early nineteenth century. Furthermore, members of the co-operative community would "have no masters," and hence would "not be liable to be discharged and cast out to starve on the wide world to make room for machines." Communities would eliminate profit and extinguish the profit-maker.[2]

This grand absorption of capitalist roles promised greater economic productivity. The distributional inefficiencies in agriculture and manufacture, as well as the waste of one cook per family, would be remedied by establishing all "dwellings, manufactures and agricultural concerns, *contiguous to each other*."[3] A co-operative publication, noting the great weekly production of cotton in Manchester, went on to promise that "wonderful as this is . . . it is comparatively nothing, to what might, under another system of society, be effected. Cotton might then be spun in a week, sufficient to girt the universe, and to make garments for all the inhabitants of all the planets!" [4]

A final object of concern was the inequality between the sexes. In 1825 William Thompson issued a small book, the title of which indicates its contents: *Appeal of One Half of the Human Race, Women, against the Pretensions of the Other Half, Men, to retain them in Political, and thence in Civil and Domestic, Slavery*. Women, he complained, were "isolated and stultified with their children, with their fire and food-preparing processes" and thereby unprepared intellectually and emotionally for the world. From childhood they were systematically excluded from educational and vocational opportunities. The custom of marriage, further, made the wife the "literal unequivocal *slave* of the man who may be styled her husband." The aim of the co-operators' Social Science, according to Thompson, was to "supersede the pursuit of wealth, the confined object of Political Economy" and to produce "a real equality of happiness between the sexes, raising both equally in the scale of wisdom, virtue, and enjoyments." The co-operative community,

1 W. Thompson, *Labor Rewarded* (London, 1827), pp. 108–9.

2 *Ibid.*, p. 109. Beatrice Potter described the disappearance of profits as the "keystone of Robert Owen's Co-operative system of industry." *The Cooperative Movement in Great Britain* (London, 1930), p. 21.

3 Thompson, *Labor Rewarded*, pp. 93–4.

4 *The Crisis*, Oct. 27, 1832.

moreover, was the avenue for minimizing the conventional differences between the sexes.[1]

Often co-operators foresaw a mystical absorption of the individual into a grand collectivity which would erase all conflicts. The literature glorified "union" or "co-operation" in itself. Thompson asked, "by what means can we secure to labor the whole products of its exertions?" and answered, "it is impracticable to secure to *individual* laborers the whole product of their own exertions: it can only be done collectively, or in large numbers." In fact, Thompson prefaced every paragraph of advice to co-operators with the phrase "UNITE IN LARGE NUMBERS."[2] This great union would override and eventually absorb all other working-class organizations. William King, a leading co-operator in the 1820's and 1830's, granted friendly societies and trade unions a place in the contemporary imperfect world, but co-operation would one day "[swallow] up every other plan of benefiting the workman, and providing for him in want of employment, sickness, and old age."[3]

Much of the early literature leads to the impression that the principle of union would re-create the unity and warmth of family and friends by removing the basis of all conflict of interest. In one passage William King spoke of the family as "the place where we are to look for the purest and happiest feelings which man is permitted to enjoy upon earth," in which "all have a common lot, either in prosperity or adversity." A few paragraphs later he outlined some of the more general advantages of co-operation:

... the sweetest of all bonds is that which is formed not merely by a common science, but by a congenial disposition and heart. It is from the heart that every valuable feeling springs, and every source of pleasure and happiness. No kind of pursuit, or knowledge, becomes a source of happiness to a man, till it takes fast hold of the heart and affections ...

It is oppressive to contemplate the picture of man ... approaching to friendless destitution. The heart mourns over it, and seeks relief in imagining the possibility of a state of things, in which we may open our bosom, and receive into our arms, all who wear the fair form and features of man. Such is the state which Co-operation

[1] W. Thompson, *Appeal of One Half of the Human Race* (London, 1825), pp. iii–iv, 41, 66, 177–81. Also *The Position of Women in Harmony* (London, 1841).

[2] *Labor Rewarded*, pp. 37, 108–14. Also *Lancashire Cooperator*, July 9, 1832, in which a writer suggested that "the only effective remedy for national distress is UNION."

[3] *The Co-operator*, Aug. 1, 1829. Also May 1, 1828, Apr. 1, May 1, July 1, and Aug. 1, 1829. *The Co-operator* is reproduced in full in T. W. Mercer, *Co-operation's Prophet* (Manchester, 1947).

holds out, and Co-operation alone. Co-operation removes the almost insurmountable obstacles to friendship, namely—self-interest, rivalry, jealousy, and envy. When two persons have an inclination to cultivate a friendship for each other, they seldom proceed far without finding their interests clash . . . Men must have different pursuits, and be wholly independent of each other, in order to stand any chance of a real and sincere friendship.[1]

On occasion this state of union had overtones of religious bliss. " [Men will establish communities] very soon. The mist of ignorance is disappearing from before the beautiful scenes of social happiness, and they will not be long before they are in possession. Gracious Father of universal nature! hasten the glorious day; let thy kingdom come upon earth that all men may love Thee, and love one another!"[2] These were not unread words of philosophers, but were circulated among the body of co-operators.

How did such doctrines succeed among the working classes? Before 1825 the interest in co-operation was limited to the well-to-do and the aristocracy of several lands. About 1825, however, co-operation spread to the working classes, and the movement mushroomed fully into its "enthusiastic period" which endured until approximately 1830.[3] All inferences as to the selective interest of the early co-operative ideology are necessarily indirect. It seems, however, that its appeal was strongest among the craftsmen and artisan classes which were gradually slipping from the industrial scene. In the co-operative literature, the power-loom was a favourite example of the evils of machinery. Much of the "straight" news in these journals, moreover, dealt with the weavers' misery.[4] In 1830 a speaker on co-operation prefaced his remarks to a Bolton audience as follows:

About one-third of our working population . . . consists of weavers and labourers, whose average earnings do not amount to a sum sufficient to bring up and maintain their families without parochial assistance. It is this portion of the community, for the most part decent and respectable in their lives, which is suffering most from the depression of wages, and the hardships of the times. It is to this

[1] *The Co-operator*, Nov. 1, 1828.
[2] *Lancashire and Yorkshire Cooperator*, Oct. 1, 1831. Owen himself, however, rejected all the organized religions of mankind.
[3] Podmore, *Robert Owen*, pp. 242–3; Cole, *A Short History of the British Working Class Movement*, pp. 82–3; Holyoake, *The History of Cooperation in England*, pp. 103–55. Also Prentice, *Historical Sketches and Personal Recollections of Manchester*, p. 114.
[4] *Lancashire Cooperator*, July 23, Aug. 20, 1831; *Lancashire and Yorkshire Cooperator*, Dec. 8, 1831, Jan. 7, 1832.

class of my poor fellow-creatures in particular, that I desire to recommend the system of co-operation, as the only means which, at present, seem calculated to diminish the evils under which they live.[1]

A speaker in Runcorn recommended in the following year that

. . . arrangements might easily be made for producing cheap, comfortable, and durable clothing for Co-operators; by their working a loom of their own: the fabrics necessary for comfort and durability, are easily produced in the present day, and if Co-operators can only be rational in their proceedings, and moderate in their desires, they have the power of clothing themselves and families without much difficulty.[2]

At a meeting of delegates in 1829, the advocates of co-operation resolved unanimously to employ the distressed Spitalfields weavers on the principles of co-operation.[3] From such sketchy evidence we might conclude that co-operators were certainly interested in the weaving population, and if we may rely on the kind of advice and news given to various audiences, the weavers probably reciprocated with an interest in co-operation. Before 1833–4, on the other hand, when the factory operatives were drawn briefly into the Society for National Regeneration, there is little evidence of their interest in Utopian co-operative principles. In 1833 a former operative from Stockport said that among the factory workers in that town "there is one or two [shops] upon the cooperative system, but the number of members belonging to them is not very great." [4]

What was the institutional basis for this selective appeal? For the weavers the picture was as black as it had ever been. Overcrowding and the power-loom forced weavers' average wages, which had stabilized at something like 8s. 3d. between 1818 and 1825, to something nearer to 6s. per week between 1825 and 1831. Apprenticeship in weaving proved unprofitable in most branches, and weavers were sending their wives and children into the factories in greater numbers. While dependents' employment might relieve the weaver's financial position, it aggravated the pressures weighing upon him by displacing him as economic head of the family. As a result of their deteriorating position, furthermore, weavers were gradually withdrawing from

[1] F. Baker, *First Lecture on Co-operation* (Bolton, 1830).
[2] *An Address to the Working Classes on Practical Co-operation* (Runcorn, 1831), p. 6.
[3] *Report of Proceedings . . . of the Society for the Promotion of Co-operative Knowledge*, p. 19.
[4] *Parliamentary Papers*, 1833, VI, Manufactures, Commerce and Shipping, p. 629.

religious, educational, and community life. In the light of these economic and social pressures, the symbolic appeal of the Utopian co-operative ideology seems clear. Co-operation promised to eliminate capital and capitalistic machinery by absorbing capitalists and profit-makers. The "artificial" gains of these classes would thereby be transferred, by all justice, to those workpeople who actually provided the labour. Furthermore, the co-operative community promised to eliminate the vagaries of the market and distribution system simply by eliminating all middlemen. In addition to these economic prospects, co-operation promised to reduce the differences between the sexes, thus liquidating at a blow all the income and status problems faced by the hand-worker in the days of his decline. If violence, pleas for assistance, and demands for reform had fallen on deaf or unsympathetic ears, why not therefore remove the evils of the contemporary world by absorbing them into a community of love and co-operation which had none of the real world's economic hardships, conflicts of interest, and withering status?

In general the spinners were not so drawn into co-operation in those years (1825–32) as the weavers and other groups. By 1833–5, however, the factory population faced disturbances which were, if not economically dire, certainly disequilibrating for the family economy. Strikes and factory agitation had failed to maintain the withering economic ties in the family; the Factory Act of 1833 recently had accentuated their failure. Co-operation provided a ready solution: to eliminate the master, to gain his artificial profit, and to restore the ideal family life of the recent past, all by a rapid National Regeneration. For the weavers who were chronically ill and for the factory operatives who were momentarily disturbed, co-operation was a sort of magic which promised to erase those evils which practical means could not move.

In summary, both Owenism and Cobbettism were "regressive" symptoms of disturbance which appealed selectively to groups under institutional pressure in the cotton industry. Both had their non-rational elements because they proposed gigantic solutions based upon social de-differentiation which were clearly unattainable, given the historical circumstances and trends of the time.* Both ideologies were, however, later brought to bear upon more realistic lines of action which gave rise to the formation of new and more solid social units.** The early stages of each nevertheless fit analytically into Step 2 of the sequence of structural change by which the family life

* This represents a denial of the "given data" of the social environment (*A*-1). Above, p. 38.
** Cf. especially the course of co-operation, Chapter XIII.

of both weavers and spinners was being eased—in different ways and by different institutional conditions—toward a higher level of differentiation.

Chartism. Before hand-loom weaving died, it emitted a final gasp in the form of extreme Chartism. Not only were the hand-loom weavers more attracted to the movement than factory operatives, but they embraced the more desperate elements of violence and Utopianism, particularly in the depression periods of 1838–9 and 1841–2.

Though the aim of Chartism was relatively simple—to achieve the six principles of the People's Charter [1]—its means, its types of adherents, and its Utopian results were diverse and confused. Perhaps the deepest split in the Chartist ranks concerned the use of moral and physical force as means for obtaining the Charter. The advocates of the former favoured processions, demonstrations, petitions, etc., whereas the physical-force advocates pressed for the use of arms, drilling, destruction of property, etc. This conflict, which dated from the outbreaks of 1838, appeared time and time again in the Chartist assemblies, and contributed to the failure of unified group action.[2] While the evidence illustrating the interest of various occupations in each faction is necessarily indirect, it appears that hand-loom weavers were well represented among the adherents of physical force.

We have noted Taylor's remark that the division between moral and physical force corresponded to the division between factory operatives on the one hand and the weavers and block printers [3] on

[1] Universal manhood suffrage, annual parliaments, vote by ballot, no property qualification, payment of members, and equal voting districts.

[2] R. G. Gammage, *History of the Chartist Movement 1837–1854* (London, 1894), pp. 83 ff., 90 ff., 106 ff., 193 ff., 267–8. For a description of the adherents of physical and moral force, respectively, cf. *Parliamentary Papers*, 1840, Hand-loom Weavers, p. 71. In addition to the basic split concerning means of agitation, various other schemes commanded the attention of small sub-groups of Chartists from time to time: the plan to establish a great complex of propagandistic organs such as schools, libraries, paid missionaries, etc., in order to educate the public; the idea for universal suffrage for women as well as men; and a land scheme adopted by later Chartists which was reminiscent of the earlier Owenite schemes. Each splinter group which formed around one of these issues initiated a sequence of criticism and mutual accusation within the Chartist ranks. It seemed, in fact, that many Chartists were committed only to "a passionate negation" which attached itself to one scheme after another. Cf. *Parliamentary Papers*, 1843, XXVII, Factory Inspectors, p. 299; Alfred, *The History of the Factory Movement*, Vol. II, p. 84; Morris, *The History of the Labour Movement in England*, pp. 669–70, 838–40.

[3] The printers also were suffering the pangs of technological displacement at this time. G. Turnbull, *A History of the Calico Printing Industry of Great Britain* (Altrincham, 1951), pp. 190–94.

the other, in one Lancashire community. The historian of the Chartist movement noted the close association between the "distressed and starving Spitalfields weavers" and the explosive formation of a "Democratic Association" at a Chartist conference in London. The leader of this group was George Harney, a notorious advocate of physical force. It seemed that the weavers were ready to accept any-thing promising the "shortest termination to their miseries." [1] There is prominent reference to the weavers' suffering in speeches of other advocates of physical force, such as the Rev. J. R. Stephens. Further, in communities devoted to weaving, such as Colne, Chartism was reported "to be advancing with fearful rapidity." [2] First-hand and historical accounts show that the weavers were amply represented in the rioting connected with the Plug Plot of 1842. [3] Finally, the concentration of Irish among the Chartist leaders and the appearance of Irish issues in the Chartist movement provide indirect evidence of the weavers' interest, because of the great attraction of poor Irish immigrants to hand-loom weaving. [4]

Failure of Trade Unionism among the Weavers. The short-lived and abortive attempts at combination among the weavers after 1818 justify the judgment that "organized action" was dead by that date. [5] Several scattered attempts at union in the West of Scotland, Man-chester, and Bolton in 1824 failed either to gain the weavers' demands or to maintain a permanent organization. [6] A similar effort by the Manchester quilting weavers illustrates the pathetic and almost pleading tone of the weavers. [7] In 1831 a meeting of weavers to

[1] Gammage, *History of the Chartist Movement*, pp. 53–4.
[2] F. F. Rosenblatt, *The Chartist Movement in its Social and Economic Aspects* (New York, 1916), p. 126; Taylor, *Notes of a Tour in the Manufacturing Districts of Lancashire*, p. 84. The *Manchester Guardian* reported on Aug. 12, 1840, that riots broke out against a solicitor in Colne who was working openly against Chartism. See also *Annual Register*, 1840, p. 66 (Chr.).
[3] One major disturbance following the strikes was the march of some 20,000 weavers from Stalybridge to Manchester after a wage reduction. The whole series of disturbances in 1842 was surrounded by Chartist symbols. J. West, *A History of the Chartist Movement* (London, 1920), pp. 186–8. For first-hand accounts, cf. B. Brierley, *Home Memories, and Recollections of a Life* (Manchester, 1886), pp. 23–4, and *Tales and Sketches of Lancashire Life* (Manchester, 1862–3), pp. 83–93.
[4] Redford, *Labour Migration in England*, p. 113; Gammage, *History of the Chartist Movement*, pp. 297–8.
[5] Hammond, *The Skilled Labourer*, p. 119.
[6] *Rules for the Union of Weavers* (Manchester, 1824); *Manchester Guardian*, Oct. 20, 1824; *Webb Manuscripts on Trade Unionism*, Vol. VII, p. 172; Vol. XXXVII, p. 13 ff.; *Parliamentary Papers*, 1825, IV, Combinations, pp. 550–52.
[7] The address preceding the Rules of this organization complains: "The name of Weaver, is becoming almost synonymous with that of vagrant, and although

prevent reductions of wages and to form an organization drew only 150 or 200 persons. Apparently all such attempts since 1826 had met a similar fate. In 1830–31 several weavers' unions paid fees to the National Association for Protection of Labour, but most of these were power-loom weavers' organizations.[1] Those who attributed the weavers' failure in unionism to their dispersion over the countryside [2] forgot the masses of weavers concentrated in Manchester and forgot the eighteenth century when weavers' clubs were reasonably effective. The weavers' inability to organize, while hindered by their dispersion, was primarily a symptom of the larger institutional process by which their trade was being eased forcibly from the industrial scene.

Step 3. Handling and Channelling. Such were the disturbances which seized the hand-loom weavers in the early nineteenth century. Initially these were met by various stop-gap measures which always predate the actual appearance of new, more differentiated forms. The police and military, for instance, grappled immediately with each outburst of workers' violence and property destruction. Simultaneously, particularly in the case of destruction of machinery, community leaders issued appeals to the dissident to be patient and to recognize the long-term promises of the detested machines.[3]

The parliamentary bodies on emigration in 1826 and 1827 and on hand-loom weavers in 1834, 1835, and 1839–41 also cushioned the weavers' disturbed displays. The very formation of such investigatory bodies and their patient attention to the weavers' complaints, appeals, and suggestions show the "handling" process at work. These bodies also "channelled" the tensions, though not usually to the weavers' satisfaction. The Select Committee in 1834 hesitated to endorse any particular remedy suggested by the weavers, but merely called vaguely for some legislative attention. In the following year the committee also recorded the weavers' complaints, but recommended only

the produce of the Loom forms the most important branch of trade in this great commercial nation, and produces more wealth and splendor than any other branch of the Kingdom, yet still the POOR WEAVERS (as we are often tauntingly called) are not allowed to occupy a place in decent society . . ." *Articles, Rules and Regulations . . . of Quilting Weavers in Manchester and Neighbourhood* (Manchester, 1829).

[1] *Manchester Guardian*, Nov. 5, 1831; *Parliamentary Papers*, 1835, XIII, Hand-loom Weavers, p. 202; *Webb Manuscripts on Trade Unionism*, Vol. XXXVII, p. 44.

[2] *Parliamentary Papers*, 1834, X, Hand-loom Weavers, p. 441.

[3] E.g., Ramsbotham, *Thoughts on the Use of Machines*, which followed the 1779 outrages; E. Baines, *An Address to the Unemployed Workmen of Yorkshire and Lancashire* (London, 1826), which followed the destruction of power-looms. Also H. Martineau, *The Rioters* (Wellington, 1827), for a literary representation of the futility of machine destruction.

minor legislation such as the tightening of embezzlement laws and more exact means of specifying the length and breadth of woven materials to minimize fraud. Finally, the Commissioners on Hand-loom Weavers in 1841 repeated some of these recommendations, but above all encouraged emigration and education as the only means of decreasing the number of weavers.[1] The effect of these recommendations was to maintain a delicate balance between (*a*) tolerating the complaints and schemes of the distressed groups and (*b*) simultaneously easing them into other trades. As such, the Parliamentary bodies were typical of agencies specializing in social control.

Formally, hand-loom weaving completed its process of structural differentiation when the domestic weaving population died out. This occurred as the younger members of weavers' families moved gradually into other occupational roles more attuned to the growing industrialization of society. It is difficult to trace the course of particular families into new occupations. In fact, very few weavers went into power-loom weaving. It is nevertheless clear that through the gradual and painful process of dispersion and emigration, the hand-loom weavers were transferred from the outmoded structure which fused the family's economic activities with other family activities into occupations which called for a more differentiated family structure.

[1] *Parliamentary Papers*, 1834, X, Hand-loom Weavers, pp. 3–4; 1835, XIII, Hand-loom Weavers, p. 19; 1841, Hand-loom Weavers, pp. 118–24.

CHAPTER XI

DIFFERENTIATION OF THE FAMILY STRUCTURE: FACTORY LEGISLATION

Introduction. Heretofore we have treated the factory question solely in its significance for the factory operatives. Their agitation in the 1820's and 1830's was one avenue taken to protect the traditional relationship between adult and child, to perpetuate the structure of wages, to limit the recruitment of labourers into the industry, and to maintain the father's economic authority.

Limiting our discussion of the factory question to a conservative movement which was stymied by factory legislation, however, does not exhaust the matter. The factory legislation, as it developed between 1833 and 1847, had more far-reaching implications: (1) It led the family economy toward a greater differentiation of economic roles and thus supplemented the concurrent technological changes which precipitated the agitation in the first place. By this process the economic role of the head of the family became more specialized in so far as this role no longer implied co-operation with, training of, and authority over dependent family members. (2) It hastened the establishment of new lines of differentiation between the family economy and such spheres as education and religion. In this chapter we shall analyse these processes, which guided the family economy of the factory operatives to a level of *structural differentiation* more in harmony with the new industrial world.

In general, factory legislation has been hailed as a working-class victory over the capitalists, who, either through natural interest or malice, had been grinding the workers into deeper and deeper misery. Such an approach [1] contains, however, several paradoxes which we shall examine more thoroughly later. First, the miseries of the workers were *not* those claimed by the factory agitators, such as bad health and overwork. The social environment for responding to illness and the social context of work changed, but working conditions in a physical sense were probably improving in the 1820's and

[1] We shall consider this and several other approaches to working-class matters in Chapter XIV.

265

1830's. Second, factory agitation was regressive in so far as it attempted to restore the family economy to a less differentiated structure; factory legislation utilized this agitation to ease the family to a *more differentiated* level. Hence the legislation was not a simple victory for the operatives. Third, a shorter factory day was hardly a simple defeat for the capitalists, since in the end factory legislation brought the conditions of labour more in harmony with the evolving capitalist system. Finally, even though factory legislation "turned the tables" on the workers in one sense, the factory population found that the once-abhorred consequences of this legislation constituted a more satisfactory *modus vivendi* in the new industrial scene.

Factory legislation bristles, therefore, with misconceptions, confusions, and unanticipated consequences. By utilizing the model of structural differentiation, we hope to iron out some of these knotty paradoxes. This model represents historical change as a sequence of "value-added" in which early symptoms of disturbance are pared gradually and brought into line to produce a new and more differentiated social structure. Hence the ten hour agitation in the 1820's was largely a "regressive" disturbance, while the agitation for the same legislation in the 1840's was by and large a movement to complete a well-advanced process of differentiation. Furthermore, by using the logic of regressive disturbances, we may shed some light on the mass of claims, counterclaims, exaggerations, and distortions concerning the evils of the factory system.

The Values underlying the Factory Question. In our previous discussion of values we assigned great weight to the independence and responsibility of the individual in the realm of his chosen calling. Any restriction of his choice in these occupational matters would infringe on his freedom and independence. One such infringement would be the interference with the terms of employment between master and man. If a man found his work or hours uncongenial, he had the right and ability—because he was independent and responsible—to leave his master or even his industry for another. Correspondingly, to limit conditions of employment *for* the individual would impose on his basic independence.

Time and again this "inborn sentiment of Englishmen" for independence [1] touched the problem of limiting work-people's hours. For those who opposed such limitations, the strongest argument was that this interfered with the independence of the adult

---

[1] J. M. Baernreither, *English Associations of Working Men* (London, 1889), p. 298.

male.[1] Proponents as well realized that "it was against principle to interfere with labour."[2] Hence the advocates of factory legislation had to demonstrate that those affected by the legislation—namely women and children—were not free agents anyway, and that limitations of hours did not actually interfere with independent labour decisions.[3] Frederick Robinson said of impending legislation in 1818: "If the bill went directly to interfere with the labour of adults, he thought it would be objectionable; but it would be going too far to say, that by protecting the children the adults might be incidentally interfered with and that therefore the children should be left as they were."[4] A quarter-century later Leonard Horner defended the 1844 restrictions on women's hours on the grounds that "no instances have come to my knowledge of adult women having expressed any regret at their *rights* being thus far interfered with."[5]

In fact the direct restriction on adult males' hours never passed into law; rather it remained a by-product of restrictions on those who were not "free agents." In 1849 an active supporter of factory legislation admitted that

it had been anticipated that the passing of the factory act would have the effect of preventing the unwilling toil of a great many adults; but the fact was that very many adult males were being employed 14 hours, and, he understood, even 15 hours per day, and if it were to be proposed in the house of commons to pass an act to protect adult males in factories, it would be answered that it was an invasion of the rights of an Englishman to prevent him from working as long as he pleased; and the house of commons would not listen to the proposal for a moment.[6]

The value of independence, therefore, set clear limits on restricting the conditions of labour.

[1] When all was said and done on the matter of health and the rest, Kirkman Finlay "put it to the House, whether, with the contradictory testimony before it, it was prepared to legislate upon the subject—to regulate free labour, and to interpose between the father and his child?" *Parliamentary Debates*, First Series, XXXVIII, 1818, col. 369; also XXXIV, 1816, col. 3.

[2] *Ibid.*, First Series, XXXIII, 1816, col. 884.

[3] *Ibid.*, First Series, XXXVII, 1818, cols. 1262–3; Third Series, XLVIII, 1839, col. 1071. Also *Information Concerning the State of Children Employed in Cotton Factories* (Manchester, 1818), pp. 3–4; *Answers to certain Objections to Sir Robert Peel's Bill* (Manchester, 1819), pp. 17–20.

[4] *Parliamentary Debates*, First Series, XXXVIII, 1818, col. 371.

[5] *Parliamentary Papers*, 1845, XXV, Factory Inspectors, pp. 444–5; for the rationale for limiting women's hours in the first place, cf. *Parliamentary Debates*, Third Series, LXXIII, 1844, col. 1118; LXXIV, 1844, cols. 657–8.

[6] *Manchester Guardian*, Jan. 10, 1849. Speech of Charles Hindley.

Differentiation of the Family Structure: Factory Legislation

Closely allied with the value of adult male independence was the traditional division of the respective roles of man and wife. The husband was chief breadwinner in the economic market, even though his dependents might assist him substantially. Correspondingly, women carried more responsibility for the emotional aspects of child-rearing and the management of psychological tensions.[1] A late eighteenth-century commentator on the duties of women summarized the female character thus:

> In three particulars, each of which is of extreme and never-ceasing concern to the welfare of mankind, the effect of the female character is most important.
> First, in contributing daily and hourly to the comfort of husbands, of parents, of brothers and sisters, and of other relations, connections and friends, in the intercourse of domestic life, under every vicissitude of sickness and health, of joy and affliction.
> Secondly, in forming and improving the general manners, dispositions, and conduct of the other sex, by society and example.
> Thirdly, in modelling the human mind during the early stages of its growth, and fixing, while it is yet ductile, its growing principles of action; children of each sex being, in general under maternal tuition during their childhood, and girls until they become women.[2]

Even before the Victorian era this skewing of responsibility led to a double standard of morality.

> It is *this* that renders the Crime of Adultery, so particularly heinous in Women. When a married *Man* commits it, he throws out *no* defiance to the World—for the World thinks too lightly of the Offense. He makes no Sacrifice of Character. A Man cannot *sink* to a Level with an Adultress, *till he has forsaken his Post in Battle.* Courage is the *male* point of Honour—Chastity the female.[3]

As chief economic agent for the family, the father was responsible for his son's economic training and education. While apprenticeship had decayed in the eighteenth century, the tradition of training one's son into a trade held firm, even in the early factory environment.[4] The relationship between master and apprentice, or father and son, dealt with non-technical matters as well, especially "the forma-

---

[1] This is an instance of division of roles between husband and wife on the "instrumental-expressive" axis. Parsons, Bales, *et al.*, *Family, Socialization, and Interaction Process*, pp. 46–7.

[2] T. Gisborne, *An Enquiry into the Duties of the Female Sex* (London, 1797), pp. 12–13.

[3] F. Foster, *Thoughts on the Times* (London, 1779), pp. 73–4.

[4] Above, pp. 181–2 and 188–90.

tion of character and training for adult life and citizenship." [1] In the early factory setting, therefore, this diffuse relationship between adult and child—as well as the nature of the early machinery—assured a solid linkage between the labour of different ages.

Thus the nineteenth century opened with a number of institutionalized "givens"—a premium on the value of labour's economic independence; a division of roles between husband and wife in the "economic" and "emotional" spheres, respectively; and an economic link between father and child which included much socialization in the broader sense.

Early Factory Legislation. In the late eighteenth century the long hours and disease in the manufactories began to injure the health of children. Yet because of the peculiar technology of the industry and the complex set of "givens" outlined in the last section, the problem could not be resolved automatically by reducing children's hours. In the first place, to limit children's hours would have been awkward technically, since many machines required an attendant and several assistants to work together continuously. In the name of the value of independence, it was unthinkable to legislate a reduction for all classes of labour.   At the same time there was widespread apprehension that a limitation of the hours of child labour would occasion the complete dismissal of children.[2] Such a consequence not only would subtract from the family income, but also would break the traditional ties between adult and child labour. The fear of these consequences, moreover, was not simple propaganda from capitalists; the operative class itself was "largely committed to the system of child labour and long hours." [3]

With this background we might assess the genesis and consequences of the factory legislation of 1802, which applied to apprentices, and that of 1819, which applied to children in general. Public interest in the treatment of apprentices was not new. Individual cases of cruelty were treated as criminal, and restrictive legislation—e.g., the act concerning chimney-sweepers and their apprentices in 1788—was not unusual.[4] When it appeared in the late eighteenth century, therefore, that disease and cruelty were widespread in

---

[1] O. J. Dunlop, *English Apprenticeship and Child Labour* (London, 1912), p. 182.

[2] Peel and Huskisson hesitated on this basis in 1824. *Parliamentary Debates,* Second Series, XIII, cols. 422, 1010. Also First Series, XXXVIII, 1818, cols. 347–8, 350; Third Series, IV, 1831, cols. 501–2. Also Clapham, *An Economic History of Modern Britain*, p. 378, and Taylor, *Factories and the Factory System*, p. 22.

[3] Hutchins and Harrison, *A History of Factory Legislation*, p. 38.

[4] *Annual Register*, 1762, p. 95 (Chr.); 1764, p. 69 (Hist.); 1766, p. 89 (Hist.); 1767, p. 115 (Hist.); 1817, pp. 302–7 (State Papers).

manufactories employing apprentice children,[1] a legislative means for correcting such evils was available.

For this reason the Health and Morals of Apprentices Act of 1802 marked the end rather than the beginning of a legislative era; by attempting to enforce good behaviour on masters, it reinforced rather than revolutionized the traditional relationship between master and parish apprentice.[2] Applying to cotton and woollen factories employing more than twenty persons, the Act restricted apprentices' hours to twelve per day and stipulated a gradual discontinuation of night work. It required minimal sanitation, adequate ventilation of the mill, provision of clothes, and a certain amount of educational and religious instruction, all under the inspection of the justices of the peace.

As it turned out, this Act was almost completely ineffective. Magistrates seldom visited the mills, and when they did, they seemed to cause insubordination among the apprentices. At best the Act was casually and sporadically enforced. In fact it may have encouraged some employers to hire free labour because of the nuisance of the apprenticeship clauses. The most important reason for its failure, however, was the decline of apprenticeship based on the rise of urban steam factories, which removed the Act's scope of applicability. By the 1820's "the apprentice problem had fallen into the background" and "free labour" had come to predominate in the cotton industry.[3] The social problems created by this last development lay behind the debates and legislation between 1815 and 1819.

Let us examine a few central features of the long political process which culminated in the Factories Regulation Act in 1819.[4] In the first place the initiators were not operatives but rather employers known for their humanitarianism under the apprenticeship system—men like Robert Owen and Sir Robert Peel. These men wished to guarantee a measure of that humanity for free labour that they had

[1] W. Clerke, *Thoughts upon the Means of Preserving the Health of the Poor* (London, 1790), pp. 7 ff.; G. Holyoake, *Self-Help a Hundred Years Ago* (London, 1888), p. 14; Aiken, *A Description of the Country from thirty to forty Miles round Manchester*, pp. 219–20; Alfred, *History of the Factory Movement*, Vol. I, pp. 27–9; Eden, *State of the Poor*, Vol. I, pp. 420–22; *Proceedings of the Board of Health of Manchester* (Manchester, 1805), pp. 6, 17–20, 26–33.

[2] 42 Geo. III, c. 73; Clapham, *An Economic History of Modern Britain*, p. 372.

[3] *Ibid.*, pp. 373–4; Society for Bettering the Condition of the Poor, *Report . . . on the late Act respecting Cotton Mills* (London, 1802), pp. 5–6, 9; *Lords Sessional Papers*, 1819, XIII, Cotton and Woollen Mills, pp. 77–136; Dunlop, *English Apprenticeship and Child Labour*, p. 270; Hammond, *The Town Labourer*, Vol. I, pp. 161–2.

[4] 59 Geo. III, c. 66. For details, Hammond, *The Town Labourer*, Vol. I, pp. 161–9.

granted to their own apprentice labour. Furthermore, the agitation from below was not very active. While the operatives' petitions supported the measure to limit children's hours—except if it meant the dismissal of children—their support never assumed the proportions of a movement.[1]

Second, the bill lost its teeth during the years of parliamentary processing. Earlier recommendations had included a 10½-hour limit on the working day, a minimum working age of ten, and salaried factory inspectors to enforce the law. In the end the legislators dropped the last clause, reduced the minimum age to nine, and raised the limit on hours to twelve. Again and again, the manufacturers and members of parliament mobilized the arguments against interfering with the independence of labour. In the sense the restrictions of 1819 did not inhibit current industrial practices, therefore, the Act was a "victory for the millowners."[2] Furthermore, completely ineffective enforcement permitted widespread evasion of even these minimum restrictions.

In general, then, the Act of 1819 did not hasten the differentiation of child from adult labour. It merely established nominal outside limits beyond which the semi-differentiated family structure in the factory could not be stretched. In 1833 the Factory Commission concluded that "the children employed in all the principal branches of manufacture throughout the kingdom work during the same number of hours as the adults."[3] Given the institutional conditions of the working-class family between 1815 and 1820, however, the limited restrictions of the 1819 legislation are not too surprising. In these years the family economy was resting in a sort of transitional equilibrium. Several traditional elements of the family economy remained despite the fact that the domestic economy in spinning was extinct. Notwithstanding long hours and other difficult conditions, this transitional system of family-in-factory yielded both higher family income and the maintenance of many traditional values.[4] Hence the low level of the operatives' interest in modifying the structure of employment. Hence also the compromising nature of

[1] Podmore, *Robert Owen*, pp. 188–9, 214–15; Alfred, *History of the Factory Movement*, Vol. I, pp. 36–8, 44; *Parliamentary Debates*, First Series, XXXIX, 1819, col. 656. Above, p. 238.

[2] Marshall, *The Development of Public Opinion in Manchester*, p. 72; above, pp. 266–7; Stewart, *Progress of Glasgow*, pp. 98–9; *Parliamentary Debates*, First Series, XXXVIII, 1818, cols. 359–60.

[3] *Parliamentary Papers*, 1833, XX, First Report of the Factory Commissioners, pp. 35–6.

[4] For a detailed discussion of this transitional equilibrium between 1790 and 1820, above, pp. 186–93.

the Act of 1819, which disturbed neither the independence of the adult male nor the tie between him and his child. Because such ties still existed, moreover, drastic legislation was not essential at this time.

THE DIFFERENTIATION OF THE FAMILY ECONOMY THROUGH FACTORY LEGISLATION

Between the 1820's and the late 1840's the transitional family-in-factory system gave way to a more fully differentiated type of industrial family structure. In the same years factory legislation grew more decisive and consequential in its effects on the organization of labour. Together these two long-term phenomena—the changing family system and the course of factory laws—constitute a complex sequence of *structural differentiation* which passed through its steps in order. For purposes of completeness, we shall review Step 1 as outlined in Chapter IX; next we shall analyse Step 2—the factory agitation itself—in much more detail than in Chapter X; finally we shall trace the course of factory legislation itself (Steps 3–7) and show how it eased the family economy of the working classes toward a new structure.

Step 1. Dissatisfaction. The 1820's ended the transitional equilibrium of the family economy. Many earlier trends continued or accelerated—the growth and centralization of population; the weakening of community ties associated with urbanization; the relative displacement of country mills by city factories, etc. More directly, the increasing size of mules displaced some adult spinners and increased the number of their assistants, thereby weakening the factory apprentice system and reducing the spinners' authority. Power-looms brought many young persons and females into a factory from outside. For the *adult spinner*, these changes threatened his authority within a stabilized way of life; for the *family economy in general*, they brought great numbers of young into the factories without traditional safeguards. Clearly such trends imperilled the older family organization.

Step 2. Symptoms of Disturbance. We have traced the course of factory agitation and its significance for the operative spinners. Now we must widen our horizons a little, and consider the agitation of the early and middle 1830's from the standpoint of the family economy as a whole. Naturally our story becomes more complex. Many groups *besides* the factory operatives supported factory legislation, e.g., certain classical economists and certain manufacturers.[1] The

---

[1] K. O. Walker, "The Classical Economists and the Factory Acts," *Journal of Economic History*, I (1941), pp. 170 ff.

most fervent agitators in the 1830's and 1840's, however, were humanitarians, mostly Tory and mostly Evangelical (e.g., Richard Oastler, Michael Sadler, Rev. G. S. Bull, and Lord Ashley). It goes without saying that factory legislation meant many different things to these groups. Some looked forward, while others looked further in the past than the operatives themselves. All these attitudes may be traced, however, to the family-community crisis between the 1820's and the 1840's. Let us now attempt to unscramble these confused components of the factory agitation by reference to its institutional background.

The outbursts for a ten hour bill in the early and middle 1830's were much broader than a simple demand for shorter hours. The leaders of the movement launched a multi-pronged attack upon the factories, the factory-owners, and the whole factory system. In this movement one finds the characteristics typical of generalized symptoms of disturbance.

The agitators divided the "evils of the factory system" into the physical and the moral.[1] The former included long hours, early ages, physical hardships of employment, cruelty to children, and bad health. The moral evils included the severance of family ties, the operatives' immorality and drunkenness, the masters' immorality in the mills, and the disintegration of education and religion. I shall examine each set of charges—considering their degree of realism when possible—and attempt to relate it to the institutional conditions of the times.

Physical Evils. Proponents of the ten-hour day maintained that children laboured "sixteen hours and upwards [a day], with few and trifling intermissions . . . a portion of the Sabbath." Manufacturers and political economists, furthermore, were accused of wishing to lengthen the general working day to "fifteen or sixteen hours." Frequently the children's long hours were contrasted with the relatively favourable conditions of criminals and slaves.[2]

We cannot assess the exact average hours worked in the Lancashire cotton factories in the early and middle 1830's—the period when the accusations were made. Certainly the outrageous treatment of apprentice labour in the late eighteenth century justified some of the agitators' claims. In 1819 working-class witnesses complained almost universally of long hours and short mealtimes. Proprietors said that

[1] C. Wing, *Evils of the Factory System* (London, 1837), pp. xx ff.
[2] Alfred, *The History of the Factory Movement*, Vol. I, pp. 21, 197–8; J. Fielden, *The Curse of the Factory System* (London, 1836), pp. 56–7; R. Cruikshank, *The Condition of the West India Slave contrasted with that of the Infant Slave in our English Factories* (London, 1833).

the working-day was normally twelve hours at this time. In country mills children sometimes worked from 5 a.m. until 9 or 10 p.m. up to three weeks at a time. Masters required some night work, especially in factories with parish apprentices. In 1825 the hours around Manchester were said to be 12, 12½, 13 and 14, plus bits stolen from mealtimes and the end of the day. In general, however, the length of the workday began to shorten gradually with the advent of the urban, steam-driven mills, so that the number of hours regularly worked in Manchester in 1833 was probably close to twelve per day.[1]

Between 1816 and 1819 children began to work at eight or nine years of age, but no evidence is available to verify the claim that this age was lowered frequently to six and even younger. The Factory Commissioners found instances of this, but "the greater number [of children] are nine." [2]

Uttered in the 1830's, therefore, the colourful atrocity stories were exaggerated. The brutal and long hours had perhaps characterized the manufactories twenty to fifty years earlier. Such mills were dwindling in proportion in the 1830's, and the apprenticeship mills—the worst of all offenders—were virtually dead. The passionate concern with long hours is even more curious when we observe that in other industries such as calico-printing and hand-loom weaving, children and young persons worked even longer hours.[3] Why, in the 1830's and not earlier, and in the cotton industry and not elsewhere, should long hours have been swept into a gigantic onslaught, when hours were gradually diminishing?

Witnesses in 1819 and 1832 also complained of accidents from machinery, cotton dust, excessive heat in spinning rooms, overcrowding of mills, and physical over-exertion.[4] The problem of accidents concerned the Factory Inspectors sufficiently after 1833 for

1 Hammond, *The Town Labourer*, Vol. I, pp. 146–50; *Lords Sessional Papers*, 1819, XVI, Children Employed in the Cotton Manufactures; 1818, IX, Cotton Factories Bill, p. 198; *Parliamentary Papers*, 1816, III, Children employed in the Manufactories, pp. 242, 286, 416–17; 1833, XX, First Report of the Factory Commissioners, p. 11; Society for Bettering the Condition of the Poor, *Report . . . on the late Act respecting Cotton Mills*, pp. 2–3; *A Sketch of the Hours of Labour, Meal Times, &c., in Manchester and its Neighbourhood* (London, 1825).

2 *Parliamentary Papers*, 1816, III, Children employed in the Manufactories, p. 493a; *Lords Sessional Papers*, 1818, IX, Cotton Factories Bill, p. 64; C. Richardson, *A Short Description of the Factory System* (Bawtry, 1831), p. 2; *Parliamentary Papers*, 1833, XX, First Report of the Factory Commissioners, p. 19.

3 L. Horner, *On the Employment of Children* (London, 1840), pp. 121–2; Clapham, *An Economic History of Modern Britain*, pp. 184–5; above, pp. 207–8.

4 *Lords Sessional Papers*, 1819, XVI, Children employed in the Cotton Manufactories; *Parliamentary Papers*, 1831–2, XV, Bill to regulate the Labour of Children in Mills and Factories.

certain restrictions to be passed into law in 1844. On the other hand, accidents were much more common in small water-mills than in steam-mills between 1819 and 1833, which meant that this situation was probably improving as the latter began to predominate. The dust problem, while severe in some mills, varied according to the original cleanliness of the cotton and was limited mainly to the carding-room.[1]

Claims and counter-claims garble the question of overwork. One proponent of ten hours calculated elaborately that piecers walked an average of thirty miles a day; an opponent answered with a calculation showing a figure of eight miles. W. Cooke Taylor, more dispassionate than either of these parties, felt that, outside of spinning, "batting" was the only really arduous labour in the factory. He commented equally moderately on the "overcrowding" charge; particularly when, compared to the cottage industries, factories scarcely hoarded men, women and children into tiny places.[2] Finally, only 10% of the mills—those engaged in fine spinning—required rooms heated up to 80°.[3] For the physical evils in general, however, each rested on a thread of evidence, but the best instances were to be found either in vanishing sectors of the industry or in times past.

Another frequent charge was cruelty to employees. "It is far from being unusual to drag the poor little defenceless sufferers out of their beds at four o'clock in the morning, winter as well as summer. . . . The overlooker always holds in his hand a leathern strap, which is used to urge them on with their work." Again, such descriptions applied to smaller mills, especially in Scotland, rather than to the more modern ones. When, however, witnesses spoke of cruelty and beating in general, they usually added that it was parents—spinners or overlookers—who beat their own children.[4]

[1] *Lords Sessional Papers*, 1819, XVI, Children employed in the Cotton Manufactories, p. 107; *Parliamentary Papers*, 1816, III, Children employed in the Manufactories, pp. 297, 490a; 1833, XX, First Report of the Factory Commissioners, p. 35.

[2] Fielden, *Curse of the Factory System*, pp. 39–40; R. H. Greg, *The Factory Question* (London, 1837), pp. 70–73; Taylor, *Factories and the Factory System*, pp. 35, 38; above, pp. 204–5.

[3] H. Hoole, *A Letter to . . .Althorp* (Manchester, 1832), pp. 6–7; R. Oastler, *A Letter to . . . Hoole* (Manchester, 1832), p. 13.

[4] Richardson, A *Short Description of the Factory System*, pp. 1–2; *Parliamentary Papers*, 1833, XX, First Report of the Factory Commissioners, pp. 22–9; 1831–2, XV, Bill to regulate the Labour of Children in the Mills and Factories, p. 414; 1834, XIX, Supplementary Report of the Factory Commissioners, pp. 498, 573–4; *Lords Sessional Papers*, 1818, IX, Cotton Factories Bill, pp. 110–11; Manchester Statistical Society, *Analysis of the Evidence taken Before the Factory Commissioners* (Manchester, 1834), p. 19; W. H. Hutt, "The Factory System of the Early Nineteenth Century," in Hayek, *Capitalism and the Historians*, pp. 161–6.

Finally, how did factory employment affect the children's health? We can make no exact statement. Before Peel's committee in 1816, "the disagreement of the witnesses examined was distinct and irreconcilable. Men of the highest respectability gave evidence on the same subject, leading to opposite conclusions." [1] This discrepancy rested partially on the absence of medical knowledge. Doctors who had never seen a cotton mill were asked for opinions on the hypothetical effects of factory employment.[2] Because the knowledge of symptoms of disease was primitive, medical men could say only that "the children *appeared* to look *unhealthy*," rather than base their judgments on medical facts.[3] Even such impressionistic surveys of cotton mills and Sunday Schools yielded contradictory evidence.[4] Other findings smacked of vested interests. All the surgeons who visited cotton-spinning factories in and around Manchester at the request of the Committee of (master) Cotton Spinners passed favourable judgment on the operatives' health.[5] In short, the medical opinions of the early nineteenth century are almost undecipherable.

In the ten hour propaganda, however, the evidence was universally black. Members of Sadler's committee distributed a placard containing a list of twenty-one selected doctors and surgeons who had testified on the adverse health of the operatives, but the evidence of none of those medical men who disagreed. Some writers attributed the symptoms of "general lassitude, debility, dyspepsia, and gastralgia" in great part to the conditions of factory labour in cotton.[6]

Of all the information, claim, counter-claim, and exaggeration on the medical question, the evidence before the Factory Commission in 1833 is probably the most trustworthy. The Medical Commissioners

---

1 Alfred, *The History of the Factory Movement*, Vol. I, p. 59.

2 *Ibid.*, Vol. I, pp. 49–59, 77–82; *Parliamentary Papers*, 1816, III, Children employed in the Manufactories, pp. 264–5, 266–7, 268, 275, 277, 279, 429–40; *Lords Sessional Papers*, 1818, IX, Cotton Factories Bill, p. 19; 1819, XVI, Children employed in the Cotton Manufactures, pp. 21, 22, 25, 249–50, 303, 306, 328.

3 *An Inquiry into . . . the Bill now pending in Parliament*, pp. 17–21; Hutt, "The Factory System of the Early Nineteenth Century," *op . cit.*, pp. 166–9; *Information Concerning the State of Children Employed in Cotton Factories*, pp. 5–29, especially p. 19.

4 *Lords Sessional Papers*, 1818, IX, Cotton Factories Bill, pp. 98, 108–11, 120, 135, 155; 1819, XVI, Children employed in the Cotton Manufactures, pp. 255, 265, 268, 288, 300, 311, 356, 454, 485.

5 For these reports cf. *Lords Sessional Papers*, 1818, IX, Cotton Factories Bill, pp. 6, 25, 36–59, 85–90, 92, 141, 224.

6 Alfred, *The History of the Factory Movement*, Vol. I, pp. 312–15; W. R. Greg, *An Enquiry into the State of the Manufacturing Population* (London, 1831), pp. 8–18.

did in fact trace sleepiness and fatigue, pains in various limbs, back and loins, swelling of the feet, etc., to factory labour. Factory workers displayed symptoms of disease and general susceptibility to disease.[1] Hence *on absolute grounds* they sustained some of the ten hour advocates' charges. To this conclusion we must add, however, several instructive corrections and comparisons.

First, certain evidence must be attributed to facts other than factory labour itself. Several witnesses testified that factory children were smaller than others. In fact, since children had to crawl under machinery, smallness was a desirable characteristic for recruitment. Further, factory children often came from families—e.g., hand-loom weavers'—which relied upon their earnings for subsistence. Children in these poverty-stricken families probably were susceptible to disease on dietary and other grounds not related to factory labour.[2] Naturally such observations are meant not to contradict, but to correct our impressions of the "evils" of the factory system as such.

Second, the Factory Commissioners commented that the larger, newer, modern buildings were "without exception" more advantageous with regard to location, size of workrooms, heat, dust, and facilities for cleanliness. The adverse influences on health were worst in the old, small mills—in many ways passing phenomena.[3]

Third, the health of all cotton factory operatives was as good as or superior to that of persons in other trades. Observers—some partisan but others less partisan—never tired of reminding that conditions were as bad if not worse in dock labour, coal-mining, hand-loom weaving, pin-heading, and agriculture. Turner Thackrah, who had no affection for the factory system, saw the medical dangers of factory employment but outlined equally serious hazards to health in other occupations.[4]

The question of the physical evils of the factory system is therefore

---

[1] *Parliamentary Papers*, 1833, XX, First Report of the Factory Commissioners, pp. 29–33.

[2] *Lords Sessional Papers*, 1818, IX, Cotton Factories Bill, pp. 17, 24.

[3] *Parliamentary Papers*, 1833, XX, First Report of the Factory Commissioners, pp. 16–21; 1834, XIX, Supplementary Report of the Factory Commissioners, p. 504; Manchester Statistical Society, *Analysis of the Evidence taken Before the Factory Commissioners*, p. 6.

[4] Greg, *The Factory Question*, pp. 43–4; *Parliamentary Papers*, 1842, XV–XVII, for voluminous documentation on conditions in the mines; 1840, Hand-loom Weavers, p. 43; 1843, XV, Children's Employment Commission, p. 401; 1843, XII, Employment of Women and Children in Agriculture, pp. 42–3; T. Thackrah, *The Effects of the Principal Arts, Trades, and Professions on Health and Longevity* (London, 1831), especially, pp. 14–81. Also Hutt, "The Factory System of the Early Nineteenth Century," *op. cit.*, pp. 169–70; H. Ashworth, *Letter to the Right Hon. Lord Ashley* (Manchester, 1833), pp. 27–8.

not without its paradoxical elements. Despite exaggerations, the claims that factory labour injured the health of children and possibly adults had some absolute basis in fact. On the other hand we are faced with two perplexing questions: (1) Health conditions of twenty to fifty years past were much worse than in the 1830's; health probably was improving slowly. Why had not the question loomed large fifty years before, and why was it swallowed by an almost religious movement in the 1830's? (2) Health conditions in cotton factories were no worse and in many cases better than in other occupations. Why did not the concern with health assume corresponding importance for other industries?

Part of the health issue in the 1830's may be attributed to an attempt of ten hour proponents to legitimize their aims. The legislation of 1802 and 1819 was based partially on health conditions, and the minds of men were alive to the issue of health. More important, however, in my opinion, is the fact that the factory's physical evils *themselves* were not changing (except probably for the better) but that the *social context* of such evils was changing.

In this case social context refers to certain *guarantees*—stemming from the "humane" side of the family and the community—that care and attention will be the response to physical evils such as the deterioration of health and the occurrence of injury. *This* kind of guarantee was beginning to crumble in the cotton industry, not the physical constitution of the labour force. Growing urbanization was gradually weakening community ties. Changes in spinning technology were undermining the spinner's economic authority and forcing on him assistants to whom he was not tied by kinship or community. Even more, the power-looms brought women and children into the factory without the old guarantees of the factory community. Further, the decline of country mills meant a simultaneous decline in quasi-parental guarantees in matters such as health. With an increasingly smaller proportion of children under direct parental surveillance, therefore, the issue of health became more serious than before, not because of the deterioration of health itself but because of the uncertainty surrounding the care of disease and illness. Children's conditions might have been as bad or worse in agriculture or handloom weaving, but the undifferentiated social structure of these spheres preserved some basic guarantees for a responsible social reaction to illness and disease.

Similarly, the concern with cruelty to children derived not from the fact of cruelty itself; such treatment was an ancient feature of apprenticeship and seemed equally harsh in other industries. Rather the concern stemmed from the growing impersonality of the social

278

setting of beating and cruel treatment. As long as cruelty was an adjunct of parental authority and discipline, it remained a legitimate means of socialization. When these parental controls began to weaken, the automatic safeguards over the appropriate use of beating began to weaken. Hence agitators over-reacted in claiming that cruelty was increasing in the industry. Naturally, opponents could counter-claim triumphantly that only parents were in fact guilty of beating. That the agitators could be proved wrong, however, does not deny that cruelty was emerging as a social problem. It was becoming a problem because its social environment was changing.

We must take care, therefore, not to fall into the biases of the 1830's and assume one of two stands on the charges against the factory: (1) that these charges were true and the humanitarians were right, or (2) that the claims were untrue and hence dismissible as a sort of sham or rationalization on the part of the agitators. It seems to me that a third explanation accounts for the apparent exaggerations and paradoxes connected with the factory agitation. Because the family economy was passing through the early stages of differentiation, the social context for responsible attention to physical evils was in a precarious state. Therefore oversensitive reformers were quick to generalize and attack the factory system for the *worsening physical condition* of the children. Such is the subtle emotional logic of a symptom of disturbance, which simplifies through exaggeration, scape-goating, and a denial of relevant facts.

Moral Evils. Factory reformers also levelled an attack on the factory system's moral evils. "About 1830 a whole crop of literature bemoaning the morals of the people burst forth." Many such charges had appeared before, but only in the 1830's did they become engulfed in a social movement.[1] These complaints concerned three major issues—the alleged decline of family relations, the alleged collapse of general "morality," and the crisis in education.

These pamphlets of the early 1830's [2] complained frequently that the home was deteriorating generally:

The population employed in the cotton factories rises at five o'clock in the morning, works in the mills from six till eight o'clock,

[1] Hutt, "The Factory System of the Early Nineteenth Century," *op. cit.*, pp. 173–4; for an earlier complaint, cf. Aiken, *A Description of the Country from thirty to forty Miles round Manchester*, p. 220; also Alfred, *The History of the Factory Movement,* Vol. I, p. 260.

[2] These include Greg, *An Enquiry into the State of the Manufacturing Population*; J. P. Kay, *The Moral and Physical Condition of the Working Classes* (London, 1832); P. Gaskell, *The Manufacturing Population of England* (London, 1833), and a revision of this, *Artisans and Machinery*, in 1836; G. S. Bull, *The Evils of the Factory System* (Bradford, 1832).

and returns home for half an hour to breakfast. This meal generally consists of tea or coffee with a little bread. Oatmeal porridge is sometimes, but of late rarely used, and chiefly by the men; but the stimulus of tea is preferred, and especially by the women. . . . The family sits round the table, and each rapidly appropriates his portion on a plate, or, they all plunge their spoons into the dish, and with an animal eagerness satisfy the cravings of their appetite . . . [after lunch] they are all again employed in the work-shops or mills, where they continue until seven o'clock or a later hour, when they generally again indulge in the use of tea, often mingled with spirits accompanied by a little bread.[1]

Home was "chiefly . . . a scene of physical exhaustion." All ages and both sexes crowded into small rooms. Sometimes the parents stayed in bed when the children arose to file to the factories.[2] In sum, commentators claimed,

a household thus constituted, in which all the decencies and moral observances of domestic life are constantly violated, reduces its inmates to a condition little elevated above that of the savage. Recklessness, improvidence, and unnecessary poverty, starvation, drunkenness, parental cruelty and carelessness, filial disobedience, neglect of conjugal rights, absence of maternal love, destruction of brotherly and sisterly affection, are too often its constituents, and the results of such a combination are moral degradation, ruin of domestic enjoyments, and social misery.[3]

Several themes emerged from this story of general misery. One was the reversal of domestic roles. "What," asked Richard Oastler in 1831, "is the most debasing principle of human nature, nurtured by 'African Slavery'? That a parent is so dreadfully demoralized as to sell his child for gold!! Yes, this is the most hateful part of that hateful system!" He had also witnessed "full-grown athletic men, whose only labour was to carry their little ones to the mill long before the sun was risen, and bring them home at night long after he had set."[4] Concomitantly the agitators deplored the children's welfare within the factory walls. Engels attributed the high death-

---

[1] Kay, *The Moral and Physical Condition of the Working Classes*, pp. 8–9; also Gaskell, *Artisans and Machinery*, p. 11.
[2] Kay, *The Moral and Physical Condition of the Working Classes*, p. 11; Greg, *Enquiry into the State of the Manufacturing Population*, pp. 30–31; Alfred, *The History of the Factory Movement*, Vol. II, p. 11.
[3] Gaskell, *Artisans and Machinery*, p. 89.
[4] Quoted in Alfred, *The History of the Factory Movement*, Vol. II, pp. 223, 234. Also Gaskell, *Artisans and Machinery*, pp. 144–5. Above, p. 190.

rate among working-class children to negligent treatment by parents employed in factories.[1]

To Richard Oastler, the consequent destruction of parental authority and filial piety was "*the greatest curse . . . the very acme of the evil, of the factory system.*" By counting the hours in the day, G. S. Bull calculated that the child spent only four and one-quarter hours per week with his parents. For Bull as well, the chief domestic and social evils of the factory lay in "the loss or absence of parental influence and filial affection, in consequence of the very early age at which the children are sent to work, and the coercion, more or less, with which it is attended, both on the part of the parents and on the part of those who overlook the child." This complaint, while not completely new, seemed to draw the most forceful language from the ten hour agitators.[2]

The woman's role was a final sore spot attributed to the factory system. Some charged that the infant death-rate in cotton districts was higher because factory employment injured the female's health and child-bearing abilities. From the limited and unsatisfactory census evidence, it is clear that Lancashire had a higher death-rate than the rest of England and Wales in 1851. It is difficult to say whether this resulted from female factory employment or from bad sanitation, infection, etc., in the new industrial cities. In addition, married female factory operatives had smaller families than the average married woman. This small family size applied, however, to all married women occupied outside the home. The small families may not have resulted, furthermore, from infant mortality but from the facts that barren women went to work and that women with large families quitted their work. In short, the problem of the female cotton operative and infant mortality is so shrouded in faulty statistics and a multiplicity of causes that we cannot answer the question satisfactorily.[3]

If the factory woman did have children, it was asserted that her factory labour annihilated "the great and beautiful principle [of maternal affection] in woman's moral organization." Her own early

[1] Alfred, *The History of the Factory Movement*, Vol. II, p. 5; E. G. Wakefield, *England and America* (London, 1833), pp. 55–6; Engels, *The Condition of the Working-Class in England in 1844*, pp. 107–8.

[2] R. Oastler, *The Factory Bill* (London, 1833), p. 10; Bull, *The Evils of the Factory System*, pp. 9–10; *Parliamentary Papers*, 1831–2, XV, Bill to regulate the Labour of Children in the Mills and Factories, p. 412; for a similar complaint, cf. 1816, III, Children employed in the Manufactories, p. 338.

[3] The summary statements in this paragraph rely on the research of Hewitt in *The Effect of Married Women's Employment in the Cotton Textile Districts on the Home in Lancashire*, pp. 124–5, 143–4, 169–70. Above, pp. 208–9.

factory work, moreover, had ruined any chances for her to acquire the domestic duties and skills of a wife and mother.[1] Her traditional role, in short, like the roles of her children and her husband, was being twisted beyond recognition by the moral evils of the factory. Since these charges were both general and intangible, it is difficult to assess their basis in fact. Certainly, however, the proponents of ten hours claimed too much. We must temper their charges of deterioration by the fact that only 20 to 25% of the factory females were married, and these tended to drop out of employment as their families increased in size. There is no proof, moreover, of the minor charge of increasing shabbiness of dress; market-purchased clothes were certainly cheaper and possibly better than home-manufactured garments. And most important, some of the conditions of domestic misery and woman's domestic incompetence have been shown to apply equally in industries which passed less noticed before the eyes of the agitators—e.g., pottery-making, hand-loom weaving, and agricultural labour.[2] Hence the moral charges were not without their exaggerated elements.

In general, however, opponents of factory legislation could not rebuff the complaints about the family so successfully as they could the complaints of bad health, deteriorating morals, and overwork. W. Cooke Taylor, who expressed impatience with the majority of the ten hour agitators' claims, admitted that

there are, indeed, serious evils connected with the employment of women in factories, and, indeed, everywhere save in their own homes, which must not be passed over without notice. The girl employed all day in the factory has little opportunity of learning the details of domestic economy and of the management of a household. When she marries she is far from being well qualified to fulfil the duties of a wife and mother, and she often neglects both from not knowing how to set about them.[3]

[1] Gaskell, *Artisans and Machinery*, pp. 86–7; Bull, *The Evils of the Factory System*, pp. 17–19. Bull found the habit of wearing ready-made clothes particularly objectionable. Also Kay, *The Moral and Physical Condition of the Working Classes*, pp. 42–3; *Parliamentary Papers*, 1833, XX, First Report of Factory Commissioners, p. 682; 1831–2, XV, Bill to regulate the Labour of Children in Mills and Factories, pp. 308–9, 326; *Parliamentary Debates*, Third Series, LXXIII, 1844, cols. 1092–6, 1383–4; for the story of a tragic marriage of an untutored factory girl, cf. R. Oastler, *Infant Slavery* (Preston, 1833), p. 9.

[2] Above, p. 208; Pinchbeck, *Women Workers in the Industrial Revolution*, p. 107; Hewitt, *The Effect of Married Women's Employment in the Cotton Textile Districts on the Home in Lancashire*, pp. 107, 91 ff; *Parliamentary Papers*, 1840, Hand-loom Weavers, p. 44; 1843, XII, Women and Children in Agriculture, pp. 26–7.

[3] *Factories and the Factory System*, pp. 45–6.

Hutt, a modern opponent of the factory legislation of the 1830's, could lay a reasonably convincing case on the problems of health, overwork, crime, and immorality by referring to some of the paradoxes we have outlined. Yet Hutt did not even *mention* the domestic charges, much less attempt to refute them; but these were among the noisiest and most persistent claims of the factory agitators.[1]

In my opinion, the strongest arguments for factory regulation could be made by referring to the contemporary institutional pressures on the family division of labour. We have attempted to outline this institutional crisis in the family economy, and to read some meaning into the operatives' activities in the 1820's and 1830's by referring to this pressure. The agitators' accusations of deterioration stem from the same crisis. Yet we need not accept their almost hysterical attacks. In most cases they did not perceive what was happening to the family division of labour because they were convinced that the whole family structure was collapsing. While the family life of the cotton operatives had by no means "fallen apart," the charges of deteriorating domestic roles—even though they were frequently exaggerated and misdirected—touched an institutional sore spot and therefore cannot be dismissed out of hand.

Also instructive were charges of "immorality" in the sexual and other emotional spheres. Agitators painted the factories as dens of vice in which masters seduced female operatives freely; in Parliament Sadler described the mills as "little better than brothels." In addition, they charged that factory women drifted into prostitution more easily than other women. Such charges were rounded out by accusations of "general licentiousness and illicit intercourse between the sexes," illegitimacy, and free cohabitation among the operatives.[2]

Richard Oastler added the operatives' drunkenness to those moral evils of the factory system:

> . . . some people will strenuously maintain that [the cause of our general distress] is to be found in the "INTEMPERANCE" and "DRUNKENNESS" of the people. No doubt this is a very great

[1] "The Factory System of the Early Nineteenth Century," *op. cit.*
[2] R. Oastler, "Mr. Sadler's Bill," in *Poor Man's Advocate*, Mar. 24, 1832; *Report . . . of a Public Meeting . . . in . . . Oldham* (Oldham, 1836), pp. 31–2; Bull, *The Evils of the Factory System*, pp. 11–13; Alfred, *The History of the Factory Movement*, Vol. I, p. 185; Gaskell, *Artisans and Machinery*, pp. 106–7; *Parliamentary Papers*, 1831–2, XV, Bill to regulate the Labour of Children in the Mills and Factories, pp. 218, 467; Kay, *The Moral and Physical Condition of the Working Classes*, p. 23; Greg, *Enquiry into the State of the Manufacturing Population*, pp. 24–5; P. Gaskell, *Prospects of Industry* (London, 1835), p. 21; C. Shaw, *Replies to Lord Ashley* (London, 1843), p. 23.

evil—it is not the *cause*,—it is one of the *effects* of our present system! . . . let every friend of *"temperance,"* look to the *causes*, and endeavour to remove them. Go with me to Manchester if you will, and, at "leaving off time,"—take your stand by a large "gin temple," in the neighbourhood of an enormous mill; and see the poor over-worked, forlorn, emaciated "Factory girl," of nine years old—the renowned "British labourer!" All in rags, and tatters; see her "slur" past you, to the door of the "gin temple."—Enter with her, and you will hear her ask for a "ha'p'orth of gin, to help her to walk home;" enquire the cause, and she will tell you,—"she is faint, and sickly, with heat, and dust, and toil!" This is the way thousands of industrious females are made into "drunkards." These injured females, are the very foundation on which our great manufacturing interest rests! LET ENGLAND BLUSH! And, oh, ye sincere haters of "drunkenness," do help me to save *these* poor industrious female children.[1]

Greg, Kay, and Gaskell all echoed this charge, attributing it to the horrors of factory life, the decline of domestic life, or both. The accusations of drunkenness—and sometimes addiction to opium—appeared in miscellaneous pamphlets and in a discourse on the English nation.[2]

The charges of sexual immorality of master and operative stand unsubstantiated in the light of historical research. The statistics of birth and illegitimacy shed no light on the problem of female immorality. Similar stories of immorality appear from time to time in statements relating to other trades. Of fifty-three witnesses asked to comment on the comparative morality by the Factory Commission, forty-six felt there was no substantial difference, and seven stated the operatives' morality was worse. In any case the Commissioners found "no evidence to show that vice and immorality are more prevalent amongst these people, considered as a class, than amongst any other portion of the community in the same station, and with the same limited means of information." Probably the cities—with their transient population and anonymity—confirmed these charges more than village or rural districts, but this would follow from urbanism in general and not particular employments.[3]

[1] *Letter to the Editor of the Agricultural and Industrial Magazine* (London, 1835), pp. 144–5.

[2] Kay, *The Moral and Physical Condition of the Working Classes*, pp. 12, 35; Greg, *Enquiry into the State of the Manufacturing Population*, p. 10; Gaskell, *Artisans and Machinery*, pp. 124–5; W. Dodd, *The Factory System Illustrated* (London, 1842), pp. 134–43; E. L. Bulwer, *England and the English* (London, 1833), Vol. I, pp. 203–5.

[3] Hewitt, *The Effect of Married Women's Employment in the Cotton Textile Districts on the Home in Lancashire*, p. 66; Manchester Statistical Society, *Analysis of the Evidence taken Before the Factory Commissioners*, p. 22; *Parlia-*

Differentiation of the Family Structure: Factory Legislation

Since per capita consumption of alcohol rose in the 1830's—though at all times it remained much lower than it had been in the mid eighteenth century[1]—the drinking charge bears closer examination. Perhaps, as W. Cooke Taylor suggested, the public houses were the only "safety-valves for mind" deadened by long and tedious factory labour. Whether this was the case, or whether alcohol consumption rose because of the beer tax repeal of 1830, because of the increasing real wages of operatives, or because of the growing numbers of Irishmen[2] is difficult to determine. We may conclude only that the rising consumption of alcohol, while lost in a maze of determinants, was not so extreme as to lead to a judgment of moral and psychological degeneration of a whole occupational class.

All these moral charges, however exaggerated, touched those kinds of behaviour which *would have* appeared if the family actually had passed into a state of extreme disorganization. The family is the chief direct controlling agency over sexual and criminal deviance, alcoholism, etc. In fact the agitators' charges were generally unfounded; operatives were neither more nor less guilty of moral infractions than comparable groups. Yet because the family structure of this class was under institutional pressure from various sides, reformers were quick to seize upon the family's specialty—morality—

mentary Papers, 1833, XX, First Report of the Factory Commissioners, p. 36; 1837–8, XIX.1, Poor Law Amendment Act, pp. 485–6; Taylor, *Factories and the Factory System*, p. 41.

[1] Porter's figures yield a rough idea of per capita consumption for the relevant years:

Malt Consumption (England)		Spirit Consumption (UK)	
Year	Bushels per head	Year	Gallons per head
1830	1·37	1802	0·56
1835	1·70	1812	0·49
1840	1·60	1821	0·46
1845	1·30	1831	0·90
		1838	1·02
		1840	0·82

Because these figures do not show regional or class differences, it is even more difficult to generalize about the factory population. Furthermore, malt consumption in these years was vastly lower than between 1740 and 1780, when the range of per capita annual consumption was between 3·38 and 4·85 bushels. *The Progress of the Nation*, pp. 460, 464.

[2] These alternatives suggested in Taylor, *Notes of a Tour in the Manufacturing Districts of Lancashire*, pp. 131, 133, 134–6; E. Waugh, *Sketches of Lancashire Life and Localities* (London, 1855), pp. 184–5; Porter, *The Progress of the Nation*, p. 455; Hutt, "The Factory System in the Early Nineteenth Century," *op. cit.*, pp. 176–7.

285

and claim that morals themselves were suffering a complete break-down. Such claims expressed two classic elements of symptoms of disturbance—anxiety, or the charge that the moral fabric of society was crumbling, and aggression, or the charge that the factory master or factory system was solely responsible. Symptoms of disturbance are too quick for social reality; they stem from very definite institutional pressures, to be sure, but they gallop ahead of these pressures in claiming that a whole way of life is dead or dying.

Reformers also linked low educational standards to factory labour. In any case, education was justly a subject of concern in the early nineteenth century, because it had lagged so noticeably behind other institutions in the English industrial revolution. The Sunday Schools had surged, as had the National Schools of Bell and Lancaster, but both contemporaries and historians agree that educational standards for the young were extremely low in these years.[1]

Factory agitators attributed the working population's educational deficiencies to the factory system. G. S. Bull feared that "the most efficient system of Sunday School Instruction, cannot secure to Factory Children the blessing of an adequate religious education—they cannot from fatigue, from the limited period devoted to instruction, generally acquire the ability to understand the Holy Scriptures . . ."[2] Some attacks were merely *against* the factories. At least one writer, however, wished to generalize the masters' paternalistic concern for education.

Every capitalist might contribute much to the happiness of those in his employ, by [an] exercise of enlightened charity. He might establish provident associations and libraries amongst his people . . . Above all he should provide instruction for the children of his work-people: he should stimulate the appetite for useful knowledge, and supply it with appropriate food.[3]

Perhaps as revealing as the agitators' attack on the factories is the simultaneous interest in education on the part of many factory and laissez-faire economists. In 1834–5 the Manchester Statistical Society —laissez-faire if anything—exposed the inadequacies of educational facilities in several industrial cities. Nassau Senior, a strong antagonist of the ten hour bill in the 1830's, regretted the low standards of factory education after the 1833 legislation. Finally, R. H. Greg, a

---

1 Porter, *The Progress of the Nation*, pp. 132–4.

2 *The Evils of the Factory System*, p. 9; *Parliamentary Papers*, 1831–2, XV, Bill to regulate the Labour of Children in the Mills and Factories, p. 415; 1835, XIII, Hand-loom Weavers, p. 208; Alfred, *The History of the Factory Movement*, Vol. I, pp. 166–76.

3 Kay, *The Moral and Physical Condition of the Working Classes*, pp. 63–4.

vitriolic opponent of the ten hour bill, made education his counter-utopia: "We know but of ONE remedy for the evils of the 'Factory System,' and for the many ills which afflict society—ills so numerous, and of such magnitude, that they force themselves upon the attention every moment. . . . That remedy is of universal application; we mean EDUCATION." [1]

In general, education was becoming a problem in the early nineteenth century because the requirements for an increasingly complex and technical occupational world could no longer be met by the old system of bringing up a child, possibly illiterate, to a simple trade. This general crisis worsened when the family began to undergo further differentiation; as the tie between parent and child began to weaken in the 1820's and 1830's, the problem of establishing a new balance between the family system and an educational system rose forcefully and quickly to public attention. Because of such pressure, factory agitators assimilated the problem of education—like the problems of health and morality—to their attack on the factories. In addition, however, men who were not convinced of the collapse of the factory population also turned their attention to the problem of education.

The enemies and defenders of the factory system, however, looked in different directions; the ten hour men might look backward to the de-differentiated system of paternalistic responsibility of master or church, whereas their opponents looked forward to a family system and an educational system more differentiated than before. Indeed, it was the manufacturers themselves who suggested the adoption of an embryonic sort of formal educational system for the Act of 1833. Presently we shall trace this interesting process of differentiating family responsibility from educational responsibility through the factory legislation. To round out the picture of the ten hour disturbances, however, let us enumerate several more instances of phantasy and aggression which characterized the movement.

Utopia and Hostility in the Ten Hour Movement. Some of the ten hour literature pictured factory labour as a kind of hell-on-earth for employees. In particular, two narratives of factory cripples received wide circulation. The first recounted the experiences of William Dodd

---

[1] Manchester Statistical Society, *Report on . . . Education in . . . Manchester; Report on . . . Education in . . . Bury in 1835* (London, 1835); *Report on . . . Education in . . . Salford in 1835* (London, 1836); Senior, *Letters on the Factory Act*, p. 19; Greg, *The Factory Question*, p. 124. Some manufacturers and political economists, of course, opposed education of the children in the mills. G. Ward, "The Education of Factory Child Workers, 1833–1850," *Economic Journal (Economic History Supplement)*, III (1934–7), p. 112.

between the ages of six and fourteen (i.e., between 1810 and 1818) and linked his deformities to factory life. The other, similar in tone, showed on the cover a beaten, stunted man whose condition was traced to his experiences in the "home-cotton-slave-trade." The truth or falsity of these narratives seems less important than the fact that their appearance coincided with the generally disturbed atmosphere of the early middle decades of the nineteenth century.[1]

Another instance of negative Utopia was Oastler's dire promise in 1831 that the masters would never stop until the "*manufacture of the empire is concentrated under one large roof, and the world is supplied by one gigantic firm*. . . .Till human nature is almost physically and morally destroyed, *and all the inhabitants of this land shall be the slaves of one great manufacturing nabob*." In contrast with this gloomy prophecy were the days before "the estates of our ancient nobility [were] *spindleized*. . . . Oh, what a beautiful ship was England once! She was well built, well manned, well commanded, well laden, well provisioned, well rigged. All were *then* merry, cheerful, and happy on board." Bull would "hail with great measure" anything which might "accelerate the re-establishment of the domestic system," and Oastler listed the encouragement of domestic machinery as one of his five positive suggestions for action in 1832.[2]

Side by side with these Utopian elements there mushroomed an onslaught against persons and things connected with the factory system. Oastler felt that machinery, while in theory a blessing, was in fact the labourer's "greatest curse." Banners such as "Muzzle the Steam Monster" appeared in popular processions. Manufacturers were labelled as "sleek men, with purses well filled, and portly paunches," "slaughter-house masters," "lawbreakers, tyrants and murderers," and so on. Closely allied were the "Scotch Philosopher," the "High [Satanic] Priest Malthus," Wilberforce, and others. Bull even maintained that "*the organized opposition to the Ten-Hour Bill*, by capitalists and political economists, *is only one* (though a principal) *part of one great conspiracy* against the honest industry of this kingdom." [3]

---

[1] W. Dodd, *A Narrative of . . . William Dodd* (London, 1841); J. Brown, *A Memoir of Robert Blincoe* (Manchester, 1832). The latter appeared in Richard Carlile's *The Lion* and Doherty's *The Poor Man's Advocate*, as well as in pamphlet form.

[2] Alfred, *The History of the Factory Movement*, Vol. I, pp. 120–21; R. Oastler, *Eight Letters to the Duke of Wellington* (London, 1835), pp. 45, 99–100; *Parliamentary Papers*, 1831–2, Bill to regulate the Labour of Children in the Mills and Factories, p. 492.

[3] Oastler, *Eight Letters to the Duke of Wellington*, p. 45; Oastler, *Letter to the Editor of the Agricultural and Industrial Magazine*, pp. 141–2; Oastler, *A Letter*

A strong charismatic attachment to leaders illustrates the emotionalism of the movement. The Yorkshire and Lancashire followers of Oastler called him the "Factory King" or "King Richard" of the Crusaders. Many meetings were almost hysterical; "Mr. Oastler has oftentimes made thousands of men, women, and children to glow, tremble, and weep, because of the force of homely words, expressed with feeling and earnestness." [1] While Yorkshire showed much more fervour than Lancashire, Sadler's entry into Manchester in 1832 excited a tremendous display:

[In August, 1832] at Manchester, Mr. Sadler and Mr. Oastler were welcomed by a public procession and dinner. . . . The procession was headed by two men, bearing a flag with the representation of a deformed man, inscribed—'Am I not a man and a brother?' underneath, 'No White Slavery.' Then came a band of music; then the Committee and their friends; then a long line of Factory children bearing a great variety of banners, decorated mops, brushes, and other utensils connected with their employment, hundreds of them singing, 'Sadler for ever, Oastler for ever; six in the Morning, six in the evening.'
One of the children carried a whip, and a strap made into thongs, with the inscription, 'Behold and weep.' Next to this immense multitude of 'little victims,' as they were aptly designated, came the carriage with the visitors. A countless number of men followed, five or six deep, all staunch friends of the Ten Hours' Bill, having at short intervals bands of music, banners, &c., with mottos expressive of some sentiment, opinion, or fact connected with the great cause. We cannot pretend to give a tithe of these inscriptions. We observed, 'Cursed are they that oppress the poor'; 'Let us unite and gain by strength our right'; 'Sadler and Oastler for ever'; 'Welcome to Sadler'; 'Oastler our Champion'; 'Sadler our advocate;' 'Let us unite in laying the axe to the root of infant slavery'; 'No White Slavery'; 'Death to infant oppression'; a figure of a deformed man exclaiming, 'Excessive toil is the burden of my soul.' One person carried a very neat model of a cotton-factory, inscribed, 'The infant's Bastile.' On the other banners we remarked, 'Revere Oastler, the children's friend'; 'The Factory system is the bane of health, the source of ignorance and vice'; 'The enactment of a Ten Hours' Bill

to those *Millowners who Continue to Oppose the Ten Hours Bill* (Manchester, 1836), p. 3; Oastler, *A Speech Delivered . . . in . . . Manchester* (Huddersfield, 1833); Alfred, *The History of the Factory Movement*, Vol. I, p. 141, Vol. II, p. 61; G. Crabtree, *Factory Commission* (London, 1833), pp. 10–11; *The Day Dream, or . . . the Trial of Mr. Factory Longhours* (Leeds, 1832); *Herald of the Rights of Industry*, Feb. 15, 1834; *The Lion*, Feb. 29, 1828; G. S. Bull, *Address . . . [to] the People of Bradford* (Bradford, 1833), p. 21.

[1] Alfred, *The History of the Factory Movement*, Vol. I, pp. 206–7, 234–5, 241, 251, 257–8.

will be attended with beneficient results to both master and man.' Many of these flags and banners were of costly materials, and the devices skilfully executed; some of them were of more homely materials, but all were showy, and the effect to the eye cannot be conveyed in the most eloquent description. There were seventeen bands of music, and several hundred flags.[1]

The factory movement also produced several tracts of Factory Poetry and a few attempts at drama.[2]

Step 3. Handling and Channelling. The most explosive agitations for ten hours occurred between 1831 and 1833. By and large this agitation proceeded peacefully through the media of demonstrations, petitions, and pamphlets. One sequence of events, however—that involving the supersession of Sadler's Committee of 1832 by the Factory Commission of 1833—illustrates the process of handling the agitation and channelling it into appropriate lines.

A parliamentary opposition countered Sadler's attempt to push through a ten hour bill in 1832 by forcing the issue into an investigating committee. Sadler himself headed this committee. As opponents of the ten hour legislation were quick to assert, his procedure in the investigation was extremely irregular. The witnesses were, as Oastler blandly stated, "friends, of course to the cause." Of the eighty-nine witnesses, only eight were from Lancashire and Cheshire cotton mills, which harboured by far the largest number of operatives. The *Annual Register* claimed that at least one injury displayed to the committee did not result from factory labour, and that one witness was rejected when it was discovered that her evidence was of no use to the committee's purposes. No evidence was given under oath, and several witnesses later refused to repeat their testimony before the Factory Commission. Sadler apparently arranged, furthermore, that proponents of the bill should give evidence first, opponents later; but he published the testimony of the first without waiting for the latter.[3]

---

1 Alfred, *The History of the Factory Movement*, Vol. I, pp. 254–5; also *Manchester Guardian*, Sept. 1, 1832, and "The Commission for perpetuating Factory Infanticide," *Fraser's Magazine*, June, 1833, pp. 9–10.

2 An Operative, *The Factory Child* (First Edition: London, 1831; Second Edition: London, 1832). J. Nicholson, *The Factory Child's Mother* (Leeds, 1832); J. Ross, *The Factory Child's Father's Reply to the Factory Child's Mother* (Leeds, 1832); W. Walker, *Poetical Strictures on the Factory System* (Leeds, 1832); *Hymns for Factory Children* (Leeds, 1831). In 1832, *The Factory Girl*, a domestic drama, opened but failed at the Drury Lane Theatre in London. *Annual Register*, 1832, pp. 129–30 (Chr.). See also, *The Factory System* (Leeds, 1831), a one-act play.

3 Alfred, *The History of the Factory Movement*, Vol. II, p. 12; Ashworth, *Letter to . . . Ashley*, fn., p. 4; *Annual Register*, 1833, pp. 205–6 (Hist.); Hutt, "The Factory System of the Early Nineteenth Century," *op. cit.*, pp. 161–6.

In response, the manufacturers angrily demanded a commission to investigate the manufacturing districts on the spot. Simultaneously the factory question was infected with the antagonism between the landed gentry and the capitalists. This hostility recently had reached a boiling-point over the Reform Bill of 1832. Amidst this fury a Commission was appointed. Even those who question its political neutrality admit that the Commission's investigations were executed "much more systematically than were those of its predecessor." [1] Medical authorities accompanied the Commissioners; all publicity was forbidden during the period of investigation; and the Commissioners were instructed to examine magistrates, masters, adult operatives, and children, and particularly to re-examine under oath those witnesses who had appeared before Sadler's committee.[2] Ten hour advocates claimed that the Commission represented masters only, but on the grounds of its selection of witnesses, attempted fairness, thoroughness of evidence, and conclusions, it was much more in line with constitutional procedure than Sadler's committee. In the sense, therefore, that the Commission "rose above" the controversy which led to its formation, it clearly illustrates the mechanism of "handling" the explosive tensions generated during a disturbed period.

The Commission's conclusions and recommendations show that it was not blind to the deleterious effects of factory labour. At the same time, however, it "handled" some of the fury of the times by selecting among the wilder charges and attempting to establish them in fact.[3] Furthermore, the Commissioners were careful always to stipulate what could and could not be allowed on value grounds. On the ten hour bill, for instance, the Commissioners spoke first of the "objection . . . in principle to any compulsory interference with the hours or terms of adult labour." In addition, the ten hour law could not guarantee the health of the children, gave no "education, elementary or moral"; further, it would restrict the hours of adult labour. The proposed ten hour legislation, in short, broke the principle of independence and did not protect the children. Children's hours *alone* might be reduced because children were not free agents and hence were outside the scope of the value of independence.[4] For adult labour, however, the Commission was forced to weigh two

[1] E. von Plener, *The English Factory Legislation* (London, 1873), pp. 10–11.
[2] *Parliamentary Papers*, 1833, XX, First Report of the Factory Commissioners, pp. 7–10.
[3] Above, pp. 274, 276–7, and 284.
[4] *Parliamentary Papers*, 1833, XX, First Report of the Factory Commissioners, pp. 37–8, 55–6; above, pp. 210–12 and 266–7 for a discussion of independence.

traditional elements in conflict: (*a*) the independence of adult labour, deeply rooted in the value-system of the day; (*b*) the traditional economic relationship between parent and child, deeply rooted in the social structure of the operative class. In choosing to sacrifice the latter to the former, the Commission exemplifies still another line of "channelling"—to reaffirm the value-system, and to rule out lines of action (such as universal ten hour labour) which might threaten its integrity.

In another way the Commission "handled" the social tensions generated during its investigations. Sadler, whose committee was now superseded, published a bitter letter in 1833 demanding that all the Commission's proceedings be made public, and claiming that it was composed of "individuals personally interested in the question." Sadler's attack was one of several such protests. In response, the Commissioners publicly rebuked Sadler for attempting to interfere with constitutional inquiry. Furthermore, when the Commission entered Manchester on its business, the ten hour agitators prepared a giant demonstration similar to that which had greeted Sadler's committee one year earlier. The Commission indicated, in a chilly manner, that it was not to be influenced by such demonstrations of public opinion as appeals from children in person.[1]

Steps 4 and 5. Tolerance of New Ideas and Attempts to Specify. In the 1830's these two steps were almost simultaneous, for a proposal to limit the hours of labour (new ideas) almost always involved a plan to carry this idea into effect (institutional forms). The distinction between ideas and institutional specifications, however, parallels Nassau Senior's distinction between the substance (Step 4) and the machinery (Step 5) of the legislation.[2] We shall discuss these two aspects separately.

The ten hour advocates' major "idea" was to restrict the hours of children to ten; one effect of this would have been to limit the hours of all workers and thereby maintain a traditional organization of labour. Lord Ashley amended this proposal slightly in 1833 by suggesting the limitation of women's as well as children's hours to ten. On the other hand, some opponents of ten hour legislation opposed all interference. Others proposed limiting children's hours only, working them in shifts or relays, thus sustaining the adults'

[1] M. T. Sadler, *Protest against the Secret Proceedings of the Factory Commission* (Leeds, 1833); J. E. Drinkwater and A. Power, *Replies to Mr. M. T. Sadler's Protest* (Leeds, 1833). Also "The Commission for Perpetuating Factory Infanticide," *op. cit.*; *The Commissioner's Vade Mecum* (Leeds, 1833); Crabtree, *Factory Commission.*

[2] *Letters on the Factory Act*, p. 17.

longer work-day. Various educational schemes were in the air as well. Naturally the adherents of these schemes were not to be held responsible for their success or failure. It was a period of groping for solutions which characterizes Step 4.

The machinery of factory legislation also was the subject of suggestion and debate. In 1833 Lord Ashley suggested imprisonment for an employer who violated the proposed Act a third time. This controversial clause split the factory agitators into those favouring personal punishment (Yorkshire, roughly) and those taking a more moderate position (Lancashire). Ashley later withdrew his proposal. Meantime the Factory Commissioners were exploring various methods of enforcement. Some manufacturers favoured the appointment of officers to inspect the factories at regular intervals. The Commissioners accepted the idea of public officials, but rejected the notion of resident inspectors on grounds of economy. In the end they recommended a plan for itinerant inspectors. The Commissioners also considered a vast number of administrative methods such as posting public clocks to regulate hours, displaying the Act publicly, requiring medical certificates for the age of children, allowing inspectors to enter factories, etc.[1]

Many of these ideas and methods were not new. Several times in the past half-century the suggestion of ten hours and similar restrictions had arisen;[2] salaried inspectors had been suggested but dropped before the 1819 legislation; and various educational schemes had come before the public mind in the early nineteenth century. The important feature of Steps 4 and 5 is not the *origin* of the ideas and methods, but their serious consideration at this time. Thus the logic of social innovation follows the logic of economic innovation; one must distinguish clearly the invention, the serious consideration of the invention, and the social incorporation of the invention. Steps 4 and 5 saw the serious public consideration of the ideas and methods of factory legislation.

Step 6. Establishment of Institutional Forms. When Parliament passed the Factory Act of 1833, it selected a few of the competing ideas, methods, and recommendations for legislation. The government thereby assumed *responsibility* for the political success or failure of factory regulation, in a way which advocates, opponents, investigators, theorists, and commissioners inherently could not have

[1] Alfred, *The History of the Factory Movement*, Vol. II, p. 57; Hammond, *Lord Shaftesbury*, p. 29; Clapham, *An Economic History of Modern Britain*, Vol. I, p. 574; M. W. Thomas, *The Early Factory Legislation* (Leigh-on-Sea, 1948), pp. 57–60.

[2] Hutchins and Harrison, *A History of Factory Legislation*, pp. 43–4.

assumed in the earlier steps. Thus the movement from agitation to investigation to actual legislation is an example of social entrepreneurship, in which the sponsor of new institutional forms has to "meet the test" of public acceptance or rejection. In this sense the Factory Act of 1833 marked the abrupt transition from Steps 4 and 5 to Step 6 in the sequence of structural differentiation of the family division of labour.

The substance of the Act was that

in factories, children under nine years of age shall not be employed at all, and those under thirteen not for more than eight hours a-day; and that they shall pass two hours a-day in school. The hours of working, except on Saturday, being twelve, it was supposed that by means of relays, the services of children might be obtained for the whole twelve hours.

The machinery of the Act required that no child under thirteen could remain in a factory

without a certificate of age from a surgeon, nor for more than eight hours a-day, nor without a certificate of its having attended school for twelve hours in the preceding week; and also in the appointment of inspectors empowered to issue regulations and visit factories, and superintendents or sub-inspectors acting under their direction, and empowered to enter all school-rooms and counting-houses, but not those parts of a factory in which manufacturing processes are carried on.[1]

In addition, the Act restricted the hours of young persons (ages thirteen to eighteen) to twelve hours a day or sixty-nine a week. Inspectors could impose fines ranging from £1 to £20 on delinquent manufacturers.[2]

Because the Act marked a distinct break between Steps 4–5 and Step 6, it resulted in a greater *structural differentiation* in the family economy. This differentiation moved along two distinct lines: (1) Whereas technological innovations had been weakening the economic link between parent and child for some years, the Act of 1833 broke this link definitively by removing the possibility that the child could remain at his father's side during the entire work-day. Thus it encouraged the segregation of the economic roles of adult and child. Further, it differentiated other characteristics of the parent-child relationship—socialization, moral training, etc.—from the economic

[1] Senior, *Letters on the Factory Act*, p. 17. In order to ease the possible unemployment of children, clauses affecting the 9–13 group were to take effect over a period of three years. Senior wrote the description in 1837; some of the elements, such as superintendents and sub-inspectors, had been added since 1833.

[2] Thomas, *The Early Factory Legislation*, p. 20.

roles of family members. Previously this whole family complex had been part of the modified apprenticeship system on the factory premises. (2) The Act pushed the differentiation of formal education from the family economy to a new level. In 1833 there already existed many educational institutions separate from the family, such as Sunday Schools, Day Schools, Dame Schools, and Infant Schools. To require a manufacturer to guarantee that his child employees receive a minimum of formal education—either in a manufactory or some other school—marked an increase of educational specialization. Earlier the adult had the option of restricting his child's education solely to the acquisition of economic and other skills on the job or of sending him to school. The Act of 1833 cancelled this parental option; if the child were to work *in* a factory, he had to receive certain instruction *outside* the factory. Of course these two lines of differentiation are almost inseparable. If the Act, by restricting the child's hours of labour, removed him from his adults' care on the factory premises, it seemed natural to re-establish on another basis some of the responsibilities it took from the parents.

Contemporary observers saw the need for such a differentiation, though they did not describe it as such. Scrope, who regretted interference on laissez-faire grounds, granted that competition had burdened the children unduly. "In a more natural state of things, which afforded a competent remuneration to the labour of the working class, such interference of the legislature would be unnecessary, and the health of children might be left with safety to the natural guardianship of their parents." [1] In a sense competition had perpetuated the crisis in child labour by inducing the technological changes in spinning and weaving in the 1820's. On the other hand, the inadequate remuneration to labour did not precipitate the factory laws; indeed, the real earning power of the operatives rose significantly with the improved technology. Scrope was partially correct, however, in judging that parents could no longer guard their children's health "with safety." Because the *economic* roles of parent and child were differentiating gradually, the *other* aspects of their relationship were imperilled if the parents continued to work long hours away from their children.

The extraordinary "rewards" for the family economy which accompany Step 6—the differentiation imposed by the Act of 1833— were foreseen by Leonard Horner:

This combination of occupation in the mill for eight hours, and of daily attendance at school, with opportunity for healthful exercise, if

[1] G. P. Scrope, *Principles of Political Economy* (London, 1833), p. 358.

generally adopted, would confer signal benefits upon the working-classes connected with factories. Their children, from an early period of their lives, would be able to earn a considerable portion of their subsistence without injury to their health, they would be early trained to order and industrious habits, and, if proper schools were provided, two hours' daily instruction, continued for several years, would give them such an education as could not fail to have the most beneficial effects upon their general character, and, by developing their capacities, and increasing their intelligence, would greatly enlarge their means of improving their condition in life. Under such a system factory employment would be one of the most advantageous in which the children of the working-classes could be engaged.[1]

This classical statement of the case for limiting children's hours promised that the prerequisites for the independent pursuit of a calling—education, developing capacities, improving their condition in life, etc.—could be realized more adequately at this *new* level of differentiation. Because the working class could now reap more of the rewards associated with the dominant value-system, presumably they would be "better off" at this new level. This does not imply that workers would be "happier" in a restricted psychological sense, but simply that they would be better equipped to live a life more in accord with the dominant values of independence, self-sufficiency, personal responsibility, and so on.

In fact, the Act of 1833 succeeded only partially in completing the lines of differentiation. It was "productive of much good; it [put] an end to a large proportion of the evils which made the interference of the legislature . . . necessary [in 1833]."[2] At the same time, however, the Act underlined certain other family problems which were to create disturbances and "regressions." These persisted until the unresolved problems were ironed out. What were these problems which blocked the completion of Step 6 after 1833?

In the first place, neither master nor operative seemed to want to obey the law. We have reviewed the evasions—falsifying certificates of age, outright lying, etc.—which in effect perpetuated some of the conditions existing before 1833.[3] Furthermore, the relay system failed on several counts. It did not influence adult hours, which were always uppermost in the operatives' minds. The shortage of children

---

[1] *Parliamentary Papers*, 1837, XXXI, Factory Inspectors, p. 61.

[2] Horner, *On the Employment of Children*, p. 1.

[3] Above, p. 244. These evasions were to some extent constant, but when the demand for labour was high the number of prosecutions for evasion was higher than when trade was depressed. *Parliamentary Papers*, 1836, XLV, Factory Inspectors, p. 161; 1837, XXXI, Factory Inspectors, pp. 92, 567, 8, 60–61; 1837–8, XXVIII, Factory Inspectors, pp. 83–105.

also drove up the wages of assistants. Finally, the relay system concealed many evasions of the Act.

The causes of [evasions] are *first* that there is a range of fifteen hours within the extreme limits of which these eight hours may be taken; and *secondly*, that the child may be worked at any time of the day, at any intervals within that range. Where they work with relays of three children, each working eight hours, instead of two above thirteen, working twelve hours each, and where the system is regularly attended to, it does quite well; but in the majority of instances, at present, where they employ children under thirteen years of age, they have no relays; *they say* that they manage to do without them the remaining few hours. They are frequently sent out at the most uncertain and irregular times, according as they can be spared; and as that varies often from day to day, so it may easily be seen to what evasions such a system must give rise. . . .[1]

By 1839 Baines complained that six hours for children would have given rise to fewer confusions than eight hours had done; in 1841 and 1842 Leonard Horner recommended the legal enactment of a half-time system for children.[2]

Resistance to the educational provisions was the final headache. While some masters conscientiously provided schools themselves or assured outside training, the majority dismissed children between nine and thirteen, thus avoiding the nuisance of the educational requirements altogether. The operatives, too, often were opposed or indifferent to education either on general grounds or because it deprived them of their children's earnings.[3]

In the years after 1833, therefore, the Factory Act seemed to be creating effects which ran counter to its intended purposes. Presumably it protected children by limiting their hours and guaranteeing their minimum education. Yet masters and parents co-operated to overwork the children, and masters discharged them altogether, thus erasing any educational benefits. The old notions on what was right in family and work were lingering. The evasions in the 1830's and 1840's were trying to turn back the clock of social change to the days before the restrictions on child labour.

[1] Horner, *On the Employment of Children*, p. 7; also Senior, *Letters on the Factory Act*, pp. 18–19; *Parliamentary Papers*, 1835, XL, Factory Inspectors, p. 690; Alfred, *The History of the Factory Movement*, Vol. II, pp. 68–73.

[2] *Parliamentary Debates*, Third Series, XLV, 1839, col. 890; Hutchins and Harrison, *A History of Factory Legislation*, pp. 76–7.

[3] *Parliamentary Papers*, 1836, XLV, Factory Inspectors, p. 158; 1837, XXXI, Factory Inspectors, p. 79; 1837, XVII.2, Poor Law Amendment Act, p. 475; 1843, XIV, Children's Employment Commission, p. 208; 1837–8, VII, Education of the Poorer Classes, pp. 180 ff., 186, 279.

In many ways, therefore, inadequate enforcement of the Act of 1833 left untouched many of the conditions which gave rise to its passage. Nevertheless, the Act of 1833 had a self-propelling effect on the evolution of factory legislation. Before its passage and into the 1830's, the operatives' interest in the factory question was largely "regressive," i.e., looking back to a less differentiated family and community structure. The effect of the Act of 1833, however, was to differentiate the family economy even further, in ways we have outlined. After the Act, the child had to work either part time or not at all, thus weakening the traditional economic relationship between parent and child. If he worked full time as before, it had to be under the threat of total discharge for evasion. If he worked part time, he had to receive minimum educational instruction or face the threat of discharge for evasion of the school clauses.

These effects on child labour naturally modified the conditions of labour of other operatives as well. The Act limited the hours of young persons to twelve per day, thus normalizing the sixty-nine-hour week in the industry.[1] After the Act went into effect, furthermore, the proportion of juveniles and women increased, mostly because they were replacing the diminishing class of children under thirteen. While we do not know whether the proportion of employed married women rose after 1833, it is probable that the sheer *number* of married women working sixty-nine hours a week increased considerably after 1833.

These effects on labour changed the *social significance* of the sixty-nine-hour week. Either because of effective installation of relays or because of total discharge of young children, the child population of nine to thirteen was gradually losing its immediate economic connections with the parent population in the factory. Under such conditions the meaning of sixty-nine hours in the factory changed radically. Sixty-nine hours a week in the mill with children and relatives under one's authority is qualitatively different from sixty-nine hours a week when most of the time with one's children must be spent *outside* these hours. As the children left the factory, many of the family's non-economic functions of moral training and discipline were naturally forced outside the factory. Hence the problems of "leisure" and "education" took on a new and positive significance in the late 1830's; if the non-economic family functions were to be performed effectively, more energy and time had to be allotted outside the factory and presumably to the home and school.

[1] This uniformity of hours was consolidated, no doubt, by the continuing eclipse of the country mills—which traditionally worked longer hours and more nights—between 1830 and 1845. Above, p. 194.

Such problems entered the operatives' agitations in the 1840's. Whereas in the 1830's they were agitating violently to *retard* a process of differentiation and to preserve the multi-functional factory community, in the 1840's their interest began to turn toward the *completion* of a process of differentiation which had been started by the changes in technology and accentuated by the factory legislation of 1833. As we hope to illustrate now, this was the difference between public opinion on the factory question in Step 2 (1830's) and public opinion in Step 6 (1840's).

Factory agitation sank into the doldrums between 1837 and 1841, just after the failure of the attempts to re-establish the old labour pattern between 1833 and 1837. When the factory question emerged in the early 1840's, it seemed to follow several new lines. In the first place, the operatives assumed a new interest in education. Second, they began to agitate for limiting the hours of women. Part of this concern stemmed, no doubt, from realistic dangers to women's health in factory labour; another part may have been a fear that the increasing numbers of women were competing for occupational opportunities.[1] It seems to me, however, that this interest in women's hours—and in education—appeared primarily because of the critical problems created by the separation of adult and child in the preceding decade. This separation gave commanding importance to formal education and to the role of women in the socialization of children *in the home*.

Several themes which emerged in the literature of the factory question in the 1840's lend support to this interpretation:

(1) Public morality. The factory inspectors, who were becoming more and more responsible for informing the public on the state of the manufacturing population in the 1840's, emphasized the broad moral aspects of the limitation of hours. In 1841 Leonard Horner commented thus on the ten-hour day:

There can be little doubt that working 10 hours a-day would be more favourable to health & the enjoyment of life than 12 hours can be; but without entering into the question of health, no one will hesitate, I think, to admit that, *in a moral point of view*, so entire an absorption of the working classes, without intermission, from the early age of 13, and in trades not subject to restriction, much younger, must be extremely prejudicial, and is an evil greatly to be deplored.—For the sake, therefore, of public morals, of bringing up an orderly population, and of giving the great body of people a reasonable enjoyment of life, it is much to be desired, that in all

---

[1] Hutchins and Harrison, *A History of Factory Legislation*, p. 65; *Parliamentary Papers*, 1844, XXVIII, Factory Inspectors, p. 540; above, pp. 202–3.

trades some portion of every working-day should be reserved for rest and leisure.[1]

(2) Education. As early as 1838, many operatives "expressed . . . their satisfaction that the education of the children forms so important a part of the factory Act." The year before, the short-time committee of Manchester had petitioned for the old aim of a ten-hour day for all between ten and twenty-one years of age. Yet one of the advantages they claimed for the ten-year-old minimum was a "better chance of obtaining a little education before [the children] enter the factory." [2] Education—which had been of relatively little interest to the *operatives* ten years earlier—was beginning to creep into the factory agitation. An even stronger impression of this rationale is gained from a reading of the *Ten Hours' Advocate*, the short-time committees' official publication in 1846–7. Among the advantages which it enumerated for a ten-hour day, education occupied an important place:

Of late we have heard much of the evils to be apprehended from legislative interference with factory labour, yet there are few of our readers who cannot recollect the time when factory schools were unknown, and when mill-owners evinced little or no sympathy with the ignorant condition of their workpeople; but since the legislature did interfere, and compelled employers to provide something for their labourers besides work and wages, they seem to appreciate it themselves, and many of them, especially the most intelligent portion of that class, are making praiseworthy efforts to raise the moral condition of their workpeople.[3]

In fact, just after the passing of the Ten Hours Bill in 1847, the *Advocate* rejoiced that

. . . success has at last crowned the efforts of its friends, and we hope the factory workers of these dominions will prove themselves worthy of such a boon; and . . . we hope the youthful advocates of the cause will now set their shoulders to the wheel, and give it all the effects which its most sanguine supporters ever anticipated. . . . Schools there are in almost every locality, and the number of their scholars we trust will be sensibly increased by the factory workers.[4]

[1] *Parliamentary Papers*, 1847–8, XXVI, Factory Inspectors, pp. 152–3. Also 1844, Factory Inspectors, pp. 556–7, 540. For a similar insistence on "sleep, recreation, and attention to . . . moral, religious and domestic duties," cf. 1843, LII, Petition of Master Spinners and Manufacturers, p. 191.

[2] *Parliamentary Papers*, 1837–8, XLV, Factory Inspectors, p. 58; 1837, L, Short-time Committee of Manchester, p. 208.

[3] *Ten Hours' Advocate*, Mar. 6, 1847.

[4] *Ibid.*, June 5, 1847.

(3) The woman's role in the home.

. . . It is needless for us to say, that all attempts to improve the moral and physical condition of female factory workers will be abortive, unless their hours of toil are materially reduced. Indeed, we may go so far as to say, that married females would be much better occupied in performing the domestic duties of the household, than following the never-tiring motion of machinery. We therefore hope the day is not distant, when the husband will be able to provide for his wife and family, without sending the former to endure the drudgery of a cotton mill.[1]

(4) The higher aspirations of the operative class.

Man was made for work, and therefore *in its due degree* we regard it as a blessing. The prejudices of society have hitherto regarded hand-labour as some-thing opposed to the cultivation of the intellect; and that the poor, like women, had no business to think, might be a rule of life whilst unfit to receive a higher. All truths are "truths of periods;" yet, surely now, when the progress of principle is giving the lie to the past, and the voice of intelligence is rising loud and clear above this hiss of engines and this din of shovels, a more amplified code of duty is requisite, and a more enlarged perception of the wants of the operative.[2]

Perhaps as important as the changing content of the operatives' interest was the changing emotional tone of their agitation. The *Ten Hours' Advocate* is a far cry from the hysteria, the universal gloom, the sordid display of crippled operatives, and the predictions of moral and physical decay of the race in the 1830's. While the complaints of health reappeared from time to time, and while Lord Ashley continued his parade of extreme attacks in Parliament in the 1840's, the fever of the ten hour agitation seemed to subside in the 1840's. Even Ashley "was especially watchful to guard against being misunderstood, as believing that a Ten Hours Bill, alone, would prove a panacea for the evils of the manufacturing districts. He looked on it as 'a prelude to other healing and beneficent measures.' "[3] This change in content and emotional tone indicates that the ten hour agitation no longer reflected such extreme symptoms of disturbance as it had in the early 1830's. It was now occurring near the end of a sequence of differentiation rather than near the beginning.

Through the years the factory inspectors had been accumulating

---

[1] *Ibid.*, Oct. 24, 1846.

[2] *Ibid.*, Feb. 27, 1847.

[3] Quoted in Alfred, *The History of the Factory Movement*, Vol. II, p. 171; for a late attack on the health issue, cf. Doherty, *The Ten Hours Bill*, pp. 12, 14–15.

valuable advice and information on the factory laws; in 1843 a Commission on Children's Employment submitted its report; and finally, the workers' agitation for ten hours reached a height in 1844.[1] All these factors resulted in the Act of 1844 (7 & 8 Vict., c. 15), which mainly strengthened and rounded out the Act of 1833. The children's half-time system—limiting those under thirteen years to six and a half hours daily—came into effect, though the minimum age of entry was reduced to eight years. The time of meals was made more uniform for all workers and was to be regulated by a public clock approved by the inspectors. Fines were increased, and sub-inspectors empowered to inspect factories and schools, to certify surgeons, and to disqualify schoolmasters. Masters were required to post the Act, with the name and address of the inspector and certifying surgeon, as well as the hours for beginning, breaking, and ending work. They were required further to keep a register of children in order to discourage evasions. Finally, the Act fixed the hours of young persons *and* women at twelve, thus fixing the twelve-hour day and the sixty-nine-hour week more securely.

Paradoxically, the Act of 1844 made the ultimate enactment of a ten-hour day *more imperative* than it had been before 1844; thus it illustrates the "self-propelling" aspect of much of the factory legislation. The Act of 1833 had disengaged the labour of children under thirteen from the labour of parents fairly effectively. This, however, had led to widespread evasions and complete dismissal of children. By shortening the hours of children further and by making evasion more difficult, the Act of 1844 came nearer to completing the split between child labour and adult labour. Because the sixty-nine-hour week remained for adults, however, this meant that even *less* time with the children within the factory walls was permissible. Hence the Act of 1844 raised the responsibility for education, leisure, and domestic care to an even more critical level.

After a final agitation in 1846–7, the House of Commons passed the Act limiting the hours for women and young persons to ten. This Act meant that the family, which had begun a sequence of differentiation in the 1820's, was now at a sort of equilibrium point. In the 'twenties a number of technological changes had generated two broad sets of dissatisfactions: (*a*) the traditional family structure was inadequate in its new economic environment, and (*b*) by implication, if the labour services of the operatives were to be performed in more differentiated ways, the *other* functions of the family would have to be differentiated as well. The final ten-hour day not

[1] At least the articles reporting meetings, speeches, etc., in the *Manchester Guardian* seemed to cluster in March–July of 1844.

only continued to limit the labour of extremely young children, but also allowed the parents more time and energy to build a new family life outside the factory walls. Hence it met, through a process of *differentiation*, the problems posed by the initial dissatisfactions several decades before. By modern standards, of course, a ten-hour day and fifty-five- or sixty-hour week seem excessive. For the labouring population of the time, however, it meant a dramatic reduction of labour and an equally dramatic increase in time for leisure and private affairs.

We have traced the passage of the Ten Hours Bill of 1847 to certain long-term institutional processes of change. Of course the exact timing and the other circumstances of the legislation depended on several other factors: (1) The operatives organized their agitation very effectively, with mass meetings, travelling missionaries, fundraising efforts, branch committees, an official weekly organ, and very probably the participation of operatives representing more occupational types.[1] (2) For a large body of Tories, the Ten Hours Bill of 1847 was an act of revenge on the Free Traders (dominated by industry and commerce) for repealing the Corn Laws in the preceding year.[2] (3) In 1847, as in 1833, the presence of depressed trade conditions led operatives and others to believe that the unemployed could be absorbed if hours were shorter.[3] The arguments of opponents of the Act were weakened because many of them were employing workers on short time or discharging them altogether. These three influences on the timing of the Act of 1847, however, do not negate the long-term forces pressing toward structural differentiation.

The Act came into effect over a period of two years; from July 1, 1847 to May 1, 1848, an eleven-hour day obtained, and ten hours came into force after that. For a few years the universal principle of ten hours was not realized because of overtime work, the use of women and young persons in relays, and the manufacturers' manipulation of meal-times.[4] In 1850 Parliament raised the weekday to $10\frac{1}{2}$ hours, shortened Saturdays to $7\frac{1}{2}$ hours, and restricted the possible working hours per day to those between 6 a.m. and 6 p.m., with a minimum of $1\frac{1}{2}$ hours for meals, thus killing the relay system. This Act, plus a modifying one in 1853, brought the "normal working day" finally into existence.

[1] Driver, *Tory Radical*, pp. 464–5; *Ten Hours' Advocate*, Sept. 26, 1846; below, pp. 336–7.

[2] Hutchins and Harrison, *A History of Factory Legislation*, pp. 61–2; Hammond, *Lord Shaftesbury*, pp. 14–15; Clapham, *An Economic History of Modern Britain*, p. 577.

[3] Rostow, *British Economy in the Nineteenth Century*, pp. 118–20.

[4] Summarized in Marx, *Capital*, pp. 272–8.

Hence the Act of 1847 and its subsequent patchwork mark the successful completion of Step 6, which had begun in 1833 and had suffered a number of jolts, starts, and minor "regressions" through the 1830's and 1840's. Upon this completion, were there any evidences of "extraordinary rewards" for the family?* Naturally we must guard our judgments in this matter, for there are few convenient indices of such "rewards." We must rely on expressions of satisfaction or dissatisfaction with the new state of affairs, and the general expression of public opinion on the factory question.

In general the operatives responded satisfactorily to the new arrangements. We have indicated the expressions of satisfaction among those operatives observing the law and obeying the educational clauses in the late 1830's. Several other experiments and expressions of opinion indicate similar sentiments in the 1840's. In a Preston factory in 1845, the managers undertook an experimental reduction of hours from twelve to eleven in order to gauge its effect on production. In connection with this experiment, Leonard Horner observed that the factory spinners and weavers "enumerated the many advantages and enjoyments they derived from stopping an hour sooner at night; and, among others, they stated that whereas while they were working twelve hours, only twenty-seven people in the mill attended the night school, there [were] now ninety-six." [1] Not only were the workers pleased with additional leisure, but they also linked their satisfaction to education. After the passage of the 1847 Act two informal polls among operatives showed overwhelming preference for the reduced hours. One firm preferred eleven hours over ten by a majority of 480 to 143, whereas a second group, consisting of 838 spinners in the borough of Bolton, preferred ten hours by 829 to 5, with four not voting. The alternative of returning to twelve hours was not even suggested.[2] Contemporary observers felt that the operatives experienced "great joy" after the 1847 Act, and that they seemed, years later, "comparatively comfortable and satisfied." Leonard Horner wrote in 1850 that the ten hour act "has taken deep root in the good opinion of the operatives." [3]

By far the most convincing expression of opinion, however, was Horner's extensive "public opinion poll" of operatives sixteen months after the eleven hour restriction and seven months after the

* Above, pp. 171–2. This corresponds to profits in the industrial sphere.

[1] *Parliamentary Papers*, 1845, XXV, Factory Inspectors, p. 450.

[2] Polls reported in *Manchester Guardian*, July 4, 1849; *Parliamentary Papers*, 1847–8, XXVI, Factory Inspectors, pp. 151–2.

[3] Alfred, *The History of the Factory Movement*, Vol. II, p. 284; Waugh, *Lancashire Sketches*, p. 181; Lyell, *A Memoir of Leonard Horner*, Vol. II, pp. 158–9.

ten hour restriction took effect. Horner was attempting to assess "the general feeling among the factory operatives on this additional limitation of their hours of work." Horner and his associates conducted the interviews themselves, talking to the operatives privately and anonymously. After obtaining their marital status, age, and wages, the offcials asked the operatives the following questions:

(1) You say that you are getting 10*s.* a-week for 10 hours, and that you would get 12*s.* if you worked 12 hours; but although you only get 10*s.* you work two hours less, and so you have two hours a-day more at your own disposal. Now tell me, whether, taking all things into account you would prefer to work 10 hours for 10*s.* a-week, or go back to 12 hours to get more wages? (2) Suppose there were three mills near together, in each of which the work was the same, and all equally convenient to you, one of them working 10 hours a-day, where you would get 10*s.* a-week; another working 11 hours where you would get 11*s.*, and the other working 12 hours where you would get 12*s.*, which of the three would you like to work in? [1]

Horner recorded the answers of *only* those operatives whose wages had been reduced by the ten hour legislation; "if any were not receiving less than they would do were they working 12 hours," Horner "did not carry the conversation further." Hence we may infer that those whose wages were not influenced by the Act of 1847 probably preferred the reduced hours almost unanimously. The following results refer, moreover, only to those whose wages had been reduced by the Act. [2]

Of the 1,153 operatives interviewed, 61¾% preferred ten hours' work, even at reduced wages; 12¾% preferred eleven hours, and 25½% preferred twelve hours. Thus a total of 74½% opposed returning

[1] *Parliamentary Papers*, 1849, XXII, Factory Inspectors, p. 144. The responses were subject to some known biases. The large mills and factories were over-represented. Furthermore, some of the sub-inspectors apparently did not propose the alternatives in an identical manner, for in one division nearly 50 per cent preferred 11 hours, as opposed to the general average of 12¾ per cent; in another region the preference for 10 hours seemed extraordinarily high. Horner also pointed out that the depressed conditions of trade might have influenced some operatives to respond favourably to "twelve," with the understanding that this would tide them over the hard times. In general, however, while Horner's polling methods do not measure up to modern sampling and statistical standards, a fair impression of the labourer's opinions could be gained.

[2] Wood judged that wage reductions in 1846–9 are traceable more to piece-rate reductions in the conditions of depressed trade. "The 'Ten Hours Act' caused a slight reduction of earnings, but . . . this reduction was only temporary." G. H. Wood, "Factory Legislation, considered with reference to the Wages, etc., of the Operatives Protected thereby," *Journal of the Royal Statistical Society*, LXV (1902), pp. 292–6.

to twelve. In general, men preferred shorter hours than women. Of the men, 82¾% preferred either ten or eleven hours, as opposed to 63⅓% of the women. Wage-levels also influenced the preferences. Men receiving less than 10*s*. 10*d*. weekly voted 57% to remain at ten hours, considerably below the men's average. On the other hand, women receiving under 10*s*. weekly voted 64%, or about average for women, to continue at ten hours.

In general, then, the operatives received the reduction in hours warmly. Furthermore, a number of millowners and their agents expressed a strong belief in interviews that the majority of work-people would oppose returning to twelve hours. These responses surprised Horner, but at the same time gratified him, since "the reason for [the preference for ten hours] by so many young persons, and even adults, that it enabled them to attend evening schools, is a gratifying circumstance, as affording a good sign of the character of the factory population." [1]

In an attempt to shed more light on these responses and on our interpretive scheme, I calculated in the Appendix the distribution of responses of men and women according to (*a*) marital and parental status and (*b*) their wage-level. While all the results are not significant statistically, the following patterns of preference appeared among the operatives:

Prefer 10 hours	*Prefer more than 10 hours*
Unmarried men	Married men
Men earning more than 17*s*. 6*d*. weekly	Men earning 17*s*. 6*d*. or less weekly
Married men earning more than 17*s*. 6*d*. weekly	Married men earning 17*s* 6*d*. or less weekly
Men with 0 or 1 children	Men with 2 or more children
Men with 0 or 1 children earning more than 17*s*. 6*d*. weekly	Men with 0 or 1 children earning 17*s*. 6*d*. or less weekly
Men with 2 or more children earning more than 17*s*. 6*d*. weekly	Men with 2 or more children earning 17*s*. 6*d*. or less weekly
Married women	Unmarried women
Women earning more than 8*s*. weekly	Women earning 8*s*. or less weekly
Married women earning more than 8*s*. weekly	Married women earning 8*s*. or less weekly
Women with children earning more than 8*s*. weekly	Women with children earning 8*s*. or less weekly
Childless married women earning more than 8*s*. weekly	Childless married women earning 8*s*. or less weekly

Finally, I traced the individual responses of those women with children who preferred to work long hours (*n*=47). Of these, four

[1] *Parliamentary Papers*, 1849, XXII, Factory Inspectors, p. 146.

were widows, three had husbands in America, one had been deserted by her husband, two had unemployed husbands, and one had a husband employed as a piecer (low-wage work). Almost one-fourth of the responses thus showed unusual and pressing economic conditions, and many of the remaining responses stressed wage considerations. This last response is consistent with the general trend in the table whereby economic necessity conditioned the desire to work twelve hours strongly.

How may we interpret the complex results of the table above theoretically?* In the thirty years before 1850 the family economy of the operatives had been experiencing a long process of *structural differentiation*. One ingredient of this process was an increase in the real income of more differentiated families, i.e., factory operatives. This augmented income is significant in two senses: (*a*) as a *reward* for offering labour in the market on a more differentiated basis (e.g., as power-loom operative, spinner on improved machinery, etc.); (*b*) as a *facility* to enhance the expenditures (style of life) of the family.** Another important component of the differentiation was the need to re-define the other family functions (education, recreation, moral training, etc.). Many of these functions which had been performed hitherto *on the factory premises* were now removed outside the factory, and required attention on a new basis.

In this light we may interpret the results of the operatives' responses in 1849. Those operatives who preferred to return to more than ten hours may be accounted for as follows: (1) They were not yet in a position of family responsibility which required attention to the non-economic functions of the family. Hence unmarried women preferred to work longer than married women. True, married men preferred to return to twelve hours when compared with unmarried men. As we shall see presently, however, most of these married men either had large families and/or earned low wages. In addition, the pressure for married men to be in the home was not so great as for married women to be in the home, because the latter assumed primary responsibility for the non-economic (e.g., child-rearing) family functions. (2) Those operatives who had not yet reaped the

* In summarizing these opinions, we must keep in mind that neither sufficient controls nor statistical significance clearly justify definitive conclusions. Furthermore, we know neither the exact level of wages required to gain the necessaries of life nor the income of other family members of the operatives. Both these factors cloud any inferences from the results above. The general *direction* which appeared in the results, however, seems to justify the theoretical remarks which follow.

** For the theoretical justification of the rise in real income, cf. above, pp. 171–2. For the empirical course of real wages, above, pp. 214–15. The significance of income as rewards and facilities is discussed above, pp. 172–4.

wage benefits of the more differentiated industrial and family structure. Hence they could not even meet the basic expenditures for necessities, much less the educational, recreational, and other motivational expenditures in the family.* Thus both men and women with low wages preferred to work longer hours than those earning higher wages. Men with large families and/or lower wages preferred longer hours more than those with small families and/or higher wages. Women with children and/or lower wages preferred to work longer hours, and their individual responses show a struggle to maintain the basic necessities of life. These low-wage, large-family workers were struggling, in short, to keep the family unit together in the most basic sense. They were squeezed, as it were, by the cross-pressures of industrial and familial differentiation; they had been forced to a new level of specialization but their wages had not yet risen to the level required by a more differentiated industrial family.

On the other hand, married operatives who were earning more than enough to meet their basic and necessary expenditures were able to turn to the educational and other motivational functions of the family.** Hence the greater preference for ten hours among married persons earning higher wages.*** Hence also the link between the reduction to ten hours and the opportunities for education and "leisure" in Horner's poll, in the experiment at Preston, and in the ten hour literature of the period. These "successfully differentiated" operatives in the 1840's were able not only to meet their standard basic expenditures but also to turn to the category of "motivational spending" on a new and more differentiated basis.****

APPENDIX

STATISTICAL BREAKDOWN OF RESPONSES IN LEONARD HORNER'S POLL, 1849

In the following tables I have tabulated the responses in Leonard Horner's poll according to sex, marital status, and wage-level. To

---

* The basic expenditures for necessities refer to the standard package (E_{Aa}), whereas the educational and recreational expenditures refer to motivational spending (E_{Ag}). Above, pp. 173–7.

** There is no claim that men earning more than 17s. 6d. and women earning more than 8s. were automatically able to meet their basic expenditures. We merely broke the wage distribution at this point and hoped that the general trend, artificially obscured by the dichotomization, might appear anyway.

*** If anything, married women showed this tendency more than married men. Cf. Appendix. Perhaps this indicates their more crucial position in the non-economic functions of the family.

**** Above, pp. 173–4 for technical definitions of "basic expenditures," "motivational spending," etc.

Differentiation of the Family Structure: Factory Legislation

each table I have applied a chi-square calculation,* more for the reader's interest rather than as a rigorous statistical test, since the collection of the original information was so casual.

According to marital status of men, the married men seemed to show a slightly greater willingness to work longer hours than unmarried men ($\chi^2=1\cdot821$, significant only at the $\cdot20$ level):

$N=434$ †	Prefer 10 hours	Prefer more than 10 hours
Married	192	133
Unmarried	73	36

In addition, lower-paid male workers seemed more willing to work more than ten hours ($\chi^2=3\cdot362$, significant at the $\cdot10$ level):

$N=434$	Prefer 10 hours	Prefer more than 10 hours
More than 17s. 6d.	107	51
17s. 6d. or less	161	115

When we combine these two influences of marital status and wages, however, we find that among *married* men those earning low wages are willing to work more than ten hours ($\chi^2=5\cdot49$, significant at the $\cdot02$ level), whereas the same relationship does not obtain among *unmarried* men ($\chi^2=\cdot008$ or completely insignificant):

$N=325$	Prefer 10 hours	Prefer more than 10 hours
Married — More than 17s. 6d.	99	48
17s. 6d. or less	96	82

* G. W. Snedecor, *Statistical Methods* (Ames, Iowa, 1948), pp. 194–200.
† Of the total of 651 men interviewed, the marital status of only 434 was indicated.

Differentiation of the Family Structure: Factory Legislation

		Prefer 10 hours	Prefer more than 10 hours
	N=109		
Unmarried	More than 17s. 6d.	8	3
	17s. 6d. or less	65	33

Among married men alone, there seems to be a slight desire for more than ten hours among men with large families ($\chi=1\cdot592$, significant at the ·30 level):

	Prefer 10 hours	Prefer more than 10 hours
N=264 *		
0 or 1 children	45	23
2 or more children	112	84

For small families ($\chi^2=2\cdot795$, significant at the ·10 level) as well as large ($\chi^2=2\cdot642$, significant at the ·20 level), however, those men with higher wages seem to show a preference for shorter hours:

		Prefer 10 hours	Prefer more than 10 hours
	N=68		
0 or 1 children	More than 17s. 6d.	16	3
	17s. 6d. or less	29	20

		Prefer 10 hours	Prefer more than 10 hours
	N=196		
2 or more children	More than 17s. 6d.	74	45
	17s. 6d. or less	38	39

I also tabulated the responses of women according to marital status and wage-level. Married women seemed to prefer shorter

* Among the 325 married men, the family status of only 264 was indicated.

hours to a greater extent than unmarried women ($\chi^2=1\cdot659$, significant at the ·20 level):

$N=396$ *	Prefer 10 hours	Prefer more than 10 hours
Married	99	89
Unmarried	95	113

Furthermore, the lower the wages among women, the greater the willingness to work longer hours ($\chi^2=10\cdot863$, significant at the ·01 level):

$N=396$*	Prefer 10 hours	Prefer more than 10 hours
More than 8s.	82	52
8s. or less	113	149

For *married* women, low wages indicate a greater willingness to work longer hours ($\chi^2=14\cdot301$, significant at the ·01 level), but the same effect did not obtain for *unmarried* women ($\chi^2=0\cdot251$, or insignificant):

$N=188$		Prefer 10 hours	Prefer more than 10 hours
Married	More than 8s.	51	21
	8s. or less	48	68

$N=208$		Prefer 10 hours	Prefer more than 10 hours
Unmarried	More than 8s.	30	31
	8s. or less	65	82

* Of the 402 women interviewed, the marital status of 396 was listed.

Among the married women with children, those earning lower wages seemed more prepared to work longer hours ($\chi^2 = 2 \cdot 582$, significant at the ·20 level):

	$N=85*$	Prefer 10 hours	Prefer more than 10 hours
	More than 8s.	16	11
Children	8s. or less	22	36

The same effect holds for married women with no children ($\chi^2 = 5 \cdot 553$, significant at the ·02 level):

	$N=35*$	Prefer 10 hours	Prefer more than 10 hours
	More than 8s.	9	5
No children	8s. or less	4	17

* Of the 188 married women, the parental status of only 120 (85 plus 35) was indicated.

CHAPTER XII

NEW CONDITIONS OF EMPLOYMENT: THE EVOLUTION OF TRADE UNIONS

Introduction. In the last few chapters we followed the differentiation of roles within the family itself. The end-product in the 1840's and 1850's was a more specialized family structure. As part of this process, several of the family's functions began to slip away. To take over these old functions, complementary organizations began to appear. In particular, we witnessed the commencement of a greater interest in formal education for factory children. In this chapter and the next we shall trace the evolution of several other organizations which were geared closely to the functions of the family economy between 1770 and 1840—the trade union, the friendly society, the savings bank, the loan society, etc.

We may render the evolution of these social units more intelligible by applying the model of structural differentiation once again. Each came into existence or changed its old structure to fulfil a function more adequately. Each followed the steps of dissatisfaction, disturbance, handling and channelling, etc., in its course of development. This process is *formally* identical with the differentiation of roles in the family economy, even though we are now dealing with the appearance and change of larger organizations.

From the *economic* standpoint, the trade union is significant in so far as it controls or restricts the conditions of industrial production. We shall ignore this aspect of trade unionism in our analysis. From the standpoint of the *family*, the trade union is a specialized organization which regulates the relationship between the family unit and its industrial employment.* If there is any differentiation whatsoever between the family and the organization of production in society, such problems of regulation must arise. The trade union is thus an organization which mediates between the family and its industrial pursuits: "a continuous association of wage-earners for the purpose of maintaining or improving the conditions of their employment." [1]

Because wage problems arise so often in industrial disputes, it is

---

* That is to say, the trade union regulates, in part, the conditions of exchange at the E_G–C_G boundary. Above, pp. 163–4.

[1] Webb, *History of Trade Unionism*, p. 1.

tempting to limit the "conditions of employment" to wage-regulation. These conditions also include, however, control over plant conditions, "fringe" benefits not directly translatable into wage receipts, limitations on the master's authority, rules regarding apprenticeship, etc. In addition, some of the union's functions are clearly "social," e.g., protecting the status of labourers, expressing the solidarity of members, etc.[1]

In this chapter we shall see how the structure of the cotton-textile trade unions *changed* to fulfil the above functions. In the early nineteenth century they became more specialized, and thereby became less entangled with other roles and organizations. They pulled away from the old friendly society; they relied less and less on masters, publicans, and other tradesmen for financial aid; they achieved a degree of organizational autonomy, etc. Because information on trade unions in these early years is scarce, however, we must be less ambitious than we were in analysing the differentiation of the family.

Since we treat this sequence in the early nineteenth century as an episode in a longer history of growth, we may by-pass the question of the origin of trade unions as such. The Webbs attribute the origin of trade-unionism in cotton textiles basically to the divorce of the manual worker from the means of production and to the separation of the worker and the entrepreneur.* We should add the Webbs' qualification, however, that this is not a sufficient cause for trade unions in general, but only for trade unions of a certain type.[2] The model of structural differentiation explains how this type appeared, and why it assumed its peculiar structure.

Historical Background. As the early weaving records show, unions —in the form of trade clubs or friendly societies—existed in the cotton trade long before the onset of machinery. These organizations possessed, however, several characteristics which were to disappear in the early nineteenth century. In the first place, the eighteenth-century unions displayed a sort of community of feeling between masters and men.

Their occasional disputes with their employers resembled rather family differences than conflicts between distinct social classes. They exhibit more tendency to "stand in" with the masters against the community, or to back them against rivals or interlopers, than to join their fellow-workers of other trades in an attack upon the capitalist class.[3]

---

[1] Parsons and Smelser, *Economy and Society*, pp. 146–9.
* I.e., differentiation at the C_{Ag}–C_{Lg} and C_{Gi}–C_{Li} boundaries, respectively.
[2] *History of Trade Unionism*, pp. 26–7, 41, 43–5.
[3] *Ibid.*, p. 46.

Wages were traditionalized and standardized, and workers' concern was less with short-term bargaining and negotiation than with the "enforcement of apprenticeship rules and a definite length of piece for weaving to enforce the control of wage-levels." [1] The control of the physical conditions of production, the control of labour supply, and the control of wages were closely related aspects of trade unionism.

The interest in trade-union matters, furthermore, was an aspect of the friendly society movement. Such societies were primarily a means of insuring through savings against sickness, old age, and death. In addition, the friendly society was a centre for convivial drinking, fellowship, and solidarity. At the same time, workmen expressed their grievances and desires to masters through the friendly society. Thus "the boundary between friendly society and trade union [in the eighteenth and even into the early nineteenth century] was extremely narrow. The law did not distinguish between them, and until 1794 the same restrictions applied to both." [2]

We take the friendly society of the 1790's in the spinning branches as the starting-point for our analysis of the differentiation of trade unions.* The earliest societies are probably those of Stockport and Manchester in 1792, even though as early as 1785 the "Friendly Society of Cotton Spinners in [Stockport] was instructing its members not to work below the 'usual prices.'" [3] By 1799 "there appear to have existed local combinations, of more or less permanence in nearly every town in Lancashire." [4]

Unfortunately "the records of the existing societies offer practically no information." [5] The early rules show, however, the societies' diffuse functions, their communal intimacy, and their traditional views on labour supply. The Stockport rules, for instance, besides restricting apprenticeship to certain classes, proposed fines for members who "after having received his, her, or their wages, shall, in a boasting manner, (as hath frequently been the case) acquaint different people not being members of this society, what money they

---

[1] Chapman, *The Lancashire Cotton Industry*, p. 183; Wadsworth and Mann, *The Cotton Trade and Industrial Lancashire*, pp. 338–9.

[2] Wadsworth and Mann, *The Cotton Trade and Industrial Lancashire*, p. 375; Chapman, *The Lancashire Cotton Industry*, pp. 180–9.

* Strictly speaking, these clubs themselves represent a differentiation from the earlier years of domestic hand-spinning, for previously the spinning operatives (women and children) had not been organized at all.

[3] Morris, *The History of the Labour Movement in England*, p. 32; Chapman, *The Lancashire Cotton Industry*, p. 193.

[4] *Webb Manuscripts on Trade Unionism*, Vol. XXXIV, p. 116.

[5] *Ibid.*

have earned in a short time (which has often been very injurious to cotton Spinners)." In addition, the society was "to raise a fund for the maintenance of such as shall hereafter be in distress, and to defray the funeral expenses of those who may die members of this society." A final rule showed an interest in close co-operation with the masters. Exclusion from the society was the punishment for anyone who

shall assault or abuse any master, or other person employed as foreman, or manager in the business of Cotton Spinning, or destroy property, or make riot, or disobey summons of the Justice of the Peace, or be found guilty of any crime.

Exclusion meant that offenders could not

partake of the advantages hereby intended, for the encouragement of sobriety, industry, and peaceable behaviour; and every member of the said society doth hereby agree to observe, and strictly perform all the articles herein contained, so that peace, harmony, love and friendship may be preserved between them, and their families, and that the Cotton Manufacture may thereby flourish and increase.[1]

The Manchester rules of 1792 and 1795 and the Oldham rules in 1796 contain similar stipulations. The "friendly" character of the latter is revealed at the beginning of their printed regulations:

> We'll friendly join
> As the rose and vine
> We'll spin our threads with equal twine
> Which sheweth plain and good design.[2]

The Oldham group held meetings on Monday nights at a public house, where deposits were placed in a box for relieving sick members, those out of work involuntarily, and those lame or unemployable. The rules also contained fines for intoxication at meetings, abusive conduct, cursing, swearing, etc., and for disclosing the society's affairs to outsiders.

Over the next several decades many new institutional structures rose from these multifunctional friendly societies—the new trade union, the savings bank, the co-operative society, and other organizations of industrial England.[3] Let us first apply the model of structural

---

[1] *Articles . . . of the Friendly Associated Mule Cotton Spinners of Stockport*, Preamble, and pp. 12, 15.

[2] Quoted in *Webb Manuscripts on Trade Unionism*, Vol. XXXVI, p. 74.

[3] This general position is developed in Baernreither, *English Associations of Working Men*, pp. 156–7, 160–2.

differentiation to the rise of industrial trade unionism in the cotton-spinning branches.*

Step 1. Dissatisfaction. In the face of urbanization and centralization of machinery after 1790, the diffuse friendly society fell quickly into obsolescence as an organ for protecting the conditions of labour. Because hordes of labourers were pouring into the industry, the sporadic and local methods of preventing members from boasting and guarding the affairs of the society were completely outmoded. Even if the local societies had attempted to co-ordinate their activities, the primitive conditions of communication made a network of such clubs almost impossible. In short, in this period the friendly society was too diffuse, small, and intimate to control wage-levels, entry into the trade, and the training of the young.**

According to the model of differentiation, we would expect these dissatisfactions to give rise, in an ordered sequence, to a new kind of organization which would assume its functions on a more specialized basis. In fact this happened over the next several decades. The sequence was not smooth, however; several obstacles delayed the emergence of a new unionism, and these obstacles precipitated several "regressive" disturbances along the way.

The first obstacle to easy evolution was the political effect of the Revolutionary and Napoleonic wars. From the outbreak of the French Revolution in 1789 well into the nineteenth century the British government was extraordinarily sensitive to the possibility of conspiracy and revolution. A number of repressive attempts to eradicate any interest in reform issued from this mentality. In the 1790's the Pitt government prosecuted reform groups and in 1799 an Act made illegal national associations which corresponded with each other. Clearly such legislation discouraged friendly societies from forming any sort of central organization. Furthermore, the legislature

---

* For the failure of unionism in hand-loom weaving, above, pp. 262–3.
** Most immediately, this kind of dissatisfaction refers to the external boundary (E_G–C_G) of the family economy. Given the industrial trends of the 1790's and following years, the family was powerless to regulate the interchange at this boundary. In terms of the table of resources, the dissatisfaction refers to the transition between G-4 (occupational role) and G-5 (commitment of labour in an occupational context). Above, pp. 163–9. This general dissatisfaction, however, implied dissatisfactions at all the internal boundaries of the family's E_G sub-system: (1) a dissatisfaction with occupational role-performance and the controls over its conditions (G-5, or E_{G_g}–E_{I_g}); (2) a dissatisfaction with the control over the earning capacity of the family members (A-5 or E_{Aa}–E_{Ga}); (3) a dissatisfaction with the controls over the levels of skill and competence required for the trade (I-6, or E_{G_i}–E_{L_i}). Above, pp. 166–9, 176–9. All these dissatisfactions, however, focused on the friendly society because it was the traditional medium for guaranteeing the workman's security in these spheres.

restricted the activities of trade combinations, probably because of the long-term association in men's minds between combination and conspiracy. Through the eighteenth century numerous Acts had prohibited combinations from restricting wages in individual trades. The Combination Acts of 1799–1800 generalized such restrictions to all trades.[1]

On the other hand, the war period burdened the government not only with financing the wars but with mounting bills for supporting the poor. Hence political leaders took an interest in encouraging working-class organizations which might relieve these public burdens. In 1793 an Act granted several monetary and administrative benefits to friendly societies which registered with the justices of the peace. This encouragement initiated a rapid growth of societies, especially in Lancashire.[2]

In these ways the government, labouring under political and economic emergencies, initiated a policy of cross-pressures on the friendly society. The effect was that

the confusion between friendly societies and trade clubs became complete. The state blessed . . . with its right hand and cursed with its left. Under [the Act of 1793] it blessed only rules which had been submitted to Quarter Sessions; but some things could easily be left out of the rules, and any body called a friendly society, even if it had not submitted its rules, sounded respectable until proved subversive.[3]

The behaviour of the Manchester Friendly Associated Spinners in the 1790's reflects these cross-pressures. Both the 1792 and the 1795 rules of the organization contain restrictive clauses on labour supply and benefits for members. The emphasis on each type of clause, however, illustrates the retreat of the trade-union aspects behind the skirts of the friendly society. In March, 1795, the mule-spinners of Manchester made the following defence of their activities in a recent labour dispute in an announcement "to the Employers of Mule-Spinners, and the Public in General":

The Advertisement in this Paper on Tuesday last, in the First Few Lines mentions, with the most perfect Truth, the complicated miseries prevailing amongst us Journeymen Mule-Spinners; but to say that it arises from our own Misconduct, cannot possibly be Truth; as it is Incontestable, that the Reduction of our Wages is the real Cause. We

[1] Cole, *A Short History of the British Working Class Movement*, pp. 43–52; Fay, *Life and Labour in the Nineteenth Century*, p. 52; George, "The Combination Laws Reconsidered," *op. cit.*, pp. 222–3; Webb, *History of Trade Unionism*, p. 58.
[2] For a discussion of the poor rates and the Act of 1793, below, pp. 349–50 and 354–6.
[3] Clapham, *An Economic History of Modern Britain*, p. 296.

consider it a Duty Incumbent upon us, therefore, with Deference to you Gentlemen, to acquit ourselves of the charges laid against us. We are falsely accused of combining against our Employers; which is not the Case. Combination, it is true seldom or never creates any thing good; but Combination, a Candid Public will Easily see, is not in Question with us—the Nature of our Meeting, or Club, is not to encourage Idleness, or promote Disorder; but only to Relieve our Fellow Labourers in Distress; and to say that Numbers of Industrious People have been dragged from their Places and menaced by the Members of our Club, and compelled to loiter about the streets in Idleness, until the Encrease of Wages demanded from their Employers be granted—we deny.

No reasonable Person can suppose we wish to Encrease the Claims upon our Society, as none but ourselves, assist in the discharge thereof. We feel no Desire or Inclination for Hostility, but humbly hope you will take into Consideration the present excessive Price of Provision, and every other necessary of Life, and at your Meeting adopt some Measure of affording every honest industrious Workman Wages sufficient to maintain him and his Family with decency; which is the most certain method of securing our happiness, and the only wish of us Poor Mule-Spinners—But if our Employers choose to lay the secrets of their Business open to the Public, we cannot help it; we for our part shall keep it inviolable, until the result of your Meeting is made known to us. We are, Gentlemen, waiting your favourable decision,

Your's, &c.
MULE-SPINNERS [1]

This claim to innocence was underscored six weeks later when the Manchester Spinners submitted their Rules. By contrast with their old Rules of 1792, the 1795 version played up their "friendly society" aspects and played down their "combination" aspects on several grounds:

(1) The 1792 Rules required a spinner entering a shop to produce a ticket showing membership in the Friendly Associated Mule Spinners. In 1795 this Rule disappeared in favour of a milder one requiring members to carry tickets, with a fine for losing or lending them. Further, the 1795 Rules designated the head shopman of every master to be responsible for collecting subscriptions for the friendly society.[2] Clearly the same pressures on spinners not carrying cards were possible under the 1795 Rules; outwardly, however, the practices seemed less restrictive.

(2) The 1792 Rules prohibited members from taking employment

---

[1] *Manchester Mercury*, Mar. 3, 1795.
[2] Article XV of the 1792 Rules; Articles VI and VII of the 1795 Rules.

in shops where a turnout had occurred. In 1795 this restriction was omitted.[1]

(3) The 1792 Rules stipulated that every "Stranger . . . having learned to Spin elsewhere" should pay 10s. 6d. to the Society in order to stop "idle and wandering Persons" from coming to Manchester. Members were instructed that if this stranger refused to pay "he or she shall be deemed unworthy the Notice of any Member of the said Society." The 1795 Rules omitted this clause.[2]

(4) The 1792 Rules merely earmarked subscriptions and fines for members in distress and for members' funerals. In 1795 the benefit clauses were more elaborate, specifying benefits for sick, blind, and lame members, funerals for members and next of kin, and more comprehensive allowances.[3]

Thus in the 1790's the need for protecting the conditions of labour was becoming more critical because of the advancing technology; paradoxically, however, the societies for protecting labour, far from blossoming to maturity, were shrouding themselves under the cloak of the more popular friendly society movement. Apparently this practice was general in the war period.

these clubs were, in many instances, composed of persons working at the same trade; the habits and opportunities of association, which the Friendly Societies gave to them, doubtless afforded facilities of combination for raising wages and other purposes, all of which were then unlawful, connected with their common business.[4]

As late as the 1830's workmen hesitated to reveal anything about their benefit clubs.[5]

After the turn of the century the Combination Laws retarded the development of trade unions. The actual force of these laws in the war period and following is a subject of much controversy. On the one side is the impression that "[between 1810 and 1824] the sufferings of persons employed in the cotton manufacture were beyond credibility. They were drawn into combinations, betrayed, prosecuted, convicted, sentenced, and monstrously severe punishments were inflicted on them; they were reduced to and kept in the most

---

[1] Article XIII of the 1792 Rules.

[2] Article XVIII of the 1792 Rules.

[3] Article XXIII of the 1792 Rules; Articles XVIII and XIX of the 1795 Rules.

[4] *Parliamentary Papers*, 1825, IV, Laws Respecting Friendly Societies, p. 328. The same committee said, however, that much of this abuse was limited to the "older societies" (p. 343), indicating, no doubt, that the friendly society and trade union were beginning to be differentiated from each other. Also Aspinall, *The Early English Trade Unions*, p. 156.

[5] Clapham, *An Economic History of Modern Britain*, p. 210.

wretched state of existence." [1] On the other hand, some feel that the application of the laws was "a far less potent instrument of oppression than a prosecution for conspiracy at common law," and that it was directed more at cases of suspected conspiracy than at simple association. [2] What prosecution there was in the name of the Laws seemed to fall on the new textile unions more heavily than on others. [3] In addition to their direct effects, however, the Combination Laws symbolically discouraged, by means of "prosecution by example," the emergence of differentiated unions.

Under the pressures of the war period, the operatives' organization beyond the friendly society level was "local and short-lived." In the 1810 strike in and around Manchester, a strikers' fund of £1,500 per week was distributed to unemployed spinners. After this strike, however, the "union was . . . utterly destroyed and remained extinct for just eight years." Again, in 1818, a short and gasping attempt to form a General Union of Trades failed. The ignominious defeat suffered by the spinners in 1818 again destroyed their union, and "no union whatever existed . . . from the latter end of 1818 to the end of 1823." [4]

Nevertheless the spinners were reputed to be the strongest workers' organization. In 1816

the classes of persons in the manufactures of [Lancashire] that have been most formidable to their employers, by their combinations, are the calico printers and cotton spinners who, labouring in large numbers in print works or cotton factories under the same masters respectively, have for many years past been almost every year in a state of combination against their respective employers. [5]

A mill manager said in 1819 that he preferred women and children to men because of the "many Combinations that have taken place amongst the Men, and the Trouble they give." Again in 1824 the desperate Lancashire hand-loom weavers noted that it was by "secret combinations that the tailors, joiners, and spinners had succeeded in keeping up wages." [6]

[1] *Webb Manuscripts on Trade Unionism*, Vol. XXXIV, p. 19. Quoted from Francis Place.
[2] George, "The Combination Laws Reconsidered," *op. cit.*, pp. 216, 222–3.
[3] Webb, *History of Trade Unionism*, pp. 56–7, 65–9, 72.
[4] Clapham, *An Economic History of Modern Britain*, p. 215; *The Quinquarticular System of Organization*, p. 3; Hammond, *The Skilled Labourer*, pp. 99–103. Above, pp. 229–30 for descriptions of the 1810 and 1818 strikes.
[5] Aspinall, *The Early English Trade Unions*, p. 214.
[6] *Lords Sessional Papers*, 1819, XVI, Children employed in the Cotton Manufactories, p. 610; Webb, *History of Trade Unionism*, p. 98.

New Conditions of Employment: The Evolution of Trade Unions

The period between 1793 and 1824 was thus a period of conflicting trends. Dissatisfactions with the friendly society as a medium for protecting the conditions of labour increased as industrial changes proceeded; yet the government and other authorities encouraged the friendly societies and *discouraged* activities dealing directly with wages and other conditions of employment. The sequence of structural differentiation was thereby "stuck" at Step 1, despite some sporadic attempts at organization and despite the general strength of the spinners.*

Step 2. Symptoms of Disturbance. Since the evolution of trade-unionism was mired in its early stages, symptoms of disturbance began to appear in the war period. Because of the repressive attitude of the government, however, outright expression of disturbance was dangerous. Thus the unions—handicapped by ineffective organization, unsuccessful strikes, and the threat of repression—displayed this disturbance primarily by withdrawal and phantasy. Toward the end of the Napoleonic war the combination movement disappeared underground to avoid the Combination Laws. Sometimes, particularly in Scotland, this disappearance was accompanied by violence, vitriol-throwing, and bizarre initiation rites. Toward the end of the war, moreover, the workers and others began a campaign to repeal the Combination Laws themselves, on the grounds that the laws were responsible for the underground activities, the hard feelings among masters and workmen, etc.[1]

Step 3. Handling and Channelling. The parliamentary response to the campaign for repeal of the Combination Laws constitutes Step 3 of the sequence leading to a new form of trade union. Of course, neither the movement for repeal nor repeal itself depended solely on the case of the cotton operatives. The committees in 1824 and 1825 regarded many other trades with equal interest. We are using the cotton industry merely as a case study in structural differentiation.

The final repeal of the Laws in 1824–5 has been attributed to "the comparative failure of the Combination Acts of 1799 and 1800, a period of prosperity and quiet, the spread of a belief in a free labour market, and some very astute political management." I shall consider neither the political intricacies of the repeal nor the short-term prosperity which conditioned both the decision to repeal and the

* Interestingly enough, the war period created conflicting tendencies for the cotton industry itself. Above, pp. 118–23.

[1] Clapham, *An Economic History of Modern Britain*, pp. 214–15; Webb, *History of Trade Unionism*, p. 113; G. Wallas, *Life of Francis Place* (London, 1951) p. 203 ff.

flurry of strikes which followed the repeal.[1] I shall discuss only the "handling" of worker dissatisfaction, and the place of the basic value-system in defining the final form of the repeal.

Most of the protagonists of repeal—McCulloch, Wade and Hume, for example—felt that unalterable economic laws would bring wages to a certain level [2] and that no organization of workmen could alter these laws. This notion became attached to the laissez-faire ideology of the day, and resulted in the assumption that the effective way to achieve the natural harmony of interests in society was to allow the individual to pursue his occupation independently and without restriction. The Combination Laws restricted his independent search for appropriate labour because they led to labour disputes, violence, and intimidation. Their repeal presumably would do away with "artificial" combinations altogether and hence bring the market for labour closer to its natural state. This ideology lay behind the opinions of those who felt the laws to be both "ineffective and mischievous," and seemed, furthermore, to justify their repeal on accepted value grounds.[3]

Workers who opposed the Combination Laws accepted this ideology less uniformly. Themselves under stress, they attached their woes to a number of causes which embarrassed men like Francis Place who were arguing for repeal on laissez-faire grounds. "The workmen," Place wrote,

were not easily managed. It required great care and pains not to shock their prejudices so as to prevent them doing their duty before the Committee [Artizans and Machinery, 1824]. They were filled with false notions, all attributing their distresses to wrong causes, which I, in this state of the business, dared not to remove. Taxes, machinery, laws against combinations, the will of the masters, the conduct of magistrates—these were the fundamental cause of all their sorrows and privations. All expected a great and sudden rise of wages, when the Combination Laws should be repealed; not one of them had any idea whatever of the connection between wages and population. I had to discuss everything with them most carefully, to arrange and prepare everything, and so completely did these things occupy my time, that for more than three months I had hardly time for rest.[4]

[1] For a discussion of these aspects, cf. R. K. Webb, *The British Working Class Reader* (London, 1955), p. 137; Wallas, *Life of Francis Place*, Chapter VIII; Rostow, *British Economy in the Nineteenth Century*, pp. 116–17.

[2] Expressing the relationship between the number of wage-earners and the funds available to pay them.

[3] Halevy, *The English People in the Nineteenth Century*, Vol. II, pp. 204 ff.

[4] Quoted in Wallas, *Life of Francis Place*, pp. 213–14.

Clearly Place's activities illustrate both handling and channelling. As a leader of the working classes, he patiently received their allegedly misdirected and "irrelevant" notions as to the cause of and the cures for the ills of society and eased them into lines acceptable in terms of the dominant value-system of the day.

After a carefully-planned investigation, Parliament repealed in 1824 all the existing statutes outlawing combinations, including the general laws of 1799 and 1800. This Act permitted workers

> to enter any combination to obtain an advance or to fix the rate of wages, or to lessen or alter the hours or duration of the time of working, or to decrease the quantity of work, or to induce another to depart from his service before the end of the time or term for which he is hired, or to quit or return his work before the same shall be finished . . . [These] shall not . . . be subject or liable to any indictment or prosecution for conspiracy, or to any other criminal information or punishment whatever under the common or the statute law.

Legal punishments were permitted only for "violence to the person or property, by threats or by intimidation." [1]

This liberal Act, plus the pressure of prosperity and rising prices, triggered a flurry of strikes. Despite the efforts of the sponsors of repeal to calm the striking groups,[2] the government became apprehensive at some of the more violent aspects of the strikes, and began to feel that repeal had gone too far. The resulting committee on combinations (1825) began the work of exploration, handling, and channelling anew, in an attempt to manage the labour tensions more successfully than had outright repeal of the Combination Laws. One conclusion in particular illustrates the committee's search for legitimization for trade unions within the confines of the dominant values of independence and personal responsibility:

> In recommending that liberty of associating and co-operating together, so far as wages or hours of labour are concerned, should be preserved alike to masters and workmen, Your Committee feel it essential to the regard which is due to the free exercise of individual judgment, to propose that the resolutions of any such association should be allowed to bind only parties actually present, or personally consenting; not to impose this limitation, would be to afford a dangerous opening to the operation of influence of the most pernicious kind, and by taking away the protection of that competition which arises out of the perfect freedom of individual action,

1 5 Geo. IV, c. 95.
2 E.g., Wallas, *Life of Francis Place*, pp. 219–20; G. White, *Combination and Arbitration Laws, Artizans and Machinery* (London, 1824), pp. 3–4.

destroy the best defence possessed both by the masters and work-men, against the efforts of each other, in support of their conflicting pretensions and interests.[1]

Thus the government, in the face of continuing violence and disturb-ance in 1824 and 1825, was searching for a more appropriate practical definition of what constituted "freedom of individual action," or the value of independence when applied to trade unions.

By way of implementing this value, the subsequent Act of 1825 omitted the clause which prevented punishment by common law, and added to the punishable offence of "violence" the more compre-hensive ones of "threats," "intimidation," "molestation," and "obstruction." None of these methods could be used to force "any workman to leave his employer or to prevent him from being employed; or to belong to any club, or to contribute to any fund; or to alter the mode of carrying on any manufacture; or to limit the number of apprentices." Workmen might assemble *voluntarily* "for the sole purpose of consulting upon and determining the rate of wages and prices"; in no way, however, could coercion be used to prevent a worker from employing his talents as he chose.[2] The legislation of 1825, in short, prevented unions from imposing on the values of individual independence. William Huskisson summarized these values in 1825 by asserting that "as a general principle . . . every man had an inherent right to carry his own labour to whatever market he liked; and so to make the best of it." [3]

The Confusions of the late 1820's and early 1830's: Lancashire and Glasgow. Despite the restrictive elements of the Act of 1825, this Act concluded Step 3 and thereby allowed the combinations to come to the surface as autonomous organizations. Other things being equal, we would expect the cotton unions to have reached a higher level of differentiation in the years following the repeal of the Combination Laws. As it turned out, however, the 1820's and 1830's also consti-tuted a period of conflicting trends. In certain respects the combina-tions moved further from their fusion with the friendly society. At the same time, the great technological changes of these years fell heavily on the Lancashire unions. While they were advancing toward organizational autonomy, they nevertheless could not escape several violent outbursts in the late 1820's and early 1830's. Hence for Lancashire these years constituted in part a "regression" to Step 2 which once again had to be worked through a process of handling and

---

[1] *Parliamentary Papers*, 1825, IV, Combinations of Workmen, pp. 507–8.

[2] 6 Geo. IV, c. 129; also J. Wade, *History of the Middle and Working Classes* (London, 1833), pp. 107–8.

[3] Quoted in *Annual Register*, 1825, pp. 91–2 (Hist.).

channelling before the structure of the union finally reached an equilibrium level in the 1840's and thereafter.

To illustrate these developments in Lancashire, let us first consider its contrast with the Glasgow union, which was relatively free from the disruptive technological changes in spinning machinery between 1825 and 1837. Glasgow is, therefore, a case study in "what might have happened" generally if industrial progress had been slower. Second, we shall consider the organizational changes in the Lancashire unions—bombarded with technological changes after 1825—up to the mid-thirties. Third, we shall consider the symptoms of disturbance (Step 2) which appeared in Lancashire (after 1825) and Glasgow (after 1836–7). Fourth, we shall discuss the ways in which these disturbances were handled in these years (Step 3), and finally, we shall indicate the beginnings of new lines of differentiation in trade-unionism in the 1840's (Steps 4–6).

As we have seen, technological progress in Glasgow lagged behind the Manchester area in the 1820's and 1830's. During this period of relative industrial quiescence, the Glasgow operative spinners achieved an extraordinary degree of organization and stability. Secret before the repeal of the Combination Laws, the Glasgow Cotton Spinners' Association came into the open after 1825. Between 1825 and 1827 there was a prolonged dispute between some masters and spinners. At this time other millowners encouraged the workers to enforce equalization of spinners' pay in all mills. The operative spinners achieved this equalization in 1827, apparently to their own satisfaction, and these conditions continued until 1837.[1]

Between 1825 and 1837 the spinners maintained a continuous and semi-differentiated organization. It numbered about 1,000, or about 90% of all Glasgow spinners. Spinners entered when they got a pair of wheels. Some claimed that an operative could not spin if not a member. The entrance fee was £1 and dues 2s. per week for financing strikes, funerals, emigration, and support of members involuntarily idle. Every week a committee of delegates from each cotton mill met to conduct the union's affairs; one of its main functions was to check on the finance committee's expenditure of funds. Statements of income and expenditure were distributed among all the mills every fortnight. During the great strike of 1837 the union borrowed funds from other Glasgow unions and received £200 to £300 from the Manchester spinners.[2]

[1] Chapman, *The Lancashire Cotton Industry*, pp. 201–2; *Parliamentary Papers*, 1837–8, VIII, Combinations of Workmen, pp. 34–6, 80, 98–9. Above, pp. 234–5.
[2] *Parliamentary Papers*, 1837–8, VIII, Combinations of Workmen, pp. 5, 20, 37, 48–9, 62, 198–9, 286.

New Conditions of Employment: The Evolution of Trade Unions

As shown by its size, its partial independence from the masters, its widespread and representative organization, its organizational complexity, and its salient concern with matters of employment, the Glasgow union had advanced considerably from the convivial friendly society a quarter-century past. On the other hand, some vestiges remained. The combination attempted to maintain equalization of spinners' wages throughout the region;[1] it assumed a diffuse concern for its members' welfare; there were still instances of masters' encouragement of workers to strike against others (e.g., 1825–7); and its financial status was not secure enough to weather the union through a major strike without *ad hoc* reliance on other sources for funds.

The stability of the Glasgow union in these years is a "model" of what the Lancashire unions might have enjoyed had technological progress been slowed in that county. Indeed, the Lancashire unions were organizationally similar. Their major aim, like Glasgow's, was to maintain a traditional and equalized system of wages. Nor were the Lancashire unions free from the masters' influence. In several strikes the latter encouraged workers to strike, no doubt because of their own fears of competition from other masters' superior machinery. So intimate was this connection between masters and workmen that a student of trade unions of the late 1820's listed support from employers as the "principal supply" of operatives' funds. Besides their own resources, the unions also relied on (1) "shopkeepers, publicans, and others interested in the well-doing of the operatives," (2) other trades, (3) independent benefit or friendly societies, (4) other miscellaneous sources such as the poor-rates.[2]

As in Glasgow, the Lancashire unions were essentially local, with few exceptions. In the local strikes up to 1829, however, delegates went around the countryside to seek funds. When more strikes were planned than the funds could withstand, the unions adopted a system of balloting for priority. The degree of permanent regional organization was, however, extremely tenuous. In 1829 the first attempt at formal federation by the spinners appeared in the guise of the Grand General Union of the United Kingdom. Shortly after its formation, however, the Grand General Union shrank into a loose federation of Lancashire societies when the attempt to include Scotland and Ireland failed. In the following year John Doherty attempted to form the National Association for the Protection of Labour, which included trades besides the textile. This second

[1] *Ibid.*, p. 81.
[2] *Ibid.*, pp. 250, 256–7; *On Combinations of Trade* (London, 1831), pp. 44–8.

attempt also failed, partly because the Nottingham members withdrew when the Lancashire members refused to support a strike, partly because of a general shortage of funds, and partly because the Manchester branch turned its interest to the ten hour agitation shortly after the Ashton strike failed in 1830–31. In general, the federations were almost ineffective on the local level. The Grand General Union, for instance, did not "appear to have . . . any marked effect on the trade; the strikes and other *offensive* business of the Union, were still for the most part decided on by the local committees." [1]

From the standpoint of *level of differentiation*, therefore, Glasgow and Lancashire possessed certain vestiges of the old friendly society: (*a*) the diffuse welfare benefits; (*b*) a susceptibility to influence by the masters, and a receptivity to their financial support; (*c*) local organization and self-financing except in critical periods when the unions would gather funds from temporary and *ad hoc* sources. Yet in the 1820's and 1830's Glasgow maintained equalized wages, whereas the Lancashire unions proved archaic, unsuccessful, and prone to "regressive" symptoms of disturbance. [2]

This difference between Glasgow and Lancashire is traceable to the presence of technological pressure in the latter and its absence in the former. The long mules, as we have seen, raised real wages while lowering piece-rates; displaced a portion of the adult male operatives; multiplied the number of assistants, and introduced a disparity of wage rates throughout the trade. We have reviewed the disequilibrating effects of these adjustments on the family economy and the resulting outburst of disturbances in Chapters IX and X. From the standpoint of the unions, these changes also signalled dissatisfaction. With their semi-differentiated structure, local autonomy, and slim finances, the unions could not resist this march of machinery. They were failing in their function—to regulate the conditions of employment in the new setting. In this sense we judge the Lancashire unions archaic in the decade from the middle 1820's to the middle 1830's. For this reason the unions were the subject of mounting dissatisfaction.* If they were to protect the status of labour in a more dif-

---

[1] Tufnell, *Character, Object and Effects of Trades' Unions*, p. 2; Chapman, *The Lancashire Cotton Industry*, pp. 201–2; Webb, *History of Trade Unionism*, pp. 104–10.

[2] This is true even though Tufnell described the spinners as "the most powerful, extensive, and best organized Union in the kingdom" in 1834. *Character, Object and Effects of Trades' Unions*, p. 2.

* Formally this "dissatisfaction" represents an intensification of the pressure on the boundary-relationships which already had been placed under strain earlier: E_{Gi}–E_{Li}, E_{Gg}–E_{Ig}, and E_{Ga}–E_{Aa}. Above, p. 317, fn. (1) The changing technology in the 1820's and 1830's meant that a new "balance of skills, levels of

ferentiated market structure, their own structure had to undergo a corresponding differentiation.

As one might suspect, these dissatisfactions gave rise to some symptoms of disturbance among the Lancashire unions in the 1820's and 1830's. We shall review these outbursts presently. Let us first note, however, the persistence of certain status relationships within the unions' organization which rendered them less flexible in action and less ready to reorganize in line with the industrial innovations. These concern the hierarchical relationship between the spinner and the other operatives. His authority in the factory, reviewed above, carried over into the conduct of strikes. In almost all cases, the spinners alone resolved to strike, thereby throwing many assistants and others out of work, apparently without any attempt on the part of junior operatives to block their actions. When the new machinery —especially the self-actor mule—began to create new classes of labour which were not under the spinners' economic direction, this began to undermine their unilateral and unequivocal authority. On the other hand, these new classes of labour represented new sources of strength for organized labour. Yet the mule-spinners' attitudes were inflexible; for nearly a generation after 1829–30, "the hand-mule spinners looked down on the 'self-actor minders' as an unskilled and inferior class, and frequently refused to allow them to enter their associations."[1] The continuation of such status distinctions through the 1830's and 1840's no doubt inhibited the growth of full-scale unionism among the factory operatives.

Step 2. Symptoms of Disturbance. We analysed the symptoms of

competence, and motivation for economic performance" (E_{Gi}) was required. More particularly, it meant that the labour of women and children was brought into greater demand, and more important, that the connections among immediate family members on the factory premises were weakened. Hence there was a dissatisfaction with the "organization of socialization and tension-management in family roles" (E_{Ii}). Thus the dissatisfaction at the E_{Gi}–E_{Ii} (or *I*-5) level. (2) A related dissatisfaction dealt with the assumption of occupational roles by family members. In one sense the innovations of the 1820's and 1830's meant an opportunity (increased occupational capacity and increased earnings, or E_{Ig}) for the family economy. On the other hand, because these innovations demanded a shift of occupational roles, they meant a dissatisfaction at the E_{Gg}–E_{Ig} (or *G*-5) level. (3) Because of the possibility of technological unemployment resulting from the innovations and because of the long-term threats to labour supply, there was a new strain placed on the family's ability to guarantee a stable relationship between its earning capacity and its basic expenditures (E_{Ga}–E_{Aa}, or *A*-5). Because these pressures operated with great force on the Lancashire unions in the 1820's and 1830's—and not on the Glasgow unions until later—the former were relatively enfeebled and therefore more prone to display the classical symptoms of disturbance in these years.

[1] *Webb Manuscripts on Trade Unionism*, Vol. XXXIV, p. 143.

disturbance among the Lancashire spinning groups in the 1820's and 1830's in Chapter X. For a number of years they concentrated on "long-wheel" strikes in which they "were not hostile to erecting machinery, but to improvements which would often produce a local or partial fall of wages." [1] These strikes against larger mules were almost uniformly unsuccessful, and damaged the unions immensely. [2] In the end the outbursts against machinery melted into the ten hour agitation of the early 1830's. A few years later, when the unions became "part and parcel" of the Owenite movement, the operatives were "dreaming of a new heaven and a new earth, humanitarians, educationalists, socialists, moralists." [3]

Step 3. Handling and Channelling. In connection with the unions, the disturbances of deepest concern to the public were the strikes and their concomitants. As the flood of strikes continued through the 1820's and 1830's—reaching a high point in the violent Glasgow strike of 1836–7—authorities and others began to explore the means of encouraging certain aspects of trade unions and discouraging others. These efforts to handle and channel the labour disturbances constitute Step 3 of the development of unionism in the early nineteenth century.

The *amount* of literature on unionism in the intense 1831–4 period shows the height of public concern over union activities. [4] In many ways this literature, combined with a parliamentary interest, constitutes a *search for legitimization*, or for those grounds on which labour combinations might find a permanent place in society. Let us recapitulate this search.

The greatest interest in the unions in the 1820's and 1830's concerned the place of violence, oaths, secrecy, and intimidation. The committees of 1824 and 1825 had examined how these activities interfered with workmen's independence. In 1824 the Manchester Chamber of Commerce, usually silent on the subject of trade unions, recommended that workers and masters be punished for violence. In the same year the Manchester operative spinners denied any connection between their union and a recent vitriol-throwing incident, and deplored the practice. Pamphlets in the later 1820's and early 1830's concentrated on the issues of violence, intimidation, and

[1] *Webb Manuscripts on Trade Unionism*, Vol. XXXIV, p. 37, quoting Nassau Senior in 1829.

[2] John Doherty spoke of the "drooping spirits" which characterized the Manchester spinners as late as five years after "that fatal blow, the reduction of 1829." *Quinquarticular System of Organization*, p. 3.

[3] Webb, *History of Trade Unionism*, pp. 158, 138. Above, pp. 253–61.

[4] Summarized in Webb, *The Working-Class Reader*, pp. 138 ff.

threats. In addition, their authors suggested the discouragement or prohibition of oaths, "affording as they do without any adequate object, increased opportunities to the great moral crime of perjury." [1]

Such criticism differed from that of a quarter-century before, however, in so far as the writers did not recommend the outright abolition of combinations, but felt policy should "[retain] those beneficial influences of which unions unquestionably are not wholly deprived, and [modify], as far as possible, their injurious tendencies." Indeed, some felt that re-enactment of the Combination Laws would make union members more "ferocious and secret in their operations." [2] Such attitudes constitute the stuff of Step 3: to sift the reprehensible elements of a disturbance from those which might find a legitimate place in society.

The committee on combinations of 1837–8 also probed into the nature and extent of such excesses. Many witnesses were asked to comment on the union's degree of responsibility for violence, secrecy, etc. [3] In the meantime the governmental authorities had been "handling" these extreme features more directly. As early as 1830, when the labour disturbances were approaching a zenith, the government—primarily Lord Melbourne and Nassau Senior—suggested remedies such as prosecuting unions in the name of "restraint of trade," forbidding solicitation of funds, etc. The government declined, though, to introduce any definite legislation at this time. However, in the midst of the rapid, bizarre, and disturbed growth of the Owenite Grand National Consolidated in 1833–4, the government, by way of example, convicted and transported six Dorchester labourers. This conviction was based on an old statute against the administration of an oath by an unlawful society. [4] This sentence created a stir of protest throughout the union world. Regardless of its injustice, however, the sentence was the authorities' symbolic reminder that certain excesses carried the unions beyond the point of legitimacy.

Union leaders claimed a corresponding legitimacy for unions, and denied any responsibility for the excesses of oaths, violence, and secrecy, except in conditions of extraordinary distress. John Doherty's

---

[1] Redford, *Manchester Merchants and Foreign Trade*, p. 229; *Manchester Guardian*, Dec. 4, 1824; *On Combinations of Trades*, p. 64; Tufnell, *Character, Object and Effects of Trades' Unions*, pp. 100–1, 120, 122, 74–5.

[2] *On Combinations of Trades*, pp. 30–31; Tufnell, *Character, Object, and Effects of Trades' Unions*, p. 115.

[3] *Parliamentary Papers*, 1837–8, VIII, Combinations of Workmen, pp. 130–31, 184–5, 246. Also Webb, *History of Trade Unionism*, p. 154.

[4] Webb, *History of Trade Unionism*, pp. 123–8; *Manchester Guardian*, Apr. 12, 1834.

defence of the unions in 1838 is a classic attempt to legitimize the place of unionism in terms of the value of independence of the adult male labourer:

Have you any oath in your association?—No; we have not had since the repeal of the combination laws; we had before.

Have you any obligations to secresy?—None, since the same time.

Are you aware of any acts of violence which have been perpetrated by the association?—Not by the association.

Or those deputed by them?—Not, as deputed by the association; there have been partial fallings out and squabbles, and we have got credit for more than was our fair share. If during a strike a scrimmage took place in the streets, it was sure to be ascribed to the union, when it had no reference whatever to it.

Is any kind of intimidation permitted by the rules of your union?— It is not.

Is there anything you desire to keep secret in the business of your association?—Nothing. I should, perhaps, qualify that with respect to strikes. At the time of strikes, of course there is a natural wish that the masters should not understand the extent of our resources; but with that exception there is nothing secret.

The amount of your funds?—Yes; and the means by which we hope to continue and increase our funds.

The names of the members of the association are not kept secret? —Not at all.

Were those members who belonged to the old association absolved in any way from their secresy when that obligation became no longer necessary?—Not at all.

What is the constitution of these societies, how are they formed, and how are they governed; in the first place, how does a man become a member?—They become members . . . by paying 7*d*. a week . . . half of which he receives back, if he should be discharged at any time from his employment for anything that cannot be traced back to his own conduct.[1]

Doherty attributed the violence in 1829 to the fact that the striking workers were living on 2*s*. 2¼*d*. per week per family. Various witnesses claimed that union members entered a strike with the greatest hesitation; that the cotton-spinners were a "well-conducted class" which paid great respect to the local authorities; that the unionists were "the most respectable and intellectual and moral of that class to which they belong," and that union members were always instructed "to conduct themselves in such a way that the civil power would have no opportunity of seizing them." [2]

[1] *Parliamentary Papers*, 1837–8, VIII, Combinations of Workmen, pp. 254–5.
[2] *Ibid.*, pp. 52, 184–5, 228–9, 249, 256, 258.

The consensus of the time seemed to be summarized by the observations of a Manchester magistrate:

Combinations among workmen appear actually necessary to a certain extent, for their protection?—I have no doubt they consider it a mere matter of self-defence.

And if stripped of intimidation and violence, might work very healthfully?—I think so.

The evils are, intimidation and violence controlling the free choice of labourers to employ themselves at such wages as they please?— Yes, I consider that the prominent evil.[1]

Those searching for the legitimate and illegitimate elements of unionism also sought to prune back the unions' realm of activity to include only the conditions of labour. Thus in 1834 the *Edinburgh Review* condemned outside political and social activities of unions:

Until within the last few years, Unions among workmen had no other ostensible object than that which was the real one,—the establishment or maintenance of a fixed rate of wages in a particular employment. Now the writers and orators of these associations often assume a higher tone; they proclaim war against capitalists in general; and hold out the grand project of dividing profits among that class of producers which at present furnishes labour and receives wages,— a project which of course implies a complete social as well as political revolution. For our parts, we believe these visionary schemes, and the applause they have met with, rather to betoken the failing hopes and desperate condition of many of the combinations, the supporters of which require to have their expectations kept alive by extravagant delusion. Those Unions which have been most successful in effecting their immediate object of raising wages, and have consequently been most injurious to our manufactures, and most detrimental to the trade of the towns in which they were established, have always wrought in comparative silence and confined their exertions to the accomplishment of their particular design, avoiding, above all things, political discussion. All schemes of a more extended character have hitherto signally failed. . . .[2]

For Tufnell, however, one point in favour of the unions was that they avoided religion and politics, except when they displayed a political interest in limiting factory hours. He even criticized those

---

[1] *Ibid.*, p. 251.

[2] "On Trades'-Unions and Strikes," *Edinburgh Review*, Vol. 59 (1834), pp. 341–2. This observation coincided with the Grand National Consolidated Trades Union and the Society for National Regeneration, in both of which the principles of trade unionism were submerged to co-operative principles. Above, pp. 241–3.

who attributed the unions' vigour to "the Reform Bill, to the French Revolution, to an hostility to the Established Church, to a spread of democratical principles, and other causes of a like nature." [1] Yet whether commentators deplored the political and religious interests of the unions or congratulated the unions for their absence, such statements imply that the unions' legitimate objects should become *differentiated* from political and social activity.

Such sentiments, as well as the governmental activities in the 1820's and 1830's, show the major characteristics of handling and channelling: (*a*) to accept unionism as an integral part of society; (*b*) to make this acceptance conditional on the cessation of their irrational outbursts of violence, intimidation, and threats, and (*c*) to assure that unions' aims and activities did not violate the definition of man as a responsible and independent agent in the world of economic endeavour.* In these ways the government, the press, and other agencies sought to create a foundation for a new kind of social unit which was more satisfactory for protecting the conditions of employment.

Steps 4 and 5: Encouragement of New Ideas and Attempts to Specify. While the agencies of social control were attempting to limit the excesses of unionism, there was simultaneously an interest in redefining the sphere of union activity. Of the 1820's Francis Place wrote that there was "great dissatisfaction among the cotton workers in the North of England and the South of Scotland: *many were the schemes* to form the people into societies to 'protect,' and in some cases, to raise their wages." [2] One such scheme, of course, was John Doherty's attempt to organize the cotton trade on a national scale, the failure of which we have noted.

In the period of confusion between 1831 and 1834 trade-unionism fused with the ten hour agitation and the co-operative movement. In a way the submergence of unionism in these movements was an appearance of "new ideas," or the conviction that these methods could attain what strikes and other union activities had failed to attain. Again, in 1834, John Doherty—who had led the Manchester spinners into most of their adventures—brought forth what he called the Quinquarticular System of union organization. Under this system he recommended the establishment of a massive formal organization, with representatives at several levels and a prolifera-

---

[1] *Character, Object, and Effects of Trades' Unions*, p. 90.

* These three characteristics correspond to Level 1 of the table of resources, to which Step 3 "brings" the resources: (a) *I*-1; (b) *G*-1; and (c) *A*-1. Above, pp. 38–9 and 170.

[2] *Webb Manuscripts on Trade Unionism*, Vol. XXXIV, p. 27. Italics mine.

tion of "tithing-men," constables, wardens, and a general committee. Apparently his recommendations never materialized.[1]

In addition to these schemes for reorganization and strategy, there arose in the same years a persistent concern with the problem of relieving unemployed men. Besides relying on their own union funds, friendly society savings, and personal resources, unions had often relied on the ancient system of "tramping." Under this system workers roamed the countryside in times of distress to find labour. Apparently the unions frequently had provided relief to such men in the past. By 1834 Doherty said that "all men are agreed" that this system of casual pay was unsatisfactory. It attracted hordes of unemployed especially into Manchester "in the hope of sharing in the pittance" allowed to men on tramp. Doherty "now proposed entirely to alter this system . . . to allow a man who has been so long a regular subscriber, a certain stated sum, to be paid to him immediately on his losing his employment, in order to assist him to go elsewhere in search of work." [2]

Related to Doherty's suggestions were several other proposals to tailor unions into agencies of relief for unemployed families.* In 1833, for instance, Wade recorded the following recommendations which carry the unions into areas beyond "keeping up the price of labour":

(1) The unions should provide for workmen in distress from unemployment in depressions. Wade viewed this as a supplement to savings banks and friendly societies, by which "future provision is made for want, infirmity, old age, and death." The unions presumably would add unemployment benefits to this backlog of security.

(2) A parliamentary committee suggested in 1830 that societies for relieving the unemployed should be formed separate from the unions themselves. These societies would be like friendly societies and savings banks, but would be concerned with the contingencies of unemployment exclusively. Wade suggested individual savings as a supplement to these societies.[3]

---

[1] *Quinquarticular System of Organization*, pp. 5–7. For a discussion of the course of unionism, the ten hour movement, and early co-operation, cf. above, pp. 231–6, 238–44, and 253–61.

[2] *Ibid.*, p. 8.

* Strictly speaking, these suggestions reflect the dissatisfaction with the boundary-relationship $E_{Ga}-E_{Aa}$ (or A-5), or the relationship between the family's earning capacity and its ability to meet the minimum levels of necessary expenditures and savings. We shall discuss this dissatisfaction in detail in the next chapter. We consider it here because some of the "new ideas" for trade unions dealt with the problem of guaranteeing stability at this boundary in times of economic distress.

[3] *History of the Middle and Working Classes*, pp. 293–6; also *Parliamentary Papers*, 1830, X, Manufacturers' Employment, pp. 221–33.

All these suggestions pointed toward a *more differentiated* structure for the unions. Doherty's quinquarticular system, for instance, visualized a large, formal, and more specialized body than the older friendly society or the contemporary transitional forms in Lancashire. Further, the suggestions that unions assume responsibility only for unemployment meant a more specialized performance of function than the friendly society's concern for general economic welfare of members in earlier decades.

Step 6. Establishment of Institutional Forms. The beginning of 1834 found the unions exhausted from their vigorous but futile activity of the past few years. In October, 1834, however, the *Manchester Guardian* reported attempts to "revive amongst the working spinners of this town that spirit of combination which has heretofore produced them so much misery, but which it seems, has been well nigh extinguished by the experience which they have had of its consequences." Despite such attempts, the evolution of trade-unionism—like so many other lines of differentiation—lagged through the late 1830's and up to the collapse of the Chartist efforts of 1842. After 1837 "the membership of the surviving Trade Unions rapidly decreased. . . . The Glasgow trades had been completely disorganized by the disasters of 1837. The Lancashire textile operatives showed no sign of life." While the Manchester spinners had 1,000 members in 1838, the number had once been as high as 1,900. Further, there were "whole mills of [spinners]" who had not been members for years. The association, moreover, did not extend outside Manchester.[1]

In the early 1840's however, the cotton factory operatives' organizations began not only to revive in strength, but also to change in structure. Perhaps the most striking change was in the increasing number of occupational types admitted into the unions. In 1846 the Lancashire Central Short Time Committee—the central body for the ten hour agitation of the operatives—resolved to raise £1,000 for campaign expenses. In years past "the greater part of the expense [had been] defrayed by the cotton-spinners alone." In 1846, however, the agitators "appealed to all other branches of factory workers, and so far their efforts have been very successful."[2] This co-operative spirit began to seep into the union organizations as well. As early as 1837 the "Associated Cotton Spinners, Self-acting Minders and other factory operatives" formed in Bolton. While the self-acting minders were expelled later in both Bolton and Ashton, their original in-

[1] *Manchester Guardian*, Oct. 4, 1834; Webb, *History of Trade Unionism*, p. 157; *Parliamentary Papers*, 1837–8, VIII, Combinations of Workmen, p. 254.
[2] *Ten Hours' Advocate*, Sept. 26, 1846.

clusion constituted an advance over the previously disdainful attitude of the mule-spinners toward the minders.[1]

This movement toward consolidation extended beyond local districts. In 1845 a circular dealing with strike policy was issued to the "Operative Spinners, Self-acting Minders, Twiners and Rovers of Lancashire, Cheshire, Yorkshire and Derbyshire." In the following year it was noticed that an organization known as the Association of Operative Cotton Spinners, Twiners, and Self-acting Minders of the United Kingdom was "intimately connected with, if indeed it did not initiate and constitute" the short time committee for ten hours. This organization, which apparently had formed in 1843, had its headquarters in Bolton. Its organization was sufficiently complex to include official gatherings in local public houses every other Sunday, and the delegation of members to central meetings. Bolton and Oldham withdrew in 1848, but before then the federation was recognized "by the employers as representative of the workmen in the various localities." After 1848 the group declined, but revived shortly thereafter as the Equitable Friendly Association of Hand-mule Spinners, Self-acting Minders, Twiners, and Rovers of Lancashire, Cheshire, Yorkshire and Derbyshire, with a central committee in Manchester.[2] In 1853 the Amalgamated Association of Operative Cotton Spinners formed; its composition and membership remains unknown until 1870, but it formed the more or less permanent organization for the operative spinners.[3]

Meantime the weaving operatives in the factory were not inactive. A Manchester society formed in 1842, but collapsed two years later. This revived in 1846 and continued until the cotton famine of the 1860's. Revived again in 1865, it preceded by one year the birth of an amalgamation called the Beamers, Twisters and Drawers Association, which began in Blackburn. The Glasgow Beamers, Twisters and Drawers had formed in 1853.[4]

Both the admission of many operative classes and the continuity of regional amalgamations are instances of *structural differentiation*. In the early nineteenth century the mule-spinners had exercised a general authority both in the plant and in the union. Put another way, the spinners' control over other operatives with regard to union activities was undifferentiated from their control on the factory premises. As we have seen, the technological improvements of the 1820's and 1830's undermined this authority. For some time the

[1] *Webb Manuscripts on Trade Unionism*, Vol. XXXV, p. 3, Vol. XXXIV, p. 143.
[2] *Ibid.* Vol. XXXIV, pp. 143, 146–51, 231.
[3] Webb, *History of Trade Unionism*, p. 494.
[4] *Webb Manuscripts on Trade Unionism*, Vol. XXXVI, p. 143.

spinners were hostile toward new groups such as the self-acting minders. After a period of adjustment, however, the workers' organizations began to include a variety of occupational types in full membership. This meant that the unions were differentiating in the 1840's in the sense that they were becoming separated from the factory community. Decisions were made collectively by several types of operatives in their differentiated capacity *as union members*; earlier they had been made by unions composed only of spinners and enforced by virtue of the spinners' traditional authority *in the factory*. This differentiation, moreover, lifted the unions of the 1840's to a point of greater adequacy in the face of industrial realities which had materialized in the past two decades. No longer were the spinners attempting to perpetuate their position in an industrial arrangement where their old authority had been undermined. Now they were beginning to rely on a number of other occupational groups for political strength and funds, thus undoubtedly increasing their power beyond that of a spinners' union alone.

Regional amalgamations represented a differentiation in the sense that the union became extracted from local ties and began to exercise a certain influence beyond the local level. Such amalgamations, furthermore, enhanced the striking power, sources of funds, continuity of structure, etc., of the unions. Thus, even though the Preston strike of 1853–4 failed to gain a 10% advance for the operatives, there is evidence of a central committee which channelled sums of money coming from labourers all over the country, particularly Lancashire.[1] While similar kinds of support were apparent earlier in the nineteenth century, the Preston strike was notable for its absence of previous *ad hoc* solicitations from the master, publican, and grocer. Support for union activities, like the organization of unions themselves, was working toward a greater level of differentiation in the 1840's and 1850's.

Still another line of differentiation of union activities concerned the operatives' new interest in methods of wage payment. In the early nineteenth century, it will be recalled, wage-payments were standardized by count and were invariable as to size of mule. As the introduction of larger mules began to alter this traditionalized piece-rate system, the unions dogmatically and steadfastly demanded the same prices for all sizes of wheels through the 1820's and into the 1830's. In the later 1830's, the interest in wage-rates—like so many other

[1] J. B. Jefferys, *Labour's Formative Years* (London, 1948), pp. 61–2; Henry Ashworth spoke of the "business-like management of the strike" which drew money from several other communities. *The Preston Strike* (Manchester, 1854), pp. 49–52.

things in these years—became confused and disorganized. While certain accepted rates continued, "district lists seem to have fallen into disuse, if not to have disappeared in some places [in the late 1830's.]" Not until the 1840's and thereafter were lists reborn. Far from being simple rates for standard weights of yarn, however, these new lists dealt with gradings, length of yarns, division of gains resulting from speed of machinery, etc.[1] "In 1852 and 1853 the . . . first of the modern standard piece-work 'price lists' in the industry was adopted. The Blackburn lists of 1853 represent an important stage in the growth of that collective bargaining which has ever since dominated in the cotton trades."[2] Again, after a period of disturbance and disorganization, the unions began to assume a character which brought them to a point of greater adequacy in dealing with the new industrial arrangements.

In addition the operatives' interest in the modified apprenticeship system declined. As we have seen, from the first introduction of machinery in the late eighteenth century through the 1830's, the operatives' concern with the traditional relationship between adult and child was paramount. In our discussion of technological change and the factory question, we have seen also how this system of recruitment was endangered in the late 1820's and early 1830's. Correspondingly, there seems to have been a clear diminution of interest in *this form* of controlling the labour supply in the 1840's. The rules of the Friendly Associated Spinners in Manchester and its Neighbourhood, revised and amended in 1837, do not mention the ancient problem of controlling child labour through modified apprenticeship. In 1848 a committee of the Bolton Union discussed the question of masters' hiring apprentices; in 1856 and 1859 the committee decided to drop the "apprentice system" altogether, because of an apparent history of conflicts with employers over the conditions of their recruitment and hiring.[3] It would be too much to assert that child labour and the informal economic relationship between adult and child had died completely in the cotton industry. Clearly, however, the unions' aims and activities had become more specialized by emphasizing this system less. The unions were turning more and more to specific methods of regulating wages and assuring a certain security of family income.

[1] Chapman, "The Regulation of Wages by Lists in the Spinning Industry," *op. cit.*, p. 594. Above, pp. 188–200 and 231–5.

[2] Cole, *A Short History of the British Working Class Movement*, pp. 61–2. For an account of the Bolton union's interest in lists, cf. *Webb Manuscripts on Trade Unionism*, Vol. XXXV, pp. 5, 21.

[3] *Parliamentary Papers*, 1837–8, VIII, Combinations of Workmen, pp. 307–9; *Webb Manuscripts on Trade Unionism*, Vol. XXXV, pp. 7–8.

One method of guaranteeing this security of income concerned the provision of funds for spinners who had been discharged during slack seasons. Both the Manchester and Glasgow Rules submitted to the committee on combinations in 1838 proposed benefits to a worker "for losing employment through no fault of his own." The Manchester association also provided funeral and other benefits which illustrate the vestiges of the friendly society. In Oldham, when the self-actor was superseding the hand mule in the early 1840's, the union hired land and used unemployed spinners to work it. Finally, the tramping system was definitely in the autumn of its existence in the 1840's. In 1845 the Bolton Association supported this form of relief, and in 1846 a committee decided to draw up a plan to relieve men on tramp. Nothing seems to have come of this plan, however. In fact, the tramping system in general, having proved totally obsolete in the face of the relatively large-scale unemployment of the 1830's and 1840's, declined rapidly as newer, more specialized forms of relief began to appear.[1]

Thus by the 1840's the trade unions were beginning to accumulate new structural elements—multi-occupational representation, regional amalgamations, an interest in complex wage-lists, a decline of interest in apprenticeship, and the rise of relief schemes for unemployed members. These features naturally did not constitute the final form of unionism in the cotton industry. During the following decades trade unions evolved in new directions, and accumulated new elements, both as a result of rounding out the lines of differentiation and as a result of new industrial changes. Already by 1850, however, the unions were reaching a level of differentiation much higher than they had possessed in their evolution through the late eighteenth and early nineteenth century.* The basic function of the

---

[1] *Parliamentary Papers*, 1837–8, VIII, Combinations of Workmen, pp. 303–9, 282–3; *Webb Manuscripts on Trade Unionism*, Vol. XXXIV, p. 232; Vol. XXXV, pp. 44–54; E. J. Hobsbawm, "The Tramping Artisan," *Economic History Review*, III (1950–51), pp. 306–7.

* How were the new features related to the dissatisfactions of the 1820's and 1830's which initiated the sequence of differentiation which entered Step 6 in the early 1840's? In general, of course, the union's structure modified because of dissatisfactions with its ability to regulate the conditions of employment of its members (E_G–C_G). Above, pp. 163–4. More specifically, however, we outlined three foci of dissatisfaction within the family economy: (1) E_{Gi}–E_{Li}; (2) E_{Gg}–E_{Ig}; (3) E_{Ga}–E_{Aa}. Above, p. 317. Correspondingly, the new elements of unionism in the 1840's represented differentiations along these three axes. (1) The decline of interest in the apprenticeship problem shows that the union was meeting, on a more specialized basis, the problem of protecting the family's occupational interests (E_{Gi}–E_{Li}, or I-5). (2) The multi-occupational representation in unions, the amalgamations, and the interest in complex wage-lists meant a differentiation

trade union had not changed. It still could be defined as "a continuous association of wage-earners for the purpose of maintaining or improving the conditions of their employment." What had changed was the conditions of employment; the *structure* of the unions had risen to a new level of differentiation in order to perform their function more adequately.

of structure and interest which brought the unions more into line with the reality of the decline of the spinners' authority and the new occupational structure of the industry (E_{Gg}–E_{Ig}, or G-5). (3) The decline of the tramping system and the interest in new methods of relief in times of distress illustrate a more differentiated attack on the problem of guaranteeing a stable and steady relationship between the family's earning capacity and its basic spending necessities (E_{Ga}–E_{Aa}, or A-5).

CHAPTER XIII

STRUCTURAL CHANGE IN CONSUMPTION AND SAVINGS: THE POOR LAW, FRIENDLY SOCIETIES, SAVINGS BANKS, AND CO-OPERATIVE SOCIETIES

Introduction. In one important sense, structural differentiation maintains long-term stability in society. One social unit becomes relatively obsolete under some sort of situational pressure. After a period of disturbances, handling and channelling, and specification, the social unit differentiates, or progresses to a new equilibrium level more in keeping with its new social environment. In the process a number of more differentiated social units replace older, more diffuse ones.

In another sense, however, differentiation has its disequilibrating effects. When the cotton industry pressed to new levels of complexity during the industrial revolution, for instance, this process disrupted the social environment of the family economy. It initiated several long and painful sequences of differentiation which ultimately produced a more specialized version of the nuclear family and a more specialized version of the trade union.

These changes in the family division of labour had, in their turn, serious disequilibrating effects on the structure of family consumption.* They exaggerated existing dissatisfactions with consumption patterns and initiated several sequences of change which gave rise to new social units geared to consumption. Empirically these sequences resulted in a modification of the poor-laws, the evolution of the friendly society, the growth of the savings bank, and the rise of the early co-operative society. These developments conform, moreover, to the model of structural differentiation. In this chapter, therefore, we shall apply the model once more, this time to the structure of family consumption.

Most students of working-class welfare in this period have dis-

* Formally, family consumption is located in E_A. Above, pp. 160–61 and 173–4.

342

cussed consumption in terms of the standard of life in a quantitative or dietary sense, and in terms of economic hardship as a basis for social unrest.[1] I shall consider such elements only secondarily, since my main concern is the evolution of the *social structure* of consumption and saving between 1770 and 1840.

In this chapter we must expand our horizons beyond the cotton industry. To analyse the family division of labour, we could use the labour force of this industry as a convenient case, because of the concentrated interest of factory inspectors, Parliament, and the general public in the industry. For consumption, however, our information is not so complete. Information on saving and consumption in our period referred generally to "the working classes," and thus hid the significance of any one industry. Hence we shall not attempt to tie the development of the poor-laws, friendly societies, savings banks, and co-operative societies specifically to any industry. We shall, however, illustrate the growth of these units in Lancashire when possible.

THE EARLY POOR LAWS AND THE EARLY FRIENDLY SOCIETY

Value Background. Let us review once again the dominant value-system of the late eighteenth and early nineteenth century, this time from the standpoint of the criteria whereby consumption behaviour might be deemed satisfactory or unsatisfactory. The essence of the dominant consumption values is found in Eden's comment on the Quakers' reputation. He had heard that this group harboured no beggars. Possibly, he felt, this might be explained by the fact that the Society of Friends expelled beggars. Nevertheless,

. . . the case does not cease to be extraordinary; and, as such, it still merits consideration. For, admitting the fact to be as it is here suggested, that the Quakers have not, strictly speaking, any Poor among them, the means they take to prevent it, shew very clearly, that they consider the want of industry, and the want of frugality, not only as the natural fore-runners, but as the general causes, of poverty. The instruction, therefore, conveyed to us by this striking fact is, that, instead of exerting ourselves, as hitherto has been the

---

[1] E.g., Ashton, "The Standard of Life of the Workers in England, 1790–1830," *op. cit.*; Collier, *The Family Economy in the Cotton Industry*; Read, "The Social and Economic Background to Peterloo," *op. cit.* See also C. C. Zimmerman, *Consumption and Standards of Living* (London, 1936), pp. 385–89, for a list of British studies. Zimmerman notes the concentration of these studies on food and rent expenditures, and their preoccupation with poverty, disease and slum conditions.

case, only to relieve indigence and distress, however produced, it might not be beneath legislative wisdom to emulate the better policy of this prudent sect, and, if possible, fall on ways and means to prevent them.[1]

Thus the cardinal value of *independence* invaded the sphere of consumption as well as labour. In the field of labour, as we have seen, the independent man should seek new opportunities, follow his calling conscientiously, and labour according to the duties imposed by personal responsibility. Equally important, the independent breadwinner should follow the appropriate performance-centred values of consumption; he should gear his expenditures actively to those kinds of motivational spending and saving which would enhance his family's economic productivity, and hence render them independent of indigence. Hence the positive value placed on frugality, prudence, and caution. Hence also the emphasis on spending only for necessaries, saving, education, and health.[2] One must guard his resources conscientiously and utilize them to encourage productive activity.

Correspondingly, the value of independence underlay several admonitions against "Pride, Dress, Fashion, Borrowing and Pawning, Ale House, Dram Shops, [and] Gaming." Spending on these drained the resources of the worker and his family; it encouraged dissipation, idleness, and less work; and it diverted family spending away from the needs of self-support. In short, drinking and the rest reduced the security and independence of the family.[3]

These values lay behind a series of dissatisfactions with the family's spending patterns, the poor-laws, and the friendly society in the late eighteenth and early nineteenth centuries. Before listing these dissatisfactions, let us outline the division of roles with regard to family consumption in the late eighteenth century.

Complaints by writers around the turn of the century reveal the woman's disproportionate responsibility for economy and frugality in the family. Eden observed in 1797 that

In the greatest part of England, the acquisition of the necessaries of life, required by a labourer's family, rests entirely on the husband. If he falls sick and is not a member of a Friendly Society, his wife and children must inevitably be supported by the parish. There is no other resource; for, to whatever cause it is to be ascribed, the wife, even in such an exigency, can do nothing. . . . There are . . . various

---

[1] *State of the Poor*, Vol. I, pp. 587–9.

[2] Above, pp. 71–9, 209–13 and 266–9 for the outline of these values.

[3] Davis, *Friendly Advice to Industrious and Frugal Persons*, pp. 22–9; Warner, *The Wesleyan Movement in the Industrial Revolution*, pp. 170 ff.

occupations, which the wife of a peasant or artificer would, it is possible, be inclined to pursue, were she only allowed to have a voice as to the disposal of her earnings. As the law now stands, the moment she acquires them, they become the absolute property of the husband; so that is not to be wondered at, that she conceives she has fulfilled her duty in attending to the children; and that he, conscious that the support of the family depends on his exertions, should so often become imperious and tyrannical. The instances are not few, where a stupid, drunken, and idle man, has an intelligent and industrious wife, with perhaps both the opportunity and the ability to earn enough to feed her children; but who yet is deterred from working from a thorough conviction that her mate would, too probably, strip her of every farthing which she had not the ingenuity to conceal. There is, perhaps, no better mode of ascertaining what degree of comfort is enjoyed by a labourer's family, than by learning what portion of his weekly earnings he commits to his wife's disposal. It makes a very material difference whether he or she holds the purse-strings. That he can earn the most, is granted, but she can make those earnings go the farthest. . . . For one extravagant mother . . . there are at least twenty improvident fathers. In the humbler spheres of society, it still seldomer happens, that the welfare of the family is affected by the misconduct of a mother.[1]

From Eden's remarks we may assume that the husband was the principal earner in the family.* The responsibility for distributing his earnings was probably variable, as the phrase "whether he or she holds the purse-strings" indicates. In general, the wife seemed more responsible for managing the expenditures on basic necessities and for a minimum of personal saving.** Possibly she specialized as well in encouraging industry in the care of children.*** The father specialized in status spending, which among the working classes consisted in convivial drinking in the neighbourhood public house.****

Step 1. Dissatisfaction. The values of independence underlay certain dissatisfactions with consumption in the late eighteenth century; the division of roles in the family provided the *structural foci* for these dissatisfactions. Before outlining the concrete dissatisfactions, however, we must discard two incorrect views regarding the genesis of dissatisfactions with family consumption.

(1) The working classes were losing real income during the industrial revolution. Statistical research has shown the upward

[1] *State of the Poor*, Vol. I, pp. 625–9.
* I.e., he specialized in the "earning capacity," or E_{Ga}. Above, p. 173.
** She specialized in E_{Aa} expenditures, or rather the control over these expenditures. Above, pp. 173–5.
*** I.e., she specialized in "motivational spending," or E_{Ag}.
**** This involves spending along the E_{Ai} dimension.

course of the real earnings of the factory operatives, who were the genuine emerging proletariat.

During the period 1790–1830 factory production increased rapidly. A greater proportion of the people came to benefit from it both as producers and as consumers. The fall in the price of textiles reduced the price of clothing. Government contracts for uniforms and army boots called into being new industries, and after the war the products of these found a market among the better-paid artisans. Boots began to take the place of clogs, and hats replaced shawls, at least for wear on Sundays. Miscellaneous commodities, ranging from clocks to pocket handkerchiefs, began to enter into the scheme of expenditure, and after 1820 such things as tea and coffee and sugar fell in price substantially. The growth of trade-unions, friendly societies, savings banks, popular newspapers and pamphlets, schools, and nonconformist chapels—all give evidence of the existence of a large class raised well above the level of mere subsistence.[1]

We should not assume, however, that the mere presence of greater earnings underlay the rise of friendly societies, savings banks, etc. They rose from genuine dissatisfactions which were based, as we hope to show, on the outmoded *structure* of family consumption.

(2) Because trade cycles were greater in magnitude in the industrial revolution than before, these crises endangered the stability of consumption and hence gave rise to dissatisfactions. True, fluctuations "characteristic of the capitalist process" become more apparent as more of an economy falls under the influence of credit creation.[2] The frequent riots in the eighteenth century, however, show the precarious position of family subsistence in the face of crop failure, plague, war, etc.[3] Furthermore, the rise in operatives' real income during the industrial revolution no doubt softened the effects of trade fluctuations. At any rate, it is almost impossible to compare the eighteenth and nineteenth centuries unequivocally in terms of the effects of fluctuations on the working classes. We hope to show, by examining the social structure of the family economy, that the *type*, not the *degree* of hardship imposed by business fluctuations was changing in the industrial revolution.

Specific Complaints. From the remarks of Colquhoun, Eden, and the writers of the Nonconformist revival, we may classify the empirical dissatisfactions with family consumption in the late

---

[1] Ashton, "The Standard of Life of the Workers in England, 1790–1830," *op. cit.*, p. 158. As Ashton points out, however, transitional groups such as the hand-loom weavers tell a different story. See Appendix A, Chapter IX.

[2] Schumpeter, *Business Cycles*, Vol. I, p. 224.

[3] Hobsbawm, "Economic Fluctuations and Some Social Movements since 1800," *op. cit.*, pp. 5–6.

eighteenth century as follows: (1) Complaints of improvidence, lack of frugality, waste, etc., were linked to a concern that the family was providing neither a basic standard of living nor a minimum of personal saving.* (2) Similarly, the criticisms of the neglect of education and the extravagant expenditures on frivolities, drink, and gambling were tied to a concern that too few of the family's resources were being devoted to expenditures which might encourage the virtues of a productive life.** (3) A corollary complaint dealt with the great proportion of family resources which were going into status spending, particularly drinking, to the sacrifice of "more basic" expenditures.*** Critics felt, in short, that the family's resources were being misallocated *away* from the productive goals of the family.

Institutional Pressures underlying these Complaints. What social conditions underlay the growing pressure of these dissatisfactions in the late eighteenth century? First, the family economy of the labouring class was undergoing a process of differentiation, and was becoming more susceptible to fluctuations in employment. Second, those displaced labouring groups which had not found a place in the new industrial world created a drain on the public resources. Third, the Revolutionary and Napoleonic wars pressed hard on the working-class family. All these trends converged to send the poor-rates—the barometer of working-class welfare in these days—into an astronomic spiral. Let us review these conditions.

One effect of industrial specialization is to move economic activities *from* the household premises *to* segregated occupational roles. We observed this effect when the putting-out system evolved into the factory system. From the standpoint of family consumption, several features of the former cushioned the economic hardships which a trade fluctuation might bring: (*a*) Weaving frequently was fused with farming. In periods of low demand for textiles, the weaver-farmer might turn to his second source of income. This adaptation was not possible when all the occupational interests of the worker became concentrated in the single role of factory operative. (*b*) "Unemployment" under the putting-out system was not so clear-cut a state as in the later factory system. In periods of slack, putters-

* This dissatisfaction implies an imperfect balance between the family's earning capacity and its expenditures on necessities and savings (E_{Aa}–E_{Ga}, or *A*-5). Above, pp. 177, 179.

** Because motivational spending was deficient, this meant that the "motivational results" of the family economy were unsatisfactory (E_{Ag}–E_{Lg}, or *A*-6). Above, pp. 177, 179.

*** E_{Ai}–E_{Ii}, or *I*-6. Above, pp. 177–9. The three dissatisfactions thus touched the three boundaries of the E_A sub-system—E_{Aa}–E_{Ga}, E_{Ag}–E_{Lg}, E_{Ai}–E_{Ii}.

out supplied smaller quantities of yarn, thus reducing but not stopping the weavers' income. Sometimes the adoption of "short time" in the factories achieved the same effect. Often, however, factory operatives were discharged altogether. Thus "underemployment" in the putting-out system became "unemployment" in the factory system. A crisis in trade was likely to be more disequilibrating for the factory worker's family than for that of his predecessor in the cottage. Even more, when the same master hired several family members, the failure of his firm could mean the discharge of whole families. (*c*) The wife in the putting-out families engaged in by-occupations such as baking, sewing, and brewing. As dependent family members began to drift into the factories, more of these economic activities began to slip from the home.

Hence under the new industrial system more of the family's productive activity moved outside the home. This meant that money began to assume a larger role in two senses: first it symbolized almost entirely the *total* economic performance of the family, and second, it began to be used for a wider variety of consumers' goods and services.[1] The family economy's self-sufficiency was approximating more closely a statement of how much it earned and what these earnings could buy. In the event of a trade crisis, moreover, the relative loss of income was greater than in the old system of production. These pressures underlay the increasing interest in family savings and security.

Such changes in the structure of consumption gave rise to comments like Scrope's in 1833 that

At present, the majority of the people of the British islands consists of *labourers for hire*—persons, that is to say, who depend for their daily maintenance on the wages of their daily labour; possessing very little property, other than a trifling degree of acquired skill, and their manual strength. The land from which raw produce may be obtained by labour, the tools and machinery which are indispensable to labour, and the stock of food on which the labourers must be subsisted while at work, are all appropriated by other classes. . . . The effect—whether good or bad on the whole, we will not determine—has been *to place the great body of the people in an exceedingly precarious position*. The owners of land, and the owners of capital of every kind, are removed from all danger, or dread, of immediate want; since, in case of the failure of a profitable demand for what they bring into the market, they are sure at least of being able to exchange it for *the means of subsistence*. The labouring class, on the contrary, on any

---

[1] For a theoretical discussion of the emergence of money as a generalized symbol, cf. Parsons and Smelser, *Economy and Society*, pp. 139–43.

failure of the ordinary demand for the labour which is their only property, have no resources to fall back upon, and no other means of obtaining even a temporary subsistence.[1]

In addition, the growing anonymity of urban centres made more difficult various organized responses to unemployment and distress, thus exaggerating the family's tenuous position. This is not to say that the responsibility of providing relief disintegrated in the ruling classes during the industrial revolution; they responded frequently with charity, subscriptions, and other forms of relief. Yet this relief could not be so certain as under the paternalistic employer or landlord. This loss of community ties added to the family's dependence on its own money income; thus, though the factory operatives' real income was improving, they were feeling the hardships of business crises more acutely because their total income ceased during these periods.

Since medieval times England had relieved its destitute by poor-laws. Contributions rested on property taxes called the poor-rates. Hence the property-owning classes—and these were the ruling classes in the late eighteenth century—perceived the pinch immediately at each call for poor-relief. In the late eighteenth and early nineteenth centuries the poor-rates spiralled, even though the burden was never immense in terms of the nation's total resources.[2] A parliamentary committee of 1818 produced the following estimates of poor-law finance for England and Wales.[3]

	Raised £	Expended on Poor £
1748, 1749, 1750 (average)	730,135	689,971
1776	1,720,316	1,530,804
1783, 1784, 1785 (average)	2,167,748	2,004,237
1803	5,348,204	4,267,963
1813, 1814, 1815 (average)	8,164,496	6,129,844

Some of this rise is traceable to the wartime inflation of prices. Much, however, attaches to displaced occupational groups in the agricultural and industrial revolutions. The agricultural enclosures movement originated long before the late eighteenth century, but when the Napoleonic war blockaded imports and created food

[1] *Principles of Political Economy*, pp. 299–300.
[2] S. & B. Webb, *English Poor Law History. The Last Hundred Years* (London, 1929), pp. 1–2.
[3] *Parliamentary Papers*, 1818, V, Lords Committee on Poor Laws, p. 4.

scarcities, the government sped enclosures to increase agricultural productivity. One effect of enclosure was to drive various kinds of traditional agricultural workers from the land. In the meantime, the industrial revolution was creating similar conditions of distress. The march of spinning machinery in cotton virtually killed hand-spinning by 1800, and about the turn of the century the hand-loom weavers began their long decline. While the military was an outlet for the unemployed during the war, their families frequently were thrown on the parish without earning capacity.[1]

These displaced, transitional groups, *rather than the new industrial classes*, demanded most from the poor relief system. In 1806 Colquhoun noted that

contrary to the generally received opinion, the number of paupers in the counties which are chiefly agricultural greatly exceed those where manufactures prevail. Thus, in Kent and Surrey, where the aggregate population is 576,687, there appears to be 77,770 paupers, while in Lancashire, where the population is 762,731, the paupers relieved are only 46,200.[2]

A questionnaire sent out in 1834 indicated that the workers on the decline technologically, such as hand-loom weavers, were least self-supporting. These classes also defaulted most frequently in payment of house-owners' rates in the late 1820's.[3]

In several ways the war period aggravated the pressure on these transitional groups. The speed-up of enclosures and the movement of wage-earners into the military increased the number of families without support. In a more general way, the wars increased provision prices faster than wages, and precipitated several severe fluctuations in trade.[4]

Stop-gap Measures in the Consumption Crisis. The effects of enclosures, technological unemployment, and inflation came to a head in the 1790's, a period marked by food riots, demands for relief, and

[1] For the course of enclosures during and after the war period, cf. Gayer, Rostow, and Schwartz, *The Growth and Fluctuation of the British Economy*, pp. 15–17, 36–7, 59, 69, 95, 121, 147; E. Davies, "The Small Landowner, 1780–1832, in the Light of the Land Tax Assessments," *Economic History Review*, I (1927), pp. 87–113; J. D. Chambers, "Enclosure and the Small Landowner," *Economic History Review*, X (1940), pp. 118–27. Also Pinchbeck, *Women Workers in the Industrial Revolution*, pp. 57–9; Eden, *State of the Poor*, Vol. II, p. 351.

[2] P. Colquhoun, *A Treatise on Indigence* (London, 1806), p. 273.

[3] *Parliamentary Papers*, 1834, XXXVI, Poor Law Commission, pp. 68, 69, 71, 73, 74; 1833, XX, First Report of the Factory Commissioners, p. 880.

[4] Above, pp. 118–23 and 215–16.

spiralling poor-rates.[1] The ruling classes' first "line of defence" against this crisis was an attempt to exhaust all opportunities for relieving the consumption pinch within the *existing structure* of consumption. Three manifestations of this attempt in the 1790's were (*a*) the encouragement of frugal food-preparation in the family; (*b*) the introduction of guarantees against outright starvation by means of direct subsidy through the poor-relief system; and (*c*) the encouragement of friendly society benefits.

(*a*) In 1776 Adam Smith had noticed the difference between the diets of Lancashire and Scotland (predominantly oatmeal) and the south of England (wheaten bread).[2] Immediately after the outbreak of war in 1793 a barrage of pamphlets exhorted the working classes to adopt these economies of the north and to substitute vegetables, Indian corn, arrow-root, etc., for more expensive items in the budget.[3] Simultaneously several pamphlets explored the means of relieving the burden of the high costs of provisions.[4] Eden devoted almost forty pages of his study of the poor to the frugality of the north, and in 1806 Colquhoun promised that "a greater boon could not be conferred upon the labouring people, than a general circulation of the art of frugal cookery. Potatoes, dressed in various ways, with a small portion of meat-fat, butter, onions, and other vegetables

[1] In the food riots of 1795, women played a major role in the violence. This may be attributed to the facts that they (as unemployed spinsters and as wives of recruits) felt the pinch economically and they were responsible for managing the basic expenditures of the family. For a description of these riots, cf. J. L. and B. Hammond, *The Village Labourer, 1760–1832* (London, 1919), pp. 120–22.

[2] *Wealth of Nations*, pp. 76, 160–61.

[3] E.g., *An Enumeration of the Principal Vegetables and Vegetable Productions, that may be substituted . . . in place of Wheat* (Birmingham, 1796); A Physician, *One Cause of the Present Scarcity of Corn, pointed out* (London, 1795); T. Ryder, *Some Account of the Maranta, or Indian Arrow Root . . . a substitute for . . . Corn* (London, 1796); *Some Information respecting the Use of Indian Corn* (Birmingham, 1795); P. Colquhoun, *Useful Suggestions favourable to the Comfort of the Labouring People* (London, 1795).

[4] E.g., S. Hudson, *An Address . . . on the Present Scarcity and High Price of Provisions* (London, 1795); An Independent Gentleman, *Thoughts on the Present Prices of Provisions* (London, 1800); Dr. Lettsom, *Hints Respecting the Distresses of the Poor* (London, 1796); J. M'Phail, *Remarks on the Present Times* (London, 1795); T. Malthus, *An Investigation of the Cause of the Present High Price of Provisions* (London, 1800); An Officer of the Volunteer Corps, *Short Thoughts on the Present Price of Provisions* (London, 1800); *Thoughts on the Causes of the Present Failures* (London, 1793); *Thoughts on the Most Safe and Effectual Mode of Relieving the Poor* (London, 1795); T. Wright, *A Short Address . . . on the Monopoly of Small Farms* (London, 1795); A Suffolk Gentleman, *A Letter . . . on the Poor Rates, and the High Price of Provisions* (Ipswich, 1795).

[etc.]" [1] Such "economizing" might have increased the family's flexibility in purchasing and preparing necessities, but it certainly would not have modified the structure of consumption sufficiently to meet the crisis in the working classes. As such it illustrates an early "cushioning" response to the crisis in consumption.

(*b*) Another reaction to the critical food situation was the Speenhamland System. This originated in 1795 to relieve unemployed workers or those working for less than subsistence wages by supplementing their incomes with payment in money or in kind. Such relief, like the encouragement of frugality, was a stop-gap measure, for it did not attack the growing structural pressures on the family economy. Nevertheless, it cushioned the existing structure through subsidy. The minimum standard, however small and unsatisfactory, no doubt reduced the amount of outright disturbance, especially among distressed agricultural labourers and other transitional groups. In later years the Speenhamland System was discredited and discarded on grounds that it defied the value of economic independence by keeping labourers artificially in unproductive positions.[2]

(*c*) Before inquiring into the ways in which the government attempted to encourage the growth of friendly societies without improving their structure, let us review the earlier history of this important social unit.

Though the friendly society has been traced centuries back to the guilds, its distinct character dates from the late seventeenth century. The progress of friendly societies was relatively sluggish until mid eighteenth century, when the rate of growth was more rapid but still gradual. At this time the societies began to concentrate in the north and west of England. The early friendly society provided not only benefits for sickness, old age, and death, but relief for manufacturers and artisans, who "receive assistance from [friendly societies] when they cannot procure employment." It was indistinguishable, moreover, from the "trade club" which safeguarded some of the conditions of its members' employment.[3] Thus before the industrial revolution

[1] Eden, *State of the Poor*, Vol. I, pp. 496–535; Colquhoun, *A Treatise on Indigence*, pp. 273–4.

[2] For a description of the system, cf. Hammond, *The Village Labourer*, pp. 161–5; H. O. Horne, *A History of Savings Banks* (London, 1947), p. 17. For the Poor Law Commissioners' attack on the system, cf. *Parliamentary Papers*, 1834, XXVII, Poor Law Commissioners, pp. 12, 34–5; also 1818, V, Lords Committee on the Poor Laws, p. 99.

[3] Baernreither, *English Associations of Working Men*, pp. 160–61; Colquhoun, *A Treatise on Indigence*, p. 111; F. M. Eden, *Observations on Friendly Societies* (London, 1801), p. 3; for a discussion of the "trade union" aspects of friendly societies, above, pp. 315–20.

the friendly society was a convivial social group, a trade union, an insurance company, and a savings bank.* In 1786 it might have had the following characteristics:

. . . every Member, in Consideration of his paying Eight-pence a Month into a joint Stock, is entitled to Seven Shillings a Week, as long as Sickness or any unfortunate Accident shall confine him to his Room; and to Three Shillings and Six-pence a Week, by way of what they term Walking Pay, for any Time, that he shall be incapacitated from following his usual Employ. After having been ten Years a Member, he is likewise entitled to Two Shillings and Six-pence a Week, during Life, if either through Age or any Accident he shall be rendered incapable of Labour. Besides the above, there is in most of their Articles a very exorbitant Allowance for Burials, even so high as Five Pounds ten Shillings, to be taken out of the Stock for the Member's own Funeral, and Forty Shillings for that of his Wife. . . .[1]

Apparently about 1760 "Benefit Clubs began to multiply rapidly in number."[2] Though historical information is lacking, it seems reasonable to assume that this burst of growth is associated with the simultaneous industrial changes which were isolating the family unit. The friendly society, in short, was growing as a "buffer unit" in the family's economic environment. Its functions protected the family by providing a reservoir of funds for contingencies such as funerals, medical expenses, and retirement. Also in the latter part of the eighteenth century—and probably because of the same industrial forces—a number of schemes for insuring or relieving the poor appeared: (1) In 1772 Richard Price and Cursitor Baron Maseres suggested a plan for life annuities to be charged on parochial assessments. This proposal passed the Commons but failed in the Lords. (2) In 1786 Acland proposed a national society or club to receive weekly contributions from wage-earners and to supply various benefits. (3) In the same year the Rev. Mr. Townsend suggested the universalization of friendly societies, improving their regulations, and excluding non-members from poor relief. (4) Also in 1786 the Rev. Mr. Hawes suggested contributions from rate-payers and wage-earners

* Formally, these functions clustered at the following boundaries: (1) E_G–C_G, or protection of the conditions of labour; (2) the reinforcement of occupational status of the members, and the government of the spending patterns relative to this status (E_{Ai}–E_{Ii}, or I-5); (3) saving, or laying aside some of the family's earnings for the indivisible expenditures for old age, sickness, and death (E_{Ga}–E_{Aa}, or A-5). Apparently faulty performance at these foci subsequently gave rise to dissatisfaction with the friendly society. Below, pp. 358–61.

[1] J. Acland, *A Plan for rendering the Poor independent on Public Contribution* (Exeter, 1786), pp. 3–4.

[2] J. T. Becher, *Observations . . . respecting Friendly Societies* (Newark, 1826), pp. 3 ff.

to support friendly societies. (5) In 1787 Gilbert attempted un-
successfully to set up large-scale allocation of funds to friendly
societies. (6) In 1789 there was an attempted revival of the Price-
Maseres scheme with amendments and improved tables of calculation. This also passed the Commons but failed in the Lords.[1]

Each of these schemes has its own story. Common to all, however,
was a neglect of the value of independence and a neglect of the multi-
functional character of the friendly society itself. Eden dismissed
Acland's plan "for rendering the poor independent" because
compulsory contributions denied the value of independence; "members would not be governed by laws of their own making." In fact,
Eden felt the first principle of the friendly societies was that "they
shall be governed by rules of their own formation." The clubs, in
short, had to be constructed on the dual principles of "Honorary
Superintendence and the Voluntary Contributions, arising from the
Benevolence of the Superior Orders, co-operating with the provident
Frugality of the Working Classes."[2] For the Superior Orders to
impose a compulsory, tax-like contribution and to dictate benefits
was to interfere with the poor's independence in managing their own
consumption and saving.

Furthermore, friendly societies were "the first societies that sought
to organize a distinct side of the modern social life of the working
classes";[3] consequently one could not disregard this social side by
imposing large and impersonal national levy schemes. Eden objected
insightfully to the compulsory plans by asking, "if [the working
classes] were prohibited from tippling in the ale-house on their club
nights, could they be prevailed on to subscribe [to national schemes]
at all?"[4] Eden here perceived the fusion of the friendly society's
various functions.

For these and other reasons,[5] therefore, the authorities balked at
compulsory plans and relied on those organizations which promised
to enhance the working classes' independence. In 1793, therefore,

[1] Becher, *Observations . . . respecting Friendly Societies*, pp. 3–6; Horne,
A History of Savings Banks, pp. 6–8.

[2] Eden, *State of the Poor*, Vol. I, pp. 600–2, 614; Becher, *Observations . . .
respecting Friendly Societies*, p. 5.

[3] Baernreither, *English Associations of Working Men*, pp. 156–7.

[4] *State of the Poor*, Vol. I, p. 604.

[5] Practical objections to the compulsory schemes were also heard. For instance,
the difficulty of calculating an appropriate contribution of, say, weavers, whose
incomes fluctuated greatly; the difficulty of transferring a man's contributions
from one friendly society to another if he left his parish, etc. Eden also noticed
that in the one case of legislated compulsory contribution—that for the Thames
coal-heavers in 1757—the law was repealed in 1770, presumably because of its
ineffectiveness. For these objections, *Ibid.*, pp. 603–7.

even though a number of other plans were in the air, Parliament attacked the crisis in consumption by passing an Act to encourage friendly societies.[1] This legislation shows the concern with maintaining the workers' independence, industry, and frugality. George Rose, its author, instructed Justices that societies should be checked for using malingering, drunkenness, and debauchery as claims for relief, and for diverting funds to purposes other than the stated aims of the society. These purposes were restricted to benefits in old age, sickness, infirmity, and relief for dependents.[2]

Under the Act, friendly societies which registered with the Justices were allowed several economic and administrative benefits such as the right to sue, the right to bring negligent officers to justice, freedom from bond and stamp fees, the right to use funds in public investment, etc.[3] In the end, however, the Act of 1793 was not revolutionary from a *structural* point of view; it attempted to encourage and advance an already-differentiated social unit in an effort to meet the crisis in consumption.

In the two or three decades after 1793, the friendly societies attained their maximum rate of growth. In 1801 Eden compiled a list of 5,117 registered clubs, from which he estimated a total of 7,200 registered and unregistered societies. From 400 sample clubs he posited an average membership of 97. For all of England and Wales, therefore, the total membership in friendly societies must have been 2,592,000, or nearly one-quarter of the population.

County by county, the 1801 figures break down as follows:

County	Number of Clubs
Lancashire	820
Middlesex (London)	about 600
Yorkshire	414
West Riding	330
Suffolk	235
London	250
Essex	205
Norfolk-Norwich	203

All other counties had less than 200 registered clubs. The cotton, woollen, and worsted districts of Lancashire and the West Riding of Yorkshire account for about 22% of the total registered societies, as

[1] 33 Geo. III, c. 54. Above, pp. 317–18 for the political background.

[2] G. Rose, *Observations on the Act for . . . Friendly Societies* (London, 1794), pp. 6–9. The restriction on purposes was simultaneously a *dis*couragement of trade-union activities. Above, pp. 318–21.

[3] Discussions of the Act of 1793 may be found in Rose, *Observations on the Act . . . for Friendly Societies; Parliamentary Papers*, 1825, IV, Combination Laws, pp. 323–5; Baernreither, *English Associations of Working Men*, pp. 302–3.

355

contrasted with this region's 14% of the total population of England and Wales in 1801.[1]

Part of the growth of friendly societies in these decades may be attributed to the Act of 1793. In addition, however, the original reasons for their rise—the growing differentiation of the family economy with regard to production and consumption—continued through the war period. Finally, the growing need for organized trade unions added to the development. As we have seen, repressive legislation against combinations forced workers to organize under the protective guise of the friendly society during the war period. In any case, the 1790's and the war period generally cemented friendly societies solidly in the social structure of the working classes. Further legislation in the nineteenth century dealt with matters of administration and detail, such as the prevention of fraud and negligence, the guarantee of security to friendly society funds, the perfection of statistical calculation of benefits, etc.[2] Friendly societies had established themselves in principle long ago and were experiencing that period of routinization associated with the later stages of structural differentiation.*

[1] Eden, *Observations on Friendly Societies*, pp. 7–8; *Population Abstracts*, 1801, pp. 451, 496.

[2] The 1793 Act did not prevent fraudulent dissolution of the friendly society by a vote of young members, who would then collect the funds which older members had been accumulating for years. Furthermore, the method of collecting funds meant a build-up of optimism in the early years, but despair when these funds were found inadequate to meet the needs of old age. J. Tamlyn, *Laws of Friendly Societies and Savings Banks* (London, 1827), pp. i–iv. Eden recommended in 1797 that printed forms, certificates of sickness, entry of subscription, and other safeguards would keep members informed and prevent fraud. *State of the Poor*, Vol. I, pp. 623–4. In 1795 Parliament extended the time required for friendly societies to enrol under the 1793 Act (35 Geo. III, c. 111). In the early nineteenth century a series of Acts modified the method of appeal for members' grievances (43 Geo. III, c. 111; 49 Geo. III, c. 125; 57 Geo. III, c. 39; 36 Geo. III, c. 90, and 52 Geo. III, c. 158). In 1817 friendly societies were given permission to invest their funds in savings banks at the rates provided for individual depositors (57 Geo. III, c. 130). In 1819 the previous Acts were consolidated and several clauses entered to prevent fraud and negligence. In the same Act it was required that tables of benefits or payments should be inspected and approved by two professional actuaries or others skilled in calculation (59 Geo. III, c. 128). Summaries of this legislation may be found in Baernreither, *English Associations of Working Men*, pp. 302–7; W. T. Pratt, *The Law Relating to Friendly Societies* (London, 1854); C. Ansell, *A Treatise on Friendly Societies* (London, 1835).

* The timing of the differentiation sequence of friendly societies as a whole might be somewhat as follows: (1) dissatisfactions produced by industrial conditions in the early and middle eighteenth centuries; (2) the gradual evolution of the friendly society throughout the century, with bursts around 1760 and the 1790's; (3) consolidation and routinization in the first half of the nineteenth century.

To summarize, the encouragement of frugality, the Speenhamland System, and the aid to friendly societies were stop-gap measures adopted in the face of rising poor-rates and increasing unrest among the poor. What was the effect of these measures on the poor-rates? Some saw many beneficial effects. In 1801 Eden

[did] not find . . . that any parish has been burthened with the maintenance of a member of any Friendly Society; nor are the instances numerous of families of members becoming chargeable . . . the active energies . . . which the possession of land never fails to excite, may be supplied by Friendly Societies, or similar institutions.[1]

Years later the *Manchester Guardian* noticed the concentration of friendly societies in Lancashire and the dearth in Devonshire (a county dependent on agriculture); correspondingly, the *Guardian* observed the reversal of this ratio with regard to institutions of charity.[2]

Nevertheless, the poor-rates continued to mount through the war, just when the friendly society was advancing most rapidly. It seems to me that these two rates of growth—one which dismayed the ruling classes, and one which pleased them—were not causally related; rather they reflected the *same* broad industrial trend. Friendly societies predominated in the manufacturing districts. They grew as the family economy became more differentiated in these districts. Such families would have leaned *less* on the poor-rates *in any case*, because the greatest need for poor-relief was among displaced agricultural labourers and other transitional groups. Thus the encouragement of friendly societies in the 1790's rested partly on insight and partly on confusion. It was wise because the new industrial workers were in need of such a cushion in their new industrial environment. Yet to hope to relieve the transitional poor by such a measure was to misunderstand both the friendly society and the poor-rates.

For such reasons the stop-gap measures of the 1790's failed to relieve the precarious position of consumption in the family economy of the distressed transitional groups. Dissatisfactions continued and disturbances mounted. Food riots reached a high pitch between 1795 and 1801, and erupted again in the Luddite violence of 1811–12.[3] At first these disturbances were countered with a mixed policy of repression and relief. In the end, however, the consumption crisis

[1] *Observations on Friendly Societies*, pp. 10–11; also *State of the Poor*, Vol. I, p. 615.

[2] Oct. 9, 1844.

[3] Webb, *English Poor Law History. The Last Hundred Years*, p. 32; Darvall, *The Luddite Disturbances and the Machinery of Order*, pp. 2, 236, 238.

gave rise to several new, differentiated social units. In the remainder of this chapter we shall trace the evolution of the savings banks (including the loan and building societies) and the co-operative stores.

THE RISE OF SAVINGS BANKS

Early Steps. The Victimization of the Friendly Society. Despite some claims that friendly societies relieved the problem of the poor, the rates continued to rise, and complaints mounted. In 1805, George Rose, later to introduce savings bank legislation, said that

with the increase in the population of the country, and in the price of provisions, the number of the poor, and the expense of maintaining them has necessarily been greater; and unfortunately the burden on the other classes of the community has also become considerably heavier; while, at the same time, the situation of the poor has been far from improving.[1]

Invariably this state of affairs was blamed on something. Rose felt that the laws of settlement immobilized labour.[2] Others blamed the poor-laws for encouraging a "habitual conviction of the certainty of parish support, in the failure of other resources," which was gradually sapping the independent spirit of the British labourer.[3] Various attacks on the poor continued; they were improvident by nature, the poor-laws made them improvident, or they had no opportunity to save funds securely.[4]

The most frequently abused body, however, was the friendly society itself. "I have no where seen," wrote Rose in 1816, "the Banks for Savings commended without unfavourable remarks on [Friendly Societies.]"[5] Many critics felt that the clubs were failing in the matter of saving.* As early as 1786 Acland asserted that a quarter of the society's subscription was spent, "by the laws of the society itself," at the ale-house on meeting nights; that the capital of such societies, remaining in a locked box, was not productive but idle money; that allowances for burials were exorbitant, etc. Worst of all, "during

---

[1] G. Rose, *Observations on the Poor Laws* (London, 1805), pp. 3, 20.
[2] *Ibid*., pp. 19–20.
[3] "On Improving the Condition of the Poor," *Quarterly Review*, XII (1814), p. 147; "On Frugality Banks," *The Philanthropist*, IV (1818), pp. 17–18.
[4] F. Burdett, *Annals of Banks for Savings* (London, 1818), p. 1; "On Frugality Banks," *op. cit*., p. 14; and H. Duncan, *An Essay on . . . Parish Banks* (Edinburgh, 1815), p. 7.
[5] G. Rose, *Observations on Banks for Savings* (London, 1816), p. 27.
* Formally this touches the E_{Aa}–E_{Ga} boundary. Above, pp. 176–7.

long and general Insurrections on Account of Wages, [the friendly societies] have almost annihilated their Capitals in Support of such mutinous Secessions from Labour."[1] Saving in the societies was suffering, in short, because they had too many functions, some of which impinged on savings; both convivial drinking and trade-union activities drained their resources.

Thirty years later Patrick Colquhoun levelled a similar attack. Friendly societies, he argued, enriched the mercer, undertaker, and milliner by their extravagant funerals. The practice of drinking on meeting-nights had "fascinating charms" which were likely to seduce the members:

Their character often assumes a new form; the irresistible gratifications to be found in convivial songs in cheerful company, allure them from their business and their families, and frequently produce idleness and dissolute habits among individuals, who, but for their temptations, would have continued to live sober and exemplary lives.[2]

Again, the diffuse social functions were reducing the economic "independence" of the members.

Not only were savings squandered, critics felt, but also the *form* of saving was inflexible. Because savings were tied to sickness, death, old age, and similar contingencies, and because expenditures on drinking were almost ritualized, all the funds were locked. "The benefits [the friendly societies] offer are too remote," said Eden, indicating perhaps that the clubs were helpless in the face of unpredictable economic crises.[3] Henry Duncan, the father of savings banks, felt that

Friendly Societies, excellent as they are, do not supply the lower classes facilities for bettering their pecuniary condition adequate to their circumstances. They provide a desirable resource in sickness and old age, but they do not accommodate themselves so much as could be wished to the varying situation and abilities of their members.[4]

Another critic contrasted the friendly societies, which limited coverage to "disease and disaster," with the "higher aim" of savings banks,

---

[1] *A Plan for rendering the Poor independent of Public Contribution*, p. 5.

[2] *A Treatise on Indigence*, pp. 115–16. Colquhoun entered some technical objection as well, such as the failure of the societies' calculations to yield an appropriate relationship between contributions and benefits.

[3] *Observations on Friendly Societies*, p. 11. Eden also objected to friendly societies' administrative procedures on technical grounds.

[4] Quoted in Horne, *A History of Savings Banks*, p. 42.

which might promote children's education and other goals.[1] Thus friendly societies' resources were not *general* enough; they could not go beyond a few fixed and indivisible expenditures.

The critics of friendly societies added a flurry of miscellaneous complaints to these objections in principle. The sickness benefits gave rise to malingering and claims for partial sickness, they felt. This in turn gave rise to a system of spying on members who claimed the right to be added to the sick-list. In addition, the organization of the clubs led to human pettiness and dishonesty. One critic felt that officers were illiterate and interested in misappropriating funds; that automatic rotation assured their position in office; that there were no auditors of funds; that the treasurer was a publican, who might lend to members and throw them into debt. Another complained that members were "scratched" if payments were not made with absolute regularity. Or young persons might dissolve the society arbitrarily, thus depriving the old contributors of their long-time savings.[2]

Equally vigorous denials met these criticisms. Rose maintained that the charges of drunkenness and extravagance were exaggerated and that no "bad and dangerous purposes" were being pursued by the clubs. In 1817 a secretary of a friendly society denied charges of dishonesty among officers and praised the clubs' collective ability to supply comfort in crisis.[3] We may agree that these attacks were exaggerated in many ways. The exaggerations, moreover, rested on the continuing crisis in consumption. *Ad hoc* measures such as the Speenhamland System, the encouragement of dietary frugality, and the assistance to friendly societies had not reduced the poor-rates. It would therefore seem a natural reaction to blame the friendly society and its members for the crisis. Some of the more extreme attacks on the friendly society system and the integrity of its members

[1] E. Christian, "General Observations on Provident Banks," *The Pamphleteer*, XVII (1820), p. 277.

[2] For these and similar objections, cf. B. Beaumont, *An Essay on Provident or Parish Banks* (London, 1816), pp. 30–31; J. T. Becher, *The Constitution of Friendly Societies* (London, 1824), pp. 50–52; J. W. Cunningham, *A Few Observations on Friendly Societies* (London, 1817), p. 24; J. Count de Salis, *A Proposal for Improving the System of Friendly Societies* (London, 1814), pp. 13–14; J. Woodrow, *Remarks on Banks for Savings and Friendly Societies* (London, 1818), p. 2; Ansell, *A Treatise on Friendly Societies*, pp. 23–4; C. Hardwick, *Friendly Societies* (Preston, 1851), p. 37; W. Lewins, *A History of Banks for Savings* (London, 1866), pp. 85–9; J. Wright, *A Treatise on the Internal Regulations of Friendly Societies* (London, 1828), pp. 13–23.

[3] Rose, *Observations on Banks for Savings*, p. 30; A Secretary and Member of a Friendly Benefit Society, *A Vindication of the Present Order of Friendly Benefit Societies* (London, 1817).

—who were no doubt as honest as any comparable group—were thus symptoms of disturbance which erupted periodically in this extended period of dissatisfaction.

On the other hand, the old friendly society was clearly anachronistic in the new world of consumption and savings. The significance of fluid money resources for the family economy had become much greater. Rather than fall back on farming or domestic labour in slack seasons, the working family now had to fall back on *savings*. Rather than manufacture basic items such as clothes, bread, and beer in the home, the working class was now spending *money* for these items. Rather than bring an illiterate son up to a simple trade, one now had to *save* small amounts for his training. Money, since it now represented more and more family needs, required a greater degree of generalizability, or transferability from one situation to another.

In the old friendly society, however, savings were placed in a box unavailable to contributors except on specified occasions such as mourning, old age, sickness, and sometimes involuntary unemployment. The friendly society also drew some family income into ritualized drinking on meeting-nights. To be sure, such expenditures are extremely important; spending for death, sickness, and community solidarity touch the deepest human sentiments. Because savings were *inflexibly tied* to such occasions, however, members and their families were less manoeuvrable in the unpredictable crises of the industrial and market world. The friendly society had *too many* functions to permit it to become a general repository for funds, payable on demand. Such limitations gave rise to the barrage of complaints in the late eighteenth and early nineteenth centuries.*

This background of dissatisfaction gave rise to the savings banks, which represented an institutional attempt to render the family economy's resources more general and more flexible than in the friendly society. If its resources could be so generalized, it would be more independent of economic hardship and parish support. Some kind of repository for general funds which were freely accessible therefore promised not only to relieve the pocket-books of the ruling classes, but also to maximize the value of independence.

Analytically, the dissatisfactions, disturbances, and *ad hoc* measures of the late eighteenth and early nineteenth centuries constitute the first three steps of structural differentiation. Now we turn

---

* Analytically, we might say that because of certain inflexibilities in the realm of motivational spending, e.g., health, old age, etc. ($E_{Ag}-E_{Lg}$, or A-6), and in the realm of status spending ($E_{Ai}-E_{Ii}$, or I-5), the new and pressing need to adjust the expenditures for basic necessities and a minimum level of savings ($E_{Aa}-E_{Ga}$, or A-5) could not be easily and freely met.

to Step 4 in the emergence of savings banks—the appearance and encouragement of new ideas. This step overlapped frequently with Steps 5 and 6 in the following way: some individual would generate a certain idea (Step 4); either the individual author or others then would supply various details (Step 5); then certain influential citizens would initiate a local bank and assume responsibility for its success (Step 6). Hence to divide the three steps in the following discussion segments the historical development of savings banks artificially; it also illustrates the necessary overlapping of steps when we apply an analytical scheme to an historical sequence in which it is impossible to control all the factors controlling change.

Step 4. Encouragement of New Ideas. A general encouragement of schemes to improve the welfare of the poor appeared as early as 1796 with the formation of the Society for Bettering the Condition of the Poor. This society

published and circulated very general information about a wide variety of social reform—improved conditions for friendly societies, village shops for supplying necessaries at cheap prices, workshops for the unemployed, model workhouses, educational reforms. . . . The Society's contribution was to circulate information about these early experiments among people who had the means, the influence, and the disposition to make practical use of the information.[1]

Such encouragement, often from "the most distinguished writers of the age," continued through the first two decades of the nineteenth century. Both Jeremy Bentham and T. R. Malthus commended the idea of a savings bank in 1797–8. Several years later Colquhoun proposed to centralize friendly societies' deposits into a National Savings Bank, and to devote its funds to welfare purposes.[2] In 1818 Burdett recommended several "tracts, adapted for the use of the Lower Classes," all of which recommended this form of saving.[3] From such banks, workers were to enjoy "the propriety of frugality

[1] Horne, *A History of Savings Banks*, p. 23; also Burdett, *Annals of Banks for Savings*, pp. 2–3.

[2] "Extract from an Account of the Provident Institutions for Savings," *Report of the Society for Bettering the Condition and Increasing the Comforts of the Poor* (London, 1817), p. 110; Horne, *A History of Savings Banks*, pp. 27–8; Colquhoun, *A Treatise on Indigence*, pp. 122–38.

[3] *Annals of Banks for Savings*, pp. 118–19. The names of the pamphlets indicate the contents: *A Friendly Address to the Industrious on the Advantages of a Provident or Savings Bank; The Savings Bank: a Dialogue between Ralph Ragged and Will Wise; Remarks* (an appendix to the rules of the Hertfordshire Saving Bank). Davis, *Friendly Advice to Industrious and Frugal Persons.* Eight thousand of the first pamphlet were sold in and about London. See also F. Wrangham, *The Savings Bank : in Two Dialogues* (Scarborough, 1800).

—of reserving *part* of their earnings when *prosperous, unincumbered,* and *healthy,* to meet the future claims of *a family,* of *sickness,* and of *old age*," to relieve them from "unhappy marriages, neglected educations, and increased poor rates," to allow apprentices and unmarried labourers to lay aside funds for their married years, and so on.[1] Implicitly these advantages promised a security through savings which contrasted with the more limited achievements of the friendly society.

These new promises, furthermore, always received the stamp of legitimacy by reference to the value of independence. When Parliament assumed a supportive interest in savings banks toward the end of the war period, the committees of both its houses underlined the value-basis for the banks:

... it is expedient to recommend the adoption of provident or saving banks, as likely to increase the comforts and improve the condition of the Poor, and to render them less dependent on parochial relief; which, under the best and most considerate administration of it, can never be so satisfactory to the person who is the object of it, or so consistent with those honourable feelings of pride and independence which are implanted in the heart of man, as that resource which is the result of his own industry and the produce of his own exertions.

.   .   .   .   .   .

The encouragement of frugal habits would, in any state of society, be an object of importance; but your Committee are strongly impressed with the opinion, that, in the present situation of the poor of this country, it is chiefly by the gradual restoration of a feeling of reliance upon their own industry, rather than upon the parochial assessments, that the transition to a more wholesome system can be effected.

Your Committee have the satisfaction of seeing that institutions for the secure and profitable deposit of the earnings of the industrious, which was heretofore projected, are now by the spontaneous exertions of individuals in actual and successful operation; and from the growth of the system of Saving Banks, they are inclined to expect very beneficial results, not only in affording to the industrious poor a secure deposit for their savings, but in familiarizing them with a practice, of which the advantage will be daily more apparent.[2]

[1] Beaumont, *An Essay on Provident or Parish Banks,* pp. 4–5; *Observations on Banks for Savings* (London, 1818), pp. 2–3; Rose, *Observations on Banks for Savings,* p. 19. Also, Burdett, *Annals of Banks for Savings,* p. 8, and "Extract from an Account of the Provident Institution for Savings," *op. cit.,* p. 113.

[2] *Parliamentary Papers,* 1818, V, Lords Committee on the Poor Laws, p. 101; 1817, VI, Select Committee on the Poor Laws, p. 12.

Other supporters joined in this praise on value grounds. The Edinburgh Savings Bank contrasted its own method of savings with a grant of simple aid to the poor, which proved so often "a bribe to the idle and dissolute to indulge in habits which inevitably lead to poverty."[1] Henry Duncan asserted that

the only way . . . by which the higher ranks can give aid to the lower in their temporal concerns, without running the risk of aiding them in their ruin, is by affording every possible encouragement to industry and virtue,—by inducing them to provide for their *own* support and comfort,—by cherishing in them that spirit of independence, which is the parent of so many virtues,—and by judiciously rewarding extraordinary efforts of economy, and extraordinary instances of good conduct.[2]

Finally, when Parliament contemplated legislation for the savings banks in 1817, the probable effects of such legislation on the independence of the poor excited "more discussion than any other [element] in the bill." The point of debate was whether persons depositing in banks should be prohibited from parish relief. The issue itself is less interesting than the arguments on each side. Those who favoured prohibiting savers from relief claimed that it would *encourage* independence by making people save on their own; those who opposed prohibition felt it would *discourage* independence by punishing those who had already exercised the initiative to open accounts. The point of debate was not the worth of the value of independence itself, but the optimum means for realizing the implications of this value.[3]

In Step 4, therefore, we find an encouragement of some sort of savings banks on the grounds that they were more in keeping with the encouragement of the values of independence among the poor than many other plans, such as the friendly society and relief from public authorities.

Step 5. Attempts to Specify. Overlapping with this encouragement was what an historian of savings banks has called the "campaign of words."[4] Concentrated between 1800 and 1810 and extending up to the 1817 legislation, this campaign involved a search for appropriate models of some sort of savings bank for the poor, and initiated a number of prolonged controversies over methods (as opposed to

---

[1] *A Short Account of the Edinburgh Savings Bank* (Edinburgh, 1815), p. 3.

[2] *An Essay on . . . Parish Banks*, p. 5; Horne, *A History of Savings Banks*, pp. 41, 49.

[3] *Parliamentary Debates*, First Series, XXXVI, 1817, cols. 681–2, 833–5. The clause for not excluding the savers from poor relief was finally adopted (col. 835).

[4] Horne, *A History of Savings Banks*, p. 38.

principles, which concentrate in Steps 3 and 4). Said Joseph Hume in 1816:

> The public mind is at present very much alive to Institutions for assisting the Poor to manage their small pecuniary affairs; and it is very desirable that every establishment formed with that intention should be so constituted as to prevent the probability of failure, and possess all the advantages, with as few as possible of the disadvantages attendant on such institutions. So many publications have lately appeared, and such different opinions have been offered on the various plans for Economic Institutions, that considerable doubts have arisen as to which of them were preferable.[1]

Let us sample some of the explorations and controversies in this campaign of words.

Some searched for existing models, such as the Penny Societies for purchasing Bibles and Testaments, or Sunday Banks. The latter, which were appendages to churches, gathered sums from the poor, and returned them on festive occasions such as Christmas celebrations. Both Malthus and Eden turned enviously toward the Scottish poor-laws, but Rose qualified their envy by claiming that the Scottish system as such was not superior, but that its management was better than that of the English system. Whatever the particular model, the most serious consideration was given to local and voluntary methods.* For this reason Samuel Whitbread's scheme in 1807 for a national system of savings through the post office found little public favour, and local schemes like those of Twiss and Adams were pondered more seriously.[2]

When early private experiments in savings banks began—e.g., Ruthwell, Edinburgh, Bath, and London—controversies over the details of management and the guarantee of security flared. *The Philanthropist*, for instance, deemed the following as necessary elements of savings banks "for the benefit of the labouring part of the community":

> 1. . . . the completeness of security . . . savings . . . ought to be placed as far beyond the reach of those failures, which are apt to arise from the accidents of business, from the improbity or from the blunders of managers, as it is possible to place them . . .

---

[1] J. Hume, *An Account of the Provident Institution for Savings* (London, 1816), p. 16.

* The consistency of this interest with the value of maximizing the independence of the poor should be evident.

[2] Davis, *Friendly Advice to Industrious and Frugal Persons*, p. v; Horne, *A History of Savings Banks*, pp. 23-6, 36-9; Rose, *Observations on the Poor Laws*, pp. 12-17.

2. . . . those banks should deal in the minutest sums. . . . If it were only a shilling, it ought to be readily received.

3. The mode of transacting business should be as commodious as possible; so as neither to perplex the customer, nor to consume his time.

4. The places should be commodious. . . . Under proper regulations at the post-office, much might be done by letter.

5. These banks should be enabled to pay interest upon the sums of the labouring classes deposited with them. . . .

6. To preserve the precious fund deposited in these banks from the cruel absorption under which it would suffer in the courts of law, every dispute should, under an act of parliament, be determined finally by a jury of twelve men, one half to be chosen by each of the parties.[1]

Should there be a delay before any depositor could withdraw funds, thus discouraging the impetuous actions of the irresponsible? Should the funds of savers be invested in government bonds? Should speculation in these bonds be permitted? Should banks be for savings alone, or should they include annuity schemes for the poor? These and other questions were argued energetically.[2]

On the question of the security of savings, *The Philanthropist* recommended publicity of transactions, including public books, general meetings of all contributors, etc. Furthermore, "it would be desirable that a beginning should be made by obtaining the contributions of well-disposed [persons] to constitute a fund for paying an interest on the deposits for those whose benefit the bank is intended. The invitation to the people to come with their savings would then act with peculiar force."[3] Several writers echoed this sentiment; Haygarth added a recommendation that "we particularly solicit the female sex to exert the beneficent and persuasive influence, which they fortunately possess in society. They are endowed with the largest share of the milk of human kindness."[4] Before 1817, in fact, most banks relied on private guarantees of security by responsible

---

[1] "On Frugality Banks," *op. cit.*, pp. 7–8.

[2] *Ibid.*, pp. 4–5; Hume, *An Account of the Provident Institution for Savings*, pp. 11, 38, 44–5, 48; Beaumont, *An Essay on Provident or Parish Banks*, pp. 33–6, 43.

[3] "On Frugality Banks," *op. cit.*, pp. 11–13.

[4] J. Haygarth, *An Explanation of . . . the Provident Institution at Bath, for Savings* (Bath, 1816), pp. 37–8. His sentiment reflects the apparent division of responsibility in the family economy. The wife was more responsible for savings and the standard package; thus the appropriateness of a female leadership figure in the matter of savings. In fact, women were instrumental in the initiation of several early savings banks. Below, p. 368. Also Beaumont, *An Essay on Provident or Parish Banks*, pp. 39, 41.

local community leaders.[1] Others, however, found private support unsatisfactory as a permanent basis for security. Hume complained of the "hazard of private security," particularly if funds should be loaned to persons of affluence in the community, and Burdett called for some kind of legislative support as banks became more numerous.[2]

The nature of possible governmental support itself was another bone of contention. The *Edinburgh Review* held out for local autonomy in management to avoid the "infinite confusion, trouble, and expense" of governmental enactments. The *Quarterly Review*, on the other hand, felt that "the assistance of the legislature might [in no other way] be more usefully employed." Part of this dispute stems from the differences between English and Scottish investment. The Chartered Banks in Scotland were in a position to give great security of funds locally, but private investment in England was "so formidable as to deter gentlemen from undertaking [Savings Banks]." [3]

We have not attempted to exhaust these controversies between 1800 and 1817, but rather to illustrate the *kind* of issues which appear in Step 5. Step 4 is a "campaign of principles" on values and basic directions of change. Step 5 involves the next step in specification; controversies in this step concern the means to carry out these general principles. In terms of structural differentiation, therefore, the social system has moved one step closer to the incorporation of a new social unit.

Step 6. Establishment of Institutional Forms. "The campaign of words was not ended when the real action began." [4] This real action was the "entrepreneurial" phase of the sequence of differentiation. While overlapping with Step 5, it differs from the earlier steps in so

1 Lewins, *A History of Banks for Savings*, pp. 45–6. George Rose was instrumental in forming the Southampton Bank for Savings in 1815 and the trustees included Lord Palmerston, the Rt. Hon. Sturges Bourne, and the Earl of Cavan. Horne, *A History of Savings Banks*, pp. 64–5. The roster of the London Provident Institution included the Duke of Somerset as President, eighteen peers and two bishops as vice-presidents, and the names of managers included Sir T. Baring, Patrick Colquhoun, Joseph Hume, Rev. T. Malthus, George Rose, David Ricardo, Major Torrens, Nicholas Vansittart, J. C. Villiers, and W. Wilberforce. Hume, *An Account of the Provident Institution for Savings*, pp. 7–8. Even after legislative support was forthcoming in 1817, the same kinds of lists dominated the boards of banks. Cf., for instance, the list of the Manchester and Salford Bank in the *Manchester Guardian*, Aug. 11, 1821; also J. G. Shaw, *History of the Blackburn Savings Bank, 1831–1931* (Blackburn, 1931), p. 11.

2 Hume, *An Account of the Provident Institution for Savings*, p. 40; Burdett, *Annals of Banks for Savings*, p. 47.

3 "Publications on Parish or Savings Banks," *Edinburgh Review*, XXV (1815), pp. 145–6; "On Improving the Condition of the Poor," *op. cit.*, p. 155; Hume, *An Account of the Provident Institution for Savings*, pp. 54, 57.

4 Horne, *A History of Savings Banks*, p. 38.

far as specific agents assume responsibilities for the success or failure of a concrete project. The initiators of savings banks had to meet the test in the world of action; the earlier planners and theorists in the world of ideas. For the latter, failure meant dispute, unpopularity, and intellectual discredit; for the former it meant collapse and financial loss.

The types of pioneer savings banks established were almost as numerous as the suggestions for their establishment in Step 5. The first institution was a small enterprise in Tottenham in 1798. Several ladies were the patrons of this organization, which combined a female benefit club, a loan society to prevent the use of pawnshops, and a bank for the earnings of young children. In 1804 the Charitable Bank for Children was extended to include the savings of adults. Trustees handled the savings, which yielded 5% interest. In 1799 the Rev. Joseph Smith began to accept weekly contributions from parishioners, which were repaid at Christmas with a bounty for economy, or earlier in cases of distress. Several years later John Bone established a bank entitled "Tranquillity" in London, the plan of which he publicized widely. The bank, run by "five highly respectable Gentlemen, wholly unconnected with the contrivance of the Plan," was open to both sexes and to children, and received deposits as small as 6*d*. In 1808 "four Ladies and four Gentlemen" formed the Bath institution "to enable Servants . . . to preserve what part of their wages they could spare." Having noticed, however, that the Tottenham bank had lost funds at 5%, the Bath trustees allowed only 4%.[1]

Savings banks spread more rapidly in Scotland than in England, no doubt because of the former's superior investment system. Henry Duncan began his famous parish savings bank in Ruthwell on the friendly society model in 1810. This tiny bank had an elaborate procedure for deposits and withdrawals in an effort to encourage frugality and independence among the depositors. It was an immediate success, its assets growing from £152 in 1810 to £922 in 1814. The Edinburgh Bank, formed in 1818, had less complex management; all depositors received the same interest, with no rewards for the exceptionally virtuous; and again the interest rate was fixed more

---

[1] For information on these early attempts, cf. Burdett, *Annals of Banks for Savings*, pp. 11, 13; J. T. Pratt, *The History of Savings Banks* (London, 1842), p. xvi; Clapham, *An Economic History of Modern Britain*, pp. 298–9; J. Bone, *Outline of a Plan for Reducing the Poor's Rate* (London, 1805); J. Bone, *The Principles . . . of Tranquillity* (London, 1806); J. Bone, *The Friend of the People* (London, 1807), especially p. 28; Haygarth, *An Explanation . . . of the Provident Institution at Bath, for Savings*, p. 1.

sensibly at 4%. During the next few years Scotland "was covering itself with savings banks," adding as many as fifteen in 1815 alone. Some followed the Edinburgh and some the Ruthwell model. Generally, however, the simpler, more differentiated Edinburgh system began to prevail.[1]

Meantime, the lack of security for investment had limited England's progress to a few pioneer institutions. This obstacle was met in several ways, none completely satisfactory: (1) Personal guarantors safeguarded investments. Such a method was restricted to localities, however. (2) Some banks invested, guarding against loss through fluctuations by giving depositors returns smaller than those yielded by the investments. Even this protection, however, could not weather extreme fluctuations. (3) The Bath and Panton Street banks transferred the risks of fluctuation to the depositors.[2] Each of these methods protected the security of funds to a degree, but each fell short of safeguarding, in a permanent way, the security required by the family economy.

Notwithstanding these limitations, savings banks advanced after 1810, and accelerated between 1815 and 1817. By this time there were seventy savings banks in England, four in Wales, four in Ireland, plus a great number in Scotland.[3] Banking activities, furthermore, were becoming more and more *differentiated*. The early banks were appendages of churches or were assimilated to the friendly society. As the years moved on, the Edinburgh model, which broke away from the communal aspects of earlier forms, began to predominate. The English banks, moreover, were larger and deviated more from the friendly society. This trend toward the differentiation of savings as such was the ultimate outcome of the original dissatisfactions with the savings functions of the friendly society.*

Curiously enough, however, the peculiar legislative arrangements of the day slowed this trend toward greater differentiation. Because of the Friendly Societies Act of 1793, savings banks could reap administrative and financial benefits by calling themselves friendly societies. The banks at Ruthwell, Kelso, Dumfries, and elsewhere filed as benefit clubs.

The regulations have accordingly been submitted to, and approved of by the Justices of the Peace of the districts. We applaud Mr. Duncan

---

[1] Horne, *A History of Savings Banks*, pp. 44–7; S. Hall, *Dr. Duncan of Ruthwell* (Edinburgh, 1910), pp. 57–8, 60–61; Lewins, *A History of Banks for Savings*, pp. 40–51.

[2] Horne, *A History of Savings Banks*, pp. 59–64.

[3] Pratt, *The History of Savings Banks*, pp. xix–xx.

* Above, pp. 358–61.

for his ingenuity in so framing the constitution of his little banks as to obtain for them the benefit which the law affords, and at the same time to place them under the inspection of the civil magistrate.[1]

There were good reasons for a structural segregation of "savings" from the more diffuse aspects of the friendly society, just as there were good reasons for segregating the "trade union" from the friendly society. Yet the legislative encouragements and discouragements of the war period postponed both.

Before 1817 the "entrepreneurs" of the savings banks were local community leaders who volunteered their prestige and sometimes their financial backing for the savers. The Act of 1817 (57 Geo. III, c. 130) transferred this responsibility from private to public hands, and thereby solidified the security of the deposits. Trustees were forbidden to profit from the banking operation by this Act. After the deposits of a local bank reached £50, the trustees passed them to the Commissioners for the Reduction of the National Debt, who established a "fund for the banks of savings," invested the deposits, and paid, in the beginning, an interest of £4 11s. 3d. a year per £100. To prevent banks from becoming solely a haven for secure and high-paying investments, the Act limited depositors to £100 deposits in the first year and £50 in any succeeding year.[2] Of course this limit was well beyond the saving capacities of the working people, and probably explains the fact that banks were not entirely working-class institutions, especially in their early days.

The encouragement by legislative protection of funds is reflected in the accumulation of banks after 1817:

	England	Wales	Ireland	Total
Established before 1816	6	—	—	6
Established during 1816	74	4	4	82
1817	57	5	1	63
1818	119	6	7	132
1819	30	2	7	39
1820	3	—	5	8

It is said that Scotland had 182 banks by 1819.[3]

Up to 1827 the savings banks in England had £16,000,000 in deposits. The rate of growth decreased after this date, so that by 1837, thirty years after the first legislation, just over £30,000,000 had accumulated. This general upward course conceals a few jerks and

[1] Burdett, *Annals of Banks for Savings*, p. 18.
[2] Clapham, *An Economic History of Modern Britain*, pp. 298–9; Horne, *A History of Savings Banks*, pp. 79–80.
[3] Horne, *A History of Savings Banks*, p. 80.

starts, especially in panics and depressions, and the withdrawals associated with the Reform agitation in 1831–2. After 1832, the growth of total deposits continued to be "eminently satisfactory," dipping only in severe depression years such as 1837 and 1839. Such reversals, furthermore, were minuscule when compared with the general business crises in these years.[1] This fact indicates that savings banks were oriented primarily toward *security* rather than speculation, even though they were not exclusively repositories of working-class family savings. This accent on security follows from our assumption that savings banks were agencies geared primarily to the family economy, in which considerations of security are paramount.*

One sequence in particular illustrates the importance of security considerations in connection with savings banks. From an early period Joseph Hume had urged a lower rate of interest in savings banks so that the government would not continue to lose money. An attempt to lower the rate occurred in 1824, and four years later, under pressure from Hume, Parliament lowered the rate from £4 11s. 3d. to £3 16s. 0½d. The banks continued to lose, and Hume continued to insist that security counted more than money gains to savers. Parliament again reduced the maximum rate payable to trustees to £3 0s. 10d. in 1844. In one sense these reductions reflect the pressure of the falling general interest rates from 1815 to mid-century. They also show, however, the salience of security for the family. Through the successive reductions, the depositors and deposits continued to rise, thus tending to justify the comment in 1818 that "it would be better that the interest should be £1 11s. 3d. than £4 11s. 3d. From his [General Thornton's] knowledge of the lower orders of the people, he was convinced that all they wanted was security for their money." [2]

How adequately did the savings banks fulfil their promise to resolve the crisis in consumption in the working-class family? To shed light on this question we shall examine the kinds of depositors, both in terms of income level and in terms of occupational type.

[1] Horne, *A History of Savings Banks*, pp. 116–18; Lewins, *A History of Banks for Savings*, pp. 89–97. For a background to the 1831–2 withdrawals, cf. Wallas, *Life of Francis Place*, Chapters IX–XI, especially pp. 308–23.

* In formal terms the savings bank is an agency specializing in the stabilization of the interchange at the E_{Aa}–E_{Ga} boundary, namely the interchange between the family's earning power and its spending needs. Above, pp. 166–7.

[2] For these developments, cf. Horne, *A History of Savings Banks*, pp. 98, 101–3; Lewins, *A History of Banks for Savings*, pp. 60–61, 68–9; Rostow, *British Economy of the Nineteenth Century*, pp. 8, 17–19; *Parliamentary Debates*, Second Series, XVIII, 1828, cols. 258–9; Third Series, XLIII, 1838, cols. 1283–91; LXIV, 1842, cols. 1096, 1104–5; First Series, XXXVII, 1818, cols. 1156, 1177–8.

One major criticism of the savings bank in the early nineteenth century was that it did not appeal to the lowest income brackets, and thus failed to reduce the poor-law burden and to stimulate the economic independence of the working classes. If we examine the average size of deposits, the charge seems justified. Between 1817 and 1827, only 400,000 persons had deposited the £16,000,000 with an average deposit of £40, a sum as great as a total year's earnings for many in the working classes. In 1824 Parliament passed a law limiting deposits to £50 in the first year and £30 in succeeding years, and prohibiting interest on amounts over £200. This reduction, plus the gradually improving condition of the working classes, reduced the average level of deposits in the next few decades. For all banks in England, Scotland, Wales, and Ireland the national registrar found an average account per depositor of £29 in 1841 and £27 18s. 0d. in 1844, which marked a considerable fall from the 1820's.[1]

A related criticism dealt with the character of the depositors. Early it was felt that "the various classes of *artificers* and *handicraftsmen* have it fully in their power to make a comfortable provision for their declining years; nay, even *agricultural labourers*, whose earnings are upon the lowest scale of remuneration, have *their* opportunity for saving." [2] Did such groups live up to this reputation? An analysis of the ledgers of some early banks shows that

from a quarter to a half . . . were domestic servants, the remainder mainly artisans, small tradesmen, women, and children. There were few unskilled labourers. The number of richer people depositing was not substantial; their individual contributions were naturally larger, but the statutory limits of deposit prevented any serious abuse.[3]

In Bolton, for instance, the first 200 depositors in 1818 included 57 from industrial occupations (including 12 weavers), 44 servants, 53 children, 14 women and 5 friendly societies.[4] Clearly the depositors

[1] For these developments, cf. Lewins, *A History of Banks for Savings*, p. 89; R. Vivian, *A Letter on Friendly Societies and Savings Banks* (London, 1816), p. 14; Horne, *A History of Savings Banks*, pp. 98–9; *Parliamentary Papers*, 1833, VI, Manufactures, Commerce and Shipping, p. 33; 1852, V, Friendly Societies, p. 33; J. T. Pratt, *A Summary of the Savings Banks* (London, 1846), p. 321; Pratt, *The History of Savings Banks*, p. 79. The number of friendly societies depositing in the banks was increasing (8,264 in 1841 and 10,203 in 1844). This meant that the average size of deposits was decreasing still faster in the 1840's, since the deposit of a friendly society included the deposits of a great number of individual members.

[2] J. Bowles, *Reasons for the Establishment of Provident Institutions, Called Savings' Banks* (London, 1817), p. 5.

[3] Horne, *A History of Savings Banks*, p. 97.

[4] *Ibid.*, p. 95.

were not of the same groups—such as weavers, labourers, etc.—
who turned chronically to the poor-law authorities for relief. An
occupational breakdown of depositors in the Manchester and Salford Savings Bank, summarized in Table 14, shows the same results.
The proportion of domestic servants declined after 1820, possibly
because of their general decline in numbers, and possibly because of
the increasing prosperity of other classes. Another feature of the table
is the slow change in the respective fortunes of those "in factories,
warehouses, as porters, etc." and "weavers" (presumably hand-loom).
While the proportion of neither is exceptionally high in comparison
with groups like tradesmen, the proportion of weavers is particularly
small.[1] Factory operatives, furthermore, increased slightly or held
their own while weavers gradually declined. In a bank report for 1843,
the category "weavers" disappeared altogether, and the new category
became "cotton spinners, weavers, their assistants and wives." [2]

Hence the savings banks, like the friendly societies, seem to have a
paradoxical side. Both received encouragement because of dissatisfactions with the mounting poor-rates and with the structure of
consumption and savings in the working classes.

Presumably the founders felt these banks would relieve the poor.
In each case, however, the primary participants were *not* those
dependent on poor-law relief. Indeed, transitional groups like
weavers and agricultural labourers progressively *withdrew* from
friendly societies, education, and other "new" social forms. In fact
the savings banks did not help these sick groups, which struggled
helplessly to their deaths. Because of the growing differentiation of
the family under industrial conditions, however, the friendly society
and to a lesser extent the savings bank appealed to the "healthy"

[1] In 1819, the time of Peterloo, there were some 40,000 weavers in and around
Manchester and some 20,000 cotton factory workers. Read, "The Social and
Economic Background to Peterloo," *op. cit.*, p. 3. As the factory system continued
its rise, and hand-loom weaving gradually died, of course, these proportions
gradually reversed.

[2] In general, savings banks flourished more in rural than in industrial areas.
In 1831 the number of depositors in several manufacturing counties was 1/45 of
the counties' total population. The deposit per head of total population in these
counties was £13 7s. In several agricultural counties, the ratio was one depositor to
twenty-seven inhabitants, and the average deposit per head was £24 1s. H. D.
Morgan, *The Beneficial Operation of Banks for Savings* (London, 1834), Appendix
III, p. 58. Several factors undoubtedly accounted for such differences: (a) the
greater proportion of domestic servants in the rural areas, heavy savers in any
case; *Ibid.*, pp. 16–17; (b) the tendency for city capital to flow into industrial
investment; (c) the tightness of rural organization which permitted more direct
influence of community leaders over the poor than in the more anonymous urban
centres.

TABLE 14

PERCENTAGE DISTRIBUTION OF CLASSES OF DEPOSITORS, MANCHESTER AND SALFORD SAVINGS BANK, 1821–39 [1]

Description	Year								
	1821	1822	1824	1825	1826	1827	1828	1830	1831
Tradesmen, Shop-keepers, Arti-ficers, Publicans, or their wives, etc.	21·2	24·4	30·0	32·9	33·1	33·3	34·1	35·0	35·0
In Factories, Warehouses, as Porters, etc.	13·0	12·0	13·0	14·4	14·8	15·7	15·9	15·9	15·8
Domestic Servants	29·0	28·1	23·8	21·6	21·1	20·2	19·0	18·4	18·4
Widows	1·1	1·6	2·1	2·4	2·6	2·6	2·6	2·6	2·5
Minors	16·6	17·2	14·4	12·2	11·7	11·5	11·4	11·6	11·1
Weavers	2·0	2·3	4·0	4·7	4·8	5·2	5·7	5·6	5·5
Labourers	1·4	1·7	2·4	2·9	3·0	2·8	2·8	2.6	2·5
Farmers	1·1	1·2	1·7	1·8	1·7	1·8	1·9	1·8	1·9
Others not speci-fied	14·6	11·4	8·2	7·0	7·0	6·7	6·4	5·9	6·4
Friendly and Charitable Societies	—	—	0·4	0·1	0·1	0·1	0·1	0·4	0·5
Total number depositors	1,679	2,438	4,877	6,952	8,100	9,985	12,425	16,480	18,423

Description	Year							
	1832	1833	1834	1835	1836	1837	1838	1839
Tradesmen, Shop-keepers, Arti-ficers, Publicans, or their wives, etc.	35·4	35·3	35·6	34·6	34·0	33·3	32·8	32·5
In Factories, Warehouses, as Porters, etc.	15·7	15·8	15·9	16·1	15·6	15·4	15·7	15·8
Domestic Servants	18·4	18·3	18·2	17·9	17·6	17·5	17·5	17·6
Widows	2·5	2·6	2·7	2·7	2·7	2·8	2·8	2·8
Minors	11·4	11·3	11·1	11·0	10·9	11·0	11·0	11·2
Weavers	5·3	5·2	5·1	5·0	5·1	5·0	4·8	4·6
Labourers	2·5	2·4	2·3	2·4	2·4	2·3	2·4	2·4
Farmers	1·9	1·9	1·8	1·8	1·7	1·6	1·6	1·5
Others not speci-fied	6·0	6·5	6·6	7·9	9·3	10·4	10·7	10·9
Friendly and Charitable Societies	0·7	0·7	0·7	0·7	0·7	0·7	0·7	0·8
Total number depositors	20,254	22,251	24,610	27,344	30,250	32,557	35,903	38,794

[1] Calculated from the annual reports of the Manchester and Salford Savings Bank in the *Manchester Guardian*.

elements of industrial society which were not dependent on the poor-law *in any case*. Thus the paradox: savings banks had their genesis in dissatisfactions with the condition of the poor; because of the transitional and desperate condition of the really poor, however, the savings bank could not assist them; yet the banks provided, after all, a cushion of stability in the sphere of consumption and savings for the new, more differentiated elements of industrial society.*

Loan Societies, Building Societies and Annuity Plans. Along with the savings banks these three arrangements began to appear. All three are essentially specialized elements built on the principle of the friendly society or the savings bank. Saving, as we have conceived it, renders the relationship between a family's earning power and its day-to-day consumption standards more stable and flexible. It allows spending to proceed even though income may be somewhat irregular. Furthermore, the principle of *credit* extends this stability and flexibility by providing purchasing power temporarily in the absence of earnings. The loan society, therefore, extends the principle of savings one step further. The building and annuity societies, on the other hand, are units specialized according to *goals*. One of the friendly society's main goals was to provide for the contingencies of sickness, old age, and burial. The annuity society specializes in old-age relief alone, and in this sense is more differentiated than the friendly society. Similarly, the building society specializes in housing —a large and inflexible expenditure.

George Rose, the framer of the 1817 legislation on savings banks, felt that loan societies should not be an aspect of the banks. "Let us apply our whole exertions in support of the Banks; the other, however benevolent and useful, is a subordinate object."[1] Nonetheless, an interest in supporting loan societies stayed alive. Woodrow launched a plan in 1818, which was followed in 1831 by Maitland's suggestion for associations "whereby the industrious classes could borrow, as well as deposit savings." Osborne suggested similar reforms in 1835. In the end Parliament supported loan societies only indirectly by enacting in 1834 that societies could be formed for any legal object. In 1835 the Loan Societies Act made the support more

---

* As Table 14 shows, the greatest proportion of depositors came from classes not *directly* influenced by the industrial revolution—tradesmen, publicans, domestic servants, etc. Yet even for these groups the growing significance of money and money-bought products made the need for money savings greater. The very extension of the market made these service groups more dependent on money income.

[1] Rose, *Observations on Banks for Savings*, p. 33. Apparently several persons had brought the possibility of connecting the two to his attention. *Parliamentary Debates*, First Series, XXXIV, 1816, col. 516.

direct.[1] From a legal standpoint, therefore, loan societies were indistinguishable from friendly societies; from a structural standpoint they pushed the specialization of these clubs further.

Building societies, originating in the early nineteenth century, also were encouraged indirectly by the general 1834 legislation concerning friendly societies' purposes, and directly by legislation in 1836. Though these societies had grown rapidly in the early 1830's, these acts accelerated their progress. By the end of 1848, 2,000 such societies had registered in the United Kingdom.[2] Thus, while both loan and building societies were just emerging, their place among friendly societies was not insignificant in the 1840's. Of the 486 friendly societies registered in Lancashire for 1842, their names indicate that some 109 were devoted explicitly to loan and 136 to building purposes.[3]

Several annuity schemes were alive in the eighteenth century, but all had been discarded for one reason or another. Around the turn of the century a pamphlet addressed to the poor praised the advantages of annuity societies over benefit societies in general. In 1822 Ricardo entered a petition calling for governmental support of an annuity system. A decade later Maitland suggested that savings banks be extended to include annuity arrangements. These sample suggestions were underscored by the fact that friendly societies apparently were ceasing to provide old-age benefits for their members. By an Act in 1833, therefore, depositors were allowed to purchase governmental annuities through savings banks. Annuity payments could commence at any age, benefits were freed from income tax, and payments and benefits were calculated on the basis of standardized tables. Thus the annuity establishments became a differentiated aspect of savings banks.[4]

These outgrowths from the friendly society illustrate the major

[1] Woodrow, *Remarks on Banks for Savings and Friendly Societies*, especially pp. 3, 7; J. Maitland, *Considerations addressed to all Classes on . . . a National Banking and Annuity System* (London, 1831), pp. 18–19, 28–30; S. G. Osborne, *The Prospects and Present Condition of the Labouring Classes* (London, 1835), pp. 7–8; Baernreither, *English Associations of Working Men*, p. 305.

[2] A. Scratchley, *A Treatise on Benefit Building Societies* (London, 1849), pp. 5–6. Building societies often combined the financing of housing arragements with old-age benefits, fees for placing boys as apprentices, etc., thereby retaining some of the general functions of the old friendly societies. Nevertheless, their emergence marks a differentiation within the friendly society movement.

[3] *Parliamentary Papers*, 1842, XXVI, Friendly Societies, pp. 289, 294. Possibly these numbers should be increased, since the name of a friendly society did not always reveal its purpose.

[4] *Moral Instruction Addressed to the Working Classes*, pp. 186–9; Maitland, *Considerations addressed to all Classes on . . . a National Banking and Annuity*

theme of our analysis, namely that as the expenditures for family consumption moved from the home into the market, new social units differentiated as buffers for the family's tenuous market position. The rise of these units—savings banks, loan, building, and annuity benefits, as well as the consolidation of the friendly societies themselves—conforms roughly to the sequence of structural differentiation. To conclude this chapter, let us analyse the rise of still another buffer unit in the sphere of consumption—the co-operative store.

THE RISE OF THE CO-OPERATIVE STORE FROM THE EARLY CO-OPERATIVE MOVEMENT

Early Steps. We have outlined the "disturbed" elements of co-operation in the 1820's and 1830's. This regressive movement promised to erase a multitude of working-class ills by a massive process of absorbing the whole of industrial society into small, compact, multi-purpose communities. Our treatment in Chapter X, however, was limited to the disturbances traceable to the family's division of labour, and co-operation's promise to return to less differentiated forms of economic endeavour.

Co-operative thinkers also found friendly societies—which specialized in consumption and savings—as unsatisfactory as most other parts of capitalist society. William Thompson considered the insurance schemes against disabilities to be mere "palliatives." For him they were

necessarily imperfect, inevitably excluding the very poor, the most in need, from their benefits, and inapplicable to many of the most grievous casualties of life, such as the permanent impotence of a greater or less degree of intensity, unequal capabilities of exertion of women, casualties of orphanage, miscalculations in trade, etc.[1]

Naturally the co-operative community not only would prove superior, but also would supersede these imperfect agencies. In fact, the next two decades did bring forth new co-operative units; far from superseding the old friendly society, however, they were a further differentiation of a buffer unit in the family's new market environment. These new units were the co-operative stores.

Step 5. Attempts to Specify. Shortly after the "campaign of principles" of the co-operative movement had reached a pitch in the

System, pp. 38–40. Lewins, *A History of Banks for Savings*, pp. 69–70. For an account of the annuities granted through savings banks, cf. *Parliamentary Papers*, 1842, XXVI, Return of Annuities, pp. 269–70.
[1] *Labor Rewarded*, p. 64.

middle 1820's, outlines of several means to hasten the millennium began to appear (Step 5), and attempts to establish co-operative communities materialized (Step 6). Intermingled as these two steps were in the late 1820's and early 1830's, we shall discuss them separately.

In earlier times an occasional group had tried to relieve uncertain spheres of consumption* by the establishment of co-operative enterprises. These associations, mostly corn-mills and baking societies among working-class persons, were relatively rare, purely commercial, limited to skilled artisans in seaport towns, and apparently directed toward resisting the high prices of private traders. In any case, working-class attempts to organize the marketing of the basic necessities were sporadic before the 1828–32 surge.[1]

The co-operative "campaign of principles" (Step 4) continued through the 1820's with tracts, books, and periodicals promising the millennium in the form of co-operative communities. Toward the end of this period a concern with more practical problems (Step 5) emerged, e.g., how to obtain capital to rent plots of land for communities. In 1827 the *Co-operative Magazine* suggested, in an article entitled "How to procure funds for a Co-operative Community," that members of societies sell articles to each other wholesale and utilize the profits to establish full-scale co-operative communities. William Thompson formulated these ideas more systematically several years later in a book entitled *Practical Directions for the Speedy and Economical Establishment of Communities*. He defined the method of co-operation as "the voluntary union of the industrious or productive classes, in such numbers as to afford a *market to each other*, by working *for each other*, for the mutual supply, directly by themselves, of all their most indispensable wants."[2]

Such a mutual trading association was, of course, a half-way house in terms of co-operation's ultimate ideals. The full division of labour among members remained intact, and benefits consisted of gains via the establishment of monopolistic buyer–seller agreements in a small

* Analytically the basic consumption items—bread, sugar, clothes, etc.—belong in the standard package (E_{Aa}), and the problem of maintaining a stable and steady supply of them is a problem of assuring stability at the $E_{Aa}-E_{Ga}$ boundary. Hence it is analytically parallel to the savings bank, loan society, and friendly society, even though its focus is on the "standard package" rather than the "personal savings" aspect of this interchange. Above, pp. 173–7.

[1] Potter, *The Co-operative Movement in Great Britain*, p. 44.

[2] *Practical Directions*, p. 1. For a list of periodicals beginning in 1822 and flourishing particularly between 1826 and 1832, cf. Holyoake, *The History of Co-operation in England*, pp. 106–7, 115, 118, 123, 125–6, 129, 132–3, 135, 177–82. Also Podmore, *Robert Owen*, pp. 383–4.

sector of the market. Theorists themselves recognized this compromise, but reminded members that mutual trading was only an expedient:

All [trading associations have] the intention of ultimately forming themselves into complete Co-operative Communities as soon as they shall have saved out of their trading fund . . . an additional sum sufficient to stock and rent the land necessary to afford them wholesale food.[1]

So the Utopian elements remained, even though co-operators were now turning to more practical problems.

Most of these practical projects developed in the absence of Robert Owen, who was engaged in co-operative experimentation in Indiana. Not long after his return to England, he produced two gigantic schemes for realizing the co-operative ideals quickly and completely. The first promised to defeat the capitalist system by establishing a National Labour Exchange. Labour notes, or promises to work so much time in return for another's labour, were to replace money, thus eliminating middlemen and profit-makers from the contemporary scene. The second scheme was the Grand National Consolidated Trades Union, which, like the labour exchanges, touched off a supercharged but fleeting response.[2]

Step 6. Establishment of Institutional Forms. In addition to the schemes, there were several attempts to create societies which might realize, more or less imperfectly, the ideals of co-operation. In the 1820's and 1830's, the co-operative organizations were of three types:

(1) purely educational and propagandist bodies, preaching the whole social gospel of Owenism, and including a great many Owenite sympathizers who were not of the working class. . . . (2) Co-operative Stores or Shops, mostly run by enthusiastic Owenites. . . . (3) societies of producers, aiming at Co-operative production of goods and looking to the Stores to provide them with a market.[3]

The third type blended with several attempts to establish full-scale co-operative communities, such as the Orbiston Community begun in 1825, the Dowlands Devon Community of 1827, and Thompson's projected plan for a community in Cork. Most of these attempts at complete co-operation collapsed shortly after their initiation.[4]

[1] Thompson, *Practical Directions*, p. ii.
[2] M. Kaufmann, *Utopias; or Schemes of Social Improvement* (London, 1879), pp. 102–3; above, pp. 253–4.
[3] Cole, *A Short History of the British Working Class Movement*, pp. 114–15.
[4] The history of these communities is described by Podmore, *Robert Owen*, pp. 347–91, and by Holyoake, *The History of Co-operation in England*, pp. 271–93.

In the late 1820's co-operative societies began to increase rapidly in number. By the beginning of 1830 there were about 300 small stores, trading asociations, and resident communities in the United Kingdom. After two more years, this figure was between 400 and 500. "England, Ireland, and Scotland were studded, England especially, in Yorkshire and Lancashire, with co-operative manufacturing and provision associations." Congresses began in Manchester in 1830. In the following year Robert Owen spoke to a meeting of forty-six co-operative societies from the north of England, at which time a general union of societies of the north was proposed.[1]

These small co-operative societies rested on shaky foundations, however, partly because of the persons involved and partly because of difficult situations:

Several . . . stores were destroyed by success. The members for a time made money, but having no idea of capitalising their profits . . . the shareholders simply found success monotonous. Some betook themselves to other enterprises more adventurous, and their places not being filled the society in time dwindled away. In other cases insufficient capital prevented profitable competition with shop-keepers; in some cases want of religious toleration broke up the society. Others fell through when their novelty wore off, the members having ulterior objects. In more cases bad management ruined the concern. In possibly quite as many instances scoundrel managers extinguished the society.[2]

Since the stores possessed no legal status, embezzlers of funds could not be prosecuted. Most of those attracted to co-operative communities were described as persons "already degraded by starvation and idleness" and "poets, enthusiasts, dreamers; reformers of all things, and the baser sorts of disbelievers in any." On the market side, women complained about having to limit their purchases to one shop.[3]

Thus the societies contained the seeds of their own failure. The Equitable Labour Exchange of 1832–3 and the Grand National Consolidated in 1833–4, however, applied the finishing touch. In the former, the issuance of labour notes from a central office in London began in September, 1832. If a craftsman worked one hour and turned his product over to the central exchange, he received a labour

[1] Podmore, *Robert Owen*, pp. 396–7; Holyoake, *The History of Co-operation in England*, p. 188; *Manchester Guardian*, May 28, 1831.
[2] Holyoake, *The History of Co-operation in England*, pp. 188–9.
[3] Potter, *The Co-operative Movement in Great Britain*, pp. 51–2, 29–30; Holyoake, *The History of Co-operation in England*, p. 347; Owen, *Threading My Way*, p. 228; Podmore, *Robert Owen*, p. 421.

note, which represented a demand on another tradesman for one hour's work. In the first few days products flooded the central warehouse, and some tradesmen began to accept labour notes as a medium of exchange. Participants in the scheme soon began to discover, however, that their labour notes were less valuable than conventional money; the problem of calculating differential wage rates also arose. Deposits continued to accumulate in the warehouse, however, and the labour exchange struggled along until its ignominious collapse in 1833. The demoralizing effects of this and later failures in provincial cities were compounded by the collapse of the Grand National Consolidated in the following year. "The disastrous year 1834 broke up many of the Co-operative Societies and reduced those that survived into quiescence." [1]

So much for the ill-fated "entrepreneurial" attempts at co-operation in the late 1820's and early 1830's. Except for a few in Scotland, the co-operative stores remained inactive between 1834 and 1844. The general disorganization of working-class aims (especially between 1837 and 1842) applied as well to the aims of the early co-operative leaders. Owen himself, who had become "a visionary pure and simple," organized a series of plans to achieve the millennium— "New Age," "New Moral Worlds," and a "Universal Community of Rational Religionists." William Lovett, James Watson, and Henry Hetherington turned their energies from co-operation to the People's Charter.[2]

As the economy pulled out of a depression in the early 1840's, working-class interest in co-operation revived. The monumental date in this revival was 1844, when a small group formed the Rochdale Equitable Pioneers. This store survived as a model for the co-operative movement throughout the nineteenth century. The Pioneers, it should be noted, were committed firmly to the ideals of earlier "disturbed" movements such as Chartism, Socialist Co-operation, and Teetotalism. In fact, one of their objects was to establish "as soon as practicable . . . a self-supporting home colony of united interests, or to assist other societies in establishing such colonies." [3]

Besides these ideals, however, was a direct and hard-headed

---

[1] Podmore, *Robert Owen*, pp. 402–23, 452.

[2] Clapham, *An Economic History of Modern Britain*, p. 316; Fay, *Life and Labour in the Nineteenth Century*, p. 64; Holyoake, *The History of Co-operation in England*; Potter, *The Co-operative Movement in Great Britain*, p. 56.

[3] Potter, *The Co-operative Movement in Great Britain*, pp. 60–62; G. Holyoake, *The History of the Rochdale Pioneers* (London, 1893), pp. 9–10; Bland, Brown, and Tawney, *English Economic History*, p. 643.

attention to practical details. One object in Rochdale was to establish a store for basic provisions, clothing, etc.* Housing and land were to be acquired for residence and employment of unemployed members. The store's administrative arrangements showed an even closer attention to practical detail. Profits were to be divided quarterly among members after deducting for expenses of management, interest on loans, capitalization, etc. The society demanded high-quality staples, and insisted on cash payments both for goods bought and merchandise sold, thus safeguarding the credit position and liquidity of the organization.[1]

Hence the co-operative stores of the 1840's differed qualitatively from the ideal communities of the late 1820's and 1830's. The latter promised a community responsible for *all* of man's economic and social needs, a community which would absorb capitalism in a great process of de-differentiation. The Rochdale model assumed, on the other hand, a differentiated market structure. Rather than absorb the economic institutions of society, the store operated as a buffer to safeguard the security of the family by ensuring quality, low cost, savings in the form of dividends, and presumably distributional efficiency. The new co-operative store, like the old co-operative community, wished to eliminate the conventional middleman. It would eliminate him, however, by *becoming a better middleman* in the new industrial market structure. Far from *de*-differentiating the economic roles of society, the new co-operative store added a new social unit to join the friendly society, savings bank, and trade union as a buffer between the new family and its economic environment. The society's policy of relief shows the same acceptance of a differentiated market structure. In the Rochdale system, the plot of land was no longer felt to be the medium whereby the whole division of labour might be erased; co-operative work on the land now tided over periods of unemployment in the *existing* industrial system.

After its formation the Rochdale store expanded rapidly. By the end of 1845 there were eighty members and a capital of £181 12s. 3d. In this year the store also allowed small dividends, thus assuming a function similar to the savings banks. In the depression years between 1846 and 1849, not only did the Rochdale store thrive, but other stores opened, e.g., in Bacup, Todmorden, Leigh, Salford, Padiham, and Middleton. By 1851 there were 130 stores on the Rochdale

---

* The content of objects sold in these stores was uniformly part of the "standard package" of necessaries. Luxuries and non-essential services were avoided.

[1] Holyoake, *The History of the Rochdale Pioneers*, p. 47; Potter, *The Co-operative Movement in Great Britain*, p. 62.

model, with an estimated total membership of something like 15,000.[1]

Nearly all the early stores were in the north or the Scottish midlands, both manufacturing districts. Though aloof from the more fanciful schemes two decades earlier, the factory operatives gave warm support to the co-operative movement after the Rochdale experiment. In some cases trade unions took a direct interest, e.g., when the Oldham spinners' association took a piece of land to support unemployed members, and when the Bolton union established a store in 1851.[2]

In 1850 a small conference of several co-operative societies was held in Rochdale. Meetings continued regularly during the next decade, and in 1863 the Lancashire co-operatives were instrumental in forming the "North of England Co-operative Wholesale Society," which later became the "English Wholesale Society," with an elaborate national organization. By 1871 there were almost 1,000 co-operative stores in England. Three-fourths of these—i.e., those making complete returns to Parliament—had 260,000 members, a capital of £12,500,000, an annual business of £47,000,000, and an annual profit of £4,000,000.[3]

Co-operative stores, therefore, like the new unions and the savings banks, had their greatest days after our period ends. Nevertheless, it is possible to observe how the stores established their foothold in a process of structural differentiation. Beginning with a period of disturbance, the co-operative movement began to concern itself with several institutional problems which had resulted from the gradual differentiation of the family unit from industrial production and marketing. The resulting gulf between the family and economic processes required social units to stabilize the family's position in the market. Having been pushed into disequilibrium through a process of differentiation in the industrial revolution, therefore, the working classes in turn initiated several sequences of differentiation which produced new social units to protect the family in its new industrial environment.

[1] Holyoake, *The History of the Rochdale Pioneers*, p. 16; Clapham, *An Economic History of Modern Britain*, p. 599.

[2] Clapham, *An Economic History of Modern Britain*, p. 599; Chapman, *The Lancashire Cotton Industry*, pp. 230–31; *Webb Manuscripts on Trade Unionism*, Vol. XXXV, pp. 72–4; Vol. XXXVI, p. 66.

[3] Potter, *The Co-operative Movement in Great Britain*, pp. 88–9; Owen, *Threading My Way*, p. 227.

CHAPTER XIV

THE QUESTION OF EXPLANATION IN
WORKING-CLASS HISTORY

In the past five chapters we have covered many important sectors of British working-class history—the history of strikes and the development of trade-unionism; the rise of factory agitation and the pattern of factory legislation; the excesses of early co-operation and the emergence of co-operative stores; the occurrence of violence and pleas for assistance, and so on. Furthermore, we have related these and other phenomena to *one* major explanatory principle, namely that the family economy of several classes of labour was undergoing a process of structural differentiation.

To appreciate this explanation, we must consider it on several levels. First we constructed an abstract model of change which proposed that under appropriate historical pressure, the units of a social system would differentiate by a determinate sequence—dissatisfaction, disturbance, handling and channelling, encouragement of ideas, attempts to specify new social units, attempts to establish new social units, and routinization of established units. Second, we phrased this model in terms of the family as a social system, thus specifying the precise units of the family which are subject to historical pressure and which might differentiate structurally. Finally, we examined the course of working-class history in the late eighteenth and early nineteenth centuries in order to illustrate that much social turmoil, unrest, experimentation, and legislation fitted into appropriate sequences by which the family economy was emerging as a more specialized social unit. Hence the nature of our "explanation" was to relate a multitude of complex social phenomena to a single set of analytical propositions without varying the logic of the propositions themselves.

The scheme of structural differentiation certainly is not meant to encompass all other possible explanations of the same phenomena. To be sure, it overlaps with some explanations—e.g., that which traces the factory operatives' unrest to their desire to maximize their short-term wages and protect their long-term economic

384

position. On the other hand, the model of differentiation conflicts in places with explanations such as the Marxist or that based on laissez-faire presumptions. I shall compare and contrast the value of four competing accounts of early nineteenth-century working-class history: (1) the "economic" explanation which refers social turmoil to wage and welfare conditions; (2) the Marxist explanation in *Capital*; (3) the approach of the "British Socialist" school; (4) the approach of a revisionist laissez-faire historian.

Social Unrest and the Workers' Economic Conditions. Is not the model of structural differentiation too elaborate and cumbersome as an explanation of the factory operatives' outbursts in the 1820's and 1830's? Were not these disturbances simply manifestations of the operatives' desire to maximize their short-term economic welfare and to protect their long-term earning power? Because a simple explanation is preferable to a complex one, should we not prefer the "economic" explanation to the "structural differentiation" scheme?

Several disturbances do fit plausibly into the "economic" explanation. In Chapter X, for instance, we isolated two types of strikes among the factory operatives: (*a*) those attempting to advance wages in times of business prosperity; (*b*) those attempting to resist introduction of superior machinery. In the first the operatives were attempting to maximize their short-term wage position; in the second they were trying to protect their occupational position by resisting long-term displacement. Even here the two elements of the economic explanation conflict a little, because the spinners *not* discharged by the improved mules enjoyed a wage advance. In spite of this, they opposed the new machines. Since the cotton operatives opposed the machinery consistently and uniformly, however, we might suggest safely that when the two principles of the economic explanation conflicted, the desire to protect long-term economic security was stronger than the desire for short-term gain.

Again the agitation for ten hours is reducible to the spinners' attempt to protect their own economic position. To limit child labour to ten hours would have prevented children from flooding the industry and displacing adult males. To reduce adults' hours to ten, moreover, not only would spread the work among more employees, but also would produce the same wages for less labour (short-term economic gain). To keep the children at work was also essential, however, because children contributed to the income of the adult spinner. The evasions of the Factory Act of 1833 also reflect the operatives' economic position; spinners overworked their own children both to augment their own wages and to avoid paying two relays of children.

All these disturbances make sense in terms of the twin economic principles of short-term economic gain and long-term economic security. The model of structural differentiation, far from conflicting with such an explanation, provides a criterion for determining *which* of the two economic principles was salient at any given time. When the operatives' position was under *structural pressure*, their desire to maintain their long-term economic security predominated over their desire to maximize their short-term wage position. By referring to the logic of differentiation, therefore, we may distinguish between the two types of strikes consistently and sort out the several causes of the factory agitation. Hence the model of structural differentiation supplements rather than conflicts with the economic explanation in this case.

Yet the original question remains. Why choose the model of structural differentiation when the economic explanation seems to explain the same phenomena equally plausibly? Why load the simpler explanation with the excess baggage of the more complex one? To answer these questions we must turn to some of the phenomena which pose greater analytical difficulties for the economic explanation.

The economic explanation seems to require "stretching," for instance, if it is to account for the factory agitations after the Factory Act of 1833. These agitations were, we may recall, (*a*) to reduce children's and adults' hours to eight under a gigantic plan for national regeneration; (*b*) to raise children's hours to twelve; (*c*) to raise children's hours to ten and simultaneously to reduce adults' hours to the same; and (*d*) to ensure a ten-hour day and avoid relays by restricting the motive power of machinery. The spinners' interest in shortening their own hours and thereby spreading the work among more workmen lay plausibly behind the efforts to reduce adult labour to eight, and later to ten hours. But why the agitation for *twelve* hours (1835) which was sandwiched between the demand for *eight* (1834) and that for *ten* (1835-7)? Perhaps the interest in twelve hours stemmed from the short-term prosperity and a demand for labour. Yet the demands for eight, twelve, and ten, respectively, all occurred in the period of rising prosperity between 1834 and 1836. Presumably, furthermore, the operatives' interest in reducing hours to ensure employment for all was strongest *not* in prosperity, but in depression periods, such as 1833, 1837, and again in 1846-7.[1] The common element in these post-1833 agitations seems not to be a desire for short-term gain so much as a desire to *equalize* the hours of children and adults, thus re-establishing, to a degree, the older, less differentiated structure of the family economy.

[1] Above, pp. 217-19.

Perhaps, on the other hand, the activity between 1834 and 1837 manifested the operatives' attempt to re-employ children at low wages, thus avoiding the relay system and the higher-paid adolescent assistants. This explanation, while feasible for the mid-1830's, is less convincing for the early 1840's, when the agitation for ten hours revived but the question of linking the labour of adults and children dropped out entirely. Perhaps we might account for the operatives' strategy in the 1840's by saying that the spinners "gave up" their attempt to restore the adult–child relationship and resigned themselves to the adult–adolescent relationship. To say this, however, is to take leave of the "economic" explanation, and to slip into a vague sort of psychological explanation based on "fatigue" or "frustration." The scheme of structural differentiation, on the other hand, treats the changing strategy of the operatives in the 1840's as one part of the same sequence of social change; in the early 1840's the family economy was approaching a new level of differentiation of the nuclear family unit in which the major economic significance of young children had been removed from the family.

Perhaps, to return to the economic explanation, the ten hour agitation was a function of the wage-level in the sense that the turmoil intensified when wages were either falling or rising. Yet in the 1820's, when real wages were rising rapidly, the ten-hour day became a subject of the operatives' interest. In the 1830's, when real wages were stationary or falling slightly, this interest continued. Between 1837 and 1841, periods of depression and unemployment, their interest lagged completely, even though the desire to "spread" employment among as many workmen as possible should have been great in these years. Finally, in the early and middle 1840's the agitation for ten hours reached new heights, even though the industry prospered between 1843 and 1846 and the operatives' real wages began to rise rapidly again.[1]

Not only does the economic explanation lose force in the face of these positive instances of social turmoil in the absence of economic determinants, but the early nineteenth century produces several negative instances as well. The years of unemployment and distress between 1837 and 1842, for instance, were apparently not years of vigorous political turmoil among the cotton *factory* operatives. They embraced the Chartist principles, to be sure, but not the more violent and activist variety. Their trade-union activity and factory agitation floundered. Yet this period imperilled their earning power directly. Why was their political activity less evident in this period

[1] Chapter IX, Appendix A, for a discussion of wage trends and fluctuations.

than in others—e.g., 1829 to 1834—particularly when many other working groups were politically impassioned in the late 1830's and early 1840's?

Another negative instance concerns the changing character of the factory agitation. Whereas operatives agitated furiously to link the labour of adults with that of children under thirteen throughout the 1830's, they dropped this interest entirely in the 1840's and took up the ten-hour day for adolescents and women. Why did the interest in using the labour of young children apparently die?

In my opinion the model of structural differentiation overcomes some of these explanatory shortcomings of the economic model. Basically, the former treats the receipt of wages as an integral part of the division of labour. *Within* a given division of labour the operatives maximize short-term wages. When, however, the *structure* of labour is endangered, their interest in augmenting short-term wages is overshadowed by longer-term forces. The first of these forces is a set of "symptoms of disturbance" among the groups under pressure, the aims of which are to *safeguard* or *restore* those elements of the division of labour which are directly under pressure. In the case of the cotton factory operatives the elements under pressure were the apprenticeship system, the traditional wage structure, the control of labour recruitment by kinship and community ties, the limitation of assistants, etc.—in short, the *fusion* between the family's economic functions and its more general moral and educational functions. The disturbances between 1823 and 1837—the "structural strikes," the factory agitation of 1831-3, the evasions of the Factory Act of 1833, the attitudes expressed toward female and child labour, the flirtation with co-operative Utopianism, etc.—represent an attempt to safeguard and restore the fusion between the family economy and other family functions. Through the 1830's and into the 1840's, however, as the family progressed through its later stages of differentiation, the operatives' interest in these "disturbed" movements waned. Hence they were not drawn fully into the Chartist agitation in the late 1830's. In addition, when the ten hour agitation revived in the 1840's, it lacked the "regressive" elements of the earlier turbulence. In the 1840's, in short, the family economy of the factory operatives, having reached a *later stage* in the sequence of differentiation, was looking not toward restoring the older family form but toward consolidating the new.

In addition to its greater explanatory consistency, the model of structural differentiation promises to explain a *wider range* of phenomena than the economic argument. Two sets of phenomena from our period come to mind: (*a*) In the eight hour agitation connected with National Regeneration in 1834, the elements of co-operative Utopia commanded the operatives' attention. Why? (*b*) During the factory agitation, the symbols of health, morals, sexual behaviour, parental authority, etc., were used as arguments for ten hour legislation. Why these symbols and not others? If one remains within the confines of the economic explanation, he often assumes either an indifferent or cynical attitude toward these symbols, i.e., either that they were unimportant or that they were rationalizations to cover the operatives' more basic economic aims. Both attitudes, however, can yield only *ad hoc* explanations of the content of these symbols. They cannot explain why these particular "rationalizations" appeared rather than others. To utilize the model of structural differentiation of the family, however, promises an intelligible interpretation of these *particular* symbols. According to this model, the early co-operative ideology and the "rationalizations" for factory legislation bore an *appropriate symbolic relationship* to the contemporary structural pressures on the family of the factory operatives.[1]

Marx' Capital. One of the major *historical* problems to which Karl Marx addressed his theory of economics concerned the conditions of labour under classical capitalism. I shall sketch briefly some of the "theoretical boxes" which Marx constructed, then attempt to assess their success in interpreting the working-class history of the late eighteenth and early nineteenth centuries. I shall not recapitulate Marx' entire theory of capitalism, but only those segments relevant to the conditions of labour.

Marx' key concept is that of *surplus-value* generated by capitalist production. The "value" element lies in the famous Marxist assumption that "the products of labour, so far as they are values, are but material expressions of the human labour spent in their production." A commodity is "only the material envelope of the human labour spent upon it." [2] This is the Marxist version of the labour theory of value. The exchange of commodities, furthermore, is an exchange of these labour values as imparted to objects. When a weaver sells his linen and buys a Bible,

> The result of the whole transaction, as regards the weaver, is this, that instead of being in possession of the linen, he now has the Bible; instead of his original commodity, he now possesses another of the same value but of different utility. In like manner he procures his

[1] Chapter X explores this symbolic connection between disturbance and structural pressure in detail.
[2] *Capital*, pp. 45, 37, 63.

other means of subsistence and means of production. From his point of view, the whole process effectuates nothing more than the exchange of the product of his labour for the product of someone else's, nothing more than an exchange of products.[1]

Such is the basis for producing and exchanging commodities. The "surplus" component of surplus-value arises when a capitalist buys a commodity (valued at so much by the labour theory of value) and sells it with the object not of using the commodity but of money gain. The way to create such a surplus, moreover, lies only in purchasing labour power from the workers directly, applying it to production, and pushing it to excess. " . . . The surplus-value results only from a quantitative excess of labour, from a lengthening-out of one and the same labour-process. . . ." This exploitation underlies capitalist profits, and the rate of profit (as well as surplus-value) is "an exact expression for the degree of exploitation of labour-power by capital, or of the labourer by the capitalist." [2]

The creation of surplus-value through exploitation also determines the capitalist's motivation. "The directing motive" of capitalist production is "to extract the greatest possible amount of surplus-value, and consequently to exploit labour-power to the greatest possible extent." Marx referred again and again to the "passion of capital for limitless draining of labour-power," the "blind eagerness for plunder," the "capitalist greed for surplus-labour," the "lust for gain," and the "appetite for more profit." [3]

How does the capitalist maximize his surplus-value? In an *absolute* sense, he merely extends the work-day beyond that portion necessary to produce goods worth the labour-value of the workers. "To appropriate labour during all the 24 hours of the day is . . . the inherent tendency of capitalist production." [4] To maximize his *relative* surplus-value, the capitalist can increase the productivity of his plant, thus reducing the labour-time necessary to produce his commodities. Then he can depress his prices, undercut his competitors, and thereby enhance his profits. Furthermore, by employing women and children, the capitalist reaps the surplus labour of the entire family by forcing all its members to work for subsistence. Finally, to intensify the work in a given hour—sometimes as a reaction to legal restrictions on hours—achieves the same exploitative end.[5] The capitalist thus presses for long hours, intensively worked by all ages and both sexes.

[1] *Capital*, p. 78.
[3] *Ibid.*, pp. 321, 222–3, 267, 404.
[5] *Ibid.*, pp. 304–9, 365–92, 404.

[2] *Ibid.*, pp. 123–33, 179, 200–1.
[4] *Ibid.*, pp. 219–20, 241, 400–7.

The Question of Explanation in Working-class History

The effect on the labourers is the physical and moral deterioration so often linked with the industrial revolution in Great Britain:

> The capitalistic mode of production . . . produces . . . with the extension of the working day, not only the deterioration of human labour-power by robbing it of its normal, moral and physical, conditions of development and function. It produces also the premature exhaustion and death of this labour-power itself.[1]

The workers' natural reaction to exploitation is to range themselves in *opposition*. "The contest between the capitalist and the wage-labourer dates back to the very origin of capital."[2] The form of this opposition depends, of course, on the exact conditions of production; under capitalism in the early nineteenth century, for instance, the workers attempted to resist long hours, the intensification of labour, the displacement of male by female and child labour, etc.

If we are to convert this characterization of capitalism into an *explanatory device*, we should assume that many phenomena resolve into attempts of the workers and capitalists to maximize their respective positions—the capitalist to augment surplus-value through exploitation and the workers to resist this exploitation to the best of their ability. Thus, according to Marx, the evasions of the Factory Acts represent the capitalists' attempt to regain their exploitative position prior to 1833. Again, Marx referred to the legislation before 1833 as the "purely nominal . . . concessions conquered by the workpeople" who were beginning to group into a class movement. The later Acts, furthermore, were "not at all the products of Parliamentary fancy. They developed gradually out of the circumstances as natural laws of the modern mode of production. Their formulation, official recognition, and proclamation by the State, were the result of a long struggle of classes."[3] Phenomena are rendered intelligible, in short, by reference to the struggle between capitalists and workers.

According to this explanatory device, the behaviour and attitudes of the working classes in the late eighteenth and early nineteenth centuries should resolve into reactions against the several exploitative tactics of capitalists—displacement of adult males, intensification of labour, long hours, injustices to women and children, etc. How effective is exploitation and its resistance as an explanatory device?

Let us consider the conditions of labour leading up to the first factory legislation in 1833. Marx described the last third of the eighteenth century as "a violent encroachment like that of an

[1] *Capital*, pp. 250–51, 393–400. [2] *Ibid.*, p. 427.
[3] *Ibid.*, pp. 264–9.

391

avalanche in its intensity and extent. All bounds of morals and nature, age and sex, day and night, were broken down. . . . Capital celebrated its orgies." Exploitation was at its highest. Marx asserted further that "as soon as the working class, stunned at first by the noise and turmoil of the new system of production, recovered, in some measure, its senses, its resistance began."[1] As we have seen, however, working-class agitation to shorten hours and improve conditions did not appear until several decades after the bitterest exploitation of the early factory system. Further, when the antagonism between master and worker flared over the question of hours in the 1830's and 1840's, the conditions of exploitation—hours, wages, health, etc.—were improving. Finally, after the Factory Act of 1833 was passed, it was *both* workers and capitalists who co-operated to evade the Act, lengthen hours, overwork children, and thereby increase the level of worker exploitation in the Marxist sense. The workers' agitations throughout the 1830's display this same interest in perpetuating the system of child labour.[2]

Hence we meet several positive instances of exploitation which did not manifest themselves in worker resistance, and several negative instances of diminishing exploitation accompanied by violent worker opposition to the capitalists and to the government. May we account for these instances within the Marxist scheme? In the case of the workers' delayed resistance to exploitation in the early days of the industrial revolution, we might rely on the frequent assertion that the workers were "unawakened" in some sense. "It took both time and experience before the workpeople learnt to distinguish between machinery and its employment by capital, and to direct their attacks, not against the material instruments of production, but against the mode in which they are used."[3] To fall back on this qualification, however, is to "stretch" the original explanatory principle based on the inherent characteristics of capitalism by introducing an indeterminate "learning principle" as an appendage to the original explanation.

Again, in connection with the workers' evasion of the Factory Acts, it is possible that they were so exploited that they were forced in turn to exploit their own children. This explanation also seems to stretch the original picture of two classes ranged chronically against each other, for it introduces the possibility of co-operative exploitation of the very lowest workers by both capitalists and workers. Furthermore, those workers who broke the law (primarily the adult

1 *Capital*, p. 264.
2 Above, pp. 238–41, 243–4, and 214–15.
3 *Capital*, p. 429.

male spinners) were improving in welfare during the whole period of exploitative capitalism.

A third possible qualification of the explanatory device based on "class struggle" is that the capitalists yielded on the question of factory legislation because of their own exploitative desires. Marx held that

apart from the working-class movement that daily grew more threatening, the limiting of factory labour was dictated by the same necessity which spread guano over the English fields. The same blind eagerness for plunder that in one case exhausted the soil, had, in the other, torn up by the roots the living force of the nation.[1]

Possibly the capitalists had begun to discover that shorter hours contributed to productivity. To accept this argument, however, strikes at the very heart of the Marxist definition of capitalist motivation: "to extract the greatest possible amount of surplus-value, and consequently to exploit labour-power to the greatest possible extent." The capitalists may have continued to be driven by the first aim, but if we admit their new insight into the nature of shorter hours, the "and consequently" is exploded.

Even granting these "stretched" or "weak" elements of the explanation based on the class struggle, a still more serious explanatory problem arises within the Marxist scheme. This concerns the concept of exploitation itself. Using Marx' assumptions, we are able to discover a clear element of exploitation as a backdrop for the factory agitation of the 1820's and 1830's—the increase of productivity by the introduction of superior machines, and the displacement of adult male labourers (hence the increase of *relative* surplus-value). Yet at the same time certain other kinds of exploitation were apparently diminishing. The production of *absolute* surplus-value was decreasing with the gradual diminution of hours, and real wages were rising. Which kind of exploitation do we choose as the genesis of factory agitation among the operatives? And why was not the absolute exploitation through long hours the subject of a similar agitation earlier? If we wish to explain the factory agitation on the basis of exploitation, in short, we must define exploitation *sufficiently precisely* to be able to determine when it is present and when it is absent. In the Marxist conception the components of exploitation are long hours, displacement of adult labour, increasing productivity, overwork of females and children, etc. Since these are not ranked in degree of exploitativeness, it is possible to discover *some* kind of exploitation at *all* times in the late eighteenth and early nineteenth

[1] *Capital*, p. 222.

393

centuries. Yet the workers acted as if they were engaging in a class struggle only on very specific occasions. These occasions, moreover, cannot be discriminated from less warlike occasions by utilizing the loose category of "exploitation."

The same problem arises in connection with female and child labour. Marx interpreted this in terms of the capitalist's search for surplus-value. "Compulsory work [of every member of the workman's family, without distinction of age or sex] for the capitalist usurped the place, not only of the children's play, but also of free labour at home within moderate limits for the support of the family."[1] Despite Marx' exaggeration of the "free" character of labour and the "moderate" limits of work in the domestic system, the switch to factory labour should have constituted exploitation for the factory workpeople and evoked corresponding resistance. Yet while domestic textile workers resisted entering factory labour in the eighteenth century, it is clear that neither long hours nor female and child labour were the subject of violent resistance until the family divison of labour began to crack.

In my application of the model of structural differentiation, I have not denied that the working classes were the victims of exploitation in the Marxist sense. I should like to reject the notion, however, that "exploitation," which existed in certain measure all through the industrial revolution, can be converted into a satisfactory *explanatory principle* governing the attitudes and behaviour of the working classes. In many cases it simply misses the facts; in other cases it must be stretched to include the facts; and above all, its categories are so general and inclusive as to occasion a weakening of the explanatory power of the scheme. It seems to me that it is less embarrassing analytically to interpret cases of outright conflict between the classes as disturbed *reactions* to specific structural pressures rather than as the manifestations of a permanent state of war between them.

The Approach of the British Socialists. In this category I rather rashly include the Webbs, the Hammonds, G. D. H. Cole, and Hutchins and Harrison. Perhaps one or more of them would disagree with this grouping. All are similar, however, in the sense that their sympathy is in certain respects "on the side" of the working classes of the period, and their explanation of many historical events rests on the assumption that the workers were fighting their way out of misery. In this assumption they are not far from Marx.

In other ways, of course, these historians differ radically from

[1] *Capital*, pp. 391–2.

Marx. Their outlook is neither so explicit nor so elaborate, and one finds no long streams of logic to connect notions such as "surplus-value," "exploitation," etc., even though these and similar words are used by socialist historians. Furthermore, because these scholars are perhaps more nearly "straight" historians than Marx, it is more difficult to locate their guiding assumptions. One must look to the byways of their research, such as the introductory or concluding remarks on subjects like the Combination Laws.

How does the notion of *misery*—which characterizes all these historians' writings—operate as an explanatory principle in working-class history? Basically, the workers rioted because they were miserable; they fought for short hours in justified response to miserable conditions; they struck because the capitalists and ruling classes joined to increase their misery. Thus G. D. H. Cole, in assessing the effects of the industrial revolution, said,

The period of the Napoleonic wars, and the economic crises which succeeded it, is the blackest chapter in the whole history of the British working class. Driven from the land by enclosures, made redundant or exposed to the competition of child-labour by the new machines, exposed to relentless persecution because of the fears engendered in the mind of the governing classes, both by the misery and by the "awful portent" of the Revolution in France, and enwalled in the hideous, stinking purlieus of the new factory towns, the workers underwent a long agony, from which they emerged at length exhausted and docile, into the Victorian era. In this age of misery, and as the child of misery, the British Labour Movement was born.[1]

Hutchins and Harrison agreed that "socially and industrially the first two or three decades of the nineteenth century form a gloomy period, in which . . . it took twenty-five years of legislation to restrict a child of nine to sixty-nine hours a week, and that only in cotton mills." The Webbs found the same gloominess in the Combination Acts of 1799–1800, and the Hammonds judged the early conditions of labour to be so bad that "in respect of hours and general conditions [the apprenticeship children] were indeed worse off than slaves of a different colour."[2] In another place they described the witnesses before Sadler's Committee in 1832 as

A long procession of workers, men and women, girls and boys. Stunted, diseased, deformed, degraded, each with the tale of his

[1] *A Short History of the British Working Class Movement*, p. 39.
[2] Hutchins and Harrison, *A History of Factory Legislation*, p. 21; Webb, *The History of Trade Unionism*, p. 64; Hammond, *Lord Shaftesbury*, p. 10.

wronged life, they pass across the stage, a living picture of man's cruelty to man, a pitiless indictment of those rulers who in their days of unabated power had abandoned the weak to the rapacity of the strong.[1]

What was the nature of this misery? In general it was economic— depression of wages, displacement of adult males by women and children, speeding up machinery, slum conditions, long hours, filth, etc. Political suffering was its complement, however, for the workers were victimized politically when they attempted either to relieve their economic miseries directly or to join political movements. What caused this misery? The Hammonds spoke of the "fashionable philosophy of the day: the creed which held that human happiness was best secured by giving to capital absolute control over the lives and liberties of men and women." Cole seemed to accept the Marxist notion that the capitalists pressed directly upon the proletarian class.[2] While the authors differ, however, they all assume that the causes of misery came from above, very likely from a league between the capitalists and the governing classes.

Hence the British Socialist definition of the early industrial society became semi-Marxist in the end; on the one hand there existed a body of neglectful or positively exploitative groups, while on the other there was a corresponding body of workers which was miserable (though the term was not defined so explicitly as Marx' term "exploited"). Justifiable hostility thus governed the workers' behaviour. Their social movements manifested a struggle to over-come the conditions of misery. In addition, the humanitarianism of Shaftesbury and others was largely a justified and natural response to the workers' conditions:

Ashley, whose name comes to every mind that dwells on the dark passages of the Industrial Revolution, has outlived nine out of ten of the Cabinet Ministers with whose ambitions and fears he wrestled for the children of the mill and the pit. He was not a constructive thinker, but by sheer persistence he shamed his age out of its prin-ciples, and the Factory Acts and the Mines Act, that preserve his reputation for humanity and patience, are events of the Victorian age not less decisive than the measures that removed from the government of England some of the worst of its ancient abuses.[3]

[1] *The Town Labourer*, p. 171.

[2] Hammond, *Lord Shaftesbury*, p. 14; Cole, *A Short History of the British Working Class Movement*, p. 130.

[3] Hammond, *Lord Shaftesbury*, p. 9. Of course, the Hammonds do not con-sider that the humanitarian drive was the *only* force behind the factory movement. *Ibid.*, p. 24.

To explain working-class reforms of the period as a product of the opposing forces of misery on the one hand and humanitarian indignation on the other seems to penetrate the problem only partially. True, humanitarian sentiment occupied an important place in the factory agitation; further, humanitarians were bitten with a sense of disgust with the conditions of the factories. Yet the embarrassing paradoxes of the early factory system reappear. Why did the humanitarian indignation with hours and other conditions "wait" through fifty years of factory horrors? Certainly humanitarianism was strong before 1830. It seemed, however, to concentrate only secondarily on industrial conditions, particularly when compared, for instance, with its focus on the abolition of slavery. Why, furthermore, did humanitarians choose the factory conditions in the 1830's when misery (as defined by the humanitarians themselves) was greater in many other trades? The appearance of humanitarianism, in short, like the social movements which it charged with energy, was very irregular in the early nineteenth century. It was not correlated perfectly with certain "objective" conditions of misery upon which it was based. Humanitarianism thus cannot be reduced to a natural reaction to the miserable conditions of the age; it requires an independent explanation.

More generally, to treat misery as a condition which initiated the labour movement is to employ a term which, like Marx' "exploitation," is so general as to be omnipresent in the industrial revolution. Yet its presumed consequences—the fight for short hours, union activity, etc.—were sporadic and even non-existent for long periods. Furthermore, since misery had a number of components such as long hours, low wages, accelerated machinery, slum conditions, etc., any one of these can be located if another is not present. For instance, when Cole discovered that the factory operatives' real wages in the early nineteenth century had actually risen, he countered with the explanation that their *general* level of welfare had nevertheless fallen:

Changes of [the workman's] character cannot be measured by the recital of mere figures about wages. . . . Moreover, the most drastic change caused by machinery had little to do with wages. The crying evil of the first half of the nineteenth century was less the low wages than the horrible factory and housing conditions and the inhumanly long working day. The working day not only grew longer, but was also made, under factory conditions, far more intense. Especially in the case of women and children, there was nothing to check remorseless speeding-up throughout a working day in itself intolerably prolonged. And at the end of it the lodging to which the workers returned was usually a stifling and insanitary den, rushed up with no regard for comfort or sanitation to meet the rapid expansion of population in the factory towns.[1]

Such logic explains both too much and too little about working-class history. It explains too much in so far as it traces all sorts of phenomena, by painfully extended reasoning, to a general misery, when these phenomena clearly had more specific roots in the social structure. It explains too little in so far as (*a*) it reduces all movements to a response to misery and therefore cannot account for the divergent directions of these social movements; (*b*) it does not explain why these movements did not occur at *other* times when the components of misery were equally stark. Hence the "misery" logic is confronted with negative instances in so far as the operatives were very selective and irregular in attempting to work their way out of misery.

My position does not deny misery. Indeed, the working classes suffered the most basic kinds of physical and psychological deprivations in the industrial revolution. On the other hand, terms like "misery" are too general as *explanatory concepts*. They cannot explain why misery erupts into disturbance only now and then, and only in certain directions and not in others. They cannot explain why humanitarianism arises to correct misery only at certain times and in certain contexts. It seems to me that to characterize the pressures on the working classes in more specific structural terms accounts more adequately for the timing and direction of both social movements and humanitarianism than to rely on extremely general terms like "exploitation" and "misery."

A corollary of the explanatory principle based on some sort of class struggle is the treatment of many workers' actions simply in terms of *tactics*. Hutchins and Harrison, while they did not stress the misery of the workers unduly, assumed that they agitated for short hours primarily to spread the work among adult males and thereby control the labour market.[2] While this was an element of the agitations which occurred in depressions, we have observed the weakness of this explanation to account consistently for the operatives' behaviour.[3] At any rate, given this motive, the authors adopted a "tactical" explanation for many of the operatives' manoeuvres. Concerning their agitation for women's hours in 1841, for instance, Hutchins and Harrison reflected as follows on the operatives' attitudes:

We have seen that, prior to 1833, concern for the children had been the alleged reason for the desire for a ten hours day. After 1833,

[1] *A Short History of the British Working Class Movement*, pp. 186–7.
[2] *A History of Factory Legislation*, p. 48.
[3] Above, pp. 238–41 and 385–9.

when it was found that the reduction of the hours for children had been effected, but in such a way as not to limit the labour of adults, concern for the children could no longer be used as an argument for a ten hours day, and the reformers openly demanded the regulation of all factory labour enforced by a restriction on the motive power. In 1841, when they began to realise that it was hopeless to get the hours of children again increased to ten hours, and that a restriction on the motive power was not yet within the sphere of practical politics, they turned their attention to the women and fought the battle "behind the women's petticoats" . . .[1]

The reason the operatives omitted motive power in 1841 was "probably due only to the fear of alienating the sympathy of the Government." The authors admitted that the pressure to limit women's hours in 1841 rested on the growing numbers of female factory operatives, but the real weight behind their argument seemed to lie in "some fear that the women were displacing the men."[2] The men were fighting for their own hours, in short, and in this connection they were "using" children and women.

This "tactical" explanation leaves several questions unanswered. Why did the workers drop the children's argument in the 1840's? Why had they not "hidden behind the women's petticoats" before? Why did the arguments concerning women's labour continue through 1843–6, when prosperity was continuous and the threat of displacement weaker? In the end, in fact, the "tactical" explanation must assume, like the straight "economic" explanation, an *ad hoc* position with regard to the content of the workers' agitations. We have attempted, on the other hand, to interpret the changing direction of the operatives' agitation in terms of the changing structure of the family, the changing significance of women's and children's roles in the home, and the changing significance of leisure. Such an interpretation seems to generate more specific solutions to the question of how and why the operatives changed their behaviour during the 1830's and 1840's than the straight "tactical" approach.

Modern Laissez-faire. A number of historians have reacted against these gloomy interpretations of capitalist history. Perhaps the most explicit rejection may be found in a small volume entitled *Capitalism and the Historians*, edited by F. A. Hayek, and containing essays by T. S. Ashton, W. H. Hutt, and others. While the authors devote much of their effort to establishing the fact that the factory operatives' real income was improving, Hutt's

[1] *A History of Factory Legislation*, p. 65.
[2] *Ibid.*, pp. 65–6.

essay on the factory system also touches on the problem of social structure.

Hutt is concerned in part with rescuing early capitalists from the ill-deserved reputation of cruelty and inhumanity smeared upon them by the literary sentimentality and the Tory anti-business circles of the age. By comparing the factory workers with those in other occupations, and by examining the limited evidence of the period, Hutt concludes that the millowners were not only innocent, but in many cases were "men of humanity." [1]

Perhaps more important, Hutt questions the alleged misery of the working classes from the standpoint of health and morals. In particular, he disputes the authenticity of the Sadler Committee's evidence and the reliability of the contemporary medical testimony, and passes favourably on the operatives' health, physical condition, and morality, particularly in comparison with other working groups. Hutt's "negative contribution," then, is to cast doubt on conventional historical assumptions and explanations.

Having discovered the questionable basis for the claims of the antagonists of the factory system, however, Hutt proceeds to deny *all* bases for the Factory Acts which limited working hours. Indeed, the supposed benefits of these Acts were "largely illusory" and sometimes positively harmful, because they drove children from well-managed factories into "workshops and the smaller factories" or into domestic industry where "conditions were at their worst." [2] Even for children remaining in the cotton factories, the Acts were useless. The incorporation of larger, improved machinery, Hutt claims, was eliminating child labour in any case. In addition, "there would have been *some* fall in hours and some elimination of child labour following increasing real wages, legislation or no legislation. Both are expressions of a demand for leisure, and leisure is only demanded after the more primary of human wants are amply satisfied." [3] On the question of improved machinery, Hutt seems to have missed the facts; the bigger, better mules and the power-looms of the 1820's and 1830's called forth children, young persons, and women. Furthermore, while higher wages led to the general reduction of child labour, we discovered a positive *structural* basis for removing work-people to the home. The new machinery was threatening

---

[1] "The Factory System of the Early Nineteenth Century," *op. cit.*, pp. 165–6, 179–82.

[2] *Ibid.*, p. 185. Marx agreed that in domestic industries and workshops, conditions were worse from the standpoint of overwork and exploitation. *Capital*, pp. 464–5.

[3] "The Factory System of the Early Nineteenth Century," *op. cit.*, p. 184.

family functions by modifying the work arrangements in the factory, and these family functions were being re-established, by a process of differentiation, in the home.[1]

Hutt concludes his critique of orthodox social historians as follows:

... first ... there has been a general tendency to exaggerate the "evils" which characterized the factory system before the abandonment of laissez faire and, second ... factory legislation was not essential to the *ultimate* disappearance of those "evils." Conditions which modern standards would condemn were then common to the community as a whole, and legislation not only brought with it disadvantages, not readily apparent in the complex changes of the time, but also served to obscure and hamper more natural and desirable remedies.[2]

I would suggest that the first conclusion is a contribution to historical research. The second, however—which is a reaffirmation of the laissez-faire ideology that either there were no evils or that the evils would have disappeared anyway—is incorrect, primarily because Hutt ignores the strains imposed by the changing factory system on the family and community life of the working classes. Because he can find that the agitators' claims were not *literally* true, he assumes that their literal falsity implied a complete absence of reasons for factory legislation. Consequently the agitators' statements are viewed implicitly as sham, rationalization, or error. It apparently did not occur to Hutt that an explanation for the Factory Acts might be found outside the realm of health and morals as conceived in the ideologies of the day—namely that physical and moral evils justified the Acts, *or* that there was no justification. Hutt, in short, accepts the dimension of "laissez-faire" vs. "correction of evils" as the only possible basis for accounting for the rise of factory legislation. As we have seen, to rest upon either end of this dimension leaves us without a satisfactory explanation for the progress of factory agitation and factory legislation. This is not to say that this ideological dimension was not important in the minds of thinkers and politicians in the early nineteenth century. Yet to convert it into an *explanatory scheme* for analysing the social history of the period is an illegitimate analytical exercise which underlies Hutt's misconceptions of the early factory system.

[1] Above, pp. 196–201 and 293–308, also Appendix B, Chapter IX.
[2] "The Factory System of the Early Nineteenth Century," *op. cit.*, p. 188.

CHAPTER XV

SUMMARY OF THE ANALYSIS

Our basic problem in this research has been to characterize and explain the growth or development of social systems. To this end we have attempted to apply in two separate structural contexts—the industry and the family—a model of differentiation which posits a typical sequence of events which occurs when the system increases in complexity. The sequence begins when members of the system in question (or some larger system) express *dissatisfaction* with some aspect of the system's functioning (Step 1). This dissatisfaction may concern role-performance in the system, the utilization of its resources, or both. In either case the dominant values governing the system legitimize the expression of the initial dissatisfaction. Accompanying the dissatisfaction, furthermore, is the prospect of facilities to overcome the source of dissatisfaction. The immediate responses to the dissatisfactions (Step 2) are undirected or misdirected symptoms of disturbance—phantasy, aggression, and anxiety. Even though non-specific with regard to concrete methods of overcoming the dissatisfactions, these symptoms are related symbolically to the original foci of dissatisfaction. Gradually these disturbances are brought into line by mechanisms of social control (Step 3), and their energy turned to the generation of more specific solutions for the original problems giving rise to the dissatisfactions. In this way future lines of action are encouraged (Step 4), specified (Step 5), and tried (Step 6). The social units which emerge, if the sequence is successful, constitute a structure *more differentiated* than the old. The new units, being more specialized, function more effectively than the old. Finally, after a period of extraordinary progress, the new units are consolidated into the social system and thereby routinized (Step 7).

In order to make this abstract statement more determinate theoretically, we had to face several difficult analytical problems connected with social change. How to identify the units of the social system in question, both before and after the differentiation has occurred? How to characterize the initial dissatisfactions? How to describe the directions of change, and how to relate these directions to the original dissatisfactions? How to describe the path of change in a determinate way? These questions lay behind our extended concern with (*a*) the functional analysis of the social system, and (*b*) the table of resources utilized in the social system.

(*a*) By characterizing a social system in terms of invariant functions—goal-attainment, adaptation, integration, and pattern-maintenance—we thereby created a set of reference points whereby the more concrete units of social structure could be classified. More important perhaps, the fact that these functions remain constant throughout a sequence of change means that we possessed a number of dimensions by which to characterize the directions along which the changing structure of the units moves. To choose a simple example, the control of fixed capital (C_A) was not differentiated from the processes of production (C_L) in the putting-out industry. Both were aspects of the household. When the factory system invaded the textile industries late in the eighteenth century, one of its directions of change involved a greater differentiation of units specialized in these two functions. The *functional* problems of capital control and production remained invariant; the *structure* of the industry differentiated, however, along the C_A–C_L axis. The functional analysis of a social system, therefore, provides us with a set of stable reference points to analyse a social system in flux.

(*b*) By characterizing the structure of resources in a social system, we provided first a statement of the foci of dissatisfaction with the performance of the units of the system. At the same time, these foci provided a set of reference points for characterizing the precise points at which the resources undergo change in a sequence. For example, we found that the problems of discipline and authority (*I-5*) were salient foci of dissatisfaction with the putting-out system. Correspondingly, we found the concern with discipline to be paramount in the early factory system. Furthermore, because the resources of a social system are organized in a system of diminishing generality, we were able to outline a point-for-point correspondence between the seven steps of structural differentiation and the state of the system's resources in each step. For instance, in Step 2, the resources generalize "beyond Level 1" as the regressive symptoms of disturbance break out; in Step 3 the resources are brought back to Level 1 by the exercise of various kinds of social control; and so on. Hence the table of resources provides not only a statement of reference points for the beginning and end of a sequence of differentiation, but provides a set of categories for describing the path of change at each step.

Our concern with the functional analysis of a social system and with the table of resources was therefore to enhance the *theoretical determinacy* of the model of structural differentiation. To examine

403

the model's *empirical workability*, however, we had to bring this abstract formulation "down to earth" to interpret some aspects of the British industrial revolution. First we re-phrased the functional analysis of a social system in industrial terms—with control over production as "goal-attainment," control over capital as "adaptation," and so on. On these bases we could classify the roles involved in industrial production at any given moment. In addition, we outlined the structure of industrial resources, both in terms of their genesis outside the industry and their utilization in the industry.

The starting-point for a sequence of structural differentiation of these roles (and reorganization of the resources) is the historical appearance of dissatisfactions with industrial production (Step 1). This dissatisfaction may be directed at classes of economic agents, or may be phrased in terms of the misallocation or misuse of the resources of labour, capital, and organization. Whatever the specific foci of dissatisfaction, however, it is justified and legitimized in terms of the current values relating to production. Before any specific action is taken to overcome the sources of dissatisfaction, diverse symptoms of disturbance appear (Step 2). Next a number of agencies of social control engage in a series of holding operations against these disturbances to prevent them from reaching disruptive proportions (Step 3). Simultaneously there is a reaffirmation of the basic values governing production and an encouragement of ideas designed to implement these values in new, more effective ways (Step 4). Inventions and experiments in rearranging the division of labour carry these ideas to a still greater degree of specification (Step 5). Finally, entrepreneurs translate these suggestions into concrete attempts to reorganize the basis of production (Step 6). If successful, the entrepreneurial attempts lead to an explosive growth of production, capitalization, profits, and reorganization, which return gradually to routine levels as the new methods become consolidated in the industrial structure (Step 7).

In Chapters IV–VII we applied this formal statement to the cotton industry of Great Britain during the industrial revolution of the late eighteenth and early nineteenth centuries. Our structural starting-point was the putting-out and domestic system of manufacture—treated as a social system—of the mid eighteenth century. We first observed the fusions between this system of manufacture and the family-community structure of the time. The initial signs of dissatisfaction with these methods of production appeared in various complaints concerning productive bottlenecks, imbalances between spinning and weaving, and the masters' inability to control the workpeople under the putting-out system (Step 1). The expanding foreign and domestic markets for cotton textiles in the middle and late eighteenth century aggravated such dissatisfactions. The complaints were legitimized, furthermore, by the values invigorated by the recent burst of Wesleyan Methodism, particularly in the manufacturing districts. Initially the complex of growing demand, complaints, and favourable legitimizing values gave rise to a period of scapegoating the working classes and dreams of immediate fortunes (Step 2).

After this initial period of confusion, inventors and entrepreneurs turned to the more practical business of overhauling the productive apparatus. Over the next several decades the factory system conquered the cotton industry gradually and irregularly with the successive introduction of the spinning jenny, the water-frame, the mule, the power-loom, the steam-engine, and the organizational changes accompanying each. To each of these innovations we applied the model of differentiation. By its logic we traced the structural modifications of production, the behaviour of economic indices such as production, capitalization, and innovation, and the occurrence of "regressive" symptoms of disturbance such as movements for protectionism and favouritism among various classes of manufacturers. We qualified each sequence of differentiation, furthermore, by reference to the influence of "external" factors such as the Revolutionary and Napoleonic war period.

For our second major field of empirical application of the model of differentiation, we turned to the family of the working classes. The *principles* of applying the model to a family economy are identical with those of applying it to an industry, even though a family is in no sense an industry except in so far as both are social systems. First we refilled the abstract concepts of a social system with categories appropriate to the family economy. In this operation we identified the major functions of the family economy as the generation of motivation appropriate to occupational performance (goal-attainment), the utilization of family income to this end (adaptation), the organization of family roles (integration), and the processes of socialization and tension-management (latency). In addition, we classified the several resources which the family economy utilizes in fulfilling these functions.

As for the dynamics of family reorganization, a sequence of structural differentiation begins when dissatisfaction is expressed over the performance of familial roles or the utilization of familial resources (Step 1). Frequently industrial pressures on the family generate such dissatisfactions. As in the industrial case, the expression of these dissatisfactions is given the weight of legitimization by reference to the dominant family values of the time. When these conditions, plus a sense of opportunity, are present, the stage is set for the differentiation of the family economy. The first reaction to the dissatisfactions is the appearance of symptoms of disturbance, which are classifiable into phantasy, aggression, and anxiety, and which are traceable to the original foci of dissatisfaction with the family (Step 2). At first these disturbances are handled by mechanisms of social control (Step 3). Only after these more explosive elements are brought into line is it possible to take the more positive steps of encouraging ideas (Step 4), specifying lines of social action (Step 5), and translating these ideas into definite social experiments (Step 6). If these latter steps are successful, one or more new social units takes its place in the social structure (Step 7). In the family economy, as in the industry, the salient directions of the final differentiation correspond to the salient foci of dissatisfaction with the older units.

We applied this model of differentiation to two subsectors of the family economy: (*a*) the family division of labour; (*b*) the structure of family consumption.

(*a*) In the early nineteenth century the technological changes in the cotton industry created the conditions of urbanization, industrial centralization, and depersonalization of the factory community. More specifically, the enlargement of mules and the introduction of power-looms threatened to separate the labour of children from that of adults (often parents). These technological pressures, while long in the making, reached a critical point in the mid-1820's. For the family economy of the factory operatives, the pressures represented a serious dissatisfaction (Step 1). The worker and his family could no longer work on the old basis which fused the family economy with other, more general family functions. If the worker refused to accept the new conditions of employment, he could no longer support his family satisfactorily; if he accepted labour on the new basis, certain non-economic relations in his family—particularly the rearing of children—might suffer. These pressures, magnified by an appeal to independence and personal responsibility as a family value, pressed for a thoroughgoing reorganization of family relationships.

The factory operatives, especially the adult male spinners, reacted immediately and fiercely to this pressure in a number of disturbed social movements (Step 2)—a series of vigorous but unsuccessful strikes to resist the improved machinery; a commitment to the ten hour agitation of the 1830's, one effect of which would have been to preserve the old work structure; a prolonged attempt to subvert the Factory Act of 1833, which threatened to separate the labour of adult and child even further; and a brief though intensive flirtation with the Utopian co-operative movement.

Summary of the Analysis

To outline how these disturbances eventually led to new and more differentiated family units, we analysed first the course of factory legislation in the 1830's and 1840's. Parliamentary investigation of the factory question represented a process of "handling and channelling" the disturbed elements of factory agitation (Step 3). Factory legislation between 1833 and 1847, in its turn, gradually eased the family structure into more differentiated directions (Steps 4–6). The working-class family which emerged about the time that the ten-hour day became normal was more specialized than the factory family of a quarter-century earlier; the economic performance of adults and children was segregated definitively, and certain minimum educational responsibilities had slipped from the family to an embryonic school system under the Factory Acts.

Meantime, the domestic hand-loom weavers were slowly differentiated "out" of the industry by the more productive hand-loom and power-loom factories. Until the hand-loom weavers were absorbed into other trades—a process which took many decades—their history was a story of one symptom of disturbance after another (Step 2)—pleas for assistance; schemes for artificial perpetuation of hand-loom weaving by means of permanent legislative support; violence; heavy emigration; withdrawal from community functions; and attraction to a sequence of Utopian schemes.

We also traced the history of trade-unionism in the early nineteenth century as a simultaneous though distinct line of differentiation in the family economy. Thrown into disorganization by the technological changes of the 1820's and 1830's (Step 1), the unions displayed several symptoms of disturbance in these years (Step 2). Gradually, however, through police activity, governmental investigations, public debate, and journalistic controversy, these disturbances were brought into line (Step 3). Later, by a sequence of exploration, debate, speculation, and social experimentation (Steps 4–6), the unions rose to a point of greater specialization in the 1840's than, for instance, as friendly societies in the eighteenth century or as the embryonic unions of the Napoleonic war period. In the important respects, therefore, this evolution of unions conformed to the model of structural differentiation.

(b) The signs of dissatisfaction with the structure of consumption in the late eighteenth century (Step 1) dealt with the inability of the poor-laws and the friendly society to safeguard the economic welfare of the working classes. The resulting symptoms of disturbance (Step 2) took the form primarily of attacks upon the friendly society, though occasionally food riots broke out, e.g., in the lean years of the 1790's and the remainder of the war period. The earliest social response to these troubles was to encourage the working classes in the art of frugality; to prevent outright starvation by subsidizing families through the poor-laws; and to encourage the further development of the friendly societies. Dissatisfactions continued, however, and in the end gave rise to several social units geared to stabilizing the economic welfare of the family in its new social environment. The most important of these were the savings banks, which developed most rapidly in the first thirty years of the nineteenth century, and the co-operative stores, which—after a period of experimentation in the 1820's and 1830's—became solidly established among the working classes in the 1840's and thereafter. We applied the model of differentiation to the rise of both, tracing in each case the parade of dissatisfactions, disturbances, new ideas, suggestions for implementation, social experimentation, and finally successful incorporation.

To apply this model to the cotton industry and to the family economy of its working classes by no means exhausts the social changes of the industrial revolution. In fact, it would be instructive to follow other instances of structural differentiation—the segregation of education from religion through a process of secularizing the schools; the segregation of political parties from the system of aristocratic family cliques; the segregation of the military and civil service from the earlier system of political and class patronage, and so on. It seems possible, by examining a series of closely-linked processes of differentiation, to contrast the *relative* stability and institutional calm of the era preceding the industrial revolution with the storm and confusion of the period of the industrial revolution itself, and again with the *relative* stability of the prosperous and optimistic Victorian period, say after 1850. The eighteenth century was a period of growing pressure on the rural-aristocratic society— pressure generated by the train of domestic and international events and by the strength of the Nonconformist ideology, which seemed conducive to the initiation of social change on so many fronts. Some time after the middle of the century the pressure broke unevenly into a number of violent disturbances which signalled the early stages of structural differentiation—the debates, the uncertainty, the anxiety and gloom, the uneasy theorizing, and the grand projects. After this period of disturbed transition, new social forms began to find a solid place in the social structure—the new industrial organization, the reformed parliament, the beginnings of a formal educational system, modern political parties, and a new family and community life. The whole society thereby levelled into the relatively quiescent state of optimistic Victorianism, dominated by urbanism and the new middle classes.

BIBLIOGRAPHY

GENERAL WORKS, THEORETICAL AND HISTORICAL

American Economic Association, *Readings in Price Theory* (London: George Allen and Unwin, 1953).

Ashley, W. J., *The Economic Organization of England* (London: Longmans, Green & Co., 1914).

Ashton, T. S., *The Industrial Revolution 1760–1830* (London: Oxford University Press, 1954).

Bland, A. E., Brown, P. A., & Tawney, R. H. (eds.), *English Economic History, Select Documents* (London: G. Bell & Sons, 1914).

Bowden, W., *Industrial Society in England towards the End of the Eighteenth Century* (New York: Macmillan, 1925).

Brinton, C., *English Political Thought in the Nineteenth Century* (London: Ernest Benn, 1949).

Bryant, A., *The Age of Elegance, 1812–22* (London: Collins, 1950).

Bulwer, E. L., *England and the English* (London: Richard Bentley, 1833).

Clapham, J. H., *An Economic History of Modern Britain*. Vol. I: *The Early Railway Age* (Cambridge: The University Press, 1926).

Deane, P., "The Implications of Early National Income Estimates for the Measurement of Long-term Economic Growth in the United Kingdom," *Economic Development and Cultural Change*, IV (1955), pp. 3–38.

Erikson, E. H., *Childhood and Society* (London: Imago Publishing Co., 1951).

Gayer, A. D., Rostow, W. W., and Schwartz, A. J., *The Growth and Fluctuation of the British Economy 1790–1850* (Oxford: The Clarendon Press, 1953).

Halevy, E., *A History of the English People in the Nineteenth Century* (London: Ernest Benn, 1949–51).

Hoffman, W., *British Industry 1700–1950* (Oxford: Basil Blackwell, 1955).

Hopkins, T., *Great Britain for the Last 40 Years* (London: 1834).

Hoselitz, B. F., *Pamphlet for Social Science Research Council Conference on the Role of the State in Economic Growth: Economic Policy and Economic Development* (1956).

Keynes, J. M., *General Theory of Employment, Interest, and Money* (London: Macmillan, 1936).

Levy, M., *The Family Revolution in Modern China* (Cambridge, Mass.: Harvard University Press, 1949).

McCulloch, J. R., *A Descriptive and Statistical Account of the British Empire* (London: Longman, Brown, Green, and Longmans, 1847).

Bibliography

Macpherson, D., *Annals of Commerce, Manufactures, Fisheries, and Navigation* (London: Nichols & Son, etc., 1805).

Mantoux, P., *The Industrial Revolution in the Eighteenth Century* (London: Jonathan Cape, 1955).

Marx, K., *Capital* (London: George Allen & Unwin, 1949).

Matthews, R. C. O., *A Study in Trade-Cycle History: Economic Fluctuations in Great Britain 1833–1842* (Cambridge: The University Press, 1954).

Moffitt, L. W., *England on the Eve of the Industrial Revolution* (London: P. S. King, 1925).

Parsons, T., *The Social System* (Glencoe, Ill.: The Free Press, 1951).

——, Bales, R. F., *et al.*, *Family, Socialization, and Interaction Process* (Glencoe, Ill.: The Free Press, 1955).

——, Bales, R. F., and Shils, E. A., *Working Papers in the Theory of Action* (Glencoe, Ill.: The Free Press, 1953).

——, and Shils, E. A. (eds.), *Toward a General Theory of Action* (Cambridge, Mass.: Harvard University Press, 1951).

——, and Smelser, N. J., *Economy and Society* (London: Routledge & Kegan Paul, and Glencoe, Ill.: The Free Press, 1956).

Postlethwayt, M., *The Universal Dictionary of Trade and Commerce* (London: John and Paul Knapton, 1751).

Porter, G. R., *The Progress of the Nation*, revised by F. W. Hirst (London: Methuen & Co., 1912).

Rostow, W. W., *British Economy of the Nineteenth Century* (Oxford: The Clarendon Press, 1949).

——, "The Take-off into Self-sustained Growth," *Economic Journal*, LXVI (1956), pp. 25–48.

Schumpeter, J. A., *Business Cycles* (New York: McGraw Hill, 1939).

——, *The Theory of Economic Development*, translated by Redvers Opie (Cambridge, Mass.: Harvard University Press, 1934).

Scrope, G. P., *Principles of Political Economy, Deduced from the Natural Laws of Social Welfare, and Applied to the Present State of Britain* (London: Longman, Rees, Orme, Brown, Green, and Longman, 1833).

Smith, A., *The Wealth of Nations* (New York: The Modern Library, 1937).

Snedecor, G. W., *Statistical Methods* (Ames, Iowa: State College Press, 1948).

Toynbee, A., *Lectures on the Industrial Revolution of the Eighteenth Century in England* (London: Longmans, Green & Co., 1908).

Ure, A., *The Philosophy of Manufactures: or an Exposition of the Scientific, Moral, and Commercial Economy of the Factory System of Great Britain* (London: Charles Knight, 1835).

Usher, A. P., *A History of Mechanical Inventions* (New York: McGraw Hill, 1929).

——, *An Introduction to the Industrial History of England* (London: George C. Harrap, 1921).

Wade, J., *History of the Middle and Working Classes* (London: Effingham Wilson, 1833).

Bibliography

Wakefield, E. G., *England and America. A Comparison of the Social and Political State of Both Nations* (London: Richard Bentley, 1833).

Weber, M., *From Max Weber: Essays in Sociology*, translated, edited, and with an introduction by H. H. Gerth and C. Wright Mills (London: Kegan Paul, Trench, Trubner & Co., 1947).

———, *The Theory of Social and Economic Organization*, translated by A. R. Henderson and Talcott Parsons (London: William Hodge & Co., 1947).

Westerfield, R. B., "Middlemen in English Business, 1660–1770," *Transactions of the Connecticut Academy of Arts and Sciences*, XIX (1915), pp. 111–445.

Wisdom, J. O., *Foundations of Inference in Natural Science* (London: Methuen, 1952).

WORKS RELATING TO THE COTTON INDUSTRY

Andrew, S., *Fifty Years' Cotton Trade*, Read before the Economic Section of the British Association (Oldham: Oldham Standard Office, 1887).

Armitage, G. W., *The Lancashire Cotton Industry from the Great Inventions to the Great Disasters* (Manchester: The Manchester Literary and Philosophical Society, 1951).

Ashworth, H., *Cotton: Its Cultivation, Manufacture, and Uses* (Manchester: James Collins, 1858).

Baines, E., jun., *History of the Cotton Manufacture in Great Britain* (London: H. Fisher, R. Fisher, and P. Jackson, 1835).

Barlow, A., *The History and Principles of Weaving by Hand and Power* (London: Sampson Low, Marston, Searle, and Rivington, 1878).

Bonami (pseud.), *The Doom of the Cotton Trade and the Fall of the Factory System* (Manchester: John Heywood, 1896).

Bremner, D., *The Industries of Scotland: Their Rise, Progress, and Present Condition* (Edinburgh: Adam and Charles Black, 1869).

Burn, R., *Statistics of the Cotton Trade* (London: Simpkin, Marshall, and Co., 1847).

Butterworth, J., *A Complete History of the Cotton Trade, with Remarks on their Progress in Bolton, Bury, Stockport, Blackburn, and Wigan* (Manchester, C. W. Leake, 1823).

Chambers, J. D., "Enclosure and The Small Landowner," *Economic History Review*, X (1940), pp. 118–27.

Chapman, S. J., *The Lancashire Cotton Industry* (Manchester: University Publications, 1904).

———, *The Cotton Industry and Trade* (London: Methuen, 1905).

Colquhoun, P., *Case of the British Cotton Spinners and Manufacturers of Piece Goods, Similar to the Importations from the East Indies* (London: 1790).

———, *Considerations Relative to a Plan of Relief for the Cotton Manufactory, By the Establishment of a General Hall in the City of London* (London: 1788).

411

Bibliography

Colquhoun, P., *An Important Crisis, in the Callico and Muslin Manufactory in Great Britain, Explained* (London: 1788).

——, *An Important Question, shortly stated: Relative to the Present Competition between the Callico and Muslin Manufactures of Great Britain; and the same Species of Goods Imported from the East Indies* (1788).

——, *Observations on the Means of extending the Consumption of British Callicoes, Muslins and other Cotton Goods, and of giving pecuniary Aids to the Manufacturers, under Circumstances of the highest Respectability and Advantage* (London: 1788).

——, *A Representation of Facts Relative to the Rise and Progress of the Cotton Manufacture in Great Britain, with Observations on the Means of Extending and Improving this valuable Branch of Trade* (London: H. Reynell, 1789).

Daniels, G. W., "The Cotton Trade During the Revolutionary and Napoleonic Wars," *Transactions of the Manchester Statistical Society*, 1915–16, pp. 53–84.

——, "The Cotton Trade at the Close of the Napoleonic War," *Transactions of the Manchester Statistical Society*, 1917–18, pp. 1–29.

——, *The Early English Cotton Industry* (Manchester: The University Press, 1920).

——, "Samuel Crompton's Census of the Cotton Industry in 1811," *Economic Journal* (*Economic History Supplement*), II (1930), pp. 107–10.

Davies, E., "The Small Landowner, 1780–1832, in the Light of the Land Tax Assessments," *Economic History Review*, I (1927), pp. 87–113.

Dodd, G., *The Textile Manufactures of Great Britain* (London: Charles Knight & Co., 1844).

Donnell, D. J., *Chronological and Statistical History of Cotton* (New York: James Sutton & Co., 1872).

Dumbell, S., "Early Liverpool Cotton Imports and the Organization of the Cotton Market in the Eighteenth Century," *Economic Journal*, XXXIII (1923), pp. 362–73.

Fairbairn, W., *Treatise on Mills and Millwork* (London: Longman, Green, Longman, and Roberts, 1861).

Farnie, D. A., *The English Cotton Industry, 1850–96* (M.A. Dissertation, Manchester University, 1953).

Graham, A., *The Impolicy of the Tax on Cotton Wool, as Aggravated by the Progress and Capabilities of Foreign Countries in Cotton Manufactures* (Glasgow: Associated Cotton Spinners, 1836).

Guest, R., *A Compendious History of the Cotton Manufacture* (Manchester: Joseph Pratt, 1823).

Jewkes, J., "The Localisation of the Cotton Industry," *Economic Journal* (*Economic History Supplement*), II (1930), pp. 91–106.

Kennedy, J., "Observations on the Rise and Progress of the Cotton Trade, in Great Britain, particularly in Lancashire and the adjoining Counties," *Memoirs of the Literary and Philosophical Society of Manchester*, Second Series, III, pp. 115–37 (read Nov., 1815).

Bibliography

Leigh, E., *The Science of Modern Cotton Spinning* (Manchester: Palmer & Howe, 1873).

Lord, J., *Capital and Steam-Power, 1750–1800* (London: P. S. King & Son, 1923).

McCulloch, J. R., "An Essay on the Rise, Progress, Present State, and Prospects of the Cotton Manufacture," *Edinburgh Review*, XLVI (1827), pp. 1–39.

Macdonald, D. K., *Fibres, Spindles and Spinning-Wheels* (Toronto: Royal Ontario Museum of Archaeology, 1944).

MacIntyre, R., "Textile Industries," in McLean, A. (ed.), *Local Industries of Glasgow and the West of Scotland* (Glasgow: Local Committee for the Meeting of the British Association, 1901), pp. 133–57.

Mann, J. A., *The Cotton Trade of Great Britain* (London: Simpkin, Marshall, & Co., 1860).

Marsden, R., *Cotton Weaving: Its Development, Principles, and Practice* (London: George Bell & Sons, 1895).

Mercator, *A Letter to the Inhabitants of Manchester on the Exportation of Cotton Twist* (Manchester: 1800).

——, *A Second Letter to the Inhabitants of Manchester on the Exportation of Cotton Twist* (Manchester: 1800).

——, *A Third Letter to the Inhabitants of Manchester on the Exportation of Cotton Twist* (Manchester: 1803).

Montgomery, J., *The Cotton Manufacture of the United States of America and the State of the Cotton Manufacture of that Country Contrasted and Compared with that of Great Britain* (Glasgow: John Niven, 1840).

——, *The Cotton Spinner's Manual* (Glasgow: John Niven, 1850).

——, *The Theory and Practice of Cotton Spinning* (Glasgow: John Niven, 1836).

Moore, F., *The Contrast, or, a Comparison between our Woollen, Linen, Cotton, and Silk Manufactures* (London: J. Buckland, 1782).

Mortimer, J., *Cotton Spinning: The Story of the Spindle* (Manchester: Palmer, Howe, & Co., 1895).

——, *Mercantile Manchester Past and Present* (Manchester: Palmer, Howe, & Co., 1896).

Muggliston, W., *A Letter on the Subject of Wool Interspersed with Remarks on Cotton, Addressed to the Public at Large; but more particularly to the Committee of Merchants and Manufacturers at Leeds* (Nottingham: H. Cox, 1782).

Nasmith, J., "The Inventive Epoch in the Cotton Trade," *Transactions of the Manchester Association of Engineers* (Manchester: Herald & Walker Printers, 1897), pp. 1–32.

Price, W. H., "On the Beginning of the Cotton Industry in England," *Quarterly Journal of Economics*, XX (1905–6), pp. 608–13.

Radcliffe, W., *Origin of the New System of Manufacture* (Stockport: James Lomax, Advertiser-Office, 1828).

——, *Exportation of Cotton Yarns the Real Cause of the Distress that has fallen upon the Cotton Trade for a Series of Years Past* (Stockport: D. Dean, 1811).

Bibliography

Redford, A., *Manchester Merchants and Foreign Trade, 1794–1858. By Students in the Honours School of History in the University of Manchester* (Manchester: The University Press, 1934).

Robson, R., *Structure of the Cotton Industry: A Study in Specialization and Integration* (Ph.D. Dissertation, London University, 1950).

Schulze-Gaevernitz, G. von, *The Cotton Trade in England and on the Continent*, translated by Oscar S. Hall (London: Simpkin, Marshall, Hamilton, Kent, and Co., 1895).

Sharp, J. B., *Letters on the Exportation of Cotton Yarns* (London: 1817).

Snell, D. W., *The Manager's Assistant* (Hartford: Case, Tiffany & Co., 1850).

Taylor, A. J., "Concentration and Specialization in the Lancashire Cotton Industry, 1825–1850," *Economic History Review*, Second Series, I (1949), pp. 114–22.

Taylor, W. C., *The Hand Book of Silk, Cotton, and Woollen Manufactures* (London: Richard Bentley, 1843).

Thornely, T., *Cotton Waste, Its Production, Manipulation, and Uses* (London: Scott, Greenwood and Son, 1912).

Turnbull, G., *A History of the Calico Printing Industry of Great Britain* (Altrincham: John Sherratt and Son, 1951).

Ure, A., *The Cotton Manufacture of Great Britain* (London: H. G. Bohn, 1861).

Wadsworth, A. P., and Mann, J. deL., *The Cotton Trade and Industrial Lancashire, 1600–1780* (Manchester: University of Manchester, 1931).

Walker, G., *Observations founded on Facts upon the Propriety or Impropriety of Exporting Cotton Twist, for the Purpose of Being Manufactured into Cloth by Foreigners* (London: J. Debrett, 1803).

White, G., *A Practical Treatise on Weaving by Hand and Power Looms* (Glasgow: John Niven, 1846).

Wood, L. S., and Wilmore, A., *The Romance of the Cotton Industry in England* (Oxford: The University Press, 1927).

Wright, J., *An Address to the Members of Both Houses of Parliament on the late Tax laid on Fustian, and other Cotton Goods; Setting Forth, that it is both Reasonable and Necessary to Annul that Impost* (Warrington: W. Eyres, 1785).

BIOGRAPHY

Bamford, S., *Early Days* (London: T. Fisher Unwin, 1843).

Crabtree, J. H., *Richard Arkwright* (London: The Sheldon Press, 1923).

Cole, G. D. H., *The Life of William Cobbett* (London: W. Collins, 1924).

Dakeyne, J., *Samuel Crompton* (Bolton: Gledsdale Brothers, 1921).

Dictionary of National Biography (Oxford University Press).

Driver, C., *Tory Radical: The Life of Richard Oastler* (New York: Oxford University Press, 1946).

Espinasse, F., *Lancashire Worthies* (London: Simpkin, Marshall, & Co., First Series, 1874; Second Series, 1877).

414

Bibliography

French, G. J., *Life and Times of Samuel Crompton* (London: Simpkin, Marshall, & Co., 1859).

Hammond, J. L., & B., *Lord Shaftesbury* (London: Longmans, Green & Co., 1936).

Iatros (*pseud.*), *The Life and Writings of Patrick Colquhoun* (London: G. Smeeton, 1818).

Kennedy, J., "A Brief Memoir of Samuel Crompton, with a description of his Machine called the Mule, and of the subsequent improvement of the Machine by others," *Memoirs of the Literary and Philosophical Society of Manchester*, Second Series, V (1831), pp. 318–53.

Lyell, K. M., *Memoir of Leonard Horner* (London: Women's Printing Society, Ltd., 1890).

One Formerly a Teacher at New Lanark, *Robert Owen at New Lanark* (Manchester, 1839).

Owen, R., *The Life of Robert Owen, Written by Himself* (London: Effingham Wilson, 1857).

Owen, R. D., *Threading my Way* (London: Trubner & Co., 1874).

Podmore, F., *Robert Owen* (London: Hutchinson, 1906).

Pole, W., *The Life of Sir William Fairbairn, Partly written by Himself* (London: Longmans, Green, and Co., 1877).

Scholes, J. C., *Memoir of the Rev. Edward Whitehead* (Bolton: Tillotson & Son, 1889).

Smiles, S., *Industrial Biography: Iron Workers and Tool Makers* (London: John Murray, 1863).

Strickland, M., *A Memoir of the Life, Writings, and Mechanical Inventions of Edmund Cartwright* (London: Saunders and Otley, 1843).

Taussig, F. W., *Inventors and Money-Makers* (New York: Macmillan, 1915).

Unwin, G., Hulme, A., and Taylor, G., *Samuel Oldknow and the Arkwrights* (Manchester: The University Press, 1924).

Wallas, G., *The Life of Francis Place* (London: George Allen & Unwin, 1951).

Tours, Local History, Religious and Scientific Development

Abram, W. A., *A History of Blackburn* (Blackburn: J. G. & J. Toulmin, 1877).

Aiken, J., *A Description of the Country from thirty to forty Miles round Manchester* (London: John Stockdale, 1795).

Ainsworth, R., *History and Associations of Altham and Huncoat* (Accrington: Wardleworths, Ltd., 1932).

Ashworth, H., "Statistical Illustrations of the Past and Present State of Lancashire," read before the British Association in Manchester in 1840–41.

Ashton, T. S., *Economic and Social Investigations in Manchester, 1833–1933* (London: P. S. King & Co., 1934).

Aston, J., *The Manchester Guide* (Manchester: Joseph Aston, 1804).

415

Bibliography

Axon, W. E. A., *The Annals of Manchester* (Manchester: John Heywood, 1886).

Baines, E., jun., *The History of the County Palatine and Duchy of Lancaster* (London: George Routledge and Sons, 1868).

——, *The Social, Educational, and Religious State of the Manufacturing Districts* (London: Simpkin, Marshall, & Co., 1843).

Baines, T., and Fairbairn, W., *Lancashire and Cheshire, Past and Present* (London: William Mackenzie, 1868).

Barnes, T., "On the AFFINITY between the ARTS, with a PLAN for promoting and extending MANUFACTURES, by ENCOURAGING THOSE ARTS, on which MANUFACTURES principally depend." *Memoirs of the Literary and Philosophical Society of Manchester*, Vol. I (Warrington: W. Eyres, 1785), pp. 72–89.

Bebb, E. D., *Nonconformity and Social Life, 1660–1800* (London: Epworth Press, 1935).

Brierley, B., *Home Memories, and Recollections of a Life* (Manchester: Abel Heywood & Son, 1886).

——, *Tales and Sketches of Lancashire Life* (Manchester: John Heywood, 1862–3).

Butterworth, E., *An Historical Account of the Towns of Ashton-under-Lyne, Stalybridge, and Dukinfield* (Ashton: T. A. Phillips, 1842).

——, *Historical Sketches of Oldham* (Oldham: John Hirst, 1856).

Butterworth, J., *A History and Description of the Towns and Parishes of Stockport, Ashton-under-Lyne, Mottram-longden-Dale, and Glossop* (Manchester: W. D. Varey, 1827).

Clayton, J., *Friendly Advice to the Poor; Written and Published at the Request of the late and present Officers of the Town of Manchester* (Manchester: 1755).

Cobbett, W., *Rural Rides*, edited by G. D. H. & M. Cole (London: Peter Davies, 1930).

Corry, J., *The History of Lancashire* (London: G. B. Whittaker, 1825).

Fishwick, H., *The History of the Parish of Preston* (Rochdale: James Clegg, 1900).

——, *History of the Parish of Rochdale* (Rochdale: James Clegg, 1889).

Foster, F., *Thoughts on the Times, but Chiefly on the Profligacy of our Women, and It's Causes* (London: C. Parker, 1779).

George, M. D., *London Life in the Eighteenth Century* (London: Kegan Paul, Trench, Trubner & Co., 1930).

Halley, R., *Lancashire: Its Puritanism and Nonconformity* (Manchester: Tubbs & Brook, 1869).

Hardwick, C., *History of the Borough of Preston* (Preston: Worthington & Co., 1857).

Heginbotham, H., *Stockport: Ancient and Modern* (London: Sampson Low, Marston, Searle, and Rivington, 1882).

Helm, E., *Chapters in the History of the Manchester Chamber of Commerce* (London: Simpkin, Marshall, Hamilton, Kent & Co., 1902).

Bibliography

Knox, V., *Family Lectures; or Domestic Divinity, being a copious Collection of Sermons, Selected from the polite Writers and found Divines, of the present Century; For the Use of Schools on Sunday Evenings and of Young Students in Divinity* (London: C. Dilly, 1791).

Love, B., *Manchester as It Is* (Manchester: Love and Barton, 1839).

Manchester Statistical Society, *Report on the State of Education in the Borough of Bury, Lancashire, in July, 1835* (London: James Ridgway & Son, 1835).

——, *Report on the State of Education in the Borough of Manchester in 1834* (London: James Ridgway & Son, 1835).

——, *Report on the State of Education in the Borough of Salford in 1835* (London: James Ridgway & Son, 1836).

Marshall, L. S., *The Development of Public Opinion in Manchester, 1780–1820* (Syracuse: The University Press, 1946).

Mattley, R. D., *Annals of Rochdale* (Rochdale: The Aldine Press, 1899).

Mendelsohn, E., Seminar Paper for History 234a, Harvard University, January, 1956, entitled "The Scientific Spirit and the Industrial Revolution: A Study of the Origins of the Manchester Literary and Philosophical Society."

Merton, R. K., *Science, Technology and Society in Seventeenth Century England* (Bruges: St. Catherine Press, 1938).

Miller, G. C., *Blackburn: The Evolution of a Cotton Town* (Blackburn: The Times, 1951).

Ogden, J., *A Description of Manchester by a Native of the Town* (Manchester: M. Faulkner, 1783).

Percival, T., *Observations on the State of Population in Manchester and other Adjacent Places* (Manchester: The Author, 1773).

The Plan of the Society for the Encouragement of Arts, Manufactures and Commerce (London: 1755).

Prentice, A., *Historical Sketches and Personal Recollections of Manchester (Intended to Illustrate the Progress of Public Opinion from 1792 to 1832)* (London: Charles Gilpin, 1851).

Rowbottom, W., *Chronology or Annals of Oldham, 1797–1830*, Vols. 93–101 of Giles Shaw Manuscripts, Manchester Central Library.

Shaw, W. A., *Manchester Old and New* (London: Cassell & Co., 1894).

Society for the Encouragement of Arts, Manufactures and Commerce, *A Register of the Premiums and Bounties Given, 1754–1776* (London: James Phillips, 1778).

Stot, J., *A Sequel to the Friendly Advice to the Poor of Manchester* (Manchester: 1756).

Stewart, G., *Progress of Glasgow: As Shown in the Records of the Glasgow Chamber of Commerce, and other Authentic Documents* (Glasgow: Printed for Private Circulation, 1883).

Tawney, R. H., *Religion and the Rise of Capitalism* (New York: New American Library, 1954).

Taylor, W. C., *Illustrated Itinerary of the County of Lancaster* (London: How & Parsons, 1842).

417

Bibliography

Taylor, W. C., *Notes of a Tour in the Manufacturing Districts of Lancashire; in a Series of Letters to His Grace the Archbishop of Dublin* (London: Duncan & Malcolm, 1842).

Thom, W., *Rhymes and Recollections of a Hand-Loom Weaver* (London: Smith, Elder, & Co., 1844).

Transactions of the Society for the Encouragement of Arts, Manufactures and Commerce, Vols. 1–52 (1783–1840).

Tupling, G. H., *The Economic History of Rossendale* (Manchester: The University Press, 1927).

The Victoria History of the Counties of England. Lancashire, Vol. II (London: Archibald Constable, 1908).

Wadsworth, A. P., "The First Manchester Sunday Schools," *Bulletin of the John Rylands Library*, Vol. 33 (1950–51), pp. 299–326.

Warner, W. J., *The Wesleyan Movement in the Industrial Revolution* (London: Longmans, Green & Co., 1930).

Waugh, E., *Sketches of Lancashire Life and Localities* (London: Whittaker & Co., 1855).

Wearmouth, R. F., *Methodism and the Common People of the Eighteenth Century* (London: The Epworth Press, 1945).

——, *Methodism and the Working-Class Movements of England, 1800–1850* (London: The Epworth Press, 1937).

Weber, M., *The Protestant Ethic and the Spirit of Capitalism*, translated by Talcott Parsons, introduction by R. H. Tawney (London: George Allen & Unwin, 1930).

Wheeler, J., *Manchester: Its Political, Social and Commercial History, Ancient and Modern* (Manchester: 1836).

Whitehead, E., *The Duty of bearing one another's Burdens. A Sermon preached before a Society of Weavers . . . in Bolton* (Manchester: J. Prescott, 1784).

Whittle, P. A., *Blackburn as it Is* (Preston: H. Oakey, 1852).

Wood, H. T., *A History of the Royal Society of Arts* (London: John Murray, 1913).

Young, A., *A Six Months Tour Through the North of England* (London: W. Strahan, 1770–71).

Works Relating to the Condition of Labour, Trade Unions, and Factory Legislation

Adshead, J., *Distress in Manchester. Evidence of the State of the Labouring Classes in 1840–42* (London: Henry Hooper, 1842).

"Alfred" (Samuel Kydd), *The History of the Factory Movement* (London: Simpkin, Marshall, & Co., 1857).

Answers to certain Objections made to Sir Robert Peel's Bill, for Ameliorating the Condition of Children employed in Cotton Factories (Manchester: R. & W. Dean, 1819).

Artizan, *Machinery: Its Tendency; viewed particularly in Reference to the Working Classes* (London: Charles Fox, 1843).

418

Bibliography

Articles of Agreement. Rules, Orders and Regulations . . . of the Friendly Associated Cotton Spinners . . . of Manchester (Manchester: 1792).

Articles, Rules, Orders, and Regulations . . . of the Friendly Associated Cotton Spinners . . . of Manchester (Manchester: 1795).

Articles, Rules, Orders, and Regulations . . . of the Friendly Associated Mule Cotton Spinners . . . of Stockport (Stockport: 1795).

Articles, Rules, and Regulations of the Friendly Associated Society of Quilting Weavers of Manchester and Neighbourhood (Manchester: 1829).

Ashworth, H., *An Inquiry into the Origin, Progress, and Results of the Strike of the Operative Spinners of Preston* (Manchester: 1838).

——, *Letter to the Right Hon. Lord Ashley on the Cotton Factory Question and the Ten Hours' Factory Bill, by a Lancashire Cotton Spinner* (Manchester: Henry Smith, 1833).

——, *The Preston Strike, an Enquiry into its Causes and Consequences* (Manchester: George Simms, 1854).

Ashworth, W., "British Industrial Villages in the Nineteenth Century," *Economic History Review*, III (1950), pp. 378–87.

Aspinall, A., *The Early English Trade Unions. Documents from the Home Office Papers in the Public Record Office* (London: The Batchworth Press, 1949).

Baines, E., jun., *An Address to the Unemployed Workmen of Yorkshire and Lancashire on the Present Distress and on Machinery* (London: James Ridgway, 1826).

Bayne-Powell, R., *The English Child in the Eighteenth Century* (London: John Murray, 1939).

Bobbinwinder, S. (*pseud.*), *A Conversation between Peter Pickingpeg, and Harry Emptybobbin, carefully reported* (Barnsley: J. Ray, 1838).

Bowley, A. L., *Wages in the United Kingdom in the Nineteenth Century* (Cambridge: The University Press, 1900).

Brown, J., *A Memoir of Robert Blincoe, An Orphan Boy; sent from the Workhouse of St. Pancras, London, at Seven Years of Age, to Endure the Horrors of a Cotton-Mill, through his Infancy and Youth, with a Minute Detail of his Sufferings, Being the First Memoir of the Kind Published* (Manchester: J. Doherty, 1832).

Bruton, F. A., *The Story of Peterloo* (Manchester: The University Press, 1919).

Bull, G. S., *Address at the Proceedings of a Public Meeting of the People of Bradford* (Bradford: T. Inkersley, 1833).

——,*The Evils of the Factory System* (Bradford: T. Inkersley, 1832).

Chadwick, D., "On the Social and Educational Statistics of Manchester and Salford," *Transactions of the Manchester Statistical Society*, 1861–2, pp. 1–48.

Chapman, S. J., "The Regulation of Wages by Lists in the Spinning Industry," *The Economic Journal*, IX (1899), pp. 592–9.

Clerke, Rev. Sir W., *Thoughts upon the Means of Preserving the Health of the Poor, by Prevention and Suppression of Endemic Fevers* (London: J. Johnson, 1790).

419

Cole, G. D. H., *A Short History of the British Working Class Movement, 1797–1937* (London: George Allen & Unwin, 1937).

———, and Filson, A. W., *British Working Class Movements: Select Documents 1789–1875* (London: Macmillan, 1951).

Collier, F., "An Early Factory Community," *Economic Journal (Economic History Supplement)*, II (1930), pp. 117–24.

———, *The Family Economy in the Cotton Industry* (M.A. Dissertation, Manchester University, 1921).

"The Commission for Perpetuating Factory Infanticide," *Fraser's Magazine*, June, 1833.

The Commissioner's Vade Mecum, whilst Engaged in Collecting Evidence for the Factory Masters (Leeds: R. Inchbold, 1833).

Crabtree, G., *Factory Commission: The Legality of its Appointment Questioned, and the Illegality of its Proceedings Proved* (London: L. B. Seeley and Sons, 1833).

Cruikshank, R., *The Condition of the West India Slave contrasted with that of the Infant Slave in our English Factories* (London: W. Kidd, 1833).

Darvall, F. O., *The Luddite Disturbances and the Machinery of Order* (Ph.D. Dissertation, University of London, 1932).

The Day-Dream, or a Letter to King Richard, Containing a Vision of the Trial of Mr. Factory Longhours (Leeds: T. Inchbold, 1832).

Dodd, W., *The Factory System Illustrated; in a series of Letters to the Right Hon. Lord Ashley* (London: John Murray, 1842).

———, *A Narrative of the Experience and Sufferings of William Dodd, A Factory Cripple, Written by Himself* (London: L. & G. Seeley, 1841).

Doherty, J., *The Ten Hours Bill. A Letter to the Factory Operatives of Lancashire, on the Necessity of Petitioning Parliament in Favour of the Ten Hours Bill* (Manchester: 1845).

Drinkwater, J. E., and Power, A., *Replies to Mr. M. T. Sadler's Protest against the Factory Commission* (Leeds: Baines and Newsome, 1833).

Dunlop, O. J., *English Apprenticeship and Child Labour* (London: T. Fisher Unwin, 1912).

Eden, F. M., *State of the Poor* (London: J. Davis, 1797).

Engels, F., *The Condition of the Working-Class in England in 1844* (London: George Allen & Unwin, 1926).

The Factory System; or Frank Hawthorn's Visit to his Cousin, Jemmy Cropper, of Leeds (Leeds: T. Inchbold, 1831).

Fay, C. R., *Life and Labour in the Nineteenth Century* (Cambridge: The University Press, 1947).

Fielden, J., *The Curse of the Factory System* (London: A. Cobbett, 1836).

———, "Letter to Mr. Fitton," in *National Regeneration* (London: 1834), pp. 5–21.

Gammage, R. G., *History of the Chartist Movement 1837–1854* (Newcastle upon Tyne: Browne & Browne, 1894).

Gaskell, P., *Artisans and Machinery: The Moral and Physical Condition of the Manufacturing Population* (London: John W. Parker, 1836).

———, *The Manufacturing Population of England* (London: Baldwin & Cradock, 1833).

Bibliography

Gaskell, P., *Prospects of Industry; being a Brief Exposition of the Past and Present Conditions of the Labouring Classes* (London: Smith, Elder & Co., 1835).

George, M. D., "The Combination Laws Reconsidered," *Economic Journal (Economic History Supplement)*, I (1929), pp. 214–28.

Gisborne, T., *An Enquiry into the Duties of the Female Sex* (London: T. Cadell, 1797).

——, *An Enquiry into the Duties of Men in the Higher and Middle Classes of Society* (London: J. Davis, 1794).

Grant, P., *The Ten Hours' Bill. The History of Factory Legislation* (Manchester: John Heywood, 1866).

Greg, R. H., *The Factory Question* (London: James Ridgway & Sons, 1837).

Greg, S., *Two Letters to Leonard Horner, Esq., on the Capabilities of the Factory System* (London: Taylor and Walton, 1840).

Greg, W. R., *An Enquiry into the State of the Manufacturing Population, and the Causes and Cures of the Evils Therein Existing* (London: James Ridgway, 1831).

Hall, W., *Vindication of the Chorley Spinners' Turn-out* (Manchester: 1825).

Hammond, J. L. & B., *The Skilled Labourer, 1760–1832* (London: Longmans, Green & Co., 1920).

——, *The Town Labourer, 1760–1832* (London: Longmans, Green & Co., 1949).

——, *The Village Labourer, 1760–1832* (London: Longmans, Green & Co., 1919).

Hewitt, M., *The Effect of Married Women's Employment in the Cotton Textile Districts on the Home in Lancashire, 1840–1880* (Ph.D. Dissertation, University of London, 1953).

Hobsbawm, E. J., "Economic Fluctuations and Some Social Movements since 1800," *Economic History Review*, V (1952), pp. 1–25.

——, "The Tramping Artisan," *Economic History Review*, Second Series, III (1950–51), pp. 299–320.

Hoole, H., *A Letter to the Right Honourable Lord Viscount Althorp . . . in Defence of the Cotton Factories of Lancashire* (Manchester: T. Sowler, 1832).

Horner, L., *On the Employment of Children, in Factories and Other Works in the United Kingdom and in some Foreign Countries* (London: Longman, Orme, Brown, Green, and Longman, 1840).

Hovell, M., *The Chartist Movement* (Manchester: The University Press, 1925).

Hutchins, B. L., *Women in Modern Industry* (London: G. Bell & Sons, 1915).

——, and Harrison, A., *A History of Factory Legislation* (London: P. S. King and Son, 1903).

Hutt, W. H., "The Factory System of the Early Nineteenth Century," in Hayek, F. A., *Capitalism and the Historians* (London: Routledge & Kegan Paul, 1954), pp. 160–88.

421

Bibliography

Hymns for Factory Children, Original and Paraphrased; to which are Added, Three Songs and a Short Heroic (Leeds: 1831).

Information Concerning the State of Children Employed in Cotton Factories (Manchester: J. Gleave, 1818).

An Inquiry into the Principle and Tendency of the Bill now pending in Parliament, for imposing Certain Restrictions on Cotton Factories (London: Baldwin, Craddock, & Joy, 1818).

Jefferys, J. B., *Labour's Formative Years* (London: Lawrence & Wishart, 1948).

Kaufmann, M., *Utopias; or, Schemes of Social Improvement, From Sir Thomas More to Karl Marx* (London: C. Kegan Paul, 1879).

Kay, J. P., *The Moral and Physical Condition of the Working Classes employed in the Cotton Manufacture in Manchester* (London: James Ridgway, 1832).

Kelly, T., *Thoughts on the Marriages of the Labouring Poor: containing Instructions for their Conduct before and after entering into that Important State* (London: G. Kearsley, 1806).

Kennedy, J., "Observations on the Influence of Machinery upon the Working Classes of the Community," *Memoirs of the Literary and Philosophical Society of Manchester*, Second Series, V (London: Baldwin & Cradock, 1831), pp. 318–53.

A Letter Addressed to the Members of both Houses of Parliament, on the Distresses of the Hand Loom Weavers . . . of Bolton (Bolton: A. R. Martin, 1834).

A Looker-on, *A Letter addressed to Farmers and Manufacturers* (York: Gazette-Office, 1826).

Maden, J., *Observations on the Use of Power Looms, by a Friend to the Poor* (Rochdale: J. Hartley, 1823).

"Man Versus Machine," *The New Anti-Jacobin*, I (1833), pp. 16–25.

Manchester Statistical Society, *Analysis of the Evidence taken Before the Factory Commissioners, as far as it relates to the Population of Manchester and the Vicinity, Engaged in the Cotton Trade* (Manchester: Bancks and Co., 1834).

Martineau, H., *The Rioters, Or a Tale of Bad Times* (Wellington, Salop: Houlston & Son, 1827).

Maxwell, J., *Manual Labour versus Machinery* (London: Cochrane & M'Crone, 1834).

Moral Instruction Addressed to the Working Classes (London: Simpkin & Marshall, 1834).

Morris, D. C., *The History of the Labour Movement in England, 1825–1852. The Problem of Leadership and the Articulation of Demands* (Ph.D. Dissertation, University of London, 1952).

Nicholson, J., *The Factory Child's Mother; or the Voice of True Humanity* (Leeds, 1832).

To the Nobility, Gentry, and Representatives in Parliament . . . The Petition of the Poor Spinners (Leicester: 1788).

Oastler, R., *Eight Letters to the Duke of Wellington* (London: James Cochrane & Co., 1835).

Bibliography

Oastler, R., *The Factory Bill. Lord Ashley's Ten-Hour Bill and the Scheme of the Factory Commissioners Compared* (London: Mills, Jowett, & Mills, 1833).

——, *Infant Slavery. Report of a Speech, Delivered in Favour of the Ten Hours Bill . . . at Preston* (Preston: J. Livesey & J. Walker, 1833).

——, *Letter to the Editor of the Agricultural and Industrial Magazine* (London: James Cochrane & Co., 1835).

——, *A Letter to those Millowners who Continue to Oppose the Ten Hours Bill, and who Impudently Dare to Break the Present Factories Act* (Manchester: John Doherty, 1836).

——, *A Letter to Mr. Holland Hoole, in Reply to his Letter to the Right Hon. Lord Viscount Althorp . . . in Defence of the Cotton Factories of Lancashire* (Manchester: Alexander Wilkinson, 1832).

——, *"Mr. Sadler's Bill," a Letter to the Poor Man's Advocate*, Mar. 24, 1832.

——, *A Speech Delivered . . . at a Meeting held in the Manor Court-Room, Manchester* (Huddersfield: J. Hobson, 1833).

On Combinations of Trades (London: James Ridgway, 1831).

An Operative, *The Factory Child* (London: 1831 and 1832).

Pinchbeck, I., *Women Workers in the Industrial Revolution, 1750–1850* (London: George Routledge & Sons, 1930).

Plener, E. von, *The English Factory Legislation*, translated by F. L. Weinmann (London: Chapman and Hall, 1873).

Proceedings of the Board of Health of Manchester (Manchester: S. Russell, 1805).

The Quinquarticular System of Organization. To the Operative Spinners of Manchester and Salford (by John Doherty) (Manchester: 1834).

Ramsbotham, D. (attributed to the Rev. Thomas Barnes in the copy of the Goldsmith Collection, University of London), *Thoughts on the Use of Machines in the Cotton Manufacture* (Manchester: 1780).

Read, D., "The Social and Economic Background to Peterloo," *Transactions of the Lancashire and Cheshire Antiquarian Society*, LXIV (1954), pp. 1–18.

Redford, A., *Labour Migration in England, 1800–1850* (Manchester: The University Press, 1926).

A Report on the Important proceedings of a Public Meeting . . . in . . . Oldham . . . on . . . shortening . . . Labour in the . . . Factories (Oldham: J. Dodge, 1836).

A Report on the Proceedings of a Delegate Meeting of the Operative Spinners of England, Ireland, and Scotland, assembled at Ramsay, Isle of Man (Manchester: M. Wardle, 1829).

Richardson, C., *A Short Description of the Factory System* (Bawtry: J. Wilson, ?1831?).

Rose, H., *Manual Labour, versus Brass and Iron: Reflections in Defense of the Body of Cotton Spinners, Occasioned by a Perusal of the Description of Mr. Roberts' Self-Acting Mule* (Manchester: J. Pratt, 1825).

Rosenblatt, F. F., *The Chartist Movement in its Social and Economic Aspects* (New York: Columbia University, 1916).

Ross, J., *The Factory Child's Father's Reply to the Factory Child's Mother* (Leeds: 1832).

Rules for the Union of Weavers, associated for the Purpose of Obtaining a proper Remuneration for their Industry (Manchester: 1824).

Sadler, J. H., *The New Invention of Double and Quadruple, or British National Looms* (London: Snell, 1831).

Sadler, M. T., *Protest against the Secret Proceedings of the Factory Commission, in Leeds* (Leeds: F. E. Bingley & Co., 1833).

Senior, N. W., *Letters on the Factory Act, as it affects the Cotton Manufacture* (London: B. Fellowes, 1837).

——, Loyd, S. J., Hickson, W. E., and Leslie, J., *Instructions from the Central Board of the Hand-loom Weavers' Inquiry Commission to their Assistant Commissioners* (London: 1839).

Shaw, C., *Replies to Lord Ashley, M.P., regarding the Education, and Moral and Physical Condition of the Labouring Classes* (London: John Ollivier, 1843).

Shuttle, T., *The Worsted Small-Ware Weavers' Apology, Together with all their Articles which either concern their Society or Trade* (Manchester: 1756).

A Sketch of the Hours of Labour, Meal Times, &c., in Manchester and its Neighbourhood (London: J. Harrison & Son, 1825).

Society for Bettering the Condition of the Poor, *Report of a Select Committee of the Society upon some Observations on the late Act respecting Cotton Mills* (London: W. Bulmer & Co., 1802).

A Statement from the Master Cotton Spinners; in Support of the Factories' Act Amendment Bill (London: 1836).

Taylor, W. C., *Factories and the Factory System: from Parliamentary Documents and Personal Examination* (London: Jeremiah How, 1844).

Thackrah, C. T., *The Effects of the Principal Arts, Trades, and Professions . . . on Health and Longevity* (London: Longman, Rees, Orme, Brown, & Green, 1831).

Thomas, M. W., *The Early Factory Legislation. A Study in Legislative and Administrative Evolution* (Leigh-on-Sea: The Thames Bank Publishing Co., 1948).

Torrens, R., *On Wages and Combination* (London: Longman, Rees, Orme, Brown, Green, and Longman, 1834).

"On Trades-Unions and Strikes," *Edinburgh Review*, Vol. 59, 1834, pp. 341–58.

Trades Union Congress, *Women in the Trade Union Movement* (London: 1955).

Tufnell, E. C., *Character, Object, and Effects of Trades' Unions with Some Remarks on the Law Concerning Them* (London: James Ridgway & Sons, 1834).

Twiss, T., *Two Lectures on Machinery* (Oxford: John Henry Parker, 1844).

Walker, K. O., "The Classical Economists and the Factory Acts," *Journal of Economic History*, I (1941), pp. 168–77.

Walker, W., *Poetical Strictures on the Factory System and Other Matters* (Leeds: 1832).

424

Ward, G., "The Education of Factory Child Workers, 1833–1850," *Economic Journal* (*Economic History Supplement*), III (1934–37), pp. 110–24.

Wearmouth, R. F., *Some Working-Class Movements of the Nineteenth Century* (London: The Epworth Press, 1948).

Webb, R., *The British Working Class Reader 1790–1848: Literacy and Social Tension* (London: George Allen & Unwin, 1955).

Webb Trade Union Collection, Library of the London School of Economics and Political Science:

  Vol. VII: General History, etc.

  XXXIV: Cotton Spinners, History 1700–1896.

  XXXV: Cotton Spinners, Local Histories.

  XXXVI: Cotton Spinners, Local Histories and Miscellaneous.

  XXXVII: Cotton Weavers.

Webb, S. & B., *The History of Trade Unionism* (London: Longmans, Green, & Co., 1894).

West, J., *A History of the Chartist Movement* (London: Constable & Co., 1920).

White, G., *Combination and Arbitration Laws, Artizans, and Machinery* (London: 1824).

Wing, C., *Evils of the Factory System* (London: Saunders & Otley, 1837).

Wood, G. H., "Factory Legislation, considered with Reference to the Wages, &c., of the Operatives Protected Thereby," *Journal of the Royal Statistical Society*, LXV (1902), pp. 284–321.

——, *The History of Wages in the Cotton Trade During the Past Hundred Years* (London: Sherratt & Hughes, 1910).

WORKS REFERRING TO POOR-LAWS, FRIENDLY
SOCIETIES, SAVINGS BANKS, AND CO-OPERATION

Acland, J., *A Plan for rendering the Poor independent of Public Contribution; founded on the Basis of the Friendly Societies* (Exeter: R. Thorn, 1786).

An Address to the Working Classes on Practical Co-operation (Runcorn: 1831).

Ansell, C., *A Treatise on Friendly Societies* (London: Baldwin & Cradock, 1835).

Ashton, T. S., "The Standard of Life of the Workers in England, 1790–1830," in Hayek, F. A., *Capitalism and the Historians* (London: Routledge & Kegan Paul, 1954).

Baernreither, J. M., *English Associations of Working Men*, translated by Alice Taylor (London: Swan Sonnenschein & Co., 1889).

Baker, F., *First and Second Lectures on Co-operation Delivered . . . at . . . Bolton*, April 19, 1830, and May 3, 1830. Published in the *Universal Pamphleteer*.

Beaumont, B., *An Essay on Provident or Parish Banks* (London: 1816).

Becher, J. T., *The Constitution of Friendly Societies* (London: W. Simpkin & R. Marshall, 1824).

Bibliography

Becher, J. T., *Observations upon the Report from the Select Committee of the House of Commons on the laws respecting Friendly Societies* (Newark: S. & J. Ridge, 1826).

Bone, J., *The Friend of the People: or, Considerations addressed principally to Persons of Small Incomes, and Members of Friendly Societies* (London: 1807).

——, *Outline of a Plan for Reducing the Poor's Rate . . . in a Letter to the Right Hon. George Rose* (London: 1805).

——, *The Principles and Regulations of Tranquillity, an Institution Commenced in the Metropolis, for encouraging and enabling industrious and prudent Individuals . . . to Provide for themselves* (London: 1806).

Bowles, J., *Reasons for the Establishment of Provident Institutions, Called Savings' Banks, with a Word of Caution Respecting their Formation* (London: 1817).

Burdett, F., *Annals of Banks for Savings* (London: Luke Hansard & Sons, 1818).

Christian, E., "General Observations on Provident Banks," *The Pamphleteer*, XVII (1820), pp. 275–88.

Colquhoun, P., *A Treatise on Indigence* (London: J. Hatchard, 1806).

——, *Useful Suggestions favourable to the Comfort of the Labouring People, and to Decent Housekeepers, explaining How a small income may be made to go far in a family so as to occasion a considerable saving in the Article of Bread* (London: 1795).

Cunningham, J. W., *A Few Observations on Friendly Societies, and their Influence on Public Morals* (London: 1817).

Davis, W., *Friendly Advice to Industrious and Frugal Persons, recommending Provident Institutions, or, Saving Banks* (London: Bensley and Son, 1817).

Count de Salis, J., *A Proposal for Improving the System of Friendly Societies, or, of Poor Assurance Offices* (London: W. & P. Reynolds, 1814).

Duncan, H., *An Essay on the Nature and Advantages of Parish Banks* (Edinburgh: Oliphant, Waugh & Innes, 1815).

Dunlop, J., *Artificial Drinking Usages of North Britain* (Greenock: K. Johnston, 1836).

Eden, F. M., *Observations on Friendly Societies, for the Maintenance of the Industrious Classes, during Sickness, Infirmity, Old Age and Other Exigencies* (London: J. White, 1801).

An Enumeration of the Principal Vegetables and Vegetable Productions, that may be substituted, either in part or wholly, in place of Wheat and other Bread-Corn, in times of Scarcity (Birmingham: 1796).

"Extract from an Account of the Provident Institution for Savings, established in the Western part of the Metropolis," *The Fortieth Report of the Society for Bettering the Condition and Increasing the Comforts of the Poor* (London: 1817), pp. 93–113.

"On Frugality Banks," *The Philanthropist*, IV (1818), pp. 1–17.

Gregson, H., *Suggestions for Improving the Condition of the Industrious Classes, by Establishing Friendly Societies and Savings' Banks, in Co-operation with Each other* (London: J. Hatchard, 1830).

426

Bibliography

Hall, S., *Dr. Duncan of Ruthwell. Founder of Savings Banks* (Edinburgh: Oliphant, Anderson & Ferrier, 1910).

Hardwick, C., *Friendly Societies: Their History, Progress, Prospects and Utility* (Preston: Dobson & Son, 1851).

Haygarth, J., *An Explanation of the Principles and Proceedings of the Provident Institution at Bath, for Savings* (Bath: 1816).

Holyoake, G. J., *The History of Cooperation in England: Its Literature and its Advocates. Volume I: The Pioneer Period—1812 to 1844* (London: Trubner & Co., 1875).

——, *The History of the Rochdale Pioneers* (London: Swan Sonnenschein & Co., 1893).

——, *Self-Help a Hundred Years Ago* (London: Swan Sonnenschein & Co., 1888).

Horne, H. O., *A History of Savings Banks* (London: Oxford University Press, 1947).

Hudson, S., *An Address to the Different Classes of Persons in Great Britain, on the Present Scarcity and High Price of Provisions* (London: 1795).

Hume, J., *An Account of the Provident Institution for Savings, Established in the Western Part of the Metropolis* (London: 1816).

"On Improving the Condition of the Poor," *Quarterly Review*, XII (1814–15), pp. 146–59.

An Independent Gentleman, *Thoughts on the Present Prices of Provisions, their Causes and Remedies* (London: 1800).

Lettsom, Dr., *Hints Respecting the Distresses of the Poor* (London: 1796).

Lewins, W., *A History of Banks for Savings in Great Britain and Ireland* (London: Sampson, Low, Son, and Marston, 1866).

M'Phail, J., *Remarks on the Present Times, exhibiting the Causes of the High Price of Provisions, and Propositions for their Reduction* (London: 1795).

Maitland, J., *Considerations addressed to all Classes on the Necessity and Equity of a National Banking and Annuity System* (London: Smith, Elder & Co., 1831).

Malthus, T., *An Investigation of the Cause of the Present High Price of Provisions* (London: 1800).

Mercer, T. W., *Co-operation's Prophet: The Life and Letters of Dr. William King of Brighton with a Reprint of The Co-operator, 1828–1830* (Manchester: Co-operative Union Limited, 1947).

Morgan, H. D., *The Beneficial Operation of Banks for Savings* (London: Henry Wix, 1834).

Observations on Banks for Savings (London: 1818).

An Officer of the Volunteer Corps, *Short Thoughts on the Present Price of Provisions* (London: 1800).

Osborne, S. G., *The Prospects and Present Condition of the Labouring Classes* (London: T. & W. Boone, ?1835?).

Owen, R., *A New View of Society, or Essays on the Principle of the Formation of the Human Character* (London: Cadell & Davies, 1813).

427

Bibliography

A Physician, *One Cause of the Present Scarcity of Corn, pointed out, and earnestly recommended to the Serious Consideration of the People* (London: 1795).

The Position of Women in Harmony (London: 1841).

Potter, B., *The Co-operative Movement in Great Britain* (London: George Allen & Unwin, 1930).

Pratt, J. T., *The History of Savings Banks in England, Wales, Ireland, and Scotland* (London: Printed for the Author, 1842).

———, *A Summary of the Savings Banks in England, Scotland, Wales, and Ireland* (London: W. Clowes & Sons, 1846).

Pratt, W. T., *The Law relating to Friendly Societies* (London: Shaw & Sons, 1854).

"Publications on Parish or Savings Banks," *Edinburgh Review*, XXV (1815), pp. 135–46.

Report of the Proceedings at the Second, Third and Fourth Quarterly Meetings of the Society for the Promotion of Co-operative Knowledge (London: Cowie & Strange, 1829).

Rose, G., *Observations on the Act for the Relief and Encouragement of Friendly Societies* (London: 1794).

———, *Observations on Banks for Savings* (London: 1816).

———, *Observations on the Poor Laws, and on the Management of the Poor in Great Britain* (London: 1805).

Ryder, T., *Some account of the Maranta, or Indian Arrow Root, in which it is considered and recommended as a substitute for Starch Prepared from Corn* (London: 1796).

Scratchley, A., *A Treatise on Benefit Building Societies* (London: John W. Parker, 1849).

A Secretary and Member of a Friendly Benefit Society, *A Vindication of the Present Order of Friendly Benefit Societies* (London: 1817).

Shaw, J. G., *History of the Blackburn Savings Bank, 1831–1931* (Blackburn: The Times Printing Works, 1931).

A Short Account of the Edinburgh Savings Bank (Edinburgh: 1815).

Some Information respecting the Use of Indian Corn (Birmingham: 1795).

A Suffolk Gentleman, *A Letter . . . on the Poor Rates, and the High Price of Provisions, with some Proposals for reducing both* (Ipswich: 1795).

Tamlyn, J., *A Digest of the Laws of Friendly Societies and Savings Banks* (London: Joseph Butterworth & Son, 1827).

Thompson, W., *Appeal of one half of the Human Race, Women, against the Pretensions of the Other Half, Men, to retain them in Political, and thence in Civil and Domestic, Slavery* (London: Longman, Hurst, Rees, Orme, Brown, and Green, 1825).

———, *Labor Rewarded. The Claims of Labor and Capital Conciliated: or, How to Secure to Labor the Whole Products of Its Exertions* (London: Hunt & Clarke, 1827).

———, *Practical Directions for the Speedy and Economical Establishment of Communities, on the principles of mutual co-operation, united possessions and equality of enjoyment* (London: 1830).

Thoughts on the Causes of the Present Failures (London: 1793).

Bibliography

Thoughts on the Most Safe and Effectual Mode of Relieving the Poor during the Present Scarcity (London: 1795).

Vivian, R., *A Letter on Friendly Societies and Savings Banks, occasioned by Mr. Rose's Letter* (London: Ridgway & Sons, 1816).

Webb, S. & B., *English Local Government: English Poor Law History. Part I: The Old Poor Law* (London: Longmans, Green and Co., 1927); *Part II: The Last Hundred Years* (London: Longmans, Green and Co., 1929).

Woodrow, J., *Remarks on Banks for Savings and Friendly Societies; with an Original Plan Combining the Principles of Both Institutions; A Friendly Loan Fund, and other Important Advantages* (London: Richard and Arthur Taylor, 1818).

Wrangham, F., *The Savings-Bank: in Two Dialogues* (Scarborough: ?1800?).

Wright, J., *A Treatise on the Internal Regulations of Friendly Societies* (London: Saunders and Benning, 1828).

Wright, T., *A Short Address to the Public on the Monopoly of Small Farms, a Great Cause of the Present Scarcity and Dearness of Provisions* (London: 1795).

Zimmerman, C. C., *Consumption and Standards of Living* (London: Williams and Norgate, 1936).

GOVERNMENT PUBLICATIONS

PARLIAMENTARY PAPERS

1780   V, Paper 38, *Report from the Committee to whom the Petition of Cotton Spinners, and others, in and adjoining to the County of Lancaster; and also the Petition of John Hilton, Agent for the Cotton Manufacturers of the Town and Neighbourhood of Manchester, on Behalf of the Said Manufacturers; were referred.*

1793   XXXVIII, Paper 774c., *Report of the Select Committee appointed by the Court of Directors to take into Consideration the Export Trade from Great Britain to the East Indies, on the Cotton Manufacture of this Country.*

1802–3 VIII, *Evidence before the Committee on Petitions on the Law relating to Disputes between Masters and Workmen in the Cotton Manufacture*, pp. 889–999.

1803–4 V, *Committee on Adjusting Differences between Masters and Workmen in the Cotton Manufacture*, pp. 211–13.

1808   II, *Committee on Petitions of Cotton Manufacturers and Journeymen Cotton Weavers*, pp. 95–134.

1809   III, *Committee on Petitions of Cotton Manufacturers and Journeymen Cotton Weavers*, pp. 311–13.

1810–11 II, *Report on the Petition of Several Weavers*, pp. 389–406.

1814–15 V, *Committee on Parish Apprentices*, pp. 1567–76.

1816   III, *Select Committee on the State of the Children employed in the Manufactories of the United Kingdom*, pp. 235–521.

1817   IV, *Committee on Secrecy*, pp. 1–7, 9–14, 17–20.

VI, *Committee on Poor Laws*, pp. 1–170.

XIV, *Copies of all Memorials . . . during the present and last Year, on the Exportation of Cotton Yarns*, pp. 355–60.

1818   V, *Lords Committee on Poor Laws*, pp. 1–90, 91–298.

1824   V, *Select Committee on Artizans and Machinery*, pp. 620.

1825   IV, *Select Committee on Combination Laws*, pp. 499–989.

IV, *Select Committee on the Laws respecting Friendly Societies*, pp. 323–498.

1826   IV, *Select Committee on Emigration*, pp. 1–382.

1826–7   V, *Select Committee on Emigration*, pp. 890.

1830   X, *Report from Select Committee on Manufacturers' Employment*, pp. 221–33.

1831   VIII, *Select Committee (Lords) on the Poor Laws*, pp. 421.

1831–2   XV, *Select Committee on the "Bill to regulate the Labour of Children in the Mills and Factories of the United Kingdom,"* pp. 682.

1833   VI, *Committee on Manufactures, Commerce and Shipping*, pp. 801.

XX, *First Report of the Factory Commissioners*, pp. 1125.

1834   X, *Committee on Hand-Loom Weavers' Petitions, with Minutes of Evidence*, pp. 717.

XIX, *Supplementary Report of Factory Commissioners*, pp. 259–612.

XX, *Supplementary Report of Factory Commissioners*, pp. 1080.

XXVII, *Commissioners on Administration and Practical Operation of the Poor Laws.* Appendix (A), Part 1, pp. 949.

XXXVI, *Commissioners on Administration and Practical Operation of the Poor Laws*, Appendix (B.2), Parts III, IV, VI, pp. 551 and 281.

1835   XIII, *Select Committee on Hand-Loom Weavers' Petitions*, pp. 1–342.

XXXV, *First Annual Report of the Poor Law Commissioners*, pp. 107–364.

XL, *Reports of Factory Inspectors*, pp. 689–704.

1836   XXIX.1, *Second Annual Report of the Poor Law Commissioners*, pp. 574.

XLV, *Returns of Number of Power-Looms as collected in the Returns of the Factory Commissioners*, pp. 145–54.

XLV, *Reports of Factory Inspectors*, pp. 155–68.

1837   XVII (2 vols.), *Report from the Select Committee on the Poor Law Amendment Act.*

XXXI, *Reports of Factory Inspectors*, pp. 53–122.

XXXI, *Third Report of Poor Law Commissioners*, pp. 127–586.

L, *Memorial from the Short-time Committee of Manchester*, pp. 203–8.

Bibliography

1837-8 VII, *Select Committee on Education of the Poorer Classes,* pp. 157–344.

VIII, *Reports from the Select Committee on Combinations of Workmen,* pp. 639.

XVIII (3 vols.), *Select Committee on the Poor Law Amendment Act.*

XIX (2 vols.), *Report from the Select Committee (Lords) on the Poor Law Amendment Act.*

XXVIII, *Report of Factory Inspectors,* pp. 81–144.

XLV, *Reports of Factory Inspectors,* pp. 55–66.

1839 XIX, *Reports of Factory Inspectors,* pp. 433–538, 589–661.

Reports of Assistant Hand-loom Weavers' Commissioners (pagination from bound volumes in the Goldsmith Collection, University of London Library).

1840 X, *Select Committee on the Regulation of Mills and Factories,* pp. 914.

Reports of Assistant Hand-loom Weavers' Commissioners (pagination from bound volumes in the Goldsmith Collection, University of London Library).

1841 *Reports of the Commissioners of the Hand-loom Weavers* (pagination from bound volumes in the Goldsmith Collection, University of London Library).

(Sess. 2) VI, *Reports of Factory Inspectors,* pp. 235–46.

1842 XV–XVII, *Children's Employment Commission (Mines).*

XIX, *Eighth Annual Report of the Poor Law Commissioners,* pp. 1–439.

XXII, *Reports of Factory Inspectors,* pp. 337–440; 441–79.

XXVI, *A Return Relating to Friendly Societies enrolled in the Several Counties of England and Wales,* pp. 275–324.

XXVI, *A Return of Number of ... Annuities granted through the Savings Banks,* pp. 269–70.

XXXV, *Report addressed to the Poor Law Commissioners by E. C. Tufnell, Assistant Poor Law Commissioner, on Distress in Rochdale,* pp. 171–9.

XXXV, *Copy of Evidence taken, and Report made, by the Assistant Poor Law Commissioners sent to inquire into the State of the Population of Stockport,* pp. 193–324.

1843 XII, *Reports of Special Assistant Poor Law Commissioners on the Employment of Women and Children in Agriculture,* pp. 1–394.

XIII–XV, *Children's Employment Commissioners (Trade and Manufactures).*

XXI, *Ninth Annual Report of the Poor Law Commissioners,* pp. 1–339.

XXVII, *Reports of Factory Inspectors,* pp. 289–334; 335–84.

LII, *Petition of Master Spinners and Manufacturers of the West Riding of York, praying for a further Limitation of Hours of Labour of Persons employed in Factories,* p. 191.

Bibliography

1844   XXVIII, *Reports of Factory Inspectors*, pp. 533–64; 565–83.
1845   XVIII, *Commissioners on State of Large Towns and Populous Districts*, pp. 746.
        XXV, *Reports of Factory Inspectors*, pp. 431–92.
1846   XX, *Reports of Factory Inspectors*, pp. 565–610; 611–42.
1847   XV, *Reports of Factory Inspectors*, pp. 441–88; 489–515.
1847–48 XXVI, *Reports of Factory Inspectors*, pp. 105–48; 149–200.
1849   XXII, *Reports of Factory Inspectors*, pp. 131–282; 283–348.
1850   XLII, *Returns on Number of Factories, etc.*, pp. 455–76.
1852   V, *Select Committee on Friendly Societies*, pp. 295–436.
        XI, *Select Committee on Manchester and Salford Education*, pp. 615.
1852–53 LXXXIX, *Census of Religious Worship*, pp. v–ccc.

LORDS SESSIONAL PAPERS

1818   IX, *Minutes of Evidence taken before the Lords Committee on Cotton Factories Bill*, pp. 1–376.
1819   XIII, *Account of Cotton and Woollen Mills and Factories entered in pursuance of the Act of Parliament 42 Geo. 3, Cap. 73 from 1803 to 1818 inclusive with a return of the several Visitors, &c.*, pp. 77–136.
        XVI, *Minutes of Evidence on the State of the Children employed in the Cotton Manufactories of the United Kingdom*, pp. 610.

PARLIAMENTARY DEBATES

Hansard's First Series, 1803–1820, Vols. I–XLI.
Hansard's New Series, 1820–30, Vols. I–XXVI.
Hansard's Third Series, 1830–46, Vols. I–LXXXVIII.

PERIODICALS, ETC.

Annual Register, 1758–1850.
The Crisis, 1832–34.
The Herald of the Rights of Industry, published by the Society for Promoting National Regeneration, Nos. 1–16, Feb. 8 to May 24, 1834.
The Lancashire Co-operator, Nos. 1–6, June 11 to Aug. 20, 1831.
The Lancashire and Yorkshire Co-operator, Nos. 1–12, Sept. 3, 1831, to Feb. 4, 1832.
The Lion (London: Richard Carlile, 1828), Vol. I, Nos. 1–26, from Jan. 4 to June 27, 1828; Vol. IV, July 3 to Dec. 25, 1829.
The Manchester Guardian, 1821–50.
The Manchester Mercury (incomplete series, 1754–1820, Manchester Central Library).
The Pioneer, or Grand National Consolidated Trades' Union Magazine, Vol. I, from Sept. 7, 1833, to June 28, 1834.
The Poor Man's Advocate, and People's Library, Nos. 1–19, 25–30, from Jan. 1 to Aug. 11, 1832.

Bibliography

The Ten Hours' Advocate, Nos. 1–38, Sept. 26, 1846, to June 12, 1847.

The Union Pilot, and Co-Operative Intelligencer, Vol. I, Nos. 9–12, 14, 16, from Mar. 10, 1832, to Apr. 28, 1832.

The United Trades' Co-operative Journal, Vol. I, No. 1 to Vol. II, No. 30. Mar. 6, 1830, to Oct. 2, 1830.

USEFUL BIBLIOGRAPHIES

Blackburn Public Library, *Catalogue of Books on Textiles and the Textile Industry* (Blackburn: County Borough of Blackburn, 1930).

Chapman, S. J., *The Lancashire Cotton Industry* (Manchester: University Publications, 1904).

Gayer, A. D., Rostow, W. W., and Schwartz, A. J., *The Growth and Fluctuation of the British Economy 1790–1850* (Oxford: The Clarendon Press, 1953).

Halkett, S., and Laing, J., *A Dictionary of the Anonymous and Pseudonymous Literature of Great Britain* (Edinburgh: William Paterson, 1882).

Hewitt, M., *The Effect of Married Women's Employment in the Cotton Textile Districts on the Home in Lancashire, 1840–1880* (Ph.D. Dissertation, University of London, 1953).

Horne, H. O., *A History of Savings Banks* (London: Oxford University Press, 1947).

Hutchins, B. L., and Harrison, A., *A History of Factory Legislation* (London: P. S. King & Son, 1903).

Mantoux, P., *The Industrial Revolution in the Eighteenth Century* (London: Jonathan Cape, 1955).

Pinchbeck, I., *Women Workers in the Industrial Revolution 1750–1850* (London: George Routledge & Sons, 1930).

The Textile Institute, *Library Catalogue* (Manchester: 1930).

Webb, S. & B., *The History of Trade Unionism* (London: Longmans, Green & Co., 1894).

INDEX

Hargreaves, James, 57, 85–6, 98
Harney, George, 262
Harrison, A., 394, 395, 398
Hawes, Rev. Mr., 353
Hayek, F. A., 399
Haygarth, J., 366
health of operatives, 276–8
Health and Morals of Apprentices Act (1802), 270
Hetherington, Henry, 381
Highs, Thomas, 87, 90
Hindley, Charles, 267
Horne, H. O., 362
Horner, Leonard, 150, 218–19, 267, 295–6, 297, 299–300, 304–5
Horrocks, William, 146
hours of work, 385 ff.; in factories, 238, 239, 266 ff.; weavers, 208; workers' preferences, 306 ff.
humanitarianism, 397
Hume, Joseph, 323, 365, 367, 371
Huskisson, William, 325
Hutchins, B. L., 394, 395, 398
Hutt, W. H., 283, 399 ff.
hybrid products, 23

immorality, 283, 284
imports, competition of, 53–4
independence, 210 ff., 247, 266, 344
Industrial Revolution, causes of, 61
integration, 12
interest rates, 78
inventors, 83
Ireland, migration from, 139, 207
Irish, in Chartist movement, 262
Isle of Man Conference, 237

Jacquard, 146
Jeffrey, James, 145
jenny, 85 ff.; results of introduction, 184
Johnson, Thomas, 145

Kay, John, 57, 60, 65, 98, 280, 284
Kelley, William, 116, 126
Kennedy, J., 55–6, 147
Kenworthy, William, 146
King, William, 257
kinship, and marriage, 2
knobsticks, 229, 230

labour, 33–4
Labour Exchange, National, 379, 380
labour notes, 379, 380–1
labour supply, for new factories, 102
Lancashire, trade unions in, 326 ff.
Lancashire Central Short Time Committee, 336
Large Towns, Commission on, 194
Lees, John, 98
legislation, factory, effects of, 202
loan societies, 375
loom: dandy, 142–3; Dutch, 56; *see also* power-looms
Lovett, William, 381
Luddite movement, 249, 357

McConnell, James, 185, 187
McCulloch, 323
machinery, violence against, 227 ff., 248 ff.
Macpherson, D., 98
Maitland, J., 375, 376
Malthus, T. R., 362
Manchester: *passim*; growth of, 188, 193–4
Manchester Chamber of Commerce, 330
Manchester Friendly Associated Spinners, 318
Manchester Literary and Philosophical Society, 76
Manchester and Salford Savings Bank, 373–4

property, destruction of, 227 ff., 248 ff.
propositions, analytical and empirical, 8
Protection of Labour, National Association for, 263, 327
Protestantism, and capitalism, 67
Puritanism, 67–8
putting-out system: 52, 58; defects of, 65–6, 142; in weaving, 130

Quakers, 343
Quinquarticular system, 334–5, 336

Radcliffe, William, 131–3, 135, 139, 144, 145, 205
Raikes, Robert, 75
Redford, A., 103, 124
reeling, 204
reform, Parliamentary, 230, 250
regression, 31
relay system, 241
reorganization, 17
resources: dissatisfactions and, 16; four types of, 33; levels of generality, 167; utilization of, 10
responsibility, personal, 67
Returns, Laws of, 7
Ricardo, D., 367
riders-out, 57
Roberts, Richard, 126–7, 146
Robertson, James Lewis, 147
Robinson, Frederick, 267
Rochdale Pioneers, 381–3
roles: 10 ff.; in analysis of industry, 21; differentiation of, 58–9; functions of, 11–12
roller-spinning, 90 ff.
Rose, George, 355, 358, 360, 365, 375
Rossendale, 142
roving, 51
Ruthwell, savings bank, 368

Sadler, Michael, 239, 240, 273, 283, 289, 290, 292
savings, 173, 181–2
savings banks: 165, 358 ff.; depositors, 372 f.; statistics, 370
Scotland, 103
scutching, 51
Scrope, G. P., 295, 348–9
Secrecy, Committee on, 251
Senior, Nassau, 246, 286, 292, 331
Seven Years War, 78
Sharp, J. B., 132
Sidmouth, 135
singeing, 51
slubbing, 51
Smith, Adam, 75, 173, 351
Smith, Rev. Joseph, 368
social systems, functional analysis of, 11 ff.
Society of Arts, 6, 82 ff., 117, 144
Society for Bettering the Condition of the Poor, 362
Speenhamland System, 352
spindles, statistics, 121
spinners: displacement of men by women, 236–7; eclipse of women, 184
spinning, 51
spinning machine, 56, 86; *see also* jenny
spreading, 51
Stalybridge, 228, 233
Stanway, Samuel, 200
steam power, introduction, 117 ff.
Stephens, Rev. J. R., 262
Stockport, 230, 235
Stot, Joseph, 73
strikes, 229 ff., 242, 321, 324, 338 ; "long-wheel", 330; two types, 231
Strutt, Jedediah, 91
Strutt, William, 126
sub-systems, relations between, 14
Sunday Schools, 75–6, 286

Index

surplus value, 389–90
symptoms, of disturbance, 4, 38

tailoring, 23
Taylor, W. Cooke, 78, 244, 275, 282, 285
technology, and factory system, 100
Ten Hours Act, 302 ff.
ten hours movement, 385; *see* hours of work
tension-management, 11
Thackrah, Turner, 277
theft of materials, 65–6; *see also* embezzlement
theory, role in economics, 7–8
Thompson, William, 255–7, 377, 378, 379
Tottenham, savings bank, 368
Townsend, Rev. Mr., 353
Toynbee, A., 62
trade unionism, weavers and, 262–3
trade unions: 182, 313 ff.; consolidation, 336 ff.; differentiation of, 338; search for legitimization, 330 ff.
training, evaluation of, 163
tramping, 335, 340
truncation, 31–2
Tufnell, 333
twist, weight consumed, 149

unemployed, relief of, 335
unemployment, 215 ff.
units of analysis: 12; of family economy, 159; in industry, 21 ff.
units of social system, relations, 13 ff.
Unwin, G., 140
Ure, A., 62, 123, 197
Usher, A. P., 61

value-system: 11, 25 ff.; family, 165 ff.; interpretation of, 17; performance-centred and sanction-centred, 26; place of, in structural differentiation, 16
values, change of, 16

Wade, —., 323, 335
Wadsworth, A. P., 51
wage-fixing, 246–7
wage-payment, methods, 338–9
wages: effects of longer mules on, 196–7; of hand-loom weavers, 139–40, 143; minimum, 246; trends and fluctuations, 213 ff.; weavers', decline, 205–6
Walker, G., 132
Warner, W. J., 71
warping, 51
water-frame, 90 ff.
water power, disadvantages, 117
Watson, James, 381
weavers: power-loom, numbers, 149; town and country, 141; *see also* hand-loom weavers
weaving, 52, 129 ff., *et passim*
Webb, S. and B., 4, 314, 394, 395
Weber, 163
Weber thesis, 67, 100–1
Wesley, John, 68, 70, 75
wheat, price of, 216
Whitbread, Samuel, 365
Whitehead, Rev. Edward, 71, 72, 74–5
wife and husband, roles, 268–9
Wigan, 235
winding, 51
women, and factory system, 281–2
Wood, Kinder, 142
Woodrow, —., 375
Wyatt, Paul and John, 56, 60

yarn, shortage of, 65
Young, Arthur, 57, 136

440